Professional Multicore

MW00637568

Professional
Multicore Programming

Professional
Multicore Programming
Design and Implementation for C++ Developers

Cameron Hughes

Tracey Hughes

WILEY

Wiley Publishing, Inc.

Professional Multicore Programming:
Design and Implementation for C++ Developers

Published by
Wiley Publishing, Inc.
10475 Crosspoint Boulevard
Indianapolis, IN 46256
www.wiley.com

Published simultaneously in Canada

ISBN: 978-0-470-28962-4

Manufactured in the United States of America

10 9 8 7 6 5 4 3 2 1

Library of Congress Cataloging-in-Publication Data

Hughes, Cameron, 1960-
   Professional multicore programming : design and implementation for C++ developers/Cameron Hughes, Tracey Hughes.
      p. cm.
      Includes index.
      ISBN 978-0-470-28962-4 (paper/website)
   1. Parallel programming (Computer science)   2. Multiprocessors.   3. C++ (Computer program   language)
4. System design.   I. Hughes, Tracey.   I. Title.
      QA76.642.H837   2008
      005.13'3—dc22   2008026307

We would like to dedicate this book to Vera and Mary, our inspiration.

About the Authors

Cameron Hughes is a professional software developer. He is a software engineer at CTEST Laboratories and a staff programmer/analyst at Youngstown State University. With over 15 years as a software developer, Cameron Hughes has been involved in software development efforts of all sizes, from business and industrial applications to aerospace design and development projects. Cameron is the designer of the Cognopaedia and is currently project leader on the GRIOT project that runs on the Pantheon at CTEST Laboratories. The Pantheon is a 24 node multicore cluster that is used in the development of multithreaded search engine and text extraction programs.

Tracey Hughes is a senior graphics programmer at CTEST Laboratories, where she develops knowledge and information visualization software. Tracey Hughes is the lead designer for the M.I.N.D, C.R.A.I.G, and NOFAQS projects that utilize epistemic visualization at CTEST Laboratories. She regularly contributes to Linux development software efforts. She is also a team member on the GRIOT project.

Cameron and Tracey Hughes are also the authors of six books on software development, multithreaded, and parallel programming: *Parallel and Distributed Programming Using C++* (Addison Wesley, 2003), *Linux Rapid Application Development* (Hungry Minds, 2000), *Mastering the Standard C++ Classes* (Wiley, 1999), *Object-Oriented Multithreading Using C++* (Wiley, 1997), *Collection and Container Classes in C++* (Wiley, 1996), and *Object-Oriented I/O Using C++ Iostreams* (Wiley, 1995).

Credits

Executive Editor
Carol Long

Senior Development Editor
Kevin Kent

Technical Editor
Andrew Moore

Production Editor
Christine O'Connor

Copy Editor
Foxxe Editorial Services

Editorial Manager
Mary Beth Wakefield

Production Manager
Tim Tate

Vice President and Executive Group Publisher
Richard Swadley

Vice President and Executive Publisher
Joseph B. Wikert

Project Coordinator, Cover
Lynsey Stanford

Proofreader
Christopher Jones

Indexer
Robert Swanson

Acknowledgments

As with all of the projects that we are fortunate to be involved with these days, we could not have made it to the finish line without the help, suggestions, constructive criticisms, and resources of our colleagues and friends. In particular, we would like to thank the YSU student chapter of the ACM for suffering through some of the early versions and rough drafts of the material presented in this book. They were single-handedly responsible for sending us back to the drawing board on more than one occasion. We are indebted to Shaun Canavan for providing us with release time for this project and for picking up the slack on several of the colloquiums and conferences where we had major responsibilities but not enough time to execute them. We would like to thank Dr. Alina Lazar for excusing us from many missed meetings and deadlines. A big thanks goes to Trevor Watkins from Z Group who gave us free and unrestricted access to Site B and for helping us with Linux and the Cell processors. We owe much gratitude to Brian Nelson from YSU who patiently answered many of our pesky questions about the UltraSparc T1 Sun-Fire-T200 and for also giving us enough disk quota and security clearance to get the job done! Thanks to Dr. Kriss Schueller for his inspiring presentation to our group on multicore computing and the UltraSparc T1 and also for agreeing to review some of the early versions of the hardware material that we present in the book. A special thanks goes to CTEST Labs who gave us full access to their Pantheon cluster, multicore Opterons, and multicore Macs. The CTEST Pantheon provided the primary testing resources for much of the material in this book. We would like to thank Jacqueline Hansson from IEEE for her help with the POSIX standards material. Thanks to Greg from Intel who helped us get off to a good start on the Intel Thread Building Blocks library. Thanks to Carole McClendon who saw value in this project from the very beginning and who encouraged us to see it through. A book of this nature is not possible without the input from technical editors, development editors, and reviewers. We have to extend much appreciation to Kevin Kent, our senior development editor, who helped sculpt the material and for providing us with very useful criticism and input throughout the project; to Carol Long, our executive acquisitions editor for her support as we tip-toed past our share of deadlines; to Andrew Moore, our technical editor; and to Christine O'Connor, our production editor.

Contents

Contents

Contents

Contents

Contents

Introduction

The multicore revolution is at hand. Parallel processing is no longer the exclusive domain of supercomputers or clusters. The entry-level server and even the basic developer workstation have the capacity for hardware- and software-level parallel processing. The question is what does this mean for the software developer and what impact will it have on the software development process? In the race for who has the fastest computer, it is now more attractive for chip manufacturers to place multiple processors on a single chip than it is to increase the speed of the processor. Until now the software developer could rely on the next new processor to speed up the software without having to make any actual improvements to the software. Those days are gone. To increase overall system performance, computer manufacturers have decided to add more processors rather than increase clock frequency. This means if the software developer wants the application to benefit from the next new processor, the application will have to be modified to exploit multiprocessor computers.

Although sequential programming and single core application development have a place and will remain with us, the landscape of software development now reflects a shift toward multithreading and multiprocessing. Parallel programming techniques that were once only the concern of theoretical computer scientists and university academics are in the process of being reworked for the masses. The ideas of multicore application design and development are now a concern for the mainstream.

Learn Multicore Programming

Our book *Professional Multicore Programming: Design and Implementation for C++ Developers* presents the ABCs of multicore programming in terms the average working software developer can understand. We introduce the reader to the everyday fundamentals of programming for multiprocessor and multithreaded architectures. We provide a practical yet gentle introduction to the notions of parallel processing and software concurrency. This book takes complicated, almost unapproachable, parallel programming techniques and presents them in a simple, understandable manner. We address the pitfalls and traps of concurrency programming and synchronization. We provide a no-nonsense discussion of multiprocessing and multithreading models. This book provides numerous programming examples that demonstrate how successful multicore programming is done. We also include methods and techniques for debugging and testing multicore programming. Finally, we demonstrate how to take advantage of processor specific features using cross-platform techniques.

Different Points of View

The material in this book is designed to serve a wide audience with different entry points into multicore programming and application development. The audience for this book includes but is not limited to:

- ❑ Library and tool producers
- ❑ Operating system programmers

- ❑ Kernel developers
- ❑ Database and application server designers and implementers
- ❑ Scientific programmers and users with compute-intensive applications
- ❑ Application developers
- ❑ System programmers

Each group sees the multicore computer from a somewhat different perspective. Some are concerned with bottom-up methods and need to develop software that takes advantage of hardware-specific and vendor-specific features. For these groups, the more detailed the information about the nooks and crannies of multithreaded processing the better. Other groups are interested in top-down methods. This group does not want to be bothered with the details of concurrent task synchronization or thread safety. This group prefers to use high-level libraries and tools to get the job done. Still other groups need a mix of bottom-up and top-down approaches. This book provides an introduction to the many points of view of multicore programming, covering both bottom-up and top-down approaches.

Multiparadigm Approaches are the Solution

First, we recognize that not every software solution requires multiprocessing or multithreading. Some software solutions are better implemented using sequential programming techniques (even if the target platform is multicore). Our approach is solution and model driven. First, develop the model or solution for the problem. If the solution requires that some instructions, procedures, or tasks need to execute concurrently then determine which the best set of techniques to use are. This approach is in contrast to forcing the solution or model to fit some preselected library or development tool. The technique should follow the solution. Although this book discusses libraries and development tools, it does not advocate any specific vendor library or tool set. Although we include examples that take advantage of particular hardware platforms, we rely on cross-platform approaches. POSIX standard operating system calls and libraries are used. Only features of C++ that are supported by the International C++ standard are used.

We advocate a component approach to the challenges and obstacles found in multiprocessing and multithreading. Our primary objective is to take advantage of framework classes as building blocks for concurrency. The framework classes are supported by object-oriented mutexes, semaphores, pipes, queues, and sockets. The complexity of task synchronization and communication is significantly reduced through the use of interface classes. The control mechanism in our multithreaded and multiprocessing applications is primarily agent driven. This means that the application architectures that you will see in this book support the multiple-paradigm approach to software development.

We use object-oriented programming techniques for component implementation and primarily agent-oriented programming techniques for the control mechanism. The agent-oriented programming ideas are sometimes supported by logic programming techniques. As the number of available cores on the processor increase, software development models will need to rely more on agent-oriented and logic programming. This book includes an introduction to this multiparadigm approach for software development.

Why C++?

There are C++ compilers available for virtually every platform and operating environment. The ANSI American National Standards Institute (ANSI) and International Organization for Standardization (ISO) have defined standards for the C++ language and its library. There are robust open-source implementations as well as commercial implementations of the language. The language has to be widely adopted by researchers, designers, and professional developers around the world. The C++ language has been used to solve problems of all sizes and shapes from device drivers to large-scale industrial applications. The language supports a multiparadigm approach to software development. We can implement Object-Oriented designs, logic programming designs, and agent-oriented designs seamlessly in C++. We can also use structured programming techniques or low-level programming techniques where necessary. This flexibility is exactly what's needed to take advantage of the new multicore world. Further, C++ compilers provide the software developer with a direct interface to the new features of the multicore processors.

UML Diagrams

Many of the diagrams in this book use the Unified Modeling Language (UML) standard. In particular, activity diagrams, deployment diagrams, class diagrams and state diagrams are used to describe important concurrency architectures and class relationships. Although a knowledge of the UML is not necessary, familiarity is helpful.

Development Environments Supported

The examples in this book were all developed using ISO standard C/C++. This means the examples and programs can be compiled in all the major environments. Only POSIX-compliant operating system calls or libraries are used in the complete programs. Therefore, these programs will be portable to all operating system environments that are POSIX compliant. The examples and programs in this book were tested on the SunFire 2000 with UltraSparc T1 multiprocessor, the Intel Core 2 Duo, the IBM Cell Broadband Engine, and the AMD Dual Core Opteron.

Program Profiles

Most complete programs in the book are accompanied by a program profile. The profile will contain implementation specifics such as headers required, libraries required, compile instructions, and link instructions. The profile also includes a notes section that will contain any special considerations that need to be taken when executing the program. All code is meant for exposition purposes only.

Testing and Code Reliability

Although all examples and applications in this book were tested to ensure correctness, we make no warranties that the programs contained in this book are free of defects or error or are consistent with any particular standard or mechantability, or will meet your requirement for any particular application. They should not be relied upon for solving problems whose incorrect solution could result in injury to person or loss of property. The authors and publishers disclaim all liability for direct or consequential damages resulting from your use of the examples, programs, or applications present in this book.

Conventions

To help you get the most from the text and keep track of what's happening, we've used a number of conventions throughout the book.

> *Notes, tips, hints, tricks, and asides to the current discussion are offset and placed in italics like this.*

As for styles in the text:

❑ We *highlight* new terms and important words when we introduce them.

❑ We show keyboard strokes like this: Ctrl+A.

❑ We show filenames, URLs, and code within the text like this: `persistence.properties`.

❑ We present code in two different ways:

```
We use a monofont type with no highlighting for most code examples.
```

```
We use gray highlighting to emphasize code that's particularly important in the
present context.
```

This book contains both code listings and code examples.

❑ Code listings are complete programs that are runnable. As previously mentioned, in most cases, they will be accompanied with a program profile that tells you the environment the program was written in and gives you a description and the compiling and linking instructions, and so forth.

❑ Code examples are snippets. They do not run as is. They are used to focus on showing how something is called or used, but the code cannot run as seen.

Source Code

As you work through the examples in this book, you may choose either to type in all the code manually or to use the source code files that accompany the book. All of the source code used in this book is available for download at `www.wrox.com`. Once at the site, simply locate the book's title (either by using the Search box or by using one of the title lists) and click the Download Code link on the book's detail page to obtain all the source code for the book.

Because many books have similar titles, you may find it easiest to search by ISBN; this book's ISBN is 978-0-470-28962-4.

Once you download the code, just decompress it with your favorite decompression tool. Alternately, you can go to the main Wrox code download page at www.wrox.com/dynamic/books/download.aspx to see the code available for this book and all other Wrox books.

Errata

We make every effort to ensure that there are no errors in the text or in the code. However, no one is perfect, and mistakes do occur. If you find an error in one of our books, such as a spelling mistake or faulty piece of code, we would be very grateful for your feedback. By sending in errata, you may save another reader hours of frustration, and at the same time you will be helping us provide even higher-quality information.

To find the errata page for this book, go to www.wrox.com and locate the title using the Search box or one of the title lists. Then, on the book details page, click the Book Errata link. On this page, you can view all errata that has been submitted for this book and posted by Wrox editors. A complete book list including links to each book's errata is also available at www.wrox.com/misc-pages/booklist.shtml.

If you don't spot "your" error on the Book Errata page, go to www.wrox.com/contact/techsupport.shtml and complete the form there to send us the error you have found. We'll check the information and, if appropriate, post a message to the book's errata page and fix the problem in subsequent editions of the book.

p2p.wrox.com

For author and peer discussion, join the P2P forums at p2p.wrox.com. The forums are a Web-based system for you to post messages relating to Wrox books and related technologies and interact with other readers and technology users. The forums offer a subscription feature to e-mail you topics of interest of your choosing when new posts are made to the forums. Wrox authors, editors, other industry experts, and your fellow readers are present on these forums.

At http://p2p.wrox.com, you will find a number of different forums that will help you not only as you read this book but also as you develop your own applications. To join the forums, just follow these steps:

1. Go to p2p.wrox.com and click the Register link.
2. Read the terms of use and click Agree.
3. Complete the required information to join as well as any optional information you wish to provide and click Submit.
4. You will receive an e-mail with information describing how to verify your account and complete the joining process.

You can read messages in the forums without joining P2P, but in order to post your own messages, you must join.

Once you join, you can post new messages and respond to messages other users post. You can read messages at any time on the Web. If you would like to have new messages from a particular forum e-mailed to you, click the Subscribe to this Forum icon by the forum name in the forum listing.

For more information about how to use the Wrox P2P, be sure to read the P2P FAQs for answers to questions about how the forum software works as well as many common questions specific to P2P and Wrox books. To read the FAQs, click the FAQ link on any P2P page.

1

The New Architecture

The most recent advances in microprocessor design for desktop computers involve putting multiple processors on a single computer chip. These multicore designs are completely replacing the traditional single core designs that have been the foundation of desktop computers. IBM, Sun, Intel, and AMD have all changed their chip pipelines from single core processor production to multicore processor production. This has prompted computer vendors such as Dell, HP, and Apple to change their focus to selling desktop computers with multicores. The race to control market share in this new area has each computer chip manufacturer pushing the envelope on the number of cores that can be economically placed on a single chip. All of this competition places more computing power in the hands of the consumer than ever before. The primary problem is that regular desktop software has not been designed to take advantage of the new multicore architectures. In fact, to see any real speedup from the new multicore architectures, desktop software will have to be redesigned.

The approaches to designing and implementing application software that will take advantage of the multicore processors are radically different from techniques used in single core development. The focus of software design and development will have to change from sequential programming techniques to parallel and multithreaded programming techniques.

The standard developer's workstation and the entry-level server are now multiprocessors capable of hardware-level multithreading, multiprocessing, and parallel processing. Although sequential programming and single core application development have a place and will remain with us, the ideas of multicore application design and development are now in the mainstream.

This chapter begins your look at multicore programming. We will cover:

❑ What is a multicore?

❑ What multicore architectures are there and how do they differ from each other?

❑ What do you as a designer and developer of software need to know about moving from sequential programming and single core application development to multicore programming?

What Is a Multicore?

A *multicore* is an architecture design that places multiple processors on a single die (computer chip). Each processor is called a core. As chip capacity increased, placing multiple processors on a single chip became practical. These designs are known as *Chip Multiprocessors (CMPs)* because they allow for single chip multiprocessing. Multicore is simply a popular name for CMP or single chip multiprocessors. The concept of single chip multiprocessing is not new, and chip manufacturers have been exploring the idea of multiple cores on a uniprocessor since the early 1990s. Recently, the CMP has become the preferred method of improving overall system performance. This is a departure from the approach of increasing the clock frequency or processor speed to achieve gains in overall system performance. Increasing the clock frequency has started to hit its limits in terms of cost-effectiveness. Higher frequency requires more power, making it harder and more expensive to cool the system. This also affects sizing and packaging considerations. So, instead of trying to make the processor faster to gain performance, the response is now just to add more processors. The simple realization that this approach is better has prompted the multicore revolution. Multicore architectures are now center stage in terms of improving overall system performance.

For software developers who are familiar with multiprocessing, multicore development will be familiar. From a logical point of view, there is no real significant difference between programming for multiple processors in separate packages and programming for multiple processors contained in a single package on a single chip. There may be performance differences, however, because the new CMPs are using advances in bus architectures and in connections between processors. In some circumstances, this may cause an application that was originally written for multiple processors to run faster when executed on a CMP. Aside from the potential performance gains, the design and implementation are very similar. We discuss minor differences throughout the book. For developers who are only familiar with sequential programming and single core development, the multicore approach offers many new software development paradigms.

Multicore Architectures

CMPs come in multiple flavors: two processors (dual core), four processors (quad core), and eight processors (octa-core) configurations. Some configurations are multithreaded; some are not. There are several variations in how cache and memory are approached in the new CMPs. The approaches to processor-to-processor communication vary among different implementations. The CMP implementations from the major chip manufacturers each handle the I/O bus and the Front Side Bus (FSB) differently.

Again, most of these differences are not visible when looking strictly at the logical view of an application that is being designed to take advantage of a multicore architecture. Figure 1-1 illustrates three common configurations that support multiprocessing.

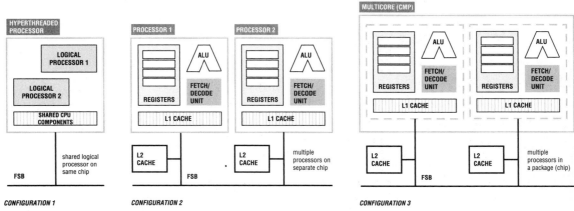

Figure 1-1

❑ Configuration 1 in Figure 1-1 uses hyperthreading. Like CMP, a hyperthreaded processor allows two or more threads to execute on a single chip. However, in a hyperthreaded package the multiple processors are logical instead of physical. There is some duplication of hardware but not enough to qualify a separate physical processor. So hyperthreading allows the processor to present itself to the operating system as complete multiple processors when in fact there is a single processor running multiple threads.

❑ Configuration 2 in Figure 1-1 is the classic multiprocessor. In configuration 2, each processor is on a separate chip with its own hardware.

❑ Configuration 3 represents the current trend in multiprocessors. It provides complete processors on a single chip.

As you shall see in Chapter 2, some multicore designs support hyperthreading within their cores. For example, a hyperthreaded dual core processor could present itself logically as a quad core processor to the operating system.

Hybrid Multicore Architectures

Hybrid multicore architectures mix multiple processor types and/or threading schemes on a single package. This can provide a very effective approach to code optimization and specialization by combining unique capabilities into a single functional core. One of the most common examples of the hybrid multicore architecture is IBM's Cell broadband engine (Cell). We explore the architecture of the Cell in the next chapter.

What's important to remember is that each configuration presents itself to the developer as a set of two or more logical processors capable of executing multiple tasks concurrently. The challenge for system programmers, kernel programmers, and application developers is to know when and how to take advantage of this.

The Software Developer's Viewpoint

The low cost and wide availability of CMPs bring the full range of parallel processing within the reach of the average software developer. Parallel processing is no longer the exclusive domain of supercomputers or clusters. The basic developer workstation and entry-level server now have the capacity for hardware- and software-level parallel processing. This means that programmers and software developers can deploy applications that take advantage of multiprocessing and multithreading as needed without compromising design or performance. However, a word of caution is in order. Not every software application requires multiprocessing or multithreading. In fact, some software solutions and computer algorithms are better implemented using sequential programming techniques. In some cases, introducing the overhead of parallel programming techniques into a piece of software can degrade its performance. Parallelism and multiprocessing come at a cost. If the amount of work required to solve the problem sequentially in software is less than the amount of work required to create additional threads and processes or less than the work required to coordinate communication between concurrently executing tasks, then the sequential approach is better.

Sometimes determining when or where to use parallelism is easy because the nature of the software solution demands parallelism. For example, the parallelism in many client-server configurations is obvious. You might have one server, say a database, and many clients that can simultaneously make requests of the database. In most cases, you don't want one client to be required to wait until another client's request is filled. An acceptable solution allows the software to process the clients' requests concurrently. On the other hand, there is sometimes a temptation to use parallelism when it is not required. For instance, you might be tempted to believe that a keyword word search through text in parallel will automatically be faster than a sequential search. But this depends on the size of text to be searched for and on the time and amount of overhead setup required to start multiple search agents in parallel. The design decision in favor of a solution that uses concurrency has to consider break-even points and problem size. In most cases, software design and software implementation are separate efforts and in many situations are performed by different groups. But in the case where software speedup or optimal performance is a primary system requirement, the software design effort has to at least be aware of the software implementation choices, and the software implementation choices have to be informed by potential target platforms.

In this book, the target platforms are multicore. To take full advantage of a multicore platform, you need to understand what you can do to access the capabilities of a CMP. You need to understand what elements of a CMP you have control over. You will see that you have access to the CMP through the compiler, through operating system calls/libraries, through language features, and through application-level libraries. But first, to understand what to do with the CMP access, you need a basic understanding of the processor architecture.

The Basic Processor Architecture

The components you can access and influence include registers, main memory, virtual memory, instruction set usage, and object code optimizations. It is important to understand what you can influence in single processor architectures before attempting to tackle multiprocessor architectures. Figure 1-2 shows a simplified logical overview of a processor architecture and memory components.

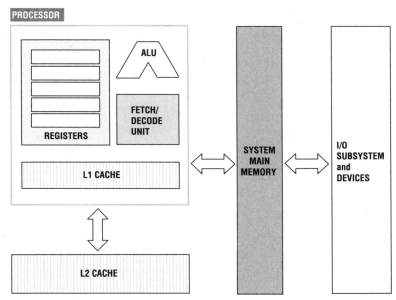

Figure 1-2

There are many variations on processor architecture, and Figure 1-2 is only a logical overview. It illustrates the primary processor components you can work with. While this level of detail and these components are often transparent to certain types of application development, they play a more central role in bottom-up multicore programming and in software development efforts where speedup and optimal performance are primary objectives. Your primary interface to the processor is the compiler. The operating system is the secondary interface.

In this book, we will use C++ compilers to generate the object code. Parallel programming can be used for all types of applications using multiple approaches, from low to high level, from object-oriented to structured applications. C++ supports multiparadigm approaches to programming, so we use it for its flexibility.

Table 1-1 shows a list of categories where the compiler interfaces with the CPU and instruction set. Categories include floating-point, register manipulation, and memory models.

Table 1-1

Compiler Switch Options	Description	Examples of Usage
Vectorization	This option enables the vectorizer, a component of the compiler that automatically uses Single Instruction Multiple Data (SIMD) instructions in the MMX registers and all the SSE instruction sets.	`-x    -ax` Enables the vectorizer.
Auto parallelization	This option identifies loop structures that contain parallelism and then (if possible) safely generates the multithreaded equivalent executing in parallel.	`-parallel` Triggers auto parallelization.

Parallelization with OpenMP	With this option the compiler generates multithreaded code based on OpenMP directives in the source code added by the programmer.	```#pragma omp parallel```
		```{```
		``` #pragma omp for```
		``` // your code```
		```}```

Fast	This option detects incompatible processors; error messages are generated during execution.	`-O1`
		Optimized to favor code size and code locality and disables loop unrolling, software pipelining, and global code scheduling.
		`-O2`
		Default; turns pipelining ON.

Floating point	Set of switches that allows the compiler to influence the selection and use of floating-point instructions.	`-fschedule-insns`
		Tells the compiler that other instructions can be issued until the results of a floating-point instruction are required.
		`-float-store`
		Tells the compiler that when generating object code do not use instructions that would store a floating-point variable in registers.

Compiler Switch Options	Description	Examples of Usage

Loop unrolling	This option enables loop unrolling. This applies only to loops that the compiler determines should be unrolled. If n is omitted, lets the compiler decide whether to perform unrolling or not.	`-unroll<n>`
		Enables loop unrolling; <n> sets the maximum time to unroll the loop.
		`n = 0`
		Disables loop unrolling, only allowable value for 64-bit architectures.

Memory bandwidth	This option enables or disables control of memory bandwidth used by processors; if disabled, bandwidth will be well shared among multiple threads. This can be used with the auto parallelization option. This option is used for 64-bit architectures only.	`-opt-mem-bandwidth<n>`
		`n = 2`
		Enables compiler optimizations for parallel code such as pthreads and MPI code.
		`n = 1`
		Enables compiler optimizations for multithreaded code generated by the compiler.

Code generation	With this option code is generated optimized for a particular architecture or processor; if there is a performance benefit, the compiler generates multiple, processor-specific code paths; used for 32- and 64- bit architectures.	`-ax<processor>`
		Generates optimized code for the specified processor.
		`-axS`
		Generates specialized code paths using SIMD Extensions 4 (SSE4) vectorizing compiler and media accelerators instructions.

Thread checking	This option enables thread analysis of a threaded application of program; can only be used with Intel's Thread Checker tool.	`-tcheck` Enables analysis of threaded application or program.
Thread library	This option causes the compiler to include code from the Thread Library; The programmer needs to include API calls in source code.	`-pthread` Uses the pthread library for multithreading support.

The CPU (Instruction Set)

A CPU has a native instruction set that it recognizes and executes. It's the C++ compiler's job to translate C++ program code to the native instruction set of the target platform. The compiler converts the C++ and produces an object file that consists of only instructions that are native to the target processor. Figure 1-3 shows an outline of the basic compilation process.

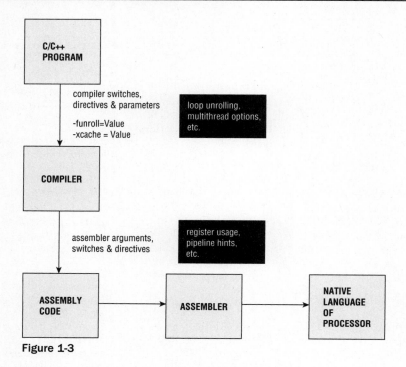

Figure 1-3

During the process of converting C++ code into the native language of the target CPU, the compiler has options for how to produce the object code. The compiler can be used to help determine how registers are used, or whether to perform loop unrolling. The compiler has options that can be set to determine whether to generate 16-bit, 32-bit, or 64-bit object code. The compiler can be used to select the memory model. The compiler can provide code hints that declare how much level 1 (L1) or level 2 (L2) cache is present. Notice in Table 1-1 in the floating-point operations category that switches from this category allow the compiler to influence the selection of floating-point instructions. For example, the GNU gcc compiler has the `--float-store` switch. This switch tells the compiler that when generating object code it should not use instructions that would store floating-point variable in registers. The Sun C++ compiler has a `-fma` switch. This switch enables automatic generation of floating-point and multi-add instructions. The `-fma=none` disables generation of these instructions. The `-fma=fused` switch allows the compiler to attempt to improve the performance of the code by using floating-point, fused, and `multiply=add` instructions. In both cases, the switches are provided as options to the compiler:

```
gcc  -ffloat-store my_program.cc
```

or

```
CC -fma=used  my_program.cc
```

Other switches influence cache usage. For instance the Sun C++ compiler has a `-xcache=c` that defines the cache properties for use by the optimizer. The GNU gcc compiler has the `-Funroll -loops` that specifies how loops are to be unrolled. The GNU gcc compiler has a `-pthread` switch that turns on support for multithreading with pthreads. The compilers even have options for setting the typical memory reference interval using the -mmemory-latency=time switch. In fact, there are compiler options and switches that can influence the use of any of the components in Figure 1-2.

The fact that the compiler provides access to the processor has implications for the developer who is writing multicore applications for a particular target processor or a family of processors. For example, The UltraSparc, Opteron, Intel Core 2 Duo, and Cell processors are commonly used multicore configurations. These processors each support high-speed vector operations and calculations. They have support for the Single Instruction Multiple Data (SIMD) model of parallel computation. This support can be accessed and influenced by the compiler.

Chapter 4 contains a closer look at the part compilers play in multicore development.

It is important to note that using many of these types of compiler options cause the compiler to optimize code for a particular processor. If cross-platform compatibility is a design goal, then compiler options have to be used very carefully. For system programmers, library producers, compiler writers, kernel developers, and database and server engine developers, a fundamental understanding of the basic processor architecture, instruction set and compiler interface is a prerequisite for developing effective software that takes advantage of CMP.

Memory Is the Key

Virtually anything that happens in a computer system passes through some kind of memory. Most things pass through many levels of memory. Software and its associated data are typically stored on some kind of external medium (usually hard disks, CD-ROMs, DVDs, etc.) prior to its execution. For example, say you have an important and very long list of numbers stored on an optical disc, and you need to add those numbers together. Also say that the fancy program required to add the very long list of numbers is also stored on the optical disc. Figure 1-4 illustrates the flow of programs and data to the processor.

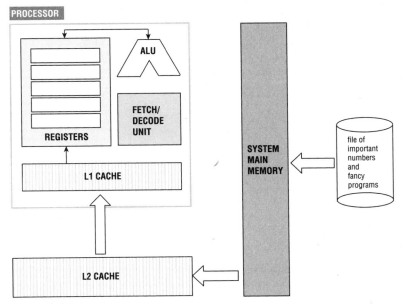

Figure 1-4

In the maze of different types of memory, you have to remember that the typical CPU operates only on data stored in its registers. It does not have the capacity to directly access data or programs stored elsewhere. Figure 1-4 shows the ALU reading and writing the registers. This is the normal state of affairs. The instruction set commands (native language of the processor) are designed to primarily work with data or instructions in the CPU's registers. To get your long list of important numbers and your fancy program to the processor, the software and data must be retrieved from the optical disc and loaded into primary memory. From primary memory, bits and pieces of your software and data are passed on to L2 cache, then to L1 cache, and then into instruction and data registers so that the CPU can perform its work. It is important to note that at each stage the memory performs at a different speed. Secondary storage such as CD-ROMs, DVDs, and hard disks are slower than the main random access memory (RAM). RAM is slower than L2 cache memory. L2 cache memory is slower than L1 cache memory, and so on. The registers on the processor are the fastest memory that you can directly deal with.

Besides the speed of the various types of memory, size is also a factor. Figure 1-5 shows an overview of the memory hierarchy.

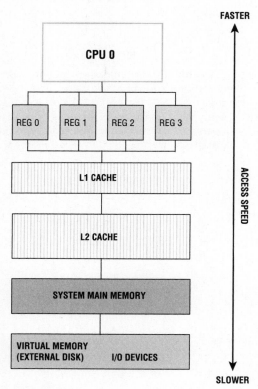

Figure 1-5

The register is the fastest but has the least capacity. For instance, a 64-bit computer will typically have a set of registers that can each hold up to 64 bits. In some instances, the registers can be used in pairs allowing for 128 bits. Following the registers in capacity is L1 cache and if present L2 cache. L2 cache is currently measured in megabytes. Then there is a big jump in maximum capacity from L2 to the system main memory, which is currently measured in gigabytes. In addition to the speeds of the various types of memory and the capacities of the various types of memory, there are the connections between the memory types. These connections turn out to have a major impact on overall system performance. Data and instructions stored in secondary storage typically have to travel over an I/O channel or bus to get to RAM. Once in RAM, the data or instruction normally travels over a system bus to get to L1 cache. The speed and capacity of the I/O buses and system buses can become bottlenecks in a multiprocessor environment. As the number of cores on a chip increases, the performance of bus architectures and datapaths become more of an issue.

We discuss the bus connection later in this chapter, but first it's time to examine the memory hierarchy and the part it plays in your view of multicore application development. Keep in mind that just as you can use the influence that the compiler has over instruction set choices, you can use it to manipulate register usage and RAM object layouts, give cache sizing hints, and so on. You can use further C++ language elements to specify register usage, RAM, and I/O. So, before you can get a clear picture of multiprocessing or multithreading, you have to have a fundamental grasp of the memory hierarchy that a processor deals with.

Registers

The *registers* are special-purpose, small but fast memory that are directly accessed by the core. The registers are volatile. When the program exits, any data or instructions that it had in its registers are gone for all intents and purposes. Also unlike swap memory, or virtual memory, which is permanent because it is stored in some kind of secondary storage, the registers are temporary. Register data lasts only as long as the system is powered or the program is running. In general-purpose computers, the registers are located inside the processor and, therefore, have almost zero latency. Table 1-2 contains the general types of registers found in most general-purpose processors.

Table 1-2

Registers	Description
Index	Used in general computations and special uses when dealing with addresses.
Segment	Used to hold segment parts of addresses.
IP	Used to hold the offset part of the address of the next instruction to be executed.
Counter	Used with looping constructs, but can also be used for general computational use.
Base	Used in the calculation and placement of addresses.
Data	Used as general-purpose registers and can be used for temp storage and calculation.
Flag	Shows the state of the machine or state of the processor.
Floating point	Used in calculation and movement of floating-point numbers.

Most C/C++ compilers have switches that can influence register use. In addition to compiler options that can be used to influence register use, C++ has the `asm{ }` directive, which allows assembly language to written within a C++ procedure or function, for example:

```
void my_fast_calculation(void)
{
   ...
     asm{
             ...
           mov 2 , %r3
           inc(%r3)
             ...
       }
        ...
}
```

`my_fast_calculation()` loads a 2 into the `%r3` general-purpose register on an UltraSparc processor. While cache is not easily visible for C++, registers and RAM are visible. Depending on the type of multiprocessor software being developed, register manipulation, either through the compiler or the C++ `asm{}` facility, can be necessary.

Cache

Cache is memory placed between the processor and main system memory (RAM). While cache is not as fast as registers, it is faster than RAM. It holds more than the registers but does not have the capacity of main memory. Cache increases the effective memory transfer rates and, therefore, overall processor performance. Cache is used to contain copies of recently used data or instruction by the processor. Small chunks of memory are fetched from main memory and stored in cache in anticipation that they will be needed by the processor. Programs tend to exhibit both temporal locality and spatial locality.

❑   **Temporal locality** is the tendency to reuse recently accessed instructions or data.

❑   **Spatial locality** is the tendency to access instructions or data that are physically close to items that were most recently accessed.

One of the primary functions of cache is to take advantage of this temporal and spatial locality characteristic of a program. Cache is often divided into two levels, level 1 and level 2.

A complete discussion of cache is beyond the scope of this book. For a thorough discussion of cache, see [Hennessy, Patterson, 2007].

Level 1 Cache

Level 1 cache is small in size sometimes as small as 16K. L1 cache is usually located inside the processor and is used to capture the most recently used bytes of instruction or data.

Level 2 Cache

Level 2 cache is bigger and slower than L1 cache. Currently, it is stored on the motherboard (outside the processor), but this is slowly changing. L2 cache is currently measured in megabytes. L2 cache can hold an even bigger chunk of the most recently used instruction, data, and items that are in the near vicinity than L1 holds. Because L1 and L2 are faster than general-purpose RAM, the more correct the guesses of what the program is going to do next are, the better the overall system performance because the right chunks of data will be located in either L1 or L2 cache. This saves a trip out to either RAM or virtual memory or, even worse, external storage.

Compiler Switches for Cache?

Most developers doing multicore application development will not be concerned with manually managing cache unless, of course, they are doing kernel development, compiler development, or other types of low-level system programming. However, compiler options that give the compiler a hint as to how much L1 or L2 cache is available or a hint about the properties of the L1 or L2 cache can be found in most of the mainstream compilers in use. For example, the Sun C++ compiler has an xcache switch. The man page for that switch shows the syntax and its use.

-xcache=c defines the cache properties that the optimizer can use. It does not guarantee that any particular cache property is used. Although this option can be used alone, it is part of the expansion of the -xtarget option; its primary use is to override a value supplied by the -xtarget option.

-xcache=16/32/4:1024/32/1 specifies the following:

Level 1 cache has:	Level 2 cache has:
16K bytes	1024K bytes
32-byte line size	32-byte line size
4-way associativity	Direct mapping

Developing software to truly take advantage of CMP requires careful thought about the instruction set of the target processor or family of processors and about memory usage. This includes being aware of opportunities for optimizations, such as loop unrolling, high-speed vector manipulations, SIMD processing, and MP compiler directives, and giving compilers hints for values such as the size of L1 or L2 cache.

Main Memory

Figure 1-2 shows the relative relationship between registers, cache, the ALU, and main memory. Outside of external storage (for example, hard disks, CD-ROMs, DVDs, and so on), RAM is the slowest memory the developer works with. Also RAM is located physically outside the processor, and data transfers across a bus to the processor slow things down a little more. On the other hand, RAM is the most visible to you as a software developer of multithreaded or multiprocessing applications. The data shared between processors and tasks in most cases is stored in RAM. The instructions that each processor has to execute are kept in RAM during runtime. The critical sections that must be synchronized among multiple processors are primarily stored in RAM. When there is task or processor lockup, it is normally due to some memory management violation. In almost every case, the communication between processors and tasks, or multiple agents, will take place through variables, message queues, containers, and mutexes that will reside in RAM during runtime. A major element in the software developer's view of multicore application programming is memory access and management. Just as was the case with the other logical components shown in Figure 1-2 that have been discussed so far, you have access to compiler switches that influence how memory is handled by an application. The memory model selected is important. Objects created by the `new()` operator in C++ end up in either the free store (heap) or in virtual memory (if the data object is large enough). The free store is logically in RAM. Virtual memory is mapped from external storage.

We take a closer look at how a process or thread uses RAM in Chapter 5.

The Bus Connection

Typically the subsystems in a computer communicate using buses. The *bus* serves as a shared communication link between the subsystems [Hennessy, Patterson, 1996]. The bus is a channel or path between components in a computer. Traditionally, buses are classified as CPU-memory buses or I/O buses. A basic system configuration consists of two main buses, a system bus also referred to as the Front Side Bus (FSB), and an I/O bus. If the system has cache, there is also usually a Back Side Bus (BSB) connected to the processor and the cache. Figure 1-6 shows a simplified processor-to-bus configuration.

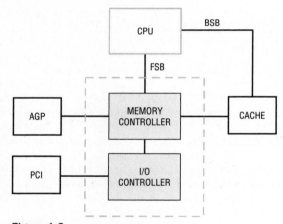

Figure 1-6

In Figure 1-6 the FSB is used to transport data to or from the CPU and memory. The FSB is a CPU-memory bus. The I/O bus generally sends information to and from other peripherals. Notice in Figure 1-6 that the BSB is used to move data between the CPU, cache, and main memory. The Peripheral Component Interconnect (PCI) is an example of an I/O bus. The PCI provides a direct connection to the devices that it is connected to. However, the PCI is usually connected to the FSB through some type of bridge technology. Since the buses provide communication paths between the CPU, the memory controller, the I/O controller, cache, and peripherals, there is the potential for throughput bottlenecks. Configurations with multiple processors can put a strain on the FSB. The trend is to add more processors to a chip. This puts more communication demands on bus-based architectures. The performance of the system is constrained by the maximum throughput of the buses used between the CPU, memory, and other system peripherals. If the bus is slower than the CPU or memory or the buses do not have the proper capacity, timing, or synchronization, then the bus will be a bottleneck, impeding overall system performance.

From Single Core to Multicore

In single core configurations you are concerned only with one (general-purpose) processor, although it's important to keep in mind that many of today's single core configurations contain special graphic processing units, multimedia processing units, and sometimes special math coprocessors. But even with single core or single processor computers multithreading, parallel programming, pipelining, and multiprogramming are all possible. So this section can help clear the air on some of the basic ideas that move you from single core to multicore programming.

Multiprogramming and Multiprocessing

Multiprogramming is usually talked about in the context of operating systems as opposed to applications. *Multiprogramming* is a scheduling technique that allows more than one job to be in an executable state at any one time. In a multiprogrammed system, the jobs (or processes) share system resources such as the main system memory and the processor. There is an illusion in a single core system that the processes are executing simultaneously because the operating system uses the technique of time slices. In the time slice scheme, each process is given a small interval to execute. After that interval, the operating system switches contexts and lets another process execute for an interval. These intervals are called time slices, and they are so small that the operating system switches the context fast enough to give the illusion that more than one process or job is executing at the same time. So in a scenario where you have single core architecture and two major tasks are being performed concurrently (for example, burning a DVD and rendering a computer graphic), you say that the system is multiprogramming.

Multiprogramming is a scheduling technique. In contrast, a *multiprocessor* is a computer that has more than one processor. In this case, you are specifically referring to the idea of having two or more general-purpose processors. Technically speaking, a computer with a CPU and a GPU is a multiprocessor. But for the purposes of this discussion, we focus instead on multiple general-purpose processors. Consequently, *multiprocessing* is a technique of programming that uses more than one processor to perform work concurrently. In this book we are interested in techniques that fall under the category of parallel programming.

Parallel Programming

Parallel programming is the art and science of implementing an algorithm, a computer program, or a computer application, using sets of instructions or tasks designed to be executed concurrently. Figure 1-7 illustrates the parts of each type and what is executed in parallel.

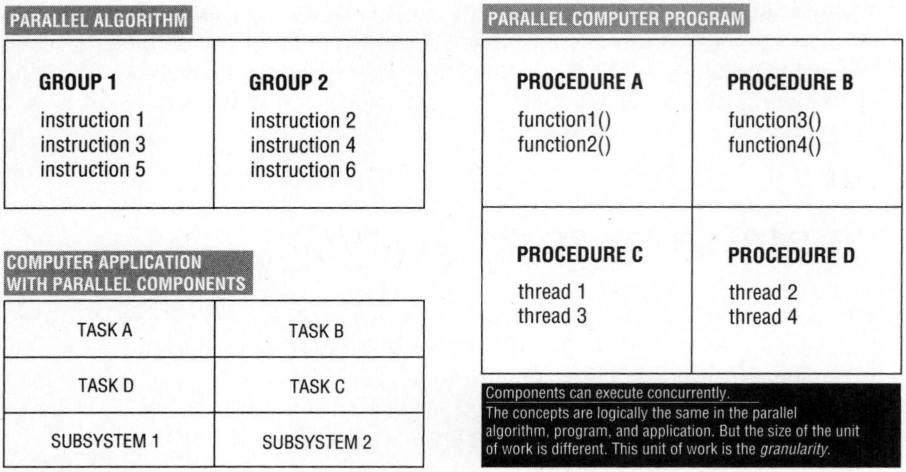

PARALLEL ALGORITHM	
GROUP 1	**GROUP 2**
instruction 1	instruction 2
instruction 3	instruction 4
instruction 5	instruction 6

PARALLEL COMPUTER PROGRAM	
PROCEDURE A	**PROCEDURE B**
function1()	function3()
function2()	function4()
PROCEDURE C	**PROCEDURE D**
thread 1	thread 2
thread 3	thread 4

COMPUTER APPLICATION WITH PARALLEL COMPONENTS	
TASK A	TASK B
TASK D	TASK C
SUBSYSTEM 1	SUBSYSTEM 2

Components can execute concurrently.
The concepts are logically the same in the parallel algorithm, program, and application. But the size of the unit of work is different. This unit of work is the *granularity*.

Figure 1-7

The parallel algorithm in Figure 1-7 can execute a set of instructions in parallel. Instruction 1 and Instruction 2 can both be executed concurrently. Instruction 5 and 6 can both be executed concurrently. In the algorithm, the parallelism happens between two instructions. This is in contrast to the computer program in Figure 1-7, where the unit of work is a procedure or function, or thread. Procedure A and Procedure B can execute simultaneously. In addition to the concurrency between Procedure A and B, they may both have concurrency within themselves. Procedure A's functions may be able to execute in parallel. So for the computer program that contains parallelism, the unit of work is larger than the algorithm.

The application in Figure 1-7 has the largest unit of work. Task A and Task B may consist of many procedures, functions, objects, and so on. When you look at the parallel programming at the application level, you are talking about larger units of work. Besides tasks, the application might contain subsystems, for example, background network components or multimedia components that are executing simultaneously in background to the set of tasks that the user can perform. The key idea here is that each structure in Figure 1-7 uses parallel programming; the difference is the unit of work, sometimes called *granularity*.

We talk more about levels of parallelism in Chapter 4.

Multicore Application Design and Implementation

Multicore application design and implementation uses parallel programming techniques to design software that can take advantage of CMP. The design process specifies the work of some task as either two or more threads, two or more processes, or some combination of threads and processes. That design can then be implemented using template libraries, class libraries, thread libraries, operating system calls, or low-level programming techniques (for example, pipelining, vectorization, and so on). This book introduces the basics of multithreading, multiprocessing, Interprocess Communication, Interthread Communication, synchronization, thread libraries, and multithreading class libraries or template libraries. The low cost of CMP implementations has brought parallel programming and its very close cousin multithreading within the reach of the average developer. The focus on this book is on developing multicore applications using multiprocessing and multithreading techniques that are portable across operating system environments. We use only libraries and language features that are part of the POSIX standard for operating systems and only C++ features that are part of the ISO standard.

Summary

This chapter has covered key concepts that you need to understand as you consider developing multicore application. Some of the important considerations this chapter introduced are:

❑ A multicore chip is a chip that has two or more processors. This processor configuration is referred to as CMP. CMPs currently range from dual core to octa-core.

❑ Hybrid multicore processors can contain different types of processors. The Cell broadband engine is a good example of a hybrid multicore.

❑ Multicore development can be approached from the bottom up or top down, depending on whether the developers in question are system programmers, kernel programmers, library developers, server developers, or application developers. Each group is faced with similar problems but looks at the cores from a different vantage point.

❑ All developers that plan to write software that takes advantage of multiprocessor configurations should be familiar with the basic processor architecture of the target platform. The primary interface to the specific features of a multicore processor is the C/C++ compiler. To get the most from the target processor or family of target processors, the developer should be familiar with the options of the compiler, the assembler subcomponent of the compiler, and the linker. The secondary interface comprises the operating system calls and operating system synchronization and communication components.

❑ Parallel programming is the art and science of implementing an algorithm, a computer program, or a computer application using sets of instructions or tasks designed to be executed concurrently. Multicore application development and design is all about using parallel programming techniques and tools to develop software that can take advantage of CMP architectures.

Now that you have in mind some of the basic ideas and issues surrounding multicore programming, Chapter 2 will take a look at four multicore designs from some of the computer industry's leading chip manufacturers: AMD, Intel, IBM, and Sun. We look at each approach to CMP for the Dual Core Opteron, Core 2 Duo, Cell Broadband Engine architecture, and UltraSparc T1 multiprocessor cores.

Four Effective Multicore Designs

In this chapter we take a closer look at four multicore designs from some of the computer industry's leading chip manufacturers:

❑   The AMD Multicore Opteron

❑   The Sun UltraSparc T1

❑   The IBM Cell Broadband Engine (CBE)

❑   The Intel Core 2 Duo

Each of these vendors approaches the Chip Multiprocessor (CMP) differently. Their approaches to multicore design are implemented effectively with each design having its advantages, strengths, and weaknesses in comparison to the other designs. We will use these designs for all of the examples in this book. The program examples in this book have been compiled and executed on one or more of these multicore processor designs. In this chapter, we introduce you to the basics of each design, and throughout the book we fill in the necessary detail as it pertains to multicore application development and design.

In many mass market software applications, the differences among hardware implementations are abstracted away because often one of the primary design goals is to make the software compatible with as many different hardware platforms as possible. So there is a conscious effort to avoid platform-specific features. In these scenarios, the software designer and developer appropriately rely on the operating system to hide any platform differences that the applications might encounter. The developers move happily and blissfully through the development process without the burden of having to worry about hardware-specific issues. This is a good thing! One of the primary jobs of the operating system is to hide and manage hardware details. And this approach works for an entire class of mass market or wide vertical market applications.

However, not every kind of software developer is so lucky. For example, those developing high-transaction database servers, web servers, application servers, hardware-intensive game engines, compilers, operating system kernels, device drivers, and high-performance scientific modeling and visualization software are practically forced to look for and exploit platform features that will make their applications acceptable to the end user. For this class of developer, familiarity with a specific processor or family of processors is a prerequisite for effective software development. Table 2-1 lists the types of applications that can require platform-specific optimization.

Table 2-1

Software Type	Developer Type
High transaction software servers • Database • Financial transaction servers • Application servers and so on	• Software architects • Software vendors • Software manufacturers
Kernels	• System programmers
Game engines	• System programmers • Software designers • Game developers • Graphics programmers
Device drivers	• System programmers
Large-scale matrix and vector computations	• Scientific programmers • Mathematicians • Scientific application developers
Compilers	• System programmers
Database engines	• Software vendors • Database architects
High-definition computer animation	• Graphics programmers • Game developers
Scientific visualization modeling	• Scientific programmers

In Table 2-1, we have also listed some of the types of developers involved with these types of applications. System programmers, graphics programmers, application developers, and software engineers who are trying to optimize the performance of a piece of software need to be aware of the capabilities of the target platform. In the cases where cross-platform portability is the primary consideration, platform-specific optimizations should be approached with caution. In other cases, cross-platform compatibility is not a concern, and the best performance on the target platform is the goal. In these situations the more the developer knows about the target processor or family of processors the better.

In this book, we look at top-down and bottom-up approaches to multiprocessor application design and implementation. To take advantage of bottom-up approaches to multiprocessor programming requires a fundamental understanding of the CMP architecture, the operating system's support for multithreading and multiprocessing, and the C/C++ compiler for the target platform. In Chapter 4, we take a closer look at operating system and compiler support for multicore development. But first here in this chapter we explore the four effective multicore designs we mentioned at the start of the chapter. Table 2-2 shows a comparison of the Opteron, UltraSparc T1, CBE, and Core 2 Duo processors.

Table 2-2

Processor Name	Hyperthreaded/SMT	Use FSB	Shared Memory	Cache 2 Location	# Cores
Opteron	No	No	No	motherboard	2
UltraSparc T1	Yes	No	No	die	8
CBE	Yes	No	Yes	die	9
Core 2 Duo	No	Yes	Yes	die	2

The AMD Multicore Opteron

The dual core Opteron is the entry level into AMD's multicore processor line. The dual core Opteron is the most basic configuration, and it captures AMD's fundamental approach to multicore architectures. The Opteron is source and binary code compatible with Intel's family of processors, that is, applications written for the Intel processors can compile and execute on Opterons. Figure 2-1 shows a simple block diagram of a dual core Opteron.

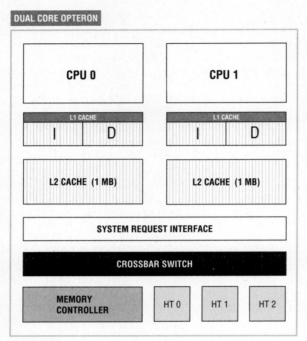

Figure 2-1

The dual core Opteron consists of two AMD 64 processors, two sets of level 1 (L1) cache, two sets of level 2 (L2) cache, a System Request Interface (SRI), a crossbar switch, a memory controller, and HyperTransport technology. One of the key architectural differences between the Opteron and other designs is AMD's Direct Connect Architecture (DCA) with HyperTransport technology. The Direct Connect Architecture determines how the CPUs communicate with memory and other I/O devices.

> *To understand the value of AMD's approach to subsystem communication, it's important to remember what part bus technology plays in the processor architecture. See the section "The Bus Connection" in Chapter 1 for more information on bus technology.*

Opteron's Direct Connect and HyperTransport

The Opteron processor moves away from this bus-based architecture. It uses a Direct Connect Architecture (DCA) in conjunction with HyperTransport (HT) technology to avoid some of the performance bottlenecks of the basic Front Side Bus (FSB), Back Side Bus (BSB), and Peripheral Component Interconnect (PCI) configurations.

The Direct Connect Architecture

The DCA is a point-to-point connection scheme. It does not use the FSB. Instead the processors, memory controller, and I/O are directly connected to the CPU. This dedicated link approach avoids the potential performance problems of the bus-based communication between the CPU and the memory controller. Also because the links are dedicated — that is, each core is directly connected to its own memory controller and has direct links to the I/O memory controller — contention issues are bypassed.

HyperTransport Technology

The HyperTransport Consortium defines HyperTransport as a high-speed, low-latency, point-to-point link designed to increase the communication speed between integrated circuits in computers, servers, embedded systems, and networking and telecommunications equipment. According to the HyperTransport Consortium, HT is designed to:

- ❑ Provide significantly more bandwidth

- ❑ Use low-latency responses and low pin counts

- ❑ Maintain compatibility with legacy buses while being extensible to new network architecture buses

- ❑ Appear transparent to operating systems and have little impact on peripheral drivers

The Opteron uses HT as a chip-to-chip interconnection between CPU and the I/O. The components connected with HT are connected in a peer-to-peer fashion and are, therefore, able to communicate with each other directly without the need of data buses. At peak throughput the HT provides 12.8 GB/s per link. The Opteron configuration comes configured with up four HT Links. I/O devices and buses such as PCI-E, AGP, PCI-X, and PCI connect to the system over HT Links. The PCIs are I/O buses, and the AGP is a direct graphics connection. The PCI, PCI-E, and AGP are used to connect the system to peripheral devices. Besides improving the connections between the processors and I/O, HT is also used to facilitate a direct connection between the processors on the Opteron. Multicore communication on the Opteron is enhanced by using HT.

System Request Interface and Crossbar

The System Request Interface (SRI) contains the system address map and maps memory ranges to nodes. If the memory access is to local memory, then a map lookup in the SRI sends it to the memory controller for the appropriate processor. If the memory access is not local (off chip), then a routing table lookup sends it to a HT port. For more see [Hughes, Conway, 2007 IEEE]. Figure 2-2 shows a logic layout of the crossbar.

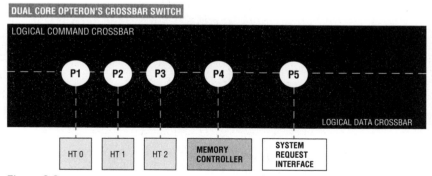

Figure 2-2

The crossbar has five ports: memory controller, SRI, and three HTs. The crossbar switch processing is logically separated into command header packet processing and data header packet processing. Logically, part of the crossbar is dedicated to command packet routing, and the other part is dedicated to data packet routing.

The Opteron Is NUMA

Opteron has a Non-Uniform Memory Access (NUMA) architecture. In this architecture, each processor has access to its own fast local memory through the processor's on-chip memory controller. NUMA architecture has a distributed but shared memory architecture. This is in contrast to the Uniform Memory Access (UMA) architecture. Figure 2-3 shows a simplified overview of a UMA architecture.

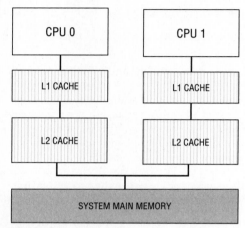

Figure 2-3

Notice in Figure 2-3 that the processors share a single memory. Each of the access times for each processor is symmetric with the other. The processor configuration in Figure 2-3 is often called a symmetric (shared-memory) multiprocessor (SMP). This arises from the fact that all processors have a uniform latency from memory even if the memory is organized into multiple banks [Hennessy, Patterson, 2007]. The single main memory and the uniform access time in the SMP makes it easier to implement than it NUMA counterpart. Also the notion of a shared address space is more straightforward in the UMA architecture because there is only one main system memory to consider.

In contrast, Figure 2-4 shows a simplified overview of a NUMA architecture.

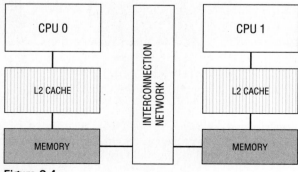

Figure 2-4

The NUMA is a distributed shared memory (DSM) architecture. Notice in Figure 2-4 that each processor has its own block memory, but each block of memory shares a single address space. That is, the same physical address on two processors refers to the same location in memory [Hennessy, Patterson, 2007]. In both cases, the UMA and the NUMA configurations, the processors share address space. However, in the NUMA architecture the address space is shared from a logical viewpoint, and in the UMA configuration the processors physically share the same block of memory. The SMP architecture is satisfactory for smaller configurations, but once the number of processors starts to increase, the single memory controller can become a bottleneck and, therefore, degrade overall system performance. The NUMA architecture, on the other hand, scales nicely because each processor has its own memory controller.

If you look at the configuration in Figure 2-4 as a simplified Opteron configuration, then the network interconnection is accomplished by the Opteron HyperTransport technology. Using the HyperTransport technology, the CPUs are directly connected to each other and the I/O is directly connected to the CPU. This ultimately gives you a performance gain over the SMP configuration.

Cache and the Multiprocessor Opteron

The dual core Opteron supports two levels of cache. L1 cache can be logically divided between I-Cache (for instructions) and D-Cache (for data). Each core has its own L1 cache. Each core in the Opteron also has its own 1MB L2 cache between the processor and main system memory.

The Sun UltraSparc T1 Multiprocessor

The UltraSparc T1 is an eight-core CMP and has support for chip-level multithreading (CMT). Each core is capable of running four threads. This is also sometimes referred to as hyperthreaded. The CMT of the UltraSparc T1 means that the T1 can handle up to 32 hardware threads. What does this mean for the software developer? Eight cores with four threads presents itself to an application as 32 logical processors. Listing 2-1 contains code that can be used to see how many processors are apparently available to the operating system (without special compilers and so on).

Listing 2-1

```cpp
// Listing 2-1
// uses sysconf() function to determine how many
// processors are available to the OS.

using namespace std;
#include <unistd.h>
#include <iostream>

int main(int argc,char *argv[])
{
    cout < < sysconf(_SC_NPROCESSORS_CONF) < < endl;
    return(0);
}
```

When appropriate, in this book listings are accompanied by a program profile stating the environment platform for the program. Anyone wishing to run code for a noncompliant OS needs to use the POSIX-compliant features for that OS.

Program Profile 2-1

Program Name:

program2-1.cc

Description:

This program uses `sysconf()` function to determine how many processors are available to the operating system.

Libraries Required:

None

Headers Required:

<unistd.h> <iostream>

Compile and Link Instructions:

g++ -o program2-1 program2-1.cc

Test Environment:

SuSE Linux 10, gcc 3.4.3

Hardware:

AMD Opteron Core 2, UltraSparc T1, CBE

Execution Instructions:

./program2-1

Notes:

None

When this program is executed on a T1, it prints 32. The `sysconf()` function provides a method for an application to get values for system limits or variables. In this case the _SC_NPROCESSORS_CONF argument asks for the number of processors configured. The _SC NPROCESSORS_MAX argument can be used to get the maximum number of processors supported. The UltraSparc T1 offers the most on-chip threads of the architectures that we discuss in the book. Each of the eight cores equates to a 64-bit execution pipeline capable of running four threads. Figure 2-5 contains a functional overview of an UltraSparc T1 multiprocessor.

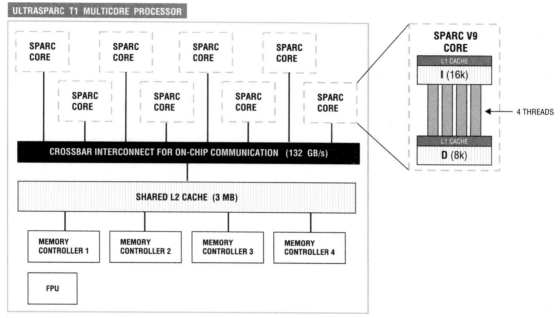

Figure 2-5

UltraSparc T1 Cores

The T1 consists of eight Sparc V9 cores. The V9 cores are 64-bit technology. Each core has L1 cache. Notice in Figure 2-5 that there is a 16K L1 instruction cache and an 8K L1 data cache. The eight cores all share a single floating-point unit (FPU). Figure 2-5 shows the access path of the L2 cache and the eight cores. The four threads share L2 cache. Each core has a six-stage pipeline:

- ❏ Fetch
- ❏ Thread selection
- ❏ Decode
- ❏ Execute
- ❏ Memory access
- ❏ Write back

Cross Talk and The Crossbar

Notice in Figure 2-5 that the cores and the L2 cache are connected through the cross-switch or crossbar. The crossbar has 132 GB/s bandwidth for on chip communications. The crossbar has been optimized for L2 cache-to-core communication and for core-to-L2 cache communication. The FPU, the four banks of L2 cache, the I/O bridges, and the cores all communicate through the crossbar. Basically the crossbar acts as the mediator, allowing the components of the T1 to communicate to each other.

DDRAM Controller and L2 Cache

The UltraSparc T1 has four separate memory controllers. Each controller is connected to one bank of L2 cache. The L2 cache is divided on the T1 into four banks. The T1 can support up to 128GB of RAM.

UltraSparc T1 and the Sun and GNU gcc Compilers

We introduce the architecture of the UltraSparc T1 to contrast it with that of the AMD Opteron, IBM Cell Broadband architecture, and the Intel Core 2 Duo. While each of these architectures is multicore, the different implementations are dramatic. From the highest level, an application designed to take advantage of multicore will see them all as a collection of two or more processors. However, from an optimization point of view, there is much more to take into consideration. Two of the most commonly used compilers for the UltraSparc T1 are the Sun C/C++ compiler (part of Sun Studio) and the GNU gcc, the standard open source C/C++ compiler. While Sun's compilers obviously have the best support for their processors, GNU gcc has a great deal of support for T1, with options that take advantage of threads, loop unrolling, vector operations, branch prediction, and Sparc-specific platform options. Virtually all of the program examples in this book have been compiled and executed on a SunFire 2000 with an eight-core T1 processor. Look at the program profiles for the program listings, and you will see which compiler switches we explored for the T1.

The IBM Cell Broadband Engine

The CBE is a heterogeneous multicore chip. It is a heterogeneous architecture because it consists of two different types of processors: PowerPC Processing Element (PPE) and Synergistic Processor Element (SPE). The CBE has one PPE and eight SPEs, one high-speed memory controller, one high-bandwidth element interconnect bus, high-speed memory, and I/O interfaces all integrated on-chip. This makes it a kind of hybird nine-core processor. Figure 2-6 shows an overview of the CBE processor.

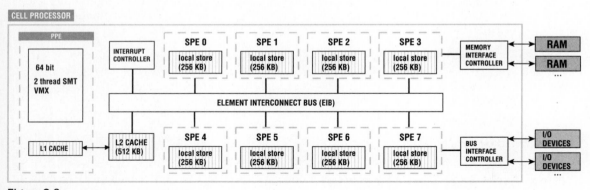

Figure 2-6

Most of the common CMPs have homogeneous processors, that is, ones with the same instruction set. The processors on the CBE have two different instruction sets. Although each of the processor elements has been optimized for certain types of operations, both types of elements can be used for general-purpose computing.

❏   The first element in the Cell processor is a 64-bit PowerPC processor. This element complies fully with the 64-bit PowerPC architecture and can execute either 32-bit or 64-bit operating systems and applications.

❏   The second type of processor element is the SPE. The SPEs have been optimized for running Single Instruction Multiple Data (SIMD) applications.

Although there are several commercial scientific uses of the CBE, its most common use is as the processor for Sony's Playstation 3.

CBE and Linux

We selected the CBE as one of our four effective multicore architecture designs because it is able to deliver so much performance in a Linux environment. The Playstation 3 is a flexible device and comes with ready-to-install Linux. Currently, there is a Fedora and a Yellow Dog distribution of Linux for the CBE. The low cost of the Playstation 3 (PS3) brings heterogeneous multicore application development into reach of virtually any software developer. The PPE element and the SPEs can be programmed using the standard GNU gcc compiler. There is a CBE SDK available for downloading from IBM that includes tools necessary to compile the SPE code. Basically, the SPE code is compiled separately and then linked with the PPE code to form a single execution unit. The PPE and SPEs act cooperatively, with both bringing specialties to the table. Typically, the SPEs use the PPE to run the operating system code and in most applications the main or top-level thread. The PPE (the general purpose processor) uses the SPEs as the application's high-performance workhorse. The SPEs have good support for SIMD operations, computer-intensive applications, and vector type operations. When you execute the code from Listing 2-1 on the CBE, the number printed to the console is 2. This is because the SPEs are directly accessible. The 2 represents the fact that the PPE is a CMT; it is a dual thread processor. So in the right configuration, you can have multiple logical processors (including the SPEs) available in a CBE configuration. The heterogeneous architecture also makes for some interesting design choices.

While standard POSIX threads (pthreads) and process management can be used with the PPE element, the SPE has to be programmed using the thread library that's available as part of the CBE SDK. The good news is the SPE thread calls are designed to be compatible with pthreads and require no learning curve for developers who are familiar with the pthread library.

CBE Memory Models

The PPE accesses memory differently than the SPEs. Although there is only a single memory flow controller, the CBE avoids the normal single bus bottleneck potentials because the SPEs each have their own local memory. Figure 2-7 shows the memory configurations for the PPE and the SPE.

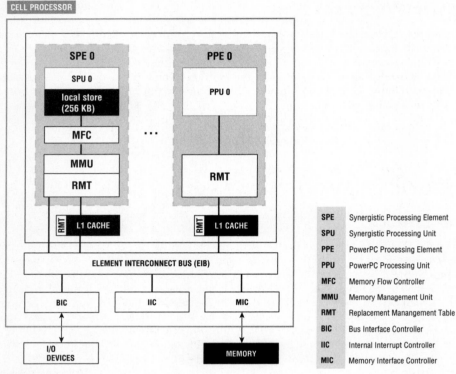

CELL PROCESSOR

SPE	Synergistic Processing Element
SPU	Synergistic Processing Unit
PPE	PowerPC Processing Element
PPU	PowerPC Processing Unit
MFC	Memory Flow Controller
MMU	Memory Management Unit
RMT	Replacement Manangement Table
BIC	Bus Interface Controller
IIC	Internal Interrupt Controller
MIC	Memory Interface Controller

Figure 2-7

The SPE configuration is where most of the savings come in. The SPE has a three-level memory access. It uses its local store, register files, and direct memory access (DMA) transfers to main memory. This three-tier memory architecture allows programmers to schedule simultaneous data and code transfers. The CBE processor can support up to 128 simultaneous transfers between the SPE local stores and main storage. Although the SPE is optimized for SIMD type operations, the PPE has support for parallel vector/SIMD operations as well.

Hidden from the Operating System

The CBE is a good example of a multicore that must be directly addressed to get the maximum performance from it. The standard Linux system calls can see the dual threads of the PPE but are not fully aware of the SPEs. The developer must explicitly develop and compile code that works with the SPEs, and then that code must be linked with the code from the PPE. At that point Linux knows how to handle the eight SPE processors. The heterogeneous architecture of the CBE also provides exciting design choices for the developer who is willing to dig a little deeper into the possibilities.

Synergistic Processor Unit

An SPE comprises a synergistic processor unit (SPU) designed to accelerate a wide range of workloads, providing an efficient data-parallel architecture, and the synergistic memory flow controller (MFC), providing coherent data transfers to and from system memory [Gschwind, Erb, Manning, and Nutter, 2007]. The SPU does not access main memory directly but rather must issue DMA commands to the MFC. The communication between the SPU and the PPU is through the interconnect bus (EIB). Since each SPE has its own memory management unit (MMU), this means that it can execute independently from the PPE. But that independence has limits. The SPUs are primarily optimized for data manipulation and calculation.

Intel Core 2 Duo Processor

Intel's Core 2 Duo is only one of Intel's series of multicore processors. Some have dual cores and others have quad cores. Some multicore processors are enhanced with hyperthreading, giving each core two logical processors. The first of Intel's multicore processors was the Intel Pentium Extreme Edition introduced in 2005. It had dual cores and supported hyperthreading, giving the system eight logical cores. The Core Duo multicore processor was introduced in 2006 and offered not only multiple cores but also multiple cores with a lower power consumption. Core 2 Duo, also introduced in 2006, has dual cores; it has no hyperthreading but supports a 64 bit architecture.

Figure 2-8 shows a block diagram of Intel's Core 2 Duo's motherboard. The Core 2 Duo processor has two 64-bit cores and 2 64K level 1 caches, one for each core. Level 2 cache is shared between cores. Level 2 cache can be up to 4MB. Either core can utilize up to 100 percent of the available L2 cache. This means that when the other core is underutilized and is, therefore, not requiring much L2 cache, the more active core can increase its usage of L2.

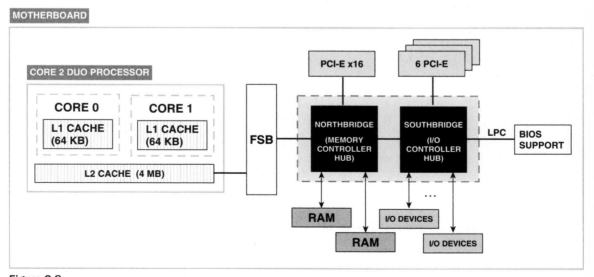

Figure 2-8

Northbridge and Southbridge

Besides the CPUs, the next most important component of the motherboard is the chipset. The *chipset*, shown in Figure 2-8, is a group of integrated circuits designed to work together that connects the CPUs to the rest of the components on the motherboard. It is an integrated part of the motherboard and, therefore, cannot be removed or upgraded. It is manufactured to work with a specific class or series of CPUs in order to optimize its performance and the performance of the system in general. The chipset moves data back and forth from CPU to the various components of the motherboard, including memory, graphics card, and I/O devices, as diagrammed in Figure 2-8. All communication to the CPU is routed through the chipset.

The chipset comprises two chips: Northbridge and Southbridge. These names were adopted because of the locations of the chips on the motherboard and the purposes they serve. The Northbridge is located in the northern region, north of many the components on the motherboard, and the Southbridge is located in the southern region, south of some components on the motherboard. Both serve as bridges or connections between devices; they bridge components to make sure that data goes where it is supposed to go.

❑   The **Northbridge**, also called the **memory controller hub**, communicates directly with the CPU via the Front Side Bus. It connects the CPUs with high-speed devices such as main memory. It also connects the CPUs with Peripheral Component Interconnect Express (PCI-E) slots and the Southbridge via an internal bus. Data is routed through the Northbridge first before it reaches the Southbridge.

❑   The **Southbridge**, also called the **I/O controller**, is a slower than the Northbridge. Because it is not directly connected to the CPUs, it is responsible for the slower capabilities of the motherboard like the I/O devices such as audio, disk interfaces, and so on. The Southbridge is connected to BIOS support via the Serial Peripheral Interface (SPI), six PCI-E slots, and other I/O devices not shown on the diagram. SPI enables the exchange of data (1 bit at a time) between the Southbridge and the BIOS support using a master-slave configuration. It also operates with a full duplex, meaning that data can be transferred in both directions.

Intel's PCI Express

PCI-E or PCI Express is a computer expansion card interface. The slot serves as a serial connection for sound, video, and network cards on the motherboard. Serial connections can be slow, sending data 1 bit at a time. The PCI-E is a high-speed serial connection, which works more like a network than a bus. It uses a switch that controls many point-to-point full-duplex (simultaneous communication in both directions) serial connections called lanes. There can be 4, 8, of 16 lanes per slot. Each lane has two pairs of wires from the switch to the device — one pair sends data, and the other pair receives data. This determines the transfer rate of the data. These lanes fan out from the switch directly to the devices where the data is to go. The PCI-E is a replacement of the PCI and provides more bandwidth. Devices do not share bandwidth. The Accelerated Graphics Port (AGP) is replaced with a PCI-E x16 (16 lanes) slot that accommodates more data transferred per second (8 GB/s).

Core 2 Duo's Instruction Set

The Core 2 Duo has increased performance of its processor by supporting Streaming SIMD Extensions (SSE) and special registers to perform vectorizable instructions. SSE3 provides a set of 13 instructions that are used to perform SIMD operations on packed integers and floating-point data elements. This speeds up applications that utilize SIMD operations such as highly intensive graphics, encryption, and mathematical applications. The processor has 16 registers used to execute SIMD instructions: 8 MMX and 8 XMM registers. The MMX registers support SIMD operations on 64-bit packed byte, word, and doubleword integers. The XMM data registers and the MXCSR registers support execution of SIMD operations on 128-bit packed single-precision and double-precision floating-point values and 128-bit packed byte, word, doubleword, and quadword integers. Table 2-3 gives a brief description of the three registers, XMM, MMX, MXCSR, involved in executing SIMD operations.

Table 2-3

Register Set	Description
MMX	Set of eight registers used to perform operations on 64-bit packed integer data types
XMM	Set of eight registers used to perform operations on 128-bit packed single- and double-precision floating-point numbers
MXCSR	Register used with XMM registers for state management instructions

There are many compiler switches that can be used to activate various capabilities of the multicore processors. For the Intel C\C++ compiler, there are compiler switches that activate vectorization options to utilize the SIMD instructions, auto parallelization options, loop unrolling, and code generation optimized for a particular processor.

You might recall that Chapter 1, Table 1-1 lists the categories of compiler switches that interface with the CPU and instruction set that affect how your program or application performs and utilizes core resources.

Summary

Although one of the primary jobs of the operating system is to encapsulate the details of the hardware and provide a hardware-independent interface, certain types of developers need to be aware of hardware specifics. These include library developers, compiler designers, system programmers, kernel programmers, server developers, game designers and developers, and others who have maximum system performance as a primary design goal. Four effective yet different designs for multicore architectures are the

- ❑ Opteron
- ❑ UltraSparc T1
- ❑ Cell Broadband Engine
- ❑ Core 2 Duo

As we have shown, each of these designs has unique features that you as a developer can leverage when you consider programming from a multicore perspective. The C/C++ compiler is the first-level interface to these designs. Homogeneous CMP designs have identical cores. Heterogeneous designs have cores with different instruction sets and architectures. The CBE is a good example of a heterogeneous CMP.

Chapter 2: Four Effective Multicore Designs

This chapter has now introduced the four architectures that we shall reference throughout this book. All of the code examples have been compiled and tested in one or more of these architectures. Most of the examples have been compiled and tested in all these environments. The program profiles for the program listings contain specific compiler switches and linking options when required. Although each of these architectures is different, we demonstrate methods for dealing with them all in a standard fashion. We want you to be able to take advantage of hardware specifics in the most general way if it's possible. For many software applications, the differences between hardware implementations are hidden because one of the primary design goals is to make the software compatible with as many different hardware platforms as possible. So there is an effort to avoid platform-specific features, as that is one of the primary jobs of the operating system. But with some applications you need to know the specifics of the hardware implementation so that you can optimize the code. Optimization for these applications becomes more important than compatibility. These applications include high-transaction database servers, web servers, application servers, hardware-intensive game engines, compilers, operating system kernels, device drivers, and high-performance scientific modeling and visualization software. Developers of these applications are practically forced to look for and exploit platform features that make their applications acceptable to the end user. So if you are this class of developer, familiarity with a specific processor or family of processors is a prerequisite for effective software development.

In Chapter 3 we turn to the challenges of multicore programming.

The Challenges of Multicore Programming

3

Assume we're facing multiple enemies and disperse the sets . . . Split up into four groups and activate the threshold triggers!

— **Shirow Masamune**, *Ghost in the Shell*

Until recently, the most accessible tools and techniques used for software development were centered on notions from the sequential model of computer program execution. The basic (and often unstated) assumption in Information Technology (IT) and Computer Science programs at universities, colleges, and technical schools was that the software developer would be working in the context of single processor computers. This is evidenced by the fact that until recently educational institutions placed very little emphasis on the ideas of parallel programming. Two of the primary reasons for the lack of focus on parallel programming were cost and tradition.

❑   **Cost**: First, single processor computers were considerably cheaper and enjoyed a much wider availability than multiple-processor computers. Cost and availability made single processor computers the configuration of choice for most businesses, academic institutions, and government agencies.

❑   **Tradition**: Second, the fundamental ideas behind software development and computer programming were worked out decades ago within the constraints of single processor environments. Basic algorithms for searching, sorting, counting, parsing, and retrieving were developed, refined, and perfected under a sequential programming model. These same basic algorithms, data structures, programming models, and software engineering methodologies form the basis of most software development approaches in use today.

Sequential programming techniques are important and will always have their place. However, multiprocessor computer configurations are now widely available. This opens up a host of very different approaches to program decomposition and software organization. Software architectures that include a mix of sequential programming, multiprocessing, and multithreading will become common place. For the majority of developers these hybrid software architectures will be uncharted waters. The trend is that multiprocessor computers will in most cases replace single processor configurations in business, academia, and government. To take advantage of the multiprocessor environments, you as a software developer must add a new set of tools and techniques to your repertoire. Software projects that require multicore or parallel programming present unique challenges to software developers who are only accustomed to the sequential programming model, and this chapter addresses the challenges that developers face as they move into projects requiring multicore or parallel programming. We discuss the Software Development Life Cycle (SDLC) and methodologies as they apply to the concurrency model. Also, we discuss decomposing a problem as well as a solution, and procedural and declarative models.

What Is the Sequential Model?

In the basic *sequential* model of programming, a computer program's instructions are executed one at a time. The program is viewed as a recipe, and each step is to be performed by the computer in the order and amount specified. The designer of the program breaks up the software into a collection of tasks. Each task is performed in a specified order, and each task stands in line and must wait its turn. In the sequential model computer programs are set up in almost story form. The programs have a clear beginning, middle, and end. The designer or developer envisions each program as a simple linear progression of tasks. Not only must the tasks march in single file, but the tasks are related in such a way that if the first task cannot complete its work for some reason, then the second task may never start. Each task is made to wait on the result of previous task's work before it can execute. In the sequential model, tasks are often serially interdependent. This means that A needs something from B, and B needs something from C, and C needs something from D and so on. If B fails for some reason, then C and D will never execute. In a sequential world, the developer is accustomed to designing the software to perform step 1 first, then step 2, and then step 3. This "one -at-time" model is so entrenched in the software design and development process that many programmers find it hard to see things any other way. The solution to every problem, the design of every algorithm, the layout of every data structure — all rely on the computer accessing each instruction or piece of data one at a time.

This all changes when the software requirements include multithreading or multiprocessing components. When parallel processing is called for, virtually every aspect of the software design and implementation is affected. The developer is faced with what we call the 10 challenges of concurrency:

1. Software decomposition into instructions or sets of tasks that need to execute simultaneously

2. Communication between two or more tasks that are executing in parallel

3. Concurrently accessing or updating data by two or more instructions or tasks

4. Identifying the relationships between concurrently executing pieces of tasks

5. Controlling resource contention when there is a many-to-one ratio between tasks and resource

6. Determining an optimum or acceptable number of units that need to execute in parallel

7. Creating a test environment that simulates the parallel processing requirements and conditions

8. Recreating a software exception or error in order to remove a software defect

9. Documenting and communicating a software design that contains multiprocessing and multithreading

10. Implementing the operating system and compiler interface for components involved in multiprocessing and multithreading

What Is Concurrency?

Two events are said to be *concurrent* if they occur within the same time interval. Two or more tasks executing over the same time interval are said to *execute concurrently*. For our purposes, concurrent doesn't necessarily mean at the same exact instant. For example two tasks may execute concurrently within the same second but with each task executing within different fractions of the second. The first task may execute for the first tenth of the second and pause. The second task may execute for the next tenth of the second and pause. The first task may start again executing in the third tenth of a second and so on. Each task may alternate executing. However, the length of a second is so short that it appears that both tasks are executing simultaneously.

We may extend this notion to longer time intervals. Two programs performing some task within the same hour continuously make progress on the task during that hour. They may or may not be executing at the same exact instant. We say that the two programs are executing concurrently for that hour. Tasks that exist at the same time and perform in the same time period are concurrent. They may or may not perform at the same exact instant. Concurrent tasks can execute in a single- or multiprocessing environment. In a single-processing environment, concurrent tasks exist at the same time and execute within the same time period by context switching. In a multiprocessor environment, if enough processors are free, concurrent tasks may execute at the same instant over the same time period. The determining factor for what makes an acceptable time period for concurrency is relative to the application. In this book, we will deal with the challenges of concurrency in terms of three categories:

- ❑ Software development
- ❑ Software deployment
- ❑ Software maintenance

While there are many other ways to think about and group the issues related to multiprocessing and parallel programming, we chose these categories because in our experience most of the heavy lifting involved in multicore programming falls into at least one of these categories.

In this chapter, we primarily discuss software development. In Chapter 10, we discuss maintenance and deployment.

Software Development

The software development effort comes in all shapes and sizes, from device driver development to the construction of large-scale *N* tier enterprise applications. Although the software development techniques involved vary with the size and scope of the application, there is a set of challenges that any application that uses multiprocessing, or multithreading, have in common. These challenges present themselves in every phase of the SDLC. It is important for you to understand the connection between multicore programming and the SDLC well. This is because the easiest way to deal with the complexity, demands, and potential pitfalls of multicore programming is to tackle the issues during the appropriate stage in the SDLC. The SDLC describes the necessary activities that designers and developers perform in the process of producing high-quality software. Since the act of creating good software is part art, part engineering, and part science, there are competing theories for exactly what makes up the SDLC. Table 3-1 lists the major activities that are found in most versions of the SDLC.

Table 3-1

Major SDLC Activities	Description
Specifications	Documents the agreement between the developer and the client by specifying what the software must do and the constraints of the software.
Design	Specifies how the software will fulfill what has been stated in the specifications. The design determines the internal structure of the software. The design can be broken down into two approaches: architectural design (system broken down into modules) and detailed design (description of the modules).
Implementation	The translation of the detailed design into code.
Testing and evaluation	The process of exercising the software in order to judge its quality by determining how well the software has met the fulfillment of the specified requirement.
Maintenance	The modification of a software product after delivery in order to correct faults, improve performance, improve attributes, or adapt the software to a changed environment.

There are many ways to think about and organize the activities in Table 3-1. Further, the activities listed in Table 3-1 are just the core activities that most versions of the SDLC have in common. Each approach to organizing the activities in the SDLC has spawned its own software development methodology. Once a software development methodology has been established, tool sets, languages, and software libraries are created to support that methodology. For example the object-oriented software revolution spawned the notions of:

- ❏ Object-Oriented Software Engineering (OOSE)
- ❏ Object-Oriented Analysis (OOA)
- ❏ Object-Oriented Design (OOD)
- ❏ Object-Oriented Programming (OOP)
- ❏ Object-Oriented Database Management Systems (OODBMS), and so on

These software development methodologies have dedicated languages such as Eiffel, Smalltalk, C++, Objective C, Java, Python, and CLOS. From these languages and methodologies have sprung libraries and tools, such as the Standard Template Library (STL), Unified Modeling Language (UML), Common Object Request Broker Architecture (CORBA), Rational Rose, Together, and Eclipse. These languages, libraries, and tools sets are very different from those used in logic programming or software development using structured programming techniques. Table 3-2 lists some commonly used software development methodologies.

Table 3-2

Software Development Methodologies	Description	Activities/Phases
Agile	Software is developed in short time intervals. Each interval or iteration is a miniature development project that delivers some part of the functionality of the software.	• Planning • Requirement analysis • Design • Coding • Testing • Documentation
Build and fix	Software is developed and built and then reworked as many times as necessary until the client is satisfied with the product.	• Build first version • Modify until client is satisfied • Maintenance phase • Retirement
Extreme programming	Model based on the incremental model; the developer informs the client how long it will take to implement and the cost of each feature, and the client selects which features are to be included in each successive build.	• Specifications • Design • Implementation/ integration • Delivery
Incremental	The software is built in increments or steps; the software is designed, implemented, and integrated module by module. For each build the modules are assembled to fulfill a specified functionality.	• Requirements • Specification • Architectural design • Build loop • Maintenance • Retirement
Object-oriented	Software development based on the identification of the objects in the system; a bottom-up approach.	• Requirements • OO analysis • OO design • Implementation/ integration • Operations mode • Maintenance

Table continued on following page

Software Development Methodologies	Description	Activities/Phases
Rapid prototyping	With the model a prototype is created of the system. After that the SDLC continues based on the acceptance of the prototype. At each phase, there is interaction with the client to either test or verify the progression of the product.	• Rapid prototype • Specification • Design • Implementation • Integration • Maintenance • Retirement
Spiral	The spiral model is similar to the incremental model with an emphasis on risk analysis and verification in each phase. Each pass through these phases occurs iteratively (called spirals).	• Planning • Risk analysis • Evaluation • Engineering
Structured	A top-down approach to software development in which the system is iteratively decomposed by functionality, starting from the highest levels of abstractions into its lowest functionality.	• Requirements • Design • Implementation • Testing • Deployment
Waterfall	Most common and classic of the models. Also called the linear-sequential model. With this model, each phase must be completed in its entirety before moving to the next phase.	• Requirements • Specifications • Design • Implementation • Integration • Maintenance • Retirement

Selecting a software development methodology is a challenge in itself, and once a methodology is selected, the possible tool sets and techniques come along by default. The choice of methodology has critical implications for how multiprocessing and multithreading are implemented in a piece of software. The developer who has multicore programming requirements needs to proceed with caution when selecting a particular approach because the tool sets and techniques of that methodology might restrict the developer to awkward and error prone implementations of multiprocessing or multithreading. Software approaches that are procedure driven handle multithreading and multiprocessing very differently from methodologies that are object or data driven. Object-Oriented Programming approaches present a very different set of options to the developer than what is available in logic programming. It is also the case that once the software development effort has begun and human resources and tools are in place, it is difficult to change paradigms in midstream or after the software has been deployed. In some software development efforts, tools sets, languages, and libraries are selected even before software requirements or specifications are understood. This is unfortunate because this often leads to a software implementation that is forced into the selected languages and tool sets whether it fits or not. Again, understanding the relationship between the various activities in the SDLC and multicore programming is important, and we emphasize this relationship throughout this book.

Although there can be (and are!) disagreements about which is the best direction to take, there are basic activities that are common to all of the approaches. These activities are present in one form or another in every software development effort regardless of size. For example, every approach has some process for getting the requirements and specifications for a project. Every approach has activities centered on designing a solution prior to actually coding the finished product. Another example of a basic activity is the testing of software prior to its release. These type of common activities may occur in different places and amounts among the various software development methods, but they are present in each. If you deal with the 10 challenges of concurrency during the appropriate activities in the SDLC, the chances of producing correct and reliable programs are greatly increased. If the software you have to develop requires some kind of concurrency, then some portion of every activity in Table 3-1 is affected. We focus on the SDLC here because we advocate a software engineering approach to multicore application development as opposed to some trial and error, ad hoc plug-in methods that are being used to get "multicore-aware" applications to market quickly. While there are ways to hide and abstract away some complexity of parallel programming and multithreading, there are no real shortcuts. The deployment of robust, correct, and scalable software applications that can take advantage of Chip Multiprocessors (CMPs) requires sound software engineering and an effective solid understanding of the SDLC.

Determining when, where, and how to incorporate multiprocessing and multithreading into the software development effort is the major theme of this book — which brings us to two of the primary questions that we will answer:

1. How do you know when your software application needs multicore programming?

2. How do you know where to put the multicore programming in your piece of software?

These questions are related to the first challenge in our list of 10 challenges presented earlier in this chapter. Both questions are central to the challenge of software decomposition.

Challenge #1: Software Decomposition

The need or opportunity for multithreading or multiprocessing is most often discovered during the decomposition activity. For our purposes, *decomposition* is the process of breaking down a problem or solution into its fundamental parts. Sometimes the parts are grouped into logical areas (that is, searching sorting, calculating, input, output, and so on). In other situations, the parts are grouped by logical resource (processor, database, communication, and so on). The decomposition of the software solution amounts to the Work Breakdown Structure (WBS) or its Architectural Artifacts (AAs).

❑   The WBS determines which piece of software does what.

❑   The AA determines what concepts or things a software solution is divided into.

The WBS typically reflects a procedural decomposition, whereas the AA represents an object-oriented decomposition. Unfortunately, there is no cookbook approach to identifying the WBS or the AA of a software solution.

> *We can say that model-driven decomposition is one of the most practical approaches, and we will have much to say about models throughout this book.*

You cannot talk about where to use threads or whether to use simultaneously executing processes in the software solution until you have decomposed both the problem and the solution. Problem and solution decompositions are typically performed during the analysis and design activities in the SDLC.

A successful decomposition is one of the primary ingredients of a successful software development effort. On the other hand, a poor or inappropriate problem and solution breakdown almost certainly leads to failed software.

An Example of Decomposition

To show you what we mean by decomposition, we take as a simple example the problem of painting the house before the guests arrive for the holidays. Of course, we will take this opportunity to use the latest craze — software-automated painters. Take a look at how you might decompose the problem of painting the house, as well as the solution.

Decomposition #1

The **problem** could be broken down into:

❑ Deciding paint color and type

❑ Acquiring paint and painters tools

❑ Determining which rooms to paint first

❑ Identifying which type of automated painter to use

❑ Choosing which days of the week to paint

❑ Figuring out when to start painting

This is one decomposition of the problem of painting the house.

A decomposition of the **solution** might look like this:

❑ Select and purchase the paint that matches the furniture.

❑ Use the neighbor's software-automated painter.

❑ Have the automated painter start at the front of the house and work to the back.

❑ Only paint during the hours of 6:00 A.M. to 1:00 P.M. on weekdays.

❑ Start the painting on the next available weekday.

You can quickly see part of the challenge of decomposition. The first thing you might notice is that there is typically more than one way to decompose the problem. As you look at the problem and solution breakdown, you may have had a very different set of steps in mind. In fact you could have chosen an entirely different approach to the problem of painting the house before the guests arrive for the holidays:

Decomposition #2

Consider the following alternate **problem** decomposition:

❑ Identifying rooms that would be better off with wallpaper

❑ Finding walls where windows could be added to reduce wall surface area

❑ Verifying if cleaning the walls could be a substitute for paint

❑ Determining how much paint the neighbors have to donate

- ❑ Figuring out which walls can be removed instead of painted
- ❑ Obtaining the travel plans of the guests
- ❑ Acquiring demo software-automated painters for a free 30-day trial

You might use the solution decomposition from the first approach, or you could choose an entirely different **solution** decomposition:

- ❑ Strategically use lighting to showcase the best-looking walls.
- ❑ Where lighting is not appropriate, the judicious use of mirrors is acceptable.
- ❑ Add windows to external walls.
- ❑ In the event that mirrors are inconvenient, use wallpaper.
- ❑ Use as many demo painters as can be obtained.
- ❑ Delay guests' arrival until software-automated painters are done.

The second observation you can make is that a decomposition might be incomplete or inappropriate! Ideally, the fundamental parts of a decomposition should collectively represent the initial problem or solution. It's like putting the pieces of a puzzle back together again. If the pieces don't collectively represent the whole, then the decomposition is incomplete. This means you haven't captured the entire problem, and you won't have the entire solution. In the painting the house problem, was identifying the amount or cost of the paint part of the original problem? You can't tell from the statement of the problem. So you don't know if Decomposition #1 or #2 is incomplete. On the other hand, clearly you need to paint the house before the guests arrive. The problem and solution in Decomposition #1 do not address the guests' arrival at all. So it is not clear whether the solution in Decomposition #1 will be acceptable. While Decomposition #2 does attempt to address the arrival of the guests, the problem and solution are geared toward finding ways not to paint the house at all or to paint as few walls as possible. This decomposition may be inappropriate. It might reflect a poor understanding of the intent of the initial problem.

You can also see that in the solution for Decomposition #1, a single software-automated painter is suggested, and in Decomposition #2 multiple software-automated painters were chosen. So not only does Decomposition #2 seek to minimize the number of walls to be painted, but it also attempts to do so as fast as possible. Appropriate decomposition is a primary challenge for applications based on the sequential model. It is even more of an issue where parallel processing is called for. There are software tools and libraries that can help the developer with implementing a decomposition; however, the process itself remains part of the problem solving and design activity. Until you get the problem and solution breakdown right, the application of multithreading or multiprocessing will be murky.

Earlier, we defined decomposition as the process of breaking down a problem or solution into its fundamental parts. But what are the fundamental parts of a problem or solution? The answer depends on what model you use to represent the problem and the solution. One of the challenges of software decomposition is that there are multiple ways to represent a problem and its solution. It could also be reasonably argued that *there is no one right way* to decompose a problem or a solution. So which decomposition should you choose? Another challenge is making sure that the decomposition is complete, appropriate, and correct. But how will you know if the breakdown is right? In some cases, it's not a matter of choosing between multiple and possibly conflicting WBSs; it is a matter of coming up with any decomposition at all. This might be due to the complexity of the original problem.

The decomposition issue is front and center in any software development effort. It's especially important where parallel processing tools or techniques will be deployed. But the WBS or AA chosen rely on the idea of models. Wherever decomposition takes place, there is always one or more models in the vicinity. Hiding beneath the surface of the choices in Decomposition #1 and #2 is an assumed and shared model.

Finding the Right Model

Models are the stuff decomposition is made of! Complicating the challenges of decomposition is the selection of a suitable model that appropriately represents problem, task, or solution.

What Is a Model?

Software development is the process of translating concepts, ideas, patterns of work, rules, algorithms, or formulas into sets of instructions and data that can be executed or manipulated by a computer. It is a process that relies heavily on the use of *models.* For our purposes a *model* is a scaled artificial representation of some real process, thing, concept, or idea. The scaled representation is some smaller, simpler, or easier to deal with approximation of the process, thing, concept, or idea.

The primary function of the model is to imitate, describe, or duplicate the behavior and characteristics of some real-world entity. The model is to be a stand-in containing enough information to allow analysis and decision making. The better the model represents the real-world entities, the more natural the decomposition, WBS, or Architectual Artifacts will be.

One of the challenges to multicore programming is to select the appropriate model of the problem and solution. In terms of parallel programming, multiprocessing, and multithreading, you succeed when the appropriate model is used and fail when the wrong model is selected. The question of how to break up an application into concurrently executing parts can often be answered during an analysis of the solution model or the problem model. The selected model affects what decomposition choices are available.

For example, in the house-painting problem we assumed one familiar model of a house:

❑ **Model #1**: The house as something that has walls, rooms, and support for windows. You should add to this model ceilings, doors, archways, floors, banisters, a roof, and so on.

This is probably one of the models that immediately comes to mind when you are thinking about the house-painting problem. But as was the case with decomposition, there is more than one model for a given problem or solution. You could have selected a totally different model for the house:

❑ **Model #2**: The house as a dwelling measured in square feet, having an entry and an exit, having reasonable space for a family of two or more, providing protection from the weather, offering a modicum of privacy, and having a place to rest for all inhabitants.

While Model #2 might be good for certain scenarios (for example, igloo selection), Model #1 appears to be more helpful for the house-painting problem.

What this shows is that the notion of decomposition is closely related to models. In fact, the decomposition follows the parts, processes, and structure of the model used. Specifically, the decomposition is limited by the underlying model of the problem and solution. So part of the challenge of decomposition is the challenge of model selection.

Procedural Models or Declarative Models?

Earlier in the chapter we introduced the idea of a Work Breakdown Structure (WBS) and Architectural Artifacts (AAs) of a solution. The WBS breaks a problem or solution down into the tasks that need to be performed or the work that needs to be done. On the other hand, the AA divide a problem or solution into a set of persons, places, things, or ideas. Table 3-3 shows the differences between the WBS and AA approaches.

Table 3-3

Attributes	WBS	AA
Definition	Breaks a problem or solution down into the tasks that need to be performed or the work that needs to be done	Divides a problem or solution into a set of persons, places, things, or ideas
Model used	Uses task-driven models	Uses object-oriented or relational-driven models
Decomposition model	Uses procedural models	Uses declarative models
Scalability/complexity	Does not scale well; difficulty with very complex system	Can scale well; works best with complex system

As you can see, whereas WBS decomposes the problem and solution into a set of actions, AAs break down problems and solutions into a set of things. Whereas the WBS uses task-driven models, AAs use object-oriented or relational-driven models. And most significant, whereas WBS decompositions follow from procedural models, AA follows from declarative models.

Perhaps the most important and critical decision that can be made for a software design that will include multiprocessing or parallel programming is whether to use procedural models or declarative models or some combination of the two. The fundamental differences in approach, technique, design, and implementation between procedural models and declarative models are so dramatic that they require radically different paradigms of computer programming [Saraswat, 1993]. In some cases, these paradigms are supported by very different languages. In other cases, the paradigms are supported by using familiar languages in extremely different ways. As the trend moves toward more processors on a single chip, toward single-chip massive multiprocessors (with 100s or 1000s) of processors on a chip, procedural models and their corresponding WBS will not be able to scale. They will collapse under the complexities of synchronization and communication. Declarative models and decompositions will have to be used.

The transition to declarative models is a major challenge because the procedural model and its WBS are based in the traditional sequential approach to programming discussed in the "What Is the Sequential Model?" section earlier in this chapter. The sequential model of computation currently has the most commonly used languages, tools, and techniques. Until very recently, the sequential model of computation was also the most frequently taught model in universities, colleges, trade schools, and so on. Although the declarative models have been with us for some time, they are not as widely used or taught (with the exception of OOP). Table 3-4 shows a list of declarative programming paradigms and some commonly used languages in that paradigm.

Table 3-4

Declarative Programming Paradigms	Commonly Used Languages
Object-oriented	C++ Java Eiffel SmallTalk Python
Functional	C++ Haskell Lisp ML Scheme
Concurrent constraint	C++ Prolog Prolog-based languages
Constraint	Prolog Prolog-based languages

One of the advantages that the C++ programmer has in the new world of CMPs is the fact that C++ supports multiparadigm development. That is, unlike languages like Java where everything must be an object, C++ supports object-oriented, parameterized, and imperative (procedural) programming. Because of C++'s power of expressiveness and flexibility, it can be used to implement ideas from all of the programming paradigms listed in Table 3-4. We will have much to say about declarative approaches to parallelism versus procedural approaches to parallelism throughout this book. As with most problems and solutions, the challenge is learning to use the right tool for the job.

One Room at a Time or All at Once?

Earlier in the chapter for the problem of painting the house before the guests arrive for the holidays, you saw two problem and solution WBS. Decomposition #1 chose to use a single software-automated painter, and Decomposition #2 chose to use as many software-automated painters as possible. Note that the solution in Decomposition #1 specified that the software-automated painter start at the front of the house and work to the back. However, Decomposition #2 does not mention how the multiple software-automated painters should proceed.

Does it make sense to paint the house one room at a time? Or is it best to paint as many rooms simultaneously as possible? If you do attempt to paint more than one room at a time, will you need multiple paint brushes? Will each of the software-automated painters share a brush, or a bucket, or an elevation device? How many automated painters are enough — one for each room? One for each wall? Do the automated painters need to communicate with each other? What if some are done before others, should they proceed to help any painter that is not yet finished? What if some but not all rooms can be painted simultaneously? What if the rooms that can be painted simultaneously change from day to day? How is this communicated and coordinated with the software-automated painters? What if there is so much time between the recognition that the house needs painting and guests arriving for the holidays that a single automated painter can easily get the job done satisfactorily? Do you use multiple painters anyway? So, how do you perform a declarative decomposition for the house-painting problem? These are the types of problems that you run into during problem and solution decomposition. And as you will soon see, the decomposition problems lead to other challenges.

It is one thing for a software solution or architecture to require multiprocessing or multithreading as a result of design decisions or user specifications. That's different from the case where insightful analysis of an existing piece of software or software design reveals opportunities to exploit multiprocessing where it was otherwise not required or included. In this book, we focus our attention on software solutions or architectures that require multiprocessing as result of design decisions or user specifications.

Challenge #2: Task-to-Task Communication

If you have two tasks, A and B, that are concurrently executing and one of the tasks is dependent on the other for information, then the tasks need to have some way to communicate the information. If the tasks need to share some resource (that is, file, memory, object, a device, or so on) and that resource supports only one at a time access, then the tasks need to have some way to pass on information that the resource is available or that the resource is requested. If the tasks involved are separate operating system processes, the communication between the tasks is called *Interprocess Communication (IPC)*.

Processes have separate address spaces. These separate address spaces serve to isolate processes from each other. This isolation is a useful protection mechanism, and this protection is sometimes a reason to choose multiprocessing over multithreading. The operating system keeps the resources of processes separate. This means that if you have two processes, A and B, then the data declared in process A is not visible to process B. Furthermore, the events that happen in process A are unknown by process B, and vice versa. If process A and B are working together to accomplish some task, information and events must be explicitly communicated between the two processes. The data and events for each process are local to process. In Chapter 5, we discuss the anatomy of a process in more detail, but for now we use Figure 3-1 to show the basic layout of two processes and their resources.

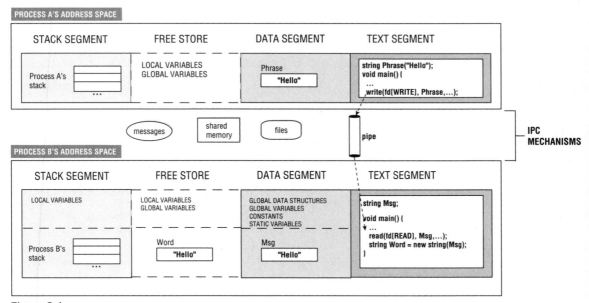

Figure 3-1

Note that in Figure 3-1 the resources of process A are isolated from the resources of process B. The processes have a text, data, and stack segment. Processes may also have other memory allocated from the free store. The data that a process owns is generally in the data segment, the stack segment, or the process's own dynamically allocated memory. This data is protected from other processes by the operating system. In order for one process to have access to another process's data, special IPC mechanisms must be used. Likewise, in order for one process to be made aware of what happens within the text segment of another process, a means of communication must be established between the processes. This also requires the assistance of operating-system-level IPCs. One of the primary challenges for the multiprocessing program is the management of IPC. The number of IPC mechanisms increases as the number of the number of processes involved in a single application increases. More processes almost always mean more IPC mechanisms and usage. In many instances, coordinating the communications among multiple processors is the real challenge.

Managing IPC Mechanisms

The POSIX specification supports six basic mechanisms used to accomplish communication between processes:

❑ Files with lock and unlock facilities

❑ Pipes (unnamed, named also called FIFOs — First-In, First-Out)

❑ Shared memory

❑ POSIX message queues

❑ Sockets

❑ Semaphores

Table 3-5 contains simple descriptions of the POSIX IPC mechanisms for processes.

Table 3-5

POSIX Interprocess Communication	Description
Command-line arguments	Can be passed to the child process during the invocation of the exec or spawn functions.
Environment variables/file descriptors	Child processes can receive a copy of the parent's environment data and file descriptors. The parent process can set the variables, and the child process can read those values. The parent process can open files and advance the location of the file pointers, and the child process can access the file using the same offset.
Files with locking facilities	Used to transfer data between two processes. Locking facilities are used to synchronize access to the file between the processes.

POSIX Interprocess Communication	Description
Pipes	A form of communication channel between related or unrelated processes. Normally accessed with file read and write facilities.
Shared memory	A block of memory accessed by processes that resides outside of their address space.
Message queues	A linked list of messages that can be shared between processes.
Semaphores	A variable used to synchronize access between threads or processes of a resource.
Sockets	A bidirectional communication link between processes that utilizes ports and IP addresses.

Each of these IPC mechanisms has strengths, weaknesses, traps, and pitfalls that the software designer and developer must manage in order to facilitate reliable and efficient communication between two or more processes. We cover these in detail in Chapter 5, but we want to mention here some of the primary challenges of using these IPC mechanisms:

❑ They must be correctly created or the application will fail.

❑ They require the proper user permissions for use.

❑ They require the proper file permissions for use.

❑ In some cases they have stringent naming conventions.

❑ They are not object-friendly (that is, they use low-level character representations).

❑ They must be properly released or they'll cause lockups and resource leaks.

❑ Source and destination processes are not easily identified in their use.

❑ Initial deployments of the software can be tricky because all environments are not compliant.

❑ Mechanisms are very sensitive to correct size of data sent and received.

❑ Wrong data type or size can cause lockups and failures.

❑ Flushing the mechanisms is not always straightforward.

❑ Some of the mechanisms are not visible use user utilities.

❑ Depending on type, the number of IPCs that a process can access may be limited.

These IPC mechanisms can be used as bridges between concurrently executing processes. Sometimes the bridge is a two-way bridge, sometimes it's not. For instance, a POSIX message queue might be created with the permission allowing processes to read messages and to write messages. Some processes might open the queue up for reading, some for writing, and some for both. The software developer has to keep track of which process opens up which queue for what. If a process opens up the queue for read-only access, then later tries to write the queue, it can cause problems. If the number of concurrently executing tasks involved is small, this can be readily managed. However, once you move beyond a dozen or so concurrently executing processes, then managing the IPC mechanisms become a challenge. This is especially true for the procedural models of decomposition mentioned earlier in the chapter. Even when the two-way or one-way traffic requirements are properly managed, you face issues of the integrity of the information transmitted between two or more processes. The message passing scheme might encounter issues such as interrupted transmissions (partial execution), garbled messages, lost messages, wrong messages, wrong recipients, wrong senders, messages that are too long, messages that are too short, late messages, early messages, and so on.

It is important to note that these particular communication challenges are unique to processes and don't apply to threads. This is because each process has its own address space and the IPC mechanisms are used as a communication bridge between processes. Threads, on the other hand, share the same address space. Simultaneously executing threads share the same data, stack and text segments. Figure 3-2 shows a simple overview of the anatomy of a thread in comparison to that of a process.

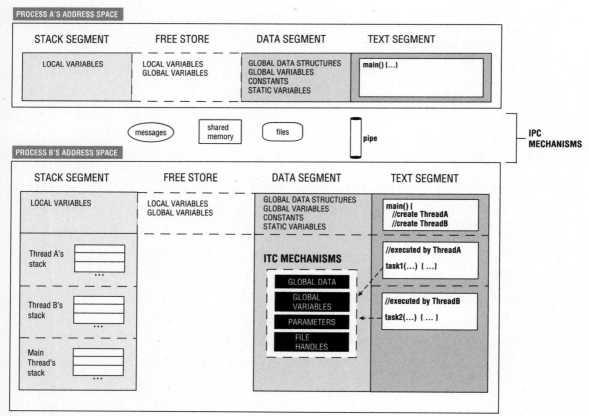

Figure 3-2

Communication between two or more threads (sometimes called lightweight processes) is easier because threads don't have to worry about address space boundaries. This means that each thread in the program can easily pass parameters, get return values from functions, and access global data. As you see in Figure 3-2, threads of the same process access the global variables of its process stored in the data segment. Here we highlight the basic difference between Interprocess Communication (IPC) and Interthread Communication (ITC) mechanisms: IPC mechanisms reside outside the address space of processes, whereas ITC mechanisms reside within the address space of a process. That's not to say that threads don't have their own challenges; it's just that they are immune from the problems of having to cross address spaces.

How Will the Painters Communicate?

Earlier in the chapter, in the example problem of painting the house before the guests arrive for the holidays, Decomposition #2 used as many software-automated painters as possible in its approach. But if the painters are in different rooms how will they communicate with each other? Do they need to communicate with each other? What if they are sharing a single bucket — how many painters can access it simultaneously? What happens when it needs to be refilled? Do the painters wait until the bucket is filled or do other work while the bucket is being refilled? What happens when multiple painters need the elevation device at the same time? Should you add more elevation devices? How many devices are enough? How does one painter let another painter knows that an elevation device is available? These kinds of questions plague multiprocessing and multithreading efforts. If they are not dealt with during the appropriate stages in the SDLC, then an application that requires multiprocessing or multithreading is in jeopardy before it is even installed. If the communication is not appropriately designed, then deadlock, indefinite postponement, and other data race conditions can easily occur. Data race, deadlock, and indefinite postponement are among the most notorious issues that multithreading or multiprocessing face, and they are the problems at the core of Challenge #3.

Challenge #3: Concurrent Access to Data or Resources by Multiple Tasks or Agents

Three common problems appear when concurrently executing instructions, tasks, or applications have been required to share data, devices, or other resources. These problems can result in the corruption of the data, the stalling of the task, or the freezing of the agent. The three problems are:

- ❏ Data race
- ❏ Deadlock
- ❏ Indefinite postponement

Problem #1: Data Race

If two or more tasks attempt to change a shared piece of data at the same time and the final value of the data depends simply on which tasks get there first, then a race condition has occurred. When two or more tasks are attempting to update the same data resource at the same time, the race condition is called a *data race*. Information that is subject to race conditions is not reliable. This goes for input values as well as output values. The status of the paint bucket in the house-painting problem using Decomposition #2 is a candidate for data race.

Consider the following description of the update process for the paint bucket: Each painter's bucket routines include a get instruction for getting 1 or more gallons from the bucket. A read instruction for reading the status of the bucket and a write instruction for updating the status of the bucket after gallons have been removed. So a bucket process for a painter might look like this:

```
Read  Bucket Status into Total
If N is <= Total
   Get N Gallons of Paint
   Total = Total - N
   Write Total to Bucket Status
end if
```

In this process, each painter once it removes paint from the bucket records how much paint is left based on the bucket's previous paint status. Say that two of the painters, Painter A and Painter B, get to the bucket at the same time, and Painter A starts the bucket routines and removes 20 gallons of paint. Before Painter A can update the status of the bucket, Painter B removes 10 gallons of paint from the bucket and updates the status first. It's possible since Painter B's paint requirement was smaller than Painter A's that Painter B finished first and, therefore, updated the Bucket Status first. Painter B has updated the status of the paint bucket with an incorrect amount. This is because, although Painter A removed 20 gallons of paint first, the update status had not yet been stored. In addition to this, Painter B has already read the value in Bucket Status prior to Painter A's update. Further, the monitor for the software-automated painters that is responsible for filling the bucket based on the Bucket Status happens to look at the status before Painter A has updated the status but after Painter B's update. Any decisions that the monitor makes based on bucket status will be incorrect. Painter A is totally unaware of Painter B's activity and updates the Bucket Status with a value of 10 gallons. At this point as a result of Painter A's paint removal and Painter B's paint removal, the bucket is actually empty, but the Bucket Status variable reads 10. Figure 3-3 shows the data race scenario for Painter A and Painter B.

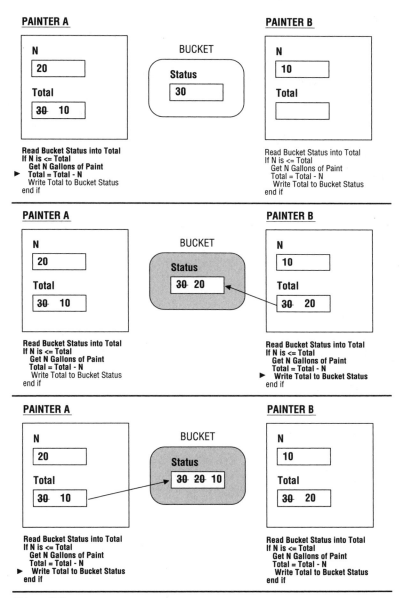

Figure 3-3

In a multithreading or multiprocessing environment, this is entirely possible because of the way that the operating system schedules threads and processes. It can all boil down to clock cycles. Since in this scenario the process of taking paint out of the bucket is separate from the process of updating the bucket status, the events can be separated by the operating system schedule. The painter that gets to the bucket status first turns out to be a matter of operating system scheduling, processor states, latency, and chance. This situation creates a race condition. Under these circumstances what will be the real status of the paint bucket?

Distinguishing shared modifiable resources from read-only resources is important. If multiple threads or processes are attempting to simultaneously access a resource that cannot be modified (that is, read-only memory or const objects), then data race is not a concern. Likewise, if multiple threads or processes are simply attempting to read a block of data simultaneously, data race does not occur. In order for a race condition to exist, the resource under consideration must be modifiable, and multiple threads or processes must be trying to simultaneously access the resource with at least one of the threads or processes attempting to modify the resource.

Whenever tasks concurrently share a modifiable resource, rules, and policies have to be applied to the task's access. For instance, for the bucket routine you may have to deploy Exclusive Read Exclusive Write (EREW) policies so that when one painter starts other painters have to wait until the entire routine is completed. Or you might have to set up a painter whose only job is to update the bucket status. If more than one painter needs the bucket at the same time, then the requests must be held and organized according to some rule and then the painters must be granted access one at a time. But if you set up the bucket status so that only one painter at a time can access it, then aren't you defeating the purpose of having multiple threads or processes? Will not the shared bucket status become a performance bottleneck? Identifying data race conditions can be tricky because the precise order in which the concurrently running processes or threads can execute is determined by what else the operating system is doing at the point. It depends on the other potentially unrelated processes or threads that are executing. Even computers with multiprocessors will be reduced to multiprogramming if the number of threads or processes that the operating system is managing is greater than the number of available processors. This means that the operating system will suspend and resume threads or processes as necessary. And, what to suspend and when to suspend it is typically up to the operating system. This introduces a degree of uncertainty when a collection of processes or threads are executing.

We will have more to say about this in Chapters 5, 6, and 7. Here, we just want to bring your attention to the fact that a data race is one of the potential pitfalls of multicore programming.

Problem #2: Deadlock

Deadlock is another waiting-type pitfall. To illustrate an example of deadlock, assume that the three painters (A, B, C) in the house-painting problem are working with two buckets (1, 2) of paint (different colors) instead of one. Painter A is responsible for updating the bucket statuses for both buckets of paint. Painter A, B, and C can perform their work concurrently. However, Painters B and C may only use one bucket of paint at a time. Painter A grants bucket status update access on a first come, first serve basis. Say that Painter B has exclusive access to Bucket 1, and Painter C has exclusive access to Bucket 2. However, Painter B needs access to Bucket 2 to complete its painting, and Painter C needs access to Bucket 1 to complete its processing. Painter B decides to hold on to Bucket 1 waiting for Painter C to release Bucket 2, and Painter C decides to hold on to Bucket 2 waiting for Painter B to release Bucket 1. Painter B and Painter C are engaged in a deadly standoff also known as a *deadlock*. Figure 3-4 shows the deadlock situation between Painter B and Painter C.

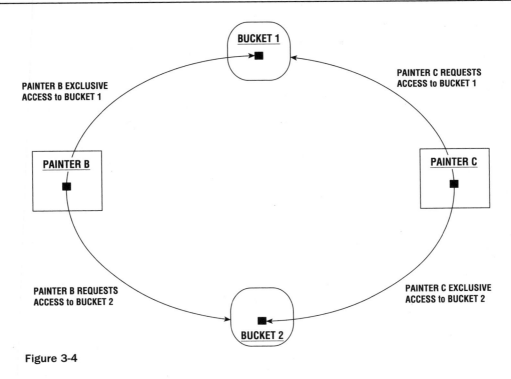

Figure 3-4

The form of deadlock shown in Figure 3-4 requires concurrently executing tasks that have access to some shared modifiable resource, which they must wait for each other to finish using before they can access. In Figure 3-4, the shared resources are Bucket 1 and Bucket 2. Both Painters have access to these buckets. It happens that instead of one Painter getting access to both buckets at the same time, by the luck of the draw each Painter got access to one of the buckets. Since Painter B can't release Bucket 1 until it gets Bucket 2, and Painter C can't release Bucket 2 until it gets Bucket 1, the software-automated painting process is locked. Notice that Painter B and C can drive another task(s) into indefinite postponement (which is discussed in more detail in the next section). For example, Painter A, who is responsible for updating the bucket status, is also waiting for Painter B or Painter C to issue a write or read request. If other tasks are waiting for access to Bucket 1 or Bucket 2 and Painter B and Painter C are engaged in a deadlock, then those tasks are waiting for a condition that will never happen.

In your attempts to coordinate concurrently executing tasks, deadlock and indefinite postponement are two of the ugliest obstacles that you must overcome. To make matters worse, it's not always clear when it has occurred. The tasks involved may be waiting for legitimate events to happen. It could also be the case that Task A is simply taking a little longer than expected. So identifying legitimate deadlocks also poses another challenge on the road to multicore programming. The steps involved in identifying deadlocks (deadlock detection), preventing deadlocks, and avoiding deadlocks are critical to applications that use multiprocessing or multithreading.

We discuss techniques for deadlock detection, prevention, and avoidance in Chapter 7.

Problem #3: Indefinite Postponement

Scheduling one or more tasks to wait until some event or condition occurs can be tricky. First, the event or condition must take place in a timely fashion. Second, it requires carefully placed communications between tasks. If one or more tasks are waiting for a piece of communication before they execute and that communication either never comes, comes too late, or is incomplete, then the tasks may never execute. Likewise, if the event or condition that you assumed would eventually happen actually never occurs, then the tasks that you have suspended will wait for ever. If one or more tasks are suspended, waiting for some condition or event that never occurs, this is known as indefinite postponement. In the software-automated painting solution, if Painter B does not release Bucket 1 until it has Bucket 2, Painter C does not release Bucket 2 until it has Bucket 1, Painter B and Painter C both do not request a `Bucket Status` update until they are finished, and Painter A waits for Painter B and C, then the work of all the involved painters is headed for *indefinite postponement*.

Data race, deadlock, and indefinite postponement are examples of synchronization problems. These types of problems take the form of competition for the same resource by two or more tasks at the same time. Resources can be software or hardware.

❑ **Software resources** include files, records within files, fields within records, shared memory, program variables, pipes, sockets, and functions.

❑ **Hardware resources** include interrupts, physical ports, and peripherals such as printers, modems, displays, storage, and multimedia devices.

Some of these resources are easily sharable such as disks or files. Other resources require that access be carefully managed as in the case of interrupts. When two or more tasks attempt to change the state of the same resource at the same time, there is the possibility of data loss, incorrect program results, system failure, and in some cases, device damage.

Challenge #4: Identifying the Relationships between Concurrently Executing Tasks

The synchronization problems of data race, deadlock, and indefinite postponement are sometimes magnified by the challenges involved in setting up the right execution relationships between threads or processes.

The Basic Synchronization Relationships

There are four basic synchronization relationships between any two threads in a single process or any two processes in a single application. Table 3-6 lists the four basic synchronization relationships and their descriptions.

Table 3-6

Synchronization Relationship	Description
Start-to-start (SS)	One task cannot start until another task starts.
Finish-to-start (FS)	One task cannot finish until another starts.
Start-to-finish (SF)	One task cannot start until another task finishes.
Finish-to-finish (FF)	One task cannot finish until another task finishes.

So, if you have two tasks, A and B:

❑ In a **start-to-start (SS)** relationship, Task A cannot start until Task B starts. Task B may start at the same time that Task A starts or after A starts, but never before Task A starts.

❑ In a **finish-to-start (FS)** relationship Task B cannot start until Task A finishes or completes a certain operation. For example, if Task B is reading from the POSIX message queue that Task A is writing to, Task A needs to write at least one element in the queue before Task B can process it. Again if Task B needs to perform a binary search on a list that Task A has to sort, Task B should be synchronized with Task A so that Task B does not start the search until Task A has finished the sort. Finish-to-start relationships normally suggest information dependencies.

❑ The **start-to-finish (SF)** synchronization relationship says that Task A cannot start until Task B finishes. This kind of relationship is common in situations where a parent process requires IPC from a child process to complete, or when a process or thread recursively calls itself after it has supplied the parent with the information or event needed.

❑ Finally, you have the **finish-to-finish (FF)** synchronization relationship, which says that Task A cannot finish until Task B finishes. Whereas Task A may finish after Task B finishes, Task A is not allowed to finish before Task B.

Figure 3-5 shows the four synchronization relationships. The SS, FS, SF, and FF synchronization relationships are present in multithreaded or multiprocessing applications. Sometimes these relationships are very subtle, and discovering all of the variations of them during the various activities in SDLC can be perplexing. Some of the relationships between tasks are obvious, while others are only implied and require careful examination. There are timing considerations in addition to the synchronization relationships.

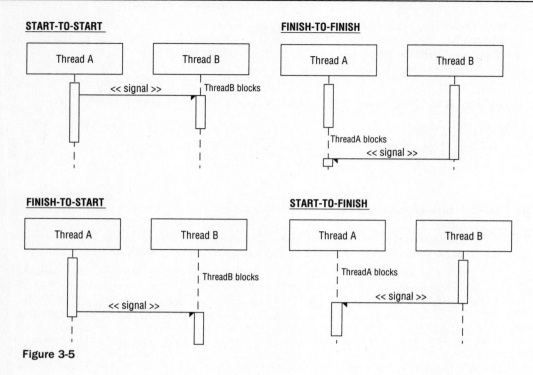

Figure 3-5

Timing Considerations

If you have more than one of the software-automated painters in the room, should the ceiling painter start first? Should the wall painters wait until the ceiling painters are finished? Should both start at the same time? Or are you happy as long as they all finish at the same time? Perhaps the wall painters should wait 15 minutes before starting. It's not just a matter having as many automated painters as possible; there has to be some kind of synchronization relationship among the painters.

Sometimes the synchronization relationships need to be augmented with timing-specific information. This means that in designing the synchronization relationship, time and events need to be considered. For example, if you have Task A and Task B executing concurrently, where Task A is performing a communication task and Task B is a monitor watching for a timeout, Task A and Task B might be synchronized with a start-to-start relationship. There is no need for Task B to begin checking for a timeout condition until Task A has started a communication task. However, once Task A starts its communication task and continues for so many milliseconds without any activity, Task B might issue a timeout message. In this case, Task B is using a *lag time* before it issues a timeout message. A lag time is used to define a synchronization relationship further. Lag times require that an element of time be added to the specification of a synchronization relationship. For instance, you might say that Task A and Task B have a start-to-start synchronization with the additional requirement that Task B has to wait 10 nanoseconds after Task A starts before starting.

These types of timing considerations are another major reason to give close attention to multiprocessing or multithreading requirements during the appropriate activities in the SDLC. Also, the implementation of the synchronization relationships and timing considerations are dramatically impacted by whether a procedural model or declarative model of decomposition is chosen.

Challenge #5: Controlling Resource Contention Between Tasks

Resource contention occurs when multiple tasks compete for the use of the same resource. This topic is covered in Chapter 7.

Challenge #6: How Many Processes or Threads Are Enough?

There is a point where the overhead in managing multiple processors outweighs the speed improvement and other advantages gained from parallelization. The old adage "you can never have enough processors" is simply not true. Communication between threads or synchronization between processors comes at a cost. The complexity of the synchronization or the amount of communication between processors can require so much computation that the performance of the tasks that are doing the work can be negatively impacted. In these cases, it's more effective to write a program based on a sequential model. For example, if you want to sort a list of 100 numbers, you could attempt to divide up the list of 100 into groups of 10, sort each group in parallel, and then merge the groups of 10 into one sorted list. But the time it would take to divide the list into groups of 10, then communicate that list to each group, and then merge the results into a single group all while trying to avoid a data race requires more effort and time than it would take to simple sort the numbers using a sequential method. On the other hand, if you have a few terabytes of numbers, the parallel approach could be more productive.

The question is how many processes, tasks, or threads should a program be divided into? Is there an optimal number of processors for any given parallel program? At what point does adding more processors or computers to the computation pool slow things down instead of speeding them up? It turns out that the numbers change depending on the program. Some scientific simulations may max out at several thousand processors, while for some business applications several hundred might be sufficient. For some client server configurations, eight processors are optimal and nine processors would cause the server to perform poorly.

The limit of software processes might be reached before you've reached the optimum number of processors or computers. Likewise, you might see diminishing returns in the hardware before you've reached the optimum number of concurrently executing tasks.

Ideally, something in the model decomposition of the problem or the model decomposition of the solution can help determine how many threads or processes are necessary. However, the actual implementation of the model can introduce so much complexity and overhead that a new model may have to be selected. Remember some of the challenges of IPC mechanisms between processes mentioned earlier in the chapter. These IPC mechanisms have to be synchronized. If the communication between two or more tasks is not properly synchronized, then data race conditions, deadlock, or indefinite postponement can be introduced into a piece of software.

While we are strong advocates for the notion that the techniques, tools, languages, and software libraries should follow the decomposition model and not the other way around; the complexity of implementing the solution decomposition model has to be considered. You also can face many varieties of halting problems in applications that include multithreading and multiprocessing. As the number of cooperating tasks in an application increases, the complexity of the interdependencies increases as well. This can lead to very fickle and brittle software implementations. When multiple tasks are cooperating to provide the solution to some problem, what happens if one or more of the tasks fail. Should the program halt or should the work be redistributed somehow? This is a problem if you have only two concurrently executing tasks. The difficulty in resolving possible task failures rise exponentially as the number and interdependencies of threads or processes in a single application increase.

Challenges #7 and #8: Finding Reliable and Reproducible Debugging and Testing

When you test a sequential program, you can trace the logic of a program in a step-by-step manner. If you start with the same data and make sure that the system is in the same state, then the outcome or flow of the logic is predictable. You can find bugs in the software by starting the program in the necessary state, using the appropriate input, and then tracing through the logic step by step. Testing and debugging in the sequential model depends on the predictability of program's initial state and current state, given the specified input.

This changes in multiprocessing and multithreaded environments. It is difficult to reproduce the exact context of parallel or concurrent tasks because of operating system scheduling policies, dynamic workloads on the computer, processor time slices, process and thread priorities, communication latency, execution latency, and the random chance involved in parallel contexts. Add to the workloads the issue of the tasks working with different data sets and the changing semantics of data as it is processed by the tasks. To reproduce the exact state of the environment during testing and debugging requires that every task the operating system was working on be recreated. The processor scheduling state must be known. The status of virtual memory and context switching must be reproduced exactly. Interrupt and signal conditions must be recreated. In some cases, even networking traffic would have to be recreated! Data must be set and reset to its original values and states. Even the testing and debugging tools impact the exact environment. This creates a debugging or testing atmosphere of nondeterminism. A situation is nondeterministic if for some initial state, the final state is not unambiguously determined [Gries, Scheider, 1993].

In our experience, all but the most trivial multiprocessing and multithreaded applications have the look and feel of nondeterminism. This means that recreating the same sequence of events in order to test or debug a program is often out of the question. The reason that these things would have to be recreated is that they can all help to determine which process or thread can execute and on which processor they can execute. And it is the particular mix of executing processes and threads that could be the reason for a deadlock, indefinite postponement, data race, or other problem. Although some of these issues also affect sequential programming, they don't disrupt the assumptions of the sequential model. The kind of predictability that is present in the sequential model is simply not available in concurrent programming. This forces the developer to acquire new tactics for testing and debugging programs. It also requires that the developer find new ways to prove program correctness. Again, the issues involved with testing and debugging are viewed through very different prisms when declarative models are chosen over procedural models. Program correctness can be a very elusive concept for programs that involve complex parallel-processing schemes.

This nondeterminism also has consequences for cross-platform development. The operating system treatment of processes and threads in different operating system environments such as Linux, Solaris, Darwin, and so on can vary. Some systems have threads that are have high-, medium-, and low-priority options. Some systems have user-defined priority levels. Some systems have mission critical priorities, real-time priorities, normal priorities, background priorities, and so on. Operating systems can have different types of schedulers, different implementations of IPC mechanisms, and different implementations of kernel threads versus user threads.

Finding the Right Debugger and Profiler

Many debuggers and profilers that are commonly in use were developed under the assumption of single processor computers. Multicore application development requires debuggers and profilers that can see all of the physical and logical processors that are available. You need the debugger to be as intrusive as possible to the operating system workload. Debuggers need to have a clear window into kernel processes and system calls. The debugger needs to be able attach or detach a process or thread. It needs to be able to see all of the processor states or thread states that the operating system may put a process or thread in. A good debugger for multithreaded or multiprocessing applications should be able to start and stop threads and processes. It should be able to examine the thread stacks and free store.

Challenge #9: Communicating a Design That Has Multiprocessing Components

You also face the challenge of how to accurately capture a parallel design in documentation. You must be able to describe the WBS as well as the synchronization and communication between tasks, objects, processes, and threads. Designers must be able to effectively communicate to developers. Developers must be able to communicate with those who must maintain and administer the system. Ideally, this should be done using a standard notation and representation that is readily available to all concerned. However, finding a single documentation language that is broadly understood and can clearly represent the multiparadigm nature of some of these systems is elusive. We have chosen the Unified Modeling Language (UML) for this purpose. Table 3-7 lists the UML diagrams that are helpful for multithreaded and parallel programs.

Table 3-7

UML Diagrams	Descriptions
Structural/Architectural Diagrams	
Component diagram	A diagram that shows the dependencies and organization among a set of physical modules of code (packages) in a system.
Deployment diagram	A diagram that shows the runtime configuration of processing nodes, hardware, and software components in a system.

Table continued on following page

UML Diagrams	Descriptions
Behavioral Diagrams	
State/Concurrent State diagram	A diagram that shows the sequence of an object's transformation as it responds to events in the system. With a concurrent state diagram, these transformations can occur during the same time interval.
Sequence diagram	An interaction diagram that shows the organization of the structure of objects that sends and receives messages.
Collaboration diagram	An interaction diagram that shows the time ordering of messages.
Activity diagram	A diagram that shows the flow from one activity to another; similar to a flowchart but can show the activities of several objects and the flow of several parallel activities.

The diagrams in Table 3-7 are only a subset of the diagram types available in the UML. But these diagrams are immediately applicable to what you want to capture in currency designs. In particular, the UML's Activity, Deployment, and State diagrams are very useful in communicating parallel-processing behavior.

Since the UML is the de facto standard for communicating object-oriented and agent-oriented designs, we rely upon its use in this book. Appendix A contains a description and explanation for the notation and symbols used in these diagrams.

Challenge #10: Implementing Multiprocessing and Multithreading in C++

How can software developers that use C++ take advantage of the new CMPs? How can you implement multiprocessing in C++? The C++ language does not include any keyword primitives for parallelism. The C++ ISO standard is for all intents and purposes mute on the topic of multithreading. There is no way within the language to specify that two or more statements should be executed in parallel. Other languages use built-in parallelism as a selling feature. Bjarne Stroustrup, the inventor of the C++ language, had something else in mind. In Stroustrup's opinion:

It is possible to design concurrency support libraries that approach built-in concurrency support both in convenience and efficiency. By relying on libraries, you can support a variety of concurrency models, though, and thus serve the users that need those different models better than can be done by a single built-in concurrency model. I expect this will be the direction taken by most people and that the portability problems that arise when several concurrency-support libraries are used within the community can be dealt with by a thin layer of interface classes. [Stroustrup, 1994]

Further, Stroustrup says, "I recommend parallelism be represented by libraries within C++ rather than as a general language feature." We have found Stroustrup's position and recommendation on parallelism as a library the most practical option. This book is only made possible because of the availability of high-quality libraries that can be used for parallel and distributed programming. The libraries that we use to enhance C++ implement national and international standards for parallelism and distributed programming and are used by thousands of C++ programmers worldwide.

C++ Developers Have to Learn New Libraries

Although there are special versions of C++ that implement parallelism, we present methods on how parallelism can be implemented using the ISO (International Organization for Standardization) standard for C++. As we implied at the end of the previous section, the library approach to parallelism is the most flexible. System libraries and user-level libraries can be used to support parallelism in C++. System libraries are those libraries provided by the operating system environment. For example, the POSIX threads library is a set of system calls that can be used in conjunction with C++ to support parallelism. The Portable Operating System Interface (POSIX) threads are part of the new Single Unix Specification. The POSIX threads are included in the IEEE Std. 1003.1-2001. The Single Unix Specification is sponsored by the Open Group and developed by the Austin Common Standards Revision Group. According to the Open Group, the Single Unix Specification:

❑ Is designed to give software developers a single set of APIs to be supported be every Unix System

❑ Shifts the focus from incompatible Unix system product implementations to compliance to a single set of APIs

❑ Is the codification and dejure standardization of the common core of Unix system practice

❑ Has the basic objective of portability for both programmers and application source code

The Single Unix Specification Version 3 includes the IEEE Std. 1003.1-2001 and the Open Group Base Specifications Issue 6. The IEEE POSIX standards are now a formal part of the Single Unix Specification and vice versa. There is now a single international standard for a portable operating system interface. C++ developers benefit because this standard contains APIs for creating threads and processes. Excluding instruction-level parallelism, dividing a program up into either threads or processes is the only way to achieve parallelism with C++. The new standard provides the tools to do this. The developer can use:

❑ POSIX threads (also referred to as pthreads)

❑ POSIX `spawn` function

❑ The `exec()` family of functions

These are all supported by system API calls and system libraries. If an operation system complies with the Single UNIX Specification Version 3, then these APIs will be available to the C++ developer.

These APIs are discussed in Chapter 5, 6, and 7. They are used in many examples in this book. In addition, the relevant portions of the POSIX standard are included in Appendixes C and D.

Processor Architecture Challenges

We looked at four effective multicore architectures in Chapter 2. They were the Opteron, the Cell, the UltraSparc T1, and the Intel Core 2. While these processors each offer multicore capabilities, they have different architectures. These different architectures translate to difference sets of compiler switches, and directives. To get the most out of those different architectures, the developer has to be familiar with compiler- and linker-specific features. In this book, we look at the compiler multicore support in the GNU C++ compiler, Intel C/C++ compiler, and the Sun C/C++ compiler. Each has its own set of switches and directives that supports multithreading and multiprocessing. In some cases (for example, the Cell processor), multiple types of compilers are needed to generate a single executable program. The danger is that taking advantage of a particular architecture can make the software nonportable. While portability is not an issue for all applications, it is for many. How can you take the most advantage of some multicore architecture without using features that will hurt portability? That is another key question you have to answer as you develop multicore applications.

Summary

Parallel and distributed programming present challenges in several areas. New approaches to software design and architectures must be adopted. Many of the fundamentals assumptions that are held in the sequential model of programming don't apply in the realm of parallel. The developer is faced with a number of challenges of concurrency that we outlined in this chapter. Some of the keys points covered include:

❑ Four primary coordination problems — data race, indefinite postponement, deadlock, and communication synchronization — are among the major obstacles to programs that require concurrency.

❑ Every aspect of the Software Development Life Cycle (SDLC) is impacted when the requirements include parallelism or distribution — from the initial design down to the testing and documentation. Opportunities for parallelism and multiprocessing will be identified during various activities in the SDLC. It is important that the software developer understand the relationship between multicore programming and the SDLC.

❑ Perhaps the most important and critical decision that can be made for a software design that will include multiprocessing or parallel programming is whether to use procedural models or declarative models. The fundamental differences in approach, technique, design, and implementation between procedural models and declarative models are so dramatic that they require radically different paradigms of computer programming.

In this book, we present architectural approaches to many of these problems. In addition to the architectural approach, we take advantage of the multiparadigm capabilities of C++ to provide techniques for managing the complexity of parallel and distributed programs.

The trend is that multiprocessor computers will in most cases replace single processor configurations in business, academia, and government. As we have shown you in this chapter, to take advantage of the multiprocessor environments, you as a software developer must expand on the tools and techniques you already possess. Software projects that require multicore or parallel programming present unique challenges to those who are only accustomed to the sequential programming model. While hiding and abstracting away some of the complexity of parallel programming and multithreading, you have no real shortcuts around this idea. The deployment of robust, correct, and scalable software applications that can take advantage of CMPs requires sound software engineering and an effective a solid understanding of the SDLC. The chapters that follow will take on the challenges laid out in this chapter and show you what you, as the software developer, can do to overcome them.

The Operating System's Role

So far we've described some of the primary challenges of multicore programming. We've briefly covered some of the notions of multithreading, multiprocessing, and multiprogramming. In Chapter 2, we introduced the Multicore Opteron, Cell, Duo Core 2, and UltraSparc T1. These chips represent four effective but very different approaches to multicore architectures. We explained how hardware-specific compiler switches are sometimes necessary to get to certain specific features of a Chip Multiprocessor (CMP). But we've said very little about the operating system's role in the design, development, and execution of multicore programs and applications. This chapter now turns to that topic. In this chapter we:

- ❑ Provide an overview of the operating system
- ❑ Discuss the developer's interface to the multiprocessor
- ❑ Explore how threads, processes, and processors are connected through the operating system
- ❑ Examine how the operating system Application Program Interfaces (APIs) and system calls are used in conjunction with C++ for multicore programming and application development
- ❑ Explain how the operating system functions as the gatekeeper of the multiprocessor
- ❑ Discuss how to use the Portable Operating System Interface (POSIX) standard to design and implement multicore applications that work on all major hardware and operating system platforms

What Part Does the Operating System Play?

Our focus on the operating system is the role it plays as a development tool. In this book, we discuss multicore programming from both the system programmer's and the application programmer's point of view. From these viewpoints, the operating system's role can be divided into two primary functions:

❑ **Software interface**: Providing a consistent and well-defined interface to the hardware resources of the computer

❑ **Resource management**: Managing the hardware resources and other executing software applications, jobs, and programs

Providing a Consistent Interface

Prior to the advent of operating systems, programmers had to be familiar with the particular instruction sets and idiosyncrasies of each device. Video adapters, disk drives, printers, keyboards — all have specific and different instruction sets and command sets. Not only is the access to each device different; the same kinds of devices made by different manufacturers have different instructions sets and peculiarities. This led to programmers constantly having to rewrite the same functionality using different instruction sets. For example, if a developer had written a program that sorted a file to disk, that program could not be reused on another manufacturer's disk until the device id, instruction set, device modes, and so on were all updated to reflect those from the new manufacturer's device! In addition to unique instruction sets, each device connected to the computer had a specific address, port, or interrupt. Prior to the advent of operating systems, the programmer would have to know a device's physical address, port, or interrupt before the device could be accessed. So, programs contained device ids, hardware addresses, port numbers, and interrupts. The programmer had to virtually write a device driver for each piece of hardware the program accessed. Program and software portability were out of the question!

The notion of the operating system changed all of this. Operating systems provided the programmer with common interfaces to similar devices. The operating system encapsulated internal structures for devices, like video adapters, sound cards, keyboards, monitors, disk drives, printers, and so on. Instead of forcing the programmer to use peculiar device specific instructions, the operating system provided the programmer with a couple of layers of software between the developer's program and the hardware resources connected to the computer. These layers are called the *Application Program Interface (API)* and the *System Program Interface (SPI)*. It became the operating system's job to directly address hardware resources and all of their peculiarities. So, now the programmer only has to use the simplified API and SPI, and the operating system deals with all of the device-specific translation.

Managing Hardware Resources and Other Software Applications

In addition to providing an API and SPI to the developer, the operating system negotiates the access to processors, memory, I/O ports, interrupts, and storage on behalf of a program's processes or threads. In most workstation environments and server environments, there are multiple programs being executed or waiting for execution at any one instant. Since the number of processors and amount of memory are limited, it's the operating system's job to decide which programs get access to which processor, for how long, and when. The operating system determines how much memory a process or collection of processes is allowed to hold and for how long. For programs that are too large to fit in main storage, the operating system manages the process of switching in pieces of the software for execution. The operating system assigns hardware resources to processes. The operating system then protects one processor's resources from access or violation by another process. In general, the operating system manages all of the hardware resources in a computer. In addition to managing hardware resources it also schedules and manages processes and threads.

The Developer's Interaction with the Operating System

Regardless of whether you use class libraries, high-level function libraries, or application frameworks for your multicore development, the operating system still plays the role of gatekeeper to the processors, memory, filesystems, and so on connected to the computer. This means that the multithreading or multiprocessing functionality that is contained in class libraries, high-level function libraries, or application frameworks still needs to pass through operating system APIs or SPIs. Figure 4-1 shows the developer's view of the software layers and the operating system.

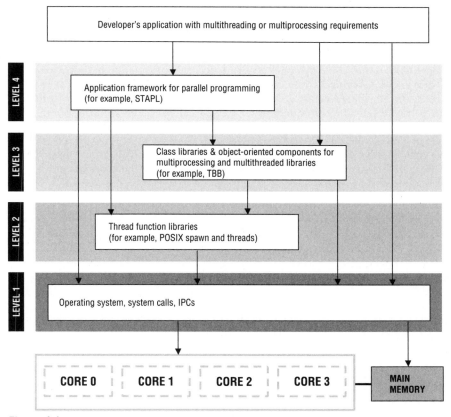

Figure 4-1

Figure 4-1 shows the software layers that can be used to provide multithreading or multiprocessing functionality to a software application. Notice the levels for each software layer in Figure 4-1. In Figure 4-1, the lower the level, the more details of the parallel programming mechanisms the developer has control over, has responsibility for using correctly, and has to have knowledge of. The lower the level, the more design and programming skill required to implement the software correctly.

❏ **Level 4** is the highest level. This level provides the most insulation from the details of parallel programming for the developer. The Standard Template Adaptive Parallel Library (STAPL) is an example of this kind of application framework. STAPL is a framework for developing parallel programs in C++. The goal of a framework like STAPL is to allow the developer to provide parallelism in a software application while not having to worry about all of the specific implementation-related issues that are involved with parallel programming.

We take a closer look at STAPL in Chapter 8.

❏ **Level 3** in Figure 4-1 is represented by template or class libraries like Intel Threading Building Blocks (TBB) library. The Intel Threading Building Block library is a set of high-level generic components that also encapsulate much of the detail of multiprocessing and multithreading. Developers using the TBB invoke high-level algorithm templates and synchronization objects that do the low-level work.

We also take a look at TBB in Chapter 8.

❏ Both STAPL and the TBB library allow the programmer to focus more on the software solution that is being implemented rather than on how the parallelism for the solution is implemented. Keep in mind that while this type of abstraction and information hiding is good for certain types of application developers, it may not be desirable for certain classes of system programmers, library developers, or server development. In Chapter 3 we stressed the fact that modeling and the Software Development Lifecycle (SDLC) are critical in determining where, when, or if multithreading or multiprocessing is needed. High-level application frameworks and thread building block libraries do not change this fact. They do not replace the job of modeling or any of the steps in the SDLC. However, if used correctly, they can make modeling and some of the steps in the SDLC easier to implement. We cannot stress enough the fact that parallel programming techniques and tools should come after problem and solution decomposition and modeling.

❏ **Level 2** in Figure 4-1 includes thread and process APIs provided by the operating system environment. In this book, we use POSIX APIs to interact with the OS for process management and thread management. Level 2 provides the application and system programmer with the most flexibility, but that flexibility comes at a cost. Working with multithreading and multiprocessing at level 2 requires detailed knowledge of process and thread management, Interprocess Communication, and a command of synchronization techniques. It requires intimate knowledge of operating system APIs related to process and thread management. It requires specific knowledge of the implementation of parallel algorithms. It requires knowledge of the specific compiler and linker directives that relate to multiprocessing and multithreading. In some cases, the control and flexibility of programming at level 2 is an acceptable tradeoff for the additional skill and effort required.

❏ The programming at **level 1** in Figure 4-1 requires the most knowledge of operating system internals, hardware interfaces, and kernel-level interfaces. Level 1 programming directly accesses the hardware with few or no software barriers. Programming at level 1 is in the domain of system programming.

Regardless of whether your application has been developed with tools and techniques from level 4 or from level 3, the frameworks, templates, and class libraries ultimately have to call APIs that exist at level 2 and level 1. Levels 1 and 2 provide the SPI and API gateways to the operating system, and at the end of the day, it's the operating system that controls access to the multiple cores that we are interested in exploiting.

While not every developer that is writing software to take advantage of multicore computers will or should work with level 1 and 2, a fundamental understanding of how things work at this level is very important during the SDLC. It's important to understand the fundamentals because no single library, framework, or tool provides all of the services that most applications need. Further, many of these tools have to be mixed and matched. Virtually all medium- and large-scale software applications are built using a combination of libraries. These libraries are not always *thread safe* or *multicore-aware*. When there is a problem, the software developer needs to understand at least the basics of what is going on with process and thread management. The high-level tools used in level 3 and 4 from Figure 4-1 have to be configured. Configuration requires a basic understanding of how things work. In some cases, the mixing and matching causes conflicts that need to be resolved.

In addition to this, not all high-level tools run in every environment. For instance, the TBB runs on many Intel-based processors but is not yet available on all other major non-Intel processors. To make it available for or completely compatible with your platform might require porting and so on. The nature of multithreaded and multiprocessing application requires that the developer understand the fundamental relationship between the software, the operating system, and the processors and memory. This is absolutely necessary to effectively deal with the debugging process, the testing process, and the final software deployment. High-quality, correct, reliable multiprocessing and multithreading applications require that the developer have a clear understanding of the operating system's role.

Core Operating System Services

The operating system's core services can be divided into:

- ❑ Process management
- ❑ Memory management
- ❑ Filesystem management
- ❑ I/O management
- ❑ Interprocess Communication Manager

Table 4-1 shows a brief description of these core services.

Table 4-1

Operating System's Core Services	Description
Process management	Manages the behavior and resources of a process. This includes process execution, resource allocation and protection, and synchronization.
Memory management	Manages memory allocation for processes, which includes how memory is allocated to a process and what to do when memory is fully utilized.
Filesystem management	Organizes collections of data on storage devices and provides an interface for accessing the data on those devices.
I/O management	Manages the input and output requests from and to hardware devices.
Interprocess Communication Manager	Manages the communication between processes.

While these services are of concern to all application developers, they are far more visible for developers of multithreaded or multiprocessing applications. This is because functions like process scheduling or Interprocess Communication tend to be transparent to sequential processing applications. For example, in a sequential processing application, the operating system simply loads the developer's program. The developer is usually not concerned with how the operating system breaks the application down into processes, how the processes are scheduled, or what priority the scheduled processes have. There is no worry about shared memory violations; as long as the operating system gives the application enough memory, everybody is happy. Since there are no concurrently executing substasks in a sequential processing application, Intertask Communication and synchronization are not issues. It is a very different picture for multiprocessing and multithreaded applications. In Chapter 3, we discussed the challenges that the developer faces for these types of applications. Some of the challenges that relate specifically to the operating system services from Chapter 3 are:

- ❑ Software decomposition into instructions or sets of tasks that need to execute simultaneously
- ❑ Communication between two or more tasks that are executing in parallel
- ❑ Concurrently accessing or updating data by two or more instructions or tasks
- ❑ Identifying the relationships between concurrently executing pieces of tasks
- ❑ Controlling resource contention when there is a many-to-one ratio between tasks and resource
- ❑ Determining an optimum or acceptable number of units that need to execute in parallel
- ❑ Documenting and communicating a software design that contains multiprocessing and multithreading
- ❑ Creating a test environment that simulates the parallel processing requirements and conditions
- ❑ Recreating a software exception or error in order to remove a software defect
- ❑ Involving the operating system and compiler interface components of multithreading and multiprocessing

Once the software design process determines that the application is best divided into two or more concurrently executing tasks, the transparency of the operating system is immediately brought into question. This is because automatic task decomposition is not a feature of the operating system, but process and thread creation and management are responsibilities of the operating system. Ultimately, the concurrently executing tasks have to be mapped to either processes, threads, or both. Today's operating systems and compilers are not capable of automatically doing this mapping. Someone has to be the liaison between the application's requirements for concurrency and the operating system's APIs and SPIs that support multiprocessing and multithreading. If you are working with tools and techniques taken from level 3 and 4 from Figure 4-1, then the operating system's role for the most part is transparent (but definitely present). If you are working at level 1 or 2 as shown in Figure 4-1, then specific knowledge of the operating system's APIs and SPIs is required.

To get a closer view of the operating system's role in deploying tasks that must execute concurrently, you can take a look at an application that has been decomposed into four simultaneously executing tasks. The C++ developer using any of today's modern operating systems has three basic choices for implementing the tasks. The tasks can be implemented as:

- ❑ Processes
- ❑ Threads
- ❑ A combination of processes and threads

Figure 4-2 shows a block diagram of the basic decomposition choices for the example four-task application.

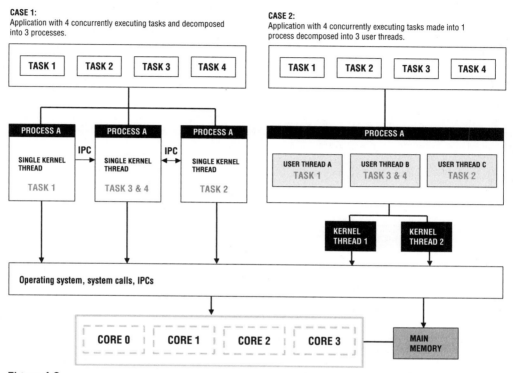

CASE 1:
Application with 4 concurrently executing tasks and decomposed into 3 processes.

CASE 2:
Application with 4 concurrently executing tasks made into 1 process decomposed into 3 user threads.

Figure 4-2

In **Case 1** in Figure 4-2 the application is divided into four tasks. These four tasks are implemented by three operating system processes. Figure 4-2 shows that the application will be deployed on a quad core computer. The fact that the four tasks are implemented by three processes means that it is possible for three of the tasks to be actually executing on three separate processors simultaneously or multiprogrammed on any number of processors. In multiprogramming, the operating system rapidly switches between processes, thus allowing multiple processes to accomplish work concurrently in a given time interval. Although only one process is actually using the processor at a time, the switching between processes is so fast that within, say, one second, two or more processes have been placed on the processor and performed work. Although we have a quad core computer in Figure 4-2, we can actually execute only three tasks simultaneously. This is because the four user tasks have been mapped to three processes. The operating system can only schedule processes or kernel threads (lightweight processes) to execute on the processor. It cannot schedule logical tasks unless they have been mapped to processes or kernel threads. Even if all four cores were free, in **Case 1** only three cores would be used by the application simultaneously. Tasks 3 and 4 share a single process. **Case 1** is using multiprocessing because it takes advantage of the operating system's multiprocessors by assigning its tasks to operating system processes. The system assigns processes to any free cores that it might have. So if the application is divided into processes, it can exploit the fact that the system can run as many processes in parallel as it has processors.

How Do You Get from Tasks to Processes?

To map a user task to a system process, you use an operating system API. In this case you use the `posix_spawn()` function. `posix_spawn()` is used to create a new operating system process. `posix_spawn()` is part of the operating system's process management API. You pass the task that you want to associate with an operating system process to `posix_spawn()`. Any task associated to a process through `posix_spawn()` can be scheduled by the operating system to run in parallel with other processes. Notice in **Case 1** that Task 1 needs one-way communication with Tasks 3 and 4, and Tasks 3 and 4 need two-way communication with Task 2. This brings up another question about interaction with the operating system. How can you pass information between concurrently executing processes? There are many ways to do this, but all of them require some kind of interaction with an operating system API. In this case, you can use a POSIX message queue. Table 4-2 contains brief descriptions for the POSIX message queue functions. These are examples of some of the POSIX API functions that allow concurrently executing processes to pass information.

Table 4-2

POSIX Message Queue Functions	Description
`mq_open()`	Establishes the connection between a process and a message queue with a message queue descriptor
`mq_close()`	Removes the association between the message queue descriptor and its message queue
`mq_send()`	Adds the message pointed to the message queue specified
`mq_receive()`	Receives the oldest of the highest priority message(s) from the message queue specified
`mq_notify()`	Registers the calling process to be notified of a message arriving at an empty message queue that is associated with the specified message queue descriptor
`mq_getattr()`	Obtains the status information and attributes of the message queue and the open message queue description associated with the message queue descriptor
`mq_setattr()`	Sets the status information and attributes of the message queue

Using the Thread Approach

The decomposition in **Case 1** in Figure 4-2 uses the process as the unit of decomposition. **Case 2** uses the thread as the unit of decomposition. Whereas the application spawns three processes in **Case 1**, the application has only one process in **Case 2**. However, that one process is divided into three user threads that can execute concurrently. In this scenario, the four concurrent tasks requirement has been implemented using three threads. Threads A, B, and C are each assigned tasks. This means that the four tasks have to be distributed among three threads. It is important to notice that **Case 2** has only two kernel threads. Since the operating system schedules processes or kernel threads for processors, this means that the single process in **Case 2** could be scheduled to a single processor or the two kernel threads could be scheduled to separate processors. Thus, if all four cores were free, at most two tasks would be executing simultaneously.

In **Case 2** Threads A, B, and C are user threads. User threads can be bound to kernel threads in some cases and unbound in others (as we discuss later in the book). In **Case 2** the user threads have to be associated with kernel threads before they are actually executed. So, you can see that in our thread approach we map the software tasks to user threads, and then the user threads are mapped to kernel threads or lightweight processes (lwp).

We explain the differences between user threads and kernel threads in Chapter 6.

How Do You Get from Tasks to Threads?

The `pthread_create()` operating system API is used to associate a software task with a thread. This function also falls under the process management duties of the operating system. We take a close look at POSIX thread API in Chapter 6. Unless you are working with tools and techniques from level 3 or 4 (as shown Figure 4-1), associating software tasks with threads requires an understanding of how to use the POSIX thread API. Notice in Figure 4-2 that the communication requirements for the tasks do not require special operating system intervention when using the thread approach for decomposition. This is because the threads share the same address space and therefore can share data structures that are kept in the data segment of the process.

The Application Programmer's Interface

It is important to note that, in both **Case 1** and **Case 2** in Figure 4-2, the software tasks had to be mapped to entities that the operating system could manage and schedule. The programmer cannot simply assign a processor to each task that must be performed. This can be done only by the operating system. The programmer has to make the software tasks comprehensible to the operating system by using execution units that the operating system can understand. The operating system is the layer of software between the developer's software and the multiple cores. The operating system provides a set of interfaces (APIs) that make hardware resources and OS services available to the application developer. To take advantage of any operating system services the developer must use an API. The problem is which OS API to use? Each operating system vendor provides its own unique API. While the functionality of these APIs is basically the same, they are not portable to different platforms. That is, software that has been developed using the Mac OS X (Darwin) API cannot be directly compiled and executed on Solaris, the Solaris API cannot be directly compiled and executed in a Windows environment, and so forth. So, programs that need to use the operating system API in order to gain full access to the multiple cores will not be portable if they use system-specific APIs. This means that applications would have to be rewritten in order to be used in a new environment. In most cases, this is not acceptable. That's why in this book we use the POSIX API.

What Is POSIX and Why Use It?

Portable Operating System Interface (POSIX) is a standard that defines a standard operating system interface and environment, including a command interpreter (or "shell") and common utility programs to support applications portability at the source code level. The standard is intended be used by both applications developers and system implementors. To make this book accessible to the broadest possible audience of system and application developers we choose to present OS API material using the POSIX standard. The major operating system environments — ZOS, Solaris, AIX, Windows, Mac OS X, Linux, HP-UX, IRIX — all claim basic support for the POSIX standard. While each of these environments has its own proprietary APIs, each also has support for the POSIX standard. Since the concepts, examples, and programs we discuss are based on the POSIX standard, you can try them out in virtually any environment. The POSIX standard plays the role of a cross-platform pseudocode that allows us to cover the main concepts of multicore programming in a language that can be implemented in all of the major environments. Further, POSIX implements a kind of "common denominator" OS interface. This means that, in most cases, it is straightforward to translate concepts, rationale, and functions calls to the proprietary OS APIs if necessary.

Because the POSIX standard aims to provide portability at the source code level, we can build class libraries, template libraries, and application frameworks on top of POSIX components that can then be compiled and used in all of the major operating system environments. Obviously, this is not the case for platform-specific OS APIs. In particular, the developers working at level 3 and 4 as shown in Figure 4-1 can benefit from this type of portability. Application frameworks for parallel processing, such as STAPL, and the template or class libraries such as TBB can be made portable by using the POSIX APIs for processes and threads for their low-level implementations. Further, mixing and matching high-level application frameworks and building block libraries in multiple environments is made practical if the POSIX APIs are used. Developers working at level 1 and 2 using POSIX APIs can write once and compile everywhere. Since large-scale computer configurations such as clusters, enterprise-class servers (mainframes), and even supercomputers have POSIX-compatible operating environments, the developer has the complete range of hardware support when scalability is a serious issue. While multicore processors are just now becoming commonplace for desktop computers, developer workstations, and small servers, they have been widely available for large-scale computer configurations for more than a decade. Therefore, when you invest in learning the POSIX API, it is applicable from small business application servers to the largest cluster-based configurations.

The POSIX standard allows us to talk about the intersection between multicore programming and core operating system services listed in Table 4-1 in a cross-platform fashion. All of the examples and programs in this book have been written and compiled in POSIX-compatible environments, and two of the appendices of this book contain POSIX reference material on process management and thread management.

Process Management

The process lifecycle is one of the important aspects of process management that we revisit throughout this book. For our purposes, the process lifecycle is summarized as:

❑   Process creation

❑   Process scheduling/execution

❑   Process termination

The standard C++ library does not provide any services that deal with the major activities in the process lifecycle. So you need to look to the OS API when you need to do programming that requires processes. Even in a CMP there are not enough processors to run all processes simultaneously. The operating system has to multitask the processes. Multitasking allows more than one process to execute at the same time, whereas multithreading allows a single process to perform more than one task at the same time. When the operating system uses a scheduling policy to allow two or more processes to share a CPU concurrently, this is called *multitasking*. Each process executes until some designated amount of time has expired or until some event has occurred. The interval of time a process is given to execute on a core is called a *quantum*. Then the operating system switches to another process. This switching happens rapidly, giving the illusion that processes are being executed simultaneously, where in fact only one process is active at a time on a core. This switching between processes occurs until each process has completed. The scheduling policy in effect determines when a process should be switched. The scheduling policy also controls what happens when:

❑   A process or thread is a running thread, and it becomes a blocked thread.

❑   A process or thread is a running thread, and it becomes a preempted thread.

❑   A process or thread is a blocked thread, and it becomes a runnable thread.

❑   A running thread calls a function that can change the priority or scheduling policy of a process or thread.

In this book, we assume that your environment supports the four basic scheduling policies supported by the POSIX standard:

```
SCHED_FIFO
SCHED_RR
SCHED_SPORADIC
SCHED_OTHER
```

Table 4-3 contains a description for each of the basic scheduling policies that you can use.

Table 4-3

POSIX Scheduling Policies	Description
SCHED_FIFO	When the quantum expires, the thread is placed at the head of the queue of its priority level.
SCHED_RR	When the quantum expires, the thread is placed at the end of the queue of its priority level.
SCHED_SPORADIC	Sporadic server scheduling policy.
SCHED_OTHER	Implementation defined; the most effective scheduling policy for general use.

Each process is controlled by an associated scheduling policy and priority. Associated with each policy is a priority range. Each policy definition specifies the minimum priority range for that policy. The priority ranges for each policy may overlap the priority ranges of other policies.

The operating system is also the transport for signals between processes. When Process A has to signal a termination to Process B, the operating system transports the signal. Each of the primary steps in the process lifecycle is in the domain of the operating system, and you have to use POSIX APIs to access these services. Keep in mind that software or programs stored on disk are not processes or threads. A process is a program that is in execution, that has a process control block and process table, and that is being scheduled by the operating system. Threads are parts of processes. Software and programs have to be loaded by the OS before any processes are created. Processes or lightweight processes have to be created before threads can be created.

Process Management Example: The Game Scenario

To illustrate how all this works, we are going to take a look at a classic game. I'm thinking of a six-character code. My code can contain any character more than once. However, my code can only contain any characters from the numbers 0–9 or characters a–z. Your job is to guess what code I have in mind. In the game the buzzer is set to go off after 5 minutes. If you guess what I'm thinking in 5 minutes, you win. You take out paper and pencil and with a little addition and a little subtraction you quickly realize that there are over 4,496,388 possibilities. So, in 2 of your 5 minutes you run through the entire SDLC and come up with the following strategy. First, as luck would have it, you just happen to have a file that contains the 4,496,388 possibilities. So, you simply write a C++ program that does something like the one in Example 4-1.

Example 4-1

```
Example 4-1

//...

  bool Found = false;
  ifstream Fin(Possibilities)
  while(!Fin.eof() && !Fin.fail() && !Found)
  {
      getline(Fin,Guess);
      if(Guess == MagicCode){
          Found = true;
      }

  }

//...
```

The problem is that you don't know where in the file of 4,496,388 possibilities the six-character code I'm thinking of occurs. Depending on where my code is in the file, it might take longer than 5 minutes to find. Sorting the file does not help because you don't know anything other than the length of my code and the possible characters that it can contain, so convenient techniques like the binary search can't be used.

However, say that in your case you just happen to have access to a dual core CMP. So, the strategy then is to divide the big file containing over four million possibilities into two files containing two million possibilities. So you develop the program called find_code. The find_code program takes as input a file containing codes, and it performs a brute-force (exhaustive/sequential) search looking for the code. The trick is that you need the OS to help you use both of the cores in the search. Ideally, you would have the two cores each searching through one of the files simultaneously. Your theory is that two heads are better than one, and if you divide the list in half, it should take half the time to find the code. So, you want the OS to run two versions of the find_code program simultaneously, with each version searching through half the original file. You use a posix_spawn() call to launch the program, as shown in Listing 4-1.

Listing 4-1

```
//Listing 4-1  Program (guess_it) used to launch find_code.

1   using namespace std;
2   #include <iostream>
3   #include <string>
4   #include <spawn.h>
5   #include <sys/wait.h>
6
7   int main(int argc,char *argv[],char *envp[])
8   {
9
10      pid_t ChildProcess;
11      pid_t ChildProcess2;
12      int RetCode1;
13      int RetCode2;
14      int Value;
15      RetCode1 = posix_spawn(&ChildProcess,"find_code",NULL,
```

```
16                              NULL,argv,envp);
17        RetCode2 = posix_spawn(&ChildProcess2,"find_code",NULL,
18                              NULL,argv,envp);
19        wait(&Value);
20        wait(&Value);
21        return(0);
22    }
```

The `posix_spawn()` call on lines #15 and #17 launches the program named `find_code`. For this to work, the program `find_code` has to be a binary executable program that the OS can locate on your computer. In this case `find_code` is a standalone program that implements the basic idea from Example 4-1. When the program in Listing 4-1 is executed, it causes the operating system to generate three processes. Recall that it is the operating system not programs that assigns processes to execute on cores and CPUs. The processes can execute simultaneously. Two processes are associated with the `find_code` program, and the third process is the process called `posix_spawn()` in the first place. The processes that are created as a result of calling `posix_spawn` are referred to as child processes.

We take a closer look at `posix_spawn()` *in Chapter 5.*

Program Profile 4-1

Program Name:

`guess_it.cc` (Listing 4-1)

Description:

`posix_spawn()` launches the program named `find_code`. `find_code` is a standalone program that implements the basic idea from Example 4-1. The program causes the operating system to generate three simultaneously executing processes. Two processes execute the `find_code` program, and the third process executes `posix_spawn()`.

Libraries Required:

None

User-Defined Headers Required:

None

Compile and Link Instructions:

```
c++ -o guess_it  guess_it.cc
```

Test Environment:

Linux Kernel 2.6

Solaris 10, gcc 3.4.3 and 3.4.6

Processors:

Multicore Opteron, UltraSparc T1, Cell Processor

Notes:

None

It is important to note that the child processes that are spawned by `posix_spawn` are always binary executables that exist outside of the calling program. Unlike `pthread_create()`, which calls a routine in the program, `posix_spawn()` uses code that exists outside of the calling program.

Each operating system environment has its own unique method of spawning child processes. The `posix_spawn()` method works in any operating environment that has the proper POSIX compliance. So, you can build cross-platform components that can be used for process creation.

The process that calls `posix_spawn()` is referred to as the parent process. So, the OS creates two child processes and a parent process. If the two cores are free, the operating system can assign two of the three processes to be executed simultaneously. Now you realize that, although you have divided the list in half and you have two simultaneous searches going on, you are not certain to find the code in the two million possibilities in time, so you need to divide the list in half once more. This gives four lists of one million codes, give or take a few that can be searched concurrently. Certainly, you can find the mystery code in a list of one million possibilities in 5 minutes. To generate four searches, you divide the `find_code` program into two threads of execution. So, the main program named `guess_it` in Listing 4-1, spawns two `child_processes` that execute the program `find_code`. The program `find_code` creates two threads called `Task1` and `Task2`. Listing 4-2 is the new multithreaded version of `find_code`.

Listing 4-2

```
//Listing 4-2  A multithreaded version of the find_code program.

1   #include <pthread.h>
2   using namespace std;
3   #include <iostream>
4   #include <fstream>
5   #include "posix_queue.h"
6   string MagicCode("yyzzz");
7   ofstream Fout1;
8   ofstream Fout2;
9   bool Found = false;
10  bool magicCode(string X)
11  {
12      //...
13
14      return(X == MagicCode);
15  }
16
17
18
19  void *task1(void *X)
20  {
21      posix_queue PosixQueue;
22      string FileName;
23      string Value;
24      if(PosixQueue.open()){
25          PosixQueue.receive(FileName);
26          ifstream Fin(FileName.c_str());
```

```
27        string FileOut(FileName);
28        FileOut.append(".out");
29        Fout1.open(FileOut.c_str());
30        while(!Fin.eof() && !Fin.fail() && !Found)
31        {
32            getline(Fin,Value);
33            if(!Fin.eof() && !Fin.fail() && !Found){
34                if(magicCode(Value)){
35                    Found = true;
36                }
37            }
38        }
39        Fin.close();
40        Fout1.close();
41    }
42    return(NULL);
43 }



47 void *task2(void *X)
48 {
49
50    posix_queue PosixQueue;
51    string FileName;
52    string Value;
53    if(PosixQueue.open()){
54        PosixQueue.receive(FileName);
55        ifstream Fin(FileName.c_str());
56        string FileOut(FileName);
57        FileOut.append(".out");
58        Fout2.open(FileOut.c_str());
59        while(!Fin.eof() && !Fin.fail()  && !Found)
60        {
61            getline(Fin,Value);
62            if(!Fin.eof() && !Fin.fail()  && !Found){
63                if(magicCode(Value)){
64                    Found = true;
65                }
66            }
67        }
68        Fin.close();
69        Fout2.close();
70    }
71    return(NULL);
72 }





78 int main(int argc, char *argv[])
79 {
80
```

(continued)

Listing 4-2 *(continued)*

```
81      pthread_t ThreadA, ThreadB;
82      pthread_create(&ThreadA,NULL,task1,NULL);
83      pthread_create(&ThreadB,NULL,task2,NULL);
84      pthread_join(ThreadA,NULL);
85      pthread_join(ThreadB,NULL);
86      return(0);
87
88  }
```

The pthread_create() functions on Lines 82 and 83 are used to create the threads for task1 and task2. (We take a closer look at the POSIX pthread functionality in Chapter 6.) The program in Listing 4-2 is for expositional purposes only. It does not contain any synchronization, exception handling, signal handling, or the like. We include it here so that you have a clear picture of the anatomy the guess_it program that we introduced in Example 4-1. Notice that task1 Line 19, and task2 Line 47 are normal C++ functions. They just happen to be used as the main routine for ThreadA and ThreadB. Also notice on Lines 24 and 53 that each thread accesses a PosixQueue. This is a user-defined object, and it contains the name of a different file that each thread will search.

So, the program in Listing 4-1 spawns two child processes. Each process executes find_code, which in turn creates two threads. This gives a total of four threads. Each thread reads a filename from the PosixQueue object. So, rather than having a one big file of 4,496,388 possibilities, you now have four smaller files containing a little more than one million possibilities. Now you use a simple brute-force search by each thread. One of the threads will find the MagicCode I was thinking about. Because of the Found variable declared on Line 9 in Listing 4-2, the file scope or global scope for ThreadA and ThreadB can be used as a control variable that causes both threads to stop. But what about the other two threads in the second process? You used the PosixQueue to communicate the filenames to both processes and all four threads. Is there a way that you can use a queue to let the three processes and four threads know that it is time to stop once one of the threads finds the MagicCode?

Program Profile 4-2

Program Name:

find_code.cc (Listing 4-2)

Description:

The program find_code creates two threads called Task1 and Task2. Each thread accesses a PosixQueue. This is a user-defined object, and it contains the name of a different file that each thread will search for the code.

Libraries Required:

pthread

User-Defined Headers Required:

```
posix_queue.h
```

Compile and Link Instructions:

```
c++ -o find_code  find_code.cc posix_queue.cc -lpthread -lrt
```

Test Environment:

Linux Kernel 2.6

Solaris 10, gcc 3.4.3 and 3.4.6

Processors:

Multicore Opteron, UltraSparc T1, Cell Processor

Notes:

None

Decomposition and the Operating System's Role

Decomposition is a theme that we revisit many times in this book for two reasons:

- ❑ The fundamental activity of software design is breaking down the problem and the solution in a way that allows the solution (and sometimes the problem) to be implemented in software.

- ❑ Parallel programming, multithreading, and multiprocessing all require that software be broken down into execution units that can be scheduled by the operating system for concurrent processing.

This makes decomposition front and center for multicore programming. Notice that, in the classic game example used in the preceding section, there is no mention of parallel programming, multithreading, operating systems, or so on. There is just a simple statement of a problem. Guess what six-character code I'm thinking of in 5 minutes or less. We started with a simple plain English description of a problem, and somehow we ended up with a multiprocessing, multithreaded program that required Interprocess Communication and operating system intervention and assistance. One of the primary links between the simple plain English description and the simultaneously executing operating system threads is the process of decomposition. Consider the example from the point of view a logical breakdown and a physical breakdown. Figure 4-3 contains a functional (logical) breakdown of the operating system components from the `guess_it` program taken from Listing 4-1 and Listing 4-2.

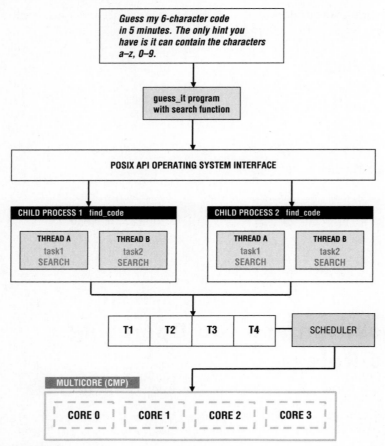

Figure 4-3

As you can see in Figure 4-3, we had six units of execution that the operating system was responsible for, two processes and four threads. Recall from Example 4-1 that we started out initially with a single program that searched a file. We used the OS API to spawn two instances of the program so that we could search two files simultaneously. Notice in Figure 4-3 that the find_code is then divided into two threads. So, the actual work components are easily visible in Figure 4-3. Missing from Figure 4-3 is the decomposition of the single data file containing the over four million possibilities into four smaller files containing one million+ possibilities. Each of the threads in Figure 4-3 worked on its own unique file. So, we had a data decomposition in addition to our work decomposition. The decomposition of our guess_it program is an example of the Single Instruction Multiple Data (SIMD) concurrency model. Recall that in this concurrency model multiple tasks execute the same sequence of instructions over different datasets. We had four threads each executing the same code (single instruction) on four different sets of data. Even if we had the benefit of the tools like STAPL or TBB, we would ultimately need to interface with the operating system to actually implement this SIMD model. This type of decomposition and OS interface is the kind of programming shown at level 1 and 2 in Figure 4-1. Although developers working at level 3 and 4 (as shown in Figure 4-1) are generally free from this level of interaction, the operating system's role should be clear.

In addition to a breakdown of the logical units that involve the OS, you also have physical units. Figure 4-4 shows a UML deployment diagram for the programs in Listing 4-1 and 4-2.

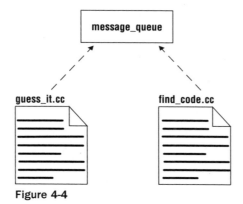

Figure 4-4

This diagram shows the physical pieces of the simple guess_it program. We have two primary executables:

❑   guess_it (Listing 4-1)

❑   find_code (Listing 4-2)

There are four files that contain the possible choices and several source files containing our simple brute-force solution to our guess my code game and a message queue. The path to all binary files must be known to the operating system at runtime. If the posix_spawn() calls on Lines 15 and 16 in Listing 4-1 can't locate the find_code programs, the guess_it program in Listing 4-2 will not work. The operating system's role of finding and loading code to be executed is one of the roles that is often overlooked and resurfaces in the form of "gotchas" when deploying multiprocessing and parallel processing applications. You can use deployment diagrams to help keep an audit trail of the physical decomposition of applications. Considering the decompositions in Figure 4-3 and Figure 4-4 along with the original statement of the problem and the first try at its solution, you can begin to see how the SDLC plays a major role in multicore application design and implementation. From the initial problem statement of "Guess what six-character code I'm thinking of in 5 minutes," we devised a solution that involved searching a list of possibilities. But since the list was sufficiently large and we were under a time constraint, we came up with a strategy that required dividing the list of possibilities up into smaller lists with the notion of searching the smaller lists simultaneously for the MagicCode.

This strategy is an example of the design activity that is part of the SDLC. The original statement of the problem is an example of requirements definitions that is part of SDLC. The implementation of the strategy using posix_spawn(), pthread_create(), and PosixQueue is part of the coding activity from the SDLC. While the operating system is not necessarily a consideration during the requirements or design activities of the SDLC, it is present for the coding, deployment, and maintenance activities of the SDLC. Our goal here is to make its function clear in terms of where it fits for applications that need to exploit multicore CMPs. In Chapters 5 and 6, we take a much closer look at processes and threads as units of execution that can be scheduled to execute simultaneously by the operating system.

Hiding the Operating System's Role

The real goal is to understand the part the operating system plays in executing multithreaded and multiprocessing programs without having your software designs bogged down with the details of thread and process implementation. One of the primary reasons that you ultimately want to get away from the details of thread and process implementation is because the trend is that CMPs are moving toward more cores on a single chip with the ultimate goal of massive parallelism (100s or 1000s) of cores on a single chip. It will be important to know the operating system's role, but you will not want to expose it in your designs. This was the case with the solution in Listings 4-1 and 4-2. As the trend moves toward more cores and more parallelism, you need to pursue two important objectives for software development:

1. Taking advantage of the operating system while making it transparent to software designs

2. Moving from procedural paradigms of parallel programming to declarative paradigms

Taking Advantage of C++ Power of Abstraction and Encapsulation

Fortunately C++'s support for Object Orientation, genericity, predicates, and multiparadigm programming give a bridge to and a way to see the future of software design and development. Object-Oriented Programming (OOP) is part of the declarative paradigms of software development [Meyer, 1988] and [Stroustrup, 1997]. As you will see in the next section, the notions of encapsulation supported by C++ aid in making the operating system level transparent to software designs. Templates can be used to implement genericity techniques found in higher-order declarative approaches to parallel programming, and ideas of classes, predicates, and assertions in C++ can be used to move toward declarative programming techniques that support massive and complex parallel programming techniques. Class and template libraries such as STAPL and the TBB are the initial components that support the move to massive parallelism on CMPs. The idea is to build classes that encapsulate lower-level procedural-driven functionality of the operating system APIs while providing higher-level declarative interfaces. C++ interface classes are ideal for providing wrappers for low-level OS APIs, synchronization mechanisms, and communication components [Stroustrup, 1997]. Also, you want to use C++ templates to capture patterns of parallelization, implementing the details while the user accesses a higher, more functional interface. You then want to build from the C++ components application frameworks that capture architectures that support parallelism. Using higher-level components, frameworks, and architectures, you can then directly implement the models that produced in the design and specification activities of the SDLC.

Interface Classes for the POSIX APIs

The easiest approach to making the POSIX APIs transparent is to provide C++ *interface classes*. Interface classes are classes that provide a wrapper for functions, data, or other classes. The interface class acts as a kind of costume that allows something to appear differently than it does normally. An interface class puts a different face on a function, piece of data, or another class. Interface classes are also called adaptor classes. The new interface provided by an interface class is designed to make the class easier to use, more functional, safer, or semantically correct. Take, for example, the POSIX thread functions shown in Lines 81–85 in Listing 4-2. We want the main line of this program to not expose operating system calls and want to add a more C++ Object-Oriented flavor to the guess_it program. Listing 4-3 contains a new format for the find_code program from Listing 4-2.

Listing 4-3

```
//Listing 4-3   A more object-oriented find_code:  ofind_code.

1  #include "thread_object.h"
2
3
4  int main(int argc, char *argv[])
5  {
6
7
8
9     user_thread Thread[2];
10    Thread[0].name("ThreadA");
11    Thread[1].name("ThreadB");
12    for(int N = 0; N < 2;N++)
13    {
14        Thread[N].run();
15        Thread[N].join();
16    }
17    return(0);
18
19 }
```

The code in Listing 4-3 replaces Lines 78–88 in Listing 4-2. While we haven't really saved any lines of code, we have changed the interface of the thread creation and execution process. We now have a user_ thread class that encapsulates the pthread_t thread id and some other pthread functions. Now we're declaring objects and invoking methods as opposed to calling POSIX API functions. The program in Listing 4-3 creates and executes two threads. It then joins with the threads prior to exiting. While we can see a little easier what the thread was supposed to do in Listing 4-2, it is not apparent in Listing 4-3 what the thread is executing. In Listing 4-2 Lines 82 and 83 call pthread_create and pass it the names of the functions task1 and task2 that will be executed by ThreadA and ThreadB. In Listing 4-3, because of encapsulation, its not apparent that ThreadA and ThreadB will execute. We can see only that the run() method has been invoked. To get a better picture of how Listing 4-3 replaces Listing 4-2, take a look at the declarations in thread_object.h from Line 1 of Listing 4-3. thread_object.h contains an abstract class named thread_object. We know this class is abstract because of the abstract virtual method declared on Line 14 in Listing 4-4.

Program Profile 4-3

Program Name:

ofind_code.cc (Listing 4-3)

Description:

The program in Listing 4-3 creates and executes two threads. It then joins with the threads prior to exiting. The run() method invokes the tasks to execute. Listing 4-3 replaces Listing 4-2; look at the declarations in thread_object.h.

Libraries Required:

rt, pthread

Additional Source Files Needed:

thread_object2.cc (Listing 4-5), user_thread.cc (Listing 4-6)

User-Defined Headers Required:

thread_object.h (Listing 4-4), posix_queue.h

Compile and Link Instructions:

```
c++ -o ofind_code ofind_code.cc user_thread.cc thread_object.cc posix_queue.cc
-lrt -lpthread
```

Test Environment:

Linux Kernel 2.6

Solaris 10, gcc 3.4.3 and 3.4.6

Processors:

Multicore Opteron, UltraSparc T1, Cell Processor

Notes:

None

Listing 4-4

```
//Listing 4-4  A declaration of a simple thread_object.


1   #ifndef __THREAD_OBJECT_H
2   #define __THREAD_OBJECT_H
3
4   using namespace std;
5   #include <iostream>
6   #include <pthread.h>
7   #include <string>
8   #include "posix_queue.h"
9
10  class thread_object{
11      pthread_t Tid;
12      string Name;
13  protected:
14      virtual void do_something(void) = 0;
15  public:
16      thread_object(void);
17      ~thread_object(void);
18      void name(string X);
```

```
19      string name(void);
20      void run(void);
21      void join(void);
22      friend void *thread(void *X);
23  };
24
25
26
27  class user_thread : public thread_object{
28      private:
29      posix_queue *PosixQueue;
30  protected:
31      virtual void do_something(void);
32  public:
33      user_thread(void);
34      ~user_thread(void);
35  };
36
37
38  #endif
```

The do_something() = 0 method prevents the user from simply declaring an object of the
thread_object. Instead, to use the thread_object class, the user has to supply functionality for
do_something() by using inheritance with thread_object and supplying an implementation
for do_something(). In the context of the program of Listing 4-2, the do_something method will have
equivalent functionality to task1 and task2 from Lines 19 and 47 in Listing 4-2. The do_something
method searches a file looking for the MagicCode. Also notice Line 22 in Listing 4-4; the friend function
is also used in conjunction with the do_something() method to provide a wrapper for the pthread_
create() functionality. The class user_thread inherits the thread_object class and provides a
definition for the do_something() method. Notice in Listing 4-4 that the user_thread class also has
posix_queue data member. This was the PosixQueue that was used in Listing 4-2 on Lines 25 and 53.
This simple example of a thread_object demonstrates a slight but real Object-Oriented departure from
the procedural only approach in Listing 4-2.

Figure 4-5 shows a UML class relationship diagram for the user_thread class.

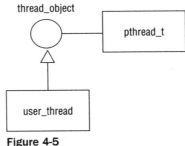

Figure 4-5

The `thread_object` class is just a simple skeleton class so far. We will fill this class's definition in as we go along. The `thread_object` class is an interface class. Its purpose is to encapsulate the POSIX thread interface and to supply Object-Oriented semantics and components so that we can implement the models we produce in the SDLC more easily. Compare the logical breakdown of the components in Figure 4-3 and Figure 4-5. The focus in Figure 4-5 is obviously different because we are doing an Object-Oriented decomposition of the `find_code` program. The `user_object` defines the `find_code` function that inherits the `thread_object`. The Object-Oriented approach hides the implementation details shown in Figure 4-3. Listing 4-5 contains some of the implementation for the simple `thread_object` class.

Listing 4-5

```
// Listing 4-5 A definition of a simple thread_object.

1   #include "thread_object.h"
2
3
4   thread_object::thread_object(void)
5   {
6
7
8
9   }
10  thread_object::~thread_object(void)
11  {
12      pthread_join(Tid,NULL);
13  }
14
15
16  void thread_object::run(void)
17  {
18      pthread_create(&Tid,NULL,thread,this);
19  }
20
21  void thread_object::join(void)
22  {
23      pthread_join(Tid,NULL);
24  }
25
26
27  void thread_object::name(string X)
28  {
29      Name = X;
30  }
31
32  string thread_object::name(void)
33  {
34      return(Name);
35  }
36
37
38  void *  thread (void * X)
39  {
40
41      thread_object *Thread;
```

```
42      Thread = static_cast<thread_object *>(X);
43      Thread->do_something();
44      return(NULL);
45
46
47  }
```

Now you can see how the run() and thread() methods together can begin to provide the functionality of the pthread_create() calls. This is just a start; we can do better. Notice that there is no implementation for the do_something() method declared in the thread_object class. This is the method that will be supplied by the user when the thread_object class is subclassed. The Thread->do_something() on Line 43 in Listing 4-5 calls the method that will be provided by a descendant class. In our case, this is defined by the definitions in Listing 4-6.

Listing 4-6

```
//Listing 4-6  The definition for the user_thread class.

1   #include "thread_object.h"
2   #include <iostream>
3   #include <fstream>
4
5   bool Found = false;
6
7
8   user_thread::user_thread(void)
9   {
10
11      PosixQueue = new posix_queue("queue_name");
12      PosixQueue->queueFlags(O_RDONLY);
13      PosixQueue->messageSize(14);
14      PosixQueue->maxMessages(4);
15
16  }
17
18
19  user_thread::~user_thread(void)
20  {
21
22      delete PosixQueue;
23
24  }
25
26
27  void user_thread::do_something(void)
28  {
29      ofstream Fout;
30      string FileName;
31      string Value;
32
33      if(PosixQueue->open()){
34          PosixQueue->receive(FileName);
35          ifstream Fin(FileName.c_str());
```

(continued)

Listing 4-6 *(continued)*

```
36          string FileOut(FileName);
37          FileOut.append(".out");
38          Fout.open(FileOut.c_str());
39
40          while(!Fin.eof() && !Fin.fail() && !Found)
41          {
42             getline(Fin,Value);
43             if(!Fin.eof() && !Fin.fail() && !Found){
44                if(Value == MagicCode){
45
46                     Found = true;
47
48                }
49
50             }
51          }
52          Fin.close();
53          Fout.close();
54       }
55
56  }
```

The main work in the user_thread class is performed by the do_something() method. By overriding the do_something() method, we can use this user_thread class to do any kind of work that can be done with the pthread_create functionality. In this case, the do_something() method performs the file search. The run() methods from the threads invoked by the user_thread object in Listing 4-3 ultimately execute the do_something() method. Since the Found variable defined on Line 5 is global and has file scope, we can use it to stop the threads from searching once the value is located.

Program Profile 4-4

Program Name:

user_thread.cc (Listing 4-6)

Description:

The user_thread class is performed by the do_something() method that does any kind of work that can be done with the pthread_create functionality. The do_something() method performs the file search. The run() methods from the threads invoked by the user_thread object execute the do_something() method. Since the Found variable is global and has file scope, it can stop the threads from searching once the value is located.

Libraries Required:

pthread

Additional Source Files Needed:

thread_object2.cc (Listing 4-6)

User-Defined Headers Required:

`thread_object.h` (Listing 4-4)

Compile Instructions:

```
cc++ -c  user_thread.cc
```

Test Environment:

Linux Kernel 2.6

Solaris 10, gcc 3.4.3 and 3.4.6

Processors:

Multicore Opteron, UltraSparc T1, Cell Processor

Notes:

None

Using interface classes in conjunction with POSIX can allow you to build cross-platform components that can help with the implementation of cross-platform multithreaded or multiprocessing applications. Certainly, the `thread_object` interface class declared in Listing 4-4 has to be fleshed out considerably before it can be used in production environments, but you can see the point we are making. The C++ interface class is heavily used in high-level component libraries and application frameworks like STAPL and TBB. If you understand how interface classes are used in conjunction with operating system APIs, the relationship between TBB, STAPL, and the operating system APIs will be more apparent. Interface classes can be used to add your own building blocks to TBB, STAPL, and other high-level libraries used for parallel processing and multithreading.

Summary

Both application developers and system developers need to have a clear understanding of the role that the operating system plays in regard to multiprocessor systems. Ideally, application programmers will not have to work directly with operating system primitives. But they still should have a grasp of the fundamentals because of the challenges that rise during testing, debugging, and software deployment. This chapter discussed the operating system's role in multicore programming. Some key points addressed include:

❑ The operating system is the gatekeeper of the CMP. Any software that wants to take advantage of multiple processors has to negotiate with the operating system. Since the C++ standard does not have direct support for process or thread management, you can use the POSIX API to access operating system services related to process and thread management.

❑ The operating system's role can be divided into two primary functions:

  ❑ **Software interface**: Providing a consistent and well-defined interface to the hardware resources of the computer

❑   **Resource management**: Managing the hardware resources and other executing software applications, jobs, and programs

❑   Instead of forcing the programmer to use particular device-specific instructions, the operating system provides the programmer with a couple of layers of software (the API and SPI) between the developer's program and the hardware resources connected to the computer.

❑   The operating system's core services can be divided into:

     ❑   Process management

     ❑   Memory management

     ❑   Filesystem management

     ❑   I/O management

     ❑   Interprocess Communication Manager

❑   The goal of a framework like STAPL is to allow the developer to provide parallelism in a software application while not having to worry about all of the specific implementation related issues that are involved with parallel programming. A library like the TBB is a set of high-level generic components that also encapsulates much of the detail of multiprocessing and multithreading.

❑   Once the software design process determines that the application is best divided into two or more concurrently executing tasks, the transparency of the operating system becomes an issue. The idea is to build classes that encapsulate lower-level procedural-driven functionality of the operating system APIs, while providing a higher-level declarative interface to the application developer.

❑   As you move toward more cores and more parallelism, you need to pursue two important steps to make software development for massive parallel CMPs practical:

     ❑   Take advantage of the operating system, while making it transparent to software designs

     ❑   Move from procedural paradigms of parallel programming to declarative paradigms

❑   Encapsulate operating system process and thread management services in C++ components. Then, from the C++ components, build application frameworks that capture architectures that support parallelism.

Ultimately, the multithreading or multiprocessing functionality contained in class libraries, high-level function libraries, or application frameworks still needs to pass through operating system APIs or SPIs. In the next two chapters, we go into more detail on the use of processes and threads in multicore programming.

5

Processes, C++ Interface Classes, and Predicates

As long as I held the Divine Spear, I had to accept debugging as my primary duty.

— **Tatsuya Hamazaki,** *.hack//AI Buster 2*

In Chapter 4, we looked at the operating system's role as a development tool for applications that required parallel programming. We provided a brief overview of the part that the operating system plays in process management and thread management. We introduced the reader to the notion of operating system Application Program Interfaces (APIs) and System Program Interfaces (SPIs), and in particular we introduced the POSIX API. In this chapter we are going to take a closer look at:

❑ Where the process fits in with C++ programming and multicore computers

❑ The POSIX API for process management

❑ Process scheduling and priorities

❑ Building C++ interface components that can be used to simplify part of the POSIX API for process management

Basically, a program can be divided into processes and/or threads in order to achieve concurrency and take advantage of multicore processors. In this chapter, we cover how the operating system identifies processes and how an application can utilize multiple processes.

We Say *Multicore*, We Mean *Multiprocessor*

Keep in mind that the name *multicore* is a popular substitution for *single chip multiprocessor* or *CMP*. Multiprocessors are computers that have more than two or more CPUs or processors. Although multiprocessor computers have been around for some time now, the wide availability and low cost of the CMP has brought multiprocessor capabilities within the reach of virtually all software developers. This raises a series of questions: How do single applications take advantage of CMPs? How do single user versus multiple user applications take advantage of CMPs? Using C++ how do you take advantage of the operating system's multiprocessing and multiprogramming capabilities? Once you have a software design that includes a requirement for some tasks to execute concurrently, how do you map those tasks to the multiple processors available in your multicore computers?

Recall from Chapter 4 that the operating system schedules execution units that it can understand. If your software design consists of some tasks that can be executed in parallel, you will have to find a way to relate those tasks to execution units the operating system can understand. Association of your tasks with operating system execution units is part of a four-stage process involving three transformations.

Each transformation in Figure 5-1 changes the view of the model, but the meaning of the model should remain intact. That is, the implementation of the application frameworks, class libraries, and templates as processes and threads should not change the meaning or semantics of what those components are doing. The execution units in stage four are what the operating system deals with directly. The execution units shown in stage four of Figure 5-1 are the only things that can be assigned directly to the cores. From the operating system's viewpoint your application is a collection of one or more processes. Concurrency in a C++ application is ultimately accomplished by factoring your program into either multiple processes or multiple threads. While there are variations on how the logic for a C++ program can be organized (for example, within objects, predicates, functions, or generic templates), the options for parallelization (with the exception of instruction level) are accounted for through the use of multiple processes and threads.

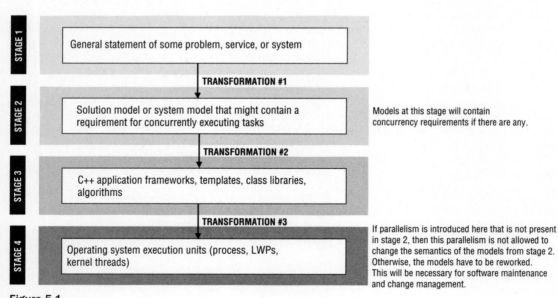

Figure 5-1

This chapter focuses on the notion of a process and how C++ applications and programs can be divided into multiple processes using the POSIX API process management services.

What Is a Process?

A *process* is a unit of work created by the operating system. It is important to note that processes and programs are not necessarily equivalent. A program may consist of multiple tasks, and each task can be associated with one or more processes. Processes are artifacts of the operating system, and programs are artifacts of the developer. Current operating systems are capable of managing hundreds even thousands of concurrently loaded processes. In order for a unit of work to be called a process, it must have an address space assigned to it by the operating system. It must have a process id. It must have a state and an entry in the process table. According to the POSIX standard, it must have one or more flows of controls executing within that address space and the required system resources for those flows of control. A process has a set of executing instructions that resides in the address space of that process. Space is allocated for the instructions, any data that belongs to the process, and stacks for functions calls and local variables. One of the important differences between a process and a thread is the fact that each process has its own address space, whereas threads share the address space of the processes that created them. A program can be broken down into one or more processes.

Why Processes and Not Threads?

When you are mapping C++ tasks to execution units that the operating system can understand, threads turn out to be easier to program. This is because threads share the same address space. This makes communication and synchronization between threads much easier. It takes the operating system less work to create a thread or to terminate a thread than it takes for processes. In general, you can create more threads within the context of a single computer than processes. The starting and stopping of threads is typically faster than processes.

So why use processes at all? First, processes have their own address space. This is important because separate address spaces provide a certain amount security and isolation from rogue or poorly designed processes. Second, the number of open files that threads may use is limited to how many open files a single process can have. Dividing your C++ application up into multiple processes instead of or in conjunction with multithreading provides access to more open file resources. For multiuser applications, you want each user's process to be isolated. If one user's process fails, the other users can continue to perform work. If you use some threading approach for multiuser applications, a single errant thread can disrupt all the users. Operating system resources are assigned primarily to processes and then shared by threads. So, in general, threads are limited to the number of resources that a single process can have. Thus, when isolation security, address space isolation, and maximum number of resources that concurrently executing tasks may have are major concerns, it is better to use processes than threads. Communication between processes and startup time are the primary tradeoffs.

The functions listed in Table 5-1 are declared in `spawn.h`. This header contains the POSIX functions used to spawn and manage processes.

Table 5-1

Types of POSIX Functions	POSIX Functions
Creating processes	`posix_spawn()` `posix_spawnp()`
Initializing attributes	`posix_spawnattr_init()`
Destroying attributes	`posix_spawnattr_destroy()`

Setting and retrieving attribute values	`posix_spawnattr_setsigdefault()`
	`posix_spawnattr_getsigdefault()`
	`posix_spawnattr_setsigmask()`
	`posix_spawnattr_getsigmask()`
	`posix_spawnattr_setflags()`
	`posix_spawnattr_getflags()`
	`posix_spawnattr_setpgroup()`
	`posix_spawnattr_getpgroup()`

Process scheduling	`posix_spawnattr_setschedparam()`
	`posix_spawnattr_setschedpolicy()`
	`posix_spawnattr_getschedparam()`
	`posix_spawnattr_getschedpolicy()`
	`sched_setscheduler()`
	`sched_setparm()`

Adding file actions	`posix_spawn_file_actions_addclose()`
	`posix_spawn_file_actions_adddup2()`
	`posix_spawn_file_actions_addopen()`
	`posix_spawn_file_actions_destroy()`
	`posix_spawn_file_actions_init()`

Using posix_spawn()

Similarly to the `fork-exec()` and `system()` methods of process creation, the `posix_spawn()` functions create new child processes from specified process images. But the `posix_spawn()` functions create child processes with more fine-grained control during creation. While the POSIX API also supports the `fork-exec()` class of functions, we focus on the `posix_spawn` functions for process creation to achieve greater cross-platform compatibility. Some platforms may have trouble implementing `fork()`, so the `posix_spawn()` functions can be used as substitution. These functions control the attributes that the child process inherits from the parent process, including:

❑ File descriptors

❑ Scheduling policy

❑ Process group id

❑ User and group id

❑ Signal mask

They also control whether signals ignored by the parent are ignored by the child or reset to some default action. Controlling file descriptors allow the child process independent access to the data stream opened by the parent. Being able to set the child's process group id affects how the child's job control relates to that of the parent. The child's scheduling policy can be set to be different from the scheduling policy of the parent.

Synopsis

```
#include <spawn.h>

int posix_spawn(pid_t *restrict pid, const char *restrict path,
                const posix_spawn_file_actions_t *file_actions,
                const posix_spawnattr_t *restrict attrp,
                char *const argv[restrict],
                char *const envp[restrict]);
int posix_spawnp(pid_t *restrict pid, const char *restrict file,
                const posix_spawn_file_actions_t *file_actions,
                const posix_spawnattr_t *restrict attrp,
                char *const argv[restrict],
                char *const envp[restrict]);
```

The difference between these two functions is that `posix_spawn()` has a `path` parameter and `posix_spawnp()` has a `file` parameter. The `path` parameter in the `posix_spawn()` function is the absolute or relative pathname to the executable program file. `file` in `posix_spawnp()` is the name of the executable program. If the parameter contains a slash, then `file` is used as a pathname. If not, the path to the executable is determined by `PATH` environment variable.

The file_actions Parameter

The `file_actions` parameter is a pointer to a `posix_spawn_file_actions_t` structure:

```
struct posix_spawn_file_actions_t{
{
    int __allocated;
    int __used;
    struct __spawn_action *actions;
    int __pad[16];
};
```

`posix_spawn_file_actions_t` is a data structure that contains information about the actions to be performed in the new process with respect to file descriptors. `file_actions` is used to modify the parent's set of open file descriptors to a set file descriptors for the spawned child process. This structure can contain several file action operations to be performed in the sequence in which they were added to the spawn file action object. These file action operations are performed on the open file descriptors of the parent process. These operations can duplicate, duplicate and reset, add, delete, or close a specified file descriptor on behalf of the child process even before it's spawned. If `file_actions` is a null pointer, then the file descriptors opened by the parent process remain open for the child process without any modifications. Table 5-2 lists the functions used to add file actions to the `posix_spawn_file_actions` object.

Table 5-2

File Action Attribute Functions	Descriptions
```int posix_spawn_file_actions_addclose (posix_spawn_file_actions_t *file_actions, int fildes);```	Adds a close() action to a spawn file action object specified by file_actions. This causes the file descriptor fildes to be closed when the new process is spawned using this file action object.
```int posix_spawn_file_actions_addopen (posix_spawn_file_actions_t *file_actions, int fildes, const char *restrict path, int oflag, mode_t mode);```	Adds an open() action to a spawn file action object specified by file_actions. This causes the file named path with the returned file descriptor fildes to be opened when the new process is spawned using this file action object.
```int posix_spawn_file_actions_adddup2 (posix_spawn_file_actions_t *file_actions, int fildes, int newfildes);```	Adds a dup2() action to a spawn file action object specified by file_actions. This causes the file descriptor fildes to be duplicated with the file descriptor newfildes when the new process is spawned using this file action object.
```int posix_spawn_file_actions_destroy (posix_spawn_file_actions_t *file_actions);```	Destroys the specified file_actions object. This causes the object to be uninitialized. The object can then be reinitialized using posix_spawn_file_actions_init().
```int posix_spawn_file_actions_init (posix_spawn_file_actions_t *file_actions);```	Initializes the specified file_actions object. Once initialized, it contains no file actions to be performed.

The attrp Parameter

The attrp parameter points to a posix_spawnattr_t structure:

```
struct posix_spawnattr_t
{
    short int __flags;
    pid_t __pgrp;
    sigset_t __sd;
    sigset_t __ss;
    struct sched_param __sp;
    int __policy;
    int __pad[16];
}
```

This structure contains information about the scheduling policy, process group, signals, and flags for the new process. The description of individual attributes is as follows:

❑   __flags: Used to indicate which process attributes are to be modified in the spawned process. They are bitwise-inclusive OR of 0 or more of the following:

     ❑   POSIX_SPAWN_RESETIDS

     ❑   POSIX_SPAWN_SETPGROUP

     ❑   POSIX_SPAWN_SETSIGDEF

     ❑   POSIX_SPAWN_SETSIGMASK

     ❑   POSIX_SPAWN_SETSCHEDPARAM

     ❑   POSIX_SPAWN_SETSCHEDULER

❑   __pgrp: The id of the process group to be joined by the new process.

❑   __sd: Represents the set of signals to be forced to use default signal handling by the new process.

❑   __ss: Represents the signal mask to be used by the new process.

❑   __sp: Represents the scheduling parameter to be assigned to the new process.

❑   __policy: Represents the scheduling policy to be used by the new process.

Table 5-3 lists the functions used to set and retrieve the individual attributes contained in the posix_spawnattr_t structure.

Table 5-3

Spawn Process Attributes Functions	Descriptions
int posix_spawnattr_getflags (const posix_spawnattr_t *restrict attr, short *restrict flags);	Returns the value of the __flags attribute stored in the specified attr object.
int posix_spawnattr_setflags (posix_spawnattr_t *attr, short flags);	Sets the value of the __flags attribute stored in the specified attr object to flags.
int posix_spawnattr_getpgroup (const posix_spawnattr_t *restrict attr, pid_t *restrict pgroup);	Returns the value of the __pgroup attribute stored in the specified attr object and stores it in pgroup.
int posix_spawnattr_setpgroup (posix_spawnattr_t *attr, pid_t pgroup);	Sets the value of the __pgroup attribute stored in the specified attr object to pgroup if POSIX_ SPAWN_SETPGROUP is set in the __flags attribute.

Table continued on following page

Spawn Process Attributes Functions	Descriptions

`int posix_spawnattr_getschedparam`
`(const posix_spawnattr_t`
`*restrict attr, struct sched_param`
`*restrict schedparam);`
	Returns the value of the __sp attribute stored in the specified `attr` object and stores it in `schedparam`.

`int posix_spawnattr_setschedparam`
`(posix_spawnattr_t *attr,`
` const struct sched_param *restrict`
` schedparam);`
	Sets the value of the __sp attribute stored in the specified `attr` object to `schedparam` if `POSIX_SPAWN_SETSCHEDPARAM` is set in the __flags attribute.

`int posix_spawnattr_getpschedpolicy`
`(const posix_spawnattr_t *restrict`
` attr, int *restrict schedpolicy);`
	Returns the value of the __policy attribute stored in the specified `attr` object and stores it in `schedpolicy`.

`int posix_spawnattr_setpschedpolicy`
`(posix_spawnattr_t *attr,`
` int schedpolicy);`
	Sets the value of the __policy attribute stored in the specified `attr` object to `schedpolicy` if `POSIX_SPAWN_SETSCHEDULER` is set in the __flags attribute.

`int posix_spawnattr_getsigdefault`
`(const posix_spawnattr_t *restrict`
` attr, sigset_t *restrict`
` sigdefault);`
	Returns the value of the __sd attribute stored in the specified `attr` object and stores it in `sigdefault`.

`int posix_spawnattr_setsigdefault`
`(posix_spawnattr_t *attr,`
` const sigset_t *restrict`
` sigdefault);`
	Sets the value of the __sd attribute stored in the specified `attr` object to `sigdefault` if `POSIX_SPAWN_SETSIGDEF` is set in the __flags attribute.

`int posix_spawnattr_getsigmask`
`(const posix_spawnattr_t *restrict`
` attr, sigset_t *restrict sigmask);`
	Returns the value of the __ss attribute stored in the specified `attr` object and stores it in `sigmask`.

`int posix_spawnattr_setsigmask`
`(posix_spawnattr_t *restrict attr,`
` const sigset_t *restrict sigmask);`
	Sets the value of the __ss attribute stored in the specified `attr` object to `sigmask` if `POSIX_SPAWN_SETSIGMASK` is set in the __flags attribute.

`int posix_spawnattr_destroy` `(posix_spawnattr_t *attr);`	Destroys the specified `attr` object. The object can then become reinitialized using `posix_spawnattr_init()`.
`int posix_spawnattr_init` `(posix_spawnattr_t *attr);`	Initializes the specified `attr` object with default values for all of the attributes contained in the structure.

A Simple posix_spawn() Example

Example 5-1 shows how the posix_spawn() function can be used to create a process.

Example 5-1

```
// Example 5-1 Spawns a process, using the posix_spawn()
// function that calls the ps utility.

#include <spawn.h>
#include <stdio.h>
#include <errno.h>
#include <iostream>
{
    //...
    posix_spawnattr_t X;
    posix_spawn_file_actions_t Y;
    pid_t Pid;
    char * argv[] = {"/bin/ps","-lf",NULL};
    char * envp[] = {"PROCESSES=2"};
    posix_spawnattr_init(&X);
    posix_spawn_file_actions_init(&Y);
    posix_spawn(&Pid,"/bin/ps",&Y,&X,argv,envp);
    perror("posix_spawn");
    cout << "spawned PID: " << Pid << endl;
    //...
    return(0);

}
```

In Example 5-1, posix_spawnattr_t and posix_spawn_file_actions_t objects are initialized. posix_spawn() is called with the arguments PID; path; Y; X; argv, which contains the command as the first element and the argument as the second; and envp, the environment list. If posix_spawn() is successful, then the value stored in Pid will be the PID of the spawned process. perror displayed:

```
posix_spawn: Success
```

and the Pid is sent to output. The spawned process, in this case, executes:

```
/bin/ps -lf
```

These functions return the process id of the child process to the parent process in the pid parameter and return 0 as the return value. If the function is unsuccessful, no child process is created; thus, no pid is returned, and an error value is returned as the return value of the function. Errors can occur on three levels when using the spawn functions.

❑   An error can occur if the `file_actions` or `attr` objects are invalid. If this occurs after the function has successfully returned (the child process was spawned), then the child process may have an exit status of 127.

❑   If the spawn attribute functions cause an error, then the error produced for that particular function (listed in Tables 5-2 and 5-3) is returned. If the spawn function has already successfully returned, then the child process may have an exit status of 127.

❑   Errors can also occur when you are attempting to spawn the child process. These errors would be the same errors produced by `fork()` or `exec()` functions. If they occur, they will be the return values for the spawn functions.

If the child process produces an error, it is not returned to the parent process. For the parent process to be aware that the child has produced an error, you have to use other mechanisms since the error will not be stored in the child's exit status. You can use Interprocess Communication, or the child can set some flag visible to the parent.

The guess_it Program Using posix_spawn

Listing 5-1 recalls the "guess the mystery code" program from Chapter 4, Listing 4-1, that spawned two child processes.

Listing 5-1

```
// Listing 5-1  Program used to launch ofind_code.

1   using namespace std;
2   #include <iostream>
3   #include <string>
4   #include <spawn.h>
5   #include <sys/wait.h>
6
7   int main(int argc,char *argv[],char *envp[])
8   {
9
10      pid_t ChildProcess;
11      pid_t ChildProcess2;
12      int RetCode1;
13      int RetCode2;
14      int Value;
15      RetCode1 = posix_spawn(&ChildProcess,"find_code",NULL,
16                              NULL,argv,envp);
17      RetCode2 = posix_spawn(&ChildProcess2,"find_code",NULL,
18                              NULL,argv,envp);
19      wait(&Value);
20      wait(&Value);
21      return(0);
22  }
```

In Example 5-1, we used posix_spawn to launch the ps shell utility. Here in Listing 5-1, we use posix_spawn to launch the ofind_code program. This illustrates an important feature of posix_spawn(); it is used to launch programs external to the calling program. Any programs that are located on the local computer can be easily launched with posix_spawn(). The posix_spawn() calls in Listing 5-1, lines 15 and 16 have a terse interface. In Chapter 4, we introduced the notion of interface classes, which can start you on the road to a more declarative style multicore programming. Interface classes are easy to implement. Listing 5-2 shows a simple interface class that you can use to encapsulate the basics of the posix_spawn() functions.

Listing 5-2

```
//Listing 5-2  An initial interface class for a posix process.

1   #ifndef __POSIX_PROCESS_H
2   #define __POSIX_PROCESS_H
3   using namespace std;
4
5   #include <spawn.h>
6   #include <errno.h>
7   #include <iostream>
8   #include <string>
9
10
11  class posix_process{
12  protected:
13      pid_t  Pid;
14      posix_spawnattr_t   SpawnAttr;
15      posix_spawn_file_actions_t   FileActions;
16      char **argv;
17      char **envp;
18      string ProgramPath;
19  public:
20      posix_process(string Path,char **av,char **env);
21      posix_process(string Path,char **av,char **env, posix_spawnattr_t X,
                       posix_spawn_file_actions_t Y);
22      void run(void);
23      void pwait(int &X);
24  };
25
26
27  #endif
28
```

This simple interface class can be used to add a more object-oriented approach to process management. It makes it easier to move from models shown in Stage 2 in Figure 5-1 to the execution units in Stage 4. It also makes the OS API calls transparent to the user. For example, the guess_it program shown in Listing 5-1 can be restated as shown in Listing 5-3.

Listing 5-3

```
//Listing 5-3  Our guess_it program using an interface class for the posix_spawn
capability.


1   #include "posix_process.h"
2
3   int main(int argc,char *argv[],char *envp[])
4   {
5      int Value;
6      posix_process  Child1("ofind_code",argv,envp);
7      posix_process  Child2("ofind_code",argv,envp);
8      Child1.run();
9      Child2.run();
10     Child1.pwait(&Value);
11     Child2.pwait(&Value);
12     return(0);
13 }
14
```

Recall from Chapter 4 that the `guess_it` program spawns two child processes. Each child process in turn spawns two threads. The resulting four threads are used to search files. The value of the interface class as a tool for converting procedural paradigms into Object-Oriented declarative approaches cannot be overstated. Once you have a `posix_process` class, it can be used like a datatype with the container classes. This means that you can have:

```
vector<posix_process>
list<posix_process>
multiset<posix_process>
etc...
```

thinking about processes and threads as objects as opposed to sequences of actions, which is a big step in the direction of the declarative models of parallel programming. Listing 5-4 shows the initial method definitions for the `posix_process` interface class.

Listing 5-4

```
// Listing 5-4 The initial method definitions for the posix_process interface class.

1   #include "posix_process.h"
2   #include <sys/wait.h>
3
4
5   posix_process::posix_process(string Path,char **av,char **env)
6   {
7
8      argv = av;
9      envp = env;
10     ProgramPath = Path;
11     posix_spawnattr_init(&SpawnAttr);
12     posix_spawn_file_actions_init(&FileActions);
13
14
```

```
15  }
16
17  posix_process::posix_process(string Path,char **av,char **env,
                    posix_spawnattr_t  X, posix_spawn_file_actions_t Y)
18  {
19      argv = av;
20      envp = env;
21      ProgramPath = Path;
22      SpawnAttr = X;
23      FileActions = Y;
24      posix_spawnattr_init(&SpawnAttr);
25      posix_spawn_file_actions_init(&FileActions);
26
27
28
29  }
30
31  void posix_process::run(void)
32  {
33
34      posix_spawn(&Pid,ProgramPath.c_str(),&FileActions,
                    &SpawnAttr,argv,envp);
35
36
37  }
38
39  void posix_process::pwait(int &X)
40  {
41
42      wait(&X);
43  }
```

The `run()` method defined on Line 31 in Listing 5-4 adapts the interface to the `posix_spawn()` function. You can build on these declarations by adding methods that adapt the interface of all of the functions listed in Table 5-2 and Table 5-3. Once completed, you can add process building blocks to your object-oriented toolkit.

Who Is the Parent? Who Is the Child?

There are two functions that return the process id (PID) of the process and parent process:

- ❑   `getpid()` returns the process id of the calling process.
- ❑   `getppid()` returns the parent id of the calling process.

These functions are always successful; therefore no errors are defined.

Synopsis

```
#include <unistd.h>

pid_t getpid(void);
pid_t getppid(void);
```

Processes: A Closer Look

When a process executes, the operating system assigns the process to a processor. The process executes its instructions for a quantum. The process is preempted, so another process can be assigned the processor. The operating system scheduler switches between the code of one process, user, or system to the code of another process, giving each process a chance to execute its instructions. There are system and user processes.

❏ Processes that execute system code are called **system processes**, also sometimes referred to as **kernel processes**. System processes administer the whole system. They perform housekeeping tasks such as allocating memory, swapping pages of memory between internal and secondary storage, checking devices, and so on. They also perform tasks on behalf of the user processes such as filling I/O requests, allocating memory, and so forth.

❏ **User processes** execute their own code, and sometimes they make system function calls. When a user process executes its own code, it is in **user mode**. In user mode, the process cannot execute certain privileged machine instructions. When a user process makes a system function call (for example, read(), write(), or open()), it is executing operating system instructions. What occurs is the user process is put on hold until the system call has completed. The processor is given to the kernel to complete the system call. At that time the user process is said to be in **kernel mode** and cannot be preempted by any user processes.

Process Control Block

Processes have characteristics that identify them and determine their behavior during execution. The kernel maintains data structures and provides system functions that allow the user to have access to this information. Some information is stored in the *process control block (PCB)*. The information stored in the PCB describes the process to the operating system. This PCB is part of the heavy weight of the process. This information is needed for the operating system to manage each process. When the operating system switches between a process utilizing the CPU to another process, it saves the current state of the executing process and its context to the PCB save area in order to restart the process the next time it is assigned to the CPU. The PCB is read and changed by various modules of the operating system. Modules concerned with the monitoring the operating system's performance, scheduling, allocation of resources, and interrupt processing all will access and/or modify the PCB. The PCB is what makes the process visible to the operating system and entities like user threads invisible to the operating system.

PCB information includes:

❏ Current state and priority of the process

❏ Process, parent, and child identifiers

❏ Pointers to allocated resources

❏ Pointers to location of the process's memory

❏ Pointer to the process's parent and child processes

❏ Processor utilized by process

❏ Control and status registers

❏ Stack pointers

The information stored in the PCB can be organized as follows:

❑ Information concerned with **process control**, such as the current state and priority of the process, pointers to parent/child PCB's, allocated resources, and memory. This also includes any scheduling related information, process privileges, flags, messages, and signals that have to do with communication between processes (IPC — Interprocess Communication). The process control information is required by the operating system in order to coordinate the concurrently active processes.

❑ The content of user, control, and status registers and stack pointers are all types of information concerned with the **state of the processor**. When a process is running, information is placed in the registers of the CPU. Once the operating system decides to switch to another process, all the information in those registers has to be saved. When the process gains the use of the CPU again, this information can be restored.

❑ Other information has to do with **process identification**. This is the process id, PID, and the parent process id, PPID. These identification numbers are unique for each process. They are positive, nonzero integers.

Anatomy of a Process

The address space of a process is divided into three logical segments: *text* (program code), *data*, and *stack* segments. Figure 5-2 shows the logical layout of a process. The text segment is at the bottom of the address space. The text segment contains the instructions to be executed called the *program code*. The data segment above it contains the initialized global, external, and static variables for the process. The stack segment contains locally allocated variables and parameters passed to functions. Because a process can make system function calls as well as user-defined function calls, two stacks are maintained in the stack segment, the *user stack* and the *kernel stack*. When a function call is made, a stack-frame is constructed and pushed onto either the user or kernel stack, depending on whether the process is in user or kernel mode. The stack segment grows downward toward the data segment. The stack frame is popped from the stack when the function returns. The text, data, and stack segments and the process control block are part of what forms the *process image*.

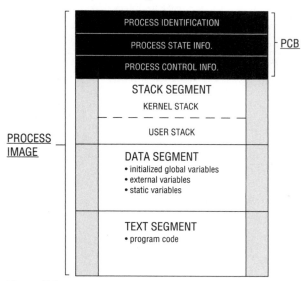

Figure 5-2

The address space of a process is *virtual*. Virtual storage dissociates the addresses referenced in an executing process from the addresses actually available in internal memory. This allows the addressing of storage space much larger than what is available. The segments of the process's virtual address space are contiguous blocks of memory. Each segment and physical address space are broken up into chunks called *pages*. Each page has a unique *page frame number*. The virtual page frame number (VPFN) is used as an index into the process's page tables. The *page tables* entries contain a physical page frame number (PFN), thus mapping the virtual page frames to physical page frames. This is depicted in Figure 5-3. As illustrated, virtual address space is contiguous but it is mapped to physical pages in any order.

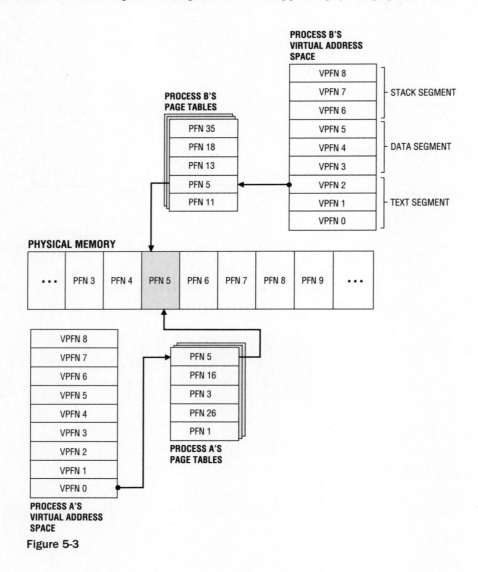

Figure 5-3

Even though the virtual address space of each process is protected to prevent another process from accessing it, the text segment of a process can be shared among several processes. Figure 5-3 also shows how two processes can share the same program code. The same physical page frame number is stored in the page table entries of both processes' page tables. As illustrated in Figure 5-3, process A's virtual page frame 0 is mapped to physical page frame 5, as is process B's virtual page frame 2.

For the operating system to manage all the processes stored in internal memory, it creates and maintains *process tables*. Actually, the operating system has a table for all of the entities that it manages. Keep in mind that the operating system manages not only processes but all the resources of the computer including devices, memory, and files. Some of the memory, devices, and files are managed on the behalf of the user processes. This information is referenced in the PCB as resources allocated to the process. The process table has an entry for each process image in memory. This is depicted in Figure 5-4. Each entry contains the process and parent process id; the real and effective user id and group id; a list of pending signals; the location of the text, data, and stack segments; and the current state of the process. When the operating system needs to access a process, the process is looked up in the process table, and then the process image is located in memory.

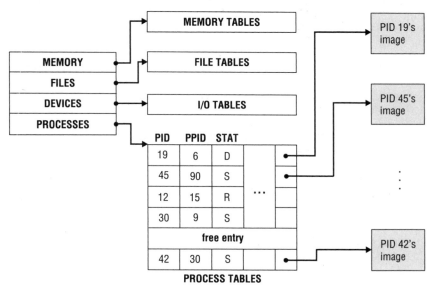

Figure 5-4

Process States

During a process's execution, it changes its state. The *state* of the process is the current condition or status of the process. In a POSIX-compliant environment, a process can be in the following states:

- ❏ Running
- ❏ Runnable (ready)
- ❏ Zombied

❑   Waiting (blocked)

❑   Stopped

The current condition of the process depends upon the circumstances created by the process or by the operating system. When certain circumstances exist, the process will change its state. *State transition* is the circumstance that causes the process to change its state. Figure 5-5 is the state diagram for the processes. The state diagram has nodes and directed edges between the nodes. Each node represents the state of the process. The directed edges between the nodes are state transitions. Table 5-4 lists the state transitions with a brief description. As Figure 5-5 and Table 5-4 show, only certain transitions are allowed between states. For example, there is a transition, an edge, between ready and running, but there is no transition, no edge, between sleeping and running. Meaning, there are circumstances that causes a process to move from the ready state to the running state, but there are no circumstances that cause a process to move from the sleeping state to a running state.

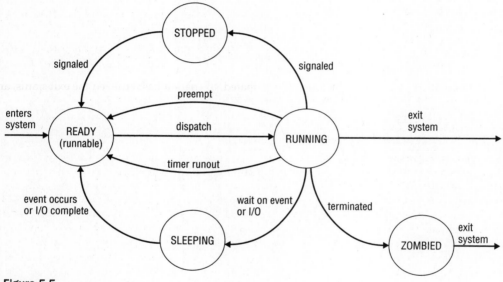

Figure 5-5

Table 5-4

State Transitions	Descriptions
READY->RUNNING (dispatch)	The process is assigned to the processor.
RUNNING-> READY(timer runout)	The time slice the process assigned to the processor has run out. The process is placed back in the ready queue.
RUNNING-> READY(preempt)	The process has been preempted before the time slice ran out. This can occur if a process with a higher priority is runnable. The process is placed back in the ready queue.

State Transitions	Descriptions
RUNNING-> SLEEPING (block)	The process gives up the processor before the time slice has run out. The process may need to wait for an event or has made a system call, for example, a request for I/O. The process is placed in a queue with other sleeping processes.
SLEEPING->READY (unblock)	The event the process was waiting for has occurred, or the system call has completed. For example, the I/O request is filled. The process is placed back in the ready queue.
RUNNING-> STOPPED	The process gives up the processor because it has received a signal to stop.
STOPPED->READY	The process has received the signal to continue and is placed back in the ready queue.
RUNNING-> ZOMBIED	The process has been terminated and awaits the parent to retrieve its exit status from the process table.
ZOMBIED->EXIT	The parent process has retrieved the exit status, and the process exits the system.
RUNNING->EXIT	The process has terminated, the parent has retrieved the exit status, and the process exits the system.

When a process is created, it is ready to execute its instructions but must first wait until the processor is available. Each process is allowed to use the processor only for a discrete interval called a *time slice*. Processes waiting to use the processor are placed in ready queues. Only processes in the ready queues are selected (by the scheduler) to use the processor. Processes in the ready queues are *runnable*. When the processor is available, a runnable process is assigned the processor by the dispatcher. When the time slice has expired, the process is removed from the processor, whether it has finished executing all its instructions or not. The process is placed back in the ready queue to wait for its next turn to use the processor. A new process is selected from a ready queue and is given its time slice to execute. System processes are not preempted. When they are given the processor, they run until completion. If the time slice has not expired, a process may voluntarily give up the processor if it cannot continue to execute because it must wait for an event to occur. The process may have made a request to access an I/O device by making a system call, or it may need to wait on a synchronization variable to be released. Processes that cannot continue to execute because they are waiting for an event to occur are in a *sleeping state*. They are placed in a queue with other sleeping processes. They are removed from that queue and placed back in the ready queue when the event has occurred. The processor may be taken away from a process before its time slice has run out. This may occur if a process with a higher priority, like a system process, is runnable. The preempted process is still runnable and, therefore, is placed back in the ready queue.

A running process can receive a signal to stop. The *stopped state* is different from a sleeping state. The process's time slice has not expired nor has the process made any request of the system. The process may receive a signal to stop because it is being debugged or some situation has occurred in the system. The process has made a transition from running to stopped state. Later the process may be awakened, or it may be destroyed.

When a process has executed all its instructions, it exits the system. The process is removed from the process table, the PCB is destroyed, and all of its resources are deallocated and returned to the system pool of available resources. A process that is unable to continue executing but cannot exit the system is in a *zombied state*. A zombied process does not use any system resources, but it still maintains an entry in the process table. When the process table contains too many zombied processes, this can affect the performance of the system, possibly causing the system to reboot.

How Are Processes Scheduled?

When a ready queue contains several processes, the scheduler must determine which process should be assigned to a processor first. The scheduler maintains data structures that allow it to schedule the processes in an efficient manner. Each process is given a priority class and placed in a priority queue with other runnable processes with the same priority class. There are multiple priority queues, each representing a different priority class used by the system. These priority queues are stratified and placed in a dispatch array called the *multilevel priority queue*. Figure 5-6 depicts the multilevel priority queue. Each element in the array points to a priority queue. The scheduler assigns the process at the head of the nonempty highest priority queue to the processor.

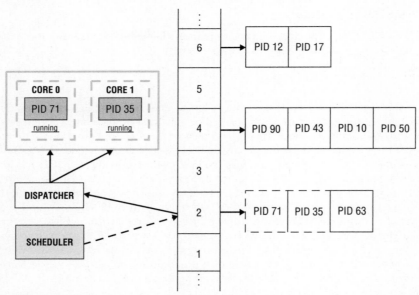

Figure 5-6

Priorities can be *dynamic* or *static*. Once a static priority of a process is set, it cannot be changed. Dynamic priorities can be changed. Processes with the highest priority can monopolize the use of the processor. If the priority of a process is dynamic, the initial priority can be adjusted to a more appropriate value. The process is placed in a priority queue that has a higher priority. A process monopolizing the processor can also be given a lower priority, or other processes can be given a higher priority than that process has. When you are assigning priority to a user process, consider what the process spends most of its time doing. Some processes are CPU-intensive. CPU-intensive processes use the processor for the whole time slice. Some processes spend most of its time waiting for I/O or some other event to occur. When such a process is ready to use the processor, it should be given the processor immediately so it can make its next request for I/O. Processes that are interactive may require a high priority to assure good response time. System processes have a higher priority than user processes.

The processes are placed in a priority queue according to a scheduling policy. Two of the primary scheduling policies used in the POSIX API are the First-In, First-Out (FIFO) and round robin (RR) policies.

❏　Figure 5-7 (a) shows the **FIFO scheduling policy**. With a FIFO scheduling policy, processes are assigned the processor according to the arrival time in the queue. When a running process time slice has expired, it is placed at the head of its priority queue. When a sleeping process becomes runnable, the process is placed at the end of its priority queue. A process can make a system call and give up the processor to another process with the same priority level. The process is then placed at the end of its priority queue.

❏　In **round robin scheduling policy**, all processes are considered equal. Figure 5-7 (b) depicts the RR scheduling policy. RR scheduling is the same as FIFO scheduling with one exception: When the time slice expires, the process is placed at the back of the queue and the next process in the queue is assigned the processor.

(a) FIFO SCHEDULING

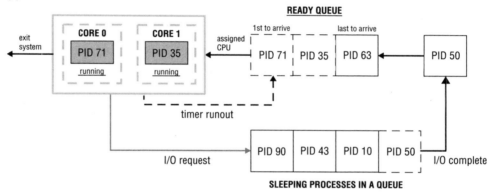

(b) RR SCHEDULING

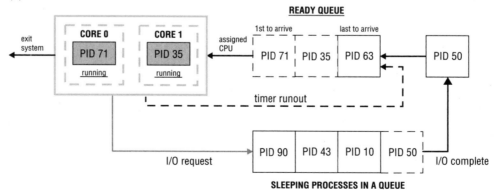

Figure 5-7

Figure 5-7 shows the behavior of the FIFO and RR scheduling policies. The FIFO scheduling policy assigns processes to the processor according to its arrival time in the queue. The process runs until completion. RR scheduling policy assigns processes using FIFO scheduling, but when the time slice runs out, the process is placed at the back of the ready queue.

Monitoring Processes with the ps Utility

The ps utility generates a report that summarizes execution statistics for the current processes. This information can be used to monitor the status of current processes. Table 5-5 lists the common headers and the meaning of the output for the ps utility for the Solaris/Linux environments.

Table 5-5

Headers	Description	Headers	Description
USER, UID	Username of process owner	TT, TTY	Process's controlling terminal
PID PPID	Process ID Parent process ID	S, STAT	Current state of the process
PGID SID	ID of process group leader ID of session leader	TIME	Total CPU time used by the process (HH:MM:SS)
%CPU	Percentage of CPU time used by the process in the last minute	STIME, START	Time or date the process started
RSS	Amount of real RAM currently used by the process in k	NI	Nice value of the process
%MEM	Percentage of real RAM used by the process in the last minute	PRI	Priority of the process
SZ	Size of virtual memory of the process's data and stack in k or pages	C, CP	Short term CPU-use factor used by scheduler to compute PRI
WCHAN	Address of an event for which a process is sleeping	ADDR	Memory address of a process
COMMAND CMD	Command name and arguments	LWP NLWP	ID of the lwp (thread) The number of lwps

In a multiprocessor environment, the ps utility is useful to monitor the state, CPU and memory usage, processor utilized, priority, and start time of the current processes executing. Command options control which processes are listed and what information is displayed about each process. In the Solaris environment, by default (meaning no command options are used), information about processes with the same effective user id and controlling terminal of the calling invoker is displayed. In the Linux environment, by default, the processes with the same user id as the invoker are displayed. In both environments, the only information that is displayed is PID, TTY, TIME, and COMMAND. These are some of the options that control which processes are displayed:

- ❏ -t term: List the processes associated with the terminal specified by term

- ❏ -e: All current processes

- ❏ -a: (Linux) All processes with tty terminal except the session leaders

- ❏ (Solaris) Most frequently requested processes except group leaders and processes not associated with a terminal

- ❏ -d: All current processes except session leaders

- ❏ T: (Linux) All processes in this terminal

- ❏ a: (Linux) All processes including those of other users

- ❏ r: (Linux) Only running processes

Synopsis

```
(Linux)
ps -[Unix98 options]
   [BSD-style options]
   --[GNU-style long options

(Solaris)
ps [-aAdeflcjLPy][-o format][-t termlist][-u userlist]
   [-G grouplist][-p proclist][-g pgrplist][-s sidlist]
```

The following lists some of the command options used to control the information displayed about the processes:

- ❏ -f: Full listings

- ❏ -l: Long format

- ❏ -j: Jobs format

This is an example of using the ps utility in Solaris/Linux environments:

```
ps -f
```

This displays information about the default processes in each environment. Figure 5-8 shows the output in the Solaris environment. The command options can also be used in tandem. Figure 5-8 also shows the output of using -1 and -f together in the Solaris environment:

```
ps -lf
```

```
//SOLARIS

$ ps -f
     UID    PID   PPID  C    STIME     TTY     TIME CMD
 cameron   2214   2212  0 21:03:35 pts/12    0:00 -ksh
 cameron   2396   2214  2 11:55:49 pts/12    0:01 nedit

$ ps -lf
F S      UID    PID  PPID  C PRI NI     ADDR  SZ    WCHAN     STIME    TTY TIME    CMD
8 S cameron   2214  2212  0  51 20 70e80f00 230 70e80f6c 21:03:35 pts/12 0:00   -ksh
8 S cameron   2396  2214  1  53 24 70d747b8 843 70152aba 11:55:49 pts/12 0:01 nedit
```
Figure 5-8

The -1 command option shows the additional headers F, S, PRI, NI, ADDR, SZ, and WCHAN.

The P command option displays the PSR header. Under this header is the number of the processor to which the process is assigned or bound.

Figure 5-9 shows the output of the ps utility using the Tux command options in the Linux environment.

```
//Linux

[tdhughes@colony]$ ps Tux
USER         PID %CPU %MEM    VSZ   RSS   TTY   STAT   START   TIME COMMAND
tdhughes   19259  0.0  0.1   2448  1356  pts/4    S    20:29   0:00 -bash
tdhughes   19334  0.0  0.0   1732   860  pts/4    S    20:33   0:00 /home/tdhughes/pv
tdhughes   19336  0.0  0.0   1928   780  pts/4    S    20:33   0:00 /home/tdhughes/pv
tdhughes   19337 18.0  2.4  26872 24856  pts/4    R    20:33   0:47 /home/tdhughes/pv
tdhughes   19338 18.0  2.3  26872 24696  pts/4    R    20:33   0:47 /home/tdhughes/pv
tdhughes   19341 17.9  2.3  26872 24556  pts/4    R    20:33   0:47 /home/tdhughes/pv
tdhughes   19400  0.0  0.0   2544   692  pts/4    R    20:38   0:00 ps Tux
tdhughes   19401  0.0  0.1   2448  1356  pts/4    R    20:38   0:00 -bash
```
Figure 5-9

The %CPU, %MEM, and STAT information is displayed for the processes. In a multiprocessor environment, this information can be used to monitor which processes are dominating CPU and memory usage. The STAT header shows the state or status of the process. Table 5-6 lists how the status is encoded and their meanings.

Table 5-6

Status of Process	Description
D	Uninterruptible sleep (usually I/O)
R	Running or runnable (on run queue)
S	Interruptible sleep (waiting for an event to complete)
T	Stopped either by a job control signal or because it is being traced
Z	"Zombie" process, terminated with no parent

The STAT header can reveal additional information about the status of the process:

- ❑ D: (BSD) Disk wait
- ❑ P: (BSD) Page wait
- ❑ X: (System V) Growing: waiting for memory
- ❑ W: (BSD) Swapped out
- ❑ K: (AIX) Available kernel process
- ❑ N: (BSD) Niced: execution priority lowered
- ❑ >: (BSD) Niced: execution priority artificially raised
- ❑ <: (Linux) High-priority process
- ❑ L: (Linux) Pages are locked in memory

These codes precede the status codes. If an N precedes the status, this means that the process is running at a lower priority level. If a process has a status S<W, this means the process is sleeping, swapped out, and has a high priority level.

Setting and Getting Process Priorities

The priority level of a process can be changed by using the nice() function. Each process has a nice value that is used to calculate the priority level of the calling process. A process inherits the priority of the process that created it. But the priority of a process can be lowered by raising its nice value. Only superuser and kernel processes can raise priority levels.

Synopsis

```
#include <unistd.h>

int nice(int incr);
```

A low nice value raises the priority level of the process. The incr parameter is the value added to the current nice value of the calling process. The incr can be negative or positive. The nice value is a non-negative number. A positive incr value raises the nice value, thus lowering the priority level. A negative incr value lowers the nice value, thus raising the priority level. If the incr value raises the nice value above or below its limits, the nice value of the process is set to the highest or lowest limit accordingly. If successful, the nice() function returns the new nice value of the process. If unsuccessful, the function returns -1, and the nice value is not changed.

Synopsis

```
#include <sys/resource.h>

int getpriority(int which, id_t who);
int setpriority(int which, id_t who, int value);
```

setpriority() sets the nice value for a process, process group, or user. getpriority() returns the priority of a process, process group, or user. Example 5-2 shows the syntax for the functions setpriority() and getpriority() to set and return the nice value of the current process.

Example 5-2

```
//Example 5-2 shows how setpriority() and getpriority() can be used.

#include <sys/resource.h>

//...
id_t pid = 0;
int which  = PRIO_PROCESS;
int value = 10;
int nice_value;
int ret;

nice_value = getpriority(which,pid);
if(nice_value < value){
    ret = setpriority(which,pid,value);
}
//...
```

In Example 5-2, the priority of the calling process is being returned and set. If the calling process's nice value is < 10, the nice value of the process is set to 10. The target process is determined by the values stored in the which and who parameters. The which parameter can specify a process, process group, or a user. It can have the following values:

❑   PRIO_PROCESS: Indicates a process

❑   PRIO_PGRP: Indicates a process group

❑   PRIO_USER: Indicates a user

Depending on the value of which, the who parameter is the id number of a process, process group, or effective user. In Example 5-2, which is assigned PRIO_PROCESS. A 0 value for who indicates the current process, process group, or user. In Example 5-2, who is set to 0, indicating that the current process value for setpriority() will be the new nice value for the specified process, process group, or user.

The range of nice value in the Linux environment is -20 to 19. In Example 5-2, the value of nice is set to 10 if the current nice value is less than 10. In contrast to how things worked with the function `nice()`, the value passed to `setpriority()` is the actual value of nice, not an offset to be added to the current nice value. In a process with multiple threads, the modification of the priority affects the priority of all the threads in that process. If successful, `getpriority()` returns the nice value of the specified process. If successful, `setpriority()` returns 0. If unsuccessful, both functions return -1. The return value -1 is a legitimate nice value for a process. To determine if an error has occurred, check the external variable `errno`.

What Is a Context Switch?

A *context switch* occurs when the use of the processor is switched from one process to another process. When a context switch occurs, the system saves the context of the current running process and restores the context of the next process selected to use the processor. The PCB of the preempted process is updated. The process state field is changed from the running to the appropriate state (runnable, blocked, zombied, or so forth). The contents of the processor's registers, state of the stack, user and process identification and privileges, and scheduling and accounting information are saved and updated.

The system must keep track of the status of the process's I/O and other resources, and any memory management data structures. The preempted process is placed in the appropriate queue.

A context switch occurs when a:

- ❑ Process is preempted
- ❑ Process voluntarily gives up the processor
- ❑ Process makes an I/O request or needs to wait for an event
- ❑ Process switches from user mode to kernel mode

When the preempted process is selected to use the processor again, its context is restored, and execution continues where it left off.

The Activities in Process Creation

To run any program, the operating system must first create a process. When a new process is created, a new entry is placed in the main process table. A new PCB is created and initialized. The process identification portion of the PCB contains a unique process id number and the parent process id. The program counter is set to point to the program entry point, and the system stack pointers are set to define the stack boundaries for the process. The process is initialized with any of the attributes requested. If the process is not given a priority value, it is given the lowest-priority value by default. The process initially does not own any resources unless there is an explicit request for resources or they have been inherited from the creator process. The state of the process is runnable, and it is placed in the runnable or ready queue. Address space is allocated for the process. How much space to be set aside can be determined by default, based on the type of process. The size can also be set as a request by the creator of the process. The creator process can pass the size of the address space to the system at the time the process is created.

Using the fork() Function Call

In addition to `posix_spawn()`, for creating processes the POSIX API also supports the `fork/exec` functions. These functions are available in all Unix/Linux derivatives. The `fork()` call creates a new process that is a duplication of the calling process, the parent. The `fork()` returns two values if it succeeds, one to the parent and one to the child process. It returns 0 to the child process and returns the PID of the child to the parent process. The parent and child processes continue to execute from the instruction immediately following the `fork()` call. If not successful, meaning that no child process was created, -1 is returned to the parent process.

Synopsis

```
#include <unistd.h>

pid_t fork(void);
```

The `fork()` fails if the system does not have the resources to create another process. If there is a limit to the number of child processes the parent can spawn or the number of systemwide executing processes and that limit has been exceeded, the `fork()` fails. In that case, `errno` is set to indicate the error.

Using the exec() Family of System Calls

The `exec` family of functions replaces the calling process image with a new process image. The `fork()` call creates a new process that is a duplication of the parent process, whereas the `exec` function replaces the duplicate process image with a new one. The new process image is a regular executable file and is immediately executed. The executable can be specified as a path or a filename. These functions can pass command-line arguments to the new process. Environment variables can also be specified. There is no return value if the function is not successful, because the process image that contained the call to the `exec` is overwritten. If the function is unsuccessful, -1 is returned to the calling process.

All of the `exec()` functions can fail under these conditions:

❑ **Permissions are denied.**

    ❑ Search permission is denied for the executable's file directory.

    ❑ Execution permission is denied for the executable file.

❑ **Files do not exist.**

    ❑ Executable file does not exist.

    ❑ Directory does not exist.

❑ **File is not executable.**

    ❑ File is not executable because it is open for writing by another process.

    ❑ File is not an executable file.

❏ **Problems with symbolic links.**

    ❏ Loop exists when symbolic links are encountered while resolving the pathname to the executable.

    ❏ Symbolic links cause the pathname to the executable to be too long.

The exec functions are used with the fork(). The fork() creates and initializes the child process with the duplicate of the parent. The child process then replaces its process image by calling an exec(). Example 5-3 shows an example of the fork-exec usage.

Example 5-3

```
// Example 5-3 Using the fork-exec system calls.

//...
RtValue = fork();
if(RtValue == 0){
    execl("/home/user/direct","direct",".");
}
```

In Example 5-3, the fork() function is called and the return value is stored in RtValue. If RtValue is 0, then it is the child process. The execl() function is called. The first parameter is the path to the executable module, the second parameter is the execution statement, and the third parameter is the argument. direct is a utility that lists all the directories and subdirectories from a given directory, which, in this case, is the current directory. There are six versions of the exec functions, each having different calling conventions and uses; those are discussed in the next sections.

The execl() Functions

The execl(), execle(), and execlp() functions pass the command-line arguments as a list. The number of command-line arguments should be known at compile time in order for these functions to be useful.

❏ int execl(const char *path,const char *arg0,.../*,(char *)0 */);

    The path parameter is the pathname to the program executable. It can be specified as an absolute pathname or a relative pathname from the current directory. The next arguments are the list of command-line arguments, from arg0 to argn. There can be *n* number of arguments. The list is to be followed by a NULL pointer.

❏ int execle(const char *path,const char *arg0,.../*,(char *)0 *, char *const envp[]*/);

    This function is identical to execl() except that it has an additional parameter, envp[]. This parameter contains the new environment for the new process. envp[] is a pointer to a null-terminated array of null-terminated strings. Each string has the form:

```
name=value
```

    where name is the name of the environment variable, and value is the string to be stored. envp[] can be assigned in this manner:

```
char *const envp[] = {"PATH=/opt/kde5:/sbin", "HOME=/home",NULL};
```

PATH and HOME are the environment variables in this case.

❑   `int execlp(const char *file,const char *arg0,.../*,(char *)0 */);`

`file` is the name of the program executable. It uses the PATH environment variable to locate the executables. The remaining arguments are the list of command-line arguments as explained for `execl()` function.

These are examples of the syntax of the `execl()` functions using these arguments:

```
char *const args[] = {"direct",".",NULL};
char *const envp[] = {"files=50",NULL};

execl("/home/tracey/direct","direct",".",NULL);
execle("/home/tracey/direct","direct",".",NULL,envp);
execlp("direct","direct",".",NULL);
```

Each shows the syntax of how the `execl()` function creates a process that executes the direct program.

Synopsis

```
#include <unistd.h>

int execl(const char *path,const char *arg0,.../*,(char *)0 */);
int execle(const char *path,const char *arg0,.../*,
           (char *)0 *,char *const envp[]*/);
int execv(const char *path,char *const arg[]);
int execlp(const char *file,const char *arg0,.../*,(char *)0 */);
int execve(const char *path,char *const arg[],
           char *const envp[]);
int execvp(const char *file,char *const arg[]);
```

The execv() Functions

The `execv()`, `execve()`, and `execvp()` functions pass the command-line arguments in a vector of pointers to null-terminated strings. The number of command-line arguments should be known at compile time in order for these functions to be useful. `argv[0]` is usually the execution statement.

❑   `int execv(const char *path,char *const arg[]);`

The `path` parameter is the pathname to the program executable. It can be specified as an absolute pathname or relative pathname to the current directory. The next argument is the null-terminated vector that contains the command-line arguments as null-terminated strings. There can be *n* number of arguments. The vector is to be followed by a NULL pointer.

`arg[]` can be assigned in this manner:

```
char *const arg[] = {"traverse",".", ">","1000",NULL};
```

This is an example of a function call:

```
execv("traverse",arg);
```

In this case, the `traverse` utility lists all files in the current directory larger than 1000 bytes.

❑   `int execve(const char *path,char *const arg[],char *const envp[]);`

This function is identical to `execv()` except that it has the additional parameter `envp[]` described earlier.

❑   `int execvp(const char *file,char *const arg[]);`

`file` is the name of the program executable. The next argument is the null-terminated vector that contains the command-line arguments as null-terminated strings. There can be *n* number of arguments. The vector is to be followed by a NULL pointer.

These are examples of the syntax of the `execv()` functions using these arguments:

```
char *const arg[] = {"traverse",".", ">","1000",NULL};
char *const envp[] = {"files=50",NULL};

execv("/home/tracey/traverse",arg);
execve("/home/tracey/traverse",arg,envp);
execvp("traverse",arg);
```

Each shows the syntax of how each `execv()` function creates a process that executes the `traverse` program.

Determining the Restrictions of exec() Functions

There is a limit on the size that `argv[]` and `envp[]` can be when passed to the `exec()` functions. The `sysconf()` can be used to determine the maximum size of the command-line arguments plus the size of environment variables for the functions that accept `envp[]`, which can be passed to the `exec()` functions. To return the size, `name` should have the value _SC_ARG_MAX.

Synopsis

```
#include <unistd.h>

long sysconf(int name);
```

Another restriction when you are using `exec()` and the other functions used to create processes is the maximum number of simultaneous processes allowed per user id. To return this number, `name` should have the value _SC_CHILD_MAX.

Working with Process Environment Variables

Environment variables are null-terminated strings that store system-dependent information such as paths to directories that contain commands, libraries, functions, and procedures used by a process. They can also be used to transmit any useful user-defined information between the parent and the child processes. They are a mechanism for providing specific information to a process without having it hardcoded in the program code. System environment variables are predefined and common to all shells and processes in that system. The variables are initialized by startup files. These are the common system variables:

- ❑ $HOME: The absolute pathname of your home directory
- ❑ $PATH: A list of directories to search for commands
- ❑ $MAIL: The absolute pathname of your mailbox
- ❑ $USER: Your user id
- ❑ $SHELL: The absolute pathname of your login shell
- ❑ $TERM: Your terminal type

They can be stored in a file or in an environment list. The environment list contains pointers to null-terminated strings. The variable:

```
extern char **environ
```

points to the environment list when the process begins to execute. These strings have the form:

```
name=value
```

as explained earlier. Processes initialized with the functions execl(), execlp(), execv(), and execvp() inherit the environment of the parent process. Processes initialized with the functions execve() and execle() set the environment for the new process.

There are functions and utilities that can be called to examine, add, or modify environment variables. getenv() is used to determine whether a specific variable has been set. The parameter name is the environment variable in question. The function returns NULL if the specified variable has not been set. If the variable has been set, the function returns a pointer to a string containing the value.

Synopsis

```
#include <stdlib.h>

char *getenv(const char *name);
int setenv(const char *name, const char *value, int overwrite);
void unsetenv(const char *name);
```

126

For example:

```
string Path;

Path = getenv("PATH");
```

the string `Path` is assigned the value contained in the predefined environment `PATH`.

`setenv()` is used to change or add an environment variable. The parameter `name` contains the name of the environment variable added with the value stored in `value`. If the `name` variable already exists, then the value is changed to `value` if the `overwrite` parameter is non-zero. If `overwrite` is 0, the content of the specified environment variable is not modified. `setenv()` returns 0 if it is successful and -1 if it is unsuccessful. The `unsetenv()` removes the environment variable specified by `name`.

Using system() to Spawn Processes

`system()` is another function that is used to execute a command or executable program. `system()` causes the execution of `fork()`, `exec()`, and a shell. The `system()` function executes a `fork()`, and the child process calls an `exec()` with a shell that executes the given command or program.

Synopsis

```
#include <stdlib.h>

int system(const char *string);
```

The `string` parameter can be a system command or the name of an executable file. If successful, the function returns the termination status of the command or return value (if any) of the program. Errors can happen at several levels; the `fork()` or `exec()` may fail, or the shell may not be able to execute the command or program.

The function returns a value to the parent process. The function returns 127 if the `exec()` fails and -1 if some other error occurs. The return code of the command is returned if the function succeeds. This function does not affect the wait status of any of the child processes.

Killing a Process

When a process is terminated, the PCB is erased, and the address space and resources used by the terminated process are deallocated. An exit code is placed in its entry in the main process table. The entry is removed once the parent has accepted the exit code. The termination of the process can occur under several conditions:

❑ All instructions have executed. The process makes an explicit return or makes a system call that terminates the process. The child processes may automatically terminate when the parent has terminated.

❑ The parent sends a signal to terminate its child processes.

Abnormal termination of a process can occur when the process itself does something that it shouldn't:

❑ The process requires more memory than the system can provide it.

❑ The process attempts to access resources it is not allowed to access. The process attempts to perform an invalid instruction or a prohibited computation.

The termination of a process can also be initiated by a user when the process is interactive.

The parent process is responsible for the termination/deallocation of its children. The parent process should wait until all its child processes have terminated. When a parent process retrieves a child process's exit code, the child process exits the system normally. The process is in a zombied state until the parent accepts the signal. If the parent never accepts the signal because it has already terminated and exited the system or because it is not waiting for the child process, the child remains in the zombied state until the `init` process (the original system process) accepts its exit code. Many zombied processes can negatively affect the performance of the system.

The exit(), and abort() Calls

There are two functions a process can call for self-termination, `exit()` and `abort()`. The `exit()` function causes a normal termination of the calling process. All open file descriptors associated with the process will be closed. The function flushes all open streams that contain unwritten buffered data then the open streams are closed. The `status` parameter is the process's exit status. It is returned to the waiting parent process that is then restarted. The value of status may be 0, EXIT_FAILURE, or EXIT_SUCCESS. The 0 value means that the process has terminated successfully. The waiting parent process only has access to the lower 8 bits of status. If the parent process is not waiting for the process to terminate, the zombied process is adopted by the `init` process. The `abort()` function causes an abnormal termination of the calling process. An abnormal termination of the process causes the same effect as `fclose()` on all open streams. A waiting parent process receives a signal that the child process aborted. A process should only abort when it encounters an error that it cannot deal with programmatically.

Synopsis

```
#include <stdlib.h>

void exit(int status);
void abort(void);
```

The kill() Function

The `kill()` function can be used to cause the termination of another process. The `kill()` function sends a signal to the process or processes specified or indicated by the parameter `pid`. The parameter `sig` is the signal to be sent to the specified process. The signals are listed in the header `<signal.h>`. To kill a process, `sig` has the value SIGKILL. The calling process must have the appropriate privileges to send a signal to the process, or it has to have a real or an effective user id that matches the real or saved `set-user-ID` of the process that receives the signal. The calling process may have permission to send only certain signals to processes and not others. If the function successfully sends the signal, 0 is returned to the calling process. If it fails, −1 is returned.

The calling process can send the signal to one or several processes under these conditions:

- ❏ `pid` > 0: The signal is sent to the process whose PID is equal to the `pid`.

- ❏ `pid` = 0: The signal is sent to all the processes whose process group id is the same as the calling process.

- ❏ `pid` = −1: The signal is sent to all processes for which the calling process has permission to send that signal.

- ❏ `pid` < −1: The signal is sent to all processes whose process id group is equal to the absolute value of `pid` and for which the calling process has permission to send that signal.

Synopsis

```
#include <signal.h>

int kill(pid_t pid, int sig);
```

Process Resources

In order for a process to perform whatever task it is instructed to perform, it may need to write data to a file, send data to a printer, or display data to the screen. A process may need input from the user via the keyboard or input from a file. Processes can also use other processes such as a subroutine as a resource. Subroutines, files, semaphores, mutexes, keyboards, and display screens are all examples of resources that can be utilized by a process. A *resource* is anything used by the process at any given time as a source of data, as a means to process or compute, or as the means by which the data or information is displayed.

For a process to access a resource, it must first make a request to the operating system. If the resource is available, the operating system allows the process to use the resource. The process uses the resource then releases it so that it will be available to other processes. If the resource is not available, the request is denied, and the process must wait. When the resource becomes available, the process is awakened. This is the basic format of resource allocation. Figure 5-10 shows a resource allocation graph. The resource allocation graph shows which processes hold resources and which processes are requesting resources. In Figure 5-10, Process B makes a request for resource 2, which is held by Process C. Process C makes a request for resource 3, which is held by Process D.

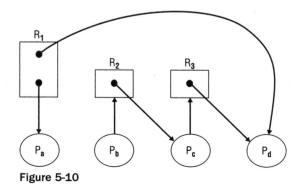

Figure 5-10

When more than one request to access a resource is granted, the resource is *sharable*. This is shown in Figure 5-10 as well. Process A shares resource 1 with Process D. A resource may allow many processes concurrent access or may allow one process only limited time before allowing another process access. An example of this type of shared resource is the processor. A process is assigned a processor for a short interval and then another process is assigned the processor. When only one request to access a resource is granted at a time and that occurs after the resource has been released by another process, the resource is *unshared*, and the process has *exclusive access* to the resource. In a multiprocessor environment, it is important to know whether a shared resource can be accessed simultaneously or only by one process at a time, in order to avoid some of the pitfalls inherent in concurrency.

Some resources can be changed or modified by a process. Other resources do not allow a process to change it. The behavior of shared modifiable or unmodifiable resources is determined by the resource type.

Types of Resources

There are three basic types of resources:

❑ Hardware

❑ Data

❑ Software

Hardware resources are physical devices connected to the computer. Examples of hardware resources are processors, main memory, and all other I/O devices including printers; hard disk, tape, and zip drives; monitors; keyboards; sound, network, and graphic cards; and modems. All these devices can be shared by several processes.

Some hardware resources are preempted to allow different processes access. For example, a processor is preempted to allow different processes time to run. RAM is another example of a shared preemptible resource. When a process is not in use, some of the physical page frames it occupies may be swapped out to secondary storage in order for another process to be swapped in to occupy those now available page frames. A range of memory can be occupied only by the page frames of one process at any given time. An example of a nonpreemptible shared resource is a printer. When a printer is shared, the jobs sent to the printer by each process are stored in a queue. Each job is printed to completion before another job starts. The printer is not preempted by any waiting printer jobs unless the current job is canceled.

Data resources such as objects; system data such as environment variables, files, and handles; globally defined variables such as semaphores; and mutexes are all resources shared and modified by processes. Regular files and files associated with physical devices such as the printer can be opened, restricting the type of access processes has to that file. Processes may be granted only read or write access, or read/write access. For processes with parent-child relationships, the child process inherits the parent process's resources and access rights to those resources existing at the time of the child's creation. The child process can advance the file pointer or close, modify, or overwrite the contents of a file opened by the parent. Shared memory and files with write permission require their access to be synchronized. Shared data such as semaphores or mutexes can be used to synchronize access to other shared data resources.

Shared libraries are examples of *software resources*. Shared libraries provide a common set of services or functions to processes. Processes can also share applications, programs, and utilities. In such a case, only one copy of the program(s) code is brought into memory. However, there are separate copies of the data, one for each user (process). Program code that is not changed (also called *reentrant*) can be accessed by several processes simultaneously.

POSIX Functions to Set Resource Limits

POSIX defines functions that restrict a process's ability to use certain resources. The operating system sets limitations on a process's ability to utilize system resources. These resource limits affect the following:

- Size of the process's stack

- Size of file and core file creation

- Amount of CPU usage (size of time slice)

- Amount of memory usage

- Number of open file descriptors

The operating system sets a hard limit on resource usage by a process. The process can set or change the soft limit of its resources. Its value should not exceed the hard limit set by the operating system. A process can lower its hard limit. This value should be greater than or equal to the soft limit. When a process lowers its hard limit, it is irreversible. Only processes with special privileges can raise their hard limit.

Synopsis

```
#include <sys/resource.h>

int setrlimit(int resource, const struct rlimit *rlp);
int getrlimit(int resource, struct rlimit *rlp);
int getrusage(int who, struct rusage *r_usage);
```

The setrlimit() function is used to set limits on the consumption of specified resources. This function can set both hard and soft limits. The parameter resource represents the resource type. Table 5-7 lists the values for resource with a brief description. The soft and hard limits of the specified resource are represented by the rlp paramater. The rlp parameter points to a struct rlimit that contains two objects of type rlim_t:

```
struct rlimit
{
    rlim_t rlim_cur;
    rlim_t rlim_max;
}
```

rlim_t is an unsigned integer type. rlim_cur contains the current or soft limit. rlim_max contains the maximum or hard limit. rlim_cur and rlim_max can be assigned any value. They can also be assigned these symbolic constants defined in the header <sys/resource.h>:

- RLIM_INFINITY: Indicates no limit

- RLIM_SAVED_MAX: Indicates an unrepresentable saved hard limit

- RLIM_SAVED_CUR: Indicates an unrepresentable saved soft limit

The soft or hard limit can be set to RLIM_INFINITY, which means that the resource is unlimited.

Table 5-7

Resource Definitions	Descriptions
RLIMIT_CORE	Maximum size of a core file in bytes that may be created by a process
RLIMIT_CPU	Maximum amount of CPU time in seconds that may be used by a process
RLIMIT_DATA	Maximum size of a process's data segment in bytes
RLIMIT_FSIZE	Maximum size of a file in bytes that may be created by a process
RLIMIT_NOFILE	A number one greater than the maximum value that the system may assign to newly created file descriptor
RLIMIT_STACK	Maximum size of a process's stack in bytes
RLIMIT_AS	Maximum size of a process's total available memory in bytes

The getrlimit() returns the soft and hard limit of the specified resource in the rlp object. Both the getrlimit() and setrlimit() functions return 0 if successful and -1 if unsuccessful. Example 5-4 contains an example of a process setting the soft limit for file size in bytes.

Example 5-4

```
//Example 5-4 Using setrlimit() to set the soft limit for file size.

#include <sys/resource.h>

//...
struct rlimit R_limit;
struct rlimit R_limit_values;

//...

R_limit.rlim_cur = 2000;
R_limit.rlim_max = RLIM_SAVED_MAX;
setrlimit(RLIMIT_FSIZE,&R_limit);
getrlimit(RLIMIT_FSIZE,&R_limit_values);
cout << "file size soft limit: " << R_limit_values.rlim_cur << endl;

//...
```

In Example 5-4, the file size soft limit is set to 2000 bytes, and the hard limit is set to hard limit maximum. R_limit and RLIMIT_FSIZE are passed to setrlimit(). getrlimit() is passed RLIMIT_FSIZE and R_limit_values. The soft value is sent to cout.

getrusage() returns information about the measures of resources used by the calling process. It also returns information about the terminated child process the calling process is waiting for. The parameter who can have these values:

- RUSAGE_SELF
- RUSAGE_CHILDREN

If the value for who is RUSAGE_SELF, then the information returned pertains to the calling process. If the value for who is RUSAGE_CHILDREN, then the information returned is pertaining to the calling process's children. If the calling process did not wait for its children, then the information pertaining to the children processes is discarded. The information is returned in r_usage. r_usage points to a struct rusage that contains information listed and described in Table 5-8. If the function is successful, it returns 0; if unsuccessful, it returns –1.

Table 5-8

struct rusage Attributes	Description
struct timeval ru_utime	User time used
struct timeval ru_sutime	System time used
long ru_maxrss	Maximum resident set size
long ru_maxixrss	Shared memory size
long ru_maxidrss	Unshared data size
long ru_maxisrss	Unshared stack size
long ru_minflt	Number of page claims
long ru_majflt	Number of page faults
long ru_nswap	Number of page swaps
long ru_inblock	Block input operations
long ru_oublock	Block output operations
long ru_msgsnd	Number of messages sent
long ru_msgrcv	Number of messages received
long ru_nsignals	Number of signals received
long ru_nvcsw	Number of voluntary context switches
long ru_nivcsw	Number of involuntary context switches

What Are Asynchronous and Synchronous Processes

Asynchronous processes execute independent of each other. Process A runs until completion without any regard to process B. Asynchronous processes may or may not have a parent-child relationship. If process A creates process B, they can both execute independently, but at some point the parent retrieves the exit status of the child. If the processes do not have a parent-child relationship, they may share the same parent.

Asynchronous processes may execute serially or simultaneously or their execution may overlap. These scenarios are depicted in Figure 5-11.

In Case 1, process A runs until completion, then process B runs until completion, and then process C runs until completion. This is serial execution of these processes.

Case 2 depicts simultaneous execution of processes. Process A and B are active processes. While process A is running, process B is sleeping. At some point both processes are sleeping. Process B awakens before process A. Then process A awakens, and now both processes are running at the same time. This shows that asynchronous processes may execute simultaneously only during certain intervals of their execution.

In Case 3, the execution of process A and the execution of process B overlap.

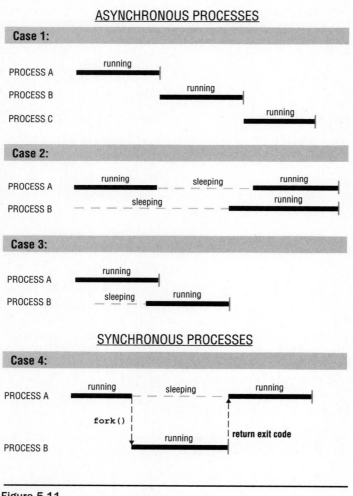

Figure 5-11

Asynchronous processes may share resources like a file or memory. This may or may not require synchronization or cooperation of the use of the resource. If the processes are executing serially (Case 1), then they will not require any synchronization. For example, all three processes, A, B, and C, may share a global variable. Process A writes to the variable before it terminates. Then, when process B runs, it reads the data stored in the variable, and before it terminates it writes to the variable. When Process C runs, it reads data from the variable. But in Case 2 and 3, the processes may attempt to modify the variable at the same time, thus requiring synchronization of its use.

For our purposes, we define *synchronous* processes as processes with interleaved execution; one process suspends its execution until another process finishes. For example, process A, the parent process, executes and creates process B, the child process. Process A suspends its execution until process B runs to completion. When process B terminates, its exit code is placed in the process table. Process A is informed process B has terminated. Process A can resume additional processing and then terminate, or it can immediately terminate. Process A and process B are synchronous processes. Figure 5-11 contrasts synchronous and asynchronous execution of processes A and B.

Synchronous vs. Asynchronous Processes for fork(), posix_spawn(), system(), and exec()

Processes created by the `fork()`, `fork-exec()`, and `posix_spawn()` functions create asynchronous processes. When you are using `fork()`, the parent process image is duplicated. Once the child process has been created, the function returns to the parent both the child's PID and a return value of 0, indicating process creation was successful. The parent does not suspend execution; both processes continue to execute independently from the statement immediately preceding the `fork()`.

Child processes created using the `fork-exec()` combination initialize the child's process image with a new process image. The `exec()` functions do not return to the parent process unless the initialization was not successful.

The `posix_spawn()` functions create the child process image and initialize it within one function call. The PID is returned to the `posix_spawn()` as well as a return value, indicating if the process was spawned successfully. After `posix_spawn()` returns, both processes are executing at the same time.

Processes created by the `system()` function create synchronous processes. A shell is created that executes the system command or executable file. The parent process is suspended until the child process terminates and the `system()` call returns.

The wait() Function Call

Asynchronous processes can suspend execution until a child process terminates by executing `wait()` system call. After the child process terminates, a waiting parent process collects the child's exit status that prevents zombied processes. The `wait()` function obtains the exit status from the process table. The status parameter points to a location that contains the exit status of the child process. If the parent process has more than one child process and several of them have terminated, the `wait()` function retrieves the exit status for only one child process from the process table. If the status information is available before the execution of the `wait()` function, the function returns immediately. If the parent process does not have any children, the function returns with an error code. The `wait()` function can also be called when the calling process is to wait until a signal is delivered and then perform some signal-handling action.

Synopsis

```
#include <sys/wait.h>

pid_t wait(int *status);
pid_t waitpid(pid_t pid, int *status, int options);
```

The waitpid() function is the same as wait(), except that it takes an additional parameter, pid. The pid parameter specifies a set of child processes for which the exit status is retrieved. Which processes are in the set is determined by the value of pid:

❑   pid > 0: A single child process

❑   pid = 0: Any child process whose group id is the same as the calling process

❑   pid < −1: Any child processes whose group id is equal to the absolute value of pid

❑   pid = −1: Any child processes

The options parameter determines how the wait should behave and can have the value of the following constants defined in the header <sys/wait.h>:

❑   WCONTINUED: Reports the exit status of any continued child process (specified by pid) whose status has not been reported since it continued.

❑   WUNTRACED: Reports the exit status of any child process (specified by pid) that has stopped whose status has not been reported since it stopped.

❑   WNOHANG: The calling process is not suspended if the exit status for the specified child process is not available.

These constants can be logically ORRED and passed as the options parameter (for example: WCONTINUED | WUNTRACED).

Both the wait() and waitpid() functions return the PID of the child process whose exit status was obtained. If the value stored in status is 0, then the child process has terminated under these conditions:

❑   The process returned 0 from the function main().

❑   The process called some version of exit() with a 0 argument.

❑   The process was terminated because the last thread of the process terminated.

Table 5-9 lists the macros in which the value of the exit status can be evaluated.

Table 5-9

Macros for Evaluating `status`	Description
WIFEXITED	Evaluates to nonzero if status was returned by a normally terminated child process.
WEXITSTATUS	If WIFEXITED is nonzero, this evaluates to the low-order 8 bits of the status argument the terminated child process passed to _exit(), exit(), or the value returned from main().
WIFSIGNALED	Evaluates to nonzero if status was returned from a child process that terminated because it was sent a signal that was not caught.
WTERMSIG	If WIFSIGNALED is nonzero, this evaluates to the number of the signal that caused the child to terminate.
WIFSTOPPED	Evaluates to nonzero if status was returned from a child process that currently stopped.
WSTOPSIG	If WIFSTOPPED is nonzero, this evaluates to the number of the signal that caused the child process to stop.
WIFCONTINUED	Evaluates to nonzero if status was returned from a child process that has continued from a job control stop.

Predicates, Processes, and Interface Classes

Recall that a predicate in C++ is a function object that returns a bool [Stroustrup, 1997]. One thing that's often overlooked in this definition is the word *object* . A predicate is not simply a function. It has object semantics. Predicates give a declarative interpretation to a sequence of actions. A predicate is a statement that can be evaluated to true or false. In a shift toward a more declarative approach to parallelism, you will find that is sometimes convenient to encapsulate a process or a thread as a C++ predicate. Enapsulating the process or thread within a predicate allows you to thread them as objects for use with containers and algorithms. This subtle use of the notion of a predicate in C++ allows you to take a big step away from the procedural approach to parallelism and toward a declarative approach.

Take, for example, the guess_it program from Listing 5-3 earlier in the chapter. Although we used an interface class to provide a more declarative interface for the posix_spawn function, we can do better. In other words, Listing 5-3 is a more declarative version of the guess_it program from Chapter 4, and now Listing 5-5 is a more declarative form of the program in Listing 5-3.

Listing 5-5

```
// Listing 5-5  A restatement of the guess_it program from Chapter 4.

1   #include "posix_process.h"
2   #include "posix_queue.h"
3   #include "valid_code.h"
4
5
6   char **av;
7   char **env;
8
9
10  int main(int argc,char *argv[],char *envp[])
11  {
12
13      valid_code  ValidCode;
14      ValidCode.determination("ofind_code");
15      cout <<  (ValidCode() ? "you win" : "you lose");
16      return(0);
17  }
```

Here, we have decided to model the code from our game as a C++ class named valid_code. We have decided to encapsulate the invocation of the posix_process.run() method within a C++ predicate. Line 15 of Listing 5-5 contains the ValidCode() predicate. If the predicate ValidCode() is true, then the user has guessed the right six-character code within the 5-minute time constraint. The program in Listing 5-5 spawns two processes using the posix_process class and four threads using the user_thread class from Chapter 4. Both the posix_process class and the user_thread class are interface classes that adapt the interface to posix_spawn() and pthread_create().

Program Profile 5-1

Program Name:

oguess_it.cc (Listing 5-5)

Description:

The program oguess_it is a more declarative form of the program in Listing 5-3. The invocation of posix_process.run() method is encapsulated within a C++ predicate. If the predicate ValidCode() is true, then the user has guessed the right six-character code within the 5-minute time constraint. The program spawns two processes using the posix_process class and four threads using the user_thread.

Libraries Required:

pthread, rt

Additional Source Files Needed:

oguess_it.cc (Listing 5-5), posix_process.cc (Listing 5-4)

User-Defined Headers Required:

posix_process.h (Listing 5-2)

Compile and Link Instructions:

c++ -o oguess_it oguess_it.cc posix_process.cc -lrt

Test Environment:

Linux Kernel 2.6

Solaris 10, gcc 3.4.3 and 3.4.6

Processors:

Multicore Opteron, UltraSparc T1, Cell Processor

Notes:

None

We take the declarative interpretation further by encapsulating the Process.run() invocation as a C++ predicate. Listing 5-6 is a declaration of the valid_code predicate class.

Listing 5-6

```
//Listing 5-6  Declaration of our valid_code predicate class.

1   #ifndef __VALID_CODE_H
2   #define __VALID_CODE_H
3   using namespace std;
4
5   #include <string>
6   class valid_code{
7   private:
8       string Code;
9       float  TimeFrame;
10      string Determination;
11      bool InTime;
12   public:
13      bool operator()(void);
14      void determination(string X);
15   };
16
17   #endif
```

We designate this as a predicate class because we have overloaded the operator() on Line 13. Notice that operator() returns a bool. This is what distinguishes the predicate from the function object. Because valid_code is a class, it has the declarative semantics that we need to build on. Because valid_code is a class, it can be used with container classes and algorithms. This use of the predicate notion for processes and threads opens up new ways of thinking about parallel programming. Listing 5-7 contains the definitions for the valid_code class.

Listing 5-7

```
//Listing 5-7  Definition of our valid_code predicate class.

1    #include "valid_code.h"
2    #include "posix_process.h"
3    #include "posix_queue.h"
4
5    extern char **av;
6    extern char **env;
7
8
9    bool valid_code::operator()(void)
10   {
11       int Status;
12       int N;
13       string Result;
14       posix_process Child[2];
15       for(N = 0; N < 2; N++)
16       {
17           Child[N].binary(Determination);
18           Child[N].arguments(av);
19           Child[N].environment(env);
20           Child[N].run();
21           Child[N].pwait(Status);
22       }
23       posix_queue PosixQueue("queue_name");
24       PosixQueue.receive(Result);
25       if((Result == Code) && InTime){
26           return(true);
27       }
28       return(false);
29   }
30
31
32   void valid_code::determination(string X)
33   {
34       Determination = X;
35   }
36
```

The definition of the predicate defined by the operator() begins on Line 9 of Listing 5-7. Notice on Line 25 that if the Result is correct and Intime, then this predicate returns true; otherwise, it returns false. Lines 16–21 cause two processes to be spawned. Line 14 from Listing 5-5 has the determination that is the name of the binary (ofind_code) that is associated with the two processes that have been spawned. In this case, each instance of ofind_code creates two threads to perform the search, causing us to have a total of four threads. But all of this talk of processes and threads is totally transparent to the program in Listing 5-5. The program in Listing 5-5 is concerned with something called ValidCode and only concerned whether the ValidCode() predicate is true or false.

You can extend the number of processes and threads without changing the declarative interpretation of the parallelism. We stress declarative semantics here because as you scale to more cores on a CMP, it gets increasingly challenging to think procedurally. You can use declarative models to help you cope with the complexity of parallel programming. Using C++ interface classes in conjunction with C++ predicates to encapsulate processes, threads, and POSIX APIs is a step in the right direction.

Summary

The bulk of this chapter has dealt with processes and how you can leverage them to aid your multicore programming. Some of the key points covered include:

- ❑ Concurrency in a C++ program is accomplished by factoring your program into either multiple processes or multiple threads. When isolation, security, address space, and maximum number of resources that concurrently executing tasks may have are major concerns, it is better to use processes than threads. Communication between processes and startup time are two of the primary tradeoffs when you decide to use processes rather than threads.

- ❑ The primary characteristics and attributes of a process are stored in the process control block (PCB) used by the operating system to identify the process. This information is needed by the operating system to manage each process. The PCB is one of the structures that makes processes heavier or more expense to use than threads.

- ❑ Processes that create other processes have a parent-child relationship with the created process. The creator of the process is the parent, and the created process is the child process. Child processes inherit many attributes from the parent. The parent's key responsibility is to wait for the child process so the parent can exit the system.

- ❑ There are several system calls that can be used to create processes: `fork()`, `fork-exec()`, `system()`, and `posix_spawn()`. The `fork()`, `fork-exec()`, and `posix_spawn()` functions create processes that are asynchronous to the parent process, whereas `system()` creates a child process that is synchronous to the parent process. Some platforms may have trouble implementing `fork()`, so the `posix_spawn()` functions can be used instead.

- ❑ Use interface classes, such as the `posix_process` class from this chapter, to build declarative interfaces for POSIX API functions that are used for processes management. If you build interface classes for processes as well as threads, then you can begin to implement your current tasks from the Object-Oriented point of view rather than the procedural viewpoint.

- ❑ In the shift toward a more declarative approach to parallelism, you can also find it sometimes useful to encapsulate a process or a thread as a C++ predicate. Encapsulating the process or thread within a predicate allows you to thread them as objects for use with containers and algorithms. This subtle use of the notion of a predicate in C++ allows you to take a big step away from the procedural approach to parallelism and toward a declarative approach.

In the next chapter, we discuss multithreading. A thread is a sequence of executable code within a process that is scheduled for execution by the operating system on a processor or core. The use of threads for parallel programming on multicore processors has a number of advantages over multiple processes. In the next chapter, we discuss those advantages and some of the pitfalls. We discuss POSIX APIs functions for creating and managing threads and show how that functionality can be encapsulated in a thread class first introduced in Chapter 4.

Multithreading

They come from a much older version of the matrix, but like so many back then, they caused more problems than they solved.

—**Persephone,** *Matrix Reloaded*

In Chapter 5, we examined how concurrency in a C++ program can be accomplished by decomposing your program into either multiple processes or multiple threads. We discussed a process, which is a unit of work created by the operating system. We explained the POSIX API for process management and the several system calls that can be used to create processes: fork(), fork-exec(), system(), and posix_spawn(). We showed you how to build C++ interface components, interface classes, and declarative interfaces that can be used to simplify part of the POSIX API for process management. In the chapter we cover:

- ❑ What is a thread?
- ❑ The pthread API for thread management
- ❑ Thread scheduling and priorities
- ❑ Thread contention scope
- ❑ Extending the thread_object to encapsulate thread attribute functionality

What Is a Thread?

A thread is a sequence or stream of executable code within a process that is scheduled for execution by the operating system on a processor or core. All processes have a primary thread. The *primary thread* is a process's flow of control or thread of execution. A process with multiple threads has as many flows of controls as there are threads. Each thread executes independently and concurrently with its own sequence of instructions. A process with multiple threads is *multithreaded.* There are user-level threads and kernel-level threads. Kernel-level threads are a lighter burden to create, maintain, and manage on the operating system as compared to a process because very little information is associated with a thread. A kernel thread is called a *lightweight process* because it has less overhead than a process.

Threads execute independent concurrent tasks of a program. Threads can be used to simplify the program structure of an application with inherent concurrency in the same way that functions and procedures make an application's structure simpler by encapsulating functionality. Threads can encapsulate concurrent functionality. Threads use minimal resources shared in the address space of a single process as compared to an application, which uses multiple processes. This contributes to an overall simpler program structure being seen by the operating system. Threads can improve the throughput and performance of the application if used correctly, by utilizing multicore processors concurrently. Each thread is assigned a subtask for which it is responsible, and the thread independently manages the execution of the subtask. Each thread can be assigned a priority reflecting the importance of the subtask it is executing.

User- and Kernel-Level Threads

There are three implementation models for threads:

❑ User- or application-level threads

❑ Kernel-level threads

❑ Hybrid of user- and kernel-level threads

Figure 6-1 shows a diagram of the three thread implementation models. Figure 6-1 (a) shows user-level threads, Figure 6-1 (b) shows kernel-level threads, and Figure 6-1 (c) shows the hybrid of user and kernel threads.

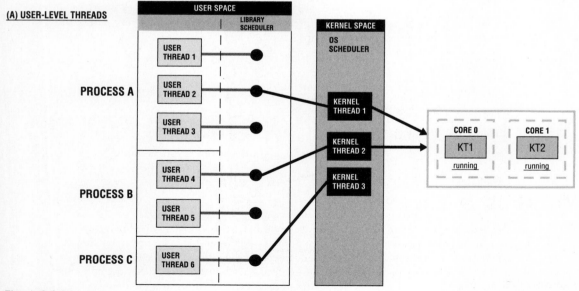

Figure 6-1 (a)

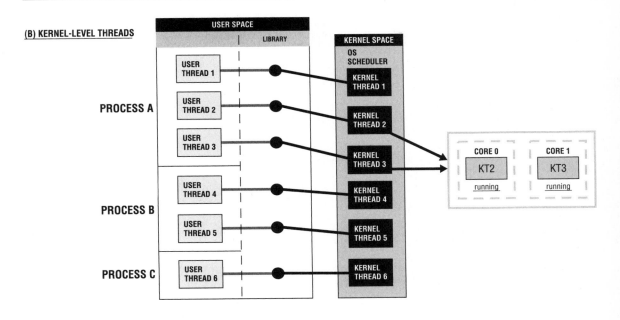

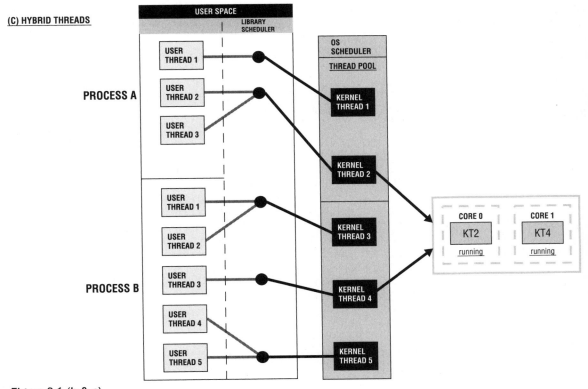

Figure 6-1 (b & c)

One of the big differences between these implementations is the mode they exist in and the ability of the threads to be assigned to a processor. These threads run in user or kernel space or mode.

❑   In **user mode**, a process or thread is executing instructions in the program or linked library. They are not making any calls to the operating system kernel.

❑   In **kernel mode**, the process or thread is making system calls such as accessing resources or throwing exceptions. Also, in kernel mode, the process or thread can access objects that are defined in kernel space.

User-level threads reside in user space or mode. The runtime library, also in user space, manages these threads. They are not visible to the operating system and, therefore, cannot be scheduled to a processor core. Each thread does not have its own thread context. So, as far as simultaneous execution of threads, there is only one thread per process that will be running at any given time and only a single processor core allocated to that process. There may be thousands or tens of thousands user-level threads for a single process, but they have no impact on the system resources. The runtime library schedules and dispatches these threads. As you can see in Figure 6-1 (a), the library scheduler chooses a thread from the multiple threads of a process, and that thread is associated with the one kernel thread allowed for that process. That kernel thread will be assigned to a processor core by the operating system scheduler. User-level threads are considered a "many-to-one" thread mapping.

Kernel-level threads reside in kernel space and are kernel objects. With kernel threads, each user thread is mapped to or *bound* to a kernel thread. The user thread is bound to that kernel thread for the life of the user thread. Once the user thread terminates, both threads leave the system. This is called a "one-to-one" thread mapping and is depicted in Figure 6-1 (b). The operating system scheduler manages, schedules, and dispatches these threads. The runtime library requests a kernel-level thread for each of the user-level threads. The operating system's memory management and scheduling subsystem must be considered for very large numbers of user-level threads. You have to know what the allowable number of threads per process is. The operating system creates a context for each thread. The context for a thread is discussed in the next section of this chapter. Each of the threads from a process can be assigned to a processor core as the resources become available.

A hybrid thread implementation is a cross between user and kernel threads and allows both the library and the operating system to manage the threads. User threads are managed by the runtime library scheduler, and the kernel threads are managed by the operating system scheduler. With this implementation, a process has its own pool of kernel threads. The user threads that are runnable are dispatched by the runtime library and are marked as available threads ready for execution. The operating system selects a user thread and maps it to one of the available kernel threads in the pool. More than one user thread may be assigned to the same kernel thread. In Figure 6-1 (c) process A has two kernel threads in its pool, whereas process B has three. Process A's user threads 2 and 3 are mapped to kernel thread 2. Process B has five threads; user threads 1 and 2 are mapped to a single kernel thread (3), and user threads 4 and 5 are mapped to a single kernel thread (5). When a new user thread is created, it is simply mapped to one of the existing kernel threads in the pool. This implementation uses a "many-to-many" thread mapping. A many-to-one mapping is suggested by some for this approach. Many user threads would be mapped to one kernel thread, as you saw in the preceding example. So, the requests for kernel threads would be less than the number of user threads.

The pool of kernel threads is not destroyed and re-created. These threads are always in the system. They are allocated to different user-level threads when necessary as opposed to creating a new kernel thread whenever a new user-level thread is created, as it is with pure kernel-level threads. A context is created only for each of the threads in the pool. With the kernel and hybrid threads, the operating system allocates a group of processor cores that the process's threads are allowed to run on. The threads can execute only on those processor cores assigned to their process.

User- and kernel-level threads also become important when determining a thread's scheduling model and contention scope. Contention scope determines which threads a given thread contends with for processor usage, and it also becomes very important in relation to the operating system's memory management for large numbers of threads.

Thread Context

The operating system manages the execution of many processes. Some of the processes are single processes that come from various programs, systems, and application programs, and some of the processes come from a single application or program that has been decomposed into many processes. When one process is removed from a core and another process becomes active, a context switch takes place between those processes. The operating system must keep track of all the information that is needed to restart that process and start the new process in order for it to become active. This information is called the *context* and describes the present state of the process. When the process becomes active, it can continue execution right where it was preempted. The information or context of the process includes:

- ❑ Process id
- ❑ Pointer to executable
- ❑ The stack
- ❑ Memory for static and dynamically allocated variables
- ❑ Processor registers

Most of the information for the context of a process has to do with describing the address space. The context of a process uses many system resources, and it takes some time to switch from the context of one process to that of another. Threads also have a context. Table 6-1 contrasts the process context, as discussed in Chapter 5, with the thread context. When a thread is preempted, a context switch between threads takes place. If the threads belong to the same process, they share the same address space because the threads are contained in the address of the process to which they belong. So, most of the information needed to reinstate a process is not needed for a thread. Although the process shares much with its threads, most importantly its address space and resources, some information is local or unique to the thread, while other aspects of the thread are contained within the various segments of the process.

Chapter 6: Multithreading

Table 6-1

Content of Context	Process	Thread
Pointer to executable	x	
Stack	x	x
Memory (data segment and heap)	x	
State	x	x
Priority	x	x
Status of program I/O	x	
Granted privileges	x	
Scheduling information	x	
Accounting information	x	
Information pertaining to resources	x	
• File descriptors		
• Read/write pointers		
Information pertaining to events and signals	x	
Register set	x	x
• Stack pointer		
• Instruction counter		
• And so on		

The information unique or local to a thread comprises the thread id, processor registers (what the state of registers is when the thread is executing, including the program counter and stack pointer), the state and priority of the thread, and thread-specific data (TSD). The thread id is assigned to the thread when it is created. Threads have access to the data segment of their process; therefore, threads can read or write to the globally declared data of their process. Any modification by one thread in the process is accessible by all threads in that process as well as by the main thread. In most cases, this requires some type of synchronization in order to prevent inadvertent updates. A thread's locally declared variables should not be accessed by any of its peer threads. They are placed in the stack of the thread, and when the thread has completed, they are removed from the stack.

Synchronization between threads is discussed in Chapter 7.

The TSD is a structure that contains data and information private to a thread. TSD can contain private copies of a process's global data. It can also contain signal masks for a thread. Signal masks are used to identify signals of a specific type that will not be received by the thread when sent to its process. Otherwise, if a process is sent a signal by the operating system, all threads in its address space also receive that signal. The thread receives all signal types that are not masked.

A thread shares text and stack segment with its process. Its instruction pointer points to some location within the process's text segment to the next executable thread instruction, and the stack pointer points to the location in the process stack where the top of the thread's stack begins. Threads can also access any environment variables. All of the resources of the process, such as file descriptors, are shared with its threads.

Hardware Threads and Software Threads

Threads can be implemented in hardware as well as software. Chip manufacturers implement cores that have multiple hardware threads that serve as *logical cores*. Cores with multiple hardware threads are called simultaneous multithreaded (SMT) cores. SMT brings to hardware the concept of multithreading, in similar way to software threads. SMT-enabled processors execute many software threads or processes simultaneously within the processor cores. Having software threads executing simultaneously within a single processor core increases a core's efficiency because wait time from elements such as I/O latencies is minimized. The logical cores are treated as unique processor cores by the operating system. They require some duplicate hardware that stores information for the context of the thread such as instruction counters and register sets. Other hardware or structures are duplicated or are shared among the threads' contexts, depending on the processor core.

Sun's UltraSparc T1, IBM's Cell Broadband Engine CBE, and various Intel multicore processors utilize SMT or chip-level multithreading (CMT), implementing from two to eight threads per core. Hyperthreading is Intel's implementation of SMT in which its primary purpose is to improve support for multithreaded code. Hyperthreading or SMT technology provides an efficient use of CPU resources under certain workloads by executing threads in parallel on a single processor core.

Thread Resources

Threads share most of their resources with other threads of the same process. Threads own resources that define their context. Threads must share other resources such as processors, memory, and file descriptors. File descriptors are allocated to each process separately, and threads of the same process compete for access to these descriptors. A thread can allocate additional resources such as files or mutexes, but they are accessible to all the threads of the process.

There are limits on the resources that can be consumed by a single process. Therefore, all the resources of peer threads in combination must not exceed the resource limit of the process. If a thread attempts to consume more resources than the soft resource limit defines, it is sent a signal that the process's resource limit has been reached.

When threads are utilizing their resources, they must be careful not to leave them in an unstable state when they are canceled. A terminated thread that has left a file open may cause damage to the file or cause data loss once the application has terminated. Before it terminates, a thread should perform some cleanup, preventing these unwanted situations from occurring.

Comparing Threads to Processes

Both threads and processes can provide concurrent program execution. The use of system resources needed for context switching, throughput, communication between entities, and program simplification is an issue that you need to consider when deciding whether to use multiple processes or threads.

Context Switching

When you are creating a process, the main thread may be the only thread needed to carry out the function of the process. In a process with many concurrent subtasks, multiple threads can provide asynchronous execution of the subtasks with less overhead for context switching. With low processor availability or a single core, however, concurrently executing processes involve heavy overhead because of the context switching required. Under the same condition using threads, a process context switch would occur only when a thread from a different process was the next thread to be assigned the processor. Less overhead means fewer system resources used and less time taken for context switching. Of course, if there are enough processors to go around, then context switching is not an issue.

Throughput

The throughput of an application can increase with multiple threads. With one thread, an I/O request would halt the entire process. With multiple threads, as one thread waits for an I/O request, the application continues to execute. As one thread is blocked, another can execute. The entire application does not wait for each I/O request to be filled; other tasks can be performed that do not depend on the blocked thread.

Communicating between Entities

Threads also do not require special mechanisms for communication with other threads of the process called *peer* threads. Threads can directly pass and receive data from other peer threads. This saves system resources that would have to be used in the setup and maintenance of special communication mechanisms if multiple processes were used. Threads communicate by using the memory shared within the address space of the process. For example, if a queue is globally declared by a process, Thread A of the process can store the name of a file that peer thread Thread B is to process. Thread B can read the name from the queue and process the data.

Processes can also communicate by shared memory, but processes have separate address spaces and, therefore, the shared memory exists outside the address space of both processes. If you have a process that also wants to communicate the names of files it has processed to other processes, you can use a message queue. It is set up outside the address space of the processes involved and generally requires a lot of setup to work properly. This increases the time and space used to maintain and access the shared memory.

Corrupting Process Data

Threads can easily corrupt the data of a process. Without synchronization, threads' write access to the same piece of data can cause data race. This is not so with processes. Each process has its own data, and other processes don't have access unless special communication is set up. The separate address spaces of processes protect the data from possible inadvertent corruption by other processes. The fact that threads share the same address space exposes the data to corruption if synchronization is not used. For example, assume that a process has three threads: Thread A, Thread B, and Thread C. Threads A and B update a counter, and Thread C is to read each update and then use that value in a calculation. Thread A and B both attempt to write to the memory location concurrently. Thread B overwrites the data written by Thread A before Thread C reads it. Synchronization should have been used to ensure that the counter is not updated until Thread C has read the data.

The issues of synchronization between threads and processes will be discussed in Chapter 7.

Killing the Entire Process

If a thread causes a fatal access violation, this may result in the termination of the entire process. The access violation is not isolated to the thread because it occurs in the address space of the process. Errors caused by a thread are more costly than errors caused by processes. Threads can create data errors that affect the entire memory space of all the threads. Threads are not isolated, whereas processes are isolated. A process can have an access violation that causes the process to terminate, but all of the other processes continue executing if the violation isn't too bad. Data errors can be restricted to a single process. Processes can protect resources from indiscriminate access by other processes. Threads share resources with all the other threads in the process. A thread that damages a resource affects the whole process or program.

Reuse by Other Programs

Threads are dependent and cannot be separated from their process. Processes are more independent than threads. An application can divide tasks among many processes, and those processes can be packaged as modules that can be used in other applications. Threads cannot exist outside the process that created them and, therefore, are not reusable.

Key Similarities and Differences between Threads and Processes

There are many similarities and significant differences between threads and processes. Threads and processes have an id, a set of registers, a state, and a priority, and both adhere to a scheduling policy. Like a process, threads have an environment that describes the entity to the operating system—the process or thread context. This context is used to reconstruct the preempted process or thread. Although the information needed for the process is much more than that needed for the thread, they serve the same purpose.

Threads and child processes share the resources of their parent process without requiring additional initialization or preparation. The resources opened by the process are immediately accessible to the threads or child processes of the parent process. As kernel entities, threads and child processes compete for processor usage. The parent process has some control over the child process or thread. The parent process can:

- ❑ Cancel
- ❑ Suspend
- ❑ Resume
- ❑ Change the priority

of the child process or thread. A thread or process can alter its attributes and create new resources, but it cannot access the resources belonging to other processes.

As we have indicated, the most significant difference between threads and processes is that each process has its own address space, and threads are contained in the address space of their process. This is why threads share resources so easily, and Interthread Communication is so simple. Child processes have their own address space and a copy of the data segment of its parent, so when a child modifies its data, it does not affect the data of its parent. A shared memory area has to be created in order for parent and child processes to share data. Shared memory is a type of *Interprocess Communication (IPC) mechanism*, which includes such things as pipes and First-In, First-Out (FIFO) scheduling policies. They are used to communicate or pass data between processes.

Interprocess Communication is discussed in Chapter 7.

Whereas processes can exercise control over other processes with which they have a parent-child relationship, peer threads are on an equal level regardless of who created them. Any thread that has access to the thread id of another peer thread can cancel, suspend, resume, or change the priority of that thread. In fact, any thread within a process can kill the process by canceling the primary thread, terminating all the threads of the process. Any changes to the main thread may affect all the threads of the process. If the priority of the main thread is changed, all the threads within the process that inherited that priority are also altered.

Table 6-2 summarizes the key similarities and differences between threads and processes.

Table 6-2

Similarities between Threads and Processes	Differences between Threads and Processes
Both have an id, set of registers, state, priority, and scheduling policy.	Threads share the address space of the process that created it; processes have their own address.
Both have attributes that describe the entity to the OS.	Threads have direct access to the data segment of their process; processes have their own copy of the data segment of the parent process.
Both have an information block.	Threads can directly communicate with other threads of their process; processes must use Interprocess Communication to communicate with sibling processes.
Both share resources with the parent process.	Threads have almost no overhead; processes have considerable overhead.
Both function as independent entities from the parent process.	New threads are easily created; new processes require duplication of the parent process.
The creator can exercise some control over the thread or process.	Threads can exercise considerable control over threads of the same process; processes can exercise control only over child processes.
Both can change their attributes.	Changes to the main thread (cancellation, priority change, and so on) may affect the behavior of the other threads of the process; changes to the parent process do not affect child processes.
Both can create new resources.	
Neither can access the resources of another process.	

Setting Thread Attributes

There is information about the thread used to determine the context of the thread. This information is used to reconstruct the thread's environment. What makes peer threads unique from one another is the id, the set of registers that defines the state of the thread, its priority, and its stack. These attributes are what give each thread its identity.

The POSIX thread library defines a thread *attribute object* that encapsulates a subset of the properties of the thread. These attributes are accessible and modifiable by the creator of the thread. These are the thread attributes that are modifiable:

❑ Contention scope

❑ Stack size

❑ Stack address

❑ Detached state

❑ Priority

❑ Scheduling policy and parameters

A thread attribute object can be associated with one or multiple threads. An attribute object is a profile that defines the behavior of a thread or group of threads. Once the object is created and initialized, it can be referenced repeatedly in calls to the thread creation function. If used repeatedly, a group of threads with the same attributes are created. All the threads that use the attribute object inherit all the property values. Once a thread has been created using a thread attribute object, most attributes cannot be changed while the thread is in use.

The scope attribute describes which threads a particular thread competes with for resources. Threads contend for resources within two contention scopes:

❑ Process scope

❑ System scope

Threads compete with other threads for processor usage according to the contention scope and the allocation domains (the set of processors to which it is assigned). Threads with process scope compete with threads within the same process, while threads with systemwide contention scope compete for resources with threads of other processes allocated across the system. A thread that has system scope is prioritized and scheduled with respect to all of the systemwide threads.

The thread's stack size and location are set when the thread is created. If the size and location of the thread's stack are not specified during creation, a default stack size and location are assigned by the system. The default size is system dependent and is determined by the maximum number of threads allowed for a process, the allotted size of a process's address space, and the space used by system resources. The thread's stack size must be large enough for any function calls; for any code external to the process, such as library code, called by the thread; and for local variable storage. A process with multiple threads should have a stack segment large enough for all of its thread's stacks. The address space allocated to the process limits the stack size, thus limiting the size of each of the thread's stacks. The thread's stack address may be of some importance to an application that accesses memory areas that have diverse properties. The important things to remember when you specify the location of a stack is how much space the thread requires and to ensure that the location does not overlap other peer threads' stacks.

Detached threads are threads that have become detached from their creator. They are not synchronized with other peer threads or the primary thread when it terminates or exits. They still share the address space with their process, but because they are detached, the process or thread that created them relinquishes any control over them. When a thread terminates, the id and the status of the terminated thread are saved by the system. By default, once the thread is terminated, the creator is notified. The thread id and the status are returned to the creator. If the thread is detached, once the thread is terminated, no resources are used to save the status or thread id. These resources are immediately available for reuse by the system. If it is not necessary for the creator of the thread to wait until a thread terminates before continuing processing or if a thread does not require any type of synchronization with other peer threads once terminated, that thread may be a detached thread.

The threads inherit scheduling attributes from the process. Threads have a priority, and the thread with the highest priority is executed before threads with lower priority. By prioritizing threads, tasks that require immediate execution or response from the system are allotted the processor for a time slice. Executing threads are preempted if a thread of higher priority is available. A thread's priority can be lowered or raised. The scheduling policy also determines when a thread is assigned the processor. FIFO, round robin (RR), and other scheduling policies are available. In general, it is not necessary to change the scheduling attributes of the thread during process execution. It may be necessary to make changes to scheduling if changes in the process environment occur that change the time constraints, causing you to need to improve the process's performance. But take into consideration that changing the scheduling attributes of specific processes within an application can have a negative impact on the overall performance of the application.

The Architecture of a Thread

We have discussed the process and the thread's relationship with its process. Figure 6-2 shows the architecture of a process that contains multiple threads. Both have context and attributes that make a process unique from other processes in the system and attributes that makes a thread unique from its peer threads. A process has a text (code), data, and stack segment. The threads share their text and stack segment with the process. A process's stack normally starts in high memory and works its way down. The thread's stack is bounded by the start of the next thread's stack. As you can see, the thread's stack contains its local variables. The process's global variables are located in the data segment. The context for Threads A and B has thread ids, state, priority, the processor registers, and so on. The program counter (PC) points to the next executable instruction in function `task1` and `task2` in the code segment. The stack pointer (SP) points to the top of their respective stacks. The thread attribute object is associated with a thread or group of threads. In this case, both threads use the same thread attribute.

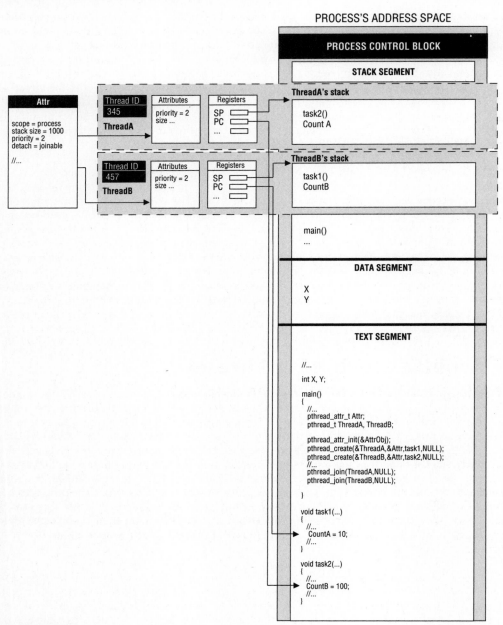

Figure 6-2

Thread States

The thread is the unit of execution when a process is scheduled to be executed. If the process has only one thread, it is the primary thread that is assigned to a processor core. If a process has multiple threads and there are multiple processors available to the process, all of the threads are assigned to processors.

When a thread is scheduled to execute on a processor core, it changes its state. A thread state is the mode or condition that a thread is in at any given time. Threads have the same states and transitions mentioned in Chapter 5 for processes. There are four commonly implemented states:

- ❏ Runnable
- ❏ Running (active)
- ❏ Stopped
- ❏ Sleeping (blocked)

There are several transitions:

- ❏ Preempt
- ❏ Signaled
- ❏ Dispatch
- ❏ Timer runout

The primary thread can determine the state of an entire process. The state of the primary thread is that same as the state of the process, if it's the only thread. If the primary thread is sleeping, the process is sleeping. If the primary thread is running, the process is running. For a process that has multiple threads, all threads of the process have to be in a sleeping or stopped state in order for the whole process to be considered sleeping or stopped. On the other hand, if one thread is active (runnable or running), then the process is considered active.

Scheduling and Thread Contention Scope

There are two types of contention scopes for threads:

- ❏ Process contention
- ❏ System contention

Threads with process contention scope contend with threads of the same process. These are hybrid threads (user- and kernel-level threads), whereby the system creates a pool of kernel-level threads, and user-level threads are mapped to them. These kernel-level threads are *unbound* and can be mapped to one thread or mapped to many threads. The kernel then schedules the kernel threads onto processors according to their scheduling attributes.

Threads with system contention scope contend with threads of processes systemwide. This model consists of one user-level thread per kernel-level thread. The user thread is bound to a kernel-level thread throughout the lifetime of the thread. The kernel threads are solely responsible for scheduling thread execution on one or more processors. This model schedules all threads against all other threads in the system, using the scheduling attributes of the thread. The default contention scope of a thread is implementation defined. For example, for Solaris 10, the default contention scope is process, but for SuSe Linux 2.6.13, the default is system scope. As a matter of fact for SuSe Linux 2.6.13, process contention scope is not supported at all.

Figure 6-3 shows the differences between process and system thread contention scopes. There are two processes in a multicore environment of eight cores. Process A has four threads, and process B has two threads. Process A has three threads that have process scope and one thread with system scope. Process

B has two threads, one with process scope and one thread with system scope. Process A's threads with process scope compete for core 0 and core 1, and process B's thread with process scope will utilize core 2. Process A and B's threads with system scope compete for cores 4 and 5. The threads with process scope are mapped to a pool of threads. Process A has a pool of three kernel-level threads and process B has a pool of two kernel-level threads.

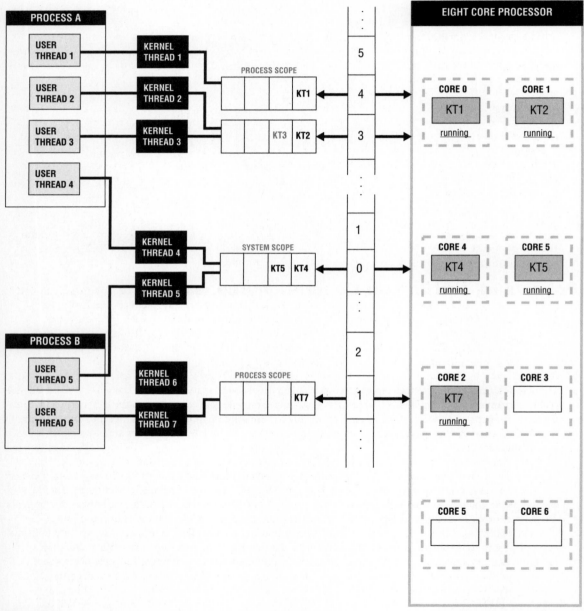

Figure 6-3

Contention scope can potentially impact on the performance of your application. The process scheduling model potentially provides lower overhead for making scheduling decisions, since there are only threads of a single process that need to be scheduled.

Scheduling Policy and Priority

The scheduling policy and priority of the process belong to the primary thread. Each thread can have its own scheduling policy and priority separate from the primary thread. The priority value is an integer that has a maximum and minimum value. When threads are prioritized, tasks that require immediate execution or response from the system are favored. In a preemptive operating system, executing threads are preempted if a thread of higher priority (the lower the number, the higher the priority) and the same contention scope is available.

For example, in Figure 6-3, process A has two threads (2, 3) with priority 3 and one thread (1) with priority 4. They are assigned to processor cores 0 and 1. The threads with priority 4 and 3 are runnable, and each is assigned to a processor. Once thread 3 with priority 3 becomes active, thread 1 is preempted and thread 3 is assigned the processor. In process B, there is one thread with process scope, and it has a priority 1. There is only one available processor for process B. The threads with system scope are not preempted by any of the threads of process A or B with process scope. They compete for processor usage only with other threads that have system scope.

The ready queues are organized as sorted lists in which each element is a priority level. This was discussed in Chapter 5 as well. In Chapter 5, Figure 5-6 shows ready queues. Each priority level in the list is a queue of threads with the same priority level. All threads of the same priority level are assigned to the processor using a scheduling policy: FIFO, RR, or another.

❑ A **round-robin scheduling policy** considers all threads to be of equal priority, and each thread is given the processor for only a time slice. Task executions are interweaved. For example, a program that filters characters from a text file is divided into three threads. Thread 1, the primary thread, reads in each line from the file and writes each to a vector as a string. Then the primary thread creates three more threads and waits for the threads to return. Each thread has its own set of characters that it is to remove from the strings. Each thread utilizes two queues, and one queue contains the strings that have been previously filtered by another thread. Once the thread has filtered a string, it is written to the second queue. The queues are global data. The primary thread is in a ready queue running preemptively until it creates the other threads; then it sleeps until all its threads return. The other threads have equal priority using a round-robin scheduling policy. A thread cannot filter a string that has not been written to a queue, so synchronized access to the source queue is required. The thread tests the mutex. If the mutex is locked, then there are no strings available, or the source queue is in use. The thread has to wait until the mutex is unlocked. If the mutex is available, then there are strings in the source queue, and the source queue is not in use. A string is read from the queue; the thread filters the string and then writes it to the output queue. The output queue serves as the source queue for another thread. At some point, Thread 2 is assigned the processor. Its source is the vector that contains all the strings to be filtered. The thread has to filter the string and then write the filtered string to its output queue so that thread 2 has something to process, then thread 3, and so on. The RR scheduling affects the execution of the threads with two processor cores. This scheduling policy inhibits the proper execution of this program. We discuss using the correct concurrency models later in this chapter.

- ❑   With **FIFO scheduling** and a high priority, there is no interweaving of the execution of these tasks. A thread assigned to a processor dominates the processor until it completes execution. This scheduling policy can be used for applications where a set of threads needs to complete as soon as possible.

- ❑   The **"other"** scheduling policy can be a customization of a scheduling policy. For example, a FIFO scheduling policy can be customized to allow random unblocking of threads, or you can use a policy with the appropriate scheduling that advances thread execution.

Scheduling Allocation Domains

The FIFO and RR scheduling policies take on different characteristics on a multiple processors. The scheduling allocation domain determines the set of processors on which the threads of a process or application may run. Scheduling policies can be affected by the number of processor cores and the number of threads in a process. As with the example of threads filtering characters from a string, if there are the same number of cores as threads, using an RR scheduling policy may result in better throughput. But it is not always possible to have same number of threads as cores. There may be more threads than cores. In general, relying on the number of cores to significantly impact the performance of your application is not the best approach.

A Simple Threaded Program

Here is an example of a simple threaded program. This simple multithreaded program has a main thread and the functions that the threads will execute. The concurrency model determines the manner in which the threads are created and managed. We will discuss concurrency models in the next chapter. Threads can be created all at once or under certain conditions. In Example 6-1 the delegation model is used to show the simple multithreaded program.

Example 6-1

```
// Example 6-1 Using the delegation model in a simple threaded program.

using namspace std;
#include <iostream>
#include <pthread.h>

void *task1(void *X) //define task to be executed by ThreadA
{
   cout << "Thread A complete" << endl;
   return (NULL);
}

void *task2(void *X) //define task to be executed by ThreadB

{
   cout << "Thread B complete" << endl;
   return (NULL);
}

int main(int argc, char *argv[])
```

```
{
    pthread_t ThreadA,ThreadB; // declare threads

    pthread_create(&ThreadA,NULL,task1,NULL); // create threads
    pthread_create(&ThreadB,NULL,task2,NULL);
    // additional processing
    pthread_join(ThreadA,NULL); // wait for threads
    pthread_join(ThreadB,NULL);
    return (0);
}
```

In Example 6-1, the primary thread is the boss thread. The boss thread declares two threads, `ThreadA` and `ThreadB`. `pthread_create()` creates the threads and associates them with the tasks they are to execute. The two tasks, `task1` and `task2`, each send a message to the standard `out`. `pthread_create()` causes the threads to immediately execute their assigned tasks. The `pthread_join` function works the same way as `wait()` does for processes. The primary thread waits until both threads return. Figure 6-4 contains the sequence diagram showing the flow of control for Example 6-1. In Figure 6-4, `pthread_create()` causes a fork in the flow of control in the primary thread. Two additional flows of control, `ThreadA` and `ThreadB`, execute concurrently. `pthread_create()` returns immediately after the threads are created because it is an asynchronous function. As each thread executes its set of instructions, `pthread_join()` causes the primary thread to wait until the thread terminates and rejoins the main flow of control.

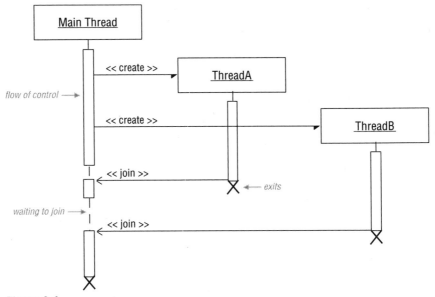

Figure 6-4

Compiling and Linking Threaded Programs

All multithreaded programs using the POSIX thread library must include this header:

```
<pthread.h>
```

In order to compile and link multithreaded applications in the Unix or Linux environments using the g++ or gcc command line compilers, be sure to link the pthread library to your application using the -l compiler switch. This switch is immediately followed by the name of the library:

```
-lpthread
```

This causes your application to link to the library that is compliant with the multithreading interface defined by POSIX 1003.1c standard. The pthread library, libpthread.so, should be located in the directory where the system stores its standard library, usually /usr/lib. If it is located in that standard directory, then your compile line would look like this:

```
g++ -o a.out test_thread.cpp -lpthread
```

If it is not located in a standard location, use the -L option to make the compiler look in a particular directory before searching the standard locations:

```
g++ -o a.out  -L /src/local/lib test_thread.cpp -lpthread
```

This tells the compiler to look in the /src/local/lib directory for the pthread library before searching in the standard locations.

As you will see later in this chapter, the complete programs in this book are accompanied by a program profile. The program profile contains implementation specifics such as headers and libraries required and compile and link instructions. The profile also includes a note section that contains any special considerations that need to be followed when executing the program. There are no program profiles for examples.

Creating Threads

The pthreads library can be used to create, maintain, and manage the threads of multithreaded programs and applications. When you are creating a multithreaded program, threads can be created any time during the execution of a process because they are dynamic. pthread_create() creates a new thread in the address space of a process.

Synopsis

```
#include <pthread.h>

int pthread_create(pthread_t *restrict thread, const pthread_attr_t *restrict attr,
            void *(*start_routine)(void*), void *restrict arg);
```

The `thread` parameter points to a thread handle or thread id of the thread to be created. The new thread has the attributes specified by the attribute object `attr`. The `thread` parameter immediately executes the instructions in `start_routine` with the arguments specified by `arg`. If the function successfully creates the thread, it returns the thread id and stores the value in `thread`. The `restrict` keyword is added for alignment with a previous IEEE standard. Here is the call to `pthread_create()` from Example 6-1:

```
pthread_create(&ThreadA,NULL,task1,NULL);
```

Here, `attr` is NULL; the default thread attributes will be used by the new thread `ThreadA`. There are no specified arguments. For new attributes for the thread, a `pthread_attr_t` object is created and initialized and then passed to the `pthread_create()`. The new thread then takes on the attributes of `attr` when it is created. If `attr` is changed after the thread has been created, it does not affect any of the thread's attributes. If `start_routine` returns, the thread returns as if `pthread_exit()` was called using the return value of `start_routine` as its exit status.

If successful, the function returns 0. If the function is not successful, no new thread is created, and the function returns an error number. If the system does not have the resources to create the thread or if the thread limit for the process has been reached, the function fails. The function also fails if the thread attribute is invalid or if the caller thread does not have permission to set the necessary thread attributes.

Passing Arguments to a Thread

Listing 6-1 shows a primary thread passing an argument from the command line to the functions executed by the threads. The command-line argument is also used to determine the number of threads to be created.

Listing 6-1

```
//Listing 6-1 Passing arguments to a thread from the command line.

1   using namespace std;
2
3   #include <iostream>
4   #include <pthread.h>
5
6
7   void *task1(void *X)
8   {
9       int *Temp;
10      Temp = static_cast<int *>(X);
11
12      for(int Count = 0;Count < *Temp;Count++)
13      {
14          cout << "work from thread: " << Count << endl;
15      }
16      cout << "Thread complete" << endl;
17      return (NULL);
18  }
19
20
21
22  int main(int argc, char *argv[])
```

(continued)

Listing 6-1 *(continued)*

```
23  {
24      int N;
25
26      pthread_t MyThreads[10];
27
28      if(argc != 2){
29          cout << "error" << endl;
30           exit (1);
31      }
32
33      N = atoi(argv[1]);
34
35      if(N > 10){
36          N = 10;
37      }
38
39      for(int Count = 0;Count < N;Count++)
40      {
41          pthread_create(&MyThreads[Count],NULL,task1,&N);
42
43      }
44
45
46      for(int Count = 0;Count < N;Count++)
47      {
48          pthread_join(MyThreads[Count],NULL);
49
50      }
51      return(0);
52
53
54  }
55
56
```

At Line 27, an array of 10 pthread_t MyThread types is declared. N holds the command-line argument. At Line 43, N MyThreads types are created. Each thread is passed N as an argument as a void *. In the function task1, the argument is cast from a void * to an int * , as follows:

```
10      Temp = static_cast<int *>(X);
```

The function executes a loop that is iterated the number of times indicated by the value passed to the function. The function sends its message to standard out. Each thread created executes this function. The instructions for compiling and executing Listing 6-1 are contained in Program Profile 6-1, which follows shortly.

This is an example of passing a command-line argument to the thread function and using the command-line argument to determine the number of threads to create. If it is necessary to pass multiple arguments to the thread function, you can create a struct or container with all the required arguments and pass a pointer to that structure to the thread function. But we show an easier way to achieve this by creating a thread object later in this chapter.

Program Profile 6-1

Program Name:

program6-1.cc (Listing 6-1)

Description:

Accepts an integer from the command line and passes the value to the thread function. The thread function executes a loop that then sends a message to standard out. The argument is used as the stopping case for the loop invariant. The argument also determines the number of threads to be created. Each thread executes the same function.

Libraries Required:

libpthread

Headers Required:

<pthread.h> <iostream>

Compile and Link Instructions:

c++ -o program6-1 program6-1.cc -lpthread

Test Environment:

Solaris 10, gcc 3.4.3 and 3.4.6

Processors:

Opteron, UltraSparc T1

Execution Instructions:

./program6-1 5

Notes:

This program requires a command-line argument.

Joining Threads

pthread_join() is used to join or rejoin flows of control in a process. pthread_join() causes the calling thread to suspend its execution until the target thread has terminated. It is similar to the wait() function used by processes. This function is called by the creator of a thread who waits for the new thread to terminate and return, thus rejoining the calling thread's flow of control. The pthread_join() can also be called by peer threads if the thread handle is global. This allows any thread to join flows of control with any other thread in the process. If the calling thread is canceled before the target thread returns, this causes the target thread to become zombied. Detached threads are discussed later in the chapter. Behavior is undefined if different peer threads simultaneously call the pthread_join() function on the same thread.

Synopsis

```
#include <pthread.h>

int pthread_join(pthread_t thread, void **value_ptr);
```

The `thread` parameter is the target thread the calling thread is waiting on. If the target thread returns successfully, its exit status is stored in `value_ptr`. The function fails if the target thread is not a joinable thread or, in other words, if it is created as a detached thread. The function also fails if the specified thread `thread` does not exist.

There should be a `pthread_join()` function called for all joinable threads. Once the thread is joined, this allows the operating system to reclaim storage used by the thread. If a joinable thread is not joined to any thread or if the thread that calls the join function is canceled, then the target thread continues to utilize storage. This is a state similar to that of a zombied process when the parent process has not accepted the exit status of a child process. The child process continues to occupy an entry in the process table.

Getting the Thread Id

As mentioned earlier in this chapter, the process shares its resources with the threads in its address space. Threads have very few of their own resources, but the thread id is one of the resources unique to a thread. The `pthread_self()` function returns the thread id of the calling thread.

Synopsis

```
#include <pthread.h>

pthread_t pthread_self(void);
```

When a thread is created, the thread id is returned to the calling thread. Once the thread has its own id, it can be passed to other threads in the process. This function returns the thread id with no errors defined.

Here is an example of calling this function:

```
pthread_t  ThreadId;
ThreadId = pthread_self();
```

A thread calls this function, and the function returns the thread id assigned to the variable `ThreadId` of type `pthread_t`.

The thread id is also returned to the calling thread of `pthread_create()`. If the thread is successfully created, the thread id is stored in `pthread_t`.

Comparing Thread Ids

You can treat thread ids as opaque types. Thread ids can be compared but not by using the normal comparison operators. You can determine whether two thread ids are equivalent by calling `pthread_equal()`:

Synopsis

```
#include <pthread.h>

int pthread_equal(pthread_t tid1, pthread_t tid2);
```

pthread_equal() returns a nonzero value if the two thread ids reference the same thread. If they reference different threads, it returns zero.

Using the Pthread Attribute Object

Threads have a set of attributes that can be specified at the time that the thread is created. The set of attributes is encapsulated in an object, and the object can be used to set the attributes of a thread or group of threads. The thread attribute object is of type pthread_attr_t. This structure can be used to set these thread attributes:

- ❑ Size of the thread's stack
- ❑ Location of the thread's stack
- ❑ Scheduling inheritance, policy, and parameters
- ❑ Whether the thread is detached or joinable
- ❑ Scope of the thread

The pthread_attr_t has several methods to set and retrieve these attributes. Table 6-3 lists the methods used to set the attributes.

Table 6-3

Types of Attribute Functions	pthread Attribute Functions
Initialization	pthread_attr_init() pthread_attr_destroy()
Stack management	pthread_attr_setstacksize() pthread_attr_getstacksize() pthread_attr_setguardsize() pthread_attr_getguardsize() pthread_attr_setstack() pthread_attr_getstack() pthread_attr_setstackaddr() pthread_attr_getstackaddr()
Detach state	pthread_attr_setdetachstate() pthread_attr_getdetachstate()

Table continued on following page

Types of Attribute Functions	pthread Attribute Functions
Contention scope	pthread_attr_setscope() pthread_attr_getscope()
Scheduling inheritance	pthread_attr_setinheritsched() pthread_attr_getinheritsched()
Scheduling policy	pthread_attr_setschedpolicy() pthread_attr_getschedpolicy()
Scheduling parameters	pthread_attr_setschedparam() pthread_attr_getschedparam()

The pthread_attr_init() and pthread_attr_destroy() functions are used to initialize and destroy thread attribute objects.

Synopsis

```
#include <pthread.h>

int pthread_attr_init(pthread_attr_t *attr);
int pthread_attr_destroy(pthread_attr_t *attr);
```

pthread_attr_init() initializes a thread attribute object with the default values for all the attributes. attr is a pointer to a pthread_attr_t object. Once attr has been initialized, its attribute values can be changed by using the pthread_attr_set functions listed in Table 6-3. Once the attributes have been appropriately modified, attr can be used as a parameter in any call to the pthread_create() function. If this is successful, the function returns 0. If it is not successful, the function returns an error number. The pthread_attr_init() function fails if there is not enough memory to create the object.

The pthread_attr_destroy() function can be used to destroy a pthread_attr_t object specified by attr. A call to this function deletes any hidden storage associated with the thread attribute object. If it is successful, the function returns 0. If it is not successful, the function returns an error number.

Default Values for the Attribute Object

The attribute object is first initialized with the default values for all of the individual attributes used by a given implementation. Some implementations do not support the possible values for an attribute. Upon successful completion, pthread_attr_init() returns a value of 0. If an error number is returned, this may indicate that the value is not supported. For example, for the contention scope, PTHREAD_SCOPE_PROCESS is not supported by the Linux environment. Calling:

```
int pthread_attr_setscope(pthread_attr_t *attr, int contentionscope);
```

returns an error code. Table 6-4 lists the default values for Linux and Solaris environment.

Table 6-4

pthread Attribute Functions	SuSE Linux 2.6.13 Default Values	Solaris 10 Default Values
pthread_attr_ setdetachstate()	PTHREAD_CREATE_JOINABLE	PTHREAD_CREATE_JOINABLE
pthread_attr_setscope()	PTHREAD_SCOPE_SYSTEM (PTHREAD_SCOPE_PROCESS **is not supported**)	PTHREAD_SCOPE_PROCESS
pthread_attr_ setinheritsched()	PTHREAD_EXPLICIT_SCHED	PTHREAD_EXPLICIT_SCHED
pthread_attr_ setschedpolicy()	SCHED_OTHER	SCHED_OTHER
pthread_attr_setschedparam()	sched_priority = 0	sched_priority = 0
pthread_attr_setstacksize()	**not specified**	NULL **allocated by system**
pthread_attr_setstackaddr()	**not specified**	NULL **1–2 MB**
pthread_attr_setguardsize()	**not specified**	PAGESIZE

Creating Detached Threads Using the Pthread Attribute Object

By default, when a thread exits, the thread system stores the thread's completion status and thread id when the thread is joined with another thread. If an exiting thread is not joined with another thread, the exiting thread is said to be *detached*. The completion status and thread id are not stored in this case. A pthread_join() cannot be used on a detached thread. If it is used, pthread_join() returns an error.

Synopsis

```
#include <pthread.h>

int pthread_attr_setdetachstate(pthread_attr_t *attr,
                                int *detachstate);
int pthread_attr_getdetachstate(const pthread_attr_t *attr,
                                int *detachstate);
```

The pthread_attr_setdetachstate() function can be used to set the detachstate attribute of the attribute object. The detachstate parameter describes the thread as detached or joinable. The detachstate can have one of these values:

❑   PTHREAD_CREATE_DETACHED

❑   PTHREAD_CREATE_JOINABLE

The PTHREAD_CREATE_DETACHED value causes all the threads that use this attribute object to be created as detached threads. The PTHREAD_CREATE_JOINABLE value causes all the threads that use this attribute object to be joinable. The default value of detachstate is PTHREAD_CREATE_JOINABLE. If it is successful, the function returns 0. If it is not successful, the function returns an error number. The pthread_attr_setdetachstate() function fails if the value of detachstate is not valid.

The pthread_attr_getdetachstate() function returns the detachstate of the attribute object. If it is successful, the function returns the value of detachstate to the detachstate parameter and 0 as the return value. If it is not successful, the function returns an error number.

Threads that are already running can become detached. For example, a thread may no longer be interested in the results of the target thread. The thread may detach to allow its resources to be reclaimed once the thread exits.

Synopsis

```
int pthread_detach(pthread_t tid);
```

In Example 6-2, the ThreadA is created as a detached thread using an attribute object. ThreadB is detached after it has been created.

Example 6-2

```
// Example 6-2 Using an attribute object to create a detached thread and changing
// a joinable thread to a detached thread.

//...

int main(int argc, char *argv[])
{

   pthread_t ThreadA,ThreadB;
   pthread_attr_t DetachedAttr;

   pthread_attr_init(&DetachedAttr);
   pthread_attr_setdetachstate(&DetachedAttr,PTHREAD_CREATE_DETACHED);
   pthread_create(&ThreadA,&DetachedAttr,task1,NULL);

   pthread_create(&ThreadB,NULL,task2,NULL);

   //...

   pthread_detach(pthread_t ThreadB);

   //pthread_join(ThreadB,NULL); cannot call once detached
   return (0);
}
```

Example 6-2 declares an attribute object `DetachedAttr`. The `pthread_attr_init()` function is used to initialize the attribute object. `ThreadA` is created with the `DetachedAttr` attribute object. This attribute object has set `detachstate` to `PTHREAD_CREATE_DETACHED`. `ThreadB` is created with the default value for `detachstate`, `PTHREAD_CREATE_JOINABLE`. Once it is created, `pthread_detach()` is called. Now that `ThreadB` is detached, `pthread_join()` cannot be called for this thread.

Managing Threads

So far we have talked about creating threads, using thread attribute objects, creating joinable and detached threads, and returning thread ids. Now we discuss managing the threads. When you create applications with multiple threads, there are several ways to control how threads behave and how they use and compete for resources. Part of managing threads is setting the scheduling policy, the priority of the threads, and so on. This contributes to the performance of the threads and, therefore, to the performance of the application. Thread performance is also determined by how the threads compete for resources, either on a process or system scope. The scheduling, priority, and scope of the thread can be set by using a thread attribute object. Because threads share resources, access to resources has to be synchronized. Thread synchronization also includes when and how threads are terminated and canceled.

Terminating Threads

A thread terminates when it comes to the end of the instructions of its routine. When the thread terminates, the pthread library reclaims the system resources the thread was using and stores its exit status. A thread can also be terminated by another peer thread prematurely before it has executed all its instructions. The thread may have corrupted some process data and may have to be terminated.

A thread's execution can be discontinued by several means:

❑ By returning from the execution of its assigned task with or without an exit status or return value

❑ By explicitly terminating itself and supplying an exit status

❑ By being canceled by another thread in the same address space.

Self-Termination

A thread can self-terminate by calling `pthread_exit()`.

Synopsis

```
#include <pthread.h>

int pthread_exit(void *value_ptr);
```

When a joinable thread function has completed executing, it returns to the thread calling `pthread_join()` for which it was the target thread. When the terminating thread calls `pthread_exit()`, it is passed the exit status in `value_ptr`. The exit status is returned to `pthread_join()`. Cancellation cleanup handler tasks that have not executed execute along with the destructors for any thread-specific data.

When this function is called, no resources used by the thread are released. No application visible process resources, including mutexes and file descriptors, are released. No process-level cleanup actions are performed. When the last thread of a process exits, the process has terminated with an exit status of 0. This function cannot return to the calling thread, and there are no errors defined for it.

Terminating Peer Threads

It may be necessary for one thread to terminate a peer thread. `pthread_cancel()` is used to terminate peer threads. The `thread` parameter is the thread to be canceled. The function returns 0 if successful and an error if not successful. The `pthread_cancel()` function fails if the `thread` parameter does not correspond to an existing thread.

Synopsis

```
#include <pthread.h>

int pthread_cancel(pthread_t thread);
```

An application may have a thread that monitors the work of other threads. If a thread performs poorly or is no longer needed, in order to save system resources it may be necessary to terminate that thread. A user may desire to cancel an executing operation. Multiple threads may be used to solve a problem, but once the solution is obtained by a thread, all of the other threads can be canceled by the monitor or the thread that obtained the solution.

A call to `pthread_cancel()` is a request to cancel a peer thread. The request can be granted immediately, granted at a later time, or even ignored. The target thread may terminate immediately or defer termination until a logical point in its execution. The thread may have to perform some cleanup tasks before it terminates. The thread also has the option to refuse termination.

Understanding the Cancellation Process

There is a cancellation process that occurs asynchronously to the returning of the `pthread_cancel()` when a request to cancel a peer thread is granted. The cancel type and cancel state of the target thread determines when cancellation actually takes place. The *cancelability state* describes the cancel condition of a thread as being *cancelable* or *uncancelable*. A thread's *cancelability type* determines the thread's ability to continue after a cancel request. The cancelability state and type are dynamically set by the thread itself.

`pthread_setcancelstate()` and `pthread_setcanceltype()` are used to set the cancelability state and type of the calling thread. `pthread_setcancelstate()` sets the calling thread to the cancelability state specified by `state` and returns the previous state in `oldstate`. `pthread_setcanceltype()` sets the calling thread to the cancelability type specified by `type` and returns the previous state in `oldtype`.

Synopsis

```
#include <pthread.h>

int pthread_setcancelstate(int state, int *oldstate);
int pthread_setcanceltype(int type, int *oldtype);
```

The values for state and oldstate for setting the cancel state of a thread are:

- ❑   PTHREAD_CANCEL_DISABLE
- ❑   PTHREAD_CANCEL_ENABLE

PTHREAD_CANCEL_DISABLE causes the thread to ignore a cancel request. PTHREAD_CANCEL_ENABLE causes the thread to concede to a cancel request. This is the default state of any newly created thread. If successful, the function returns 0. If not successful, the function returns an error number. The pthread_setcancelstate() may fail if not passed a valid state value.

pthread_setcanceltype() sets the calling thread to the cancelability type specified by type and returns the previous state in oldtype. The values for type and oldtype are:

- ❑   PTHREAD_CANCEL_DEFFERED
- ❑   PTHREAD_CANCEL_ASYNCHRONOUS

PTHREAD_CANCEL_DEFFERED causes the thread to put off termination until it reaches its cancellation point. This is the default cancelability type for any newly created threads. PTHREAD_CANCEL_ASYNCHRONOUS causes the thread to terminate immediately. If successful, the function returns 0. If not successful, the function returns an error number. The pthread_setcanceltype() may fail if not passed a valid type value.

The pthread_setcancelstate() and pthread_setcanceltype() are used together to establish the cancelability of a thread. Table 6-5 list combinations of state and type and a description of what occurs for each combination.

Table 6-5

Cancelability State	Cancelability Type	Description
PTHREAD_CANCEL_ENABLE	PTHREAD_CANCEL_DEFERRED	*Deferred cancellation.* The default cancellation state and type of a thread. Thread cancellation takes places when it enters a cancellation point or when the programmer defines a cancellation point with a call to pthread_testcancel().
PTHREAD_CANCEL_ENABLE	PTHREAD_CANCEL_ASYNCHRONOUS	*Asynchronous cancellation.* Thread cancellation takes place immediately.
PTHREAD_CANCEL_DISABLE	Ignored	*Disabled cancellation.* Thread cancellation does not take place.

Take a look at the Example 6-3.

Example 6-3

```
// Example 6-3 task3 thread sets its cancelability state to allow thread
// to be canceled immediately.

void *task3(void *X)
{
    int OldState,OldType;

    // enable immediate cancelability

    pthread_setcancelstate(PTHREAD_CANCEL_ENABLE,&OldState);
    pthread_setcanceltype(PTHREAD_CANCEL_ASYNCHRONOUS,&OldType);

    ofstream Outfile("out3.txt");
    for(int Count = 1;Count < 100;Count++)
    {
        Outfile << "thread C is working: " << Count << endl;

    }
    Outfile.close();
    return (NULL);
}
```

In Example 6-3, cancellation is set to take place immediately. This means that a request to cancel the thread can take place at any point of execution in the thread's function. So, the thread can open the file and be canceled while it is writing to the file.

Cancellation of a peer thread should not be taken lightly. Some threads are of such a sensitive nature that they may require safeguards against untimely cancellation. Installing safeguards in a thread's function may prevent undesirable situations. For example, consider threads that share data. Depending on the thread model used, one thread may be processing data that is to be passed to another thread for processing. While the thread is processing data, it has sole possession of the data by locking a mutex. If a thread is canceled before the mutex is released, this will cause deadlock. The data may be required to be in some state before it can be used again. If a thread is canceled before this is done, an undesirable condition may occur. Depending on the type of processing that a thread is performing, thread cancellation should be performed only when it is safe.

A vital thread may prevent cancellation entirely. Therefore, thread cancellation should be restricted to threads that are not vital, points of execution that do not have locks on resources or are in the process of executing vital code. Set the cancelability of the thread to the appropriate state and type. Cancellations should be postponed until all vital cleanups have taken place, such as releasing mutexes, closing files, and so on. If the thread has cancellation cleanup handler tasks, they are performed before cancellation. When the last handler returns, the destructors for thread-specific data, if any, are called, and the thread is terminated.

Using Cancellation Points

When a cancel request is deferred, the termination of the thread is postponed until later in the execution of the thread's function. When it occurs, it should be *safe* to cancel the thread because it is not in the middle of locking a mutex, executing critical code, or leaving data in some unusable state. These safe locations in the code's execution are good locations for *cancellation points*. A cancellation point is a checkpoint where a thread checks if there are any cancellation requests pending and, if so, concedes to termination.

Cancellation points are marked by a call to pthread_testcancel(). This function checks for any pending cancellation request. If a request is pending, it causes the cancellation process to occur at the location this function is called. If there are no cancellations pending, then the function continues to execute with no repercussions. This function call should be placed at any location in the code where it is considered safe to terminate the thread.

Synopsis

```
#include <pthread.h>

void pthread_testcancel(void);
```

In Example 6-3, the cancelability of the thread was set for immediate cancelability. Example 6-4 uses a deferred cancelability, the default setting. A call to pthread_testcancel() marks where it is safe for the thread to be canceled, before the file is opened or after the thread has closed the file.

Example 6-4

```
// Example 6-4 task1 thread sets its cancelability state to be deferred.


void *task1(void *X)
{
    int OldState,OldType;

    //not needed default settings for cancelability
    pthread_setcancelstate(PTHREAD_CANCEL_ENABLE,&OldState);
    pthread_setcanceltype(PTHREAD_CANCEL_DEFERRED,&OldType);

    pthread_testcancel();

    ofstream Outfile("out1.txt");
    for(int Count = 1;Count < 1000;Count++)
    {
        Outfile << "thread 1 is working: " << Count << endl;

    }
    Outfile.close();
    pthread_testcancel();return (NULL);
}
```

In Example 6-5, two threads are created and then canceled.

Example 6-5

```cpp
//Example 6-5 shows two threads being canceled.

//...
int main(int argc, char *argv[])
{
   pthread_t Threads[2];
   void *Status;

   pthread_create(&(Threads[0]),NULL,task1,NULL);
   pthread_create(&(Threads[1]),NULL,task3,NULL);


    // ...

   pthread_cancel(Threads[0]);
   pthread_cancel(Threads[1]);


   for(int Count = 0;Count < 2;Count++)
   {
      pthread_join(Threads[Count],&Status);
      if(Status == PTHREAD_CANCELED){
          cout << "thread" << Count << " has been canceled" << endl;
      }
      else{
             cout << "thread" << Count << " has survived" << endl;
      }
   }
   return (0);
}
```

In Example 6-5, the primary thread creates two threads. Then it issues a cancellation request for each thread. The main thread calls the `pthread_join()` function for each thread. The `pthread_join()` function does not fail if it attempts to join with a thread that has already been terminated. The join function just retrieves the exit status of the terminated thread. This is good because the thread that issues the cancellation request may be a different thread than the thread that calls `pthread_join()`. Monitoring the work of all the worker threads may be the sole task of a single thread that also cancels threads. Another thread may examine the exit status of threads by calling the `pthread_join()` function. This type of information can be used to statistically evaluate which threads have the best performance. In this example, the main thread joins and examines each thread's exit status in a loop. A canceled thread may return an exit status PTHREAD_CANCELED.

Taking Advantage of Cancellation-Safe Library Functions and System Calls

In these examples, cancellation points marked by a call to `pthread_testcancel()` are placed in user-defined functions. When you are calling library functions from the thread function that uses asynchronous cancellation, is it safe for the thread to be canceled?

The pthread library defines functions that can serve as cancellation points and are considered asynchronous cancellation-safe functions. These functions block the calling thread, and while the calling thread is blocked, it is safe to cancel the thread. These are the pthread library functions that act as cancellation points:

❑   `pthread_testcanel()`

❑   `pthread_cond_wait()`

❑   `pthread_timedwait`

❑   `pthread_join()`

If a thread with a deferred cancelability state has a cancellation request pending when making a call to one of these pthread library functions, the cancellation process is initiated.

Table 6-6 lists some of the POSIX system calls that are required to be cancellation points. These pthread and POSIX functions are safe to be used as deferred cancellation points, but they may not be safe for asynchronous cancellation. A library call that is not asynchronously safe that is canceled during execution can cause library data to be left in an incompatible state. The library may have allocated memory on the behalf of the thread and, when the thread is canceled, may still have a hold on that memory. In this case, before making such library calls from a thread that has asynchronous cancelability, it may be necessary to change the cancelability state before the call and then change it back after the function returns.

Table 6-6

POSIX System Calls (Cancellation Points)		
`accept()`	`nanosleep()`	`sem_wait()`
`aio_suspend()`	`open()`	`send()`
`clock_nanosleep()`	`pause()`	`sendmsg()`
`close()`	`poll()`	`sendto()`
`connect()`	`pread()`	`sigpause()`
`creat()`	`pthread_cond_timedwait()`	`sigsuspend()`
`fcntl()`	`pthread_cond_wait()`	`sigtimedwait()`
`fsync()`	`pthread_join()`	`sigwait()`
`getmsg()`	`putmsg()`	`sigwaitinfo()`

Table continued on following page

POSIX System Calls (Cancellation Points)		
lockf()	putpmsg()	sleep()
mq_receive()	pwrite()	system()
mq_send()	read()	usleep()
mq_timedreceive()	readv()	wait()
mq_timedsend()	recvfrom()	waitpid()
msgrcv()	recvmsg()	write()
msgsnd()	select()	writev()
msync()	sem_timedwait()	

For other library and systems functions that are not cancellation safe (asynchronously or deferred), it may be necessary to write code preventing a thread from terminating by disabling cancellation or deferring cancellation until after the function call has returned.

Example 6-6 is a wrapper for the library or system call. The wrapper changes the cancelability to deferred, makes the function or system call, and then resets cancelability to previous type. Now it would be safe to call pthread_testcancel().

Example 6-6

```
//Example 6-6 shows a wrapper for system functions.

int OldType;
pthread_setcanceltype(PTHREAD_CANCEL_DEFERRED,&OldType);
system_call(); //some library of system call
pthread_setcanceltype(OldType,NULL);
pthread_testcancel();

//...
```

Cleaning Up before Termination

We mentioned earlier that a thread may need to perform some final processing before it is terminated, such as closing files, resetting shared resources to a consistent state, releasing locks, or deallocating resources. The pthread library defines a mechanism for each thread to perform last minute tasks before terminating. A *cleanup stack* is associated with every thread. The cleanup stack contains pointers to routines that are to be executed during the cancellation process. The pthread_cleanup_push() function pushes a pointer to the routine to the cleanup stack.

Synopsis

```
#include <pthread.h>

void pthread_cleanup_push(void (*routine)(void *), void *arg);
void pthread_cleanup_pop(int execute);
```

The `routine` parameter is a pointer to the function to be pushed to the stack. The `arg` parameter is passed to the function. The function `routine` is called with the `arg` parameter when the thread exits under these circumstances:

❑ When calling `pthread_exit()`

❑ When the thread concedes to a termination request

❑ When the thread explicitly calls `pthread_cleanup_pop()` with a nonzero value for `execute`

The function does not return.

The `pthread_cleanup_pop()` removes `routine`'s pointer from the top of the calling thread's cleanup stack. The `execute` parameter can have a value of 1 or 0. If 1, the thread executes `routine` even if it is not being terminated. The thread continues execution from the point after the call to this function. If the value is 0, the pointer is removed from the top of the stack without executing.

For each push, there needs to be a pop within the same lexical scope. For example, `task4()` requires a cleanup handler to be executed when the function exits or canceled.

In Example 6-7, `task4()` pushes the cleanup handler `cleanup_task4()` to the cleanup stack by calling the `pthread_cleanup_push()` function. The `pthread_cleanup_pop()` function is required for each call to the `pthread_cleanup_push()` function. The pop function is passed 0, which means the handler is removed from the cleanup stack but is not executed at this point. The handler is executed if the thread that executes `task4()` is canceled.

Example 6-7

```
//Example 6-7 task4 () pushes cleanup handler cleanup_task4 () onto cleanup stack.

void *task4(void *X)
{
   int *Tid;
   Tid = new int;
   // do some work
   //...
   pthread_cleanup_push(cleanup_task4,Tid);
   // do some more work
   //...
   pthread_cleanup_pop(0);
}
```

In Example 6-8, `task5()` pushes cleanup handler `cleanup_task5()` onto the cleanup stack. The difference in this case is `pthread_cleanup_pop()` is passed 1, which means that the handler is removed from the cleanup stack but executes at this point. The handler is executed regardless of whether the thread that executes `task5()` is canceled or not. The cleanup handlers, `cleanup_task4()` and `cleanup_task5()` are regular functions that can be used to close files, release resources, unlock mutexes, and so forth.

Example 6-8

```
//Example 6-8 task5 () pushes cleanup handler cleanup_task5 () onto cleanup stack.

void *task5(void *X)
{
   int *Tid;
   Tid = new int;
   // do some work
   //...
   pthread_cleanup_push(cleanup_task5,Tid);
   // do some more work
   //...
   pthread_cleanup_pop(1);
}
```

Managing the Thread's Stack

Managing the thread's stack includes setting the size of the stack and determining its location. The thread's stack is usually automatically managed by the system. But you should be aware of the system-specific limitations that are imposed by the default stack management system. They might be too restrictive, and that's when it may be necessary to do some stack management. If your application has a large number of threads, you may have to increase the upper limit of the stack established by the default stack size. If an application utilizes recursion or calls to several functions, many stack frames are required. Some applications require exact control over the address space. For example, an application that has garbage collection must keep track of allocation of memory.

The address space of a process is divided into the text and static data segments, free store, and the stack segment. The location and size of the thread's stacks are carved out of the stack segment of its process. A thread's stack stores a stack frame for each routine it has called but that has not exited. The stack frame contains temporary variables, local variables, return addresses, and any other additional information the thread needs to finds its way back to previously executing routines. Once the routine has exited, the stack frame for that routine is removed from the stack. Figure 6-5 shows how stack frames are generated and placed onto a stack.

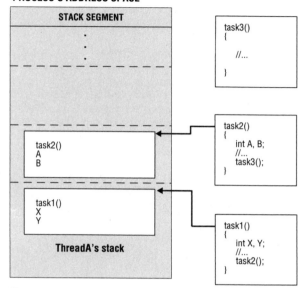

Figure 6-5

In Figure 6-5, `ThreadA` executes `task1`. `task1` creates some local variables, does some processing, and then calls `task2`. A stack frame is created for `task1` and placed on the stack. `task2` creates local variables, and then calls `task3`. A stack frame for `task2` is placed on the stack. After `task3()` has been completed, flow of control returns to `task2()`, which is popped from the stack. After `task2()` has executed, flow of control is returned to `task1()`, which is popped from the stack. Each stack must be large enough to accommodate the execution of all peer threads' functions along with the chain of routines that will be called. The size and location of a thread's stack can be set or examined by several methods defined by the attribute object.

Setting the Size of the Stack

There are two attribute methods concerned with the size of the thread's stack.

Synopsis

```
#include <pthread.h>

int pthread_attr_getstacksize(const pthread_attr_t *restrict attr,
                              size_t *restrict stacksize);
int pthread_attr_setstacksize(pthread_attr_t *attr, size_t *stacksize);
```

The `pthread_attr_getstacksize()` returns the default stack size minimum. The `attr` is the thread attribute object from which the default stack size is extracted. When the function returns, the default stack size in bytes is stored in `stacksize` and the return value is 0. If not successful, the function returns an error number.

The `pthread_attr_setstacksize()` sets the stack size minimum. The `attr` is the thread attribute object for which the stack size is set. The `stacksize` is the minimum size of the stack in bytes. If the function is successful, the return value is 0. If not successful, the function returns an error number. The function fails if `stacksize` is less than PTHREAD_MIN_STACK or exceeds the system minimum. The PTHREAD_STACK_MIN will probably be a lower minimum than the default stack minimum returned by `pthread_attr_getstacksize()`. Consider the value returned by the `pthread_attr_getstacksize()` before raising the minimum size of a thread's stack.

In Example 6-9, the stack size of a thread is changed by using a thread attribute object. It retrieves the default size from the attribute object and then determines whether the default size is less than the minimum stack size desired. If so, the offset is added to the default stack size. This becomes the new minimum stack size for this thread.

Example 6-9

```
// Example 6-9 Changing the stack size of a thread using an offset.

#include <limits.h>
//...

pthread_attr_getstacksize(&SchedAttr,&DefaultSize);
if(DefaultSize < PTHREAD_STACK_MIN){
    SizeOffset = PTHREAD_STACK_MIN - DefaultSize;
    NewSize = DefaultSize + SizeOffset;
    pthread_attr_setstacksize(&Attr1,(size_t)NewSize);
}
```

There is a tradeoff in setting the size. The stack size is fixed. A large stack means there is less of a probability there will be stack overflow. But on the other hand a large stack means more expense in terms of swap space and real memory for the stack.

Setting the stack size and stack location may make your program unportable. The stack size and location you set for your program on one platform may not match the stack size and location of another platform.

Setting the Location of the Thread's Stack

Once you decide to manage the thread's stack, you can retrieve and then set the location of the stack by using these attribute object methods:

Synopsis

```
#include <pthread.h>

int pthread_attr_setstackaddr(pthread_attr_t *attr, void *stackaddr);
int pthread_attr_getstackaddr(const pthread_attr_t *restrict attr,
                              void **restrict stackaddr);
```

The `pthread_attr_setstackaddr()` sets the base location of the stack to the address specified by `stackattr` for the thread created with the thread attribute object `attr`. This address `addr` should be within the virtual address space of the process. The size of the stack will be at least equal to the minimum stack size specified by `PTHREAD_STACK_MIN`. If successful, the function returns 0. If not successful, the function returns an error number.

`pthread_attr_getstackaddr()` retrieves the base location of the stack address for the thread created with the thread attribute object specified by the `attr`. The address is returned and stored in the `stackaddr`. If it is successful, the function returns 0. If not successful, the function returns an error number.

Setting Stack Size and Location with One Function

The stack attributes (size and location) can be set by using a single function.

Synopsis

```
#include <pthread.h>

int pthread_attr_setstack(pthread_attr_t *attr, void *stackaddr,
                          size_t stacksize);
int pthread_attr_getstack(const pthread_attr_t *restrict attr,
                          void **restrict stackaddr, size_t *restrict stacksize);
```

`pthread_attr_setstack()` sets both the stack size and location of a thread created using the specified attribute object `attr`. The base location of the stack is set to the `stackaddr`, and the size of the stack is set to the `stacksize`. `pthread_attr_getstack()` retrieves the stack size and location of a thread created using the specified attribute object `attr`. If this is successful, the stack location is stored in `stackaddr`, and the stack size is stored in `stacksize`. If successful, these functions return 0. If not successful, an error number is returned. The `pthread_setstack()` fails if the `stacksize` is less than `PTHREAD_STACK_MIN` or exceeds some implementation-defined limit.

Setting Thread Scheduling and Priorities

Threads execute independently. They are assigned to a processor core and execute the task they have been given. Each thread is given a scheduling policy and priority that dictates how and when it is assigned to a processor. The scheduling policy of a thread or group of threads can be set by an attribute object using these functions:

Synopsis

```
#include <pthread.h>
#include <sched.h>

int pthread_attr_setinheritsched(pthread_attr_t *attr, int inheritsched);
void pthread_attr_setschedpolicy(pthread_attr_t *attr, int policy);
int pthread_attr_setschedparam(pthread_attr_t *restrict attr,
                          const struct sched_param *restrict param);
```

`pthread_attr_setinheritsched()` is used to determine how the thread's scheduling attributes are set, by inheriting the scheduling attributes either from the creator thread or from an attribute object. `inheritsched` can have one of these values:

❑ PTHREAD_INHERIT_SCHED: Thread scheduling attributes are inherited from the creator thread, and any scheduling attributes of the attr are ignored.

❑ PTHREAD_EXPLICIT_SCHED:Thread scheduling attributes are set to the scheduling attributes of the attribute object `attr`.

If `inheritsched` value is PTHREAD_EXPLICIT_SCHED, then `pthread_attr_setschedpolicy()` is used to set the scheduling policy and `pthread_attr_setschedparam()` is used to set the priority.

The `pthread_attr_setschedpolicy()` sets the scheduling policy of the thread attribute object `attr`. `policy` values can be one of the following defined in the `<sched.h>` header:

❑ SCHED_FIFO: First-In, First-Out scheduling policy whereby the executing thread runs to completion.

❑ SCHED_RR: Round robin scheduling policy whereby each thread is assigned to processor only for a time slice.

❑ SCHED_OTHER: Another scheduling policy (implementation-defined). By default, this is the scheduling policy of any newly created thread.

Use `pthread_attr_setschedparam()` to set the scheduling parameters of the attribute object `attr` used by the scheduling policy. `param` is a structure that contains the parameters. The `sched_param` structure has at least this data member defined:

```
struct sched_param {
    int sched_priority;
    //...
};
```

It may also have additional data members, along with several functions that return and set the priority minimum, maximum, scheduler, parameters, and so on. If the scheduling policy is either SCHED_FIFO or SCHED_RR, then the only member required to have a value is `sched_priority`.

Use `sched_get_priority_max()` and `sched_get_priority_max()`, as follows, to obtain the maximum and minimum priority values.

Synopsis

```
#include <sched.h>

int sched_get_priority_max(int policy);
int sched_get_priority_min(int policy);
```

Both functions are passed the scheduling policy `policy` for which the priority values are requested, and both return either the maximum or minimum priority values for the scheduling policy.

Example 6-10 shows how to set the scheduling policy and priority of a thread by using the thread attribute object.

Example 6-10

```
// Example 6-10 Using the thread attribute object to set scheduling
// policy and priority of a thread.

#include <pthread.h>
#include <sched.h>

//...

pthread_t ThreadA;
pthread_attr_t SchedAttr;
sched_param SchedParam;
int MidPriority,MaxPriority,MinPriority;

int main(int argc, char *argv[])
{
   //...

   // Step 1: initialize attribute object
   pthread_attr_init(&SchedAttr);

   // Step 2: retrieve min and max priority values for scheduling policy
   MinPriority = sched_get_priority_max(SCHED_RR);
   MaxPriority = sched_get_priority_min(SCHED_RR);

   // Step 3: calculate priority value
   MidPriority = (MaxPriority + MinPriority)/2;

   // Step 4: assign priority value to sched_param structure
   SchedParam.sched_priority = MidPriority;

   // Step 5: set attribute object with scheduling parameter
   pthread_attr_setschedparam(&SchedAttr,&SchedParam);

   // Step 6: set scheduling attributes to be determined by attribute object
   pthread_attr_setinheritsched(&SchedAttr,PTHREAD_EXPLICIT_SCHED);

   // Step 7: set scheduling policy
   pthread_attr_setschedpolicy(&SchedAttr,SCHED_RR);

   // Step 8: create thread with scheduling attribute object
   pthread_create(&ThreadA,&SchedAttr,task1,NULL);

   //...
}
```

In Example 6-10, the scheduling policy and priority of ThreadA is set using the thread attribute object SchedAttr. This is done in eight steps:

1. Initialize attribute object.

2. Retrieve min and max priority values for scheduling policy.

3. Calculate priority value.

4. Assign priority value to the sched_param structure.

5. Set the attribute object with a scheduling parameter.

6. Set scheduling attributes to be determined by attribute object.

7. Set the scheduling policy.

8. Create a thread with the scheduling attribute object.

In Example 6-10, we set the priority to be an average value. But the priority can be set to be any value between the maximum and minimum priority values allowed by the scheduling policy for the thread. With these methods, the scheduling policy and priority are set in the thread attribute object before the thread is created or running. To dynamically change the scheduling policy and priority, use pthread_setschedparam() and pthread_setschedprio().

Synopsis

```
#include <pthread.h>

int pthread_setschedparam(pthread_t thread, int policy,
                          const struct sched_param *param);
int pthread_getschedparam(pthread_t thread, int *restrict policy,
                          struct sched_param *restrict param);
int pthread_setschedprio(pthread_t thread, int prio);
```

pthread_setschedparam() sets both the scheduling policy and priority of a thread directly without the use of an attribute object. thread is the id of the thread, policy is the new scheduling policy, and param contains the scheduling priority. The pthread_getschedparam() returns the scheduling policy and scheduling parameters and stores their values in policy and param parameters, respectively, if successful. If successful, both functions return 0. If not successful, both functions return an error number. Table 6-7 lists the conditions in which these functions may fail.

The pthread_setschedprio() is used to set the scheduling priority of an executing thread whose thread id is specified by the thread. prio specifies the new scheduling priority of the thread. If the function fails, the priority of the thread is not changed, and an error number is returned. If it is successful, the function returns 0. The conditions under which this function fails are listed in Table 6-7.

Table 6-7

pthread Scheduling and Priority Functions	Failure Conditions
int pthread_getschedparam (pthread_t thread, int *restrict policy, struct sched_param *restrict param);	The thread parameter does not refer to an existing thread.
int pthread_setschedparam (pthread_t thread, int *policy, const struct sched_param *param);	The policy parameter or one of the scheduling parameters associated with policy parameter is invalid. The policy parameter or one of the scheduling parameters has a value that is not supported. The calling thread does not have the appropriate permission to set the scheduling parameters or policy of the specified thread. The thread parameter does not refer to an existing thread. The implementation does not allow the application to change one of the parameters to the specified value.
int pthread_setschedprio (pthread_t thread, int prio);	The prio parameter is invalid for the scheduling policy of the specified thread. The prio parameter has a value that is not supported. The calling thread does not have the appropriate permission to set the scheduling priority of the specified thread. The thread parameter does not refer to an existing thread. The implementation does not allow the application to change the priority to the specified value.

Remember to carefully consider why it is necessary to change the scheduling policy or priority of a running thread. This may diversely affect the overall performance of your application. Threads with higher priority preempt running threads with lower priority. This may lead to starvation, a thread constantly being preempted and, therefore, not able to complete execution.

Setting Contention Scope of a Thread

The contention scope of the thread determines which set of threads a thread competes with for processor usage. The contention scope of a thread is set by the thread attribute object.

Synopsis

```
#include <pthread.h>

int pthread_attr_setscope(pthread_attr_t *attr, int contentionscope);
int pthread_attr_getscope(const pthread_attr_t *restrict attr,
                          int *restrict contentionscope);
```

The pthread_attr_setscope() sets the contention scope property of the thread attribute object specified by attr. The contention scope of the thread attribute object will be set to the value stored in the contentionscope. contentionscope can have these values:

❑   PTHREAD_SCOPE_SYSTEM: System scheduling contention scope

❑   PTHREAD_SCOPE_PROCESS: Process scheduling contention scope

System contention scope means the thread contends with others threads of other processes systemwide. pthread_attr_getscope() returns the contention scope attribute from the thread attribute object specified by the attr. If it is successful, the contention scope of the thread attribute object is returned and stored in the contentionscope. Both functions return 0 if successful and an error number otherwise.

Using sysconf()

Knowing the thread resource limits of your system is a key to having your application appropriately manage them. Examples of utilizing the system resources have been discussed in previous section. When setting the stack size of a thread, PTHREAD_MIN_STACK is the lower minimum. The stack size should not be below the value of the default stack minimum returned by pthread_attr_getstacksize(). The maximum number of threads per process places an upper bound on the number of worker threads that can be created for a process. sysconf() is used to return the current value of configurable system limits or options. Your system defines several variables and constant counterparts concerned with threads, processes, and semaphores. In Table 6-8, we list some of them to give you an idea to what is available.

Table 6-8

Variable	Name Value	Description
_SC_THREADS	_POSIX_THREADS	Supports threads
_SC_THREAD_ATTR_ STACKADDR	_POSIX_THREAD_ATTR_ STACKADDR	Supports thread stack address attribute
_SC_THREAD_ATTR_ STACKSIZE	_POSIX_THREAD_ATTR_ STACKSIZE	Supports thread stack size attribute
_SC_THREAD_STACK_MIN	PTHREAD_STACK_MIN	Minimum size of thread stack storage in bytes
_SC_THREAD_THREADS_MAX	PTHREAD_THREADS_MAX	Maximum number of threads per process

Variable	Name Value	Description
_SC_THREAD_KEYS_MAX	PTHREAD_KEYS_MAX	Maximum number of keys per process
_SC_THREAD_PRIO_INHERIT	_POSIX_THREAD_PRIO_ INHERIT	Supports priority inheritance option
_SC_THREAD_PRIO	_POSIX_THREAD_PRIO_	Supports thread priority option
_SC_THREAD_PRIORITY_ SCHEDULING	_POSIX_THREAD_PRIORITY_ SCHEDULING	Supports thread priority scheduling option
_SC_THREAD_PROCESS_ SHARED	_POSIX_THREAD_PROCESS_ SHARED	Supports process-shared synchronization
_SC_THREAD_SAFE_ FUNCTIONS	_POSIX_THREAD_SAFE_ FUNCTIONS	Supports thread safe functions
_SC_THREAD_DESTRUCTOR_ ITERATIONS	_PTHREAD_THREAD_ DESTRUCTOR_ITERATIONS	Determines the number of attempts made to destroy thread-specific data on thread exit
_SC_CHILD_MAX	CHILD_MAX	Maximum number of processes allowed to a UID
_SC_PRIORITY_SCHEDULING	_POSIX_PRIORITY_ SCHEDULING	Supports process scheduling
_SC_REALTIME_SIGNALS	_POSIX_REALTIME_SIGNALS	Supports real-time signals
_SC_XOPEN_REALTIME_ THREADS	_XOPEN_REALTIME_THREADS	Supports X/Open POSIX real-time threads feature group
_SC_STREAM_MAX	STREAM_MAX	Determines the number of streams one process can have open at a time
_SC_SEMAPHORES	_POSIX_SEMAPHORES	Supports semaphores
_SC_SEM_NSEMS_MAX	SEM_NSEMS_MAX	Determines the maximum number of semaphores a process may have
_SC_SEM_VALUE_MAX	SEM_VALUE_MAX	Determines the maximum value a semaphore may have
_SC_SHARED_MEMORY_ OBJECTS	_POSIX_SHARED_MEMORY_ OBJECTS	Supports shared memory objects

Here is an example of a call to `sysconf()`:

```
if(PTHREAD_STACK_MIN == (sysconf(_SC_THREAD_STACK_MIN))){
    //...
}
```

The constant value of `PTHREAD_STACK_MIN` is compared to the `_SC_THREAD_STACK_MIN` value returned by the `sysconf()`.

Thread Safety and Libraries

A library is thread safe or reentrant when its functions may be called by more than one thread at a time without requiring any other action on the caller's part. When designing a multithread application, you must be careful to ensure that concurrently executing functions are thread safe. We have already discussed making user-defined functions thread safe, but an application often calls functions defined by the system or a third-party supplied library. We have discussed system functions that are safe as cancellation points, but some of these functions and/or libraries are thread safe, while others are not. If the functions are not thread safe, then this means the functions:

❏   Contain static variables

❏   Access global data

❏   Are not reentrant

If the function contains static variables, then those variables maintain their values between invocations of the function. The function requires the value of the static variable in order to operate correctly. When concurrent multiple threads invoke this function, a race condition occurs.

If the function modifies a global variable, then multiple threads invoking that function may each attempt to modify that global variable. If concurrent multiple accesses to the global variable are not synchronized, then a race condition can occur here as well. Consider concurrent multiple threads executing functions that set `errno`. With some of the threads, the function fails, and `errno` is set to an error message. Meanwhile, other threads execute successfully. Depending on the compiler implementation, `errno` is thread safe, but if it's not, when a thread checks the state of `errno`, which message does it report?

Reentrant code is a block of code that cannot be changed while it is in use. Reentrant code avoids race conditions by removing references to global variables and modifiable static data. The code can be shared by multiple concurrent threads or processes without a race condition occurring. The POSIX standard defines several functions as reentrant. They are easily identified by a `_r` attached to the function name of the nonreentrant counterpart. Some are:

❏   `getgrgid_r()`

❏   `getgrnam_r()`

❏   `getpwuid_r()`

❏   `sterror_r()`

❏   `strtok_r()`

- ❑   `readdir_r()`

- ❑   `rand_r()`

- ❑   `ttyname_r()`

If the function accesses unprotected global variables, contains static modifiable variables, or is not reentrant, then the function is considered *thread unsafe*.

Using Multithreaded Versions of Libraries and Functions

System- and third-party-supplied libraries may have two different versions of their standard libraries, one version for single-threaded applications and the other version for multithreaded applications. Whenever a multithreaded environment is anticipated, link to the multithreaded versions of the library. Other environments do not require multithreaded applications to be linked to the multithreaded version of the library but only require macros to be defined for reentrant versions of functions to be declared. The application can then be compiled as thread safe.

It is not always possible to use multithreaded versions of functions. In some instances, multithreaded versions of particular functions are not available for a given compiler or environment. Some functions' interfaces cannot be made thread safe simply. In addition, you may be faced with adding threads to an environment that uses functions that were only meant to be used in a single-threaded environment. Under these conditions, mutexes can be used to wrap all such functions within the program.

For example, a program has three concurrently executing threads. Two of the threads, ThreadA and ThreadB, both concurrently execute task1(), which is not thread safe. The third thread, ThreadC, executes task2(). To solve the problem of task1(), the solution may be to simply wrap access to task1() by ThreadA and ThreadB with a mutex:

```
ThreadA
{
    lock()
    task1()
    unlock()
}

ThreadB
{
    lock()
    task1()
    unlock()
}

ThreadC
{
    task2()
}
```

If this is done, then only one thread accesses task1() at a time. But what if task1() and task2() both modify the same global or static variable? Although ThreadA and ThreadB are using mutexes with task1(), ThreadC executes task2() concurrently with either of these threads. In this situation, a race condition occurs. Avoiding race conditions requires synchronized access to the global data. We discuss this topic in Chapter 7.

Thread Safe Standard Out

To illustrate another type of race condition when dealing with `iostream` library, say that you have two threads, `Thread A` and `Thread B`, sending output to the standard output stream, `cout`. `cout` is an object of type `ostream`. Using inserters (`>>`) and extractors (`<<`) invokes the methods of the `cout` object. Are these methods thread safe? If `ThreadA` is sending the message:

Global warming is a real problem.

to `stdout` and `Thread B` is sending the message:

Global warming is not a real problem.

will the output be interleaved and produce the following message?

Global warming is a Global warming is not a real problem real problem.

In some cases, thread-safe functions are implemented as atomic functions. *Atomic* functions are functions that cannot be interrupted once they begin to execute. In the case of `cout`, if the inserter operation is implemented as atomic, then this interweaving cannot take place. When you have multiple calls to the inserter operation, they are executed as if they were in serial order. `ThreadA`'s message will be displayed, then `ThreadB`'s, or vice versa. This is an example of serializing a function or operation in order to make it thread safe.

This may not be the only way to make a function thread safe. A function may interweave operations if it has no adverse effect. For example, if a method adds or removes elements to or from a structure that is not sorted and two different threads invoke that method, interweaving their operations will not have an adverse effect.

If it is not known which functions from a library are thread safe and which are not, you have three choices:

- ❑ Restrict use of all thread-unsafe functions to a single thread
- ❑ Do not use any of the thread unsafe functions
- ❑ Wrap all potential thread unsafe functions within a single set of synchronization mechanisms

To extend the last option, you can create interface classes for all thread unsafe functions that will be used in a multithreaded application. The idea of a wrapper was illustrated when making a cancellation point for system calls earlier in this chapter. The unsafe functions are encapsulated within an interface class. That class can be combined with the appropriate synchronization objects and can be used by the host class through inheritance or composition. This approach reduces the possibility of race conditions and is discussed in Chapter 7. However, first we want to discuss the `thread_object` interface class introduced in Chapter 4 and extend it to encapsulate the thread attribute object.

Extending the Thread Interface Class

A thread interface class was introduced in Chapter 4. The interface class acts as a wrapper that allows something to appear differently than it does normally. The new interface provided by an interface class is designed to make the class easier to use, more functional, safer, or more semantically correct. In this chapter, we have introduced a number of pthread functions used to manage a thread, including the creation and usage of the thread attribute object. The `thread_object` class was a simple skeleton class. Its purpose was to encapsulate the pthread thread interface and to supply object-oriented semantics and components so that you can implement the models you produce in the SDLC more easily. Now it's time to expand the `thread_object` class to encapsulate some of the functionality of the thread attribute object. Listing 6-2 shows the declaration of the new `thread_object` and `user_thread` classes.

Listing 6-2

```
//Listing 6-2 Declaration of the new thread_object and user_thread.

1    #ifndef __THREAD_OBJECT_H
2    #define __THREAD_OBJECT_H
3
4    using namespace std;
5    #include <iostream>
6    #include <pthread.h>
7    #include <string>
8
9    class thread_object{
10        pthread_t Tid;
11
12   protected:
13        virtual void do_something(void) = 0;
14        pthread_attr_t SchedAttr;
15        struct sched_param SchedParam;
16        string Name;
17        int NewPolicy;
18        int NewState;
19        int NewScope;
20   public:
21        thread_object(void);
22        ~thread_object(void);
23        void setPriority(int Priority);
24        void setSchedPolicy(int Policy);
25        void setContentionScope(int Scope);
26        void setDetached(void);
27        void setJoinable(void);
28
29        void name(string X);
30        void run(void);
31        void join(void);
32        friend void *thread(void *X);
33   };
34
35
36   class filter_thread : public thread_object{
```

(continued)

Listing 6-2 *(continued)*

```
37   protected:
38        void do_something(void);
39   public:
40        filter_thread(void);
41        ~filter_thread(void);
42   };
43
44   #endif
45
46
```

For the `thread_object` we have included methods that set:

- ❑ scheduling policies
- ❑ priority
- ❑ state
- ❑ contention scope

of the `thread_object`. Instead of a `user_thread`, we are defining a `filter_thread` that defines the `do_something()` method. This class is used in the next chapter on synchronization.

Listing 6-3 is the class definition of the new `thread_object` class.

Listing 6-3

```
//Listing 6-3  A definition of the new thread_object class.

1    #include "thread_object.h"
2
3    thread_object::thread_object(void)
4    {
5       pthread_attr_init(&SchedAttr);
6       pthread_attr_setinheritsched(&SchedAttr,PTHREAD_EXPLICIT_SCHED);
7       NewState = PTHREAD_CREATE_JOINABLE;
8       NewScope = PTHREAD_SCOPE_PROCESS;
9       NewPolicy = SCHED_OTHER;
10   }
11
12   thread_object::~thread_object(void)
13   {
14
15   }
16
17   void thread_object::join(void)
18   {
19       if(NewState == PTHREAD_CREATE_JOINABLE){
20           pthread_join(Tid,NULL);
21       }
22   }
```

```
23
24   void thread_object::setPriority(int Priority)
25   {
26       int Policy;
27       struct sched_param Param;
28
29       Param.sched_priority = Priority;
30       pthread_attr_setschedparam(&SchedAttr,&Param);
31   }
32
33
34   void thread_object::setSchedPolicy(int Policy)
35   {
36       if(Policy == 1){
37           pthread_attr_setschedpolicy(&SchedAttr,SCHED_RR);
38           pthread_attr_getschedpolicy(&SchedAttr,&NewPolicy);
39       }
40
41       if(Policy == 2){
42           pthread_attr_setschedpolicy(&SchedAttr,SCHED_FIFO);
43           pthread_attr_getschedpolicy(&SchedAttr,&NewPolicy);
44       }
45   }
46
47
48   void thread_object::setContentionScope(int Scope)
49   {
50       if(Scope == 1){
51           pthread_attr_setscope(&SchedAttr,PTHREAD_SCOPE_SYSTEM);
52           pthread_attr_getscope(&SchedAttr,&NewScope);
53       }
54
55       if(Scope == 2){
56           pthread_attr_setscope(&SchedAttr,PTHREAD_SCOPE_PROCESS);
57           pthread_attr_getscope(&SchedAttr,&NewScope);
58       }
59   }
60
61
62   void thread_object::setDetached(void)
63   {
64       pthread_attr_setdetachstate(&SchedAttr,PTHREAD_CREATE_DETACHED);
65       pthread_attr_getdetachstate(&SchedAttr,&NewState);
66
67   }
68
69   void thread_object::setJoinable(void)
70   {
71       pthread_attr_setdetachstate(&SchedAttr,PTHREAD_CREATE_JOINABLE);
72       pthread_attr_getdetachstate(&SchedAttr,&NewState);
73   }
74
75
```

(continued)

Listing 6-3 *(continued)*

```
76  void thread_object::run(void)
77  {
78      pthread_create(&Tid,&SchedAttr,thread,this);
79  }
80
81
82  void thread_object::name(string X)
83  {
84      Name = X;
85  }
86
87
88  void *  thread (void * X)
89  {
90      thread_object *Thread;
91      Thread = static_cast<thread_object *>(X);
92      Thread->do_something();
93      return(NULL);
94  }
```

In Listing 6-3, the constructor defined at Lines 3–10 initializes a thread attribute object for this class `SchedAttr`. It sets the `inheritsched` attribute to `PTHREAD_EXPLICIT_SCHED` so that the thread that is created uses the attribute's object to define its scheduling and priorities instead of inheriting them from its creator thread. By default, the thread's state is `JOINABLE`. The other methods are self-explanatory:

```
setPriority(int Priority)
setSchedPolicy(int Policy)
setContentionscope(int Scope)
setDetached()
setJoinable()
```

The `join()` checks to see if the thread is joinable before it calls `pthread_join()` in Line 20. Now when the thread is created in Line 78, the `pthread_create()` uses the `SchedAttr` object:

```
pthread_create(&Tid,&SchedAttr,thread,this);
```

Listing 6-4 shows the definition for the `filter_thread`.

Listing 6-4

```
//Listing 6-4  A definition of the filter_thread class.

1    #include "thread_object.h"
2
3
4    filter_thread::filter_thread(void)
5    {
6        pthread_attr_init(&SchedAttr);
7
8
9    }
10
```

```
11
12   filter_thread::~filter_thread(void)
13   {
14
15   }
16
17   void filter_thread::do_something(void)
18   {
19      struct sched_param Param;
20      int Policy;
21      pthread_t thread_id = pthread_self();
22      string Schedule;
23      string State;
24      string Scope;
25
26      pthread_getschedparam(thread_id,&Policy,&Param);
27      if(NewPolicy == SCHED_RR){Schedule.assign("RR");}
28      if(NewPolicy == SCHED_FIFO){Schedule.assign("FIFO");}
29      if(NewPolicy == SCHED_OTHER){Schedule.assign("OTHER");}
30      if(NewState == PTHREAD_CREATE_DETACHED){State.assign("DETACHED");}
31      if(NewState == PTHREAD_CREATE_JOINABLE){State.assign("JOINABLE");}
32      if(NewScope == PTHREAD_SCOPE_PROCESS){Scope.assign("PROCESS");}
33      if(NewScope == PTHREAD_SCOPE_SYSTEM){Scope.assign("SYSTEM");}
34      cout << Name << ":" << thread_id << endl
35           << "---------------------" << endl
36           << " priority: "<< Param.sched_priority   << endl
37           << " policy:   "<< Schedule                << endl
38           << " state:    "<< State                   << endl
39           << " scope:    "<< Scope                    << endl << endl;
40
41   }
42
```

In Listing 6-4, the `filter_thread` constructor in Lines 4–9 initializes with the thread attribute object `SchedAttr`. The `do_something()` method is defined. In `filter_thread`, this method simply sends to `cout` thread information:

- ❏ Name of the thread
- ❏ Thread id
- ❏ Priority
- ❏ Scheduling policy
- ❏ State
- ❏ Scope

Some values may not be initialized because they were not set in the attribute object. This method will be redefined in the next chapter.

Now, multiple `filter_thread` objects can be created, and each can set the attributes of the thread. Listing 6-5 shows how multiple `filter_thread` objects are created.

Listing 6-5

```
//Listing 6-5 is main line to create multiple filter_thread objects.

1    #include "thread_object.h"
2    #include <unistd.h>
3
4
5    int main(int argc,char *argv[])
6    {
7       filter_thread  MyThread[4];
8
9       MyThread[0].name("Proteus");
10      MyThread[0].setSchedPolicy(2);
11      MyThread[0].setPriority(7);
12      MyThread[0].setDetached();
13
14      MyThread[1].name("Stand Alone Complex");
15      MyThread[1].setContentionScope(1);
16      MyThread[1].setPriority(5);
17      MyThread[1].setSchedPolicy(2);
18
19      MyThread[2].name("Krell Space");
20      MyThread[2].setPriority(3);
21
22      MyThread[3].name("Cylon Space");
23      MyThread[3].setPriority(2);
24      MyThread[3].setSchedPolicy(2);
25
26      for(int N = 0;N < 4;N++)
27      {
28         MyThread[N].run();
29         MyThread[N].join();
30      }
31      return (0);
32   }
```

In Listing 6-5, four `filter_threads` were created. This is the output for Listing 6-5:

```
Proteus:Stand Alone Complex:32

----------------------
 priority:  7
----------------------
 policy:    FIFO priority:5
 state:        policy:    DETACHEDFIFO

 scope:        state:     PROCESSJOINABLE


 scope:     SYSTEM
```

```
Krell Space:4
---------------------
priority:   3
policy:     OTHER
state:      JOINABLE
scope:      PROCESS

Cylon Space:5
---------------------
priority:   2
policy:     FIFO
state:      JOINABLE
scope:      PROCESS
```

The main thread does not wait for a detached thread (Proteus), and the output is a little messed up. Proteus starts its output, and then it is interrupted with output from Stand Alone Complex. As mentioned earlier, standard cout is not thread safe. If all the threads are joinable, then the output would be as you would expect:

```
Proteus:2
---------------------
priority:   7
policy:     FIFO
state:      JOINABLE
scope:      PROCESS

Stand Alone Complex:3
---------------------
priority:   5
policy:     FIFO
state:      JOINABLE
scope:      SYSTEM

Krell Space:4
---------------------
priority:   3
policy:     OTHER
state:      JOINABLE
scope:      PROCESS

Cylon Space:5
---------------------
priority:   2
policy:     FIFO
state:      JOINABLE
scope:      PROCESS
```

Program Profile 6-2

Program Name:

```
program6-2.cc
```

Description:

Demonstrates the use of `filter_thread` class. Four threads are created; each is assigned a name. Each invokes the methods that modify some of the attributes of the thread that will be created.

Libraries Required:

```
libpthread
```

Headers Required:

```
thread_object.h
```

Compile & Link Instructions:

```
c++ -o program6-2 program6-2.cc thread_object.cc filter_thread.cc -lpthread
```

Test Environment:

Solaris 10, gcc 3.4.3 and 3.4.6

Processors:

AMD Opteron, UltraSparc T1

Execution Instructions:

```
./program6-2
```

The `thread_object` class encapsulates some of the functionality of the thread attribute object. The `filter_thread` is the user thread. It inherits the `thread_object` and defines the `do_something()`, the function that is executed by the thread. The functionality of this class will be extended again to form the `assertion` class that is used as part of a pipeline model executed in Chapter 7.

Summary

A thread is a sequence or stream of executable code within a process that is scheduled for execution by the operating system on a processor or core. This chapter has been all about dealing with multithreading. The key things you can take away from this discussion of multithreading are as follows:

❑　All processes have a *primary thread* that is the process's flow of control. A process with multiple threads has as many flows of controls in which each executes independently and concurrently. A process with multiple threads is *multithreaded*.

❑　Kernel-level threads or lightweight processes are a lighter burden on the operating system as compared to a process to create, maintain, and manage because very little information is associated with a thread. Kernel threads are executed on the processor. They are created and managed by the system. User-level threads are created and managed by a runtime library.

❏ Threads can be used to simplify the program's structure, model the inherent concurrency using minimal resources, or execute independent concurrent tasks of a program. Threads can improve the throughput and performance of the application.

❏ Threads and processes both have an id, a set of registers, a state, and a priority, and both adhere to a scheduling policy. Both have a context used to reconstruct the preempted process or thread. Threads and child processes share the resources of their parent process and compete for processor usage. The parent process has some control over the child process or thread. A thread or process can alter its attributes and create new resources, but cannot access the resources belonging to other processes. The most significant difference between threads and processes is each process has its own address space and threads are contained in the address space of its process.

❏ The POSIX thread library defines a thread *attribute object* that encapsulates a subset of the properties of the thread. These attributes are accessible and modifiable. The thread attribute is of type pthread_attr_t. pthread_attr_init() initializes a thread attribute object with the default values. Once the attributes have been appropriately modified, the attribute object can be used as a parameter in any call to the pthread_create() function.

❏ The thread_object interface class acts as a wrapper that allows something to appear differently than it does normally. The new interface is designed to make the class easier to use, more functional, safer, or more semantically correct. The thread_object can be extended to encapsulate the attribute object.

In Chapter 7, we will discuss communication and synchronization between processes and threads. Concurrent tasks may be required to communicate between them to synchronize work or access to shared global data.130+   Very superior   about 2% of the population

    120-129 Superior   about 7% of the population

    110-119 High average   about 16% of the population

    90-109   Average about 50% of the population

    80-89   Low average   about 16% of the population

    70-79   Borderline   about 7% of the population

    Below 69 Mentally retarded   about 2% of the population

Communication and Synchronization of Concurrent Tasks

There is only one constant, one universal. It is the only real truth; causality. Action, reaction. Cause and effect.

— **Merovingian, Matrix Reloaded**

In Chapter 6, we discussed the similarities and differences between processes and threads. The most significant difference between threads and processes is that each process has its own address space and threads are contained in the address space of their process. We discussed how threads and processes have an id, a set of registers, a state, and a priority, and adhere to a scheduling policy. We explained how threads are created and managed. We also created a thread class.

In this chapter, we take the next step and discuss communication and cooperation between threads and processes. We cover among other topics:

❑   Communication and cooperation dependencies.

❑   Interprocess and Interthread Communication.

❑   The PRAM model and concurrency models.

❑ Order of execution models.

❑ Object-oriented message queues and mutexes.

❑ A simple agent model for a pipeline.

Communication and Synchronization

In Chapter 3, we discussed the challenges of coordinating the execution of concurrent tasks. The example used was software-automated painters who were to paint the house before guests arrived for the holidays. A number of issues were outlined while decomposing of the problem and solution for the purpose of determining what would be the best approach to painting the house. Some of those issues had to deal with communication and the synchronization resource usage.

❑ Did the painters have to communicate with each other?

❑ Should the painters communicate when they had completed a task or when they required some resource like a brush or paint?

❑ Should painters communicate directly with each other or should there be a central painter through which all communications are routed?

❑ Would it be better if only painters in one room communicated or if painters of different rooms communicated?

❑ As far as sharing resources, can multiple painters share a resource or will usage have to be serialized?

These issues are concerned with coordinating communication and synchronization between these concurrent tasks. If communication between dependent tasks is not appropriately designed, then data race conditions can occur. Determining the proper coordination of communication and synchronization between tasks requires matching the appropriate concurrency models during problem and solution decomposition. Concurrency models dictate how and when communication occurs and the manner in which work is executed. For example, for our software-automated painters a boss-worker model (which we discuss later in this chapter) could be used. A single boss painter can delegate work or direct painters as to which rooms to paint at a particular time. The boss painter can also manage the use of resources. All painters then communicate what resources they need in order to complete their tasks to the boss who then determines when resources are delegated to painters. Dependency relationships can be used to examine which tasks are dependent on other tasks for communication or cooperation.

Dependency Relationships

When processes or threads require communication or cooperation among each other to accomplish a common goal, they have a *dependency relationship*. Task A depends on Task B to supply a value for a calculation, to give the name of the file to be processed, or to release a resource. Task A may depend on Task B, but Task B may not have a dependency on Task A. Given any two tasks, there are exactly four dependency relationships that can exist between them:

❑ **A → B**: Task A depends on Task B.

❑ **A ← B**: Task B depends on Task A.

❑ **A ↔ B**: Task A depends on Task B, and Task B depends on Task A.

❑ **A NULL B**: There are no dependencies between Task A and Task B.

In the first and second cases the dependency is a one-way unidirectional dependency. In the third case, there is a two-way bidirectional dependency; A and B are mutually dependent on each other. In the fourth case, there is a NULL dependency between Task A and B; no dependency exists.

Communication Dependencies

When Task A requires data from Task B in order for it to execute its work, then there is a dependency relationship between Task A and Task B. A software-automated painter can be designated to fill all buckets running low on paint with paint at the behest of the boss painter. That would mean all painters (that are actually painting) would have to communicate with the boss painter that they were low on paint. The boss painter would then inform the refill painter that there were buckets of paint to be filled. This would mean that the worker painters have a communication dependency with the boss painter. The refill painter also had a communication dependency with the boss painter.

In Chapter 5, a posix_queue object was used to communicate between processes. The posix_queue is an interface to the POSIX message queue, a linked list of strings. The posix_queue object contains the names of the files that the worker processes are to search to find the code. A worker process can read the name of the file from posix_queue. posix_queue is a data structure that resides outside the address space of all processes. On the other hand, threads can also communicate with other threads within the address space of their process by using global variables and data structures. If two threads wanted to pass data between them, thread A would write the name of the file to a global variable, and thread B would simply read that variable. These are examples of unidirectional communication dependencies where only one task depends on another task. Figure 7-1 shows two examples of unidirectional communication dependencies: the posix_queue used by processes and the global variables used to hold the name of a file for threads A and B.

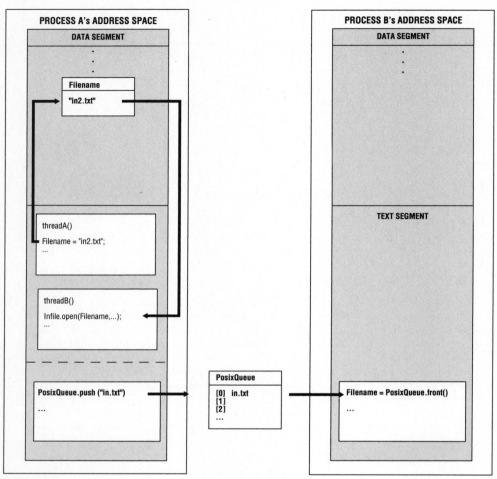

Figure 7-1

An example of a bidirectional dependency is two First-In, First-Out (FIFO) pipes. A pipe is a data structure that forms a communication channel between two processes. Process A will use pipe 1's input end to send the name of the file that process B has to process. Process B will read the name of the file from the output end of pipe 1. After it has processed the contents of the file, the result is written to a new file. The name of the new file will be written to the input end of pipe 2. Process A will read the name of the file from the output end of pipe 2. This is bidirectional communication dependency. Process B depends on process A to communicate the name of the file, and process A depends on process B to communicate the name of the new file. Thread A and thread B can use two global data structures like queues; one would contain the names of source files, and the other would be used to contain the names of resultant files. Figure 7-2 shows two examples of bidirectional communication dependencies between processes A and B and threads A and B.

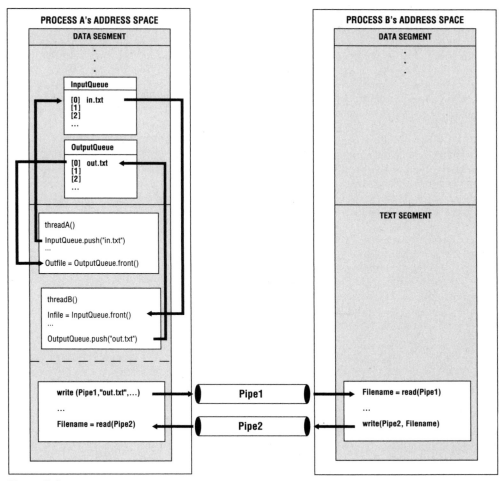

Figure 7-2

Cooperation Dependencies

When Task A requires a resource that Task B owns and Task B must release the resource before Task A can use it, this is a *cooperation dependency*. When two tasks are executing concurrently, and both are attempting to utilize the same resource, cooperation is required before either can successfully use the resource. Assume that there are multiple software-automated painters in a single room, and they are sharing a single paint bucket. They all try to access the paint bucket at the same time. Considering that the bucket cannot be accessed simultaneously by painters (it's not thread safe to do so), access has to be synchronized, and this requires cooperation.

Another example of cooperation dependency is write access to the posix_queue. If multiple processes were to write the names of the files where the code was located to the posix_queue, this would require that only one process at a time be able write to the posix_queue. Write access would have to be synchronized.

Counting Tasks Dependencies

You can understand the overall task relationships between the threads or processes in an application by enumerating the number of possible dependencies that exist. Once you have enumerated the possible dependencies and then their relationships, you can determine which threads you must code for communication and synchronization. This is similar to truth tables used to determine possible branches of decision in a program or application. Once the dependency relationships among threads are enumerated, the overall thread structure of the process is available.

For example, if there are three threads A, B, and C (three threads from one process or one thread from three processes), you can examine the possible dependencies that exist among the threads. If there are two threads involved in a dependency, use combination to calculate the possible threads involved in the dependency from the three threads: $C(n,k)$ where n is the number of threads and k is the number of threads involved in the dependency. So, for the example $C(3,2)$, the answer is 3; there are three possible combinations of threads: A and B, A and C, B and C.

Now if you consider each combination as a graph (with two nodes and one edge between them), a simple graph, meaning that there are no self-loops and no parallel edges (no two edges will have the same endpoints), then the number of edges in a graph is $n(n-1)/2$. So, for the two-node simple graph, there are $2(2-1)/2$, which is 1. There is one edge for each graph. Now each edge can have a possible four possible dependency relationships as discussed earlier:

❑　**A → B**: Task A depends on Task B.

❑　**A ← B**: Task B depends on Task A.

❑　**A ↔ B**: Task A depends on Task B, and Task B depends on Task A.

❑　**A NULL B**: There are no dependencies between Task A and Task B.

So, each individual graph has four possible relationships. If you count the number of possible dependency relationships among three threads in which two are involved in the relationship, there are 12 possible relationships.

An adjacency matrix can be used to enumerate the actual dependency relationships for two-thread combinations. An adjacency matrix is a graph $G = (V,E)$ in which V is the set of vertices or nodes of the graph and E is the set of edges such that:

$A(i,j) = 1$ if (i,j) is an element of E
　　　$= 0$ otherwise
$A(i,j) <> A(j,i)$

where i denotes a row and j denotes a column. The size of the matrix is $n \times n$, where n is the total number of threads. Figure 7-3(A) shows the adjacency matrix for three threads. The 0 indicates that there is no dependency, and the 1 indicates that there is a dependency. An adjacency matrix can be used to demarcate all of the dependency relationships between any two threads. On a diagonal, there are all 0s because there are no self-dependencies.

- ❏ A(1,2) = 1 means for A → B, A depends on B.
- ❏ A(1,3) = 0 means for A → C, A does not depend on C.
- ❏ A(2,1) = 0 means for B → A, B does not depend on A.
- ❏ A(2,3) = 1 means for B → C, B depends on C.
- ❏ A(3,1) = 1 means for C → A, C depends on A.
- ❏ A(3,2) = 0 means for C → B, C does not depends on B.

A) ADJACENCY MATRIX

	A	B	C
A	0	1	0
B	0	0	1
C	1	0	0

B) DEPENDENCY MATRIX

	A	B	C
A		S,Co	
B			S,C
C	S,C		

Figure 7-3

A dependency graph is useful for documenting the type of dependency relationship, for example, *C* for communication or *Co* for cooperation. *S* is for synchronization if the communication or cooperation dependency requires synchronization. The dependency graph can be used during the design or testing phase of the Software Development Life Cycle (SDLC). To construct the dependency graph, the adjacency matrix is used. Where there is a 1 in a row column position, it is replaced by the type of relationship. Figure 7-3(B) shows the dependency graph for the three threads. The 0s and 1s have been replaced by C or Co. Where there was a 0, no relationship exists; the space is left blank. For A(1,2), A depends on B for synchronized cooperation, A(2,3) B depends on C for synchronized communication, and A(3,2) C depends on A for synchronized communication. Bidirectional relationships like A ↔ B can also be represented, but there are none in this example. So, as you can see, all of the relationships can be represented in the matrix. For a NULL relationship a 0 is used in the adjacency matrix, and in the dependency matrix that position will be left blank. Figure 7-4 shows the Unified Modeling Language (UML) dependency for these three threads.

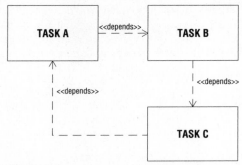

Figure 7-4

These tools and approaches are very useful. Knowing the number of possible relationships and identifying what those relationships are helps in establishing the overall thread structure of processes and the application. We have used them for small numbers of threads. The matrix is only useful when two threads are involved in the dependency. For large numbers of threads, the matrix approach cannot be used (unless it is multidimensional.) But having to enumerate each relationship for even a moderate number of threads would be unwieldy. This is why the declarative approach is very useful.

What Is Interprocess Communication?

Processes have their own address space. Data that is declared in one process is not available in another process. Events that happen in one process are not known to another process. If process A and process B are working together to perform a task such as filtering out special characters in a file or searching files for a code, there must be methods for communicating and coordinating events between the two processes. In Chapter 5, the layout of a process was described. A process has a text, data, and stack segment. Processes may also have other memory allocated in the free store. The data that the process owns is generally in the stack and data segments or is dynamically allocated in memory protected from other processes. For one process to be made aware of another process's data or events, you use operating system Application Program Interfaces (APIs) to create a means of communication. When a process sends data to another process or makes another process aware of an event by means of operating system APIs, this is called *Interprocess Communication (IPC)*. IPC deals with the techniques and mechanisms that facilitate communication between processes. The operating system's kernel acts as the communication channel between the processes. The `posix_queue` is an example of IPC. Files can also be used to communicate between related or unrelated processes.

The process resides in user mode or space. IPC mechanisms can reside in kernel or user space. Files used for communication reside in the filesystem outside of both user and kernel space. Processes sharing information by utilizing files have to go through the kernel using system calls such as `read`, `write`, and `lseek` or by using iostreams. Some type of synchronization is required when the file is being updated by two processes simultaneously. Shared information between processes resides in kernel space. The operations used to access the shared information will involve a system call into the kernel. An IPC mechanism that does reside in user space is shared memory. Shared memory is a region of memory that each process can reference. With shared memory, processes can access the data in this shared region without making calls to the kernel. This also requires synchronization.

Persistence of IPC

The *persistence* of an object refers to the existence of an object during or beyond the execution of the program, process, or thread that created it. A storage class specifies how long an object exists during the execution of a program. An object can have a declared storage class of automatic, static, or dynamic.

- ❑ **Automatic** objects exist during the invocation of a block of code. The space and values an object is given exist only within the block. When the flow of control leaves the block, the object goes out of existence and cannot be referred to without an error.

- ❑ A **static** object exists and retains values throughout the execution of the program.

- ❑ An object that was **dynamically** allocated can have no more than static storage but can have less than automatic storage. Programmers determine when an object is dynamically declared during runtime, and that object will exist for the entire execution of the program.

Persistence of an object is not necessarily synonymous with the storage of the object on a storage device. For example, automatic or static objects may be stored in external storage that is used as virtual memory during program execution, but the object will be destroyed after the program is over.

IPC entities reside in the filesystem, in kernel space, or in user space, and persistence is also defined the same way: filesystem, kernel, and process persistence.

- ❑ An IPC object with **filesystem persistence** exists until the object is deleted explicitly. If the kernel is rebooted, the object will keep its value.

- ❑ **Kernel persistence** defines IPC objects that remain in existence until the kernel is rebooted or the object is deleted explicitly.

- ❑ An IPC object with **process persistence** exists until the process that created the object closes it.

There are several types of IPCs, and they are listed in Table 7-1. Most of the IPCs work with related processes — child and parent processes. For processes that are not related and require Interprocess Communication, the IPC object has a name associated with it so that the server process that created it and the client processes can refer to the same object. Pipes are not named; therefore, they are used only between related processes. FIFO or named pipes can be used between unrelated processes. A pathname in the filesystem is used as the identifier for a FIFO IPC mechanism. A name space is the set of all possible names for a specified type of IPC mechanism. For IPCs that require a POSIX IPC name, that name must begin with a slash and contain no other slashes. To create the IPC, one must have write permissions for the directory.

Table 7-1

Type of IPC	Name space	Persistence	Process
Pipe	unnamed	process	Related
FIFO	pathname	process	Both
Mutex	unnamed	process	Related
Condition variable	unnamed	process	Related
Read-write locks	unnamed	process	Related
Message queue	Posix IPC name	kernel	Both
Semaphore (memory-based)	unnamed	process	Related
Semaphore (named)	Posix IPC name	kernel	Both
Shared memory	Posix IPC name	kernel	Both

Table 7-1 also shows that each type of IPC (FIFO and pipes) has process persistence. Message queues and shared memory mst have kernel persistence, but may also use filesystem persistence. When message queues and shared memory utilize filesystem persistence, they are implemented by using a mapping a file to internal memory. This is called mapped files or memory mapped files. Once the file is mapped to memory that is shared between processes, the contents of the files are modified and read by using a memory location.

Environment Variables and Command-Line Arguments

Parent processes share their resources with child processes. By using posix_spawn, or the exec functions, the parent process can create the child process with exact copies of its environment variables or initialize them with new values. Environment variables store system-dependent information such as paths to directories that contain commands, libraries, functions, and procedures used by a process. They can be used to transmit useful user-defined information between the parent and the child processes. They provide a mechanism to pass specific information to a related process without having it hardcoded in the program code. System environment variables are common and predefined to all shells and processes in that system. The variables are initialized by startup files.

The common environment variables are listed in Chapter 5.

Environment variables and command-line argument can also be passed to newly initialized processes.

```
int posix_spawn(pid_t *restrict pid, const char *restrict path,
                const posix_spawn_file_actions_t *file_actions,
                const posix_spawnattr_t *restrict attrp,
                char *const argv[restrict], char *const envp[restrict]);
```

`argv[]` and `envp[]` are used to pass a list of command-line argument and environment variables to the new process. This is one-way, one-time communication. Once the child process has been created, any changes to those variables by the child will not be reflected in the parent's data, and the parent cannot make any changes to the variables that are seen by its child processes.

Files

Using files to transfer data between processes is one of the simplest and most flexible means of transferring or sharing data. Files can be used to transfer data between processes that are related or unrelated. They can allow processes that were not designed to work together to do so. Of course, files have filesystem persistence; in this case, the persistence can survive a system reboot.

When you use files to communicate between processes, you follow seven basic steps in the file-transferring process:

1. The name of the file has to be communicated.

2. You must verify the existence of the file.

3. Be sure that the correct permission are granted to access to the file.

4. Open the file.

5. Synchronize access to the file.

6. While reading/writing to the file, check to see if the stream is good and that it's not at the end of the file.

7. Close the file.

First, the name of the file has to be communicated between the processes. You might recall from Chapters 4 and 5 that files stored the work that had to be processed by the workers. Each file contained over a million strings. The `posix_queue` contained the names of the files. Filenames can also be passed to child processes by means of other IPC-like pipes.

When the process is accessing the file, if more than one process can also access the same file, you need synchronization. You might recall in Chapter 4 in Listing 4-2, that a file was broken up into smaller files, and each process had exclusive access to the file. However, if there was just one file, the access to the file would have to be synchronized. One process at a time would have exclusive read capability and would read a string from the file, advancing the read pointer. We discuss read/write locks and other types of synchronization later in the chapter.

Leaving the file open can lead to data corruption and can prevent other processes from accessing the file. The processes that read or write to or from the file should know the file's file format in order to correctly process the file. The file's format refers to the file type and the file's organization. The file's type also implies the type of data in the file. Is it a text file or a binary file? The processes should also know the file layout or how the data is organized in the file.

File Descriptors

File descriptors are unsigned integers used by a process to identify an open file. They are shared between parent and child processes. They are indexes to the file descriptor table, a block maintained by the kernel for each process. When a child process is created, the descriptor table is copied for the child process, which allows the child process to have equal access to the files used by the parent. The number of file descriptors that can be allocated to a process is governed by a resource limit. The limit can be changed by `setrlimit()`. The file descriptor is returned by the `open()`. File descriptors are frequently used by other IPCs.

Shared Memory

A block of shared memory can be used to transfer information between processes. The block of memory does not belong to any of the processes that are sharing the memory. Each process has its own address space; the block of memory is separate from the address space of the processes. A process gains access to the shared memory by temporarily connecting the shared memory block to its own memory block. Once the piece of memory is attached, it can be used like any other pointer to a block of memory. Like other data transfer mechanisms, shared memory is also set up with the appropriate access permission. It is almost as flexible as using a file to transfer data. If Processes A, B, and C were using a shared memory block, any modifications by any of the processes are visible to all the other processes. This is not a one-time, one-way communication mechanism.

Pipes require that at least two processes be connected before they can be used; shared memory can be written to and read by a single process and held open by that process. Other processes can attach to and detach from the shared memory as needed. This allows much larger blocks of data to be transferred faster than when you use pipes and FIFOs. However, it is important to consider how much memory to allocate to the shared region.

When you are accessing the data contained in the shared memory, synchronization is required. In the same way that file locking is necessary for multiple processes to attempt read/write access for the same file at the same time, access to shared memory must be regulated. Semaphores are the standard technique used for controlling access to shared memory. Controlled access is necessary because a data race can occur when two processes attempt to update the same piece of memory (or file for that matter) at the same time.

Using POSIX Shared Memory

The shared memory maps:

❑ a file

❑ internal memory

to the shared memory region:

Synopsis

```
#include <sys/mman.h>

void   *mmap(void *addr, size_t len, int prot, int flags, int fd, off_t offset);
int mumap(void *addr, size_t len);
```

The function maps `len` bytes starting at offset `offset` from the file or other object specified by the file descriptor `fd` into memory, preferably at address `addr`, which is usually specified as 0. The actual place where the object is mapped in memory is returned and is never 0. It is a `void *`. `prot` describes the desired memory protection. It must not conflict with the open mode of the file. `flags` specifies the type of mapped object. It can also specify mapping options and whether modifications made to the mapped copy of the page are private to the process or are to be shared with other references. Table 7-2 shows the possible values for `prot` and `flags` with a brief description. To remove the memory mapping from the address space of a process, use `mumap()`.

Table 7-2

Flag Arguments for mmap	Description
prot	Describes the protection of the memory-based region.
PROT_READ	Data can be read.
PROT_WRITE	Data can be written.
PROT_EXEC	Data can be executed.
PROT_NONE	Data is inaccessible.
flags	Describes how the data can be used.
MAP_SHARED	Changes are shared.
MAP_PRIVATE	Changes are private.
MAP_FIXED	`addr` is interpreted exactly.

To create a shared memory, open a file and store the file descriptor; then call `mmap()` with the appropriate arguments and store the returning `void *`. Use a semaphore when accessing the variable. The `void *` may have to be type cast. depending on the data you are trying to manipulate:

```
fd = open(file_name,O_RDWR);
ptr = casting<type>(mmap(NULL,sizeof(type),PROT_READ,MAP_SHARED,fd,0));
```

This is an example of memory mapping with a file. When using shared memory with internal memory, a function that creates a shared memory object is used instead of a function that opens a file:

Synopsis

```
#include <sys/mman.h>

int shm_open(const char *name, int oflag, mode_t mode);
int shm_unlink(const char *name);
```

The `shm_open()` creates and opens a new or opens an existing POSIX shared memory object. The function is very similar to `open()`. `name` specifies the shared memory object created and/or opened. To ensure the portability of `name` use an initial slash (/) and don't use embedded slashes. `oflag` is a bit mask created by ORing together one of these flags: O_RDONLY or O_RDWR and any of the other flags listed in Table 7-3, along with the possible values for `mode` with a brief description. `shm_open()` returns a new file descriptor referring to the shared memory object. The file descriptor is used in the function call to `mmap()`.

```
fd = sh_open(memory_name,O_RDWR, MODE);
ptr = casting<type>(mmap(NULL,sizeof(type),PROT_READ,MAP_SHARED,fd,0));
```

Now `ptr` can be used like any other pointer to data. Be sure to use semaphores between processes:

```
sem_wait(sem);
... *ptr;
sem_post(sem);
```

Table 7-3

Shared Memory Arguments	Description
oflag	Describes how the shared memory will be opened.
O_RDWR	Opens the object for read or write access.
O_RDONLY	Opens the object for read-only access.
O_CREAT	Creates the shared memory if it does not exist.
O_EXCL	Checks for the existence and creation of the object. If O_CREAT is specified and the object exists with the specified name, then returns an error.
O_TRUNC	If the shared memory object exists, then truncates it to zero bytes.
mode	Specifies the permission.
S_IRUSR	User has read permission.
S_IWUSR	User has write permission.
S_IRGRP	Group has read permission.
S_IWGRP	Group has write permission.
S_IROTH	Others have read permission.
S_IWOTH	Others have write permission.

Pipes

Pipes are communication channels used to transfer data between processes. Whereas data transfer using files generally does not require the sending and receiving of data to be active at the same time, data transfer using pipes includes processes that are active at the same time. Although there are exceptions, the general rule is that pipes are used between two or more active processes. One process (the writer) opens or creates the pipe and then blocks until another process (the reader) opens the same pipe for reading and writing.

There are two kinds of pipes:

❑ Anonymous

❑ Named (also called FIFO)

Anonymous pipes are used to transfer data between related processes (child and parent). Named pipes are used for communication between related or unrelated processes. Related processes created using `fork()` can use the anonymous pipes. Processes created using `posix_spawn()` use named pipes. Unrelated processes are created separately by programs. Unrelated processes can be logically related and work together to perform some task, but they are still unrelated. Named pipes are used by unrelated processes and related processes that refer to the pipe by the name associated with it. Named pipes are kernel objects. So, they reside in kernel space with kernel persistence (as far as the data), but the file structure has filesystem persistence until it is explicitly removed from the filesystem.

Pipes are created from one process, but they are rarely used in a single process. A pipe is a communication channel to a different process that is related or unrelated. Pipes create a flow of data from one end in one process (input end) to the other end that is in another process (output end). The data becomes a stream of bytes that flows in one direction through the pipe. Two pipes can be used to create bidirectional flow of communication between the processes. Figure 7-5 shows the various uses of pipes from a single process, from to two processes using a single pipe with a one direction flow of data from Process A to Process B, and then with a bidirectional flow of data between two processes that use two pipes.

A) UNIDIRECTIONAL DATA FLOW (ONE PROCESS ONE PIPE)

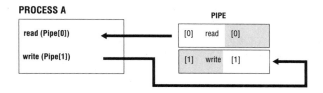

B) UNIDIRECTIONAL DATA FLOW (TWO PROCESSES ONE PIPE)

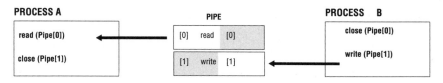

B) BIDIRECTIONAL DATA FLOW (TWO PROCESSES TWO PIPES)

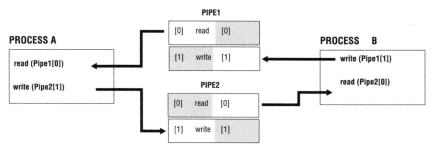

Figure 7-5

Chapter 7: Communication and Synchronization of Concurrent Tasks

Two pipes are used to create a bidirectional flow of data because of the way that pipes are set up. Each pipe has two ends, and each pipe has a one-way flow of data. So, one process uses the pipe as an input end (write data to pipe), and the other process uses the same pipe but uses the output end (read data from the pipe). Each process closes the end of the process it does not access, as shown in Figure 7-5.

Anonymous pipes are temporary and exist only while the process that created them has not terminated. Named pipes are special types of files and exist in the filesystem. They can remain after the process that created it has terminated unless the process explicitly removes them from the filesystem. A program that creates a named pipe can finish executing and leave the named pipe in the filesystem, but the data that was placed in the pipe will not be present. Future programs and processes can then access the named pipe later, writing new data to the pipe. In this way, a named pipe can be set up as a kind of permanent channel of communication. Named pipes have file permission settings associated with them, and anonymous pipes do not.

Using Named Pipes (FIFO)

Names pipes are created with `mkfifo()`:

Synposis

```
#include <sys/types.h>
#include <sys/stat.h>

int mkfifo(const char *pathname, mode_t mode);
int unlink(const char *pathname);
```

`mkfifo()` creates a named pipe using `pathname` as the name of the FIFO with permission specified by `mode`. `mode` comprises the file permission bits. They are as listed previously in Table 7-3.

`mkfifo()` is created with `O_CREAT | O_EXCL` flags, which means it creates a new named pipe with the name specified if it does not exist. If is does exist, an error `EEXIST` is returned. So, if you want to open an already existing named pipe, call the function, and check for this error. If the error occurs then use `open()` instead of `mkfifo()`.

The `unlink()` removes the filename `pathname` from the filesystem. The program in Listing 7-1 creates a named pipe with `mkfifo`.

Listings 7-1 and 7-2 are listings of programs that demonstrate how a named pipe can be used the transfer data from one process to another unrelated process. Listing 7-1 contains the program of the writer, and Listing 7-2 contains the program for the reader.

Listing 7-1

```
// Listing 7-1 A program that creates a named pipe with mkfifo().

1   using namespace std;
2   #include <iostream>
3   #include <fstream>
4   #include <sys/wait.h>
5   #include <sys/types.h>
6   #include <sys/stat.h>
7
```

```
 8  int main(int argc,char *argv[],char *envp[])
 9  {
10
11      fstream Pipe;
12
13      if(mkfifo("Channel-one",S_IRUSR | S_IWUSR
14                                      | S_IRGRP
15                                      | S_IWGRP) == -1){
16          cerr << "could not make fifo" << endl;
17      }
18
19      Pipe.open("Channel-one",ios::out);
20      if(Pipe.bad()){
21          cerr << "could not open fifo" << endl;
22      }
23      else{
24              Pipe << "2 3 4 5 6 7 " << endl;
25
26      }
27
28      return(0);
29  }
```

The program in Listing 7-1 creates a named pipe with the mkfifo() system call. The program then opens the pipe with an fstream object called Pipe in Line 19. Notice that Pipe has been opened for output using the ios::out flag. If the Pipe is not in a bad() state after the call to open, then the Pipe is ready for writing data to Channel-one. Although Pipe is ready for input, it blocks (waits) until another process has opened Channel-one for reading. When using the iostreams with pipes, it is important to remember that either the writer or reader must be opened for both input and output using ios::in | ios::out. Opening either the reader or the writer in this manner will prevent deadlock. In this case, we open the reader (Listing 7-2) for both. The program in this listing is called a *reader* because it reads the information from the pipe. The writer then writes a line of input to Pipe.

Listing 7-2

```
// Listing 7-2 A program that reads from a named pipe.

 1  using namespace std;
 2  #include <iostream>
 3  #include <fstream>
 4  #include <string>
 5  #include <sys/wait.h>
 6  #include <sys/types.h>
 7  #include <sys/stat.h>
 8
 9
10  int main(int argc, char *argv[])
11  {
12      int type;
13      fstream NamedPipe;
14      string Input;
15
16      NamedPipe.open("Channel-one",ios::in | ios::out);
```

(continued)

Listing 7-2 *(continued)*

```
17
18      if(NamedPipe.bad()){
19          cerr << "could not open Channel-one" << endl;
20      }
21
22      while(!NamedPipe.eof() && NamedPipe.good()){
23
24          getline(NamedPipe,Input);
25          cout << Input << endl;
26      }
27      NamedPipe.close();
28      unlink("Channel-one");
29      return(0);
30
31  }
```

The program in Listing 7-1 uses the << operator to write data into the pipe. Here the reader also has to open the pipe by using an fstream open, using the name of the named pipe Channel-one, and opening the pipe for input and output in Line 16. If the NamedPipe is not in a bad state after opening, then the data is read from the NamedPipe while NamedPipe is not eof() and is still good. The data is read from the pipe and stored in a string Input that is sent to cout. NamedPiped is then closed and the pipe is unlinked. These are unrelated processes. To run, each is launched separately.

Here is Program Profile 7-1 for Listings 7-1 and 7-2.

Program Profile 7-1

Program Name:

program7-1.cc (Listing 7-1)
program7-2.cc (Listing 7-2)

Description:

Listing 7-1 creates a pipe and opens the pipe with a fstream object. Before it writes a string to the pipe, it waits until another process opens the pipe for reading (Listing 7-2). Once the reader process opens the pipe for reading, the writer program writes a string to the pipe, closes the pipe, and then exits. The reader pipe reads the string from the pipe and displays the string to standard out. Run the reader and then the writer.

Libraries Required:

None

Headers Required:

<iostream> <fstream> <string> <sys/stat.h>

Compile and Link Instructions:

c++ -o program7-1 program7-1.cc program7-2.cc

Test Environment:

Solaris 10, gcc 3.4.3 and 3.4.6

Chapter 7: Communication and Synchronization of Concurrent Tasks

Processors:

Opteron, UltraSparc T1

Execution Instructions:

```
./program7-1
./program7-2
```

Notes:

Run each program in separate terminals.

The use of `fstream` simplifies the IPC making the named pipe easier to access. All of the functionality of streams comes into play for this example:

```
mkfifo("Channel-one",...);
vector<int> X( 2,3,4,5,6,7);
ofstream OPipe("Channel-one",ios::out);
ostream_iterator<int> Optr(OPipe,"\n");
copy(X.begin(),X.end(),Optr);
```

Here a vector is used to hold all the data. An `ofstream` object is used this time instead of an `fstream` object to open the named pipe. An `ostream` iterator is declared and points to the named pipe (`Channel-one`). Now instead of successive insertion in a loop, the `copy` algorithm can copy all the data to the pipe. This is a convenience if have hundreds, thousands, or even more numbers to write to the pipe.

FIFO Interface Class

Besides simplifying the use of IPC mechanisms by using iostreams, iterators, and algorithm, you can also simplify use by encapsulating the FIFO into an FIFO interface class. Remember that in doing so you are modeling a FIFO structure. The FIFO class is a model for the communication between two or more processes. It transmits some form of information between them. The information is translated into a sequence of data, inserted into the pipe, and then retrieved by a process on the other side of the pipe. The data is then reassembled by the retrieving process. There must be somewhere for the data to be stored while it is in transit from process A to process B. This storage area for the data is called a buffer. Insertion and extraction operations are used to place the data into or extract the data from this buffer. Before performing insertions or extractions into or from the data buffer, the data buffer must exist. Once communication has been completed, the data buffer is no longer needed. So, your model must be able to remove the data buffer when it is no longer necessary. As indicated, a pipe has two ends, one end for inserting data and the other end for extracting data, and these ends can be accessed from different processes. Therefore the model should also include an input port and an output port that can be connected to separate processes. Here are the basic components of the FIFO model:

- ❑ Input/output port
- ❑ Insertion and extraction operation
- ❑ Creation/initialization operation
- ❑ Buffer creation, insertion, extraction, destruction

For this example, there are only two processes involved in communication. But if there are multiple processes that can read/write to/ from the named pipe stream, synchronization is required. So, this class also requires a mutex object. Example 7-1 shows the beginnings of the FIFO class:

Example 7-1

```
// Example 7-1 Declaration of fifo class.

class fifo{
    mutex Mutex;
    //...
protected:
    string  Name;
public:
    fifo &operator<<(fifo &In, int X);
    fifo &operator<<(fifo &In, char X);
    fifo &operator>>(fifo &Out, float X);
    //...
};
```

Using this technique, you can easily create `fifos` in the constructor. You can pass them easily as parameters and return values. You can use them in conjunction with the standard container classes and so on. The construction of such a component greatly reduces the amount of code needed to use FIFOs, provides opportunities for type safety, and generally allows the programmer to work at a higher level.

Message Queue

A message queue is a linked list of strings or messages. This IPC mechanism allows processes with the adequate permissions to the queue to write or remove messages. The sender of the message assigns a priority to it. Message queues do not require more than one process to be used. With a FIFO, the writer process blocks and cannot write to the pipe until there is a process that opens it for reading. With a message queue, a writer process can write to the message queue and then terminate. The data is retained in the queue. Some other process later can read or write to it. The message queue has kernel persistence. When reading a message from the queue, the oldest message with the highest priority is returned. Each message in the queue has these attributes:

❑   A priority

❑   The length of the message

❑   The message or data

With a linked list the head of the list has the maximum number of messages allowed in the queue and the maximum size allowed for a message.

Using a Message Queue

The message queue is created with `mq_open()`:

Synopsis

```
#include <mqueue.h>

mqd_t mq_open(const char *name, int oflag,mode_t mode,
              struct mq_attr *attr);
int mq_close(mqd_t mqdes);
int mq_unlink(const char *name);
```

mq_open() creates a message queue with the specified name. The message queue uses oflag with these possible values to specify the access modes:

❑   O_RDONLY: Open to receive messages

❑   O_WRONLY: Open to send messages

❑   O_RDWR: Open to send or received messages

These flags can be ORred with the following:

❑   O_CREAT: Create a message queue.

❑   O_EXCL: If ORred with previous flag, function fails if the pathname already exists.

❑   O_NONBLOCK: Determines if queue waits for resources or messages that are not currently available.

The function returns a message queue descriptor of type mq_dt.

The last parameter is a struct mq_attr *attr. This is an attribute structure that describes the properties of the message queue:

```
struct mq_attr {
    long mq_flags;      //flags
    long mq_maxmsg;     //maximum number of messages allowed
    long mq_msgsize;    //maximum size of message
    long mq_curmsgs;    //number of messages currently in queue
}
```

mq_close() closes the message queue, but the message queue still exists in the kernel. However, the calling function can no longer use the descriptor. If the process terminates, all message queues associated with the process also close. The data is still retained in the queue.

unlink() removes the message queue specified by name from the system. The number of references to the message queue is tracked, but the queue name can still be removed from the system even if the count is greater than 0. The queue is not destroyed until all processes that utilized the queue have closed or called mq_close().

There are two functions to set and return the attribute object, as shown in the following code synopsis:

Synopsis

```
#include <mqueue.h>

int mq_getattr(mqd_t mqdes,struct mq_attr *attr);
int mq_setattr(mqd_t mqdes,struct mq_attr *attr,struct mq_attr *oattr);
```

When you are setting the attribute with mq_setattr, only the mq_flags are set in the attr structure. Other attributes are not affected. mq_maxmsg and mq_msgsize are set when the message queue is created. mq_curmsg can be returned and not set. oattr contains the previous values for the attributes.

To send or write a message to the queue, use these functions:

Synopsis

```
#include <mqueue.h>

int mq_send(mqd_t mqdes, const char *ptr, size_t len,
           unsigned int prio);
ssize_t mq_receive(mqd_t mqdes, const char *ptr, size_t len,
           unsigned int priop);
```

For mq_receive(), the len must be at least the maximum size of the message. The returned message is stored in *ptr.

posix_queue: The Message Queue Interface Class

posix_queue is a simple class that models some of the functionality of a message queue. It encapsulates the basic functions and the message queue attributes. Listing 7-3 shows the declaration of the posix_queue class.

Listing 7-3

```
// Listing 7-3 Declaration of the posix_queue class.

1  #ifndef __POSIX_QUEUE
2  #define __POSIX_QUEUE
3  using namespace std;
4  #include <string>
5  #include <mqueue.h>
6  #include <errno.h>
7  #include <iostream>
8  #include <sstream>
```

```
 9   #include <sys/stat.h>
10
11
12   class posix_queue{
13   protected:
14       mqd_t   PosixQueue;
15       mode_t  OMode;
16       int     QueueFlags;
17       string QueueName;
18       struct mq_attr  QueueAttr;
19       int   QueuePriority;
20       int MaximumNoMessages;
21       int MessageSize;
22       int ReceivedBytes;
23       void setQueueAttr(void);
24   public:
25       posix_queue(void);
26       posix_queue(string QName);
27       posix_queue(string QName,int MaxMsg, int MsgSize);
28       ~posix_queue(void);
29
30       mode_t  openMode(void);
31       void openMode(mode_t OPmode);
32
33       int queueFlags(void);
34       void queueFlags(int X);
35
36       int queuePriority(void);
37       void queuePriority(int X);
38
39       int maxMessages(void);
40       void maxMessages(int X);
41       int messageSize(void);
42       void messageSize(int X);
43
44       void queueName(string X);
45       string queueName(void);
46
47       bool open(void);
48       int send(string Msg);
49       int receive(string &Msg);
50       int remove(void);
51       int close(void);
52
53
54   };
55


     #endif
```

The basic functions performed by a message queue are encapsulated in the `posix_queue` class:

```
47      bool open(void);
48      int send(string Msg);
49      int receive(string &Msg);
50      int remove(void);
51      int close(void);
```

We have discussed what each these functions does already. Examples 7-2 through 7-6 show the definitions of these methods. Example 7-2 is the definition of `open()`:

Example 7-2

```
// Example 7-2 The definition of open().

122  bool posix_queue::open(void)
123  {
124     bool Success = true;
125     int RetCode;
126     PosixQueue = mq_open(QueueName.c_str(),QueueFlags,OMode,&QueueAttr);
127     if(errno == EACCES){
128        cerr  << "Permission denied to created " << QueueName << endl;
129        Success = false;
130     }
131     RetCode = mq_getattr(PosixQueue,&QueueAttr);
132     if(errno == EBADF){
133        cerr << "PosixQueue is not a valid message descriptor" << endl;
134        Success = false;
135        close();
136
137     }
138     if(RetCode == -1){
139        cerr << "unknown error in mq_getattr() " << endl;
140        Success = false;
141        close();
142     }
143     return(Success);
144  }
```

After the call to `mq_open()` is made in Line #126, `errno` is checked to see if message queue failed to open because a message queue by the name `QueueName.c_str()` already exists. If it does, then the call is not successful. `bool Success` is returned with a value of `false`.

In Line 131, the queue attribute structure is returned by `mq_getattr()`. To ensure that the message queue was opened and successfully initialized its attribute, `errno` is checked again in Line 132. `EBADF` means the descriptor was not a valid message queue descriptor. The return code is checked in Line 138.

Example 7-3 is the definition of `send()`.

Example 7-3

```
// Example 7-3 The definition of send().

146   int posix_queue::send(string Msg)
147   {
148
149      int StatusCode = 0;
150      if(Msg.size() > QueueAttr.mq_msgsize){
151         cerr << "message to be sent is larger than max queue
                      message size " << endl;
152         StatusCode = -1;
153      }
154      StatusCode = mq_send(PosixQueue,Msg.c_str(),Msg.size(),0);
155      if(errno == EAGAIN){
156         StatusCode = errno;
157         cerr << "O_NONBLOCK not set and the queue is full " << endl;
158      }
159      if(errno == EBADF){
160         StatusCode = errno;
161         cerr << "PosixQueue is not a valid descriptor open for
                      writing" << endl;
162      }
163      if(errno == EINVAL){
164         StatusCode = errno;
165         cerr << "msgprio is out side of the priority range for the
                      message queue or " << endl;
166         cerr << "Thread my block causing a timing conflict with
                      time out" << endl;
167      }
168
169      if(errno == EMSGSIZE){
170         StatusCode = errno;
171         cerr << "message size exceeds maximum size of message
                      parameter on message queue" << endl;
172
173      }
174      if(errno == ETIMEDOUT){
175         StatusCode = errno;
176         cerr << "The O_NONBlock flag was not set, but the time expired
                      before the  message " << endl;
177         cerr << "could be added to the queue " << endl;
178      }
179      if(StatusCode == -1){
180         cerr << "unknown error in mq_send() " << endl;
181      }
182      return(StatusCode);
183
184   }
```

In Line 150, the message is checked to ensure that its size does not exceed the allowable size for a message. In Line 154 the call to mq_send() is made. All other code checks for errors.

Example 7-4 is the definition of receive().

Example 7-4

```
//Example 7-4 The definition of receive().

187   int posix_queue::receive(string &Msg)
188   {
189
190       int StatusCode = 0;
191       char QueueBuffer[QueueAttr.mq_msgsize];
192       ReceivedBytes = mq_receive(PosixQueue,QueueBuffer,
                                      QueueAttr.mq_msgsize,NULL);
193       if(errno == EAGAIN){
194          StatusCode = errno;
195          cerr << "O_NONBLOCK not set and the queue is full " << endl;
196
197       }
198       if(errno == EBADF){
199          StatusCode = errno;
200          cerr << "PosixQueue is not a valid descriptor open for writing"
                   << endl;
201       }
202       if(errno == EINVAL){
203          StatusCode = errno;
204          cerr << "msgprio is out side of the priority range for the message
                        queue or " << endl;
205          cerr << "Thread my block causing a timing conflict with time out"
                   << endl;
206       }
207       if(errno == EMSGSIZE){
208          StatusCode = errno;
209          cerr << "message size exceeds maximum size of message parameter on
                        message queue" << endl;
210       }
211       if (errno == ETIMEDOUT){
212          StatusCode = errno;
213          cerr << "The O_NONBlock flag was not set, but the time expired
                        before the message " << endl;
214          cerr << "could be added to the queue " << endl;
215       }
216       string XMessage(QueueBuffer,QueueAttr.mq_msgsize);
217       Msg = XMessage;
218       return(StatusCode);
219
220   }
```

In Line 191, a buffer `QueueBuffer` with the maximum size of a message is created. `mq_receive()` is called. The message returned is stored in `QueueBuffer`, and the number of bytes is returned and stored in `ReceivedBytes`. In Line 216, the message is extracted from `QueueBuffer` and assigned to the string in Line 217.

In Example 7-5 is the definition for `remove()`.

Example 7-5

```
//Example 7-5 The definition for remove().

221  int  posix_queue::remove(void)
222  {
223      int StatusCode = 0;
224      StatusCode = mq_unlink(QueueName.c_str());
225      if(StatusCode != 0){
226          cerr << "Did not unlink " << QueueName << endl;
227      }
228      return(StatusCode);
229  }
230
```

In Line 224, mq_unlink() is called to remove the message queue from the system.

Example 7-6 provides the definition for close().

Example 7-6

```
//Example 7-6 The definition for close().

231  int posix_queue::close(void)
232  {
233
234      int StatusCode = 0;
235      StatusCode = mq_close(PosixQueue);
236      if(errno == EBADF){
237          StatusCode = errno;
238          cerr << "PosixQueue is not a valid descriptor open for
                        writing" << endl;
239      }
240      if(StatusCode == -1){
241          cerr << "unknown error in mq_close() " << endl;
242      }
243      return(StatusCode);
244
245  }
```

In Line 235, mq_close() is called to close the message queue.

Return briefly to Listing 7-3, notice that the bolded methods from Examples 7-2 through 7-6 encapsulate the message queue's attributes to set and return the properties of the message queue:

```
33  int queueFlags(void);
34  void queueFlags(int X);
35
36  int queuePriority(void);
37  void queuePriority(int X);
38
```

(continued)

(continued)

```
39   int maxMessages(void);
40   void maxMessages(int X);
41   int messageSize(void);
42   void messageSize(int X);
```

Some of these attributes are can also be set in the constructor. There are three constructors in Listing 7-3:

```
25   posix_queue(void);
26   posix_queue(string QName);
27   posix_queue(string QName,int MaxMsg, int MsgSize);
```

At Line 25 is the default constructor. Example 7-7 shows the definition.

Example 7-7

```
// Example 7-7 The definition of the default constructor.

 4   posix_queue::posix_queue(void)
 5   {
 6
 7
 8      QueueFlags = O_RDWR | O_CREAT | O_EXCL;
 9      OMode = S_IRUSR | S_IWUSR;
10      QueueName.assign("none");
11      QueuePriority = 0;
12      MaximumNoMessages = 10;
13      MessageSize = 8192;
14      ReceivedBytes = 0;
15      setQueueAttr();
16
17
18   }
```

This posix_queue class is a simple model of the message queue. All functionality has not been included here, but you can see a message queue class makes the message queue easier to use. The posix_queue class performs error checking for all of the major functions of the IPC mechanism. What should be added is the mq_notify function. With notification signaling, a process is signaled when the empty message queue has a message. This class does not have synchronization capabilities. If multiple processes want to use the posix_queue to write to it, a built-in mutex should be implemented and used when messages are sent or received.

What Are Interthread Communications?

We have discussed the different mechanisms defined by POSIX to perform communication between processes, related and unrelated. We have discussed where those IPC reside and their persistence. Because threads reside in the address space of their process, it is safe and logical to assume that communication between threads would not be difficult or require the use of special mechanisms just for communication. That is true. The most important issue that has to be dealt with when peer threads require communication with each other is synchronization. Data races and indefinite postponement are likely when performing Interthread Communication (ITC).

Chapter 7: Communication and Synchronization of Concurrent Tasks

Communication between threads is used to:

❏ Share data

❏ Send a message

Multiple threads share data in order to streamline processing performed concurrently. Each thread can perform different processing or the same processing on data streams. The data can be modified, or new data can be created as a result, which in turn is shared. Messages can also be communicated. For example, if an event happens in one thread, this could trigger another event in another thread. Threads may communicate a signal to other peer threads, or the main thread may signal the worker threads.

When two processes need to communicate, they use a structure that is external to both processes. When two threads communicate, they typically use structures that are part of the same process to which they both or all belong. Threads cannot communicate with threads outside their process unless you are referring to primary threads of processes. In that case, you refer to them as two processes. Threads within a process can pass values from the data segment of the process or stack segments of each thread.

In most cases, the cost of Interprocess Communication is higher than Interthread Communication. The external structures that must be created by the operating system during IPC require more system processing than the structures involved in ITC. The efficiency of ITC mechanisms makes threads a more attractive alternative in many, but not all programming scenarios that require concurrency.

We discussed some of the issues and drawbacks of using threads as compared to processes in Chapter 5.

Table 7-4 lists the basic Interthread Communications with a brief description.

Table 7-4

Types of ITC	Description
Global data, variables, and data structures	Declared outside of the main function or have global scope. Any modifications to the data are instantly accessible to all peer threads.
Parameters	Parameters passed to threads during creation. The generic pointer can be converted any data type.
File handles	Files shared between threads. These threads share the same read-write pointer and offset of the file.

Global Data, Variables, and Data Structures

An important advantage that threads have over processes is that threads can share global data, variables, and data structures. All threads in the process can access them equally. If any thread changes the data, the change is instantly available to all peer threads. For example, take three threads, ThreadA, ThreadB, and ThreadC. ThreadA makes a calculation and stores the results in a global variable Answer. ThreadB reads Answer, performs its calculation on it, and then stores its results in Answer. Then Thread C does the same thing. The final answer is to be displayed by the main thread. This example is shown in Listings 7-4, 7-5, and 7-6.

Listing 7-4

```
// Listing 7-4 thread_tasks.h.

1
2   void *task1(void *X);
3   void *task2(void *X);
4   void *task3(void *X);
5
```

Listing 7-5

```
// Listing 7-5 thread_tasks.cc.

1   extern int Answer;
2
3   void *task1(void *X)
4   {
5      Answer = Answer * 32;
6   }
7
8   void *task2(void *X)
9   {
10     Answer = Answer / 2;
11  }
12
13  void *task3(void *X)
14  {
15     Answer = Answer + 5;
16  }
```

Listing 7-6

```
// Listing 7-6 main thread.

1   using namespace std;
2   #include <iostream>
3   #include <pthread.h>
4   #include "thread_tasks.h"
5
6   int Answer = 10;
7
8
9   int main(int argc, char *argv[])
10  {
11
12     pthread_t ThreadA, ThreadB, ThreadC;
13
14     cout << "Answer = " << Answer << endl;
15
16     pthread_create(&ThreadA,NULL,task1,NULL);
17     pthread_create(&ThreadB,NULL,task2,NULL);
18     pthread_create(&ThreadC,NULL,task3,NULL);
19
```

```
20      pthread_join(ThreadA,NULL);
21      pthread_join(ThreadB,NULL);
22      pthread_join(ThreadC,NULL);
23
24      cout << "Answer = " << Answer << endl;
25
26      return(0);
27
28  }
```

In these listings, the tasks that the threads will execute are defined in a separate file. Answer is the global data declared in the main line in the file program7-6.cc. It is out of scope for use by the tasks that are in defined in thread_tasks.cc. It is declared as extern, so it can have global scope. If the threads are to process the data in the way described earlier — ThreadA, ThreadB, and then ThreadC perform their calculations — it requires synchronization. It is not guaranteed that the correct answer, 165, will be returned if ThreadA and ThreadB have other work they have to do first. The threads are transferring data from one thread to another. With, say, two multicores, ThreadA and ThreadB can be executing. ThreadA works for a time slice, and then ThreadC is given the processor. When ThreadA is preempted, it may still not execute its calculation on Answer. If ThreadC finished when it was preempted, the value of Answer would be 15. Then ThreadB finishes; the Answer is 7. Then ThreadA does its calculation; Answer is 224 not 165. Although a pipeline model of data communication is what was desired, there is no synchronization in place for it to be executed.

Threads can also share data structures in the same way that the variable was used. IPC supports only a limited set of data structures that can be used (for example, a message queue); in contrast, any type of global set, map, or so forth or any other collection or container class can be used to accomplish ITC. For example, threads can share a set. With a set, membership, intersection, union, and so forth, operations can be performed by different threads using Multiple Instruction Single Data (MISD) or Single Instruction Single Data (SISD) memory access models. The coding that it would take to implement a set container that could be used as an IPC mechanism is prohibitive.

Here is Program Profile 7-2 for Listings 7-4, 7-5, and 7-6.

Program Profile 7-2

Program Name:

program7-6.cc (Listing 7-6)

Description:

For this program, there is a global variable Answer declared in the main line in the file program7-6.cc. It is declared as extern, so it can have global scope in thread_tasks.cc. Answer is to be processed by ThreadA, ThreadB, and then ThreadC. They are to perform their calculations, which requires synchronization. The correct answer is 165. Although a pipeline model of data communication is what was desired, there is no synchronization in place for it to be executed.

Libraries Required:

libpthread

Headers Required:

```
<iostream> <pthread.h> "thread_tasks.h"
```

Compile and Link Instructions:

```
c++ -o program7-6 program7-6.cc thread_tasks.cc -lpthread
```

Test Environment:

Solaris 10, gcc 3.4.3 and 3.4.6

Processors:

Opteron, UltraSparc T1

Execution Instructions:

```
./program7-6
```

Notes:

None

Parameters for Interthread Communication

Parameters to threads can be used for communication between threads or between the primary thread and peer threads. The thread creation API supports thread parameters. The parameter is in the form of a void pointer:

```
int pthread_create(pthread_t *threadID,const pthread_attr_t *attr,
                   void *(*start_routine)(void*),
                   void *restrict parameter);
```

The void pointer in C++ is a generic pointer and can be used to point to any data type. The value of `parameter` passes values as simple as a `char *` or a complex as a pointer to a container or user-defined object. In the program in Listing 7-7 and Listing 7-8, we use two queues of strings as global data structures. One thread uses the queue as an output queue, and another thread uses that same queue as a data stream for input and then writes to the second global queue of strings.

Listing 7-7

```
// Listing 7-7 Thread tasks that use two global data structures.

1  using namespace std;
2  #include <queue>
3  #include <string>
4  #include <iostream>
5
6  extern queue<string> SourceText;
7  extern queue<string> FilteredText;
8
9  void *task1(void *X)
```

```
10   {
11       char Token = '?';
12
13       queue<string> *Input;
14
15
16       Input = static_cast<queue<string> *>(X);
17       string Str;
18       string FilteredString;
19       string::iterator NewEnd;
20
21       for(int Count = 0;Count < 16;Count++)
22       {
23           Str = Input->front();
24           Input->pop();
25           NewEnd = remove(Str.begin(),Str.end(),Token);
26           FilteredString.assign(Str.begin(),NewEnd);
27           SourceText.push(FilteredString);
28
29       }
30
31
32   }
33
34
35   void *task2(void *X)
36   {
37       char Token = '.';
38
39       string Str;
40       string FilteredString;
41       string::iterator NewEnd;
42
43       for(int Count = 0;Count < 16;Count++)
44       {
45           Str = SourceText.front();
46           SourceText.pop();
47           NewEnd = remove(Str.begin(),Str.end(),Token);
48           FilteredString.assign(Str.begin(),NewEnd);
49           FilteredText.push(FilteredString);
50
51
52       }
53
54   }
```

These tasks filter a string of text. task1 removes the (?) from a string and task2 removes a (.) from a string. task1 accepts a queue that serves as the container of strings to be filtered. The void * is type cast to a pointer to a queue of strings in Line #16. task2 does not require a queue for input. It uses the global queue SourceText that is populated by task1. Inside their loops, a string is removed from the queue, the token is removed, and the new string is pushed onto the global queues. For task1 the queue string is SourceText and for task2, the queue string is FilteredText. Both queues are declared extern in Lines 6 and 7.

Listing 7-8

```
// Listing 7-8 Main thread declares two global data structures.

1   using namespace std;
2   #include <iostream>
3   #include <pthread.h>
4   #include "thread_tasks.h"
5   #include <queue>
6   #include <fstream>
7   #include <string>
8
9
10
11
12  queue<string> FilteredText;
13  queue<string> SourceText;
14
15  int main(int argc, char *argv[])
16  {
17
18     ifstream Infile;
19     queue<string> QText;
20     string Str;
21     int Size = 0;
22
23
24     pthread_t ThreadA, ThreadB;
25
26     Infile.open("book_text.txt");
27     for(int Count = 0;Count < 16;Count++)
28     {
29        getline(Infile,Str);
30        QText.push(Str);
31
32     }
33
34     pthread_create(&ThreadA,NULL,task1,&QText);
35     pthread_join(ThreadA,NULL);
36
37     pthread_create(&ThreadB,NULL,task2,NULL);
38     pthread_join(ThreadB,NULL);
39
40     Size = FilteredText.size();
41
42     for(int Count = 0;Count < Size ;Count++)
43     {
44        cout << FilteredText.front() << endl;
45        FilteredText.pop();
46
47     }
48
49     Infile.close();
```

```
50
51      return(0);
52
53   }
```

The program in Listing 7-8 shows the code for the main thread. It declares the two global queues on Line 12 and Line 13. The strings are read in from a file into string queue QText. This is the data source queue for ThreadA in Line 34. The main thread then calls a join on ThreadA and waits for it to return. When ThreadA returns, ThreadB uses the global queue SourceText just populated by task1. When ThreadB returns, the strings in the global queue FilteredText are sent to cout by the main thread. By the main thread calling join in this way these threads are not executed concurrently. The main thread does not create ThreadB until ThreadA returns. If the threads were created one after the other, they would be executed concurrently. The threat of a core dump looms. If ThreadB starts its execution before ThreadA populates its source queue, then ThreadB attempts to pop an empty queue. The size of the queue could be checked before attempting to read it. But you want to take advantage of the multicore in doing this processing. Here you have a few strings in a queue and all you want to do is remove a single token. But if you scale this problem to thousands of string and many tokens to be removed, you realize that another approach has to exist. Again, you do not want to go to a serial solution. Access to the queue can be synchronized but filtering all the strings at once can also be parallelized. We will revisit the problem and present a better solution later in this chapter.

Here is Program Profile 7-3 for Listings 7-7 and 7-8.

Program Profile 7-3

Program Name:

program7-8.cc (Listing 7-8)

Description:

The program in Listing 7-8 shows the code for the main thread. It declares the two global queues used for input and output. The strings are read in from a file into string queue QText, the data source queue for ThreadA. The main thread then calls a join on ThreadA and waits for it to return. When ThreadA returns, ThreadB uses the global queue SourceText just populated by ThreadA. When ThreadB returns, the strings in the global queue FilteredText are sent to cout by the main thread.

Libraries Required:

libpthread

Headers Required:

<iostream> <pthread.h> <fstream> <queue> <string> "thread_tasks.h"

Compile and Link Instructions:

c++ -o program7-8 program7-8.cc thread_tasks.cc -lpthread

Test Environment:

Solaris 10, gcc 3.4.3 and 3.4.6

Processors:

Opteron, UltraSparc T1

Execution Instructions:

```
./program7-8
```

Notes:

None

With processes, command-line arguments are passed by using the `exec` family of functions or `posix_spawn`, as discussed in Chapter 5. The command-line arguments are restricted to simple data types such as numbers and characters. The parameters passed to processes are one-way communication. The child process simply copies the parameter values. Any modifications made to the data will not be reflected in the parent. With threads, the parameter is not a copy but an address to some data location. Any modification made by the thread to that data can be seen by any thread that uses it.

But this type of transparency may not be what you desire. A thread can keep its own copy of data passed to it. It can copy it to its stack, but what's on its stack will come and go. A thread can be called several times performing the same task over and over again. By using thread-specific data, data can be associated with a thread and made private and persistent.

File Handles for Interthread Communication

Sharing files between multiple threads as a form of ITC requires the same caution as using global variables. If Thread A moves the file pointer, then Thread B accesses the file at that location. What if one thread closes the files and another thread attempts to write to the file — what happens? Can a thread read from the file while another thread writes to it? Can multiple threads write to the file? Care must be taken to serialize or synchronize access to files within a multithreaded environment. Since threads can share actual read-write pointers, cooperation techniques must be used.

Synchronizing Concurrency

In any computer system, the resources are limited. There is only so much memory, and there are only so many I/O devices and ports, hardware interrupts, and, yes, even processors cores to go around. The number of I/O devices is usually restricted by the number of I/O ports and the hardware interrupts that a system has. In an environment of limited hardware resources, an application consisting of multiple processes and threads must compete for memory locations, peripheral devices, and processor time. Some threads and processes will be working together intimately using the system's limited sharable resources to perform a task and achieve a goal while other threads and processes work asynchronously and independently competing for those same sharable resources. It is the operating system's job to determine when the process or thread utilizes system resources and for how long. With preemptive scheduling, the operating system can interrupt the process or thread in order to accommodate all the processes and threads competing for the system resources. There are software resources and hardware resources. An example of software resources is a shared library that provides a common set of services or functions to processes and threads. Other sharable software resources are:

❑ Applications

❑ Programs

❑ Utilities

To share software resources requires only one copy of the program(s) code to be brought into memory. Data resources are objects, system data files (for example, environment variables), globally defined variables, and data structures. In the last section, we discussed data resources that are used for data communication. It is possible for processes and threads to have their own copy of shared data resources. In other cases, it is desirable, and maybe necessary, that data is shared. Sharing data can be tricky and may lead to race conditions (modifying data simultaneously) or data not being where it should when it is needed. Even attempting to synchronize access to resources can cause problems if this is not properly executed or if the wrong IPC or ITC mechanism is used. This can cause indefinite postponement or deadlock. Synchronization allows multiple threads and processes to be active at the same time while sharing resources without interfering with each other's operation. The synchronization process temporarily serializes (in some cases) execution of the multiple tasks to prevent problems. Serialization occurs if one-at-a-time access has to be granted to hardware or software resources. But too much serialization defeats the advantages of concurrency and parallelism. Then cores sit idle. Serialization is used as the last approach if nothing else can be done. Coordination is the key.

Types of Synchronization

We talked about the resources of the system that are shared, hardware and software resources. These are the entities in a system that require synchronization. What also should be included are tasks, which should also be synchronized. You saw evidence of this in the program in Listing 7-7 and 7-8. `task1` had to execute and complete before `task2` could begin. Therefore, there are three major categories of synchronization:

❑ Data

❑ Hardware

❑ Task

Table 7-5 summarizes each type of synchronization.

Table 7-5

Types of synchronization	Description
Data	Necessary to prevent race conditions. It allows concurrent threads/processes to access a block of memory safely.
Hardware	Necessary when several hardware devices are needed to perform a task or group of tasks. It requires communication between tasks and tight control over real-time performance and priority settings.
Task	Necessary to prevent race conditions. It enforces preconditions and postconditions of logical processes.

Synchronizing Access to Data

In this chapter thus far, we have discussed IPC and ITC. As we have discussed, the difference between data shared between processes and data shared between threads is that threads share the same address space and processes have separate address spaces. IPC exists outside the address space of the processes involved in the communication, in the kernel space or in the filesystem. Shared memory maps a structure to a block of memory that is accessible to the processes. ITC are global variables and data structures. It is the IPC and ITC mechanisms that require synchronization. Figure 7-6 shows where the IPC and ITC mechanisms exist in the layout of a process.

PROCESS A'S ADDRESS SPACE

STACK SEGMENT	FREE STORE	DATA SEGMENT	TEXT SEGMENT
local variables	local variables global variables	global data structures global variables constants static variables	

messages — shared memory — files — FIFOs/pipes — IPC MECHANISMS

PROCESS B'S ADDRESS SPACE

STACK SEGMENT	FREE STORE	DATA SEGMENT	TEXT SEGMENT
local variables	local variables global variables	global data structures global variables constants static variables	
thread A's stack		• trees • graphs	thread A's code
thread B's stack		• queues • stacks ITC MECHANISMS	thread B's code

Figure 7-6

Data synchronization is needed in order to control race conditions and allow concurrent threads or processes to safely access a block of memory. Data synchronization controls when a block of memory can be read or modified. Concurrent access to shared memory, global variables, and files must be synchronized in a multithreaded environment. Data synchronization is needed at the location in a task's code when it attempts to access the block of memory, global variable, or file shared with other concurrently executing processes or threads. This is called the *critical section*. The critical section can be any block of code that changes the writes or reads to/from a file, closes a file, reads or writes global variables or data structures.

Critical Sections

Critical sections are an area or block of code that accesses a shared resource that must be controlled because the resource is being shared by multiple concurrent tasks. Critical sections are marked by an entry point and an exit point. The actual code in the critical section can be one line of code where the thread/process is reading or writing to memory or a file. It can also be several lines of code where processing and calls to other methods involve the shared data. The entry point marks your entering the critical section and an exit point marks your leaving the critical section.

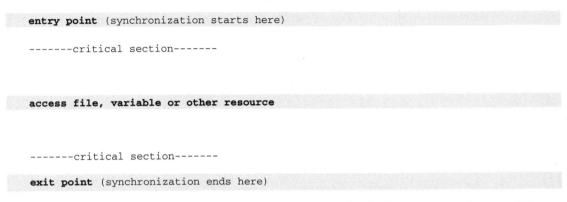

```
entry point (synchronization starts here)

-------critical section-------



access file, variable or other resource



-------critical section-------

exit point (synchronization ends here)
```

In order to solve the problems caused by multiple concurrent tasks sharing a resource, three conditions should be met:

1. If a task is in its critical section, other tasks sharing the resource cannot be executing in their critical section. They are blocked. This is called *mutual exclusion*.

2. If no tasks are in their critical section, then any blocked tasks can now enter their critical section. This is called *progress*.

3. There should be a *bounded wait* as to the number of times that a task is allowed to reenter its critical sections. A task that keeps entering its critical sections may prevent other tasks from attempting to enter theirs. A task cannot reenter its critical sections if other tasks are waiting in a queue.

These synchronization techniques are what are used to manage critical sections. It is important to determine the how these concurrently executing tasks are using the shared data. Are they writing to the data while others are reading? Are all reading from it? Are all writing to it? How they are sharing the shared data helps determine what type of synchronization is needed and how it should be implemented. Remember applying synchronization incorrectly can also cause problems like deadlock, data race conditions, and so forth.

PRAM Model

The Parallel Random-Access Machine (PRAM) is a simplified theoretical model in which there are N processors labeled P1, P2, P3, . . . PN that share one global memory. All the processors have simultaneous read and write access to shared global memory. Each of these theoretical processors can access the global shared memory in one *uninterruptible* unit of time. The PRAM model has four algorithms that can be used to access the shared global memory, concurrent read and write algorithms, and exclusive read and write algorithms that work like this:

1. Concurrent read algorithms are allowed to read the same piece of memory simultaneously with no data corruption.

2. Concurrent write algorithms allow multiple processors to write to the shared memory.

3. Exclusive read algorithms are used to ensure that no two processors ever read the same memory location at the same time.

4. Exclusive write ensures that no two processors write to the same memory at the same time.

Now this PRAM model can be used to characterize concurrent access to shared memory by multiple tasks.

Concurrent and Exclusive Memory Access

The concurrent and exclusive read-write algorithms can be combined into the following types of algorithm combinations that are possible for read-write access:

❑ Exclusive Read and Exclusive Write (EREW)

❑ Concurrent Read and Exclusive Write (CREW)

❑ Exclusive Read and Concurrent Write (ERCW)

❑ Concurrent Read and Concurrent Write (CRCW)

These algorithms can be viewed as access policies implemented by the tasks sharing the data. Figure 7-7 shows these access policies. EREW means access to the shared memory is serialized where only one task at a time is given access to the shared memory whether it is access to write or to read. An example of EREW access policy is the producer-consumer. The program in Chapter 5 in Listing 5-7 has an EREW access policy with the shared posix_queue between processes. One process writes the name of a file another process is to search for the code in. Access to the queue that contained the filenames was restricted to exclusive write by the producer and exclusive read by the consumer. Only one task was allowed access to the queue at any given time.

CREW access policy allows multiple reads of the shared memory and exclusive writes. There are no restrictions on how many tasks can read the shared memory concurrently, but only one task can write to the shared memory. Concurrent reads can occur while an exclusive write is taking place. With this access policy, each reading task may read a different value while other task is writing. The next task that reads the shared memory will see different data than some other task. This may be intended, but it also may not. ERCW access policy is direct reverse of CREW. Only one task can read the shared data, but concurrent writes are allowed. CRCW access policy allows concurrent reads and concurrent writes.

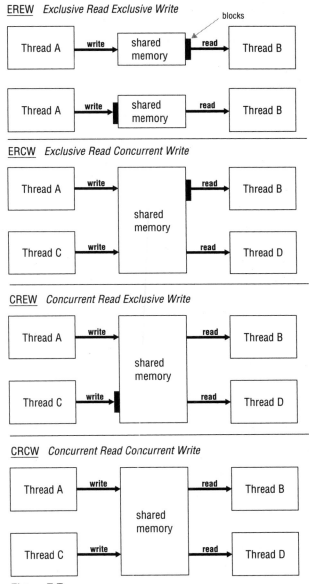

Figure 7-7

Each of these four algorithm types requires different levels and types of synchronization. They can be analyzed on a continuum with the access policy that requires the least amount of synchronization to implement on one end and the access policy that requires the most amount of synchronization at the other end. EREW is the policy that is the simplest to implement because EREW essentially forces sequential processing. You may think that CRCW is the simplest, but it presents the most challenges. It may appear that memory can be accessed without restriction. But this is the most difficult to implement and requires the most synchronization in order to meet the goal to implement a synchronization process that maintains data integrity and satisfactory system performance.

Concurrent Tasks: Coordinating Order of Execution

Synchronization is also needed to coordinate the order of execution of concurrent tasks. Order of execution was important in the program in Listings 7-5 and 7-6. If the tasks were executed out of order, the final value for Answer would be wrong. In the program in Listings 7-7 and 7-8, if task1 did not complete, task2 would attempt to read from an empty queue. Synchronization is required to coordinate these tasks so that work can progress or so that the correct results can be produced. Data synchronization (*access synchronization*) and task synchronization (*sequence synchronization*) are two types of synchronization required when executing multiple concurrent tasks. Task synchronization enforces preconditions and postconditions of logical processes.

Relationships between Cooperating Tasks

There are four basic synchronization relationships between any two tasks in a single process or between any two processes within a single application:

- ❏ Start-to-start (SS)
- ❏ Finish-to-start (FS)
- ❏ Start-to-finish (SF)
- ❏ Finish-to-finish (FF)

These four basic relationships characterize the coordination of work between threads and processes. Figure 7-8 shows activity diagrams for each synchronization relationship.

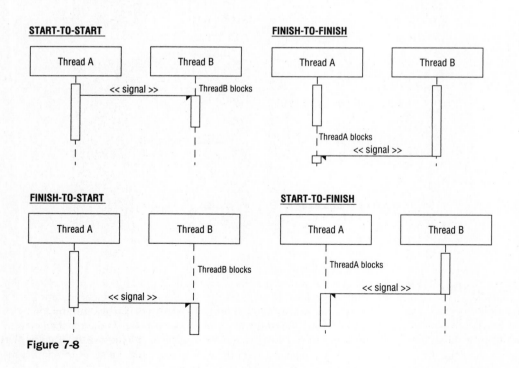

Figure 7-8

Start-to-Start (SS) Relationship

In a *start-to-start* synchronization, one task cannot start until another task starts. One task may start before the other but never after. For example, say that you have a program that implements an Embedded Conversational Agent (ECA). The ECA is a computer-generated talking head, which provides a kind of personality for software. The program that implements the ECA has several threads. Here, the focus is on the threads that controls the animation of the eyes (ECA does not have a mouth, the eyes animate) and the thread that controls the sound or voice. You want to give the illusion that the sound and eyes animation are synchronized. Ideally, they should execute at precisely the same moment. With multiple processor cores, both threads may start simultaneously. The threads have a start-to-start relationship. Because of timing conditions, the thread that produces the audio (Thread A) is allowed to start slightly before the thread that starts the animation (Thread B), but not much before for the illusion's sake. It takes a little longer for the audio to initialize, so it can start a bit early. Graphics load much faster. Figure 7-9 shows images of our ECA.

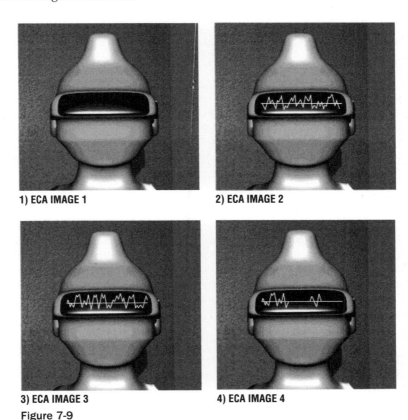

1) ECA IMAGE 1   2) ECA IMAGE 2

3) ECA IMAGE 3   4) ECA IMAGE 4

Figure 7-9

Finish-to-Start (FS) Relationship

In a *finish-to-start* synchronization, Task A cannot finish until Task B starts. This type of relationship is common with parent-child processes. The parent process cannot complete execution of some operation until it spawns a child process or it receives a communication from the child process that it has started its operation. The child process continues to execute once it has signaled the parent or supplied the needed information. The parent process is then free to complete its operation.

Start-to-Finish Relationship

A *start-to-finish* synchronization relationship is the reverse of the finish-to-start relationship. In a start-to-finish synchronization relationship, one task cannot start until another task finishes. Task A cannot start execution until Task B finishes executing or completes a certain operation. The program in Listing 7-7 and 7-8 had a start-to-finish synchronization. task2 could not start until task1 completed. The main thread used a join for synchronization. The main thread blocked until task1 returned then it created a thread that executed task2.

If process A is reading from a pipe connected to process B, process B must first write to the pipe before process A reads from it. Process B must complete at least one operation — write a single element to the pipe — before process A starts. With the pipe, there is limited synchronization built in by using blocking. But if there are multiple readers and writers, then more elaborate synchronization is required.

Finish-to-Finish Relationship

A *finish-to-finish* synchronization relationship means one task cannot finish until another task finishes. Task A cannot finish until Task B finishes. This again can describe the relationship between parent and child processes. The parent process must wait until all its child processes have terminated before it is allowed to terminate. If the parent process terminates before its child processes, those terminated child processes become zombied. The parent process calls a wait() for each of its child processes (like join for threads) or waits for a mutex or condition variable that is broadcast by child threads.

Another example of a finish-to-finish relationship is the boss-worker concurrency model. It is the boss's job to delegate work to the workers. It would be undesirable for the boss to terminate before the worker. New requests to the system would not be processed, existing threads would have no work to perform, and no new threads would be created. If the boss were a primary thread and it terminated, the process would terminate along with all the worker threads. In a peer-to-peer model, if thread A dynamically allocates an object passed to thread B and thread A terminates, the object is destroyed along with thread A. If this is done before thread B has a chance to use it, a segmentation fault or data access violation occurs. In order to prevent these kinds of errors with threads, termination of threads is synchronized by using the pthread_join(). This creates a finish-to-finish synchronization.

Synchronization Mechanisms

The synchronization mechanisms we discuss in this section cover mechanisms for both processes and threads. These mechanisms can be used to prevent race conditions and deadlocks between multiple tasks by implementing the synchronization access policies we have mentioned and managing critical sections of tasks. In this section, we introduce:

❑   Semaphores and mutexes

❑   Read-write locks

❑   Condition variables

Semaphores

A *semaphore* is a synchronization mechanism that is used to manage synchronization relationships and implement access policies. A semaphore is a special kind of variable that can be accessed only by very specific operations. It helps threads and processes synchronize access to shared modifiable memory or manage access to a device or other resource. The semaphore is like a key that grants access the resource. This key can be owned by only one process or thread at a time. Whichever task owns the key or semaphore locks the resource for its exclusive use. Locking the resource causes any other task that wishes to access the resource to wait until the resource has been unlocked. When the semaphore is unlocked, the next task waiting in the queue for the semaphore is given it, thus accessing the resource. The *next task* is determined by the scheduling policy used by the thread or process. Figure 7-10 shows the basic concept of a semaphore as described.

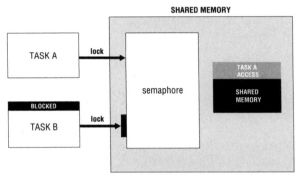

Figure 7-10

Basic Semaphore Operations

A semaphore can be accessed only by specific operations. There are two operations that can be performed on a semaphore: `P()` and `V()` operations. The `P()` operation decrements the semaphore and the `V()` operation increments the semaphore:

P(Mutex)
```
if(Mutex > 0){
   Mutex--;
}
else {
    Block on Mutex;
}
```

V(Mutex)
```
if(Blocked on Mutex N processes){
   pass on Mutex;
}
else{
    Mutex++;
}
```

Here `Mutex` is the semaphore. The actual implementation will be system dependent. These operations are indivisible. This means that once the operation is in progress, it cannot be preempted. If several tasks attempt to make a call to the `P()` operation, only one task is allowed to proceed. If `Mutex` has already been decremented, then the task blocks and is placed in a queue. The `V()` operation is called by the task that owns `Mutex`. If there are other tasks waiting on `Mutex`, it is given to the next task in the queue according the scheduling policy. If no tasks are waiting, then `Mutex` is incremented.

Semaphore operations can go by other names such as:

`P() operation`
```
lock()
wait()
own()
```

`V() operation`
```
unlock()
post()
unown()
```

The value of the semaphore depends on the type of semaphore it is. There are several types of semaphores. For example:

❑   A **binary semaphore** has the value 0 or 1. The semaphore is available when its value is 1 and not available when it is 0. When a process or thread obtains the binary semaphore, the value is decremented to 0. So, if another process or thread tests its value, it will not be available. Once the process or thread is done, the semaphore is incremented.

❑   A **counting semaphore** has some non-negative integer value. Its initial value represents the number of resources available.

The POSIX standard defines several types of semaphores. Some of these semaphores are used by threads only, and others can be used by processes or threads. Any operating system that is compliant with the Single Unix Specification or POSIX standard can supply an implementation of these semaphores. They are apart of the `libpthread` library, and the functions are declared in the `pthread.h` header.

Posix Semaphores

The POSIX semaphore defines a named binary semaphore. The name corresponds to a pathname in the filesystem. Table 7-6 lists the basic functions for using a semaphore along with a brief description.

Table 7-6

Basic Semaphore Operations	Description
Initialization	Allocates memory required to hold the semaphore and give memory initial values. Also determines whether the semaphore is private, sharable, owned, or unowned.
Request ownership	Makes a request to own the semaphore. If the semaphore is owned by a thread, then the thread blocks.

Basic Semaphore Operations	Description
Release ownership	Releases the semaphore so it is accessible to blocked threads.
Try ownership	Tests the ownership of the semaphore. If the semaphore is owned, the requester does not block but continues executing. Can wait for a period of time before continuing.
Destruction	Frees the memory associated with the mutex. The memory cannot be destroyed or closed if it is owned or others are still waiting.

Listing 7-9 shows how semaphores can be used between multiple processes.

Listing 7-9

```
// Listing 7-9 A process using a semaphore on an output file.

1   using namespace std;
2   #include <semaphore.h>
3   #include <iostream>
4   #include <fstream>
5
6
7   int main(int argc, char *argv[])
8   {
9
10      int Loop, PN;
11      sem_t *Sem;
12      const char *Name;
13      ofstream Outfile("out_text.txt",ios::app);
14
15      PN = atoi(argv[1]);
16      Loop = atoi(argv[2]);
17      Name = argv[3];
18
19      Sem = sem_open(Name,O_CREAT,O_RDWR,1);
20      sem_unlink(Name);
21
22
23      for (int Count = 1; Count < Loop; ++Count) {
24          sem_wait(Sem);
25          Outfile << "Process:" << PN << " counting " << Count << endl;
26          sem_post(Sem);
27
28      }
29      Outfile.close();
30
31      exit(0);
32
33
34
35  }
```

The program in Listing 7-9 opens a semaphore of type `sem_t` in Line 11. The named semaphore `Sem` is opened with `Name` typed in as the third argument on the command line. `O_CREATE` and `O_RDWR` are flags that specify how the semaphore is opened. In this case, the semaphore is opened only if is does not exist. With the `O_RDWR` flag set, the semaphore is opened with read and write permissions. `Sem` is initialized with a value of 1. The `sem_wait` and `sem_post` operations encapsulate the access to `Outfile`. During the execution of Line 25, no other processes should access the file. All processes that use this file for input or output should use the same semaphore. In Listing 7-10, a process that reads the file also uses the semaphore.

Listing 7-10

```
// Listing 7-10 A process using a semaphore on an input file.

1    using namespace std;
2    #include <semaphore.h>
3    #include <iostream>
4    #include <fstream>
5    #include <string>
6
7
8    int main(int argc, char *argv[])
9    {
10
11       string Str;
12       const char *Name;
13       sem_t *Sem;
14       ifstream Infile("out_text.txt");
15
16       if(Infile.is_open()){
17          Name = argv[1];
18          Sem = sem_open(Name,O_CREAT,O_RDWR,1);
19          sem_unlink(Name);
20
21          while(!Infile.eof() && Infile.good()){
22             sem_wait(Sem);
23             getline(Infile,Str);
24             cout << Str << endl;
25             sem_post(Sem);
26
27          }
28          cout << "--------------------------------" << endl;
29
30          Infile.close();
31
32       }
33
34       exit(0);
35
36
37
38   }
```

The program in Listing 7-10 the named semaphore Sem is opened with Name typed in as the first argument on the command line. O_CREATE and O_RDWR are flags that specify how the semaphore is opened, as in Listing 7-9. The sem_wait and sem_post operations encapsulate the access to Infile. During the execution of Line 23, the process in Listing 7-9 cannot write to the file.

Here is Program Profile 7-4 for Listings 7-9 and 7-10.

Program Profile 7-4

Program Name:

program7-9.cc (Listing 7-9)
program7-10.cc (Listing 7-10)

Description:

The program7-9 in Listing 7-9 opens a semaphore of type sem_t named semaphore Sem. It is opened with Name typed in as the third argument on the command line. Sem is initialized with a value of 1. The sem_wait and sem_post operations encapsulate the access to Outfile. During the execution no other processes should access the file. All processes that use this file for input or output should use the same semaphore. In Listing 7-10, a process that reads the file also uses the semaphore. From the command line the program looks for the process number, a loop invariant, and the name of the semaphore. The program writes process, process number, and the loop iteration number to the file.

In program7-10 in Listing 7-10 the named semaphore Sem is opened with Name typed in as the first argument on the command line. It should have the same name as the semaphore in program7-9 in order to coordinate access to out_text.txt. The sem_wait and sem_post operations encapsulate the access to Infile. During the execution program7-9 cannot write to the file. The program requires the name of the semaphore as a command-line argument. It uses the named semaphore. It opens the file out_text.txt and writes its contents to stout.

Libraries Required:

librt

Headers Required:

<semaphore.h> <iostream> <fstream> <string> <fcntl.h>

Compile and Link Instructions:

```
c++ -o program7-9 program7-9.cc -lrt
c++ -o program7-10 program7-10.cc -lrt
```

Test Environment:

Solaris 10, gcc 3.4.3 and 3.4.6

Processors:

Opteron, UltraSparc T1

Execution Instructions:

These programs require command-line arguments. For `program7-9`, the first argument is the process number, the second argument is the loop invariant, and the third argument is the name of the semaphore. `program7-10` requires the name of the semaphore.

```
./program7-9 3 4 /sugi & ./program7-10 /sugi
```

Notes:

Make sure that the name of the semaphore contains a "/". These programs are to execute at the same time.

Mutex Semaphores

The POSIX standard defines a mutex semaphore of type `pthread_mutex_t` that can be used by threads and processes. Mutex means *mutual exclusion*. A mutex is a type semaphore, but there is a difference between them. A mutex must always be unlocked by the thread that locked it. With a semaphore, a post (or unlock) can be performed by a thread other than the thread that performed the wait (or unlock). So, one thread or process can call `wait()` and another process/thread can call `post()` on the same semaphore.

`pthread_mutex_t` provides the basic operations necessary to make it a practical synchronization mechanism:

- ❑ Initialization
- ❑ Request ownership
- ❑ Release ownership
- ❑ Try ownership
- ❑ Destruction

Table 7-7 lists the `pthread_mutex_t` functions that are used to perform these basic operations. The *initialization* allocates memory required to hold the mutex semaphore and to give the memory some initial values. A binary semaphore has an initial value of 0 or 1. A counting semaphore has a value that represents the number of resources the semaphore is to track. It can represent the request limit a program is capable of processing in a single session. In contrast to regular variables, there is no guarantee that the initialization operation of a mutex will occur. Be sure to take precautions to ensure that the mutex was initialized by checking the return value or checking the `errno` value. The system fails to create the mutex if the space set aside for mutexes has been used, the number of allowable semaphores has been exceeded, the named semaphore already exists, or there is some other memory allocation problem.

Table 7-7

Mutex Operations	Function Prototypes/Macros #include <pthread.h>
Initialization	`int pthread_mutex_init(pthread_mutex_t *restrict mutex, const pthread_mutexattr_t *restrict attr);`
	`pthread_mutex_t mutex = PTHREAD_MUTEX_INITIALIZER;`
Request ownership	`<time.h>`
	`int pthread_mutex_lock(pthread_mutex_t *mutex);`
	`int pthread_mutex_timedlock(pthread_mutex_t *restrict mutex, const struct timespec *restrict abs_timeout);`
Release ownership	`int pthread_mutex_unlock (pthread_mutex_t *mutex);`
Try ownership	`int pthread_mutex_trylock(pthread_mutex_t *mutex);`
Destruction	`int pthread_mutex_destroy(pthread_mutex_t *mutex);`

The pthread mutex has an attribute object that encapsulates all the attributes of the mutex. This attribute object is used similarly to the attribute object for a thread. This difference is that whereas the attribute object of a thread is set, the attribute for a mutex has no set group of properties associated with it. We will discuss this later in the chapter. What is important to understand for now is that the attribute object can be passed to the initialization function creating a mutex with attributes of those set in the object. If no attribute object is used, the mutex is initialized with default values. The `pthread_mutex_t` is initially unlocked and private. A *private* mutex is shared between threads of the same process, whereas a *shared* mutex is shared between threads of multiple processes. If default attributes are to be used, the mutex can be initialized statically by using the macro:

```
pthread_mutext Mutex = PTHREAD_MUTEX_INITIALIZER;
```

This creates a statically allocated mutex object. This method uses less overhead but performs no error checking.

The *request ownership* operation grants ownership of the mutex to the calling process or thread. The mutex is either owned or unowned. Once owned, the thread or process owning it has exclusive access to the resource. If there is any attempt to own the mutex (by calling this operation) by any other processes or threads, they are blocked until the mutex is made available. When the mutex is released, this causes the next process or thread that has blocked to unblock and obtain ownership of the mutex. With the `pthread_mutex_lock()` the thread granted ownership of a given mutex is the only thread that can release the mutex.

The *try* ownership operation tests the mutex to see if it is already owned. The function returns some value if it is owned. The advantage of this operation is the thread or process does not block. It can continue executing code. If the mutex is not owned, then ownership is granted.

The *destruction* operation frees the memory associated with the mutex. The memory cannot be destroyed or closed if it is owned or a thread or process is waiting for the mutex.

Using the Mutex Attribute Object

The pthread_mutex_t has an attribute object used in a similar way as the thread attribute. As previously indicated, the attribute object encapsulates the attributes of a mutex object. Once initialized, it can be used by multiple mutex objects when passed to pthread_mutex_init(). Also, as previously indicated, in contrast to the thread attribute function, there are no mandatory attributes associated with the object. The functions that can be used to set the mutex attributes have to do with the following:

❑ Priority ceiling

❑ Protocol

❑ Shared

❑ Type

These functions are listed in Table 7-8 with a brief description.

Table 7-8

pthread_mutex_t Attribute Object Function Prototypes #include <pthread.h>	Description
Creation/Destruction	
int pthread_mutexattr_ init(pthread_mutexattr_t * attr);	Initializes a mutex attribute object specified by the parameter attr with default values for all of the attributes defined by the implementation.
int pthread_mutexattr_ destroy(pthread_mutexattr_t * attr);	Destroys a mutex attribute object specified by the attr, which causes the mutex attribute object to become uninitialized. Can be reinitialized by calling the pthread_mutexattr_init() function.
Priority Ceiling	Defines the minimum priority level of the mutex.
int pthread_mutexattr_ setprioceiling(pthread_ mutexattr_t * attr,int prioceiling);	Sets and returns the priority ceiling attribute of the mutex specified by attr. prioceiling contains the priority ceiling of the mutex. The values are within the maximum range of priorities defined by SCHED_FIFO.
int pthread_mutexattr_ getprioceiling(const pthread_ mutexattr_t*restrict attr,int *restrict prioceiling);	
Protocol	Defines how the scheduling and priority of the mutex is utilized.

pthread_mutex_t Attribute Object Function Prototypes #include <pthread.h>	Description
| ```
int
pthread_mutexattr_
setprotocol(pthread_
mutexattr_t * attr,int
protocol);

int
pthread_mutexattr_
getprotocol(const pthread_
mutexattr_t *restrict attr,
int *restrict protocol);
``` | Sets and returns the `protocol` of the mutex attrbute specified by the `attr`. `protocol` contains the value of the protocol attribute: <br><br> PTHREAD_PRIO_NONE <br><br> The priority and scheduling of the thread is not affected by the ownership of the mutex. <br><br> PTHREAD_PRIO_INHERIT <br><br> Thread blocking other threads of higher priority due to ownership of such a mutex execute at the highest priority of any of the threads waiting on any of the mutexes owned by this thread with such a protocol. <br><br> PTHREAD_PRIO_PROTECT <br><br> Threads owning such a mutex execute at the highest priority ceilings of all mutexes owned by this thread with such a protocol regardless of whether other threads are blocked on any of these mutexes. |
| **Shared** | Determines whether the mutex is for processes. |
| ```
int pthread_mutexattr_
setpshared(pthread_mutexattr_
t * attr,int pshared);

int pthread_mutexattr_
getpshared(const pthread_
mutexattr_t *restrict
attr,int *restrict pshared);
``` | Sets or returns the `shared` attribute of the mutex attribute object specified by the `attr`. `pshared` contains a value: <br><br> PTHREAD_PROCESS_SHARED <br><br> Permits a mutex to be shared by any threads that have access to the allocated memory of the mutex even if the threads are in different processes. <br><br> PTHREAD_PROCESS_PRIVATE <br><br> Mutex is shared between threads of the same process as the initialized mutex. |
| **Type** | Describes the behavior of the mutexes; determines whether deadlock is determined, error checking performed, and so on. |
| ```
int pthread_mutexattr_
settype(pthread_mutexattr_t *
attr,int type);

int pthread_mutexattr_
gettype(const pthread_
mutexattr_t *restrict
attr,int *restrict type);
``` | Sets and returns the `type` mutex attribute specified by the `attr`. `type` contains a value: <br><br> PTHREAD_MUTEX_DEFAULT <br><br> PTHREAD_MUTEX_RECURSIVE <br><br> PTHREAD_MUTEX_ERRORCHECK <br><br> PTHREAD_MUTEX_NORMAL |
```

To use a phtread mutex between threads of different processes requires the shared attribute. This attribute determines if the mutex is private or shared. Private mutexes are shared only among threads of the same process. They can be declared as global or a handle can be passed between threads. Shared mutexes, however, are used by any thread that has access to the mutex memory, and this includes threads of different processes. To do this, use `pthread_mutexattr_setshared()` and set the attribute to `PTHREAD_PROCESS_SHARED` as follows:

```
pthread_mutexattr_setpshared(&MutexAttr,PTHREAD_PROCESS_SHARED);
```

This allows `Mutex` to be shared by threads of different processes.

Figure 7-11 contrasts the idea of private and shared mutexes. If threads of different processes are to share a mutex, that mutex must be allocated in memory shared between processes. We discussed shared memory earlier in this chapter. Mutexes between processes can be used to protect critical sections that access files, pipes, shared memory, and devices.

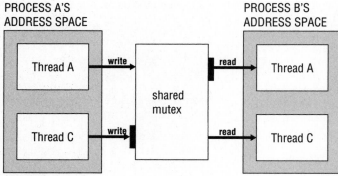

Figure 7-11

Using Mutex Semaphores to Manage Critical Sections

Mutexes can be used to manage critical sections of processes and threads in order to control race conditions. Mutexes avoid race conditions by serializing access to the critical section. Example 7-8 shows code for the new tasks defined in Listing 7-5. Mutexes are used to protect their critical sections.

Example 7-8

```
// Example 7-8 New code for tasks in Listing 7-5.

3   void *task1(void *X)
4   {
5       pthread_mutex_lock(&Mutex);
6       Answer = Answer * 32; //critical section
7       pthread_mutex_unlock(&Mutex);
8       cout << "thread A Answer = " << Answer << endl;
9
10  }
```

In Example 7-8, task1 now uses a mutex when it modifies the global variable Answer. In Line 8 the task sends the new value of Answer to cout. This is the critical section for the task. Now you can have each task execute the same code except each task sends to stout its thread name. So, now this is the output:

```
Before threads Answer = 10
thread 1 Answer = 320
thread 2 Answer = 160
thread 3 Answer = 165
After threads Answer = 165
```

Read-Write Locks

Mutex semaphores serialize the critical section. Only threads or processes that use the shared data are permitted to enter the critical section. With *read-write locks*, multiple threads are allowed to enter the critical section if they are to read the shared memory only. Therefore, any number of threads can own a read-write lock for reading, but if multiple threads are to write or modify the shared memory, only one thread is given access. No other threads are allowed to enter the critical section if one thread is given write access to the shared memory. If the application has multiple threads, mutex exclusion can be extreme. The performance of the application can benefit by allowing multiple reads. The POSIX standard defines a read-write lock of type pthread_rwlock_t. Similar to mutex semaphores, the read-write locks have the same operations. Table 7-9 lists the read-write lock operations.

Table 7-9

Read-Write Lock Operations	Function Prototypes #include <pthread.h>
Initialization	`int pthread_rwlock_init(pthread_rwlock_t *restrictrwlock, const pthread_rwlockattr_t *restrict attr);`
Request ownership	`#include <time.h>`
	`int pthread_rwlock_rdlock(pthread_rwlock_t *rwlock);`
	`int pthread_rwlock_wrlock(pthread_rwlock_t *rwlock);`
	`int pthread_rwlock_timedrdlock(pthread_rwlock_t *restrict rwlock, const struct timespec *restrict abs_timeout);`
	`int pthread_rwlock_timedwrlock(pthread_rwlock_t *restrict rwlock, const struct timespec *restrict abs_timeout);`
Release ownership	`int pthread_rwlock_unlock(pthread_rwlock_t *rwlock);`
Try ownership	`int pthread_rwlock_tryrdlock(pthread_rwlock_t *rwlock);`
	`int pthread_rwlock_trywrlock(pthread_rwlock_t *rwlock);`
Destruction	`int pthread_rwlock_destroy(pthread_rwlock_t *rwlock);`

The difference between regular mutexes and read-write mutexes is their locking request operations. Instead of one locking operation there are two:

```
pthread_rwlock_rdlock()
pthread_rwlock_wrlock()
```

pthread_rwlock_rdlock() obtains a read-lock and pthread_rwlock_wrlock() obtains a write lock. If a thread requests a read-lock, it is granted the lock as long as there are no threads that hold a write lock. If so, the calling thread is blocked. If a thread requests a write lock, it is granted as long as there are no threads that hold a read lock or a write lock. If so, the calling thread is blocked.

The read-write lock is of type pthread_rwlock_t. This type also has an attribute object that encapsulates its attributes. The attribute functions are listed in Table 7-10.

Table 7-10

pthread_rwlock_t Attribute Object Function Prototypes #include <pthread.h>	Description
int pthread_rwlockattr_init(pthread_rwlockattr_t * attr);	Initializes a read-write lock attribute object specified by attr with default values for all of the attributes defined by the implementation.
int pthread_rwlockattr_destroy(pthread_rwlockattr_t * attr);	Destroys a read-write lock attribute object specified by attr. Can be reinitialized by calling pthread_rwlockattr_init().
int pthread_rwlockattr_setpshared (pthread_rwlockattr_t * attr, int pshared);	Sets or returns the process shared attribute of the read-write lock attribute object specified by attr. The pshared parameter contains a value: PTHREAD_PROCESS_SHARED
int pthread_rwlockattr_getpshared(const pthread_rwlockattr_t * restrict attr, int *restrict pshared);	Permits a read-write lock to be shared by any threads that have access to the allocated memory of the read-write lock even if the threads are in different processes. PTHREAD_PROCESS_PRIVATE The read-write lock is shared between threads of the same process as the initialized rwlock.

The pthread_rwlock_t can be private between threads or shared between threads of different processes.

Using Read-Write Locks to Implement Access Policy

Read-write locks can be used to implement a CREW access policy. Several tasks can be granted concurrent reads, but only one task is granted write access. Using read-write locks can keep concurrent reads from occurring with the exclusive write. Example 7-9 contains tasks using read-write locks to protect critical sections.

Example 7-9

```
// Example 7-9 Threads using read-write locks.
//...

pthread_t ThreadA,ThreadB,ThreadC,ThreadD;
pthread_rwlock_t RWLock;

void producer1(void *X)
{
   pthread_rwlock_wrlock(&RWLock);
```

(continued)

Example 7-9 *(continued)*

```
    //critical section
    pthread_rwlock_unlock(&RWLock);
}

void producer2(void *X)
{
    pthread_rwlock_wrlock(&RWLock);
    //critical section
    pthread_rwlock_unlock(&RWLock);
}

void consumer1(void *X)
{
    pthread_rwlock_rdlock(&RWLock);
    //critical section
    pthread_rwlock_unlock(&RWLock);
}

void consumer2(void *X)
{
    pthread_rwlock_rdlock(&RWLock);
    //critical section
    pthread_rwlock_unlock(&RWLock);
}

int main(void)
{

    pthread_rwlock_init(&RWLock,NULL);
    //set mutex attributes
    pthread_create(&ThreadA,NULL,producer1,NULL);
    pthread_create(&ThreadB,NULL,consumer1,NULL);
    pthread_create(&ThreadC,NULL,producer2,NULL);
    pthread_create(&ThreadD,NULL,consumer2,NULL);
    //...
    return(0);
}
```

In Example 7-9 four threads are created. Two threads are producers, ThreadA and ThreadC, and two threads are consumers, ThreadB and ThreadD. All the threads have a critical section protected by the read-write lock, RWLock. ThreadB and ThreadD can enter their critical sections concurrently or serially, but neither thread can enter its critical section if either ThreadA or ThreadC is in its. ThreadA and ThreadC cannot enter their critical sections concurrently. Table 7-11 shows part of the decision table for this program.

Table 7-11

Thread A (writer)	ThreadB (reader)	ThreadC (writer)	ThreadD (reader)
N	N	N	Y
N	N	Y	N
N	Y	N	N
N	Y	N	Y
Y	N	N	N

Object-Oriented Mutex Class

Listing 7-11 is the declaration of an object-oriented mutex class.

Listing 7-11

```
// Listing 7-11 Declaration of an object-oriented mutex class.


1   #ifndef _PERMIT_H
2   #define_PERMIT_H
3   #include <pthread.h>
4   #include <time.h>
5   class permit{
6   protected:
7       pthread_mutex_t Permit;
8       pthread_mutexattr_t PermitAttr;
9   public:
10      permit(void);
11      bool available(void);
12      bool not_in_use(void);
13      bool checkAvailability(void);
14      bool  availableFor(int secs,int nanosecs);
15  };
16
17
18  #endif/* _PERMIT_H */
```

The permit class provides the basic operations for a mutex class. Listing 7-12 contains the definition of the permit class.

Listing 7-12

```
// Listing 7-12 Definition of the permit class.

1   #include "permit.h"
2
3
4   permit:: permit(void)
5   {
6      int AValue,MValue;
7      AValue = pthread_mutexattr_init(&PermitAttr);
8      MValue = pthread_mutex_init(&Permit,&PermitAttr);
9   }
10  bool permit::available(void)
11  {
12     int RC;
13     RC = pthread_mutex_lock(&Permit);
14     return(true);
15
16  }
17  bool permit::not_in_use(void)
18  {
19     int RC;
20     RC = pthread_mutex_unlock(&Permit);
21     return(true);
22
23  }
24  bool permit::checkAvailability(void)
25  {
26     int RC;
27     RC = pthread_mutex_trylock(&Permit);
28     return(true);
29  }
30  bool permit::availableFor(int secs,int nanosecs)
31  {
32     //...
33     struct timespec Time;
34     return(true);
35
36  }
```

Listing 7-12 shows only the basic operations. For the class to be a fully viable mutex class, error checking would have to be added, as was the case in the posix_queue class in Example 7-3 earlier in the chapter.

Here is Program Profile 7-5 for Listings 7-11 and 7-12.

Program Profile 7-5

Program Name:

permit.h (Listing 7-11)
permit.cc (Listing 7-12)

Description:

Listing 7-11 contains the header for `permit.h`, and Listing 7-12 contains `permit.cc`.

Libraries Required:

    libpthread

Headers Required:

    <pthread.h> <time.h> "permit.h"

Compile and Link Instructions:

    c++ -c permit.cc

Test Environment:

Solaris 10, gcc 3.4.3 and 3.4.6

Processors:

Opteron, UltraSparc T1

Execution Instructions:

N/A

Notes:

None

Condition Variables

A mutex allows tasks to synchronize by controlling access to the shared data. A *condition variable* allows tasks to synchronize on the value of the data. Condition variables are semaphores that signal when an event has occurred. There can be multiple processes or threads waiting for the signal once the event has taken place. Condition variables are typically used to synchronize the sequence of operations.

The condition variable is of type `pthread_cond_t`. These are the types of operations it can perform:

❏   Initialize

❏   Destroy

❏   Wait

❏   Timed wait

❏   Signal

❏   Broadcast

The initialize and destroy operations work in a similar manner to the other mutexes. The wait and timed wait operations suspend the caller until another process/thread signals on the condition variable. The timed wait allows you to specify a period of time the thread waits. If the condition is not signaled within the specified time, the thread is released. Condition variables are used with mutexes. If a thread or process attempts to lock a mutex, you know that it blocks until the mutex is released. Once unblocked, it obtains the mutex and then continues. If a condition variable is used, it must be associated with a mutex. A task waits for the signal, and another task signals or broadcasts that the signal has happened. Table 7-12 lists the basic operations defined for a condition variable.

Table 7-12

Condition Variables Operations	Function Prototypes/Macros#include <pthread.h>

Initialization	```int pthread_cond_init(pthread_cond_t *restrictcond, const pthread_condattr_t *restrict attr);```
	
	```pthread_cond_t cond = PTHREAD_COND_INITIALIZER;```

Signaling	```int pthread_cond_signal(pthread_cond_t *cond);```
	
	```int pthread_cond_broadcast(pthread_cond_t *cond);```

Destruction	```int pthread_cond_destroy(pthread_cond_t *cond);```

A task attempts to lock a mutex. If the mutex is already locked, then the task blocks. Once unblocked, the task releases the mutex while it waits on the signal for the condition variable. If the mutex is not locked, it releases the mutex and waits, indefinitely. With a timed wait, the task waits only for a specified period of time. If the time expires before the task is signaled, the function returns an error. It then acquires the mutex.

The signaling operation causes a task to signal to another thread or process that an event has occurred. If a task is waiting for a condition variable, it is unblocked and given the mutex. If there are several tasks waiting for the condition variable, only one is unblocked. The tasks wait in a queue and unblock according to the scheduling policy. The broadcast operation signals all the tasks waiting for the condition variable. If multiple tasks are unblocked, the tasks compete for the ownership of the mutex according to a scheduling policy. In contrast to the waiting operation, the signaling task is not required to own the mutex, although it is recommended.

The condition variable also has an attribute object. Table 7-13 lists the functions of the attribute object with a brief description.

Table 7-13

pthread_cond_t Attribute ObjectFunction Prototypes #include <pthread.h>	Description
int pthread_condattr_ init(pthread_condattr_t * attr);	Initializes a condition variable attribute object specified by attr with default values for all of the attributes defined by the implementation.
int pthread_condattr_ destroy(pthread_condattr_t * attr);	Destroys a condition variable attribute object specified by attr. Can be reinitialized by calling the pthread_condattr_init().
int pthread_condattr_ setpshared(pthread_condattr_t * attr,int pshared);	Sets or returns the process shared attribute of the condition variable attribute object specified by attr .pshared contains a value: PTHREAD_PROCESS_SHARED
int pthread_condattr_ getpshared(const pthread_ condattr_t * restrict attr,int *restrict pshared);	Permits a read-write lock to be shared by any threads that have access to the allocated memory of the condition variable even if the threads are in different processes. PTHREAD_PROCESS_PRIVATE The condition variable is shared between threads of the same process as the initialized cond.
int pthread_condattr_ setclock(pthread_condattr_t * attr,clockid_t clock_id); int pthread_condattr_getclock(const pthread_condattr_t * restrict attr,clockid_t *restrict clock_id);	Sets and returns the clock attribute for the condition variable attribute object specified by attr. clock is the clock id of the clock used to measure the timeout service of the pthread_cond_timedwait() function. The default value of clock is the system clock.

Using Condition Variables to Manage Synchronization Relationships

The condition variable and the mutex can be used to implement the synchronization relationships mentioned earlier in the chapter:

❑ Start-to-start (SS)

❑ Finish-to-start (FS)

❑ Start-to-finish (SF)

❑ Finish-to-finish (FF)

These relationships can exist between threads of the same processes or different processes. Listing 7-13 contains a program demonstrating how to implement SF synchronization relationship. There are two mutexes used in each example. One mutex is used to synchronize access to the shared data, and the other mutex is used with the condition variable.

Listing 7-13

```
// Listing 7-13 SF synchronization relationship implemented with
// condition variables and mutexes.

1   using namespace std;
2   #include <iostream>
3   #include <pthread.h>
4
5   int Number;
6   pthread_t ThreadA,ThreadB;
7   pthread_mutex_t Mutex,EventMutex;
8   pthread_cond_t Event;
9
10  void *worker1(void *X)
11  {
12      for(int Count = 1;Count < 10;Count++){
13          pthread_mutex_lock(&Mutex);
14          Number++;
15          pthread_mutex_unlock(&Mutex);
16          cout << "worker1: Number = " << Number << endl;
17          if(Number == 7){
18              pthread_cond_signal(&Event);
19          }
20      }
21
22      return(0);
23  }
24
25  void *worker2(void *X)
26  {
27      pthread_mutex_lock(&EventMutex);
28      pthread_cond_wait(&Event,&EventMutex);
29      pthread_mutex_unlock(&EventMutex);
30      for(int Count = 1;Count < 10;Count++){
31          pthread_mutex_lock(&Mutex);
32          Number = Number + 20;
33          cout << "worker2: Number = " << Number << endl;
34          pthread_mutex_unlock(&Mutex);
35
36      }
37
38      return(0);
39  }
40
41
42  int main(int argc, char *argv[])
43  {
44      pthread_mutex_init(&Mutex,NULL);
```

```
45      pthread_mutex_init(&EventMutex,NULL);
46      pthread_cond_init(&Event,NULL);
47      pthread_create(&ThreadA,NULL,worker1,NULL);
48      pthread_create(&ThreadB,NULL,worker2,NULL);
49
50      pthread_join(ThreadA,NULL);
51      pthread_join(ThreadB,NULL);
52
53      return (0);
54  }
```

In Listing 7-13, the SF synchronization relationship is implemented. ThreadB cannot start until ThreadA finishes. ThreadA signals to ThreadB once Number has a value of 7. It can then continue execution until finished. ThreadB cannot start its computation until it gets a signal from ThreadA. Both use the EventMutex with the condition variable Event. Mutex is used to synchronize write access to the shared data Number. A task can use several mutexes to synchronize different critical sections and synchronize different events. These techniques can easily be used to synchronize order of execution between processes.

Here is Program Profile 7-6 for Listing 7-13.

Program Profile 7-6

Program Name:

program7-13.cc. (Listing 7-13)

Description:

program7-13.cc (Listing 7-13) has a SF synchronization relationship. ThreadB cannot start until ThreadA finishes. ThreadA signals to ThreadB once Number has a value of 7. It can then continue execution until finished. ThreadB cannot start its computation until it gets a signal from ThreadA. Both use the EventMutex with the condition variable Event. Mutex is used to synchronize write access to the shared data Number. ThreadA and ThreadB send Number to stout. ThreadA adds 1 to the value of Number and ThreadB adds 20 to Number at each iteration through the loop.

Libraries Required:

libpthread

Headers Required:

<iostream> <pthread.h>

Compile and Link Instructions:

c++ -o program7-13 program7-13.cc -lpthread

Test Environment:

Solaris 10, gcc 3.4.3 and 3.4.6

Processors:

Opteron, UltraSparc T1

Execution Instructions:

`./program7-13`

Notes:

None

Thread-Safe Data Structures

With the synchronization primitives discussed in this chapter, it is possible to build complex data structures that are safe for concurrent use by multiple threads. A data structure can contain a mutex class used to protect access to the internal data.

Thread Strategy Approaches

The thread strategies determine the approach that can be employed when threading your application. The approach determines how the threaded application delegates its works to the tasks and how communication is performed. A strategy supplies a structure and approach to threading and helps in determining the access policies.

The purpose of a thread is to perform work on behalf of the process. If a process has multiple threads, each thread performs some subtask as part of what the application is to do. Threads are given work according to a specific strategy or approach. If the application models some procedure or entity, then the approach selected should reflect that model.

The common models are as follows:

❑   Delegation (boss-worker)

❑   Peer-to-peer

❑   Pipeline

❑   Producer-consumer

Each model has its own Work Breakdown Structure (WBS). WBS determines which piece of software does what, for example, who is responsible for thread creation and under what conditions threads are created.

WBS is discussed in more detail in Chapter 3.

With a centralized approach there is a single process/thread that creates other processes/threads and delegates work to each. An assembly line approach performs work at different stages on the same data. Once these processes/threads are created, they can perform the same task on different data sets, different tasks on the same data set, or different tasks on different data sets. Threads can be categorized to perform only certain types of tasks. There can be a group of threads that only perform computations while others perform process input or produce output.

It is also important to remember that what is to be modeled may not be homogeneous throughout the application or the process. Therefore, it may be necessary to mix models. One model may be embedded in another model. With the pipeline model, a thread or process may create other threads or processes and utilize a delegation model locally in order to process the data at that stage.

Delegation Model

In the *delegation* model, a single thread (boss) creates other threads (workers) and assigns each a task. It may be necessary for the boss thread to wait until each worker thread completes its task before it can continue its executing its code. Its code may be based on the results of the worker thread. The boss thread delegates the task each worker thread is to perform by specifying a function. As each worker is assigned its task, it is the responsibility of each worker thread to perform that task and produce output or synchronize with the boss or other thread to produce output.

The boss thread can create threads as a result of requests made to the system. The processing of each type of request can be delegated to a thread worker. The boss thread executes an event loop. As events occur, thread workers are created and assigned their duties. A new thread is created for every new request that enters the system. Using this approach may cause the process to exceed its resources or thread limits. A different approach is to have a boss thread create a pool of threads that are reassigned new requests. The boss thread creates a number of threads during initialization, and then each thread is suspended until a request is added to their queue. As requests are placed in the queue, the boss thread signals a worker thread to process the request. When the thread completes, it dequeues the next request. If none are available, the thread suspends itself until the boss signals to the thread more work is available in the queue. If all the worker threads are to share a single queue, then the threads process only certain types of request. The results from each thread are placed in another queue. The primary purpose of the boss thread is to:

1. Create all the threads
2. Place work in the queue
3. Awaken worker threads when work is available

The worker threads:

1. Check the request in the queue
2. Perform the assigned task
3. Suspend itself if no work is available

All the workers and the boss are executing concurrently. Example 7-10 contains pseudocode for the event loop for the delegation model for this approach.

Example 7-10

```
// Example 7-10 Skeleton program for delegation model where boss creates a
// pool of threads.

pthread_t Thread[N]

// boss thread
{

    pthread_create(&(Thread[1]...taskX...);
    pthread_create(&(Thread[2]...taskY...);
    pthread_create(&(Thread[3]...taskZ...);
    //...
    pthread_create(&(Thread[N]...?...);

    loop while(Request Queue is not empty
       get request
       classify request
       switch(request type)
       {
           case X :
                   enqueue request to XQueue
                   broadcast to thread XQueue request available

           case Y :
                   enqueue request to YQueue
                   broadcast to thread YQueue request available

           case Z :
                   enqueue request to ZQueue
                   broadcast to thread ZQueue request available
            //...
       }

    end loop
}

void *taskX(void *X)
{
   loop
       waiting for signal
       when signaled
       loop while XQueue is not empty
          lock mutex
          dequeue request
    release mutex
          process request
          set mutex
          enqueue results
          release queue
       end loop
   until done
}
```

```
void *taskY(void *X)
{
   loop
       waiting for signal
       when signaled
       loop while YQueue is not empty
           lock mutex
           dequeue request
     release mutex
           process request
           set mutex
           enqueue results
           release queue
       end loop
   until done
}

void *taskZ(void *X)
{
   loop
       waiting for signal
       when signaled
       loop while ZQueue is not empty
           lock mutex
           dequeue request
     release mutex
           process request
           set mutex
           enqueue results
           release queue
       end loop
   until done
}

//...
```

In Example 7-10, the boss thread creates *N* number of threads. Each task is associated with processing a request type denoted by taskX, taskY, and taskZ. In the event loop, the boss thread dequeues a request from the request queue, determines the request type, and then enqueues the request to the appropriate request queue. It broadcasts to the threads a request is available in a particular queue. The functions also contain an event loop. The thread is suspended until it receives a signal from the boss that there is a request in its queue. Once awakened, in the inner loop, the thread processes all the requests in the queue until it is empty. It removes a request from the queue, processes it, and then places the results in the result queue. A mutex is used for the input and output queues.

Peer-to-Peer Model

Whereas the delegation model has a boss thread that delegates tasks to worker threads, in the *peer-to-peer* model all the threads have an equal working status. There is a single thread that initially creates all the threads needed to perform all the tasks, but that thread is still considered a worker thread. It does no delegation of work. The worker (peers) threads have more local responsibility. The peer threads can process requests from a single input stream shared by all the threads, or each thread may have its own input stream for which it is responsible. The input can also be stored in a file or database. The peer threads may have to communicate and share resources. Example 7-11 contains the pseudocode for the peer-to-peer model.

Example 7-11

```
// Example 7-11  Skeleton program using the peer-to-peer model.
//...
pthread_t Thread[N]

// initial thread
{

    pthread_create(&(Thread[1]...taskX...);
    pthread_create(&(Thread[2]...taskY...);
    pthread_create(&(Thread[3]...taskZ...);
    //...
    pthread_create(&(Thread[N]...?...);
}

void *taskX(void *X)
{
    loop while (Type XRequests are available)
         set mutex
         extract Request
         unlock mutex
         process request
         lock mutex
         enqueue results
         unlock mutex
    end loop
    return(NULL)
}

//...
```

Producer-Consumer Model

In the *producer-consumer* model, there is a producer thread that *produces* data to be *consumed* by the consumer thread. The data is stored in a block of memory shared between the producer and consumer threads. The producer thread must produce data; then the consumer threads retrieve it. If the producer thread deposits data at a much faster rate than the consumer thread consumes it, then the producer thread may at several times overwrite previous results before the consumer thread retrieves it. On the other hand, if the consumer thread retrieves data at a much faster rate than the producer deposits data then the consumer thread may retrieve identical data or attempt to retrieve data not yet deposited. This process, like the others, requires synchronization. We discussed read-write locks earlier in this chapter and included an example of producers that write and consumers that read. Example 7-12 contains the pseudocode for the producer-consumer model. The producer-consumer model is also called the client-server model for large-scale programs and applications.

Example 7-12

```
// Example 7-12 Skeleton program using the producer-consumer model.

/...

// initial thread
{
    pthread_create(&(Thread[1]...producer...);
    pthread_create(&(Thread[2]...consumer...);
    //...
}


void *producer(void *X)
{
    loop
       perform work
         lock mutex
          enqueue data
         unlock mutex
          signal consumer
       //...
    until done
}

void *consumer(void *X)
{
    loop
       suspend until signaled
       loop while(Data Queue not empty)
           lock mutex
            dequeue data
           unlock mutex
            perform work
           lock mutex
           enqueue results
           unlock mutex
        end loop
    until done
}
```

Pipeline Model

The *pipeline* model is characterized by an assembly-line approach in which a stream of items is processed in stages. At each stage, work is performed on a unit of input by a thread. When the unit has been through all the stages in the pipeline, then the processing of the input has been completed and exits the system. This approach allows multiple inputs to be processed simultaneously. Once data has been processed at a certain stage, it is ready to process the next data in the stream. Each thread is responsible for producing its interim results or output and making them available to the next stage in the pipeline. The last stage or thread produces the result of the pipeline.

As the input moves down the pipeline, it may be necessary to buffer units of input at certain stages as threads process previous input. This may cause a slowdown in the pipeline if a particular stage's processing is slower than other stages. This may cause a backlog. To prevent backlog, it may be necessary for that stage to create additional threads to process incoming input. This is a case of mixed models. At this stage in the pipeline, the thread may create a delegation model to process its input and prevent backlogs.

The stages of work in a pipeline should be balanced so that one stage does not take more time than the other stages. Work should be evenly distributed throughout the pipeline. More stages and therefore more threads may also be added to the pipeline. This also prevents backlog. Example 7-13 contains the pseudocode for the pipeline model.

Example 7-13

```
// Example 7-13 Skeleton program using the pipeline model.
//...

pthread_t Thread[N]
Queues[N]

// initial thread
{
    place all input into stage1's queue
    pthread_create(&(Thread[1]...stage1...);
    pthread_create(&(Thread[2]...stage2...);
    pthread_create(&(Thread[3]...stage3...);
    //...
  }

void *stageX(void *X)
{
    loop
    suspend until input unit is in queue
    loop while XQueue is not empty
        lock mutex
        dequeue input unit
        unlock mutex
        perform stage X processing
        enqueue input unit into next stage's queue
      end loop
    until done
    return(NULL)
}

//...
```

SPMD and MPMD for Threads

In concurrency models, the threads may be performing the same task over and over again on different data sets or may be assigned different tasks to be performed on different data sets. Figure 7-12 shows the different models of parallelism. Concurrency models utilize *Single Instruction Multiple Data (SIMD)* or *Multiple Programs Multiple Data (MPMD)*. These are two models of parallelism that classify programs by instruction and data streams. They can be used to describe the type of work that the thread models are implementing in parallel. For purposes of this discussion, MPMD is better defined as *Multiple Threads Multiple Data (MTMD)*. This model describes a system that executes different threads processing different sets of data or data streams. In Figure 7-12 (a) you can see that thread 1 processes dataset 1, and thread 2 processes dataset 2. Likewise, SIMD (also known as *Single Program Multiple Data or SIMD*) for purposes of this discussion is better redefined as *Single Thread Multiple Data (STMD)*. This model describes a system that executes a single thread that processes different sets of data or data streams. In Figure 7-12 (b), thread 1 executes routine A and processes dataset 1 and thread 2 also executes routine A but processes dataset 2. This means several identical threads executing the same routine are given different sets of data to process. *Multiple Threads Single Data (MTSD)* describes a system where different instructions are applied to the same dataset. In Figure 7-12 (c), thread 1, which executes routine A, and thread 2, which executes routine B, both process the same dataset, dataset 1. *Single Instruction Single Data (SISD)* describes a system in which a single instruction processes a single dataset. In Figure 7-12 (d), thread 1 executes routine A, which sequentially processes datasets.

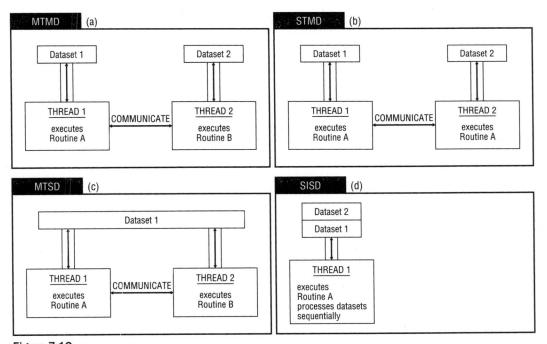

Figure 7-12

The delegation and peer-to-peer models can both use STMD or MTMD models of parallelism. As described, the pool of threads can execute different routines processing different sets of data. This approach utilizes the MTMD model. The pool of threads can also be given the same routine to execute. The requests or jobs submitted to the system could be different sets of data instead of different tasks. In this case, there would be a set of threads implementing the same instructions but on different sets of data, thus utilizing STMD. The peer-to-peer model can be threads executing the same or different tasks. Each thread can have its own data stream or several files of data that each thread is to process. The pipeline model uses the MTMD model of parallelism. At each stage, different processing is performed, so multiple input units are at different stages of completion. The pipeline metaphor would be useless if at each stage the same processing was performed.

Decomposition and Encapsulation of Work

Now we have discussed communication and cooperation between concurrently executing tasks, whether they are processes or threads. We have discussed communication relationships and the mechanisms of communication with IPC and ITC. We have also covered task cooperation, memory access models, and synchronization relationships. Data and communication synchronization was also covered along with the many techniques that can be used to avoid race conditions. Concurrency models can be used to layout an approach for communication and delegation of work. Now we want to use these techniques and models to do some work.

Problem Statement

We have a multitude of text files that requires filtering. The text files have to be filtered in order to be used in our Natural Language Processing (NLP) system. We want to remove a specified group of tokens or characters from multiple text files, characters such as [, . ? !], and we want this done in real time.

The objects that can be immediately identified are:

❑ Text files

❑ The characters to be removed

❑ The resulting filtered files

Strategy

We have over 70 files to process. Each file can contains hundreds or thousands of lines of text. To simplify this, we have a set of characters we want to remove. We want to be able specify the name of the file, have the program filter out all the unwanted characters, have it create the new filtered file, and then be able to give the program the next file. With the guess_it example we used earlier in the book, an approach to break down the problem into smaller tasks was used. The task was to search a file for a code. The file was very large with over four million codes to search. So the file was broken down into smaller files and the search was performed on the smaller files. Since there was a time constraint, the searches had to be performed in parallel.

Here with this problem the filtered files have to be the same as the original files with the unwanted characters removed. The text cannot be altered in anyway. Although deconstructing the files into smaller files can be done, reconstructing them is not something we want to do. So what approach should we take? Keep in mind these are the goals:

1. Removing all the unwanted characters has to be performed

2. Having the work done in real-time

3. Keeping the integrity of the contents of each file

We can remove characters from the whole file or remove characters from each line at a time. Here are the possibilities:

- ❑ **Approach 1**: Search the file for a character. When it is, found remove it, and then search for the next occurrence of the character. When all of those characters have been removed, search the file again for the next unwanted character. Repeat this for each file. The postcondition is met because we are working on the original file and removing the unwanted characters from it.

- ❑ **Approach 2**: Remove all occurrences of a single character from each file then repeat this process for each unwanted character. The postcondition is met in the same way as in Approach 1.

- ❑ **Approach 3**: Read in a single line of text, remove an unwanted character. Go through the same line of text and remove the next unwanted character, and so on. When all characters have been removed from the line of text, write the filtered line of text to the new file. This is done for each file. The postcondition is met because we are restructuring a new file as we go. As a line is processed, it is written to the new file.

- ❑ Approach 4: Same as Approach 3, but we remove only a single unwanted character from a line of text and then write it to a file or container. Once the whole file has been processed, it is reprocessed for the next character. When the last character has been removed, the file has been filtered. If the text is in a container, it can now be written to a file. This is repeated for each file. The container becomes important in restructuring the file.

Observation

When considering each approach, we see there are a number of passes through a file or through a single line of text. This is what has to be looked at to see how it affects performance. This filtering has to be done in real time. For Approaches 1 and 2, the file is reentered for every occurrence of the character. There is a pass through the file for each unwanted character. There are four unwanted characters. An interim result is a whole file in which a single character has been removed, then two, and so on. With Approaches 3 and 4, a single line of text is filtered. So, the interim results are a single line of text. In Approach 3, a single line of text can be completed quickly. Depending of what type of processing is to be performed, a single line of text may be useful or it may not be. Waiting for a whole file is a longer wait. What is also obvious in each approach is that, whether it is a file or a single line of text you are dealing with, they are not dependent tasks; a file can be processed independently from other files. This is also true for a single line of text. But with a single line of text (remembering that the integrity of the file has to be maintained), it has to be performed in the order in which the line appears in the file. So, the lines of text have to be filtered in order: line 1, line 2, line 3, and so forth.

Problem and Solution

We will use Approach 3. Based on the observations stated, we have concluded that this approach will give us results more quickly, even for large sets of data, and produce interim results. Now we can consider the concurrency model. The model helps determine the communication and type of cooperation to be used to solve this problem. A single line should start being processed before another line is attempted. This suggests a pipeline model. At each stage, the same single line of text and a single unwanted character are to be removed. At the end of the stages, a single line of text is completely filtered. It can then be written to a file. This is to be done very quickly, and the file keeps its integrity. Queues should be used because they have First-In, First-Out access. This ensures that the lines of text stay in order.

Each stage has an input queue and an output queue. The input queue is the output queue of the previous stage. Once the text has been processed, it is written to a queue, and the next stage retrieves the line of text from the queue. Of course, this requires synchronization. A task retrieves the text from the queue after the previous stage has placed the text in the queue. Since there are only two tasks involved in sharing any queue, a mutex (mutual exclusion) works fine. We can use the `permit` class from Listing 7-10 and Listing 7-11.

What are the communication and cooperation requirements in this solution:

❏ Queues require synchronization.

❏ EREW access policy is needed.

❏ Main agent populates the first queue and then creates the threads (one for each stage).

❏ The input and output queues and a mutex are passed to the stages.

Simple Agent Model Example of a Pipeline

We can discuss the solution of this problem as an agent model. Each stage is going to be managed by an agent. The queues are lists that contain lines of text from a file. For each list, the agent is given a permit to access the list. The new objects in this solution are now agents, lists, and permits. Figure 7-13 shows the class relationship diagram for this solution.

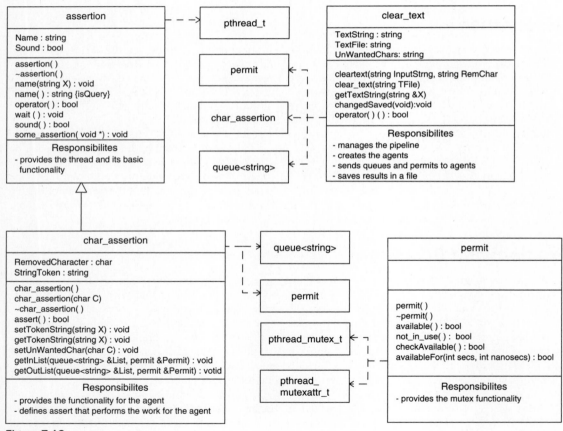

Figure 7-13

Example 7-14 is the main line for the simple agent solution.

Example 7-14

```
//Example 7-14 The main line for character removal agent.

1   #include "clear_text.h"
2   #include <iostream>
3
4
5   int main(int argc, char** argv) {
6
7      if(argc != 2){
8         cerr << "usage:  characters_removed FileName:" << endl;
9         exit(0);
10     }
11     clear_text  CharactersRemoved(argv[1]);
12     if(CharactersRemoved()){
13        CharactersRemoved.changesSaved();
14        return (1);
15     }
16     return(0);
17  }
18
```

The `CharactersRemoved` object of type `clear_text` is the main agent. It manages the pipeline. The name of the file to be filtered is the second command-line argument. `CharactersRemoved()` executes the pipeline. If it returns false, this means that one of the agents failed, and the unwanted character that was to be removed by the agent may not have been removed from the file or some of the lines of text. `changesSaved()` gets the results from the last lists (which contains all the filtered lines of text) and writes them to a file.

Example 7-15 contains the `operator()` method.

Example 7-15

```
//Example 7-15 The pipeline method for the clear_text object.

1   bool clear_text::operator()(void)
2   {
3      bool Sound = true;
4      char_assertion  CharacterRemoved[4];
5      CharacterRemoved[0].setUnWantedChar(',');
6      CharacterRemoved[1].setUnWantedChar('.');
7      CharacterRemoved[2].setUnWantedChar('?');
8      CharacterRemoved[3].setUnWantedChar('\'');
9
10     for(int N = 0; N < 3;N++)
11     {
12        CharacterRemoved[N].getInList(TextQ[N],Permit[N]);
13        CharacterRemoved[N].getOutList(TextQ[N+1],Permit[N+1]);
14     }
15
```

(continued)

Example 7-15 *(continued)*

```
16      for(int N = 0; N < 4; N++)
17      {
18          CharacterRemoved[N]();
19      }
20
21      CharacterRemoved[3].wait();
22      CharacterRemoved[0].wait();
23      CharacterRemoved[1].wait();
24      CharacterRemoved[2].wait();
25
26      for(int N = 0; N < 4;N++)
27      {
28          Sound = Sound * CharacterRemoved[N].sound();
29      }
30      return(Sound);
31
32  }
```

In Example 7-15, in Line #4 four `char_assertion` agents are declared. Each is passed the unwanted character it is to remove from the file. In Lines 10–14, the `for` loop passes to each agent the source list and its `permit` and the output list with its `permit`. The `for` loop in Lines 16–19 actually starts the agents working.

`operator()` is defined in the base class `assertion` as well as `wait()` and `sound()`. Example 7-16 contains `operator()`, `wait()`, and `sound()` as defined in the `assertion` class.

Example 7-16

```
//Example 7-16 The methods defined in the base class assertion.

1   bool assertion::operator()(void)
2   {
3       pthread_create(&Tid,NULL,some_assertion,this);
4       return(Sound);
5   }
6
7   void assertion::wait(void)
8   {
9       pthread_join(Tid,NULL);
10  }
11
12
13  bool assertion::sound(void)
14  {
15      return(Sound);
16  }
```

In Example 7-16, you see that the `assertion` class creates the threads for the `char_assertion` agents in Line 3. The threads/agents are to execute the `some_assertion` function. The assertion class is an improved version of the `user_thread` class in Chapter 6 and `some_assertion` is the `do_something` method.

Example 7-17 contains the `some_assertion` method from the `assertion` class and Example 7-18 contains the `assert` method from the `char_assertion` class.

Example 7-17

//Example 7-17 The some_assertion method defined in the base class assertion.

```
1   void *  some_assertion (void * X)
2   {
3
4       assertion *Assertion;
5       Assertion = static_cast<assertion *>(X);
6       if(Assertion->assert()){
7           Assertion->Sound = true;
8       }
9       else{
10              Assertion->Sound = false;
11      }
12      return(NULL);
13
14
15  }
```

Example 7-18

//Example 7-18 The assert method defined in the class char_assertion.

```
1   bool char_assertion::assert(void)
2   {
3
4
5       if(PermitIn.available()){
6           TokenString = ListIn.front();
7           ListIn.pop();
8           remove(TokenString.begin(),TokenString.end(),RemovedCharacter);
9           PermitIn.not_in_use();
10       }
11      if(PermitOut.available()){
12          ListOut.push(TokenString);
13          PermitOut.not_in_use();
14      }
15
16      return(true);
17  }
```

In Example 7-17, on Line 6, assert() is called. This method is where the agent does the work of its stage in the pipeline. Example 7-18 contains the definition for assert(), the work of the agent. If PermitIn is available for ListIn list, which is the source of strings of text, the string is popped, the unwanted character is removed in Line 8, and PermitIn is released. Now the new string is to be pushed on ListOut if PermitOut is available.

This example shows the use of a concurrency model (namely a pipeline) utilizing a MTSD. A single string of text is processed at each stage of the pipeline where a single unwanted character is removed from the string. Each thread at a stage can be assigned to its own processor core. This is a simple process, removing a single character from a string, but the process described (from determining the problem, decomposition of the problem, and determining an approach) can be used to solve problems on a larger scale. But we can do better. Here we have described a task-oriented software decomposition to multicore programming. In Chapter 8, we discuss a declarative and predicate-oriented decomposition for problems on a larger scale with massive cores to manage.

Summary

In this chapter, we discussed managing synchronized communication between concurrent tasks as well as synchronizing access to global data, resources, and task execution. We also discussed concurrency models that can be used to delegate the work and communication between concurrently executing tasks running on multiple processor cores. This chapter discussed the following points:

- ❑ Dependency relationships can be used to examine which tasks are dependent on other tasks for communication or cooperation. Dependency relationships are concerned with coordinating communication and synchronization between these concurrent tasks. If communication between dependent tasks is not appropriately designed, then data race conditions can occur.

- ❑ Interprocess Communications (IPC) are techniques and mechanisms that facilitate communication between processes. When a process sends data to another process or makes another process aware of an event by means of operating system APIs, it requires IPC. The POSIX queue, shared memory, pipes, mutexes/semaphores, and condition variables are examples of IPC.

- ❑ Interthread Communications (ITC) are techniques that facilitate communication between threads that reside in the same address space of their process, The most important issues that have to be dealt with concerning ITC are data races and indefinite postponement.

- ❑ You can synchronize access to data and resources and task execution. Task synchronization is required when a thread is in its critical sections. Critical sections can be managed by PRAM models such as EREW and CREW. There are four basic synchronization relationships between any two tasks in a single process or between any two processes within a single application.

- ❑ Synchronization mechanisms are used for both processes and threads. These mechanisms can be used to prevent race conditions and deadlocks between multiple tasks by implementing the synchronization access policies using semaphores and mutexes, read-write locks, and condition variables.

- ❑ The thread strategies determine the approach that can be employed when threading your application. The approach determines how the threaded application delegates its work to the tasks and how communication is performed. A strategy supplies a structure and approach to threading and helps in determining the access policies.

In the next chapter, we discuss the Parallel Application Design Layers (PADL). PADL is a five-layer analysis model used in the design of software that requires some parallel programming. It is used to help organize the software decomposition effort. PADL is meant to be used during the requirements analysis and software design activities of the Software Development Life Cycle (SDLC), which is also covered in Chapter 8.

8

PADL and PBS: Approaches to Application Design

Even if parallel processing is done on a project, there really isn't much change in actual processing efficiency — there's just a diversity of output.

—**Shirow Masamune,** *Ghost in the Shell: Man-Machine Interface*

Chapter 4 illustrated the role the operating system plays for applications that have a requirement for parallelism or multicore support. In it, we explained how the processes and kernel threads are the only execution units that the operating system schedules for processor execution. In Chapters 5 and 6, we explained how processes and threads are created and are used to gain access to Chip Multiprocessors (CMPs), but processes and threads are relatively low-level constructs. The question remains, "How do you approach application design when there is a concurrency requirement or when the design model has components that can operate in parallel?" In Chapter 7, we explored mechanisms that support Interprocess Communication (IPC): mutexes, semaphores, and synchronization. These are also low-level constructs that require intimate knowledge of operating-system-level Application Program Interfaces (APIs) and System Program Interfaces (SPIs) in order to program correctly.

So far we have discussed only scenarios that involved dual or quad core processors. But the trend in CMP production will soon replace dual and quad core processors. The UltraSparc T1, which we introduced in Chapter 2, has eight cores on a single chip with four hardware threads for each core. This makes it possible to have 32 processes or threads executing concurrently. Currently dual and quad core CMPs are the most commonly found configurations. However, dual and quad core configurations will soon be replaced by octa-core CMPs like the UltraSparc T1. So, how do you think about application design when 32 hardware threads are available? What if there are 64, 128, or 256 processors on a single CMP? How do you think about software decomposition as the numbers of available hardware threads approach the hundreds? This chapter turns to those questions by discussing:

- ❑ A design approach for applications to run on multiple processor cores
- ❑ The PADL and PBS approach to application design
- ❑ Task-oriented software decompositions and declarative and predicate-oriented decompositions
- ❑ Knowledge sources and multiagent architectures
- ❑ Intel Thread Building Blocks (TBB) and the new C++ standard that supports concurrency

Designing Applications for Massive Multicore Processors

So, how do you approach process management or IPC in application design if you can have 100s or 1000s of concurrently executing processes or threads? Considerations of large numbers of concurrently executing tasks during application design can be daunting. And we use the term *application design* here loosely. It is a loaded term that means different things to different types and levels of software developers. It means one thing for system-level programmers and another for application-level programmers. Further, there are all sorts of classifications for software and computer applications. Consider a small excerpt taken from The Association of Computing Machinery (ACM) Computing Classification System (CCS) in Table 8-1

Table 8-1

ACM Classification #	Software	Multiuser	Single User
H.4.1	Office automation	Groupware	Word processing
		Project management	Spreadsheets
		Time management	
H.4.3	Communication applications	Teleconferencing	Electronic mail
		Videoconferencing	Information browser
		Computer conferencing	
D.2.2	Software development tools	Software libraries	Editors
		Source code maintenance	Compilers
D.2.3	Coding tools and techniques		Linkers
D.2.4	Software reliability verification		
I.3.3	Picture/image generation	Advance visualization	Digitizing and scanning
		Virtual environments	Graphics packages
I.3.4	Graphics utilities	Virtual reality systems	Animation
I.3.5	3D graphics		3D rendering

This classification breakdown looks at software categories from Sections H and D from the ACM's CCS. These categories are then further grouped by multiuser and single user. In multiuser applications, two or more users can access some feature(s) of a software application simultaneously. As can be seen from Table 8-1, multiuser applications come in all shapes and sizes ranging from intranet videoconferencing to Internet-based source code management applications. Many database servers, web servers, e-mail servers, and so on are good examples of multiuser applications. Further, while a single-user application doesn't have to worry about multiple users accessing some feature, the single-user application might be required to perform multiple tasks concurrently. Single-user multimedia applications that require synchronization of audio and video are good examples.

Also, look at the diversity of the applications in Table 8-1. Software developers in each of these domains may approach application design differently. One thing that most of the application classifications in Table 8-1 will definitely have in common in the future is that they will be running on medium- to large-scale CMPs. The classification in Table 8-1 is a small excerpt from a large taxonomy that the ACM has on software and computing classifications. In addition to being only a small excerpt, it is only a single view from the multiple views that can be found in the ACM CCS. Table 8-2 contains the CCS breakdown of computer applications by area. This breakdown is taken from Section J of the CCS.

Table 8-2

(J.1) Administrative Data Processing	(J.2) Physical Sciences and Engineering
1. Business	1. Aerospace
2. Education	2. Archaeology
3. Financial	3. Astronomy
4. Government	4. Chemistry
5. Law	5. Earth and atmospheric sciences
6. Manufacturing	6. Electronics
7. Marketing	7. Engineering
8. Military	8. Mathematics and statistics
	9. Physics
(J.3) Life and Medical Sciences	**(J.4) Social and Behavioral Sciences**
1. Biology and genetics	1. Economics
2. Health	2. Psychology
3. Medical information systems	3. Sociology

(Continued)

(J.5) Arts and Humanities	(J.6) Computer-Aided Engineering
1. Architecture	1. Computer-aided design
2. Arts, fine and performing	2. Computer-aided manufacturing
3. Fine arts	
4. Language translation	
5. Linguistics	
6. Literature	
7. Music	
8. Performing arts	

As you consider software development approaches from the various areas shown in Table 8-2, it is clear that the phrase *application design* summons very different notions for different groups. If you add to the discussion multiprocessor computers and parallel programming techniques, then you have clarified at least the problem of which approach to take toward application design.

So, as you look at the applications in Table 8-1, it might be easier to visualize how to break up multiuser applications than it is to decompose single-user applications. However, decomposition complexity and task management are still issues once the number of available cores passes a certain threshold. Procedural bottom-up approaches to threading and multiprocessing become increasingly difficult as the number of available cores increases. As a developer, you will soon have cheap and widely available CMPs that can support any level of parallelism that you may need. But the question remains, "How do you approach multicore application design without getting overwhelmed by the available parallelism?"

It should be clear from the excerpt of classifications shown in Table 8-1 and the diversity of computer applications shown in Table 8-2 that there is no single tool, library, vendor solution, product, or cookbook recipe that will serve as the answer to that question. Instead, we share with you some of the approaches that we use as working software engineers. While our approaches are not meant to be one-size-fit-all, they are generic enough to be applied to many of the areas shown in Tables 8-1 and 8-2. They are for the most part platform- and vendor-neutral, or at the very least they assume ISO standard C++ implementations and POSIX-compliant operating environments. The techniques given in this chapter are not product or vendor driven. One reason for this is that no single vendor or product has produced a *magic bullet* solution, allowing all applications to exploit single chip multiprocessors.

Instead, as you have noticed, we focus on a paradigm shift for parallel programming that involves movement away from imperative task-oriented software decompositions to declarative and predicate-oriented decompositions. Our advice to you comes from a combination of our experience as software engineers and from many basic notions found in Object-Oriented software engineering and logic programming. You might be interested to know that the techniques, models, and approaches that we present in this chapter rely on the foundations of modal logic, its extensions and on situational calculus

[Fagin et al., 1995]. Chapters 5, 6, and 7 include a discussion of low-level operating system primitives and POSIX APIs that are primarily used in conjunction with imperative approaches to parallel programming. Our intention is to show that these same low-level primitives can (and ultimately must) be used with declarative approaches to parallel programming.

Now, in this chapter, we explain how to approach the process of application design when there is a concurrency requirement in the original software development request or when parallelism is explicitly called for or implied by the solution decomposition. We introduce Parallel Application Design Layers (PADL). PADL is a five-layer analysis model that we use at CTEST Laboratories during the requirements analysis, software design, and decomposition activities of the Software Development Life Cycle (SDLC). We use PADL to place concurrency and parallelism considerations in the proper context. PADL is used during the initial problem and solution decomposition. We also use the PADL model to circumvent much of the complexity that results from bottom-up approaches to parallel programming. In this chapter, we present an *architectural approach* to parallelism rather than a task-oriented procedural approach. Although concurrently executing tasks represent the basic unit of work in applications that take advantage of CMPs, we place those tasks within declarative architectures and predicate-based software models. In this chapter, we approach application design with the fundamentals of the SDLC front and center.

We also briefly introduce Predicate Breakdown Structure (PBS) decomposition. The PBS of a software design presents a view of the software as a collection of assertions, propositions, and logical predicates. The PBS gives the declarative or predicate-based view of a software design. At CTEST Laboratories we use PADL and PBS as fundamental tools for application design when multithreading, multiprocessing, or parallel programming will be used. PADL and PBS are departures from procedural and bottom-up task-oriented methods, but they are tools that can be used in conjunction with interface classes, application frameworks, predicates, and algorithm templates to move the process of application design in a direction that will be able to exploit the availability of medium- and large-scale single chip multiprocessors.

What Is PADL?

As already noted, Parallel Application Design Layers (PADL) is a five-layer analysis model used in the design of software that requires some parallel programming. PADL is used to help organize the software decomposition effort. The PADL model is a refinement model. Starting with the top layer, each lower layer contains more detail and is one step closer to operating system and compiler primitives. PADL is meant to be used during the requirements analysis and software design activities of the SDLC. The industry standard description for an SDLC is contained in the IEEE Std 1074, *Guide for Developing Software Life Cycle Processes*. IEEE Std 1074 helps clarify what the minimum set of activities are.

Table 3-1 in Chapter 3 shows some of the common activities found in the SDLC, but it is not exhaustive.

The PADL model is used to help design or decompose *patterns of work* before the software is written. That's why we place an emphasis on its use during design and analysis activities of the SDLC. Figure 8-1 shows the five layers of PADL.

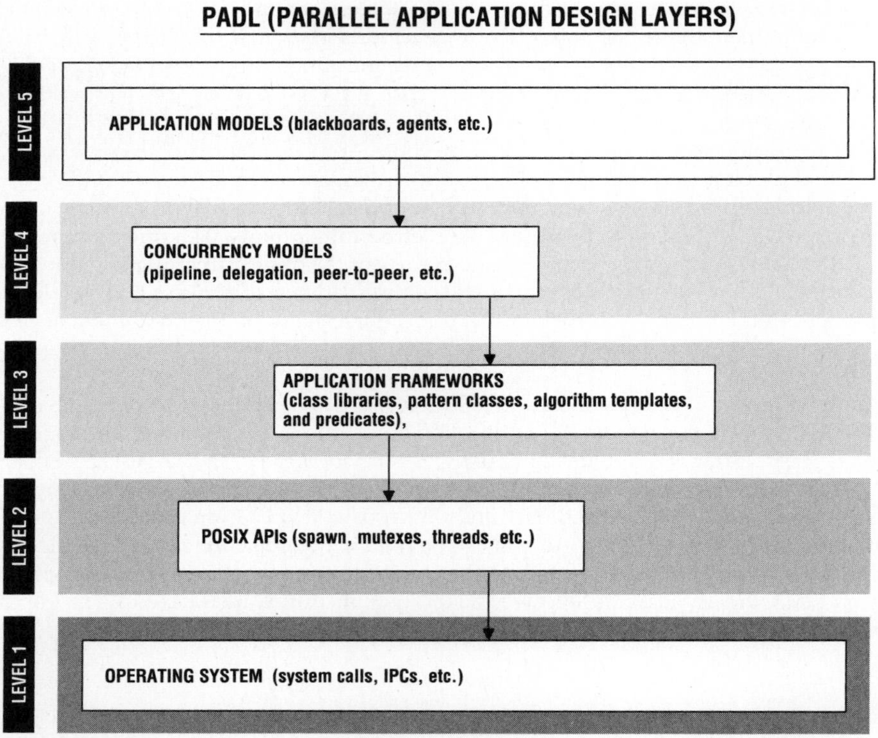

PADL (PARALLEL APPLICATION DESIGN LAYERS)

LEVEL 5 — APPLICATION MODELS (blackboards, agents, etc.)

LEVEL 4 — CONCURRENCY MODELS (pipeline, delegation, peer-to-peer, etc.)

LEVEL 3 — APPLICATION FRAMEWORKS (class libraries, pattern classes, algorithm templates, and predicates),

LEVEL 2 — POSIX APIs (spawn, mutexes, threads, etc.)

LEVEL 1 — OPERATING SYSTEM (system calls, IPCs, etc.)

Figure 8-1

❑ Layer 5 deals with application architecture selection. Selection of the application architecture is one of the most critical decisions because everything else follows the architecture, and once it is in place, it is expensive to change. The architecture allows certain functionality and features while preventing others. The architecture provides the basic infrastructure of the application.

❑ Layer 4 in Figure 8-1 identifies concurrency models that will be used for the application. The architecture should be flexible enough to use the concurrency models that are needed, and the concurrency models should be flexible enough to support the architecture selected. Table 8-3 reviews the basic concurrency models and their definitions.

Table 8-3

Thread Models	Description
Boss-worker model	A central process/thread (boss) creates the processes/threads (workers) and assigns each worker a task. The boss may wait until each worker completes its task.
Peer-to-peer model	All the processes/threads have an equal working status; there are no leaders. A peer creates all the workers needed to perform the tasks but performs no delegation responsibilities. The peer can process requests from a single input stream shared by all the threads, or each thread may have its own input stream.
Pipeline	An assembly line approach to processing a stream of input in stages. Each stage is a thread that performs work on a unit of input. When the unit of input has been through all the stages, then the processing of the input has been completed.
Producer-consumer model	A producer *produces* data to be *consumed* by the consumer thread. The data is stored in a block of memory shared by the producer and consumer threads.

The pattern of work is initially expressed within the context of the architecture chosen in Layer 5. We discuss this shortly. The architecture is then fleshed out by one or more concurrency models in Layer 4.

It is important to note that Layer 4 and Layer 5 in Figure 8-1 are strictly conceptual models. Their primary purpose is to help describe and identify the concurrency structure a software application will have.

❑ Layer 3 of the PADL starts to identify application frameworks, pattern class hierarchies, component/predicate libraries, and algorithm templates that are used to implement the concurrency models identified at Layer 4 of the analysis. Layer 3 introduces tangible software into the PADL model. Software libraries such at the Thread Building Blocks (TBB) library or STAPL would be identified in Layer 3.

❑ Layer 2 represents the application's program interface to operating system. The components in Layer 3 ultimately talk to and cooperate with the OS API. In our case the POSIX API is used for the greatest cross-platform compatibility. Many of the components in Layer 3 are interface classes or wrappers for functionality found in Layer 2.

❑ Finally, Layer 1 is the lowest level of detail that the software application can be decomposed into. At Layer 1 you are dealing with kernel execution units, signals, device drivers, and so on. The software at Layer 1 performs the actual work of the application interfaces presented in Layer 2. Layer 1 decomposition also encompasses compiler and linker switches.

Layers 4 and 5 are considered design layers. Layers 1–3 are the implementation layers. Layer 3 is usually reserved for application-level software development. Layers 1 and 2 are usually reserved system-level software development. Obviously, the barrier between Layer 2 and 3 can be (and often is) easily crossed. Once a PADL model analysis has been performed, the picture of the concurrency structure of an application is clear to all of those involved in the software development effort. The PADL analysis of an application provides the framework for the testing activities of the SDLC. The PADL analysis provides the necessary implementation and deployment targets of the SDLC for the application. At the top layers of the PADL are design concepts and models. At the lowest level of the PADL are operating system primitives. So, you have a complete picture of the concurrency of an application through the PADL model. The PADL model is meant to drive a *declarative decomposition* of the application because you proceed from architectures to operating system primitives *not* from the primitives to the architectures! But in order for PADL to ensure a declarative decomposition, it must restrict the architectures to software blueprints that have declarative, goal-oriented, or predicate-based semantics. The next sections take a closer look at how the PADL model moves you toward declarative approaches to parallel programming.

Layer 5: Application Architecture Selection

Consideration of the numbers of cores, threads, and processes is not part of the analysis in Layer 5. In fact, computers are not even visible at Layer 5. The application architectures considered in Layer 5 represent conceptual or logical structures that are platform, operating system, and computer independent. The value of these architectures is that they are known to support certain patterns of work. In the PADL model, we use two primary architectures:

❑　Multiagent architectures

❑　Blackboard architectures

It is important to note that here we are referring to the problem-solving structures and patterns of work as opposed to any specific tools or vendor products that are based on some of the ideas of multiagents and Blackboards. Our use of the terms *agent* and *Blackboard* is not to be confused with the many gimmicks that claim agent or Blackboard functionality. We use agents and Blackboards in their more formal sense. Multiagent architectures are classified in section I.2.11 of the ACM CCS, and Blackboard architectures are classified in D.2.11 of the ACM CCS. Both architectures are able to support a wide variety of concurrency models. They are well defined and well understood. Both architectures support the notion of PBS. We have chosen to use multiagent architectures to capture goal-oriented patterns of work and Blackboard architectures to capture state-oriented patterns of work. Although goals and states are sometimes used interchangeably and sometimes the goal is to reach a certain state, we differentiate between the two when using concurrency models. Goal-based decompositions and state transitions can help you in the direction of declarative models of parallel programming, and declarative models of parallel programming can help you cope with the transition to massively parallel chip multiprocessors. Multiagent architectures and Blackboard architectures can be understood using declarative semantics.

What Are Agents?

There was a lot of controversy over what constituted an object when object programming was initially introduced. There is a similar controversy over exactly what constitutes an agent. Many proponents define agents as autonomous continuously executing programs that act on behalf of a user. However, this definition can be applied to some Unix daemons or even some device drivers. Others add the requirements that the agent must have special knowledge of the user, must execute in an environment inhabited by other agents, and must function only within the specified environment. These requirements would exclude other programs considered to be agents by some. For instance, many e-mail agents act alone and may function in multiple environments. In addition to agent requirements, various groups in the agent community have introduced terms like *softbot*, *knowbot*, *software broker*, and *smart object* to describe agents. One commonly found definition defines an agent as "an entity that functions continuously and autonomously in an environment in which other processes take place and other agents exist."

Although it is tempting to accept this definition and move on, we cannot because it too easily describes other kinds of software constructions. A more formal source, the Foundation for Intelligent Physical Agents (FIFA) specification, defines the term agent as follows: "An Agent is the fundamental actor in a domain. It combines one or more service capabilities into a unified and integrated execution model which can include access to external software, human users and communication facilities."

While this definition has a more structured feel, it also needs further clarification because many servers (some Object-Oriented and some that are not) fit this definition. This definition as is would include too many types of programs and software constructs to be useful. In our PADL model we use the five-part definition of agents as stated by [Luger, 2002]:

1. **Agents are autonomous or semi-autonomous.** That is, each agent has certain responsibilities in problem solving with little or no knowledge either what other agents do or how they do it. Each agent does its own independent piece of the problem solving and either produces a result itself (does something) or reports its result back to others in the community of agents.

2. **Agents are situated.** Each agent is sensitive to its own surrounding environment and (usually) has no knowledge of the full domain of all agents.

3. **Agents are interactional.** That is, they form a collection of individuals that cooperate on a particular task. In this sense, they may be seen as a "society."

4. **The society of agents is structured.** In most views of agent-oriented problem solving, each individual, although having its own unique environment and skill set, will coordinate with other agents in the overall problem solving. Thus, a final solution will not only be seen as collective but also cooperative.

5. **Although individual agents are seen as possessing sets of skills responsibilities, the overall cooperative result of the society of agents can be viewed as greater than the sum of its individual contributors.**

What Is a Multiagent Architecture?

We use the term *multiagent architecture* when referring to an agent-based architecture that consists of two or more agents that can execute concurrently if necessary. It should be clear from Luger's definition of agents that multiagent architecture can be used as an extremely flexible approach to patterns of work that require or can benefit from concurrency. Notice in this definition of agents that there is no mention of particular computer capabilities, numbers of processors, thread management, or so forth. There is also no limit on the number of agents involved. There are no complexity constraints on the patterns of work that a collection of agents can perform. If you begin with the blueprint that is consistent with a multiagent architecture, you should be able to handle concurrency of any size.

From Problem Statements to Multiagent Architectures

Decomposition is one of the primary challenges in software development. It is more of a challenge when the software development requires parallel programming. Our approach to this challenge is to find an appropriate model of the problem and appropriate solution model. Using PADL analysis, we select an application architecture based on the solution model. To see how this works, consider again the guess-what-code-I'm-thinking problem from Chapter 4.

Recall the game scenario from Chapter 4 goes as follows: I'm thinking of a six-character code. My code can contain any character more than once. However, my code can only contain any characters from the numbers 0–9 or characters a–z. Your job is to guess what code I have in mind. In the game the buzzer is set to go off after 5 minutes. If you guess what I'm thinking in 5 minutes you win. In that chapter, we determined that you have 4,496,388 possible codes to choose from.

Now, in this simple example, we want to make the game a little more challenging. You now have only 2 minutes to guess. In addition to this, instead of making up a code, I am handed the initial code by my trusted assistant. If my assistant determines that you have made more than N incorrect guesses within a 15-second interval, my assistant hands me a new code, and the new code is guaranteed to be among the guesses that you have already made.

The Strategy

Recall from Chapter 4 that you happened to have a file that contained all of the possible six-character codes. The total number of codes is determined by samples of size r that can be selected out of n objects. The formula that calculates the possibilities is as follows:

$$(n - 1 + r)! / (n-1)!r!$$

In this case n is 36 counting (0-9, a-z) and $r = 6$. The original strategy was to the divide the file into four parts and have the parts searched in parallel. The thinking was that the longest search would be only the length of the time it took to search one-quarter of the file. But because you are given a new time constraint of 2 minutes, you now have to modify your strategy to divide the original file into eight parts and have the parts searched concurrently. Therefore, you should be able to guess correctly in the time that it takes to search one-eighth of the file. But you also make one other provision. If you are able to search all eight files, and still do not guess correctly and are not out of time, you divide the files into 64 and try again. If you fail and still have time, you divide the file into 128 and try again and so on.

An Observation

If you carefully look at the code to be guessed, you see that if the assistant determines that some unusual number of guesses are being made within a 15-second interval, then the assistant changes the code to one that has already been guessed. It is not specified what the unusual number. So, your strategy is to try to make more guesses in a shorter period of time because the time constraint is tighter. Further, if you are able to go through all of the possibilities and still do not have the correct code, you assume that the code is being changed during the 2-minute interval, and, therefore, you attempt to increase the guesses at a rate faster than that at which the code can be changed.

Problem and Solution Model as Multiagents

You can easily see from the statement of the problem that you are initially dealing with three agents. If you recast the game in terms of agents you have the following: Agent A gives the code to Agent B. Agent C tries to guess Agent B's code. If Agent C comes up with too many guesses in a 15-second interval, Agent A will give Agent B a new code that is guaranteed to be a code that Agent C has already presented. If Agent C is able to go through all of the possibilities and is still not declared the winner and if Agent C has more time left, that agent will make the same guesses only faster. Agent C realizes that in order to generate enough guesses to guarantee success within the given time limit will require help. So, Agent C recruits a team of agents to help him come up with guesses. For each pass through the total possibilities, Agent C recruits a bigger team of agents to help with the guesses.

Obviously, you could now start thinking in terms of agents mapped to either threads or processes. But we will resist this temptation. You do not want to think in terms of threads and processes at this level. In the PADL model approach, you work out a complete and correct logical statement of the application in Layers 5 and 4. So, before proceeding to Layer 4, if you are applying the PADL model to the game scenario, you refine the relationships and interactions of all of the agents involved. The assumption and conditions that the agents operated under would all be made clear. A complete picture of the multiagent interaction would be given. Figure 8-2 is a UML activity diagram that captures the interaction of the micro-multiagent society.

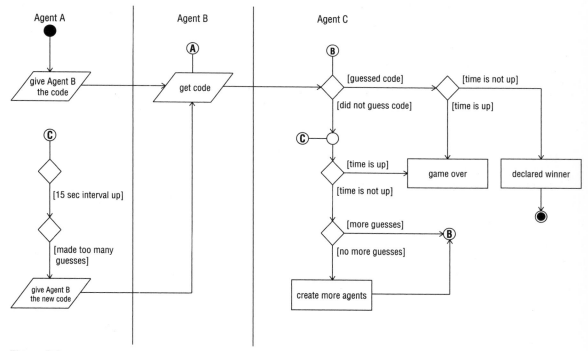

Figure 8-2

Blackboard Architectures

The Blackboard model is an approach to collaborative problem solving. The Blackboard is used to record, coordinate, and communicate the efforts of two or more software-based problem solvers. There are two primary types of components in the Blackboard model.

❑   The Blackboard

❑   The problem solvers

The *Blackboard* is a centralized object that each of the problem solvers has access to. The problem solvers may read the Blackboard and change the contents of the Blackboard. The contents of the Blackboard at any given time will vary. The initial content of the Blackboard will include the problem to be solved.

In addition to the problem to be solved, other information representing the initial state of the problem, problem constraints, goals, and objectives may be contained on the Blackboard. As the problem solvers are working toward the solution, intermediate results, hypotheses, and conclusions are recorded on the Blackboard. The intermediate results written by one problem solver on the Blackboard may act as catalyst for other problem solvers reading the Blackboard. Tentative solutions are posted to the Blackboard. If the solutions are determined not to be sufficient, these solutions are erased, and other solutions are pursued. The problem solvers use the Blackboard as opposed to direct communication to pass partial results and findings to each other. In some configurations, the Blackboard acts as a referee, informing the problem solvers when a solution has been reached or when to start work or stop work. The Blackboard is an active object, not simply a storage location. In some cases, the Blackboard determines which problem solvers to involve and what content to accept or reject. The Blackboard may also organize the incremental or intermediate results of the problem solvers. The Blackboard may translate or interpret the work from one set of problem solvers so that it can be used by another set of problem solvers.

The *problem solver* is a piece of software that typically has specialized knowledge or processing capabilities within some area or problem domain. The problem solver can be as simple a routine that converts from Celsius to Fahrenheit or as complex as a smart agent that handles medical diagnosis. In the Blackboard model, these problem solvers are called *knowledge sources* (KS). To solve a problem using Blackboards, you need two or more knowledge sources, and each knowledge source usually has a specific area of focus or specialty. The Blackboard is a natural fit for problems that can be divided into separate tasks that can be solved independently or semi-independently. In the basic Blackboard configuration each problem solver tackles a different part of the problem. Each problem solver only sees the part of the problem that it is familiar with. If the solutions to any parts of the problem are dependent on the solutions or partial solutions to other parts of the problem, then the Blackboard is used to coordinate the problem solvers and the integration of the partial solutions.

A Blackboard's problem solvers need not be homogeneous. Each problem solver may be implemented using different techniques. For instance, some problem solvers might be implemented using Object-Oriented techniques, while other solvers might be implemented as functions. Further the problem solvers may employ completely different problem-solving paradigms. For example, solver A might use a backward chaining approach to solving its problem, while solver B might use a counterpropagation approach. There is no requirement that the Blackboard's problem solvers be implemented using the same programming language.

The Blackboard model does not specify any particular structure or layout for the Blackboard. Neither does it suggest how the knowledge sources should be structured. In practice, the structure of a Blackboard is problem dependent. The implementation of the knowledge sources is also specific to the problem being solved. The Blackboard framework is a conceptual model describing relationships without describing the structures of the Blackboard and knowledge sources. The Blackboard model does not dictate the number or purpose of the knowledge sources. The Blackboard may be a single global object or a distributed object with components on multiple computers. Blackboard systems may even consist of multiple Blackboards, with each Blackboard dedicated to a part of the original problem. This makes the Blackboard an extremely flexible model for problem solving. The Blackboard model supports parallel programming and many of the concurrency models. The Blackboard can be segmented into separate parts, allowing concurrent access by multiple knowledge sources. The Blackboard easily supports Concurrent Read Exclusive Write (CREW), Exclusive Read Exclusive Write (EREW), and Multiple Instruction, Multiple Data (MIMD). The knowledge sources may execute simultaneously with each knowledge source working on its part of the problem.

Figure 8-3 shows two memory configurations for the Blackboard.

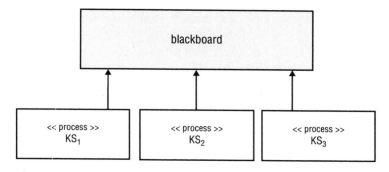

BLACKBOARD MEMORY CONFIGURATION 1:
Knowledge sources are in different address spaces.

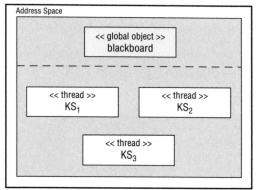

BLACKBOARD MEMORY CONFIGURATION 2:
Knowledge sources share the same address space.

Figure 8-3

In both the cases in Figure 8-3, all knowledge sources have access to the Blackboard. This configuration provides for an extremely flexible model of problem solving.

Approaches to Structuring the Blackboard

As we have indicated, there is no one way to structure a Blackboard. However, most Blackboards have certain characteristics and attributes in common. The original contents of the Blackboard typically contain some kind of partitioning of the solution space for the problem that is to be solved. The solution space contains all the partial solutions and full solutions to a problem.

A "Question and Answer Browser" Blackboard Example

Say that you need a domain-specific information browser, that is, one that allows the user to search for information only on a narrow topic or range of specified topics (for example, anime, robots, YouTube, or so on). The user should be able to browse through the available information using a graphical interface or choose advanced search features. The advance search features should allow the user to simply type a question (as long as it pertains to the topic), and the browser should return a complete answer based on the information it has access to. It is assumed that most users will prefer the advanced search because it's faster.

Where's the Parallelism? Where's the Blackboard?

In the innocent browser request above you see no mention made of multiple cores, concurrency threads, or processes. There is simply the assumption that the browser will have what the user perceives as an acceptable performance. You are immediately faced with, among other things, one of the primary challenges of software development (especially challenging for CMP deployments): *decomposition*. Decomposition begins with understanding the problem and then devising a solution that addresses the problem. In this case, browsing information using a graphical user interface is fairly well understood. On the other hand, allowing the user to type in a question and having software that can understand the user's question, search through information, find an appropriate answer, and then present it in a form that is acceptable is another challenge altogether. This problem involves determining what language the question is being asked in (perhaps, you can assume the local language). So, a quick run through of the problem yields the following challenges:

❑   Is the question in a language that is known to the software?

❑   Is the question concerning a topic that is available in the software's information?

❑   Is the question clear and unambiguously stated?

❑   Are there any unknown or misspelled words in the question? (How can it answer if so?)

❑   How will the software deal with meaning in the question?

❑   What about language grammar (syntax, semantics, morphology, pragmatics)?

After a moment of internal deliberation, you realize that to accept, understand, and appropriately respond in a timely manner (in a second or so) to a random question typed into an information browser is a challenging problem! With a little research you find out that natural language processing techniques are required. You stumble across partial solutions in computational linguistics and computational semantics. You now have a rough but somewhat complete picture of the problem.

Components of the Solution

To provide a solution to the problem, you realize that you need software components that include parsers, word experts, grammar analysis for syntax, semantics, pragmatics, and so on. As it turns out, the user's original question can be analyzed at several levels simultaneously. Determination of what language the question is asked in can be done at the same time as identification of unknown words or misspelled words. The syntax analysis that breaks down the question into its parts of speech can also be done at the same time. You also determine that once part of the syntax is figured out, the semantic analysis process can start. Likewise, once part of the question's semantics has been identified, identification of the pragmatics (context and meaning) can begin. You have now identified the parts. While there are some partial dependencies (for example, between syntax and semantics, and semantics and pragmatics), you can do most of the analysis of the user's question concurrently.

Looking at the PADL analysis model at Layer 5, it is clear that you can use both the multiagent and Blackboard architecture for the solution model. You choose the Blackboard architecture here because the semantic and pragmatic analysis can begin work with only partial solutions, and the Blackboard architecture is a good fit for incremental problem solving.

Knowledge Sources for the Browser Program

So, you place the original user's question on the Blackboard, and each of your knowledge sources has its specialties:

- ❑ Checking a dictionary for unknown or misspelled words
- ❑ Breaking down the question into parts of speech (nouns, verbs, interrogatives, and so on)
- ❑ Understanding the morphology, that is, word forms (plural, present, past)
- ❑ Semantic understanding of the meaning and use of words
- ❑ Pragmatic analysis (the use of words in context)

The knowledge source that simply checks the question for unknown or misspelled words places its candidates on the Blackboard. As they arrive, the morphology knowledge sources make any corrections that could be due to plural forms, past tense, or abbreviations. They then place corrected words back on the Blackboard. While this is happening the syntax knowledge sources are breaking down the question with the corrected words into parts of speech and are placing phrases back up on the Blackboard as it goes. As soon as there is something that the semantics and pragmatics knowledge sources can work with, they read the Blackboard as well and begin to put up a potential meaning of the user's original question in a form that the search engine can use.

This is a cooperative kind of concurrent processing because the partial solutions can be used and interpreted on many levels by different knowledge sources. Each knowledge source writes a tentative hypothesis for what it is currently dealing with on the Blackboard. Something that the semantic knowledge source uncovers may help the syntax parser refine its work. Something that the syntax parser refines may clarify something for the pragmatics knowledge source and so on. The Blackboard represents a solution space that is divided into a hierarchy of partial solutions with proper forms of questions and answers at the highest level and parts of speech and word forms at the lowest level. If some part of the solution space matches something in the rules of grammar or usage of language, that piece of the solution is written to another part of the Blackboard as a partial solution. One KS might put a verb phrase on the Blackboard. Another may put a choice of contexts on the Blackboard. Once these two pieces of information have been put on the Blackboard, another KS may uses this information to aide in identifying the real subject or object of the question. All of this has to take place within the space of a few seconds.

Is a Blackboard a Good Fit?

From the original naïve statement of the question and answer browser request that did not really hint at concurrency, you have now produced a solution that needs to use parallel models of work in order to meet the assumed speed requirements. The Blackboard solution is well suited to concurrency with knowledge sources working with incomplete or staged information. Again, it is important to note that at this level you are not concerned with threads, numbers of cores, or processes.

The Blackboard as an Iterative Shared Solution Space

The solution space is sometimes organized in a hierarchy. In the case of the question and answer processing example, valid question classifications would be at the top of the hierarchy, and the next level might consist of various views of the classifications. For example, with different forms for who, what, where, and when questions, each level describes a smaller perhaps less obvious aspect of a question classification (for example, is the verb transitive?). The knowledge sources may work on multiple levels within the hierarchy simultaneously. The solution space may also be organized as a graph where each node represents some part of the solution, and each edge represents the relationships between two partial solutions. The solution space may be represented as one or more matrices with each element of the matrix or matrices containing a solution or partial solution. The solution space representation is an important component of the Blackboard architecture. The nature of the problem will often determine how the solution space should be partitioned. This feature is critical in the PADL model because we use Layer 5 to describe the application architecture and the application architecture has to be flexible enough to map to the solution model. The structure of the Blackboard supports this flexibility.

In addition to a solution space component, Blackboards typically have one or more rule (heuristic) components. The rule component is used to determine which knowledge sources to deploy, and what solutions to accept or reject. The rule component can also be used to translate partial solutions from one level in the solution space hierarchy to another level. The rule component may also be used to prioritize the knowledge source approaches. The rule component supports concurrently among knowledge sources. This is the level where concurrency needs to be dealt with by using a declarative interpretation of parallel processing. Some knowledge sources might be going down blind alleys. The Blackboard deselects one set of knowledge sources in favor of another set. The Blackboard may use the rule component to suggest to the knowledge sources a more appropriate potential hypothesis based on the partial hypothesis already generated.

In addition to the solution space and rule component, the Blackboard often contains initial values, constraints values, and ancillary goals. In some cases, the Blackboard contains one or more event queues that are used to capture input from either the problem space or the knowledge sources. Figure 8-4 shows a logical layout for a basic Blackboard architecture.

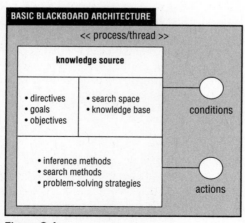

Figure 8-4

Figure 8-4 shows that the Blackboard has a number of segments. Each segment in Figure 8-4 has a variety of implementations. This suggests that Blackboards are more than global pieces of memory or traditional databases. While Figure 8-4 shows the common core components that most Blackboards have, the Blackboard architecture is not limited to these components. Other useful components for Blackboards include context models of the problem and domain models that can be used to aid the problem solvers (KS) with navigation through the solution space. The support that C++ has for Object-Oriented Design and Programming fits nicely with the flexibility requirements of the Blackboard model. Most Blackboard architectures can be modeled using classes in C++. Recall that classes can be used to model some person, place, thing, or idea. Blackboards are used to solve problems that involve persons, places, things, or ideas. So, using C++ classes to model the objects that Blackboards contain or the actual Blackboards is a natural fit. We take advantage of C++ container classes and the standard algorithms in our implementations of the Blackboard model.

The Anatomy of a Knowledge Source

Knowledge sources are represented as objects, procedures, sets of rules, logic assertions, and in some cases entire programs. Knowledge sources have a condition part and an action part. When the Blackboard contains some information that satisfies the condition part of some knowledge source, the action part of the knowledge source is activated. Robert Englemore and Tony Morgan clearly state the responsibilities of a knowledge source in their work *Blackboard Systems*:

> Each knowledge source is responsible for knowing the conditions under which it can contribute to a solution. Each knowledge source has preconditions that indicate the condition on the Blackboard that must exist before the body of the knowledge source is activated. One can view a knowledge source as a large rule. The major difference between a rule and a knowledge source is the grain size of the knowledge each holds. The condition part of this large rule is called the knowledge source precondition, and the action part is called the knowledge source body. [Englemore, Morgan, 1998]

Here, Englemore and Morgan don't specify any of the details of the condition part or the action part of a knowledge source. They are logical constructs. The condition part could be as simple as the value of some boolean flag on the Blackboard or as complex as a specific sequence of events arriving in an event queue within a certain period of time. Likewise, the action part of a knowledge source can be a simple as a single statement performing an expression assignment or as involved as forward chain in an expert system. Again, this is a statement of how flexible the Blackboard model can be. The C++ class construct and the notion of an object are sufficient for our purposes. Each knowledge source will be an object (for sophisticated uses an object hierarchy). The action part of the knowledge source will be implemented by the object's methods. The condition part of the knowledge source will be captured as data members of the object. Once the object is in a certain state then the action parts of that object will be activated.

An important attribute of the knowledge source is its autonomy. Each knowledge source is a specialist and is largely independent from the other problem solvers. This presents one of the desired qualities for a parallel program. Ideally the tasks in a parallel program can operate concurrently without much interaction with other tasks. This is exactly the case in the Blackboard model. The knowledge sources act independently, and any major interaction is through the Blackboard. So, from the knowledge source's point of view, it is acting alone, getting additional information from the Blackboard, and recording its findings on the Blackboard. The activities of the other knowledge sources, their strategies, and structures are unknown. In the Blackboard model, the problem is partitioned into a number of autonomous or semi-autonomous program solvers. This is the advantage of the Blackboard model over other concurrency models. In the most flexible configuration, the knowledge sources are *rational agents*, meaning the agent is completely self-sufficient and able to act on its own with minimum interaction with the Blackboard. Rational agents in conjunction with Blackboards present the greatest opportunity for large scale parallelism or massively parallel CMPs. This use of rational agents as knowledge sources combines the two primary architectures from Layer 5 of PADL: multiagent architectures and Blackboard architectures. A full discussion of rational agents takes us beyond the scope of this book. However, we can say that rational agents fit into the category of agents that we discussed earlier in the chapter in the section "What Are Agents?" When knowledge sources are implemented as rational agents in large-scale systems, the rule and action components of the knowledge sources are learned using Inductive Logic Programming (ILP) techniques [Bergadano, Gunetti, 1996]. The ILP techniques provide a gateway to bottom-up declarative programming.

We move away from bottom-up *procedural* programming techniques and toward PADL in order to cope with complexity as the scale of available cores on CMP increases. However, bottom-up *declarative* programming using ILP or evolutionary programming techniques [Goertzel, Pennachin, 2007] is a legitimate part of the PADL analysis model. These approaches are used in Layer 3 where we are concerned with the availability and implementation of application frameworks, class libraries, algorithm templates, and so on.

Concurrency Flexibility of the Application Architecture

Although there are many different types of software architectures that support parallelism, we use multiagent and Blackboard architectures in Layer 5 of PADL because of their general purpose nature and the range of concurrency models they support. Many different types of solutions that require concurrency can be expressed using multiagent or Blackboard architectures. Multiagent architectures and Blackboards are domain independent. They can be used in many different areas. Further, these architectures can be used for solutions of all sizes from small programs to large-scale, enterprise-wide solutions. While these architectures might be new to developers who are in the process of learning parallel or multithreaded programming techniques, they are well defined, and many useful resources that introduce the basic ideas of agents and Blackboards are available, see [Russell, Norvig, 2003], [Englemore, Morgan, 1988], [Goertzel, Pennachin, 2007], and [Fagin et al., 1996]. You will see that the selection of the architecture impacts software maintenance, testing, and debugging. Most successful software undergoes constant change. If that software has components that require concurrency and synchronization, then the natural evolution of the software can be extremely challenging if an appropriate application architecture was not selected from the start. The PADL analysis model presents two well-known and well-understood architectures that perform well under the conditions of software evolution. Ultimately, the concurrency of an application is going to be implemented by low-level operating system primitives like threads and processes. If the application architecture is clean, modular, scalable, and well understood, then the translation into manageable operating system primitives has a chance to succeed. On the other hand, selection of the wrong or a poor application architecture leads to brittle, error-prone software that cannot be readily changed, maintained, or evolved. While this is true of any kind of computer application, it is magnified when that software involves parallel programming, multithreading, or multiprocessing.

Layer 4: Concurrency Models in PADL

The applications architectures selected in Layer 5 have to flexible enough to support concurrency models selected in Layer 4. There can be more than one concurrency model needed in the application, so the architecture chosen should be able to accommodate multiple models. Layer 4 is also a design layer. We are not necessarily thinking in terms of threads or processes when we select concurrency models in Layer 4.

Whereas the architecture focuses on the language and concepts in the application domain, the concurrency model layer is concerned with picking known models of parallelism that will work. In the browser example used in the chapter so far, we have several highly specialized knowledge sources that are concurrently working on different parts of the user's question. This particular example uses a variation of the MIMD model of parallelism in combination with a peer-to-peer model. In this case, the peers communicated and cooperated through a shared Blackboard. Since each knowledge source has its own specialty and works on a different aspect of the question, we select the Multiple Instruction, Multiple Data (MIMD) concurrency model. In Chapter 7, we explained the Parallel Random-Access Machine (PRAM) and the Exclusive Read Exclusive Write (EREW), Concurrent Read Exclusive Write (CREW), Exclusive Read Concurrent Write (ERCW), and Concurrent Read Concurrent Write (CRCW) models for memory or critical section access. It is clear that in the example of the question and answer browser that you have either a CREW or CRCW requirement for the Blackboard.

The identification or selection of a MIMD/peer-to-peer model in conjunction with CREW/CRCW critical section access is important at this stage because it shapes and molds the use of threads and processes in Layers 2 and 3. This emphasizes the fact that the parallelism in the implementation model should naturally follow the concurrency in the solution model. If you allow implementation model and the solution model to drift or diverge too much, then you will not be able to guarantee that the software is correct. The simple game example discussed earlier in this chapter uses a multiagent application architecture. It uses the classic boss-worker concurrency model with a Single Instruction Multiple Data (SIMD) PRAM architecture and EREW access for the critical section. In the case of the game, the critical section is a shared queue that all of the agents used to get the names of the partial files to search. A shared queue was also used by the agents to report back to the main agent when a correct code was found. Table 8-4 shows the PADL analysis as it applies at this point to the two examples.

Table 8-4

	Architecture	Concurrency Model	PRAM Model	SIMD/MIMD
Guess-My-Code Agents	Multiagent	Peer-to-peer	CRCW or CREW	MIMD
Question and Answer Browser	Blackboard	Boss-worker	EREW	SIMD

While Table 8-4 does present a simplification of concurrency design choices for the two examples, it nevertheless gives a high-level evaluation of the concurrency infrastructure of the software. Once you've identified the concurrency models, you can plan for their strengths and weaknesses. For example, if you know that you are dealing with SIMD model, then vector optimization, loop unrolling, and pipelining all become serious contenders for implementation. You can take advantage of their strengths and plan for their weaknesses. On the other hand, if you know you're dealing with EREW critical sections, then you know ahead of time that you have potential bottleneck issues or indefinite postponement issues. One of the advantages of selecting well-known models is that you know what you're getting into before you start implementing the applications. Figure 8-5 shows a block diagram of the concurrency infrastructure of the two examples.

Q & A BROWSER BLACKBOARD

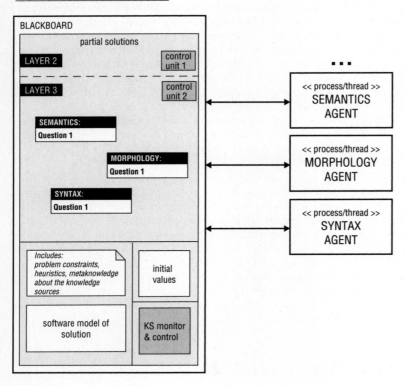

guess_my_code SIMD

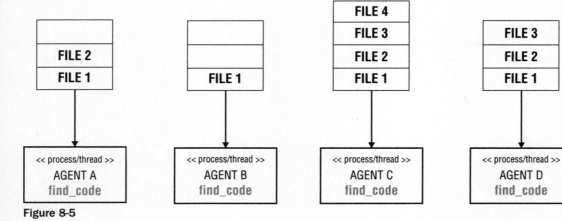

Figure 8-5

Figure 8-5 clarifies where the concurrency is in the applications. One of the major benefits of using a PADL model analysis is to identify the nature and location of concurrency in an application. Again, it is important to note that Layer 4 and 5 are conceptual design layers. We are not really concerned with threads, or processes in these layers. These layers function as a blueprint that specifies the concurrency architecture and infrastructure of the application. Layers 4 and 5 identify the primary agents, objects, components, and processes that will be involved in concurrency and where in the application the concurrency takes place. Layers 4 and 5 specify how the agents, objects, components, and processes are related in terms of concurrency models such as boss-worker, pipeline, SIMD, MIMD, and so on. After you have done the decomposition in Layers 4 and 5, you can begin to think about the implementation models in Layer 3. Figure 8-6 contains a general overview of how the PADL analysis is applied during decomposition.

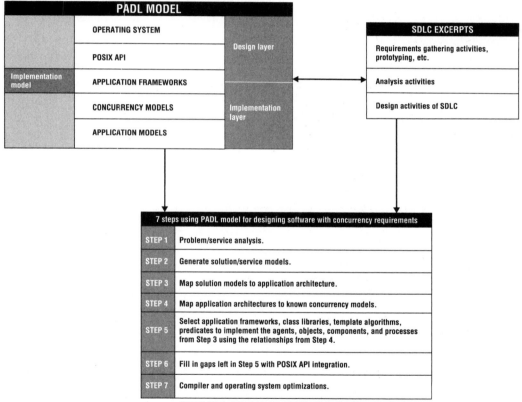

Figure 8-6

The concurrency infrastructure is identified from steps 1 through 4, as shown in the figure. Notice again that Layers 4 and 5 are design layers and that Layer 3 contains the implementation model for your application. Layer 3 plays a dual role because it is part of the design layer and the implementation layer. This is because application frameworks, pattern classes, class hierarchies, and template algorithms are useful during the design and are directly deployed at implementation. Once Layer 3 analysis is done, the application's concurrency infrastructure has a specific set of classes and template algorithms. We turn our attention to Layer 3 next.

Layer 3: The Implementation Model of PADL

Layer 3 analysis consists of selecting the application frameworks, pattern classes, class libraries, class hierarchies, algorithm templates, predicates, and container classes that are necessary to implement the agents, objects, components, predicates, and processes identified during the solution model decomposition, the application architecture selection and the concurrency model(s) identification. During Layer 3 analysis all of the primary design artifacts from Layers 4 and 5 are associated with specific Object-Oriented components, algorithms, and predicates. Once Layer 3 analysis is done, we have the clearest picture of the concurrency infrastructure and the concurrency implementation model of the application. Notice in Figure 8-6 that the items in Layer 3 are traceable back to the original statement of the problem. Since the entire PADL analysis takes place in the context of a well structured SDLC, the application that you deliver will be sound, scalable and maintainable by a software development group.

We mention development group here because the software development enterprise is a group effort. Useful software evolves over time and is changed and maintained by different individuals. Ad hoc approaches to parallel programming or multithreading hacks are virtually impossible to maintain in the long run. The work accomplished in Layers 3, 4, and 5 of the PADL analysis is the difference between software that has concurrency, allowing developers to actually manage and cope with the complexity, and software that just grows more complex and unmanageable and is finally decommissioned as the development group and the end users collapse under the strain.

C++ Components to the Rescue

Fortunately, the C++ environment has an impressive set of features, libraries, and techniques that can be deployed for *model* implementation. We emphasize the word *model* here because parallelism and concurrency are best managed in the context of models. The seven steps shown in Figure 8-6 move from models of the problem to models of the solution and finally to implementation models. If you use declarative models in your solutions, then you can reliably develop software that takes advantage of medium- to large-scale CMPs or massively parallel multicores. Although C++ does not have concurrency constructs, C++ does have excellent support for many categories of library. So, you can add support for parallel programming and multithreading to C++ through the use of libraries. There are three very important C++ component libraries that support parallel programming that we introduce in this chapter: the Parallel STL Library (STAPL), Intel Thread Building Blocks (TBB), and the new C++0x standard. Although there are many different efforts that have generated concurrency support using C++, we introduce these three because they will be soon be the most widely available and easily accessible C++ components that support concurrency, parallel programming, and multithreading.

The C++0x or C++09 Standard

As of this writing the new, standard for C++0x is on the verge of being adopted. The standard will probably be adopted in 2009, and the C++0x designation will become The C++09 Standard. C++03 adopted in 2003 is the current C++ standard. The C++0x standard includes some exciting updates to the language. Most of the improvements come in the form of new classes and libraries. The new C++ standard will have more support for parallel programming and multithreading through the addition of a concurrent programming library. This is very good news for C++ developers because prior to the new standard there was no guaranteed parallel programming facility in every C++ environment. The new standard will change this. Table 8-5 lists some of the new libraries that C++0x (C++09) will support.

Table 8-5

New Class Libraries in C++0x Standard	Description
MPI	Message Passing Interface (MPI) library for use in distributed-memory and parallel application programming.
Interprocess	Includes interprocess mechanisms such as shared memory, memory mapped files, process shared mutexes, and condition variables. Also includes containers and allocators for processes.
-asio	A portable networking library that includes sockets, timers, and hostname resolution socket iostreams.

The libraries in Table 8-5 contain some of the functionality that we discussed in Chapters 4, 5, 6, and 7, including threads, mutexes, condition variables, and Interprocess Communication (IPC) capabilities. The class libraries are essentially interface classes that wrap operating system APIs. They will be compatible with the POSIX thread management and process management facilities. Whereas the new standard provides an interface to most of the features in POSIX API, the holes can be filled by using other libraries, or providing your own interface classes to the POSIX API. Listing 8-1 shows a small part of the Boost C++ Libraries implementation of the new standard C++ thread class and some of the services that it offers developers. Boost has provided free peer-reviewed portable C++ source libraries that are compliant to the C++ Standard Library. Currently 10 of their libraries have been included in the C++ Standards Committee's Library Technical Report (TR1) and will become a part of future C++ Standards.

Listing 8-1

```
//Listing 8-1 An implementation of the new C++0x thread class.

1   #ifndef BOOST_THREAD_THREAD_PTHREAD_HPP
2   #define BOOST_THREAD_THREAD_PTHREAD_HPP
3   // Copyright (C) 2001-2003
4   // William E. Kempf
5   // Copyright (C) 2007 Anthony Williams
6   //
7   //  Distributed under the Boost Software License,
    //  Version 1.0. (See accompanying
8   //  file LICENSE_1_0.txt or copy at http://www.boost.org/LICENSE_1_0.txt)
9
10  #include <boost/thread/detail/config.hpp>
11
12  #include <boost/utility.hpp>
13  #include <boost/function.hpp>
14  #include <boost/thread/mutex.hpp>
15  #include <boost/thread/condition_variable.hpp>
16  #include <list>
17  #include <memory>
18
```

(continued)

Listing 8-1 (continued)

```
19   #include <pthread.h>
20   #include <boost/optional.hpp>
21   #include <boost/thread/detail/move.hpp>
22   #include <boost/shared_ptr.hpp>
23   #include "thread_data.hpp"
24   #include <stdlib.h>
25
26   #ifdef BOOST_MSVC
27   #pragma warning(push)
28   #pragma warning(disable:4251)
29   #endif
30
31   namespace boost
32   {
33     class thread;
34
35     namespace detail
36     {
37         class thread_id;
38     }
39
40     namespace this_thread
41     {
42         BOOST_THREAD_DECL detail::thread_id get_id();
43     }
44
45     namespace detail
46     {
47         class thread_id
48         {
49         private:
50             detail::thread_data_ptr thread_data;
51
52             thread_id(detail::thread_data_ptr thread_data_):
53                 thread_data(thread_data_)
54             {}
55             friend class boost::thread;
56             friend thread_id this_thread::get_id();
57         public:
58             thread_id():
59                 thread_data()
60             {}
61
62             bool operator==(const thread_id& y) const
63             {
64                 return thread_data==y.thread_data;
65             }
66
67             bool operator!=(const thread_id& y) const
```

```
68              {
69                  return thread_data!=y.thread_data;
70              }
71
72          bool operator<(const thread_id& y) const
73              {
74                  return thread_data<y.thread_data;
75              }
76
77          bool operator>(const thread_id& y) const
78              {
79                  return y.thread_data<thread_data;
80              }
81
82          bool operator<=(const thread_id& y) const
83              {
84                  return !(y.thread_data<thread_data);
85              }
86
87          bool operator>=(const thread_id& y) const
88              {
89                  return !(thread_data<y.thread_data);
90              }
91
92          template<class charT, class traits>
93          friend std::basic_ostream<charT, traits>&
94          operator<<(std::basic_ostream<charT, traits>& os,
                        const thread_id& x)
95              {
96                  if(x.thread_data)
97                  {
98                      return os<<x.thread_data;
99                  }
100                 else
101                 {
102                     return os<<"{Not-any-thread}";
103                 }
104             }
105         };
106     }
107
108     struct xtime;
109     class BOOST_THREAD_DECL thread
110     {
111     private:
112         thread(thread&);
113         thread& operator=(thread&);
114
115         template<typename F>
116         struct thread_data:
117             detail::thread_data_base
118         {
119             F f;
120
```

Listing 8-1 *(continued)*

```
121              thread_data(F f_):
122                  f(f_)
123              {}
124              thread_data(detail::thread_move_t<F> f_):
125                  f(f_)
126              {}
127
128              void run()
129              {
130                  f();
131              }
132          };
133
134          mutable boost::mutex thread_info_mutex;
135          detail::thread_data_ptr thread_info;
136
137          void start_thread();
138
139          explicit thread(detail::thread_data_ptr data);
140
141          detail::thread_data_ptr get_thread_info() const;
142
143      public:
144          thread();
145          ~thread();
146
147          template <class F>
148          explicit thread(F f):
149              thread_info(new thread_data<F>(f))
150          {
151              start_thread();
152          }
153          template <class F>
154          thread(detail::thread_move_t<F> f):
155              thread_info(new thread_data<F>(f))
156          {
157              start_thread();
158          }
159
160          thread(detail::thread_move_t<thread> x);
161          thread& operator=(detail::thread_move_t<thread> x);
162          operator detail::thread_move_t<thread>();
163          detail::thread_move_t<thread> move();
164
165          void swap(thread& x);
166
167          typedef detail::thread_id id;
168
169          id get_id() const;
170
171          bool joinable() const;
172          void join();
173          bool timed_join(const system_time& wait_until);
```

```
174
175        template<typename TimeDuration>
176        inline bool timed_join(TimeDuration const& rel_time)
177        {
178            return timed_join(get_system_time()+rel_time);
179        }
180        void detach();
181
182        static unsigned hardware_concurrency();
183
184        // backwards compatibility
185        bool operator==(const thread& other) const;
186        bool operator!=(const thread& other) const;
187
188        static void sleep(const system_time& xt);
189        static void yield();
190
191        // extensions
192        void interrupt();
193        bool interruption_requested() const;
194    };
195
196    inline detail::thread_move_t<thread> move(thread& x)
197    {
198        return x.move();
199    }
200
201    inline detail::thread_move_t<thread>
       move(detail::thread_move_t<thread> x)
202    {
203        return x;
204    }
205
206
207    template<typename F>
208    struct thread::thread_data<boost::reference_wrapper<F> >:
209        detail::thread_data_base
210    {
211        F& f;
212
213        thread_data(boost::reference_wrapper<F> f_):
214            f(f_)
215        {}
216
217        void run()
218        {
219            f();
220        }
221    };
222
223    namespace this_thread
224    {
225        class BOOST_THREAD_DECL disable_interruption
```

(continued)

Listing 8-1 *(continued)*

```
226          {
227              disable_interruption(const disable_interruption&);
228              disable_interruption& operator=(const disable_interruption&);
229
230              bool interruption_was_enabled;
231              friend class restore_interruption;
232          public:
233              disable_interruption();
234              ~disable_interruption();
235          };
236
237          class BOOST_THREAD_DECL restore_interruption
238          {
239              restore_interruption(const restore_interruption&);
240              restore_interruption& operator=(const restore_interruption&);
241          public:
242              explicit restore_interruption(disable_interruption& d);
243              ~restore_interruption();
244          };
245
246          BOOST_THREAD_DECL thread::id get_id();
247
248          BOOST_THREAD_DECL void interruption_point();
249          BOOST_THREAD_DECL bool interruption_enabled();
250          BOOST_THREAD_DECL bool interruption_requested();
251
252          inline void yield()
253          {
254              thread::yield();
255          }
256
257          template<typename TimeDuration>
258          inline void sleep(TimeDuration const& rel_time)
259          {
260              thread::sleep(get_system_time()+rel_time);
261          }
262      }
263
264      namespace detail
265      {
266          struct thread_exit_function_base
267          {
268              virtual ~thread_exit_function_base()
269              {}
270              virtual void operator()() const=0;
271          };
272
273          template<typename F>
274          struct thread_exit_function:
275              thread_exit_function_base
276          {
277              F f;
```

```
278
279            thread_exit_function(F f_):
280                f(f_)
281            {}
282
283            void operator()() const
284            {
285                f();
286            }
287        };
288
289        BOOST_THREAD_DECL void
           add_thread_exit_function(thread_exit_function_base*);
290    }
291
292    namespace this_thread
293    {
294        template<typename F>
295        inline void at_thread_exit(F f)
296        {
297            detail::thread_exit_function_base*
                   const thread_exit_func=new detail::thread_exit_function<F>(f);
298            detail::add_thread_exit_function(thread_exit_func);
299        }
300    }
301
302    class BOOST_THREAD_DECL thread_group
303    {
304    public:
305        thread_group();
306        ~thread_group();
307
308        thread* create_thread(const function0<void>& threadfunc);
309        void add_thread(thread* thrd);
310        void remove_thread(thread* thrd);
311        void join_all();
312        void interrupt_all();
313        size_t size() const;
314
315    private:
316        thread_group(thread_group&);
317        void operator=(thread_group&);
318
319        std::list<thread*> m_threads;
320        mutex m_mutex;
321    };
322    } // namespace boost
323
324    #ifdef BOOST_MSVC
325    #pragma warning(pop)
326    #endif
327
328
329    #endif
```

Notice on Line 302 of Listing 8-1 that the new thread class also supports thread groups. This provides much of the functionality of the POSIX pthread API. Notice on Line 19 that this implementation includes pthread.h. We covered the role of the operating system in Chapter 4 and explained that the operating system is the gatekeeper of the hardware and the multicores. Any class hierarchies, application frameworks, or pattern classes that present multithreading or multiprocessing capabilities are essentially providing interface classes to the operating system API. So, this is a welcome interface class because with standard C++ classes like the thread class shown in Listing 8-1 you get to move one step closer to declarative interpretations of parallel programming. These kinds of interface classes not only add declarative or Object-Oriented flavor to low-level operating system primitives, but they also simplify the interface. Consider Lines 308–311 and their POSIX API pthread counterparts. These methods replace direct calls to pthread calls such as pthread_create(), pthread_join(), using the attribute object to detach threads, thread cancellation functions, and so on. Interface classes as implemented in this type of library allow developers to maintain their Object-Oriented or declarative approach to application development.

A C++0x (C++09) Mutex Interface Class

In addition to thread interface classes, the C++0x standard will include mutex interface classes.

We explained the POSIX pthread_mutex() and its use in dealing with one of the primary synchronization challenges of multithreading. But pthread_mutex() is in Layer 2 of the PADL analysis. Ideally, you do not want to do most of the synchronization at Layer 2, and the important reason that you don't want to do the majority of your synchronization at Layer 2 is because the POSIX API has procedural semantics. To take advantage of the POSIX API services, you would have to provide interface classes. The new C++ standard comes to the rescue here by providing standard mutex classes. Listing 8-2 is Anthony William's implementation of the standard C++ mutex class. As you can see, the basic pthread mutex functionality of lock, unlock, destroy, timed lock, and so forth is encapsulated in the mutex class. Also, a timed mutex class is defined that encapsulates some of the functionality of a condition variable.

Listing 8-2

```
//Listing 8-2 An implementation of the new standard C++0x mutex class.

 1  #ifndef BOOST_THREAD_PTHREAD_MUTEX_HPP
 2  #define BOOST_THREAD_PTHREAD_MUTEX_HPP
 3  // (C) Copyright 2007 Anthony Williams
 4  // Distributed under the Boost Software License, Version 1.0. (See
 5  // accompanying file LICENSE_1_0.txt or copy at
 6  // http://www.boost.org/LICENSE_1_0.txt)
 7
 8  #include <pthread.h>
 9  #include <boost/utility.hpp>
10  #include <boost/thread/exceptions.hpp>
11  #include <boost/thread/locks.hpp>
12  #include <boost/thread/thread_time.hpp>
13  #include <boost/assert.hpp>
14  #ifndef WIN32
15  #include <unistd.h>
16  #endif
17  #include <errno.h>
18  #include "timespec.hpp"
19  #include "pthread_mutex_scoped_lock.hpp"
```

```
20
21   #ifdef _POSIX_TIMEOUTS
22   #if _POSIX_TIMEOUTS >= 0
23   #define BOOST_PTHREAD_HAS_TIMEDLOCK
24   #endif
25   #endif
26
27   namespace boost
28   {
29       class mutex:
30           boost::noncopyable31      {
32       private:
33           pthread_mutex_t m;
34       public:
35           mutex()
36           {
37               int const res=pthread_mutex_init(&m,NULL);
38               if(res)
39               {
40                   throw thread_resource_error();
41               }
42           }
43           ~mutex()
44           {
45               BOOST_VERIFY(!pthread_mutex_destroy(&m));
46           }
47
48           void lock()
49           {
50               BOOST_VERIFY(!pthread_mutex_lock(&m));
51           }
52
53           void unlock()
54           {
55               BOOST_VERIFY(!pthread_mutex_unlock(&m));
56           }
57
58           bool try_lock()
59           {
60               int const res=pthread_mutex_trylock(&m);
61               BOOST_ASSERT(!res || res==EBUSY);
62               return !res;
63           }
64
65           typedef pthread_mutex_t* native_handle_type;
66           native_handle_type native_handle()
67           {
68               return &m;
69           }
70
71           typedef unique_lock<mutex> scoped_lock;
72           typedef scoped_lock scoped_try_lock;
73       };
```

(continued)

Listing 8-2 *(continued)*

```
 74
 75     typedef mutex try_mutex;
 76
 77     class timed_mutex:
 78         boost::noncopyable
 79     {
 80     private:
 81         pthread_mutex_t m;
 82 #ifndef BOOST_PTHREAD_HAS_TIMEDLOCK
 83         pthread_cond_t cond;
 84         bool is_locked;
 85 #endif
 86     public:
 87         timed_mutex()
 88         {
 89             int const res=pthread_mutex_init(&m,NULL);
 90             if(res)
 91             {
 92                 throw thread_resource_error();
 93             }
 94 #ifndef BOOST_PTHREAD_HAS_TIMEDLOCK
 95             int const res2=pthread_cond_init(&cond,NULL);
 96             if(res2)
 97             {
 98                 BOOST_VERIFY(!pthread_mutex_destroy(&m));
 99                 throw thread_resource_error();
100             }
101             is_locked=false;
102 #endif
103         }
104         ~timed_mutex()
105         {
106             BOOST_VERIFY(!pthread_mutex_destroy(&m));
107 #ifndef BOOST_PTHREAD_HAS_TIMEDLOCK
108             BOOST_VERIFY(!pthread_cond_destroy(&cond));
109 #endif
110         }
111
112         template<typename TimeDuration>
113         bool timed_lock(TimeDuration const & relative_time)
114         {
115             return timed_lock(get_system_time()+relative_time);
116         }
117
118 #ifdef BOOST_PTHREAD_HAS_TIMEDLOCK
119         void lock()
120         {
121             BOOST_VERIFY(!pthread_mutex_lock(&m));
122         }
123
```

```
124         void unlock()
125         {
126             BOOST_VERIFY(!pthread_mutex_unlock(&m));
127         }
128
129         bool try_lock()
130         {
131             int const res=pthread_mutex_trylock(&m);
132             BOOST_ASSERT(!res || res==EBUSY);
133             return !res;
134         }
135         bool timed_lock(system_time const & abs_time)
136         {
137             struct timespec const timeout=detail::get_timespec(abs_time);
138             int const res=pthread_mutex_timedlock(&m,&timeout);
139             BOOST_ASSERT(!res || res==EBUSY);
140             return !res;
141         }
142 #else
143         void lock()
144         {
145             boost::pthread::pthread_mutex_scoped_lock const local_lock(&m);
146             while(is_locked)
147             {
148                 BOOST_VERIFY(!pthread_cond_wait(&cond,&m));
149             }
150             is_locked=true;
151         }
152
153         void unlock()
154         {
155             boost::pthread::pthread_mutex_scoped_lock const local_lock(&m);
156             is_locked=false;
157             BOOST_VERIFY(!pthread_cond_signal(&cond));
158         }
159
160         bool try_lock()
161         {
162             boost::pthread::pthread_mutex_scoped_lock const local_lock(&m);
163             if(is_locked)
164             {
165                 return false;
166             }
167             is_locked=true;
168             return true;
169         }
170
171         bool timed_lock(system_time const & abs_time)
172         {
173             struct timespec const timeout=detail::get_timespec(abs_time);
174             boost::pthread::pthread_mutex_scoped_lock const local_lock(&m);
175             while(is_locked)
```

(continued)

315

Listing 8-2 *(continued)*

```
176                {
177                        int const cond_res=pthread_cond_timedwait(&cond,&m,&timeout);
178                        if(cond_res==ETIMEDOUT)
179                        {
180                            return false;
181                        }
182                        BOOST_ASSERT(!cond_res);
183                }
184                is_locked=true;
185                return true;
186        }
187  #endif
188
189        typedef unique_lock<timed_mutex> scoped_timed_lock;
190        typedef scoped_timed_lock scoped_try_lock;
191        typedef scoped_timed_lock scoped_lock;
192    };
193
194  }
195
196
197  #endif
```

If you look at Lines 77–110, you can see how the services that POSIX API functions such as `pthread_mutex_init()`, `pthread_cond_init()`, `pthread_cond_destroy()`, and `pthread_mutex_destroy()` are adapted in a `timed_mutex` interface class. We explained in Chapter 4 the importance of understanding the operating system's role even though the goal is to program at higher level. This implementation of a mutex class that will be available in the new C++ standard can serve to illustrate that point. This class does not perform all of the functionality that you might want in a mutex class. Further, this mutex class might be used in conjunction with other thread libraries such as the TBB. If there are any problems at runtime, you have to have some idea of where these classes intersect with the operating system. Both the C++ thread class and the TBB threading facilities may use the POSIX pthreads differently in subtle ways. So, you deploy higher-level classes in Layer 3 of the PADL model, but you must keep in mind that those classes are ultimately mapped to operating system APIs, in our case, the POSIX API.

Obtaining Early Implementations of the C++0x Concurrent Programming Libraries

The thread class in Listing 8-1 and the mutex class in Listing 8-2 are taken from the Boost C++ libraries found at `www.boost.org`. Boost provides free peer-reviewed portable C++ source libraries. The Boost group emphasizes libraries that work well with the C++ standard Library. Boost libraries are intended to be widely usable across a broad spectrum of applications. The Boost group aims to establish "existing practice" and provide reference implementations so that Boost libraries are suitable for eventual standardization. The concurrent programming libraries that we introduced in this chapter have Boost reference implementations and can be freely downloaded.

The Intel Threading Building Blocks

Another important component that can be used in level 3 PADL analysis is the Intel Threading Building Blocks (TBB). The TBB is a set of C++ components consisting of generic algorithm templates, container classes, and Object-Oriented synchronization components, as well as other miscellaneous components that are very useful in multithreaded programming. The TBB is a runtime-based parallel programming model for C++ code that uses threads. It is designed primary to write scalable applications that:

- ❑ Specify tasks instead of threads
- ❑ Emphasize data parallel programming
- ❑ Take advantage of concurrent collections

Table 8-6 lists some of the primary template algorithms and containers that are available in the TBB library.

Table 8-6

TBB Generic Parallel Algorithms	TBB Containers with Concurrency Support
parallel_for	concurrent_queue
parallel_scan	concurrent_vector
parallel_reduce	concurrent_hash_map
parallel_while	
pipeline	
parallel_sort	

While the TBB intersects in a few areas (for example, mutexes), with the new concurrent programming library in the new C++ standard, it is largely complementary and provides a set of tools that can be used in the implementation Layer of PADL. Recall the seven steps from Figure 8-6. In Layer 4, we identified concurrency models. Layer 4 does not determine whether those concurrency models will be implemented by threads or processes. In fact, the concurrency models in Layer 4 can be implemented by clusters or other distributed computing models. The question and answer example that uses the Blackboard architecture does not indicate whether the knowledge sources should be implemented as threads or as processes. It also may be the case that one knowledge source may be implemented by a multiple threads or processes or even a combination of threads and processes. This can be necessary in order to meet the logical requirements of the knowledge source. To see how you might get to Layer 3 in the Blackboard example, you can take a closer look at the control strategies in the Blackboard architecture.

Blackboard: A Critical Section

There are several layers of control in a Blackboard implementation where the knowledge sources may be activated concurrently. At the lowest layer, there are synchronization schemes that must protect the integrity of the Blackboard. Although the Blackboard is an application architecture from Layer 5 of PADL and the discussion at that level is conceptual, you can state that the Blackboard is a critical section because ultimately it is a shared modifiable resource. In fact Table 8-4 shows that CRCW or CREW concurrency models are called for in the use of the Blackboard applied to knowledge sources. In a parallel environment, the knowledge sources' read and write access must be coordinated and synchronized. This coordination and synchronization can involve file locking, semaphores, mutexes, and so on. This layer of control is not directly involved in the solution that the knowledge sources are working toward. This is a utility layer of control and should be independent of the problem to be solved by the Blackboard. In the architectural approach for this chapter's example, this layer of control will be implemented by interface classes like the mutex and semaphore classes that we introduced in Chapter 7. You can also take advantage of the concurrent containers that the TBB has to offer to partially meet your needs for CRCW or CREW. Parts of the Blackboard could be implemented using the `concurrent_vector` class from the TBB. The `concurrent_vector` allows safe simultaneous access, and it is easy to use and easily works with components from the standard C++ library. Listing 8-3 is an excerpt from the question and answer Blackboard example.

Listing 8-3

```
//Listing 8-3   A Program that uses concurrent_vector and parallel_for from TBB.

 1   using namespace std;
 2   #include <iostream>
 3   #include <vector>
 4   #include <stdlib.h>
 5   #include <ctype.h>
 6   #include <algorithm>
 7   #include <iterator>
 8   #include <string>
 9   #include "tbb/blocked_range.h"
10   #include "tbb/parallel_for.h"
11   #include "tbb/task_scheduler_init.h"
12   #include "tbb/concurrent_vector.h"
13   #include <sstream>
14   #include <fstream>
15
16   using namespace tbb;
17   concurrent_vector<string>  Terms;
18   concurrent_vector<string>  Question;
19
20
21   class lower_case{
22
23   public:
24      char operator()(char X){
25
26          return(tolower(X));
27      }
28
29   };
30
31
32
33   void changeIt(string &X)
34   {
35      transform(X.begin(),X.end(),X.begin(),lower_case());
36   }
```

```
37
38
39
40   void tokenize(string &X)
41   {
42       stringstream Sin(X);
43       string Token;
44       while(!Sin.fail() && Sin.good())
45       {
46           Sin >> Token;
47           Terms.push_back(Token);
48       }
49   }
50
51
52   class parallel_lower_case{
53
54   public:
55
56       void operator() (const blocked_range<int> &X) const
57       {
58           for(int I = X.begin(); I != X.end(); I++)
59           {
60
61               changeIt(Terms[I]);
62
63           }
64
65       }
66
67   };
68
69   class valid_tokens{
70   public:
71       void operator() (const blocked_range<int> &X) const
72       {
73           for(int I = X.begin(); I != X.end(); I++)
74           {
75               tokenize(Question[I]);
76
77           }
78
79       }
80
81   };
82
83
84
85
86   int main(int argc,char *argv[])
87   {
88
89       task_scheduler_init Init;
90       ifstream Fin("question.txt");
```

(continued)

Listing 8-3 *(continued)*

```
 91    istream_iterator<string> Ftr(Fin);
 92    istream_iterator<string> Eof;
 93    copy(Ftr,Eof,back_inserter(Question));
 94    Fin.close();
 95    parallel_lower_case Lower;
 96    valid_tokens  Token;
 97    parallel_for(blocked_range<int>(0,Question.size(),
                                       (Question.size() /2)) ,Token);
 98    parallel_for(blocked_range<int>(0,Terms.size(),
                                       (Terms.size() /2)),Lower);
 99    ostream_iterator<string> Out(cout,"\n");
100    copy(Terms.begin(),Terms.end(),Out);
101
102
103  }
```

Part of the processing of our knowledge sources required that the individual words in a question be tagged with their part of speech or flagged as unknown, misspelled, or so forth. The program in Listing 8-3 is for exposition only. We include it here to demonstrate how TBB components can be easily mapped from Layers 4 and 5 of the PADL. The `Terms` component declared on Line 17 is a TBB `concurrent_vector<T>`. This vector permits concurrent read access by multiple knowledge sources. This satisfies part of the CREW concurrency model. Likewise, part of the processing requires that the questions be broken up into individual words or tokens and that the tokens be converted to lowercase. The call to the TBB `parallel_for` algorithm on Line 97 breaks up each `Question` that is stored in the `Question` vector into individual tokens. This is done on Lines 40–49. The `parallel_for()` algorithm on Line 97 takes `Token` as a C++ function object. The `parallel_for()` on Line 98 converts the tokens in the `Terms` vector to lowercase. The `parallel_for` algorithm does a high-level loop unrolling. It can execute components of its function object in parallel. In this example, the function calls on Lines 61 and 75 are executed in parallel. Notice on Lines 93 and 100 that the TBB `concurrent_vector<T>` is used with `ostream_iterator<string>`, `istream_iterator<string>`, and the standard C++ `copy()` algorithm.

Here is Program Profile 8-1 for Listing 8-3.

Program Profile 8-1

Program Name:

`convert_it.cc` (Listing 8-3)

Description:

The program in Listing 8-3 demonstrates how TBB components can be mapped from Layers 4 and 5 of the PADL. The `Terms` component is a TBB `concurrent_vector<T>`. This vector permits concurrent read access by multiple knowledge sources. The TBB `parallel_for` algorithm is used to break up each `Question` stored in the `Question` vector into individual tokens, takes `Token` as a C++ function object, and converts the tokens in the `Terms` vector to lowercase. The TBB `concurrent_vector<T>` is used with `ostream_iterator<string>`, `istream_iterator<string>`, and the standard C++ `copy()` algorithm.

Libraries Required:

tbb (Intel Thread Building Blocks)

Additional Source Files Needed:

None

User-Defined Headers Required:

None

Compile and Link Instructions:

```
c++ -o convert_it -I TBBIncludePath convert_it.cc -L TBBLibraryPath  -ltbb
```

Test Environment:

Linux Kernel 2.6

Processors:

Core 2 Duo

Notes:

None

Obtaining the TBB library

The TBB library is open source and can be obtained from www.threadingbuildingblocks.org. It is available for the Intel platforms and Intel-based Macs. As of this writing, it has not been ported to Solaris, HP-UX, or AIX. It does work in Linux environments.

The Parallel STL Library

As noted, concurrent programming library facilities will appear in the new C++ standard, including a long awaited thread library and synchronization components. However, another important set of C++ components that will support parallel programming is the Standard Template Adaptive Parallel Library (STAPL). Whereas TBB and the upcoming concurrent programming library in C++ are designed to work with multicore and parallel computers, STAPL is designed to work on both shared and distributed memory parallel computers. The STAPL library design goals are consistent with our PADL analysis approach to designing parallel programs. STAPL is designed to allow developers to work at a high level of abstraction. It provides interface classes and interface algorithms that hide many of the details specific to parallel programming. Throughout this book, we have made a distinction between application-level developers and system-level developers. System-level development tends to work closer to the operating system APIs and SPIs. STAPL users are divided into three groups:

- ❑ **Users:** These are the application developers who primarily use the STAPL components without having to do much extending or redefining.

- ❑ **Developers:** These developers extend the toolset of STAPL usually within the context of specific domains or applications through adding new data structures and algorithms for the users.

- ❑ **Specialists:** This group provides the users and the developers with additional programming frameworks for developing algorithms and applications.

Bjarne Stroustrup, the inventor of C++, is involved with the development of STAPL. This means that you can count on STAPL to be consistent with the philosophy of the C++ standard. STAPL consists of these primary components:

❑ **pContainers**: Containers that support concurrency.

❑ **Views**: Support the notion of iteration and object visitation for the pContainers.

❑ **pAlgorithms**: Standard Template Library (STL) algorithms that support parallelism.

❑ **pRange**: The pAlgorithms are executed over a range. The pRange allows for the Work Breakdown Structure (WBS) of the algorithm to be stated in a Task Dependency Graph.

❑ **Runtime**: Runtime system that provides performance monitoring, communication primitives, scheduling for the subviews or tasks of the pRanges, and so on.

Figure 8-7 shows a block diagram of the structure of the STAPL library.

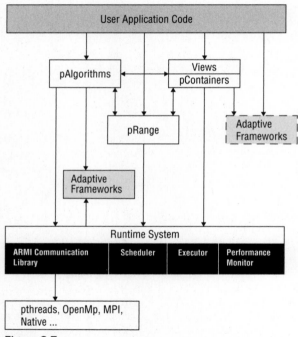

Figure 8-7

The standard C++ concurrent programming library will be complementary and compatible with STAPL.

The TBB is in part inspired by design concepts in STAPL, but STAPL is a higher-level framework that extends both the STL and TBB. Also notice in Figure 8-7 that the Runtime system can and will interface with the POSIX pthread API as well as with other operating thread and process APIs. You can see from looking at the structures of the new concurrent programming class library that will be part of C++0x, TBB, and STAPL that using interface classes and components that wrap lower-level operating system primitives is the most practical way to provide concurrency support to the C++ developer. Notice in Figure 8-7 that the user application code is at least two layers above the POSIX threads. If you look back at Figure 4-1 in Chapter 4, it shows the relationships for the developer's view of the operating system and frameworks such as STAPL. The complexity and special challenges of parallel programming as discussed in Chapter 3 require that the software developer have a clear understanding of the integration between class libraries, application frameworks, pattern classes, algorithm templates, and the concurrency and synchronization services that the operating system provides. PADL and PBS analysis (which is discussed later in the chapter) are performed in the context of a solid understanding of the relationships of all of the pieces involved.

> *More information about the STAPL library can be found at* `http://parasol.tamu.edu/stapl`.

The new standard C++ concurrent programming class libraries, TBB, and STAPL provide the bulk of the implementation domain independent components that you need in Layer 3 of the PADL analysis. Keep in mind that Layer 3 components consist of domain-specific application frameworks, class libraries, and so forth as well as domain-independent components.

The "Implementation Layer" Mapping

If you look at the Blackboard example, the segmentation of the Blackboard into parts determines whether CREW or CRCW concurrency (determined in Layer 2 of PADL) is appropriate. The most flexible model of critical section access is CRCW. CRCW can be achieved depending on the structure of the Blackboard. For instance, if 16 knowledge sources are involved in a collaborative effort and each knowledge source accesses its own segment of the Blackboard, then these knowledge sources can concurrently read and write the Blackboard without data race problems. Looking at the communication model can also help determine what Layer 3 components will be used. Obviously, containers that support concurrency such as the TBB `concurrent_vector<T>` or `concurrent_queue<T>` or `pContainers` from STAPL can be used to implement some portions of the Blackboard that require CREW. With a little planning, these structures can also support CRCW.

PADL: Layer 3 Type Control Strategies

One of the major reasons that we choose multiagent architectures and Blackboard architectures as our two fundamental application architectures for Layer 5 in PADL is that the patterns of work that can be captured by these architectures are extremely flexible and well understood. Here is an important point.

Before putting effort into the coordination and synchronization of concurrent threads or processes in your application, it is better to have a solid handle on the pattern of work at the domain and application level.

STAPL supports work at a higher level. The TBB is best used when the developer thinks in terms of tasks not threads. Here, we go a step further; think about the "story" of your application, how the actors and objects naturally interface. Work out the pattern of work at the model level in Layers 4 and 5. Understand the parallelism or concurrency in terms of a well-known architecture that supports concurrency (for example, Blackboards, multiagents).

To examine this further, take a closer look closer at the Blackboard control strategy for the example used in this chapter.

The layer of control in a Blackboard involves the selection of which knowledge sources to involve in the search for the solution and which aspects of the problem to focus on. This is a *focus* or *attention layer*. This layer of control focuses on a certain area of the problem and selects knowledge sources accordingly. Major issues to tackle in any kind of problem solving are where to start and what kind of information is needed to solve the problem. The focus/attention layer evaluates the initial conditions of the problem and then *controls* which knowledge sources to use and where they start. The available knowledge sources are known to the Blackboard, and typically the knowledge source accepts messages or parameters that dictate how it should proceed or where in the solution space it should begin the search. For parallel implementations, this layer determines the basic concurrency model for Layer 4 in PADL. Usually for Blackboards, this is the Multiple Programs Multiple Data (MPMD — a.k.a. MIMD) model because each knowledge source/problem solver has its own area of specialty. However, the nature of the problem might warrant the popular Single Program Multiple Data (SPMD or SIMD) model. If this model is used, the control layer spawns N number of the same knowledge source but pass different parameters to each.

The next layer of control involves determining what to do with the solution or partial solutions that are written to the Blackboard. This layer of control will determine whether the knowledge sources can stop work or whether the solution that was generated is acceptable, unacceptable, partially acceptable, and so on. This layer of control has complete visibility of the Blackboard and all the partial or tentative solutions. It *guides* the overall problem-solving strategies of the collective. As with the layout of the Blackboard and the structure of the knowledge sources, the Blackboard model suggests the existence of a control component but does not specify how it should be structured. Sometimes the control component is part of the Blackboard. Sometimes the control component is implemented by the knowledge sources. In some cases, the control component is implemented by modules external to the Blackboard. The control component can also be implemented by any combination of these. The knowledge sources collectively search for *a solution* to some problem. We want to emphasize *a solution* because many problems have more than one solution. Some of the solutions may be deeper in the search space than others. Some solutions may cost more to find than others. Some solutions may be deemed not good enough. The control component helps to manage the collective search strategies of the knowledge sources. The control component monitors the tentative or partial solutions to make sure that the knowledge sources are not pursuing an impractical search strategy. The control component looks out for any infinite loops, blind alleys, or recursive regression. Further, the control component is involved in selecting the best or the most appropriate knowledge sources for the problem. As the knowledge sources make progress toward a solution, the control component may relieve some knowledge sources while assigning others. The control strategy will be closely related to the search strategies used by the knowledge sources. It is important to remember that the knowledge sources may each use different search strategies and problem-solving techniques. Although they work with a common Blackboard, the knowledge sources or problem solvers are essentially autonomous and self-contained. Therefore, this layer of control has a two-way communication with the knowledge sources. Figure 8-8 shows possible control configurations and their layers in a Blackboard architecture.

CASE 1:
Control component is part of the blackboard.

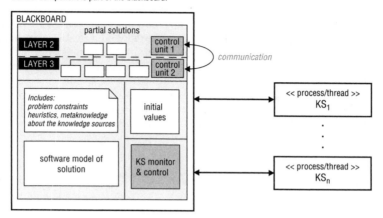

CASE 2:
Control component is part of the blackboard and the knowledge sources.

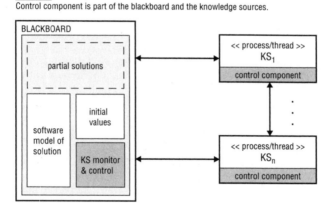

CASE 3:
Control component is external to both the blackboard and the knowledge sources.

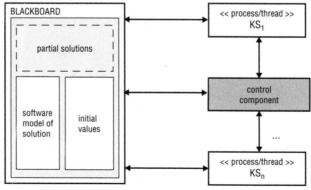

Figure 8-8

Notice the relationships between the Blackboard and the knowledge sources in Figure 8-8. If this interface is properly and completely worked out at the design level, then mapping knowledge sources or agents to tasks, threads, or processes is easier. It is not practical to attempt to optimize threads or processes and coordinate communication or synchronization at the implementation level if things are murky at the design and domain level. On the other hand, if all of the relationships are completely clear at the design level, if the patterns of work are well understood, and if the details of actor/object interaction have been worked out, then mapping to threads or processes is straightforward.

The chances for a successful software deployment are greatly increased. The "story" of the application, that is, its beginning, middle, and ending, has to be clear to all the developers involved. This understanding starts with a PADL analysis and PBS of your software application.

The Predicate Breakdown Structure (PBS)

A predicate is statement that is either true or false. A predicate makes a statement about some relationship between some person, place, thing, or idea. The Predicate Breakdown Structure (PBS) of an application breaks the application down into a set of statements that describe assertions and patterns of work of an application. The PBS of an application contains the rules, constraints, assertions, predicates, propositions, and axioms that apply to the agents, actors, and objects and their relationships within an application. The PBS captures the most declarative structure of an application or piece of software. This declarative structure is critical for software that has parallel programming or concurrency requirements. When it comes to parallel programming the old adage "Make it work, then make it fast" is a requirement for survival. The PBS helps you to understand what it truly means when you say the application works or that it's correct.

Throughout this book we've explained why if you think of multithreaded or multiprocessing programs from the bottom up as sequences of parallel instructions or parallel procedures, you will soon reach a limit because of the complexity of interactions between the instructions and procedures and the sheer number of cores that will eventually become available (that is, massively parallel CMPS). We have suggested that you need to begin the move away from thinking about parallel programming procedurally and move toward declarative programming techniques. There are many reasons why declarative interpretations of parallelism are beneficial. Today's systems are growing larger, more complex, and more integrated. Now adding to this mix are multicore capabilities of computers at the client side and server side. Imperative programming techniques buckle under this level of complexity. On the other hand, declarative techniques are scalable and have models that are designed to deal with complexity (for example, First-Order Logic analysis, model checking, Boolean algebra, and so on). Declarative interpretations describe what software systems are and what they mean as opposed to what they do and how it is done. Once you start thinking about hundreds or thousands of concurrently executing threads or processes, it is difficult to keep in mind what is going on in the system. This can make maintenance, testing, and debugging treacherous. Declarative interpretations make you consider what is true about the relationships between agents, actors, and objects in the system at any given time. Imperative approaches focus on what to do and when to do it. Declarative approaches focus on what is true or false and what conditions are necessary to cause some statement or predicate in the application to be true or false at any instant.

The PBS structure helps you capture the "meaning" of an application or piece of software. The meaning of a piece of software is important because if you understand the software, then you know how it can be scaled and evolved while at the same time keeping it reliable and correct. If you do not understand the software's meaning, then software maintenance and software evolution is hopeless. This is especially true for software that involves parallel programming. PADL analysis and PBS can be used to help make the shift away from imperative and sequential models of programming and toward declarative semantic design models.

An Example: PBS for the "Guess-My-Code" Game

You were able to write a guess-it application that used concurrently executing processes that were then broken down into currently executing threads in order to take enough guesses in the time limit to win the game. You could think about how many parallel threads or processes you would need to plow through 4 million codes in 2 minutes. You could also focus on what action the threads or processes would have to take. However, this would be more of an empirical approach to the problem. A PBS breakdown of the guess-what-code-I'm-thinking-of game would have a more goal look-and-feel. Example 8-1 is one PBS breakdown of the game.

Example 8-1: A PBS Breakdown of the Guess-What-Code Game

Breakdown 1: You've won the game if your guess is correct and in time.

Breakdown 2: Your guess is correct if it consists of a six-character code that contains only combinations of the characters (a–z, 0–9), considering duplication is allowed, and that code is the one my agent has handed me.

Breakdown 3: Your guess is in time if it is correct and it occurs within 2 minutes.

Breakdown 4: A brute force search through the codes will be successful if there are enough agents searching.

Breakdown 5: N agents are enough find the correct code from a sample of 4 million codes in 2 minutes.

Breakdown 6: 4 times N agents are required to find the correct code from a sample of 4 million codes in 2 minutes if the code is being changed every 15 seconds.

The PBS in Example 8-1 consists of the rules, statements, or predicates that make up the application.

These statements are either true or false. If you design code that correctly represents these statements, then the application will be correct and will work if the original statements are correct. On the other hand, if one or more of the statements are false, then the underlying code will also be in error. For example, Breakdown 5 states that N agents are enough. How do you know that N agents are enough? If you do your homework at this level, then later translations into concurrently executing instructions or threads are more productive and correct. How big should N be is the kind of information you want to discover during PADL analysis and the design activities of the SDLC. It should not be part of some trial-and-error process handled at the thread management level. Although the PBS presented in Example 8-1 is a simplification, it serves as a complete example of what we mean by PBS. Notice that Breakdown 6 deals with dynamically changing code and resubmission of the entire guess data set.

Connecting PBS, PADL, and the SDLC

Once the PBS is complete and the development group is satisfied with the PBS of the application, then the PBS is used to help with the application architecture selection that is done in Layer 5 and the concurrency model identification that is done in Layer 4 of the PADL. In terms of the SDLC, the PBS is done during the requirements gathering, analysis, and design activities. Ideally, it is done before Layer 5 in PADL, but sometimes it is performed concurrently with Layer 5 analysis. In an actual PBS breakdown, the statements are refined and clarified until there is no ambiguity left in the statement of the applications solution or services. Further, because the PBS consists of propositions, predicates, and statements, theorem-proving approaches and model-checking techniques can be used to determine the correctness of the application prior to any code that is developed. This ability to check for correctness, meaning, and declarative semantics prior to code implementation becomes more critical as you move toward more complex systems and massively parallel multicore computers.

Coding the PBS

Domain components, that is, the agents, actors, and objects of the application domain, should be associated with C++ application frameworks, class hierarchies, domain classes, and so on at Layer 3 in the PADL model.

For every person, place, thing, or idea mentioned in the PBS, there should be a corresponding C++ component(s) that implements the concept and the relationships between the concepts. These components will be the domain components, and they will be directly visible in the application architecture. That's because the application architecture is primarily chosen because of its fit with the PBS. The correctness and completeness of the application can be seen and proved at this level. Once the domain classes are provided, they can be supported by components from the TBB, the C++ concurrent programming library, or frameworks such as STAPL. Using PADL and PBS helps produce applications that are correct, that can evolve and that can be maintained in an efficient manner.

Summary

In this chapter, we explained how to approach the process of application design when there is a concurrency requirement in the original software development request or when parallelism is explicitly called for or implied by the solution decomposition. We discussed two main approaches:

❑ First, we introduced Parallel Application Design Layers (PADL), a five-layer analysis model that we use at CTEST Laboratories during the requirements analysis, software design, and decomposition activities of SDLC. We also use the PADL model to circumvent much of the complexity that results from bottom up approaches to parallel programming. Also in this chapter we presented a top-down architectural approach to parallelism rather than a bottom-up, task-oriented imperative approach. We also presented multiagent architectures and Blackboard architectures as two of the main and well understood paradigms for parallel programming at the application level. Most successful software undergoes constant change. If that software has components that require concurrency and synchronization, then the natural evolution of the software can be extremely challenging if an appropriate application architecture is not selected from the start. The PADL analysis model identifies multiagent and Blackboard architectures as two well-known and well-understood architectures that perform well under the conditions of software evolution. Ultimately, the concurrency of an application is going to be implemented by low-level operating system primitives like threads and processes. If the application architecture is clean, modular, scalable, and well understood, then the translation into manageable operating system primitives has a chance to succeed. On the other hand, selection of the wrong or a poor application architecture can lead to brittle, error-prone software that cannot be readily changed, maintained, or evolved. While this is true of any kind of computer application, it is magnified when that software involves parallel programming, multithreading, or multiprocessing.

❑   We also introduced the notion of a Predicate Breakdown Structure (PBS) of an application idea. The PBS of an application breaks the application down into a set of statements that describe assertions and patterns of work of an application. The PBS of an application contains the rules, constraints, assertions, predicates, propositions, and axioms that apply to the agents, actors, and objects and their relationships within an application. The PBS captures the most declarative structure of an application or piece of software. This declarative structure is critical for software that has parallel programming or concurrency requirements. The PBS structure helps capture the "meaning" of an application or piece of software. The meaning of a piece of software is important because if you understand the software, then you know how it can be scaled and evolved, while at the same time keeping it reliable and correct. If you do not understand the software's meaning, then software maintenance and software evolution are impossible.

Today's systems are growing larger and more complex and more integrated. We are now adding to this mix multicore capabilities of computers at the client side and server side. Imperative programming techniques buckle under this level of complexity. On the other hand, declarative techniques are scalable and have models that are designed to deal with complexity Declarative interpretations describe what software systems are and what they mean as opposed to what they do and how it is done. They make you consider what is true about the relationships between agents, actors, and objects in the system at any given time. It is not practical to attempt to optimize thread or processes and coordinate communication or synchronization at the implementation level if things are murky at the design and domain level. On the other hand, if all of the relationships are completely clear at the design level and the patterns of work are well understood at the design level and the details of actor/object interaction has been worked out, then mapping to threads or processes will be straightforward. The chances for a successful software deployment are greatly increased. The story of the application has to be clear to all the developers involved. This understanding starts with a PADL analysis and PBS of your software application.

In the next chapter, we discuss modeling and documenting applications using UML notation for concurrent behavior. We have used UML class, sequence, and activity diagrams in the book so far. In the next chapter, we discuss some basic UML diagramming techniques for modeling classes, gradually covering concurrent notation and behavior between classes and ultimately the architecture of systems with parallelism.

Modeling Software Systems
That Require Concurrency

The topology of perceived interconnected cyberspaces need not have any direct connection to that of the array of support computers, since the cyberspaces are perceived, not actual spaces.

— **Marcus Novak,** *Liquid Architectures in Cyberspaces*

A model of a system is the body of information gathered for the purpose of studying the system so that it can be better understood by the developers and maintainers of the system. When a system is modeled, the boundaries and identification of the entities, attributes, and activities performed by the system can be determined. Modeling is an important tool in the design process of any system. It is essential that developers fully understand the system they are developing. Modeling can reveal the hidden concurrency and opportunities where parallelism can be exploited.

In this chapter, we show you how to visualize and model your concurrent system using the UML. We will discuss diagraming techniques used to visualize and model concurrent systems from three perspectives:

❑ The structural perspective

❑ The behavioral perspective

❑ The architectural perspective

The classes, objects, processes, threads, and systems used as examples in this chapter are used for exposition purposes and may or may not necessarily reflect actual classes, objects, or structures used in an actual system. This chapter should not be considered a primer for UML but rather an introduction to the diagrams used in this book focused on the UML notation used to design and document systems that utilize concurrency.

What Is UML?

Unified Modeling Language (UML) is a graphical language used for modeling, visualizing, designing and documenting the artifacts of a system. It is the standardized specification language used to communicate and model different system paradigms such as Object-Oriented, agent-oriented, and event-driven systems. It uses symbols and notations to represent the components from different views and perspectives of the system.

The UML is called "unified" because it brought three of the most prominent modeling languages (Grady Booch's Approach, Ivar Jacobson's Object-Oriented Software Engineering (OOSE), and James Rumbaugh's Object Modeling Technique(OMT)). Although each was a complete systems, each had a particular focus. Each also had a weakness — they were not able to be a general-purpose modeling language for complex systems. Table 9-1 gives a brief definition of each of these modeling approaches and what their main contribution was to the UML standard. The purpose of the UML was to unify these methods into a definition that would provide to users a modeling system that was capable of capturing:

❑ Conceptual to executable components of a software system utilizing object-oriented techniques

❑ Simple to complicated mission-critical systems

This was true whether those users were people or machines. The first draft of the UML was released in early 1995, and a new version was released later that year. In 1997, the Object Management Group (OMG), an international consortium of companies active in the development of the Object-Oriented paradigm, made a request for proposal for a standard modeling language, and UML 1.0 was offered. Since then UML has become the de facto international standard modeling language revised and extended by OMG. Many interests over the years have contributed to the standard, and it has now been adopted for modeling not only Object-Oriented (OO) software systems but concurrent and distributed systems, engineering problems, and business structures and processes. OMG released version 2.0 in 2007.

Table 9-1

UML Language Primitives	Types	Description
Things	Structural	Nouns of the model
	• class	The static parts of the model representing elements that are conceptual or physical.
	• interface	
	• collaborations	
	• use cases	
	• active class	
	• component	
	• node	
	Behavioral	Verbs of the model
	• interaction	Dynamic parts of the model representing behavior over time.
	• state	

UML Language Primitives	Types	Description
	Grouping	Organizations parts of the model
	• package	These are highest level of the model where decomposition can occur.
	Annotational	Explanatory parts of the model
		Used for comments that describe element in the model.
Relationships	Dependency	Change to one element may affect the other.
	Association	A structural connection between elements (whole-part).
	Generalization	The child element is a specialization of the parent element.
	Realization	One element fulfills the contract of another element.
Diagrams	• class	
	• object	
	• use case	
	• sequence	
	• collaboration	
	• statechart	
	• activity	
	• component	
	• deployment	

The UML grammar is based on three language primitives:

❑ **Things**: The most basic components in a model

❑ **Relationships**: Relate things with other things

❑ **Diagrams**: Define a collection of things and their relationships

Table 9-1 shows how each of the three language primitives is broken down into its various components and types. As you can see, UML is a comprehensive language with many ways for representing a system. What we focus on in this chapter are the notations and diagrams of the language that you utilize when modeling a system with concurrent behavior.

Modeling the Structure of a System

When you are modeling the structure of a system, the focus will be on the static parts of a system such as objects, classes, and their attributes, services, organization, and composition, along with relationships those parts of the system will have with other entities in the system.

The Class Model

The *class* is the basic software component of an Object-Oriented system. A class is a model of a construct that includes its attributes and behaviors. It serves as a definition of a group or set of things that all share the same attributes and behaviors. A class can model something conceptual, a real-world physical entity, or a software construct.

❑ A class modeling something **conceptual** is a scaled representation of a process, concept, or an idea for the purpose of analysis or experimentation. It is a scaled representation because a full model would be too difficult to create or not desirable. The nature of the analysis may be focused in a specific area, and therefore, a full-scale model is not necessary. An example of a class is a model of a molecule. The structure of a molecule and the distances and angles of chemical bonds are attributes of the class, and the chemical reactions and processes are the behaviors of the model. This molecule class simulates the characteristics of the real-world counterpart for the purpose of predicting and analyzing its behavior.

❑ A class can model a **real-world physical entity**, process, task, or idea for the purpose of replacing it. In this, the model is not a scaled representation but duplicates all the functionality of the existing entity. This type of class models the real-world counterpart because the software model may be more efficient, accessible, or effective. For example, a class can model an accounting system or a calculator. A calcular class would have a display, a calculation, and an input mechanism for attributes. The calculator class would have to be able to parse the input, validate the input, perform the desired arithmetic operations, and then display the results.

❑ A class can model **software constructs**. In this case, the model only has meaning within a software system. An example of modeling a software construct is a bitmapped image class. A bitmapped image class would have a header, number of bit planes, size, and vector of bits that represents each pixel of the image. The class would have to be able to display, read, and resize the image. Other software constructs that are modeled are datatypes. Datatypes such as floats, integers, and booleans have both attributes and a set of operations. These software constructs are used as utility and support classes for modeling a larger system such as an accounting system or a simple calculator. They can be used in any system regardless of the domain.

So, as you can see, classes can be used to model various types of entities in a software system. When you are modeling, it is important to be able to identify the constructs based on the structural, behavioral, or architectural view of the system. It is even necessary to model types of classes based on how they are used in the system. Some classes are useful when used as a blueprint that provides an interface policy for other classes, whereas other classes are useful as a base or ancestor class or a class just for a particular domain. Table 9-2 lists commonly found class types.

Table 9-2

Class	Description
Abstract	A base class that defines the blueprint for all its descendants; an object cannot be declared of this type.
Concrete	A standalone class that represents the end of an ancestor-descendant lineage.
Interface	A class that modifies or enhances the interface of another class or set of classes.
Node	A class that supplies the foundation for inheritance and polymorphism and contains no pure virtual functions.
Domain	A class created to simulate reality or some entity within a domain.
Support/Utility	Useful programs for applications regardless of domain.
Collection and Containers	Generic holder of a set of objects with a defined set of operations to access them.
Template	A class in which the type is parameterized with a defined set of operations to access and manipulate the objects.
Datatypes	A type and its operations.

For instance, say that you are modeling a subsystem that identifies unrecognized words in a text file. The subsystem extracts words from a text file, determines if a word cannot be recognized, and then stores that word in a global container. Some classes in this subsystem are:

❑   **Word expert**: Determines if a word is recognized, if not writes the word to a container

❑   **Unrecognized words list**: Removes a given set of characters from a file

❑   **Dictionary lexicon**: Contains all the recognized words

❑   **Text file**: Contains the words to be recognized

❑   **Main agent**: Creates word experts

❑   **Unrecognized word container**: Contains all the unrecognized words

❑   **Misspelled and morphology agents**: Agents that filter misspelled or word forms from the unrecognized words list

Each of these classes can be identified as a type of class:

❑   **Utility and support classes**: Filtering agents, text file

❑   **Domain classes**: Dictionary lexicon, word expert

❑   **Container classes**: Unrecognized word container

Visualizing Classes

The UML provides a graphical representation of a class. The representation of the class, or *class icon*, can show the attributes, services, and semantics of the class. The UML also provides a representation of types of classes such as datatypes, interface, template, and node classes. The simplest representation of a class is a rectangular box containing the name of the class. The *simple name* is the name of the class alone; a pathname is the name of the class with the name of the package where the class is contained prefixed to the name. The class name is text containing any number of letters and numbers. Punctuation can be used except for a colon that is used to separate the package from the class name. Class names are usually nouns or noun phrases taken from the vocabulary of the system that is being modeled. Class name should have the first letter of every word capitalized:

- ❑ `DictionaryLexicon`
- ❑ `WordExpertAgent`
- ❑ `Filter::MorphologyAgent`

Visualizing Class Attributes, Services, and Responsibilities

The class icon can be divided into three horizontal compartments. The top compartment contains the class name. The next two contain the attributes and services provided to the user of the class. An additional compartment at the bottom can describe the *responsibility of the class*. The responsibilities of the class are the obligations of the class stated in a few short sentences. For example, here are the basic responsibilities of the `WordExpertAgent`, `UnrecognizedWords`, and `DictionaryLexicon` classes:

- ❑ `WordExpertAgent`
    - ❑ Determines if a word is recognized
    - ❑ Writes the unrecognized words to a global container
- ❑ `UnrecognizedWords`
    - ❑ Determines if unrecognized words are word forms or misspellings of recognized words by using `MorphologyAgent` and `MisspelledAgent`
- ❑ `DictionaryLexicon`
    - ❑ Contains all the recognized words
    - ❑ Contains the part of speech, synonyms, and word forms for each word
    - ❑ When given a word, returns TRUE if the word is in the lexicon

These responsibilities can be transformed into the attributes and services of the class. The attributes are the named properties of the class, and the services or operations describe the behaviors of the class. Figure 9-1 shows how the responsibilities of the `DictionaryLexicon` were used to create some of the attributes and services of the class. The attributes are then transformed into datatypes and data structures, and services are transformed into methods. Attributes and service names use a lowercase for the first letter of the first word and uppercase for the first letter of any additional words.

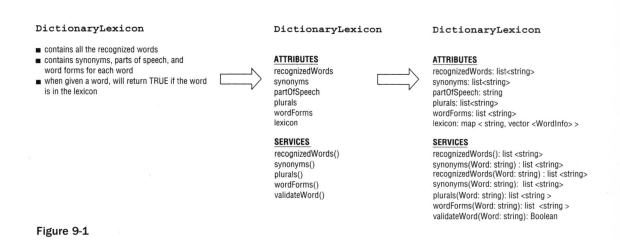

Figure 9-1

The attributes, services, and responsibilities compartments can be labeled *attributes*, *services*, and *responsibilities*, respectively, to identify each compartment. If the attributes or services are not shown, then the compartment is displayed as empty. Figure 9-2 shows the various ways that a class can be represented, using the `DictionaryLexicon` class as an example.

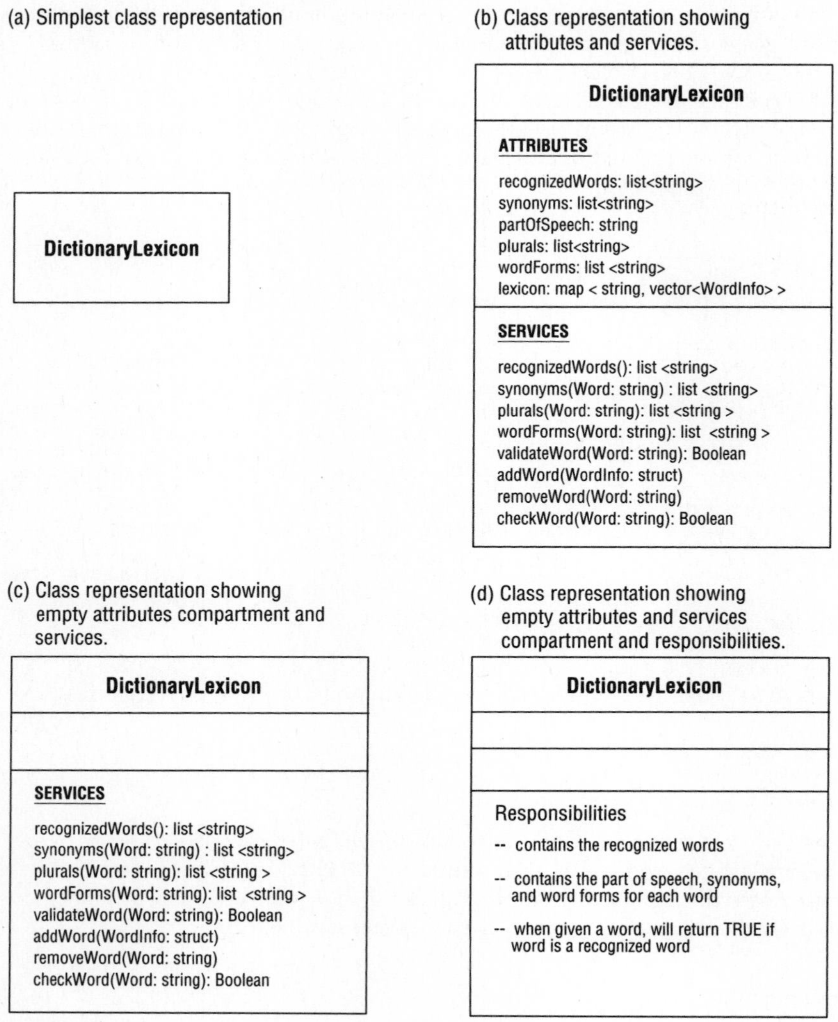

(a) Simplest class representation

(b) Class representation showing
attributes and services.

DictionaryLexicon

DictionaryLexicon
ATTRIBUTES
recognizedWords: list<string>
synonyms: list<string>
partOfSpeech: string
plurals: list<string>
wordForms: list <string>
lexicon: map < string, vector<WordInfo> >
SERVICES
recognizedWords(): list <string>
synonyms(Word: string) : list <string>
plurals(Word: string): list <string >
wordForms(Word: string): list <string >
validateWord(Word: string): Boolean
addWord(WordInfo: struct)
removeWord(Word: string)
checkWord(Word: string): Boolean

(c) Class representation showing
empty attributes compartment and
services.

DictionaryLexicon
SERVICES
recognizedWords(): list <string>
synonyms(Word: string) : list <string>
plurals(Word: string): list <string >
wordForms(Word: string): list <string >
validateWord(Word: string): Boolean
addWord(WordInfo: struct)
removeWord(Word: string)
checkWord(Word: string): Boolean

(d) Class representation showing
empty attributes and services
compartment and responsibilities.

DictionaryLexicon
Responsibilities
-- contains the recognized words
-- contains the part of speech, synonyms, and word forms for each word
-- when given a word, will return TRUE if word is a recognized word

Figure 9-2

In Figure 9-2:

❏ (a) shows the class in its simplest representation.

❏ (b) shows the class name and its attributes and services.

❏ (c) shows the class name and its services; the attributes compartment is empty to show that there are attributes but not shown.

❏ (d) lists the responsibilities of the class.

The attributes compartment can specify the datatype and/or default value (if there is one) of the attributes for objects:

```
word : string
Word : string = "Car"
```

The datatypes and data structures for the attributes of the WordExpertAgent and DictionaryLexicon classes can be displayed:

```
synonyms : map <string,vector<string> >
synonymIterator :  map <string,vector<string> >::iterator
```

Methods can be shown with parameters and return type:

```
synonym(&X : map <string,vector<string> >) : void
partOfSpeech(string &X) : string
```

The synonym() method returns the synonyms of the word. DictionaryLexicon is a class that models a dictionary for a single domain. The synonyms for each word are stored in a vector. The map container maps a string (recognized word) with the vector of synonyms. The synonym() method returns void, whereas the partOfSpeech() method returns the part of speech of a word as a string.

Using Attribute and Operation Properties

You can use properties to describe attributes and methods. These properties help describe how an attribute or method can be used. Properties for attributes can be constant or modifiable:

❑ changeable

❑ addOnly

❑ frozen

There are four properties used to defined methods:

❑ isQuery

❑ sequential

❑ guarded

❑ concurrent

These properties are listed in Table 9-3, along with a brief description of each.

Table 9-3

Properties for Attributes	Description
{changeable}	No restrictions on modifying the values of this type of attribute.
{addOnly}	For attributes with multiplicity > 1, additional values can be added; once created a value cannot be removed or changed.
{frozen}	Attribute's value cannot be changed once the object has been initialized.
Properties for Services	**Description**
{isQuery}	Execution leaves the state of the object unchanged; returns a value.
{sequential}	Uses synchronization to ensure sequential access to this method; multiple concurrent access to this method jeopardizes the integrity of the object.
{guarded}	Synchronized sequential access to this method is built into the object; integrity of the object is guaranteed.
{concurrent}	Multiple concurrent access is permitted; integrity of the object is guaranteed.

The sequential, guarded, and concurrent properties are concerned with methods involved with concurrency. For example, multiple WordExpertAgent objects can be created then passed individually to threads. Each WordExpertAgent object's method writes the unrecognized words to a shared container. The method that writes to the shared container has a critical section. *Critical sections* are regions of code where the code is accessing a shared modifiable object. When one method is in its critical section, other methods accessing that same object should not be in theirs. These properties (sequential, guarded, and concurrent) mark and manage methods that have or are critical sections by delineating whose responsible for synchronization.

❑ The sequential property describes concurrent access where synchronization is the responsibility of the callers of the method. To synchronize access to the shared object, the mutex is tested by the calling objects. If the mutex is in use, then the calling object must wait until it is available. Once it is available, the mutex is set, and the operation that modifies the object can be performed. Once the operation is completed, the mutex is reset. The sequential operations do not guarantee the integrity of the object.

❑ The guarded property describes a concurrent access where synchronization is built into the shared object; access is sequential.

❑ The concurrent property describes a method that permits simultaneous use.

Methods that are guarded and concurrent guarantee the integrity of the shared modifiable object or data. Figure 9-3 shows where the synchronization occurs for sequential, guarded, and concurrent methods.

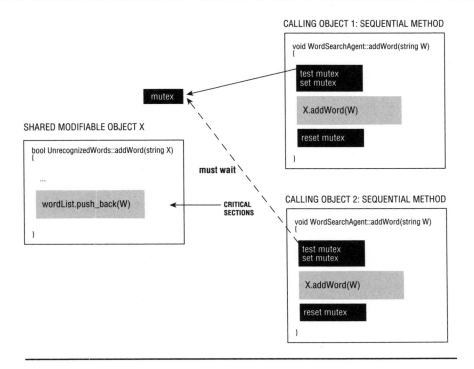

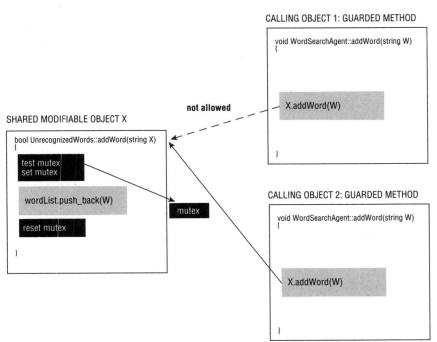

Figure 9-3 (*Continued*)

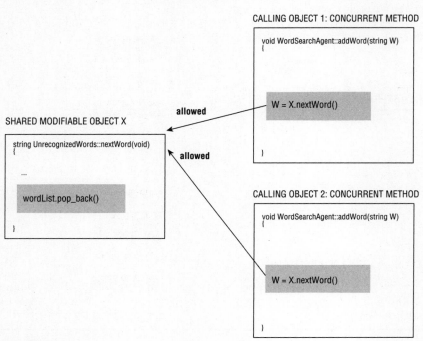

Figure 9-3

Here are examples of attributes and methods labeled with properties:

attributes

```
wordList : vector<string> {changeable}
```

operations

```
addWord(word : string) : boolean {guarded}
nextWord(void) : string {isQuery, concurrent}
```

The attributes and operations in this example are defined by the UnrecognizedWords class that contains all the unrecognizable words. WordSearchAgent objects pass a word to addWord(), which adds the word to the list and returns TRUE. addWord() changes the state of the object. UnrecognizedWords objects are shared between all the WordSearchAgent objects. So, the addWord() is guarded. Synchronization is built into the object by using mutexes. nextWord(), on the other hand, returns the next word in the list. Calling this method does not change the state of the object; thus, it can use the isQuery, concurrent properties because this operation does not change the state of the object.

Another important property you can show is the *visibility* of attributes and operations. The visibility property describes who can access the attribute or invoke the operation. A character or symbol is used to represent the level of visibility. Visibility maps to the access specifiers of C++ and other languages. Access specifiers and visibility symbols are listed in Table 9-4.

Table 9-4

Access Specifiers	Visibility Symbols
public	(+) Anyone has access.
protected	(#) The class itself and its descendants have access.
private	(-) Only the class itself has access.

The symbol is prepended to the service, method, or attribute name.

Ordering the Attributes and Services

Some classes have many attributes and operations, so it may be best to organize them within their compartments. Ordering helps identify and navigate through the attributes and operations. The organization can be:

❑   By access

❑   By category

Ordering by *access* can be very useful to users. It communicates which attributes and operations are publicly accessible. Knowing which members are protected assists users who need to extend or specialize the class through inheritance. Visibility symbols or access specifiers can be used to organize attributes and services/methods by access.

Ordering attributes and operations based on the *category* helps in the modeling of the class. Organizing by category helps you determine what the basic operations of the class will be. Are you modeling a nice class? A *nice class* provides regular functionality to the class. This is the functionality that should be defined for a nice class:

❑   Default constructor

❑   Copy constructor

❑   Assignment operator

❑   Equality operator

❑   Destructor

The copy constructor, assignment operator, and destructor can be generated by the compiler for classes that need them, but do not define them. Some software designers believe that classes that are not nice classes have severely restricted behavior. Reusable classes should have a nice interface when possible. The *minimal standard interface* defines categories that not only have the nice interface but also have these additional operations:

- ❏ Input and output
- ❏ Hash function
- ❏ Query
- ❏ Shallow and deep copy operations

Still, an argument can be made against a "minimal standard interface" or even a nice class. For example, a class may model an object that does not require any input or output operations.

Attributes and services can be categorized according to the language of the domain. If you are modeling a class, the attributes and services are dictated by what is being modeled. For example, the `DictionaryLexicon` class might have categories based on services concerned with vocabulary, word forms, synonyms, and so on. Using these categories is very useful when you are starting to determine what attributes and operations a class requires. Other categories may be based on other properties of the methods or attributes such as:

attributes
```
static
const
```

operations
```
virtual
pure virtual
friend
query
concurrent
guarded
```

To show category names, you place them within left and right double angle brackets, (<< . . . >>).

Figure 9-4 shows examples of the different ways operations can be organized for the `DictionaryLexicon` class using the visibility symbols for the attributes and minimal standard interface, or domain categories for operations/services. In 9-4 (a) services are categorized by the function they fulfill for the class. In 9-4(b) services are categorized by the domain language of the class. All attributes have private visibility.

(a) Attributes categorized by visibility and services
   categorized functionality.

DictionaryLexicon
ATTRIBUTES
- recognizedWords: list<string> {changeable} - synonyms: list<string> {changeable} - partOfSpeech: string {changeable} - plurals: list<string> {changeable} - wordForms: list <string> {changeable} - lexicon: map < string, vector<WordInfo> > {changeable}
<<constructor>> dictionaryLexicon() dictionaryLexicon(lexicon: map <string, vector<Wordinfo> > <<query>> synonyms(Word: string) : list <string> plurals(Word: string): list <string > wordForms(Word: string): list <string > recognizedWords(): list <string> partOfSpeech(Word: string): string <<assignment>> addWord(WordInfo: struct) synonyms(Word: string, s: list <string>) plurals(Word: string, p: list <string>) partofSpeech(Word: string, p: string) ... <<validation>> validateWord(Word: string): Boolean checkWord(Word: string): Boolean

(b) Attributes categorized by visibility and services
   categorized by domain language.

DictionaryLexicon
ATTRIBUTES
- recognizedWords: list<string> {changeable} - synonyms: list<string> {changeable} - partOfSpeech: string {changeable} - plurals: list<string> {changeable} - wordForms: list <string> {changeable} - lexicon: map < string, vector<WordInfo> > {changeable}
<<constructor>> dictionaryLexicon() dictionaryLexicon(lexicon: map <string, vector<Wordinfo> > <<vocabulary>> recognizedWords(): list <string> addWord(WordInfo: struct) validateWord(Word: string): Boolean checkWord(Word: string) Boolean <<word forms>> synonyms(Word: string, s: list <string>) synonyms(Word: string): list <string> plurals(Word: string, p: list <string>) wordForms(Word: string): list <string> <<part of speech>> partOfSpeech(Word: string): string partOfSpeech(Word: string, p: string)

Figure 9-4

Visualizing Instances of a Class

An *object* is an instantiation of a class. The object has an identity and gives values to attributes; this can be depicted using UML notation. The simplest representation of an object, an instance of a class, is a rectangle containing the name of the object underlined. This is called a *named instance* of a class. A named instance of a class can be shown with or without its class name:

myWordSearch	Named instance
myWordSearch:WordSearchAgent	Named instance with class name

Since the actual name of the object may be known only to the program that declares it, you may want to represent *anonymous instances* of classes in your system documentation, with or without the pathnames. An *orphan instance* does not show the class name:

```
:WordSearchAgent          Anonymous instance

myWordSearch:             Orphan instance
```

Instances of a class may also show their current state, the static properties, and the dynamic ones in their own compartments. When the object changes dynamically, the object displays the new value of its properties. For example, Figure 9-5 shows the `myWordSearch:WordSearchAgent` object's attributes changing. To show the active or current object, a heavier line is used. More specifically, Figure 9-5 shows several versions of the `myWordSearch` object:

❑   (a) shows the various notations for an instance.

❑   (b) shows the instance's attributes changing but only one is the active object.

❑   (c) denotes a collection of unintialized instances of the class called *multiobjects*.

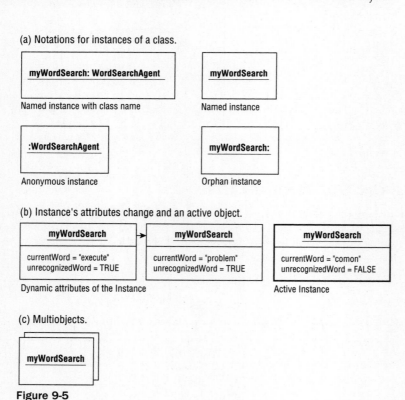

(a) Notations for instances of a class.

myWordSearch: WordSearchAgent — Named instance with class name

myWordSearch — Named instance

:WordSearchAgent — Anonymous instance

myWordSearch: — Orphan instance

(b) Instance's attributes change and an active object.

myWordSearch
currentWord = "execute"
unrecognizedWord = TRUE

myWordSearch
currentWord = "problem"
unrecognizedWord = TRUE

Dynamic attributes of the Instance

myWordSearch
currentWord = "comon"
unrecognizedWord = FALSE

Active Instance

(c) Multiobjects.

myWordSearch

Figure 9-5

Multiobjects are a way to show multiple instances of a class exist. Depending upon the nature of the class or the relationship between two classes, you may want to restrict the number of instances of a class. Multiplicity is a specification that shows the allowable range of possible instances of a class. The multiplicity of a class can be noted on the class icon or an object. The multiplicity is placed in the upper-right corner of the icon. A class may have zero to an infinite number of instances. For example, a class with 0 instances is a *pure abstract class*. It cannot have any objects explicitly declared of its type. The number of instances may have an upper or lower bound. This may also be expressed in the diagram of a class. Figure 9-6 shows how multiplicity of a class can be represented (and how it can be represented between associated classes as well).

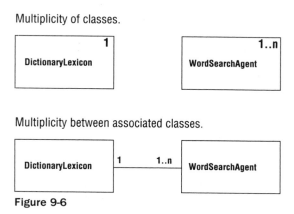

Multiplicity of classes.

Multiplicity between associated classes.

Figure 9-6

In Figure 9-6, the multiplicity of the WordSearchAgent class is 1..n, meaning that the least number of WordSearchAgent objects in a system is 1 and the most that can exist is n (depending on the amount of space available), each containing a different set of words. The DictionaryLexicon has a multiplicity of one. It is a singleton class meaning only one exists in the system. Here are more examples of multiplicity notation and their meanings:

1	One instance
1..n	One to a specified number n
1..*	One to an infinite number
0..1	0 to 1
0..*	0 to an infinite number
*	An infinite number

Multiplicity can be shown between classes with association relationships. In Figure 9-6, there is one DictionaryLexicon to 1 to many instances of WordSearchAgents. This means there can be many WordSearchAgents performing searches on a DictionaryLexicon.

Visualizing Template Classes

A *template class* is a mechanism that allows a type to be a parameter in the definition of the class. The template defines services that manipulate the datatype passed to it. The parameterized class is created in C++ by using the `template` keyword:

```
template <class Type > classname {...};
```

The `Type` parameter represents any type passed to the template. `Type` can be a built-in datatype or a user-defined class. When `Type` is declared, the template is bound by the element passed to it as the parameterized type. For example, the `Synonym` is a `map` container that contains `vectors` of `string` objects. The `map` and the `vector` are template classes:

```
map <string,vector<string> > Synonym;
```

The `map` container has `string` as a key and `vector` of strings as the value. The `vector` container contains string objects. The `map` container can map any datatype to any other datatype, and `vector` containers can contain any datatype:

```
map <int, vector <string> >    // maps a number to a vector of strings
map <int, string> >            // maps a number to a string
vector <DictionaryLexicon>     // a vector of dictionary objects
vector <map <int,string> >     // a vector of maps that maps a number to
                               // string
```

Template classes are represented as rectangular boxes like any other class. There is an added notation of a parameterized type. It is represented as a dashed box displayed in the upper-right corner of the class icon. The template class can be unbound or bound to a type. The notation for representing an unbound template class is a dashed box displaying a capital T to represent the unbound parameterized type. A bound template class can be represented with *implicit binding*, the C++ syntax for declaring and binding a template class. For example, the template `vector` is implicitly bound with a string object:

```
vector <string>
```

This can be displayed in the class icon or `<string>` can be placed in the dashed box as the type for the template. Another approach is to use the dependency stereotype `bind` and a template object. The stereotype specifies the source that instantiates the template class by using the actual named parameterized type. This is called *explicit binding*. The stereotype indicator <<bind>> refines the template class by instantiating the parameterized type. Refinement is a general term to indicate a greater level of detail of something that already exists. Next to the stereotype indicator are the actual named parameters supplied by the template object. The template object has a dependency relationship with the template class. The template object can also be considered as a *refinement* of the template class. Figure 9-7 depicts the ways a template class can be represented, unbound and bound, for a `map` container.

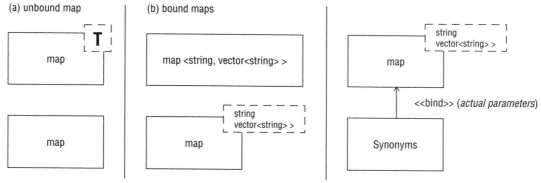

Figure 9-7

Showing the Relationship between Classes and Objects

The UML provides three classifications of relationships between classes:

- ❑ **Dependencies**: A dependency relationship between two classes means that a change to the independent class may affect the dependent class.

- ❑ **Generalizations**: A *generalization* relationship between two classes means that one is a general construct of a more specific type. The general construct is considered the *parent* or *superclass*, and the more specific construct is the *child* or *subclass*. The child inherits the properties, attributes, and operations of the parent but may define other attributes and operations of its own. The child is derived from the parent and can be used as a substitute for the parent class. A *root* or *base* class is a class with no parent.

- ❑ **Associations**: An *association* is a structural relationship that specifies that objects are connected to other objects. Associations between objects can unidirectional or bidirectional. When objects have bidrectional associations, this means that object 1 is associated with object 2 and object 2 is associated with object 1. When objects have unidirectional associations, this means that object 1 is associated with object 2 but object 2 is not associated with object 1. An association between two elements (classes and so on) is called a *binary association* where an association between *n* elements is called an *n-ary association*.

Table 9-5 shows the various stereotypes that can be used for the dependency relationships.

Table 9-5

Dependency Stereotypes `SOURCE ---> TARGET`	Description
<<bind>>	The source instantiates the template target using the actual parameters.
<<friend>>	The source has visibility into the target.
<<instanceof>>	The source is an instance of the target. The dependency is used to define relationships between classes and objects.
<<instantiate>>	The source creates instances of the target. This dependency is used to define relationships between classes and objects.
<<refine>>	The source has a greater level of detail than the target. This dependency is used to define relationships between base class and the derived class.
<<use>>	The source depends on the public interface of the target.
<<become>>	The target is the same object as the source but at a later time in the lifetime of the source object. The target may be in a different state than the source.
<<call>>	The source invokes method of the target.
<<copy>>	The source is an exact but independent copy of the target.
<<access>>	The source package is given the right to reference the elements of the target package.
<<extend>>	The target use case extends the behavior of the source use case.
<<include>>	The source use case can include the behavior of the target use case at a location named by the source use case.

Many types of dependencies, generalizations, and associations exist. Each relationship classification has its own notation. The relationship notation is a solid or dashed line segment between the elements and may be accompanied with some type of arrowhead. To further define the relationship, stereotypes or adornments are used.

These *stereotypes* are labels that further describe the nature of the relationship. They are rendered as a named enclosed by guillemets and placed above or next to the element. For example, in Figure 9-8, which appears shortly:

    <<bind>>

is placed next to the arrow depicting a dependency of the template object to the bound template class list. The <<bind>> dependency means the StrList is a list type supplying the parameter to the template string. UnrecognizedWords has a dependency with StrList in which it is an <<instanceOf>> of this type. WordSearchAgent <<use>> the UnrecognizedWords as a container of the words that it cannot recognize.

Adornments are textual or graphical items added to an element's basic representation. They are used to document details about that element's specifications. For example:

❑ An **association** is depicted as a solid line connecting the same or different constructs. Use an association relationship when one construct is structurally related to another.

❑ **Navigation** is a type of association. To depict navigation, the line between the elements becomes a dashed line with an arrow pointing to one of the elements in the association.

❑ **Dependency** is represented as dashed directed line (with an arrow) between two elements, from the source pointing to the element it depends on, the target. Use a dependency relationship when one construct uses another.

❑ A **generalization relationship** is rendered as a solid directed line with a large open arrowhead pointing to the parent or superclass. Use a generalization relationship when one construct inherits the behaviors and attributes from another construct. The child may change or modify the behaviors and attributes.

Table 9-6 and Table 9-7 list the stereotypes, constraints, and properties that can be applied to generalizations and associations, respectively.

Table 9-6

Generalization	Description
stereotype	
<<implementation>>	Child inherits the implementation of the parent but does not make public nor support the interface of the parent.
constraints	
{complete}	All children of the parent have been named and no more additional children can be derived.
{incomplete}	All children of the parent have not been named; additional children can be derived.
{disjoint}	The parent's objects may have no more than one of its children as a type.
{overlapping}	The parent's objects may have more than one of its children as a type.

Table 9-7

Association	Description
type	
OBJECT1 ----> OBJECT2 navigation	Unidirectional association where *object1* is associated with *object2*, but *object2* is not associated with *object1*. Without the arrow, the association is bidirectional.
PART <--◇ WHOLE aggregation	A containment (whole-part relationship) where part is not associated with just one whole for its lifetime.
PART <--◆ WHOLE composition	A containment (whole-part relationship) where part is associated with just one whole for its lifetime.
constraints	
{implicit}	The relationship is conceptual.
{ordered}	The objects at one end of the association have an order.
property	
{changeable}	Describes what can be added, deleted and changed between two objects.
{addOnly}	Describes new links that can be added to an object on the opposite end of the association.
{frozen}	Describes a link that once added to an object on the opposite end of the association cannot be changed or deleted.

Associations have another level of detail that can be applied to a general association or stereotype listed in Table 9-7:

❑ **Name**: An association can have a name that is used to describe the nature of the relationship. A directional triangle can be added to the name to assure its meaning. The triangle points in the direction the name is intended to be read.

❑ **Role:** A role is the face the class at the near end of the association presents to the class at the other end the association.

❑ **Multiplicity**: Multiplicity notation can be used to state how many objects may be connected across an association. Multiplicity can be shown at both ends of the association.

Figure 9-8 also shows examples of association relationships between classes. DictionaryLexicon and WordSeacrchAgent have a multiplcity association of 1 to 1... *n*. This means there is only one DictionaryLexicon to 1 or many WordSearchAgents. The DictionaryLexicon can be searched by many WordSearchAgents. The LexicalEntry is the name of the association between DictionaryLexicon and Word. In this case, the named association LexicalEntry is also a class with attributes.

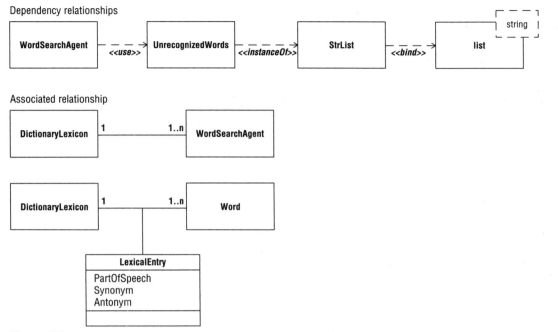

Dependency relationships

Associated relationship

Figure 9-8

Visualizing Interface Classes

The *interface* of a class defines the outside world's interaction with an object through the methods and attributes that are exposed. Once a class has been designed, implemeted, and is in use, it may be necessary to change the interface of the class to accomodate a user. It may not be practical to actually change the existing interface of the class because it is already in use and will break existing code. An *interface class* is used to modify the interface of another existing class or set of classes. The modification makes the class easier to use, more functional, safer, or more semantically correct for a set of users. An example of an interface class are the container *adaptors* that are part of the Standard Template Library. The adaptors provide a new public interface for the deque, vector, and list containers. Example 9-1 shows the stack class. It is used as an interface class to modify a vector class.

Example 9-1

```
//Example 9-1  Using the stack class as an interface class.

template < class Container >
class stack{
//...
public:
    typedef Container::value_type value_type;
    typedef Container::size_type size_type;
```

(continued)

Example 9-1 (continued)

```
protected:
    Container c;
public:
    bool empty(void) const {return c.empty();}
    size_type size(void) const {return c.size(); }
    value_type& top(void) {return c.back(); }
    const value_type& top const {return c.back(); }
    void push(const value_type& x) {c.push.back(x); }
    void pop(void) {c.pop.back(); }
};
```

The stack is declared by specifying the Container type:

```
stack < vector< T> > Stack;
```

In this case, the Container is a vector, but any container, such as a deque and list, that defines these operations:

```
empty()
size()
back()
push.back()
pop.back()
```

can be used as the implementation class for the stack interface class:

```
stack < list< T> > Stack;
stack < deque< T> > Stack;
```

The stack class supplies the semantically correct interface traditionally accepted for stacks:

```
push()
pop()
top()
```

Multiple notations can be used to represent an interface class, each showing various levels of detail. Figure 9-9 shows the multiple notations for interface classes:

❑   (a) shows the stack as an interface class.

❑   (b) shows the stereotype indicator <<interface>> displayed in the class symbol above the name of the class to denote that this is an interface class. This example shows the attributes and methods of the class. The letter I can be prepended to the name of the interface class and all of its operations to further distinguish it from other classes.

❑   (c) shows the realization of a template class. It is read as "the stack class is realized by the vector class." *Realization* can be used to show the relationship between the stack and the class with which it interfaces. Realization is a semantic relationship between classes in which one specifies a contract (interface class) and the other class carries it out (implementation class). Here, the stack class specifies the contract, and the vector class carries it out. A realization relationship is depicted as a dashed line between the two classes with a large open arrowhead pointing to the interface class or the class that specifies the contract.

❑   (d) showsthe relationship between the interface class and its implementer depicted with the interface lollipop notation.

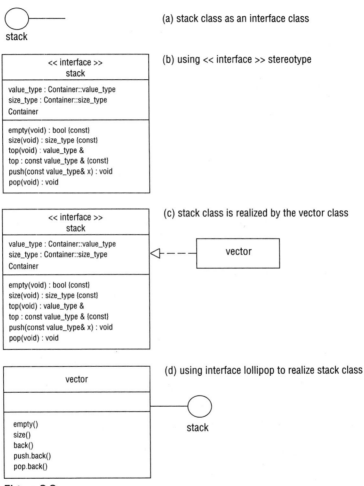

(a) stack class as an interface class

(b) using << interface >> stereotype

(c) stack class is realized by the vector class

(d) using interface lollipop to realize stack class

Figure 9-9

The Organization of Interactive Objects

As you can see, classes and interfaces can be used as building blocks to create more complex classes and interfaces. In a parallel system, you may have many large and complex structures collaborating with other structures thus creating a society of classes and interfaces working together to accomplish the goals of the system. The collection of elements together with their interactions form a *collaboration*. These building blocks can include the structural and behavioral elements of the system. A request from a user to perform a particular task may involve many objects working together. Other tasks can be accomplished by those same objects working with other elements. Understanding that certainly makes apparent the benefits of well-defined resuable classes that can be used in different ways in the same system or in completely different systems. The collaboration has two parts:

❑ A **structural part** that focuses on the way the collaborating elements are organized and constructed

❑ A **behavioral part** that focuses on the interaction between the elements

Figure 9-10 shows an example of the structural part of the agent-based Lexicon system. In this colloboration, all of the classes used have some type of dependency relationship. For example, MorphologyAgent and MisspelledAgent call methods in UnrecognizedWords, Lexicon binds the template map, and UnrecognizedWords contains a word list that binds the list template. The WordSearchAgent has a 1..n relationship with UnrecognizedWords. The structural part of a collaboration consists of any combination of classes and interfaces, components and nodes. As you can see in Figure 9-10, a system may contain many collaborations. A single collaboration is unique in the system, but the elements of a collaboration are not. The elements of one collaboration may be used in another collaboration using a different organization and performing a different functions. In this particular collaboration, WordSearchAgent is used to find unrecognized words in a list. It could also be used to find words of a particular domain if it were to use a different Lexicon.

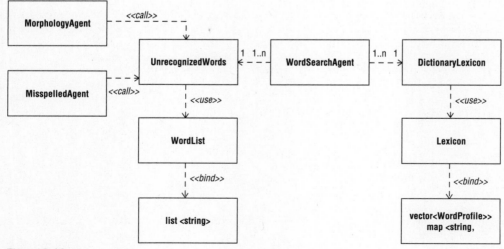

Figure 9-10

. *Depicting the behavioral part of a collaboration is accomplished by using interaction diagrams such as sequence or activity diagrams. Those are discussed in the next section.*

UML and Concurrent Behavior

The behavioral view of a system focuses on the dynamic aspects of that system. This view examines how the elements in the system behave as it interacts with other elements of the system. Here is where concurrency emerges as elements interact with other elements. The diagramming techniques discussed in this section are the ones used to model:

❑   The lifetime of the behavior of an object

❑   Behavior of objects that work together for a particular purpose

❑   Flows of control focusing on an action or a sequence of actions

❑   Synchronization and communication between elements

Collaborating Objects

Collaborating objects are objects involved with each other to perform some specific task. They do not form a permanent relationship. The same objects can be involved with other objects working together to perform other tasks. Collaborating objects can be represented in a *collaboration diagram*. Collaboration diagrams have a structural part and an interactive part. The structural part has already been discussed. The interaction part is a graph where all of the participating objects are vertices. The connections between the objects are the arcs. The arcs can be adorned with messages passed between the objects, method invocations, and stereotype indicators that express more details about the nature of the connection.

The connection between two objects is a *link*. A link is a type of association. When two objects are linked, actions can be performed between them. The action may result in a change of the state of one or both objects. The following table shows examples of the types of actions that can take place.

create	An object can be created.
destroy	An object can be destroyed.
call	An operation of an object can be invoked by another object or itself.
return	A value is returned to an object.
send	A signal may be sent to an object.

When any method is invoked, the parameters and the return value can be expressed. Other actions can take place if specified.

The following actions can take place if the receiving object is visible to the calling object. Stereotypes can be used to specify why the object is visible.

association	The object is visible because an association exists (very general).
parameter	The object is visible because it is a parameter to the calling object.
local	The object is visible because it is has local scope to the calling object.
global	The object is visible because it has global scope to the calling object.
self	The object calls its own method.

Other stereotypes and adornments appropriate for associations can be expressed.

When a method is invoked, this may cause a number of other methods to be invoked by other objects. The sequence in which the operations are performed can be shown by using a sequence number combination and a colon separator prepended to the method. The sequence number combination expresses what sequence the method is associated with and the time order number in which the operation takes place. For example, Figure 9-11 shows a collaboration diagram that uses the sequence numbers.

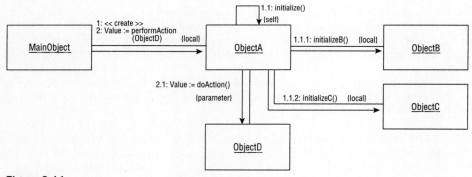

Figure 9-11

In Figure 9-11, MainObject performs two operations in sequence:

```
1: <<create>>
2: Value := performAction(ObjectF)
```

In operation 1, MainObject creates ObjectA. ObjectA is local to the MainObject by containment. This initiates the first sequence of operations in a nested flow of control. All operations that are a part of this sequence use the number 1 followed by the time order number in which the operation takes place. The first operation of sequence 1 is:

```
1.1: initialize()
```

ObjectA invokes its own operation. This is expressed by linking the object to itself and by using the {self} stereotype indicator. The ObjectA::initialize() operation also causes the beginning of another sequence of actions:

```
1.1.1: initializeB()
1.1.2: initializeC()
```

in which two other objects local to ObjectA initialize methods are called. The operation:

```
2: performAction(ObjectD)
```

is the beginning of another nested sequence. ObjectA invokes ObjectD's operation:

```
2.1: doAction()
```

ObjectA can invoke this operation because ObjectD is a parameter (passed by MainObject) as the stereotype {parameter} indicates. A value is returned to ObjectA, and a value is returned to MainObject. Besides sequence number combinations, these nested flows of controls are further enhanced by using a line with a solid arrowhead pointing in the direction of the flow of the sequence.

Multitasking and Multithreading with Processes and Threads

Concurrency within an application can be implemented by using *multitasking* or *multithreading*. Multitasking allows more than one process to execute at the same time, whereas multithreading allows a single process to perform more than one task at the same time using multiple threads. When a process is divided into multiple tasks and each task is executed by a thread, the process is said to be multithreaded. The thread is a flow of control executing within the process's address space. Each process has at least one thread, the main thread.

Diagramming Active Objects

When using the UML, each independent flow of control is considered an *active object*. An active object is an object that owns a process or thread. Each active object can initiate control activity. An *active class* is a class whose objects are active. Active classes can be used to model a group of processes or threads that share the same data members and methods. The objects of your system may not have a one-to-one correlation with active objects. When dividing your program up into processes and threads along object lines, an object's methods may execute in a separate process or execute on separate threads. Therefore, when modeling such an object, it may be represented by several active objects. This relationship between static and active objects can be represented by using an interaction diagram. Threads and processes can be represented directly as active objects.

The UML represents an active object or class the same way a static object is represented except it has a heavier line tracing the perimeter of the rectangle. Two stereotypes can also be used:

❑   process

❑   thread

These stereotype indicators can be displayed to show the distinction between the two types of active objects. Figure 9-12 shows two active objects, both are threads. Each thread executes methods of `unrecognizedWords` and `wordSearchAgent2`.

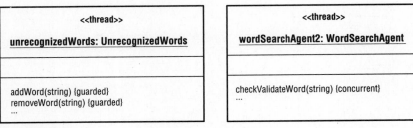

Figure 9-12

Showing the Multiple Flows of Control and Communication

In a concurrent system, you have multiple flows of control. Each flow of control is based on a process or a thread controlling the activity. These processes and threads may be executing on a single computer system with multiple processors. An active object or class is used to represent each flow of control. When the active object is created, an independent flow of control is initiated. When the active object is destroyed, the flow of control is terminated. Modeling the multiple flows of control in your system helps you with the management, synchronization, and communication among them.

In a collaboration diagram, sequence numbers and solid arrows are used to identify flows of controls. In a collaboration diagram that consists of active objects in a concurrent system, the name of the active object is preprended to the sequence numbers of the operations peformed by the active object. Active objects can invoke methods in other objects and suspend execution until the function returns or can continue to execute. Arrows are used not to show just the direction of the flow of control but also the nature of it. A solid arrowhead is used to represent a synchronous call and a half-stick arrowhead is used to represent an asynchronous call. Since more than one active object can invoke the operation of a single object, the method properties:

- ❏ sequential
- ❏ guarded
- ❏ concurrent

can be used to describe the synchronization property of that method.

Figure 9-13 shows a collaboration of several active objects. In this diagram, these objects are working together to produce a list of unknown words. The `mainAgent` is used to record and coordinate the preliminary work and resulting list of unknown words produced by the active object problem solvers.

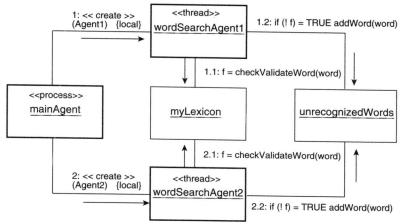

Figure 9-13

The `myLexicon` and `unrecognizedWords` objects are accessed concurrently by two agents. Both objects are visible to all the agents in this collaboration. The `wordSearchAgents` invoke the methods of the `unrecognizedWords` object:

```
wordSearchAgent1:unrecognizedWords.addWord(string word)
WordSearchAgent2:unrecognizedWords.addWord(string word)
```

The `wordSearchAgents` also invoke the methods of the myLexicon object:

```
wordSearchAgent1:myLexicon.validateWord(string &X)
WordSearchAgent2:myLexicon.validateWord(string &X)
```

The `WordSearchAgents` are concurrently invoking `unrecognizedWords` object's operation. `unrecognizedWords addWord()` has a `guarded` property and, therefore, is safe to call simultaneously. `myLexicon.validateWord()` does not modify the object and is also safe to call simultaneously.

Message Sequences between Objects

Whereas a collaboration diagram focuses on the structural organization and interaction of objects working together to perform a task or operation or to realize a use case, a *sequence diagram* focuses on the time ordering of method invocation or procedures involved in a particular task, operation, or use case. In a sequence diagram, the name of each object or construct involved is displayed in its own rectangular box. The boxes are placed at the top along the x-axis of the diagram. You should only include the major players involved and the most important function calls because the diagram can quickly become too complicated. The objects are ordered from left to right starting from the object or procedure that initiates the action to the most subordinate objects or procedures. The calls are placed along the y-axis from top to bottom in time order. Vertical lines are placed under each box representing the lifeline of the object. Solid arrowhead lines are drawn from the lifeline of one object to the lifeline of another representing a function call or method invocation from the caller to the receiver. Stick arrowhead lines are drawn from the receiver back to the caller representing a return from a function or method. Each function call is labeled at the minimum with the function or method name. The arguments and control information, like the condition in which the method is invoked can also be displayed. For example:

```
if(!Unrecognized)
checkTransposes()
```

The function or method will not be performed unless the condition is true. Methods that are to be invoked several times on an object, like reading values from a structure, are preceded by an *iteration marker* (*).

Figure 9-14 shows a sequence diagram of some of the objects involved in the Lexicon system. Only some of the objects are shown to avoid a complicated diagram. When you are using the sequence diagram for concurrent objects or procedures, activation symbols are used. An activation symbol is a rectangle that appears on the object's lifeline. This indicates the object or procedure is active. These are used when an object makes a call to another object or procedure and does not block. This shows that the object or procedure is continuing to execute or be active. If an object is not active, a dashed line is used. In Figure 9-14, the misspelledAgent object is always active whereas the mainAgent becomes inactive after it has created the misspelledAgent. Once unrecognizedWords and myLexicon have been created, they do not become active until misspelledAgent invokes nextWord() and removeWord().

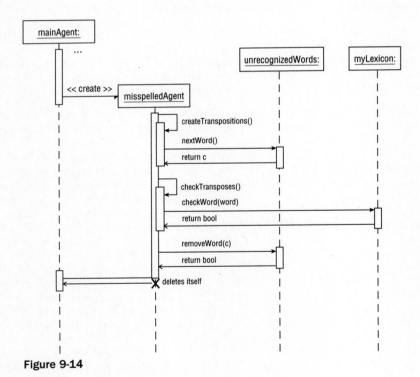

Figure 9-14

To indicate an object has called one of its own methods, a *self-delegation* symbol is used. This is a combination of an activation symbol and a call arrow. An activation symbol is overlapped on the existing activation symbol. A line proceeds from the original activation symbol with an arrow pointing to the added activation symbol. In Figure 9-14, self-delegation occurs for the `misspelledAgent` when it call its methods `createTranspositions()` and `checkTransposes()`. The `checkTransposes` method passes a transposition of the original word to `myLexicon`, which checks to see if this word is in the list of recognizable words. This method is called iteratively until `Unrecognized` is `FALSE`, which means the transposed word has been identified as the correct spelling of the original word. If the transposed word has been recognized, the original word is removed.

The Activities of Objects

The UML can be used to model the activities performed by objects involved in a specific operation or use case. This is called an *activity diagram*. It is a flowchart showing the sequential and concurrent actions or activities involved a specific task, step by step. The arrows trace the flow of the control for the activities represented in the diagram. Collaboration diagrams emphasize the flow of control from object to object, sequence diagrams emphasize the flow of control in time order, and the activity diagram emphasizes the flow of control from one action or activity to another. The actions or activities change the state of the object or return a value. The containment of the action or activity is called an *action* or *activity state*. They represent the state of the object at a particular instant in the flow of control.

Actions and activities differ.

❑ **Actions** cannot logically be decomposed or interrupted by other actions or events. Examples of actions are creating or destroying an object, invoking an object's method, or calling a function in a procedure.

❑ An **activity** can be decomposed into other activities or even another activity diagram. An example of an activity is a program, a use case, or a procedure. Activities can be interrupted by an event or other activities or actions.

An activity diagram is a graph in which the nodes are actions or activities and the arcs are triggerless transitions. Triggerless transitions require no event to cause the transition to occur. The transition occurs when the previous action or activity has completed. The diagram comprises decision branches, starts, stops, and synchronization bars that join or fork several actions or activities. Both action and activity states are represented the same way. To represent an action or activity state, the UML uses the standard flowchart symbol used to show the enter and exit point of the flowchart. This symbol is used regardless of the type of action or activity occurring. However, we prefer to use the standard flowchart symbols that distinguish input/output actions (parallelogram) from processing or transformation actions (rectangle). The description of the action or activity as a function call, expression, phrase, use case, or program name is displayed in the action symbol used. An activity state may in addition show the entry and/or exit action. The entry action is the action that takes places when the activity state is entered. The exit action is the action that takes places just before exiting the activity state. They are the first and last actions to be executed in the activity state, respectively.

Once an action has completed, a transition occurs in which the next action takes place immediately. The transition is represented as a directed line from one state with a stick arrow pointing to the next state. A transition pointing to a state is inbound and a transition leading from a state is outbound. Before the outbound transition occurs, the exit action, if it exists, executes. After an inbound transition, the entry action for the state, if it exists, executes. The start of the flow of control is represented as a large solid dot.

The first transition leads from the solid dot to the first state in the diagram. The stopping point or stop state of the activity diagram is represented as a large solid dot inside a circle.

Activity diagrams, like flowcharts, have a decision symbol. The decision symbol is a diamond with one inbound transition and two or more outbound transitions. The outbound transitions are guarded conditions that determine the path of the flow of control. The guarded condition is a simple boolean expression. All of the outbound transitions should cover all of the possible paths from the branch. Figure 9-15 shows the decision symbol used in determining whether a knowledge source should be constructed, in determining whether a word should be added to the unrecognized word list.

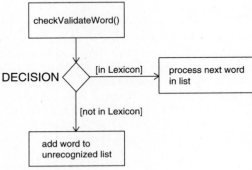

Figure 9-15

You may find that there exists more than one flow of a sequence of actions or activities occurring concurrently after an action or activity has completed. In contrast to a flowchart, the UML defines a symbol that can be used to represent the instant where multiple flows of controls occur concurrently. A *synchronization bar* is used to show where single path branches off or forks into parallel paths and where parallel paths join. It is a thick horizontal line in which there can be multiple outbound transitions (forking) or multiple inbound transitions (joining). Each transition represents a different path. Outbound transitions from a synchronization bar signify an action or activity state has caused multiple flows of control to occur. Inbound transitions into a synchronization bar signify the multiple flows of control need to be synchronized. A synchronization bar is used to show that the paths are waiting for all paths to meet and join into a single flow or path.

In Figure 9-16, `mainAgent` creates two concurrent flows of control by creating two `WordSearchAgents`. After these these agents have completed, they are joined again into a single flow of control, where the `mainAgent` then creates a `MorphologyAgent`.

The diagram is divided into separate sections called *swimlanes*. In each swimlane, the actions or activities of a particular object, component, or use case occur. Swimlanes are vertical lines that partition the diagram into sections. A swimlane for a particular object, component, or use case specifies the focus of activities. An action or activity can occur only in a single swimlane. Transitions and synchronization bars can cross one or more swimlanes. Actions or activities in the same lane or different lanes but at the same level are concurrent. Figure 9-16 shows the activity diagram with swimlanes.

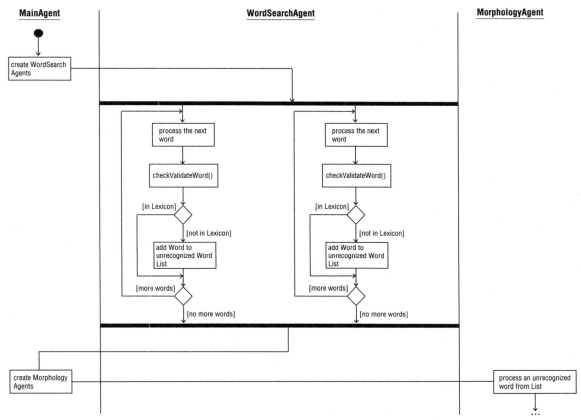

Figure 9-16

The purpose of this activity diagram is to model the sequence of actions involved in a mainAgent and other objects involved in producing the unknown word list for the agent-based Lexicon system. Concurrency occurs with the WordSearchAgents. The synchronization bar is in WordSearchAgent's swimlane. When there are no more words to process, then the flow of control for these agents is relinquished, and the flow of control returns back to the main thread, mainAgent.

State Machines

State machines depict the behavior of a single construct, specifying the sequence of transformations during its lifetime as it responds to internal and external events. The single construct can be a system, a use case, or an object. State machines are used to model the behavior of a single entity. An entity can respond to events such as procedures, functions, operations, and signals. An entity can also respond to elapses in time. Whenever an event takes place, the entity responds by performing some activity or taking some action resulting in a change of the state of the entity or the production of some artifact. The action or activity performed depends upon the current state of the entity. A *state* is a condition the entity is in during its lifetime as a result of performing some action or responding to some event.

A state machine can be represented in a table or directed graph called a *state diagram*. Figure 9-17 shows a UML state diagram for the state machine of a process.

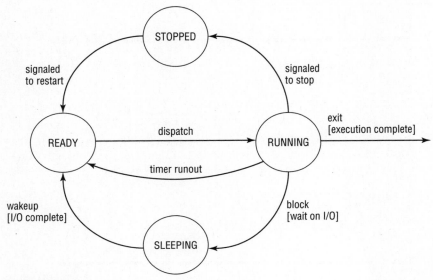

Figure 9-17

Figure 9-17 shows the states some process progresses through while it is active in the system. The process can have four states: ready, running, sleeping, and stopped. There are eight events that cause the four states of the process. Three of the events occur only if a condition is met.

❑ The **block** event occurs only if the process requests I/O or it is waiting for an event to occur. If the **block** event occurs, it triggers the process to transform from a running state to a sleeping state.

❑ The **wakeup** event occurs only if the event takes place or the I/O has been completed. If the **wakeup** event occurs, it triggers the process to transform from a sleeping state (source state) to a ready state (target state).

❑ The **exit** event occurs only if the process has executed all its instructions. If the **exit** event occurs, it triggers the process to transform from a running state to a sleeping state.

The remaining events are external events and not under the control of the process. They occur for some external reason, triggering the process to transform from a source to a target state.

The state diagrams are used to model the dynamic aspects of an object, use case, or system. The sequence, activity, interactive collaboration diagrams, and now the state diagram are used to model the behavior of the system or object when it is active. Structural collaboration and class diagrams are used to model the structural organization of an object or system. State diagrams are good to use to describe the behavior of an object regardless of the use case. They should not be used to describe the behavior of several interacting or collaborating objects. They should be used to describe the behavior of an object, system, or use case that goes through a number of transformations and that on which more than one event can cause a single transformation to occur. These are constructs that are very reactive to internal and externals events.

In the state diagram, the nodes are states, and the arcs are transitions. The states are represented as rounded-corner rectangles in which the name of the state is displayed. The transitions are lines connecting the source and target states with a stick arrow pointing to the target state. There are *initial* and *final states*.

❑   The **initial state** is the default starting point for the state machine. It is represented as a solid black dot with a transition to the first state of the state machine.

❑   The **final state** is the ending state of the state machine, indicating it has completed or the system, use case, or object has reached the end of its lifeline. It is represented as a solid dot embedded in a circle.

Representing the Parts of a State

A state has several parts. Table 9-8 lists the parts of a state.

Table 9-8

Parts of a State	Description
Name	The unique name of the state that distinguishes it from other states; a state may have no name.
Entry/exit actions	Actions executed when entering the state (entry state) or executed when exiting the state (exit action).
Substates	A nested state; the substates are the disjoint states that can be activated sequentially or concurrently. The composite or superstate is the state that contains the substates.
Internal transitions	Transitions that occur within the state that are handled without causing a change in the state.
Self-transitions	Transitions that occur within the state that are handled without causing a change in the state but that cause the exit and then the entry actions to execute.
Deferred events	A list of events that occur while the object is in that state but that is queued and handled when the object is in another state.

A state can be represented simply by displaying the name of the state at the center of the state symbol. If other actions are to be shown inside the state symbol, the name of the state should appear at the top in a separate compartment. The actions and activities are listed below this compartment and are displayed in this format:

```
label [Guard] / action or activity
```

For example:

```
do / validate(data)
```

The `do` is the label used for an activity to be performed while the object is in this state. The `validate(data)` function is called with `data` as the argument. If an action or activity is a call to a function or method, the arguments can be displayed.

The `Guard` is an expression that evaluates to true or false. If a condition evaluates to true, the action or activity takes place. For example:

```
exit [data valid] / send(data)
```

The exit action `send(data)` is guarded. The expression `data valid` is evaluated to be true or false. Upon exiting the state, if the expression is true, then the `send(data)` function is called. The `Guard` is always optional.

Transitions occur when an event takes place. This causes the object, system, or use case to transform from one state to another state. Two transitions can occur that do not cause a change in the state of the object, system, or use case. They are:

❑ **Self-transition**: With a self-transition, when a particular event occurs, this triggers the object to leave the current state. When exiting, it performs the exit action (if any) and then performs whatever action is associated with the self-transition (if any). The object reenters the state, and the entry action (if any) is performed.

❑ **Internal transition**: With an internal transition, the object does not leave the state and therefore no entry or exit actions are performed.

Figure 9-18 shows the general structure of a state with exit and entry actions and do activity along with internal and self-transitions. A self-transition is represented as a directed line that points back to the same state.

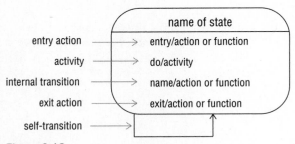

Figure 9-18

A transition between different states indicates that there is a relationship or path that exists between them. From one state an event can occur or a condition can be met that causes the object to be transformed from one state (source state) to another state (target state). The event triggers the transition of the object. A transition may have several concurrently existing source states. If so they are joined before the transition occurs. A transition may have several concurrently existing target states in which a fork has occurred. Table 9-9 lists the parts of a transition. A transition is rendered as a directed line from the source state pointing to the target state. The name of the event trigger is displayed next to the transition. Like actions and activities, events for transitions can also be guarded. A transition can be *triggerless* meaning no special event occurs that causes the transition to take place. Exiting the source state, the object immediately makes the transition and enters the target state.

Table 9-9

Parts of a Transition	Description
Target state	The state the object enters after a transition occurs.
Source state	The original state of the object; when a transition occurs, the object leaves the source state.
Event trigger	The event that causes the transition to occur. A transition may be triggerless, in which the transition occurs as soon as the object has completed all activities in the source state.
Guard condition	A boolean expression associated with an event trigger. When it evaluates to True, the transitions occurs.
Action	An action executed by the object that takes place during a transition; it may be associated with an event trigger and/or guard condition.

Diagramming Concurrent Substates

A substate can be used to further simplify the depiction of modeling the behavior of a concurrent system. A *substate* is a state contained inside another state called a *superstate* or *composite state*. This representation means a state can be further broken down into one or more substates. These substates can be sequential or concurrent. With concurrent substates, each state machine represented exists in parallel as different but concurrently existing flows of control. Each substate is separated by a dashed line. This is true for the WordSearchAgent objects in the example used throughout this chapter. Each object is processing all the words in its local list. The states for these objects are in a superstate called "building the unrecognized words list".

Each substate is contained in a separate compartment. The substates are synchronized and joined before exiting the composite state. When one substate has reached its final state, it waits for the other state to reach its final state, then the substates are joined back into one flow. Figure 9-19 shows a state diagram for Lexicon agent-based system.

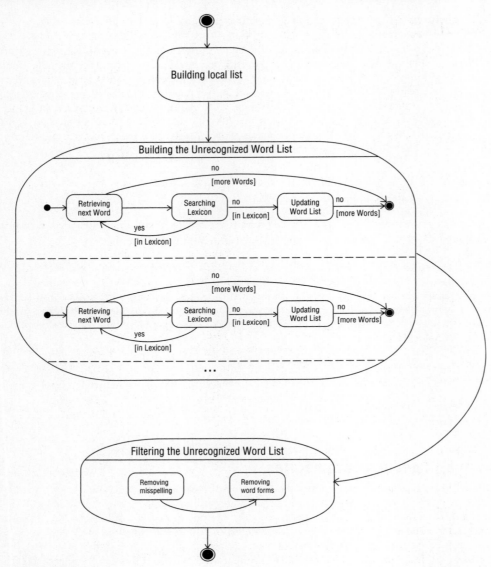

Figure 9-19

In Figure 9-19, there is another composite state called "Filtering the Unrecognized Word List". The substates in this composite state are sequential; they are not executed concurrently. First, the misspelled words are removed, and then the word forms of recognized words are removed.

Visualizing the Whole System

A system is composed of many elements, including subsystems organized into a collaboration to accomplish some purpose. It is an aggregation of constructs joined in some regular interaction. The diagraming techniques discussed in this chapter allow the developer to model a single system from different viewpoints, from different levels, and from different flows of control to assist in the design and development of the system. In this section, we discuss modeling and documenting the system as a whole, meaning that the major components or functional elements can be depicted at the highest level. The diagraming techniques discussed in this section are the ones used to model the architecture of the system.

> *Although this is the last section in this chapter, modeling and documenting the whole system would be the first level of designing and developing a system.*

When modeling and documenting the architecture of a system, the view of the system is the highest level. Grady Booch, James Rumbaugh, and Ivar Jacobson define *architecture* as:

> The set of significant decisions about the organization of a software system, the selection of the structural elements and their interfaces by which the system is composed, together with their behavior as specified in the collaboration among those elements, the composition of these structural and behavioral elements into progressively larger subsystems, and the architectural style that guides this organization — these elements and their interfaces, their collaborations, and their composition. [Booch, Rumbaugh, and Jacobson, 1999]

Modeling and documenting the architecture captures the system's logical and physical elements along with the structure and behavior of the system at the highest level.

The architecture of the system is a description of the system from a distinct view that focuses on the structure and organization of the system from that aspect. The views are as follows:

- ❑ **Use case**: Describes the behavior of the system presented to end users

- ❑ **Process**: Describes the processes and threads used in the system's mechanisms of concurrency and synchronization

- ❑ **Design**: Describes the services and functions provided to the end user

- ❑ **Implementation**: Describes the components used to create the physical system

- ❑ **Deployment**: Describes the software components and the nodes on which they are executing in the delivered system

As you can see these views overlap and interact with each other. Use cases can be used in the design view. Processes can show up as components in the implementation view. Software components are used in both implementation and deployment views. When designing the architecture of the system, diagrams that reflect each of these views should be constructed.

A system can be decomposed into subsystems and modules. The subsystems or modules will be further broken down into components, nodes, classes, objects, and interfaces. In the UML, subsystems or modules used at the architectural level of documentation are called *packages*. A package can be used to organize elements into a group that describes the general purpose of those elements. A package is represented as a rectangle with a tab on the upper-left corner. The package symbol contains the name of the package. The packages in the system can be connected by means of composition, aggregation, dependency, and association relationships. Stereotype indicators can be used to distinguish one type of package from another. Figure 9-20 shows the packages involved in the Lexicon system. The system package uses a <<system>> indicator to distinguish it from the *List Build* and *Filter* subsystems, which use the <<subsystem>> indicator. Because they are subsystems, they are related to the system by an aggregation relationship.

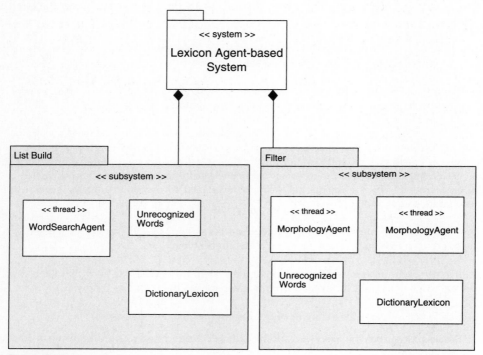

Figure 9-20

Summary

As we noted earlier, this chapter has covered some of the basic UML diagramming and notation techniques used to design and document the concurrent behavior in an application, but it is only an introduction to a very complex topic. We covered the following key points:

❑   A model of a system is the body of information gathered for the purpose of studying the system. Documentation is a tool used in modeling a system. The UML, Unified Modeling Language, is a graphical notation used to design, visualize, model, and document the artifacts of a software system created by Grady Booch, James Rumbaugh, and Ivar Jacobson. It is the de facto standard for communicating and modeling object-oriented systems. The UML can be used to model concurrent from the structural and behavioral perspectives.

❑   UML diagrams can be used to model to most basic units, the object, to the whole system. An object is the basic unit used in many UML diagrams. Dependency, inheritance, aggregation, and composition are some of the relationships that can exist between objects. Interaction diagrams are used to show the behavior of an object and identify concurrency in the system. Objects can interact with other objects by communicating and invoking methods. Collaborations diagrams depict the interactions between objects working together to perform some particular task. Sequence diagrams are used to represent the interactions between object in time sequence. Statecharts are used to depicts the actions of a single object over its lifetime.

❑   When modeling the whole system, the basic unit is a package. A package can be used to represent systems and subsystems. Packages can have relationships with other packages such as composition or some type of association.

For a more comprehensive treatment on these techniques, we recommend the book *Designing Concurrent, Distributed,* and *Real-Time Applications with UML* by Hassan Gomaa (Addison-Wesley, 2000).

In the next chapter, we turn our attention to one last area of concern for multicore programming: testing and logical fault tolerance.

10

Testing and Logical Fault Tolerance for Parallel Programs

Those are places that can't be accessed from a Chaos Gate. If you try to enter, you show up, see a warning indicator, and then you're warped back to town.

— **Miu Kawasaki,** *.hack// Another Birth*

In Chapter 8, we introduced the Predicate Breakdown Structure (PBS) of an application and the Parallel Application Design Layers (PADL) analysis model. These are top-down approaches to producing declarative architectures for applications that have a concurrency or parallel programming requirements. One of the ultimate goals of PBS and PADL is to establish a chain of possession or audit trail for the application concurrency requirements that lead from the solution model to threads or processes at the operating system level. In this chapter, we connect the PBS and PADL analysis to application software testing and exception handling. The PBS and PADL tell you what you should be testing for and what constitutes an error or an exception. You can use exception handling to provide a kind of logical fault-tolerance for declarative architectures. That is, if your application for unknown and uncontrollable reasons violates statements, assertions, rules, predicates, or constraints from the PBS, you want to throw an exception and gracefully exit because once the predicates have been violated, then the correctness, reliability, and meaning of the application has been compromised.

In this chapter, we also introduce the various types of testing that should be part of any Software Development Life Cycle (SDLC), especially ones where parallel programming will be deployed. We explain exception handling, the differences between error handling and exception handling, some of the issues for multithreading and parallel programming. We also briefly introduce the notion of model checking, the relevance of possible-world semantics to the declarative interpretation of parallel programming, and how they are used for testing and exception handling.

Specifically, in this chapter we will cover the following:

❑ Connecting the PBS and PADL analysis to application software testing and exception handling

❑ Explaining the various types of testing that should be part of any SDLC

❑ Defining exception handling and what the differences are between error handling and exception handling

❑ Introducing to the notion of model checking and the relevance of possible-world semantics to the declarative interpretation of parallel programming

Can You Just Skip the Testing?

The goal of testing software is to make sure that the software does what you want and you want what is does. An application is often requested as a list of desired features. This list can be represented as a formal specification consisting of hundreds of pages or can be as simple as verbal request from an employer detailing a dozen or so requirements. Regardless of how the list of requirements for a piece of software is generated, the testing process must make sure that the software meets those requirements and that the requirements meet the user's expectations. In many cases where parallel computers or multiprocessors are involved, the user's expectations include performance speed up or a certain level of high performance throughput. The kinds of software errors increase when multithreading or multiprocessing is added in attempt to meet the user's expectation. When the software does not perform according to the specifications, the software is in error, even if the specification violation is that the system performs too slowly. Software that requires parallel programming can be notoriously difficult to test and debug. Testing and debugging are among the top 10 challenges to parallel programming discussed in Chapter 3. Some of the main issues that are unique to testing and debugging multithreaded or multiprocessing programs are:

❑ Simulating minimum-to-maximum volume loads

❑ Duplicating the exact flow of control during debugging

❑ Duplicating race condition errors during debugging

❑ Duplicating systemwide process and thread contention

❑ Finding hidden unsafe thread functions

❑ Testing and debugging nondeterministic algorithms

❑ Proving there are no possibilities for deadlock or data race in the software

❑ Simulating boundary and average workload mixes

❑ Checking intermediate results when 100s or 1000s of threads and processes are in execution

❑ Identifying the right number of threads or processes that will generate acceptable performance

The PADL and PBS analysis covered in Chapter 8 create the primary concurrency infrastructure and implementation models that testing phases validate and verify. Declarative and predicate-based approaches lend themselves to more automated forms of model checking and testing. Declarative designs lead to declarative implementations. Declarative implementations bring the testing complexity of medium to large-scale parallel programs within reach of the software developer. Regardless of the complexity of the testing or debugging process, the goal is to deploy software that is error free and fault tolerant. The testing process must find each error and software defect and remove it.

A Public Service Announcement on Programmer Ethics and Software Reliability

The code examples in this book contain little or no error and exception handling. This is because the code examples are meant for *exposition purposes only*. We wanted to keep the code examples short, and we did not want to distract the reader from the concepts that were presented. However, real-world applications must be bulletproof. Because as software developers, we produce applications in the fields of medicine, manufacturing, homeland security, transportation, finance, education, scientific research, and all areas of business, we have an ethical and moral responsibility to produce software that is safe, correct, reliable, and fault tolerant. Anything less is malpractice.

Five Concurrency Challenges That Must Be Checked during Testing

Some of the concurrency challenges in Chapter 3 have to be checked for in the testing phase and accounted for in exception handlers. These challenges are:

1. Incorrect/inadequate communication between two or more tasks that are executing in parallel

2. Data corruption as a result of unsafe updating of data by two or more instructions or tasks

3. Resource contention when there is a many-to-one ratio between tasks and a resource

4. An unacceptable number of units that need to execute in parallel

5. Missing/incomplete documentation for communicating a software design that contains multiprocessing and multithreading

In Chapter 7, we discussed the mechanisms that are used to enable and synchronize communication and data or device access between concurrently executing threads or processes. For instance, mutexes and semaphores are used to control and prevent errors that would occur from Challenge 2 in the preceding list. Timed mutexes can be used to control and prevent errors that would result from the problems that could occur from Challenge 3 in the preceding list. Documentation in so many cases receives the least amount of attention and dedicated resources, but it is one of the most important components of a software deployment. As with everything else with parallel programming and multithreading, documentation is even more critical for these classes of application. The testing process should verify and validate that the design documentation and the postproduction documentation match! Table 10-1 shows which mechanisms discussed in Chapter 7 can be used to prevent control and prevent some of the five challenges shown in the preceding list.

Chapter 10: Testing and Logical Fault Tolerance for Parallel Programs

Table 10-1

Types of Semaphores	Description
Mutex semaphores	Mechanism used to implement mutual exclusion in a critical section of code.
Read-write locks	Mechanism used to implement read-write access policy between tasks.
Condition variables	Mechanism used to broadcast a signal between tasks that an event has taken place. When a task locks an event mutex, it blocks until it receives the broadcast.
Multiple condition variable	Same as an event mutex but includes multiple events or conditions.

The mechanisms listed in Table 10-1 are low-level mechanisms. Fortunately, using features of higher-level component libraries, such as Threading Building Blocks (TBB) or the standard C++ concurrent programming library, can take some of tedium away during the testing process. These issues are meant to be dealt with in Layer 2 and 3 of the PADL analysis model discussed in Chapter 8.

However, first, we need to establish some definitions. There are several words that are used in discussions on testing, error handling, and fault tolerance that are often used incorrectly or too loosely. Table 10-2 contains the basic definitions for the terms that we will use in this chapter.

Table 10-2

Terms	Definitions
Defect	A flaw in any aspect of software or software requirements that contributes or may potentially contribute to the occurrence of one or more failures
Error	An inappropriate decision made by a software engineer/programmer that leads to a defect in the software
Exception handling	A mechanism for managing exceptions (unanticipated conditions during the execution of a program) that changes the normal flow of the execution of a program/software
Failure	An unacceptable departure from the operation of a software element that occurs as a consequence of a fault
Fault	A defect in the software due to human error that when executed under particular conditions causes failure
Fault tolerance	A property that allows a piece of software to survive and recover from the software failures caused by faults (defects) introduced into the software as a result of human error
Reliability	The ability of the software to perform a required function under specified condition for a stated period of time

Since some of the terms in Table 10-2 such as *error*, *failure*, and *fault* are commonly used in many different ways, we have provided simple definitions for how they are used in this chapter. The extent to which software is able to minimize the effects of failure is a measure of its *fault tolerance*. Achieving fault tolerant software is one of the primary goals of any software engineering effort. However, the distinction between fault-tolerant software and well-tested software is often misunderstood and blurred. Sometimes the responsibilities and activities of software verification, software validation, and exception handling are erroneously interchanged. To work toward the goal of using the C++ exception-handling mechanism to help achieve logical fault-tolerant software, you must first be clear where exception handling fits in the scheme of things.

Failure: The Result of Defects and Faults

Failures occur at runtime during software operation. Failures are the result of a defect in hardware, software, or human operation. If the software is not running, then it cannot encounter defects. Although this is an obvious statement it is important in understanding some of the distinctions between the responsibilities and activities of the testing phase versus those of the exception handler. Ideally defects in the software are removed during the testing stages. The same would be true for hardware. As for defects in human operation, we would like to remove those defects through training and experience, but this is easier said than done. To keep matters simple, we focus our discussion on defects in software.

Basic Testing Types

Table 10-3 describes the eight basic types of testing that should be performed on a piece of software prior to its being put into operation.

Table 10-3

Types of Testing	Description
Unit testing	Requires that the software be tested one component or unit at a time. A unit might be a software module, a collection of modules, a function, a procedure, an object, an algorithm, or in some instances a computer program.
Stress testing	Designed to push a component or a system up to and sometimes beyond its limits. Stress testing includes testing boundary conditions. When boundary conditions are tested, it helps in determining what happens at the boundaries the software component or system contains.
Integration testing	Used to test the assembly of components. The components are combined into logical groups, and each group is tested as a unit. The group can be subjected to the same type of tests to which units are subjected. As each component is added to the assembly, the number of elements that must be tested grows combinatorially.
Regression testing	Used to retest modules that have changed. Regression tests ensure that the changes to the component do not cause it to lose any functionality.

Table continued on following page

Types of Testing	Description
Operational testing	Used to test the system in its full operation. This test puts the software component in a live environment to be tested under a complete system load. The tests that the component undergoes during unit, integration, and stress testing usually serve as operational tests as well. The operational tests also serve to determine how the component will behave in a totally foreign environment.
Specification testing	Used as part of the software verification process. The component is audited against the original specification. This specification dictates what components are involved in a system and what the relationships are between those components.
Acceptance testing	Used by the end user of the module, component, or system to determine performance. Acceptance testing is part of the software validation process.

As you perform the type of tests in Table 10-3 on a piece of software, you find defects and remove them from the software. The more defects you find and remove during testing, the fewer defects your software encounters during runtime. Defects encountered during runtime lead to failures in the software. Failures in the software produce exceptional conditions for the software to operate under. The exceptional conditions require exception handlers. So, the balancing act is between:

❑ *Defect removal* during the *testing stages*

❑ *Defect survival* during *exception handling*

Defect Removal versus Defect Survival

Although you can choose to favor defect survival over defect removal, the problem is that exception-handling code can become so complex that it introduces defects into the software. So, instead of providing a mechanism to help achieve fault tolerance, the exception handler becomes a source of failure. Choosing defect survival over defect removal reduces the software's chance to operate properly. Extensive and thorough testing removes defects, which reduces the strain on the exception handlers. It is also important to note that exception handlers do not occur as freestanding pieces of code. They occur within the context of the overall software architecture. The journey toward fault tolerance in our software begins by recognizing that:

❑ No amount of exception handling can rescue a flawed or inappropriate software architecture.

❑ The fault tolerance of a piece of software is directly related to the quality of its architecture.

❑ The exception-handling architecture cannot replace the testing stages.

To make this discussion about exception handling clear and meaningful, it is important to understand that the exception-handling architecture occurs within the context of the software architecture as a whole. This means that exceptions are identified by the PBS and PADL analysis. The solution model has a PBS. When you have an unavoidable, uncontrollable, unexplainable deviation from the application architecture's PBS, then you have an exception. So, the exception is defined by clearly articulated architectures. If the software architecture is inappropriate, incomplete, or poorly thought out, then any attempt at *after-the-fact* exception handling is highly questionable. Further, if shortcuts have been taken during the testing stages (that is, incomplete stress testing, incomplete integration testing, incomplete glass box testing, and so on), then the exception-handling code has to be perpetually added to and becomes increasingly complex, ultimately detracting from the software's fault tolerance and the declarative architecture of the application. On the other hand, if the software architecture is sound and the exception-handling architecture is compatible and consistent with the PBS and Layers 3, 4, and 5 of the PADL analysis, then a high degree of fault tolerance can be achieved for parallel programs. If you approach the goal of *context failure resilience* with an understanding of the roles that software application architecture and testing play, then it is obvious that you need to choose defect removal over defect survival. Defect removal takes place during testing.

How Do You Approach Defect Removal for Parallel Programs?

First, we should point out that testing should accompany every major activity in the SDLC from requirements gathering activities to software maintenance activities. However, programs that involve multithreading or multiprocessing require even more effort during the testing phase. So, you make use of PADL analysis and PBS breakdown during you test plan. You break up the testing goals of parallel programs into answering three fundamental questions:

1. Do the design models and PBS correctly and completely represent the solution model (assuming that the solution model solves the original problem)?

2. Does the implementation model map correctly to the design models (Layer 4 and 5 from PADL) and the PBS?

3. Have all of the challenges to concurrency in the implementation model been addressed?

Traditionally, most of the effort in testing parallel programs goes into answering the third question. This is what typically happens in an imperative bottom-up approach to parallel programming. However, in a declarative approach you answer Question 1 first. This is the most important test. If this test fails, there is no reason to perform any further testing. We have presented simple versions of these models in Chapter 8, but in release code these models would contain a considerable amount of detail. If the design models are sufficiently detailed and accurate, the PBS is complete, and they both accurately map to the original solution problem, then you are in good shape. Opportunities for scalability or evolution of a software application are determined by its application architecture and concurrency infrastructure. We test the quality of both during the process of answering the first question. If the answer to the second question is yes, then you have a solid application. So, answering Question 3, which has typically been thought of as the most important, becomes secondary to answering Question 1 and Question 2. Standard software engineering testing techniques are used to answer these questions. We simply use PADL and PBS to formulate the three fundamental questions. Testing will verify that our application meets PADL and PBS.

To get some idea how this works, you can take a look at the flow of process that precedes the standard testing phases.

The Problem Statement

Recall from Chapter 8 the refinement of the game scenario: My trusted assistant has handed me a six-character code. The code can contain any character more than once. However, the code can only contain any characters from the numbers 0–9, or characters a–z. Your job is to guess what code the trusted assistant has handed me. In the game the buzzer is set to go off after 2 minutes. If you guess what I'm thinking in 2 minutes, you win. If my trusted assistant determines that you have made more than N incorrect guesses within a 15-second interval, my assistant hands me a new code guaranteed to be among the guesses that you have already made.

A Simple Strategy and Rough-Cut Solution Model

From the problem statement you devised the following simple strategy: You just happened to have all 4,496,388 possible codes to choose from in a file. You could simply perform an exhaustive search on the file presenting each code as a guess. But since you are given a time constraint of 2 minutes, you aren't sure if you'll have enough time. So, your strategy is to find a way to search through multiple portions of the file simultaneously. You decide to divide the original file into eight and have it searched concurrently. Therefore, you should be able to guess correctly in the time that it takes to search one-eighth of the file. But you also make one other provision. If you are able to search all 8 files, you still did not guess correctly, and you are not out of time, you will divide the files into 64 and try again. If you fail and still have time, you will divide the file into 128, try again, and so on.

A Revised Solution Model Using Layer 5 from PADL

Since you have determined that parallelism is useful in your solution model, you now include PADL analysis as part of your SDLC. Layer 5 in PADL involves identifying an appropriate application architecture for the problem and solution model. On first take, it appears that a multiagent architecture best fits the solution model. So, you refine the solution model in the context of a multiagent application architecture.

Revised Agent Model

You can easily see from the statement of the problem that you are initially dealing with three agents. If you recast the game in terms of agents you have: Agent A gives the code to Agent B. Agent C tries to guess Agent B's code. If Agent C comes up with too many guesses in a 15-second interval, Agent A gives Agent B a new code that is guaranteed to be a code that Agent C has already presented. If Agent C is able to go through all of the possibilities and is still not declared the winner and if Agent C has more time left, Agent C will make the same guesses only faster. Agent C realizes that generating enough guesses to guarantee success within the given time limit requires help. So, Agent C recruits a team of agents to help come up with guesses. For each pass through the total possibilities Agent C recruits a bigger team of agents to help with the guesses.

The Concurrency Model for the Agents

From the revised agent model, you have identified that the concurrency models that you need to use are the boss-worker model, peer-to-peer, Single Program Multiple Data (SPMD), Single Instruction Multiple Data (SIMD), and Exclusive Read Exclusive Write (EREW). You use SPMD/SIMD here because the agents use the same search techniques over different data sets. EREW covers the agents' communication with the boss. The boss-worker model covers the relationship between guesser agent and its helpers. The peer-to-peer model covers the relationship between the code owner and the trusted assistant.

The PBS of the Agent Solution Model

Breakdown 1: You've won the game if your guess is correct and in time.

Breakdown 2: Your guess is correct if it consists of a six-character code that contains only combinations of the characters (a–z, 0–9), considering that duplication is allowed and that code is the one my agent has handed me.

Breakdown 3: Your guess is in time if it is correct and it occurs within 2 minutes.

Breakdown 4: A brute force search through the codes will be successful if there are enough agents searching.

Breakdown 5: N agents are enough find the correct code from a sample of 4 million codes in 2 minutes.

Breakdown 6: 4 times N agents are required to find the correct code from a sample of 4 million codes in 2 minutes if the code is being changed every 15 seconds.

Declarative Implementation of the PBS

Listing 10-1 follows the declarative semantics of the PBS.

Listing 10-1

```
// Listing 10-1   A declarative implementation of the guess_it program.

1   #include "posix_process.h"
2   #include "posix_queue.h"
3   #include "valid_code.h"
4
5
6   char **av;
7   char **env;
8
9
10  int main(int argc,char *argv[],char *envp[])
11  {
12
13     valid_code  ValidCode;
14     ValidCode.determination("ofind_code");
15     cout << (ValidCode() ? "you win" : "you lose)";
16  }
```

So, you have a declaration of a `ValidCode` predicate in Line 13 and 14. This predicate is used to represent the statement:

```
This is the code the trusted agent handed you.
```

On Line 14 you test this statement by invoking the predicate `ValidCode()`. The `ValidCode()` predicate spawns four processes which in turn create two threads each. So, in fact the `ValidCode` predicate is implemented using parallel programming. However, its implementation is encapsulated. Listing 10-2 shows the declaration of the `valid_code` predicate class.

Listing 10-2

```
//Listing 10-2  Declaration of the valid_code predicate class.


1   #ifndef __VALID_CODE_H
2   #define __VALID_CODE_H
3   using namespace std;
4
5   #include <string>
6   class valid_code{
7   private:
8       string Code;
9       float  TimeFrame;
10      string Determination;
11      bool InTime;
12  public:
13      bool operator()(void);
14      void determination(string X);
15  };
16
17  #endif
```

In C++ predicates are classes that have an `operator()` method that returns a boolean value. You use the C++ predicate to approximate the notion of predicates from the PBS. Since a predicate is a C++ class, it can be used in conjunction with containers and algorithms. Listing 10-3 shows the definition of the predicate class.

Listing 10-3

```
// Listing 10-3 Definition of the valid_code predicate.

1   #include "valid_code.h"
2   #include "posix_process.h"
3   #include "posix_queue.h"
4
5   extern char **av;
6   extern char **env;
7
8
9   bool valid_code::operator()(void)
10  {
11      int Status;
12      int N;
13      string Result;
14      posix_process Child[4];
15      for(N = 0; N < 2; N++)
16      {
17          Child[N].binary(Determination);
18          Child[N].arguments(av);
19          Child[N].environment(env);
20          Child[N].run();
21          Child[N].pwait(Status);
22      }
```

```
23      posix_queue PosixQueue("queue_name");
24      PosixQueue.receive(Result);
25      if((Result == Code) && InTime){
26          return(true);
27      }
28      return(false);
29   }
30
31
32   void valid_code::determination(string X)
33   {
34       Determination = X;
35   }
```

Here is Program Profile 10-1 for Listings 10-1, 10-2, 10-3, and 10-4, which appears later in the chapter.

Program Profile 10-1

Program Name:

pguess_it (Listing 10-1)

Description:

This program is a "guess it" game. You win the game if your guess is correct in 2 minutes. Your guess is correct if it consists of a six-character code that contains only combinations of the characters a–z, 0–9, considering duplication is allowed.

The declaration of a ValidCode predicate is used to represent the statement:

```
This is the code the trusted agent handed you.
```

This statement is tested by invoking the predicate ValidCode(). The ValidCode() predicate spawns four processes, which in turn create two threads each. Its implementation is encapsulated.

Libraries Required:

rt

Additional Source Files Needed:

pguess_it.cc (Listing 10-1), posix_process.cc (Listing 10-4), valid_code.cc (Listing 10-3), posix_queue.cc

> *Please note that because of its length* posix_queue.cc *is not listed in its entirety in the book. However, you can download the full* posix_queue.cc, *along with the rest of the sample code from the book, from* www.wrox.com.

User-Defined Headers Required:

posix_process.h (Listing 5-3), valid_code.h (Listing 10-2), posix_queue.h (Listing 7-3).

Compile and Link Instructions:

c++ -o pguess_it pguess_it.cc valid_code.cc posix_process.cc posix_queue.cc -lrt

Test Environment:

Linux Kernel 2.6

Solaris 10, gcc 3.4.3 and 3.4.6

Processors:

Multicore Opteron, UltraSparc T1, Cell Processor

Notes:

None

How Do You Know This Code Works?

You use standard software engineering testing techniques but within the context of PADL, PBS and those three fundamental questions mentioned earlier in the chapter. To answer this question, you see how far you can get through standard software engineering tests with the PBS as the basic measuring stick of success.

What Are the Standard Software Engineering Tests?

As we have previously noted, there are many types of software tests: tests done during the software design as well as those done during implementation phases, installation and operational tests, usability tests, and even acceptance tests done that determine whether a customer is satisfied with a delivered system. Because of the complexity of today's software systems, and their economic and social value, software testing has become a highly specialized field. The Institute of Electrical and Electronics Engineers (IEEE) publishes standards for the complete set of testing activities. IEEE, a nonprofit organization, is the world's leading professional association for the advancement of technology. Two important testing standards documents published by the IEEE are:

❏   IEEE Std 1012, which provides guidelines for software verification and validation

❏   IEEE Std 1008, which covers unit testing

Every software development group should have these documents readily available. If you do not have them, they can be downloaded from www.standards.ieee.org.

This chapter provides a brief overview of some of the issues covered in Std 1008 and Std 1012. Because testing is one of the fundamental activities in any SDLC, Std 1008 and 1012 should be part of every SDLC. If they are adhered to, the guidelines and recommendations presented in these standards considerably enhance the quality of the software that is ultimately delivered to the user. The requirements and the specifications you can glean from Std 1008 and Std 1012 help you answer two questions:

1.   Am I building the correct software?

2.   Am I building the software correctly?

The answers to these two questions deal with issues of software verification and validation.

Software Verification and Validation

Software verification and validation perform are concerned with removing defects during each of the types of testing mentioned in Table 10-3. When you engage in software validation, you are answering the first question whereas verification answers the second question. Validation is an audit of the software features against the software specification. According to IEEE Std 1012:

> Software verification and validation (V&V) is a technical discipline of systems engineering. The purpose of software V&V is to help the development organization build quality into the software during the software life cycle. The software V&V processes determine if development products of a given activity conform to the requirements of that activity, and if the software satisfies the intended use and user needs. The determination includes assessment, analysis, evaluation, review, inspection, and testing of software products and processes. The software V&V is performed in parallel with the software development, not at the conclusion of the software development.

During the requirements and analysis activities of the SDLC, software specifications are generated. For the purpose of the multicore application design that we are discussing in this book, the specifications come from the design models and implementation models of the PADL analysis and the PBS. When you perform software verification, you are examining whether the software meets these specifications. When you engage in the process of determining whether the software actually performs the work the user wants, you are answering the second question. Verification is implementing the *software right* and validation is implementing the *right software*. Much of the software-testing process can be described as a verification or validation process. Ultimately, all of the types of testing in Table 10-3 have to be performed during the SDLC.

In addition to the seven types of software testing in Table 10-3, there are also six important types of errors that you must keep in mind that relate to parallel programming. Table 10-4 lists the common parallel programming errors and their descriptions.

Table 10-4

Common Parallel Programming Errors	Description
Deadlock	A task is waiting for an event that will not occur
Priority inversion	Occurs when a lower-priority task blocks the execution of a higher-priority task when synchronization variables are being used or when they are competing for resources
Performance degradation	Occurs when a system's performance lowers or degrades in terms of responsiveness, execution time, calculation of results, and so on
Indefinite postponement	Occurs when a system indefinitely delays the scheduling of tasks while other tasks receive the attention and the allocation of resources
Mutex exhaustion	Occurs when a system has reached its maximum number of mutexes that can be created
Thread exhaustion	Occurs when a system has reached its maximum number of threads that can be allocated

The Code Doesn't Work — Now What?

For example, after performing the most basic unit tests, say you discover that the program from Listing 10-1 fails the unit tests. The program doesn't work. What does it mean for the program not work? This program fails because it does not meet the specifications of the PBS. This means that the program causes one or more of the statements in the PBS to be false. Since the PBS is meant to capture the meaning of the concurrency infrastructure, you know that the parallelism in this program will fail at some point because it does not correctly implement the assertions, statements, and predicates in the PBS. In particular PBS #6 states:

Breakdown 6: 4 times *N* agents are required to find the correct code from a sample of 4 million codes in 2 minutes if the code is being changed every 15 seconds.

Recall the user-defined predicate `valid_code()` referenced on Lines 13–15 in Listing 10-1. It states whether the search was successful or not. But in order for the search to be successful all of the assertions in the PBS must be maintained. If you look a little closer at the definition of the predicate `operator()` for `valid_code` in Lines 9–30 in Listing 10-3, you can see that it spawns four `posix_processes`. Listing 10-4 shows the definition for the user-defined `process_interface` class.

Listing 10-4

```
// Listing 10-4   Definitions for user-defined posix_process interface class.

1   #include "posix_process.h"
2   #include <sys/wait.h>
3
4
5   posix_process::posix_process(string Path,char **av,char **env)
6   {
7
8       argv = av;
9       envp = env;
10      ProgramPath = Path;
11      posix_spawnattr_init(&SpawnAttr);
12      posix_spawn_file_actions_init(&FileActions);
13
14
15  }
16
17  posix_process::posix_process(string Path,char **av,char **env,
                                 posix_spawnattr_t  X,
                                 posix_spawn_file_actions_t Y)
18  {
19      argv = av;
20      envp = env;
21      ProgramPath = Path;
22      SpawnAttr = X;
23      FileActions = Y;
24      posix_spawnattr_init(&SpawnAttr);
25      posix_spawn_file_actions_init(&FileActions);
26
27
28
29  }
```

```
30
31   void posix_process::run(void)
32   {
33
34       posix_spawn(&Pid,ProgramPath.c_str(),&FileActions,
                     &SpawnAttr,argv,envp);
35
36
37   }
38
39   void posix_process::pwait(int &X)
40   {
41
42       wait(&X);
43   }
```

The class in Listing 10-4 is an interface class that adapts the interface for the POSIX API
posix_spawn(). The posix_process class is used to spawn two copies of ofind_code. ofind_code
in turn spawns two threads. The problem is that you end up with only eight consecutive agents working
(four processes * two threads). So, the PBS #6 requirement that you quadruple the number of agents if
the code is being changed is not addressed by the valid_code predicate. In this case, you have a simple
mapping of one agent per thread. You should not get past unit tests if the predicates in the application
are not consistent with the PBS.

This matching of the PBS with C++ predicates is part of the fundamental shift to a declarative style of
parallel programming. This is a subtle but very powerful idea. You apply software verification and
validation (V&V) to the mapping of the PBS, and the C++ predicates extend the declarative style of
parallel programming to the V&V. Some of the other important objectives of V&V are:

❑   Facilitate early detection and correction of software errors

❑   Enhance management insight into process and product risk

❑   Support the software life cycle processes to ensure compliance with program performance,
    schedule, and budget requirements

If you audit the predicates against the PBS, you can find the concurrency problems early and before the
software is deployed. In fact, one of the primary objectives of PADL and PBS is to deal with the full
complexity of the concurrency requirements prior to writing any code.

One of the consequences of the PADL and PBS is that they support declarative models of testing such
as model checking and possible-worlds analysis (which are briefly discussed later in the chapter).
These models can be deployed early in the SDLC. The complexity and integrity of multithreaded and
multiprocessing programs have to be managed at the beginning of the software development effort.
The testing process must mirror this. Consider the following from IEEE Std 1012:

> Planning the V&V process, software integrity levels are generally assigned early in the development
> process, preferably during the system requirements, analysis, and architecture design activities.
> The software integrity level can be assigned to software requirements, functions, group of functions
> or software components and subsystems. The assigned software integrity levels may vary as the
> software evolves. Design, coding, procedural, and technology implementation features selected by
> the development organization can raise or lower the software criticality and the associated software
> integrity levels assigned to the software.

The V&V at the unit test level is surprisingly effective (when used), as the example of the `ValidCode()` predicate failing at the unit test level demonstrates. The unit testing process is composed of three phases that are partitioned into a total of eight basic activities:

1. Perform the test planning
   a. Plan the general approach, resources, and schedule
   b. Determine features to be tested
   c. Refine the general plan
2. Acquire the test set
   a. Design the set of tests
   b. Implement the refined plan and design
3. Measure the test unit
   a. Execute the test procedures
   b. Check for termination
   c. Evaluate the test effort and unit

We suggest that you start to integrate these basic activities at end of the Layer 4 analysis from the PADL model and after the PBS has been done. Other common types of errors that should be located in the testing phase of your Layer 4 analysis are shown in Table 10-5.

Table 10-5

Categories of Errors	Description
User interface errors	Errors in the design, functionality, or performance of the user interface. The user interface may fail in the areas of communication, command structure, or output. The program may fail to do a task that is expected by the user or it performs the task awkwardly.
Boundary related errors	A boundary of a program is anything that makes the program change its behavior. Errors may be made by incorrectly describing the boundary conditions or not detecting the limits of the program.
Calculation errors	Errors that occur during calculations. These include errors of misinterpretation of formulas or lost precision. This also includes computational errors due to the use of incorrect algorithms.
Initial and later states	Errors that occur during an initial use of a program. They occur each time the program is restarted.
Race conditions	Errors that occur when a thread or process executes before the expected thread or process.
Control flow errors	Errors that occur when the program performs the wrong thing next.

Categories of Errors	Description
Error handling	Errors made when dealing with errors. The program may fail in detecting or anticipating possible errors and fail in correcting those errors reasonably.
Errors in handling or interpreting data	Errors that occur when data is misinterpreted, corrupted, or lost when passed back and forth between modules, programs, threads or processes.
Load conditions	Errors that occur when the program is overloaded. The program may misbehave when performing a lot of work over long periods of time, or a lot of work all at once. The program may fail when it runs out of memory, or exhausts or shares its resources with other programs or routines. How well does the program meet its limits, and how badly does the program perform when its limits are surpassed?
Hardware	Errors that occur when the program does not recognize or recover from hardware failure. The program may fail to recognize error codes that are returned from a device or it may try to access a device that is not there or is already in use. The program may also send bad data to the device.
Source and version control	Errors that occur when the incorrect version of the program is used. An old version of a subroutine that contains errors may be linked to the latest version of the program.
Documentation	Errors that occur when bad documentation is being used.
Testing errors	Errors that occur during the testing of the software.

Using the declarative architecture of the application in conjunction with mapping the PBS and PADL early on in the unit testing phase will deal with the most significant challenges of a parallel programming development effort. This technique is then supported by the application using C++ exception handling and what we call *logical fault tolerance*.

What Is Logical Fault Tolerance?

You can use the C++ exception handling facilities and the exception classes to enforce the semantics of the PADL and PBS. By extending the exception and error classes through inheritance you aid the testing process in catching non sequiturs that occur in the C++ predicate implementation of the application PBS. We call this process adding logical fault tolerance to an application.

How the basics of the C++ exception-handling facility are used has at least two important implications for the software architecture:

❑ The flow of control in the software architecture can be altered by the throw mechanism.

❑ The exception classes used introduce new types and each type has its own semantics.

It is the transfer of control from the problem area to someplace that knows how to bring the system into a consistent state and knows the semantics of the exception thrown that enables you to start to reach for the goal of logical fault tolerance. The semantics of the exception thrown describes what the exceptional condition is and suggests what should be done. The transfer of control takes you to code that implements your exception strategy. The exception strategy is designed to make the software resilient to defects and system failures. In C++, the catch() mechanism either implements the exception strategy directly or creates objects and calls functions that implement the exception strategy:

```
catch(some_exception){

    //Execute exceptions strategy

}
```

The Exception Handler

The catch{} block is called the exception handler. A C++ program can contain multiple exception handlers. Each exception handler is associated with one or more types (depending on the class hierarchy of the exception). Three of the basic functions of an exception handler are:

❑ Register the type of exception(s) that it can handle

❑ Record or in some way log what exception has occurred (sometimes this requires notification)

❑ Execute an appropriate exception-handling strategy

Exception-handling strategies come in many shapes and sizes. The primary purpose of the exception-handling strategy in the termination model is to bring the software back to a consistent state so that the software can continue to function at some acceptable level. Table 10-6 contains some of the commonly used exception strategies.

Table 10-6

Exception Strategies	Description
Resource reallocation and deallocation	Attempt to: • Reallocate memory • Close files • Release mutexes • Close semaphores • Release memory • Find files • Shut down processes • Change security of the offending process
Transaction or data rollback	Undoing steps of an incomplete transaction, rolling the data back to a check point where the data was valid

Exception Strategies	Description
Operation retry	Retrying an operation: • With the original resources • With alternate resources • After a certain interval has passed • After additional conditions have been met
Redundancy and failover	Turning over processing to other threads or that are operating in parallel with the current process
Notification for outside assistance	Requesting assistance from other software agents, human users, or other systems

The exception-handling strategy(ies) that are used will greatly impact the software architecture. This means that the exception-handling strategy has to be included in the software design phase. In the approach toward declarative interpretations of parallel programming, you are moving toward logical models. Ultimately, you want nonlogical models or irrational program behavior to be considered an exception. So the exception-handling strategy flows from Layer 5 of the PADL and the PBS. It is a fundamental part of the software architecture. If the overall software architecture is brittle, the exception-handling strategy is doomed.

The semantics of the exception thrown is tied to the exception strategy implemented. Defining and understanding the semantics of an exception in the context of the software architecture is as important as deciding where to transfer control during the exception-handling process. The C++ standard defines several built-in exception classes with their own semantics. Figure 10-1 shows the class relationship diagram for the C++ exception classes.

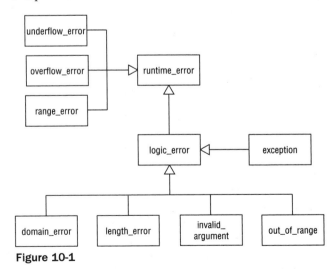

Figure 10-1

These exception classes can be extended through inheritance. C++ also supports user-defined exception classes.

The standard C++ class library has nine exception classes divided into two basic groups: the runtime error group and the logic error group. The runtime error group represents errors that are somewhat difficult to prevent, whereas the logic error group represents errors that are theoretically preventable.

The runtime_error Classes

The `runtime_error` family of classes is derived from the `exception` class. Three classes are derived from `runtime_error`: `range_error`, `overflow_error`, and `underflow_error`. The `runtime_error` classes report internal computation or arithmetic errors. The `runtime_error` classes get their primary functionality from the exception class ancestor. The `what()` method, assignment `operator=()`, and the constructors for the exception-handling class provide the capability of the `runtime_error` classes. The `runtime_error` classes provide an exception framework and architectural blueprint to build upon.

The logic_error Classes

The `logic_error` family of classes is derived from the `exception` class. In fact, most of the functionality of the `logic_error` family of classes is also inherited from the `exception` class. The `exception` class contains the `what()` method, used to report to the user a description for the error being thrown. Each class in the `logic_error` family contains a constructor used to tailor a message specific to that class.

Like the `runtime_error` classes, these classes are really designed to be specialized. Unless the user adds some functionality to these classes, they cannot do anything other than report the error and the type. So, the nine generic exception classes provide no corrective action or error handling. Take a look at how the basic exception classes work with no specialization. Example 10-1 shows how an `exception` object and a `logic_error` object can be thrown.

Example 10-1

```
// Example 10-1  Throwing an exception object and a logic_error object.

try{
    exception X;
    throw(X);
}

catch(const exception &X)
{
    cout << X.what() << endl;
}

try{
    logic_error Logic("Logic Mistake");
    throw(Logic);
}

catch(const exception &X)
{
    cout << X.what() << endl;
}
```

The basic exception classes have only construction, destruction, assignment, copy, and simple reporting capabilities. They do not contain the capability to correct a fault that has occurred. The error message returned by the `what()` method of the exception classes will be determined by the string passed to the constructor for the `logic_error` object. In Example 10-1, the string `"Logic Mistake"` passed to the constructor is returned by the `what()` message in the `catch block()`.

Deriving New Exception Classes

The exception classes can be used as is, that is, they can be used simply to report an error message describing the error that has occurred. However, this is virtually useless as an exception-handling technique. Simply knowing what the exception was doesn't do much to increase software reliability. The real value of the exception class hierarchy is the architectural road map that it provides for the designer and the developer. The exception classes provided basic error types that the developer can specialize. Many of the exceptions that occur in a runtime environment can be placed into either the `logic_error` or `runtime_error` family of classes. To see how to specialize an `exception` class, you can consider the `runtime_error` class as an example. As already noted, the `runtime_error` class is a descendant of the `exception` class. You can specialize the `runtime_error` class through inheritance. For example:

```
class  concurrent_ file_access_exception : public runtime_error{
protected:
    //...
    int ErrorNumber;
    string DetailedExplanation;
    string FileName;
    //...
public:
    virtual int takeCorrectiveAction(void)
    string detailedExplanation(void);
    //...
};
```

Here, the `concurrent_file_access_exception` inherits `runtime_error` and specializes it by adding a number of data members and member functions. Specifically, the `takeCorrectiveAction()` method is added. This method can be used to help the exception handler perform its recovery and correction work. This `file_access_exception` object knows how to identify deadlock and how to break deadlock. Recall that deadlock is one of the major challenges for parallel programming. It also has specialized logic for dealing with viruses that can damage files. It also has specialized knowledge for dealing with file transfers that get unexpectedly interrupted. Each of these situations can introduce runtime exceptions. You can use the `concurrent_file_access_exception` objects with the `throw`, `catch`, and `try` facilities of C++. For example:

```
try{
    //...
    fileProcessingOperation();
    //...
}

catch(concurrent_file_access_exception  &E)
{
    cerr << E.what() << endl;
    cerr << E.detailedExplanation() << endl;
```

(continued)

(continued)

```
        E.takeCorrectiveAction();
        // Handler Take Additional Corrective Action
        //...
    }
```

Protecting the Exception Classes from Exceptions

The exception objects are thrown when some software component encounters a software or hardware anomaly. But note, the exception objects themselves do not throw exceptions. This has many implications. Special care should be taken when designing handlers in multithreaded or multiprocessing environments. If the processing of the exception is complex enough to potentially cause another exception to be generated, then the exception processing should be redesigned and simplified where possible. The exception-handling mechanism is unnecessarily complicated when exception-handling code can generate exceptions. Therefore, most of the methods in the exception classes contain the empty `throw()` specification.

```
// Class declaration for exception class

class exception {
public:
    exception() throw() {}
    exception(const exception&) throw() {}
    exception& operator=(const exception&) throw() {return *this;}
    virtual ~exception() throw() {}
    virtual const char* what() const throw();
};
```

Note the `throw()` declarations with empty arguments. The empty argument shows that the method cannot throw an exception. If the method attempts to throw an exception, a compile-time error message is generated. If the base class cannot throw an exception, then the corresponding method in any derived class cannot throw an exception.

A Simple Strategy for Implementing Logical Fault Tolerance

In its simplest form, the implementation model creates a C++ predicate for each of the predicates in the PBS structure of the application. At that time, a predicate exception class (possibly derived from `logic_error`) is created for each predicate. If for some unknown and uncontrollable reason assumptions, assertions, or propositions concerning a predicate are contradicted, then that predicate's exception class is thrown. In most cases this means that the application will exit gracefully. It should exit at this point because once one or more of the predicates from the PBS are contradicted; therefore, the application doesn't have the same meaning. The integrity of the concurrency infrastructure has been violated. The predicate exception class acts as a logic-based invariant that guards the consistency of the PBS for the application. Obviously, the predicate exception handler will know what to do when its exception is thrown.

For example, if the `guess_it` program determines that it does not have enough agents to generate enough guesses in time to win, should it throw a `valid_code` exception? Or is the lack of enough agents a normal software error, which, therefore, should be taken care of by error handling as opposed to exception handling? The answer is a lack of enough agents in this case is not a normal software error because the fundamental operation of the software is to acquire enough agents to guess the code in time. If it cannot acquire enough agents, then it will fail its mission. The unit testing process should expose this, and the predicate exception handlers are used to aid the quality of unit testing. So, logical fault tolerance serves two important roles in this example:

1. It brings the application to a graceful exit (or other acceptable state). For multiagent and blackboard architectures this includes:

   ❑ Dismissing or retiring agents and knowledge sources

   ❑ Returning blackboard resources and communication lines

   ❑ Releasing reservations on any shared data, synchronization, or communication components

2. It prevents the application from carrying on in an irrational state and thereby prevents the application from committing further fallacies.

In particular, the second role logical fault tolerance plays here helps to build and enforce a declarative-based architecture.

Testing and Logical Fault Tolerance

Typically, the exception-handling mechanism is used to keep the program from simply crashing. The C++ exception-handling mechanism supports the termination model. A graceful exit is what is called for in the termination model. However, you usually terminate an application when something catastrophic has happened. Although it may be possible for a multithreaded or multiprocessing application to continue if the PBS is not strictly adhered to, you should classify any departure from the PBS as catastrophic because the logical consequence (or the meaning) of the application is the sum of is its predicates, propositions, axioms, and statements. These predicates form the application's logical argument. If one of the assertions or predicates turns out to be false, then the application is irrational at that point. You want to discover any irrational behavior during the testing phase, and you use logical fault tolerance semantics to help you do this. This use of C++ predicates in conjunction with predicate exceptions is an important part of achieving a declarative approach to parallel programming. While the goal is to find all of the defects in the testing phases, it is not always possible. So, you add to the typical uses for the C++ exception handling that of logical fault tolerance. The goal of logical fault tolerance is to not allow the program to have any other consequences than the consequences that are present in the PBS.

Predicate Exceptions and Possible Worlds

You might recall from the guess_it game that the agent with the code would change the code only if the number of guesses within a certain interval had been reached. In this scenario, the agent that attempted to guess the code faced two possible worlds: one world in which the code had not been changed and one where it had. The PBS had the following breakdowns for these situations:

> Breakdown 5: N agents are enough find the correct code from a sample of 4 million codes in 2 minutes.

> Breakdown 6: 4 times N agents are required to find the correct code from a sample of 4 million codes in 2 minutes if the code is being changed every 15 seconds.

The ValidCode() predicate failed the unit test because it did not provide for Breakdown 6. It is important to note that if you were in a situation where the agent luckily guessed the code before the 15 seconds were up, it would appear that the program was in good working order. But when you are evaluating the application against the PBS, you have to have a test case for each predicate in the PBS. Each predicate introduces one or more possible worlds. The notion of *possible worlds* is taken from field of logic. A possible world is used to express what is necessarily true, possibly true, or contingently true. The intuitive idea behind the possible-worlds model is that besides the true (or current) state of affairs, there are a number of other possible states of affairs, or "worlds" [Fagin et al., 1995]. Possible worlds are outcomes that an agent considers possible, in this case, the possibility of the code being changed (world 1) or not changed (world 2). The PBS of an application clearly defines what the possible worlds an agent or knowledge source will operate within. For every world that is possible for the agent, there is a set of acceptable code that the agent or knowledge source can execute. On the other hand, for worlds that are not possible (as far as the agent is concerned), there is no acceptable code that the agent can execute. Impossible worlds generate predicate exceptions!

The predicates in the PBS introduce what possible worlds there are for an application or its agents to live in. The predicate exception class represents scenarios where impossible worlds are encountered. For example, the world where the code is changed every 15 seconds but no new agents are added to accommodate that is an impossible world in the example PBS. It is exactly this problem that caused the `ValidCode()` predicate to fail. You can use a form of model checking during your unit tests to uncover these kinds of software defects in a parallel program.

What Is Model Checking?

Although a discussion of model checking is beyond the scope of this book, we introduce it here so that once you're ready to deal with validation and verification of large and potentially complex parallel programs or massively multithreaded applications, you have some idea of what tools are used. In this book, we present a brief introduction to some of the more challenging issues with multicore and multithreaded programming. But this book is just an introduction. We present declarative parallel programming techniques that move in the direction of logical models of parallelism. Logical models will ultimately help developers cope with massively parallel multicore computers. Model-checking techniques can be used to automate some of the testing multithreaded or parallel programs that have declarative architectures. Model checking is a technique for verifying finite-state concurrent systems [Huth, Ryan, 2004]. Model checking is used to determine whether the model that is presented is the model that is expected. The PBS approach used as an example in this chapter presents a logical model of the application that can be formalized and used with model checking tools. You might be interested to know that Kripke Structures are used in a formal presentation of possible worlds and model checking [Meyer, Van der Hoek, 2004].

Summary

The goal of testing software is to make sure that the software does what you want, and that you want what is does. An application is often requested as a list of desired features, and regardless to how the list of requirements for a piece of software is generated, the testing process must make sure that the software meets those requirements and that the requirements meet the user's expectations.

In many cases where parallel computers or multiprocessors are involved, the user's expectations include performance speedup or a certain level of high-performance throughput, and often the kinds of software errors you encounter increase when multithreading or multiprocessing is added in attempt to achieve the user's expectation. When the software does not perform according to the specifications, the software is in error, even if the specification violation is that the system performs too slowly.

In this chapter, we discussed using exception handling to provide a kind of *logical* fault tolerance for declarative architectures. That is, if an application for unknown and uncontrollable reasons violates statements, assertions, rules, predicates, or constraints from the PBS, you want to throw an exception and gracefully exit because once your predicates have been violated, then the correctness, reliability, and meaning of the application has been compromised. The journey toward fault tolerance in your software begins by recognizing that:

- ❏   No amount of exception handling can rescue a flawed or an inappropriate software architecture.

- ❏   The fault tolerance of a piece of software is directly related to the quality of its architecture.

- ❏   The exception-handling architecture cannot replace the testing stages.

In this approach toward declarative interpretations of parallel programming, we are moving you more toward logical models. Ultimately, you want nonlogical models or irrational program behavior to be considered an exception. So, the exception-handling strategy needs to flow from Layer 5 of the PADL and the PBS and become a fundamental part of the software architecture. User-defined C++ predicates form the application's logical argument. If one of the assertions or predicates turns out to be false, then the application is irrational at that point. The PBS of an application clearly defines what the possible worlds an agent or knowledge source will operate within. For every world that is possible for the agent, there is a piece of acceptable code that the agent or knowledge source can execute.

Software that requires parallel programming can be notoriously difficult to test and debug, which is why testing and debugging represent key challenges for software that has a concurrency requirement. Ideally, this chapter has given you a good foundation for how to approach some of those testing and debugging challenges in your own parallel programming, just as this book has grounded you in the everyday fundamentals of programming for multiprocessor and multithreaded architectures, the very kind of application design and development that is now a mainstream concern. We wish you the best of luck with your future multicore programming projects.

> **Finally, we want to leave you with a reiteration of a point we made toward the beginning of this chapter: As software developers, we produce applications in the fields of medicine, manufacturing, homeland security, transportation, finance, education, scientific research, and all areas of business, we have an ethical and moral responsibility to produce software that is safe, correct, reliable, and fault tolerant. Anything less is malpractice.**

UML for Concurrent Design

This appendix provides a quick reference to the UML diagrams used throughout this book. The Unified Modeling Language (UML) is a graphical notation used to design, visualize, model, and document the artifacts of a software system. It is the de facto standard for communicating and modeling object-oriented systems. The modeling language uses symbols and notations to represent the artifacts of a software system from different views and with different focuses. Although there are other graphical notations and artifacts used in this book, this appendix provides a quick way the reader can become familiar with the basic UML notations and symbols they may require in documenting their software systems.

The following web sites are online resources and quick reference PDFs for UML documentation:

- ❑   www.uml.org
- ❑   www.acmesoffware.com/acme/default.asp
- ❑   www.oio.de/uml-1-4-reference.htm
- ❑   www.quantum-leaps.com/resources/UML_Reference.pdf

Class and Object Diagrams

Class and object diagrams are the most common diagrams used in modeling an object-oriented system. Class diagrams can be use to represent each type of class in your system including:

- ❑   Template classes
- ❑   Interface classes

Class diagrams can include the details of the class (for example, attributes and services). Class and object diagrams can show the data type, value of variables, and return types of functions. Object diagrams can show the object name. Both types of diagrams can depict the number of classes or objects used in the system along with the relationships between classes and objects.

Figure A-1 illustrates the various ways to represent classes and objects, including active classes and objects. Class diagrams can show as much detail as needed, including attributes, services, initial values, return types, and visibility. Active classes or objects use a heavier line.

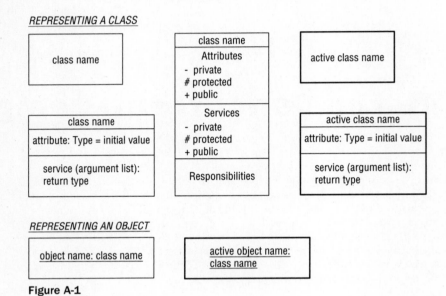

Figure A-1

Figure A-2 shows multiple instances of classes and objects. Multiple instances can be shown graphically or by using multiplicity notation.

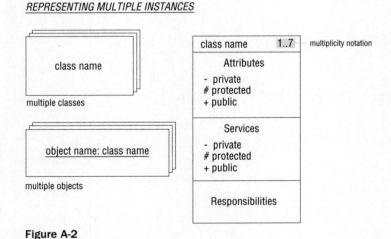

Figure A-2

Figure A-3 illustrates the ways to represent bound or unbound templates or parameterized classes.

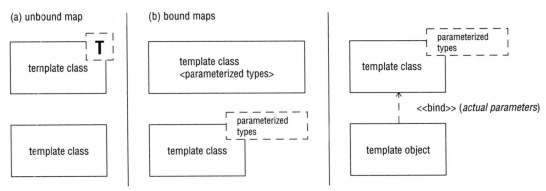

(a) unbound map

(b) bound maps

Figure A-3

Figure A-4 shows the ways to represent an interface class. An interface class can be represented using a lollipop symbol or can be represented as a regular class displaying the <<interface>> stereotype. The relationship between the interface class and the realization of the class can also be depicted.

REPRESENTING AN INTERFACE CLASS

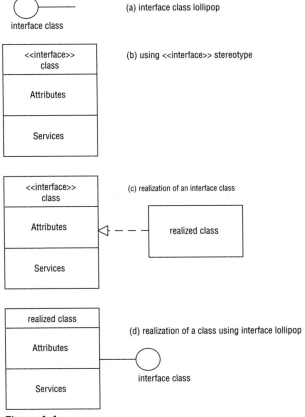

(a) interface class lollipop

(b) using <<interface>> stereotype

(c) realization of an interface class

(d) realization of a class using interface lollipop

Figure A-4

Appendix A: UML for Concurrent Design

Figure A-5 shows the ways to represent single and multiple inheritance. Two target styles can be used when multiple classes are involved in a relationship: shared and separate.

❑ With the shared target style, multiple classes are tied to a single inheritance symbol that points to the target class.

❑ With the separate target style, each class has its own inheritance symbol.

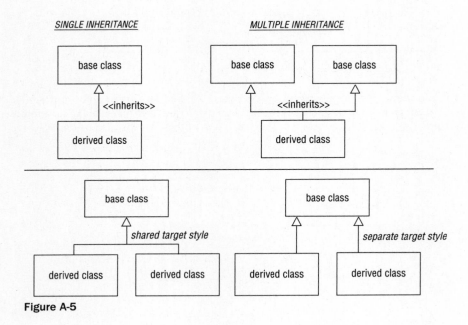

Figure A-5

Figure A-6 shows examples of the multiple relationships that can be depicted in a class diagram. Multiplicity notation can be used to show the number of instances between classes and objects.

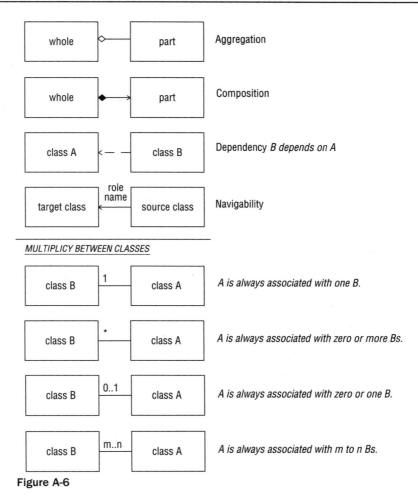

Figure A-6

Interaction Diagrams

Interaction diagrams show the interaction between objects. They consist of a set of objects, their relationship, and the messages exchanged between them. Interaction diagrams include collaboration, sequence, and activity diagrams.

Collaboration Diagrams

Collaboration diagrams are used to show a set of objects working together to perform some work. The collaboration in the system is a temporary cooperation between a set of objects. Collaboration diagrams can depict the organization of the collaboration or can depict the structure of the collaboration. This involves showing all the objects in the set, their links, and the messages sent and received between them.

Figure A-7 is a collaboration diagram showing the organization of collaborations within a system and the structural relationship of objects within a collaboration.

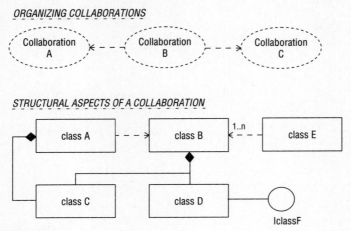

Figure A-7

Sequence Diagrams

Sequence diagrams are used to emphasize the time ordering of messages received and sent by objects in a system.

In Figure A-8 a sequence diagram is used to emphasize the time ordering of messages passed between objects. The active objects are placed at the top on the x-axis of the diagram. The messages passed between the objects are placed on the y-axis of the diagram. The diagram can depict synchronous and asynchronous messaging. The time ordering of messages is demonstrated by reading the messages from top to bottom along the y-axis.

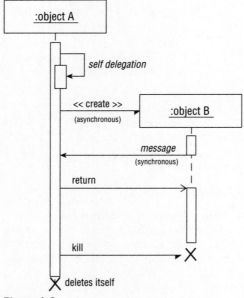

Figure A-8

Activity Diagrams

Activity diagrams show the flow of control from one activity to another. Activities are actions performed by objects. Actions include processing input/output, creating or destroying objects, or performing computations. Activity diagrams are similar to flowcharts.

In Figure A-9 the activity diagram shows the actions of objects as it flows from the focus of control of one object to another. It depicts the forking of multiple flows of control (concurrency) and joining of flows of control with a synchronization bar. Swimlanes are used to show which object is performing the action. Transitions may cut across swimlanes. A synchronization bar may also cut across swimlanes, indicating that multiple flows of controls reside in different objects performing actions concurrently.

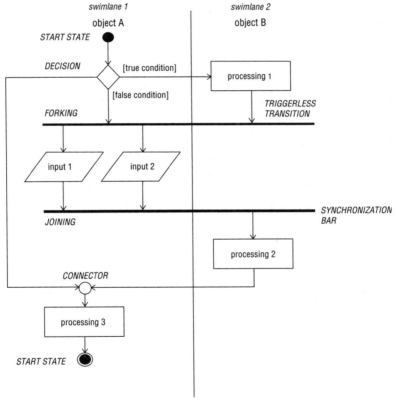

Figure A-9

State Diagrams

State diagrams are used to emphasize the state of objects and their transitions to those states. A state is a condition that an object occupies at some point in its lifetime. An object can be transformed into many different states in its lifetime. The object transform into a state if some condition is met, some action is performed, or some event has taken place.

The Figure A-10 state diagrams show the states and transitions of an object during its lifetime. A state diagram has an initial state and a final state. A state has several parts. States can also be a composite of other states or even another state diagram. Substates that execute in parallel within a single entity are called concurrent substates.

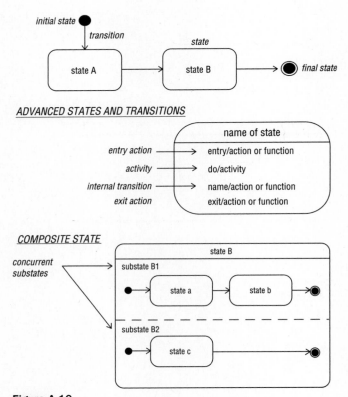

Figure A-10

Package Diagrams

Package diagrams are used to organize entities into groups.

Figure A-11 shows how package diagrams can be used to organize elements of a system. The stereotypes <<system>> or <<subsystem>> can be used. The tab on the left can hold the name of the package if the package contains other entities.

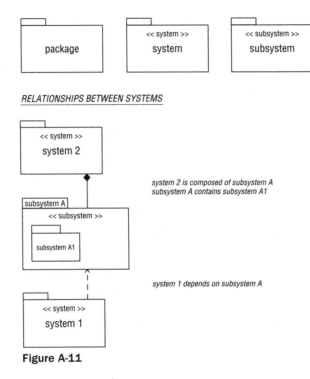

Figure A-11

B

Concurrency Models

This appendix provides a quick reference to the concurrency models used in this book. Concurrency models determine how concurrent tasks delegate work to the tasks and how communication is performed. The models can also supply a structure and approach that will assist you in determining the access policies. Here, we compiled the concurrency models with a short definition and diagram for each model.

Interprocess and Interthread Communication

With *Interprocess* Communication (IPC), communication between processes is performed by mechanisms that exist outside both address spaces of the processes.

With *Interthread* Communication (ITC), communication between threads occurs within the address space of the process the communicating threads exist.

In Figure B-1, you see that the IPC resides outside the address space of both processes. IPC allows for communication and the transference of data between related or unrelated processes. ITC resides within the address space of a process. As you can see, ITC mechanisms allow threads of the same process to access global data and variables, parameters, and file handles.

See Figure B-1 for an example of both.

INTERPROCESS and INTERTHREAD COMMUNICATION:

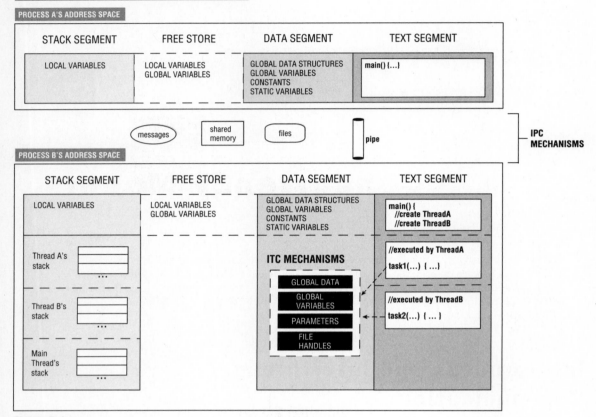

Figure B-1

Boss/Worker Approach 1 with Threads

The boss thread creates a new thread for each task. The threads can then execute their tasks simultaneously. The threads are active. Interthread Communication (ITC) is used for communicating between threads and synchronizing access to shared resources, data, and objects. See the top portion of Figure B-2 for an example.

Boss/Worker Approach 1 with Processes

The boss process creates a new process for each task. The processes can then execute their tasks simultaneously. The processes are active. Interprocess Communication (IPC) is used for communicating between processes and synchronizing access to shared resources, data, and objects. See the bottom portion of Figure B-2 for an example.

BOSS/WORKER APPROACH 1 with THREADS:

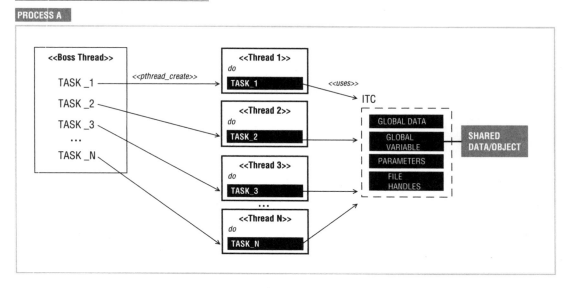

BOSS/WORKER APPROACH 1 with PROCESSES:

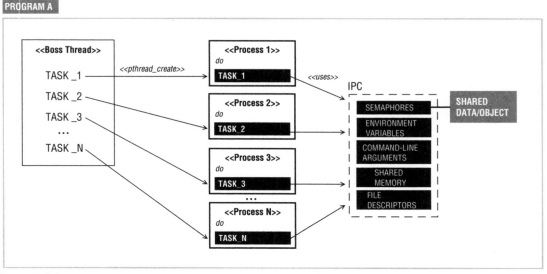

Figure B-2

Boss/Worker Approach 2 with Threads

The boss thread creates a pool of threads in which each thread has its own queue of data. For shared data or objects, ITC is used to synchronize access. See the top portion of Figure B-3 for an example.

Boss/Worker Approach 3 with Threads

The boss thread creates a pool of threads that processes data from a shared queue of data. Each thread will process a type of data. For shared data or objects, ITC (Interprocess Communication) is used to synchronize access. See the bottom portion of Figure B-3 for an example.

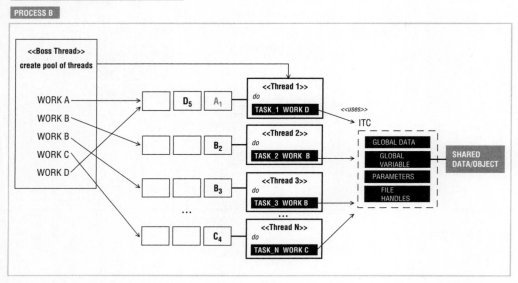

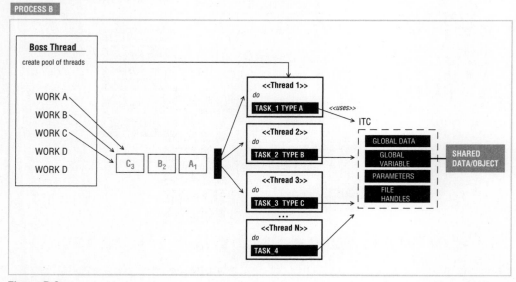

Figure B-3

414

Peer-to-Peer Approach 1 with Threads

A peer thread creates a pool of peer threads in which each thread has its own queue of data. For shared data or objects, ITC is used to synchronize access. See the top portion of Figure B-4 for an example.

Peer-to-Peer Approach 1 with Processes

A peer process spawns a pool of peer processes in which each has its own queue of data. For shared data or objects, IPC is used to synchronize access. See the bottom portion of Figure B-4 for an example.

PEER-TO-PEER APPROACH 1 with THREADS:

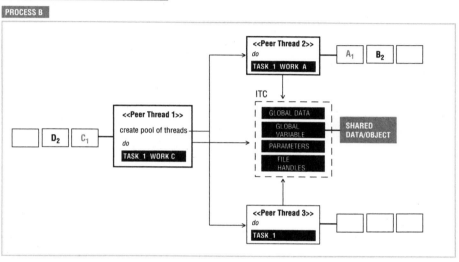

PEER-TO-PEER APPROACH 1 with PROCESSES:

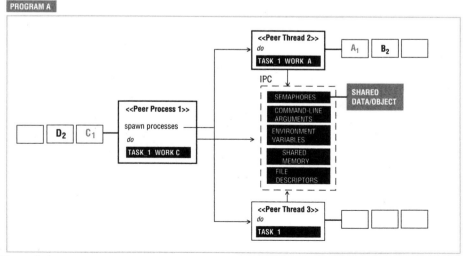

Figure B-4

Peer-to-Peer Approach 2 with Threads

A peer thread creates a pool of peer threads in which the threads share a queue of data. For shared data or objects, ITC is used to synchronize access. See the top portion of Figure B-5 for an example.

Peer-to-Peer Approach 2 with Processes

A peer process spawns a pool of peer processes in which the processes share a queue of data. For shared data or objects, IPC is used to synchronize access. See the bottom portion of Figure B-5 for an example.

PEER-TO-PEER APPROACH 2 with THREADS:

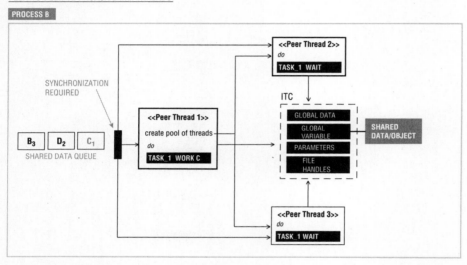

PEER-TO-PEER APPROACH 2 with PROCESSES:

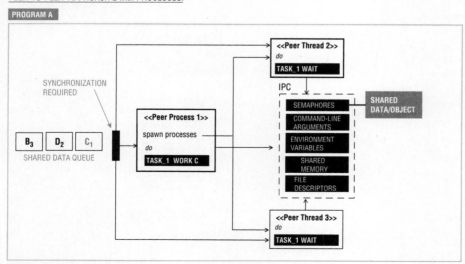

Figure B-5

Workpile Approach 1

Workpile requires multiple workers to process data from the workpile (a shared data queue). The controller creates a pool of workers and creates a workpile. The controller manages the workpile by assigning work to the workers. The workers then store the results of their work in an output queue that requires synchronization. See the top portion of Figure B-6 for an example.

Workpile Approach 2

With Workpile Approach 2, threads can also produce work that can be placed in the workpile. See the bottom portion of Figure B-6 for an example.

WORKPILE APPROACH 1

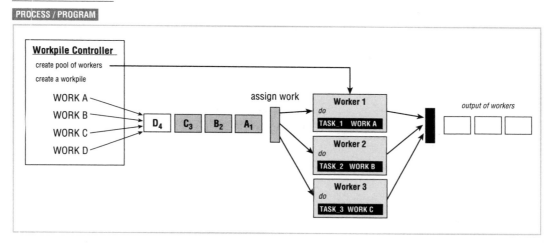

WORKPILE APPROACH 2

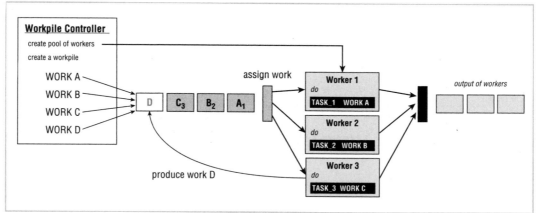

Figure B-6

Pipeline Approach with Threads

Each thread in the pipeline performs work on input from the queue. Once a thread has performed the work, it is passed to the next thread in the pipeline. Each thread represents a stage in the pipeline, performing interim results. This allows multiple inputs to be processes simultaneously. The last thread produces the final result of the pipeline. A buffer can be used between threads if one thread is slower than the proceeding thread. See the top portion of Figure B-7 for an example.

Producer/Consumer Approach 1 with Threads

A producer thread produces data to be consumed by the consumer thread. The data is stored in a block of memory shared between them. Storing the data in memory and retrieving the data from memory will require synchronization. See the bottom portion of Figure B-7 for an example.

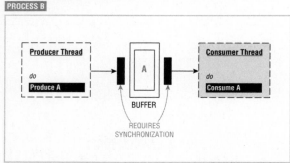

Figure B-7

Producer/Consumer Approach 2 with Threads

Multiple producer threads produce data to be consumed by one consumer thread. The data is stored in a block of memory shared between them. Storing the data in memory and retrieving the data from memory will require synchronization. See the top portion of Figure B-8 for an example.

Producer/Consumer Approach 3 with Threads

Multiple producer threads produce data to be consumed by multiple consumer threads. The data is stored in a block of memory shared between them. Storing the data in memory and retrieving the data from memory will require synchronization. See the bottom portion of Figure B-8 for an example.

PRODUCER/CONSUMER APPROACH 2 with THREADS:

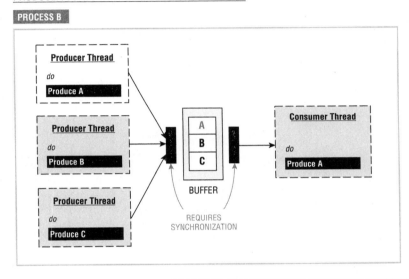

PRODUCER/CONSUMER APPROACH 3 with THREADS:

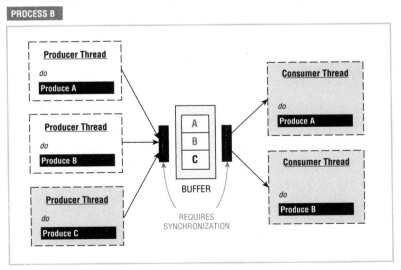

Figure B-8

Monitor Approach

Monitor contains both data and methods needed to synchronize access to serially reusable shared resources, data, or objects. The worker must enter the monitor and gain access to a condition variable in order to access the shared resource. See Figure B-9 for an example.

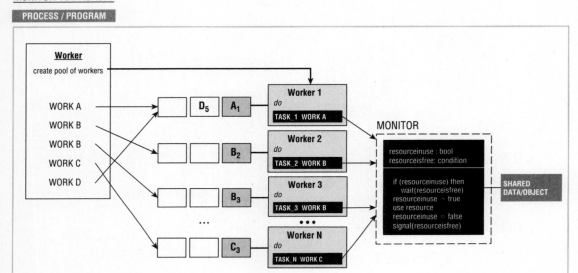

Figure B-9

Blackboard Approach with Threads

The Blackboard is a centralized object that each thread has access to. Access to the Blackboard has to be synchronized. Each thread can post preliminary results or data. The threads can also process those results or data in order to create partial solutions. See Figure B-10 for an example.

BLACKBOARD APPROACH with THREADS:

PROCESS B

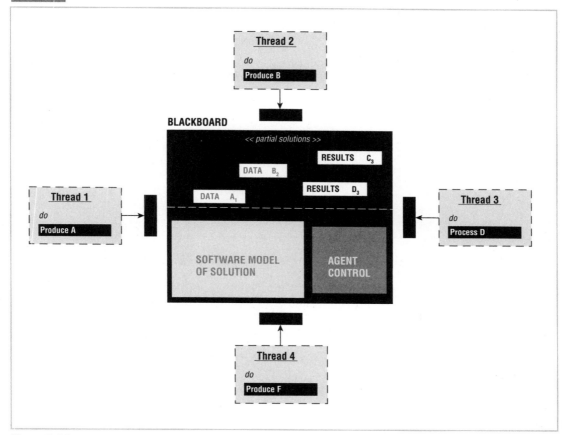

Figure B-10

Data Level Parallelism: SIMD Approach

Single Instruction Multiple Data (SIMD) means a single instruction is performed on different data or sets of data. One thread or process can perform the same task or different threads/processes can perform the same task. See the top portion of Figure B-11 for an example.

Data Level Parallelism: MIMD Approach

Multiple Instruction Multiple Data (MIMD) means multiple instructions are performed on different data or sets of data. Multiple threads or processes are used to execute the different tasks. See the bottom portion of Figure B-11 for an example.

DATA-LEVEL PARALLELISM: SIMD (SINGLE INSTRUCTION MULTIPLE DATA) APPROACH:

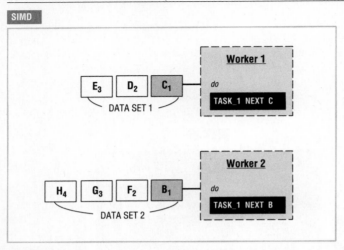

DATA-LEVEL PARALLELISM: MIMD (MULTIPLE INSTRUCTION MULTIPLE DATA) APPROACH:

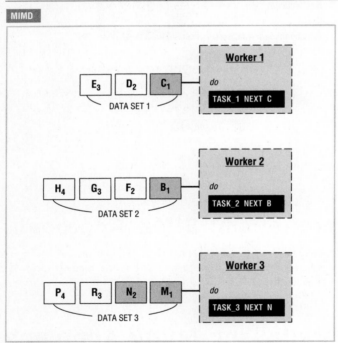

Figure B-11

PRAM Model

Parallel Random Access Machine (PRAM) is a theoretical model for multiple processors sharing one global memory. All the processors have simultaneous read and write access to the shared global memory. The PRAM model can be used for tasks that have simultaneous access to shared global memory. These are the four algorithms that can be used to access the shared global memory:

1. Concurrent read algorithms are allowed to read the same piece of memory simultaneously with no data corruption.

2. Concurrent write algorithms allow multiple processors to write to the shared memory.

3. Exclusive read algorithms are used to ensure that no two processors ever read the same memory location at the same time.

4. Exclusive write ensures that no two processors write to the same memory at the same time.

See the top portion of Figure B-12 for an example.

The PRAM model can be used to characterize concurrent access to shared memory by multiple tasks. The next sections explain the concurrent and exclusive read-write algorithms combinations that are possible for read-write access.

CRCW — Concurrent Read Concurrent Write

CRCW is the most difficult access policy to implement and requires the most synchronization. With this access policy, unrestricted access is allowed but the integrity of the data and satisfactory system performance still has to be maintained. See the bottom portion of Figure B-12.

PRAM (PARALLEL RANDOM ACCESS MACHINE) MODEL:

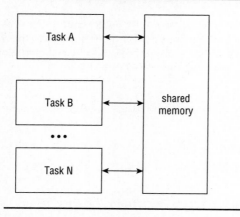

CRCW   *Concurrent Read Concurrent Write*

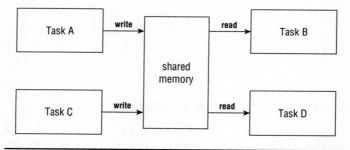

Figure B-12

EREW — *Exclusive Read Exclusive Write*

EREW means access to the shared memory is serialized where only one task at a time is given access to the shared memory, whether it is access to write or to read. An example of EREW access policy is the producer-consumer. This is the most restrictive access policy. See the top portion of Figure B-13.

ERCW — *Exclusive Read Concurrent Write*

ERCW access policy allows multiple writes to shared memory and exclusive reads. There are no restrictions on how many tasks can write to the shared memory concurrently, but this policy allows only one task to read the shared memory. This access policy is normally not implemented. See the middle portion of Figure B-13.

CREW — Concurrent Read Exclusive Write

CREW access policy allows multiple reads of the shared memory and exclusive writes. There are no restrictions on how many tasks can read the shared memory concurrently, but the policy allows only one task to write to the shared memory. Concurrent reads can occur while an exclusive write is taking place. With this access policy, each reading task may read a different value while the other task is writing. The next task that reads the shared memory will see different data than some other task sees. See the bottom portion of Figure B-13.

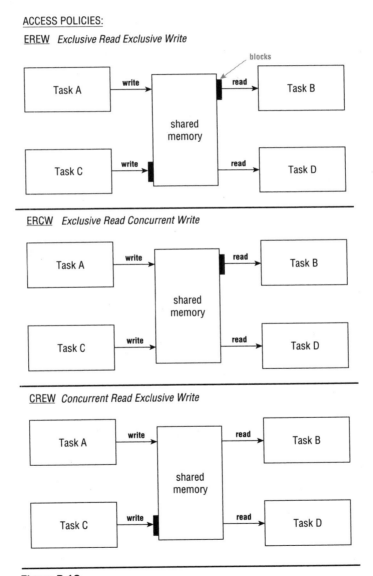

ACCESS POLICIES:

EREW *Exclusive Read Exclusive Write*

ERCW *Exclusive Read Concurrent Write*

CREW *Concurrent Read Exclusive Write*

Figure B-13

C

POSIX Standard
for Thread Management

This appendix contains sections from the POSIX Standard for Thread Management. Portable Operating System Interface (POSIX) is the open operating system interface standard accepted worldwide. It is produced by IEEE and recognized by ISO and ANSI. Support of POSIX standards ensures code portability between systems and is increasingly mandated for commercial applications and government contracts. The POSIX Standard is the most widely available method for cross-platform multicore development. It is compatible with high-level thread libraries such as Solaris Threads, Intel Thread Building Block, and the new Standard C++0x. The POSIX Standard is voluminous, containing thousands of pages. Here, for your convenience, are sections from the standard on thread management. The API functions contained in these sections are either covered in this book or are of concern when developing multicore applications.

NAME

pthread_atfork — register fork handlers

SYNOPSIS

THR   #include <pthread.h>

```
int pthread_atfork(void (*prepare)(void), void (*parent)(void),
    void (*child)(void));
```

DESCRIPTION

The *pthread_atfork*( ) function shall declare fork handlers to be called before and after *fork*( ), in the context of the thread that called *fork*( ). The *prepare* fork handler shall be called before *fork*( ) processing commences. The *parent* fork handle shall be called after *fork*( ) processing completes in the parent process. The *child* fork handler shall be called after *fork*( ) processing completes in the child process. If no handling is desired at one or more of these three points, the corresponding fork handler address(es) may be set to NULL.

The order of calls to *pthread_atfork*( ) is significant. The *parent* and *child* fork handlers shall be called in the order in which they were established by calls to *pthread_atfork*( ). The *prepare* fork handlers shall be called in the opposite order.

RETURN VALUE

Upon successful completion, *pthread_atfork*( ) shall return a value of zero; otherwise, an error number shall be returned to indicate the error.

ERRORS

The *pthread_atfork*( ) function shall fail if:

[ENOMEM]   Insufficient table space exists to record the fork handler addresses.

The *pthread_atfork*( ) function shall not return an error code of [EINTR].

EXAMPLES

None.

APPLICATION USAGE

None.

RATIONALE

There are at least two serious problems with the semantics of *fork*( ) in a multi-threaded program. One problem has to do with state (for example, memory) covered by mutexes. Consider the case where one thread has a mutex locked and the state covered by that mutex is inconsistent while another thread calls *fork*( ). In the child, the mutex is in the locked state (locked by a nonexistent thread and thus can never be unlocked). Having the child simply reinitialize the mutex is unsatisfactory since this approach does not resolve the question about how to correct or otherwise deal with the inconsistent state in the child.

It is suggested that programs that use *fork*( ) call an *exec* function very soon afterwards in the child process, thus resetting all states. In the meantime, only a short list of async-signal-safe library routines are promised to be available.

Unfortunately, this solution does not address the needs of multi-threaded libraries. Application programs may not be aware that a multi-threaded library is in use, and they feel free to call any number of library routines between the *fork*( ) and *exec* calls, just as they always have. Indeed, they may be extant single-threaded programs and cannot, therefore, be expected to obey new restrictions imposed by the threads library.

On the other hand, the multi-threaded library needs a way to protect its internal state during *fork*( ) in case it is re-entered later in the child process. The problem arises especially in multi-threaded I/O libraries, which are almost sure to be invoked between the *fork*( ) and *exec* calls to effect I/O redirection. The solution may require locking mutex variables during *fork*( ), or it may entail simply resetting the state in the child after the *fork*( ) processing completes.

The *pthread_atfork*( ) function provides multi-threaded libraries with a means to protect themselves from innocent application programs that call *fork*( ), and it provides multi-threaded application programs with a standard mechanism for protecting themselves from *fork*( ) calls in a library routine or the application itself.

The expected usage is that the *prepare* handler acquires all mutex locks and the other two fork handlers release them.

For example, an application can supply a *prepare* routine that acquires the necessary mutexes the library maintains and supply *child* and *parent* routines that release those mutexes, thus ensuring that the child gets a consistent snapshot of the state of the library (and that no mutexes are left stranded). Alternatively, some libraries might be able to supply just a *child* routine that reinitializes the mutexes in the library and all associated states to some known value (for example, what it was when the image was originally executed).

When *fork*( ) is called, only the calling thread is duplicated in the child process. Synchronization variables remain in the same state in the child as they were in the parent at the time *fork*( ) was called. Thus, for example, mutex locks may be held by threads that no longer exist in the child process, and any associated states may be inconsistent. The parent process may avoid this by explicit code that acquires and releases locks critical to the child via *pthread_atfork*( ). In addition, any critical threads need to be recreated and reinitialized to the proper state in the child (also via *pthread_atfork*( )).

A higher-level package may acquire locks on its own data structures before invoking lower-level packages. Under this scenario, the order specified for fork handler calls allows a simple rule of initialization for avoiding package deadlock: a package initializes all packages on which it depends before it calls the *pthread_atfork*( ) function for itself.

FUTURE DIRECTIONS
None.

SEE ALSO
atexit( ), *fork*( ), the Base Definitions volume of IEEE Std 1003.1-2001, **<sys/types.h>**

CHANGE HISTORY
First released in Issue 5. Derived from the POSIX Threads Extension.

IEEE PASC Interpretation 1003.1c #4 is applied.

Issue 6

The *pthread_atfork*( ) function is marked as part of the Threads option.

The **<pthread.h>** header is added to the SYNOPSIS.

NAME

pthread_attr_destroy, pthread_attr_init — destroy and initialize the thread attributes object

SYNOPSIS

THR   #include <pthread.h>

int pthread_attr_destroy(pthread_attr_t *attr);
int pthread_attr_init(pthread_attr_t *attr);

DESCRIPTION

The *pthread_attr_destroy( )* function shall destroy a thread attributes object. An implementation may cause *pthread_attr_destroy( )* to set *attr* to an implementation-defined invalid value. A destroyed *attr* attributes object can be reinitialized using *pthread_attr_init( )*; the results of otherwise referencing the object after it has been destroyed are undefined.

The *pthread_attr_init( )* function shall initialize a thread attributes object *attr* with the default value for all of the individual attributes used by a given implementation.

The resulting attributes object (possibly modified by setting individual attribute values) when used by *pthread_create( )* defines the attributes of the thread created. A single attributes object can be used in multiple simultaneous calls to *pthread_create( )*. Results are undefined if *pthread_attr_init( )* is called specifying an already initialized *attr* attributes object.

RETURN VALUE

Upon successful completion, *pthread_attr_destroy( )* and *pthread_attr_init( )* shall return a value of 0; otherwise, an error number shall be returned to indicate the error.

ERRORS

The *pthread_attr_init( )* function shall fail if:

[ENOMEM]   Insufficient memory exists to initialize the thread attributes object.

These functions shall not return an error code of [EINTR].

EXAMPLES

None.

APPLICATION USAGE

None.

RATIONALE

Attributes objects are provided for threads, mutexes, and condition variables as a mechanism to support probable future standardization in these areas without requiring that the function itself be changed.

Attributes objects provide clean isolation of the configurable aspects of threads. For example, "stack size" is an important attribute of a thread, but it cannot be expressed portably. When porting a threaded program, stack sizes often need to be adjusted. The use of attributes objects can help by allowing the changes to be isolated in a single place, rather than being spread across every instance of thread creation.

Attributes objects can be used to set up "classes' of threads with similar attributes; for example, "threads with large stacks and high priority" or "threads with minimal stacks". These classes can be defined in a single place and then referenced wherever threads need to be created. Changes to "class" decisions become straightforward, and detailed analysis of each *pthread_create( )* call is not required.

The attributes objects are defined as opaque types as an aid to extensibility. If these objects had been specified as structures, adding new attributes would force recompilation of all multithreaded programs when the attributes objects are extended; this might not be possible if different program components were supplied by different vendors.

Additionally, opaque attributes objects present opportunities for improving performance. Argument validity can be checked once when attributes are set, rather than each time a thread is created. Implementations often need to cache kernel objects that are expensive to create. Opaque attributes objects provide an efficient mechanism to detect when cached objects become invalid due to attribute changes.

Since assignment is not necessarily defined on a given opaque type, implementation-defined default values cannot be defined in a portable way. The solution to this problem is to allow attributes objects to be initialized dynamically by attributes object initialization functions, so that default values can be supplied automatically by the implementation.

The following proposal was provided as a suggested alternative to the supplied attributes:

1. Maintain the style of passing a parameter formed by the bitwise-inclusive OR of flags to the initialization routines (*pthread_create*( ), *pthread_mutex_init*( ), *pthread_cond_init*( )). The parameter containing the flags should be an opaque type for extensibility. If no flags are set in the parameter, then the objects are created with default characteristics. An implementation may specify implementation-defined flag values and associated behavior.

2. If further specialization of mutexes and condition variables is necessary, implementations may specify additional procedures that operate on the **pthread_mutex_t** and **pthread_cond_t** objects (instead of on attributes objects).

The difficulties with this solution are:

1. A bitmask is not opaque if bits have to be set into bitvector attributes objects using explicitly-coded bitwise-inclusive OR operations. If the set of options exceeds an **int**, application programmers need to know the location of each bit. If bits are set or read by encapsulation (that is, get and set functions), then the bitmask is merely an implementation of attributes objects as currently defined and should not be exposed to the programmer.

2. Many attributes are not Boolean or very small integral values. For example, scheduling policy may be placed in 3-bit or 4-bit, but priority requires 5-bit or more, thereby taking up at least 8 bits out of a possible 16 bits on machines with 16-bit integers. Because of this, the bitmask can only reasonably control whether particular attributes are set or not, and it cannot serve as the repository of the value itself. The value needs to be specified as a function parameter (which is non-extensible), or by setting a structure field (which is non-opaque), or by get and set functions (making the bitmask a redundant addition to the attributes objects).

Stack size is defined as an optional attribute because the very notion of a stack is inherently machine-dependent. Some implementations may not be able to change the size of the stack, for example, and others may not need to because stack pages may be discontiguous and can be allocated and released on demand.

The attribute mechanism has been designed in large measure for extensibility. Future extensions to the attribute mechanism or to any attributes object defined in this volume of IEEE Std 1003.1-2001 has to be done with care so as not to affect binary-compatibility.

Attributes objects, even if allocated by means of dynamic allocation functions such as *malloc*( ), may have their size fixed at compile time. This means, for example, a *pthread_create*( ) in an implementation with extensions to **pthread_attr_t** cannot look beyond the area that the binary application assumes is valid. This suggests that implementations should maintain a size field in the attributes object, as well as possibly version information, if extensions in different directions (possibly by different vendors) are to be accommodated.

FUTURE DIRECTIONS

None.

SEE ALSO

pthread_attr_getstackaddr( ), *pthread_attr_getstacksize( )*, *pthread_attr_getdetachstate( )*, *pthread_create( )*, the Base Definitions volume of IEEE Std 1003.1-2001, **<pthread.h>**

CHANGE HISTORY

First released in Issue 5. Included for alignment with the POSIX Threads Extension.

Issue 6

The *pthread_attr_destroy( )* and *pthread_attr_init( )* functions are marked as part of the Threads option.

IEEE PASC Interpretation 1003.1 #107 is applied, noting that the effect of initializing an already initialized thread attributes object is undefined.

NAME

pthread_attr_getdetachstate, pthread_attr_setdetachstate — get and set the detachstate attribute

SYNOPSIS

THR   `#include <pthread.h>`

```
int pthread_attr_getdetachstate(const pthread_attr_t *attr,
    int *detachstate);
int pthread_attr_setdetachstate(pthread_attr_t *attr, int detachstate);
```

DESCRIPTION

The *detachstate* attribute controls whether the thread is created in a detached state. If the thread is created detached, then use of the ID of the newly created thread by the *pthread_detach*( ) or *pthread_join*( ) function is an error.

The *pthread_attr_getdetachstate*( ) and *pthread_attr_setdetachstate*( ) functions, respectively, shall get and set the *detachstate* attribute in the *attr* object.

For *pthread_attr_getdetachstate*( ), *detachstate* shall be set to either PTHREAD_CREATE_DETACHED or PTHREAD_CREATE_JOINABLE.

For *pthread_attr_setdetachstate*( ), the application shall set *detachstate* to either PTHREAD_CREATE_DETACHED or PTHREAD_CREATE_JOINABLE.

A value of PTHREAD_CREATE_DETACHED shall cause all threads created with *attr* to be in the detached state, whereas using a value of PTHREAD_CREATE_JOINABLE shall cause all threads created with *attr* to be in the joinable state. The default value of the *detachstate* attribute shall be PTHREAD_CREATE_JOINABLE.

RETURN VALUE

Upon successful completion, *pthread_attr_getdetachstate*( ) and *pthread_attr_setdetachstate*( ) shall return a value of 0; otherwise, an error number shall be returned to indicate the error.

The *pthread_attr_getdetachstate*( ) function stores the value of the *detachstate* attribute in *detachstate* if successful.

ERRORS

The *pthread_attr_setdetachstate*( ) function shall fail if:

[EINVAL]   The value of *detachstate* was not valid

These functions shall not return an error code of [EINTR].

EXAMPLES

None.

APPLICATION USAGE

None.

RATIONALE

None.

FUTURE DIRECTIONS

None.

SEE ALSO

pthread_attr_destroy( ), *pthread_attr_getstackaddr*( ), *pthread_attr_getstacksize*( ), *pthread_create*( ), the Base Definitions volume of IEEE Std 1003.1-2001, **<pthread.h>**

CHANGE HISTORY

First released in Issue 5. Included for alignment with the POSIX Threads Extension.

Issue 6

The *pthread_attr_setdetachstate*( ) and *pthread_attr_getdetachstate*( ) functions are marked as part of the Threads option.

The DESCRIPTION is updated to avoid use of the term ''must'' for application requirements.

NAME

pthread_attr_getguardsize, pthread_attr_setguardsize — get and set the thread guardsize attribute

SYNOPSIS

XSI
```
#include <pthread.h>

int pthread_attr_getguardsize(const pthread_attr_t *restrict attr,
    size_t *restrict guardsize);
int pthread_attr_setguardsize(pthread_attr_t *attr,
    size_t guardsize);
```

DESCRIPTION

The *pthread_attr_getguardsize*( ) function shall get the *guardsize* attribute in the *attr* object. This attribute shall be returned in the *guardsize* parameter.

The *pthread_attr_setguardsize*( ) function shall set the *guardsize* attribute in the *attr* object. The new value of this attribute shall be obtained from the *guardsize* parameter. If *guardsize* is zero, a guard area shall not be provided for threads created with *attr*. If *guardsize* is greater than zero, a guard area of at least size *guardsize* bytes shall be provided for each thread created with *attr*.

The *guardsize* attribute controls the size of the guard area for the created thread's stack. The *guardsize* attribute provides protection against overflow of the stack pointer. If a thread's stack is created with guard protection, the implementation allocates extra memory at the overflow end of the stack as a buffer against stack overflow of the stack pointer. If an application overflows into this buffer an error shall result (possibly in a SIGSEGV signal being delivered to the thread).

A conforming implementation may round up the value contained in *guardsize* to a multiple of the configurable system variable {PAGESIZE} (see **<sys/mman.h>**). If an implementation rounds up the value of *guardsize* to a multiple of {PAGESIZE}, a call to *pthread_attr_getguardsize*( ) specifying *attr* shall store in the *guardsize* parameter the guard size specified by the previous *pthread_attr_setguardsize*( ) function call.

The default value of the *guardsize* attribute is {PAGESIZE} bytes. The actual value of {PAGESIZE} is implementation-defined.

If the *stackaddr* or *stack* attribute has been set (that is, the caller is allocating and managing its own thread stacks), the *guardsize* attribute shall be ignored and no protection shall be provided by the implementation. It is the responsibility of the application to manage stack overflow along with stack allocation and management in this case.

RETURN VALUE

If successful, the *pthread_attr_getguardsize*( ) and *pthread_attr_setguardsize*( ) functions shall return zero; otherwise, an error number shall be returned to indicate the error.

ERRORS

The *pthread_attr_getguardsize*( ) and *pthread_attr_setguardsize*( ) functions shall fail if:

[EINVAL]   The attribute *attr* is invalid.

[EINVAL]   The parameter *guardsize* is invalid.

These functions shall not return an error code of [EINTR].

EXAMPLES

None.

APPLICATION USAGE

None.

RATIONALE

The *guardsize* attribute is provided to the application for two reasons:

1. Overflow protection can potentially result in wasted system resources. An application that creates a large number of threads, and which knows its threads never overflow their stack, can save system resources by turning off guard areas.

2. When threads allocate large data structures on the stack, large guard areas may be needed to detect stack overflow.

FUTURE DIRECTIONS

None.

SEE ALSO

The Base Definitions volume of IEEE Std 1003.1-2001, **<pthread.h>**, **<sys/mman.h>**

CHANGE HISTORY

First released in Issue 5.

Issue 6

In the ERRORS section, a third [EINVAL] error condition is removed as it is covered by the second error condition.

The **restrict** keyword is added to the *pthread_attr_getguardsize*( ) prototype for alignment with the ISO/IEC 9899: 1999 standard.

NAME

pthread_attr_getinheritsched, pthread_attr_setinheritsched — get and set the inheritsched attribute (**REALTIME THREADS**)

SYNOPSIS

THR TPS `#include <pthread.h>`

```
int pthread_attr_getinheritsched(const pthread_attr_t *restrict attr,
    int *restrict inheritsched);
int pthread_attr_setinheritsched(pthread_attr_t *attr,
    int inheritsched);
```

DESCRIPTION

The *pthread_attr_getinheritsched*( ), and *pthread_attr_setinheritsched*( ) functions, respectively, shall get and set the *inheritsched* attribute in the *attr* argument.

When the attributes objects are used by *pthread_create*( ), the *inheritsched* attribute determines how the other scheduling attributes of the created thread shall be set.

PTHREAD_INHERIT_SCHED
> Specifies that the thread scheduling attributes shall be inherited from the creating thread, and the scheduling attributes in this *attr* argument shall be ignored.

PTHREAD_EXPLICIT_SCHED
> Specifies that the thread scheduling attributes shall be set to the corresponding values from this attributes object.

The symbols PTHREAD_INHERIT_SCHED and PTHREAD_EXPLICIT_SCHED are defined in the **<pthread.h>** header.

The following thread scheduling attributes defined by IEEE Std 1003.1-2001 are affected by the *inheritsched* attribute: scheduling policy (*schedpolicy*), scheduling parameters (*schedparam*), and scheduling contention scope (*contentionscope*).

RETURN VALUE

If successful, the *pthread_attr_getinheritsched*( ) and *pthread_attr_setinheritsched*( ) functions shall return zero; otherwise, an error number shall be returned to indicate the error.

ERRORS

The *pthread_attr_setinheritsched*( ) function may fail if:

[EINVAL]   The value of *inheritsched* is not valid.

[ENOTSUP]   An attempt was made to set the attribute to an unsupported value.

These functions shall not return an error code of [EINTR].

EXAMPLES

None.

APPLICATION USAGE

After these attributes have been set, a thread can be created with the specified attributes using *pthread_create*( ). Using these routines does not affect the current running thread.

RATIONALE

None.

FUTURE DIRECTIONS

   None.

SEE ALSO

   pthread_attr_destroy( ), *pthread_attr_getscope*( ), *pthread_attr_getschedpolicy*( ),
   pthread_attr_getschedparam( ), *pthread_create*( ), the Base Definitions volume of
   IEEE Std 1003.1-2001, **<pthread.h>**, **<sched.h>**

CHANGE HISTORY

   First released in Issue 5. Included for alignment with the POSIX Threads Extension.

   Marked as part of the Realtime Threads Feature Group.

Issue 6

   The *pthread_attr_getinheritsched*( ) and *pthread_attr_setinheritsched*( ) functions are marked as part
   of the Threads and Thread Execution Scheduling options.

   The [ENOSYS] error condition has been removed as stubs need not be provided if an
   implementation does not support the Thread Execution Scheduling option.

   The **restrict** keyword is added to the *pthread_attr_getinheritsched*( ) prototype for alignment with
   the ISO/IEC 9899: 1999 standard.

NAME

pthread_attr_getschedparam, pthread_attr_setschedparam — get and set the schedparam attribute

SYNOPSIS

THR   #include <pthread.h>

```
int pthread_attr_getschedparam(const pthread_attr_t *restrict attr,
    struct sched_param *restrict param);
int pthread_attr_setschedparam(pthread_attr_t *restrict attr,
    const struct sched_param *restrict param);
```

DESCRIPTION

The *pthread_attr_getschedparam*( ), and *pthread_attr_setschedparam*( ) functions, respectively, shall get and set the scheduling parameter attributes in the *attr* argument. The contents of the *param* structure are defined in the **<sched.h>** header. For the SCHED_FIFO and SCHED_RR policies, the only required member of *param* is *sched_priority*.

TSP   For the SCHED_SPORADIC policy, the required members of the *param* structure are *sched_priority*, *sched_ss_low_priority*, *sched_ss_repl_period*, *sched_ss_init_budget*, and *sched_ss_max_repl*. The specified *sched_ss_repl_period* must be greater than or equal to the specified *sched_ss_init_budget* for the function to succeed; if it is not, then the function shall fail. The value of *sched_ss_max_repl* shall be within the inclusive range [1,{SS_REPL_MAX}] for the function to succeed; if not, the function shall fail.

RETURN VALUE

If successful, the *pthread_attr_getschedparam*( ) and *pthread_attr_setschedparam*( ) functions shall return zero; otherwise, an error number shall be returned to indicate the error.

ERRORS

The *pthread_attr_setschedparam*( ) function may fail if:

[EINVAL]   The value of *param* is not valid.

[ENOTSUP]   An attempt was made to set the attribute to an unsupported value.

These functions shall not return an error code of [EINTR].

EXAMPLES

None.

APPLICATION USAGE

After these attributes have been set, a thread can be created with the specified attributes using *pthread_create*( ). Using these routines does not affect the current running thread.

RATIONALE

None.

FUTURE DIRECTIONS

None.

SEE ALSO

pthread_attr_destroy( ), *pthread_attr_getscope*( ), *pthread_attr_getinheritsched*( ), *pthread_attr_getschedpolicy*( ), *pthread_create*( ), the Base Definitions volume of IEEE Std 1003.1-2001, **<pthread.h>**, **<sched.h>**

CHANGE HISTORY

First released in Issue 5. Included for alignment with the POSIX Threads Extension.

Issue 6

The *pthread_attr_getschedparam*( ) and *pthread_attr_setschedparam*( ) functions are marked as part of the Threads option.

The SCHED_SPORADIC scheduling policy is added for alignment with IEEE Std 1003.1d-1999.

The **restrict** keyword is added to the *pthread_attr_getschedparam*( ) and *pthread_attr_setschedparam*( ) prototypes for alignment with the ISO/IEC 9899: 1999 standard.

NAME

pthread_attr_getschedpolicy, pthread_attr_setschedpolicy — get and set the schedpolicy attribute (**REALTIME THREADS**)

SYNOPSIS

THR TPS `#include <pthread.h>`

```
int pthread_attr_getschedpolicy(const pthread_attr_t *restrict attr,
    int *restrict policy);
int pthread_attr_setschedpolicy(pthread_attr_t *attr, int policy);
```

DESCRIPTION

The *pthread_attr_getschedpolicy*( ) and *pthread_attr_setschedpolicy*( ) functions, respectively, shall get and set the *schedpolicy* attribute in the *attr* argument.

The supported values of *policy* shall include SCHED_FIFO, SCHED_RR, and SCHED_OTHER, which are defined in the **<sched.h>** header. When threads executing with the scheduling policy
TSP   SCHED_FIFO, SCHED_RR, or SCHED_SPORADIC are waiting on a mutex, they shall acquire the mutex in priority order when the mutex is unlocked.

RETURN VALUE

If successful, the *pthread_attr_getschedpolicy*( ) and *pthread_attr_setschedpolicy*( ) functions shall return zero; otherwise, an error number shall be returned to indicate the error.

ERRORS

The *pthread_attr_setschedpolicy*( ) function may fail if:

[EINVAL]   The value of *policy* is not valid.

[ENOTSUP]   An attempt was made to set the attribute to an unsupported value.

These functions shall not return an error code of [EINTR].

EXAMPLES

None.

APPLICATION USAGE

After these attributes have been set, a thread can be created with the specified attributes using *pthread_create*( ). Using these routines does not affect the current running thread.

RATIONALE

None.

FUTURE DIRECTIONS

None.

SEE ALSO

pthread_attr_destroy( ), *pthread_attr_getscope*( ), *pthread_attr_getinheritsched*( ), *pthread_attr_getschedparam*( ), *pthread_create*( ), the Base Definitions volume of IEEE Std 1003.1-2001, **<pthread.h>**, **<sched.h>**

CHANGE HISTORY

First released in Issue 5. Included for alignment with the POSIX Threads Extension.

Marked as part of the Realtime Threads Feature Group.

Issue 6

The *pthread_attr_getschedpolicy*( ) and *pthread_attr_setschedpolicy*( ) functions are marked as part of the Threads and Thread Execution Scheduling options.

The [ENOSYS] error condition has been removed as stubs need not be provided if an implementation does not support the Thread Execution Scheduling option.

The SCHED_SPORADIC scheduling policy is added for alignment with IEEE Std 1003.1d-1999.

The **restrict** keyword is added to the *pthread_attr_getschedpolicy*( ) prototype for alignment with the ISO/IEC 9899: 1999 standard.

NAME

pthread_attr_getscope, pthread_attr_setscope — get and set the contentionscope attribute (**REALTIME THREADS**)

SYNOPSIS

THR TPS `#include <pthread.h>`

```
int pthread_attr_getscope(const pthread_attr_t *restrict attr,
    int *restrict contentionscope);
int pthread_attr_setscope(pthread_attr_t *attr, int contentionscope);
```

DESCRIPTION

The *pthread_attr_getscope*( ) and *pthread_attr_setscope*( ) functions, respectively, shall get and set the *contentionscope* attribute in the *attr* object.

The *contentionscope* attribute may have the values PTHREAD_SCOPE_SYSTEM, signifying system scheduling contention scope, or PTHREAD_SCOPE_PROCESS, signifying process scheduling contention scope. The symbols PTHREAD_SCOPE_SYSTEM and PTHREAD_SCOPE_PROCESS are defined in the **<pthread.h>** header.

RETURN VALUE

If successful, the *pthread_attr_getscope*( ) and *pthread_attr_setscope*( ) functions shall return zero; otherwise, an error number shall be returned to indicate the error.

ERRORS

The *pthread_attr_setscope*( ) function may fail if:

[EINVAL]   The value of *contentionscope* is not valid.

[ENOTSUP]   An attempt was made to set the attribute to an unsupported value.

These functions shall not return an error code of [EINTR].

EXAMPLES

None.

APPLICATION USAGE

After these attributes have been set, a thread can be created with the specified attributes using *pthread_create*( ). Using these routines does not affect the current running thread.

RATIONALE

None.

FUTURE DIRECTIONS

None.

SEE ALSO

pthread_attr_destroy( ), *pthread_attr_getinheritsched*( ), *pthread_attr_getschedpolicy*( ), *pthread_attr_getschedparam*( ), *pthread_create*( ), the Base Definitions volume of IEEE Std 1003.1-2001, **<pthread.h>**, **<sched.h>**

CHANGE HISTORY

First released in Issue 5. Included for alignment with the POSIX Threads Extension.

Marked as part of the Realtime Threads Feature Group.

Issue 6

The *pthread_attr_getscope*( ) and *pthread_attr_setscope*( ) functions are marked as part of the Threads and Thread Execution Scheduling options.

The [ENOSYS] error condition has been removed as stubs need not be provided if an implementation does not support the Thread Execution Scheduling option.

The **restrict** keyword is added to the *pthread_attr_getscope*( ) prototype for alignment with the ISO/IEC 9899:1999 standard.

NAME

pthread_attr_getstack, pthread_attr_setstack — get and set stack attributes

SYNOPSIS

THR `#include <pthread.h>`

TSA TSS
```
int pthread_attr_getstack(const pthread_attr_t *restrict attr,
    void **restrict stackaddr, size_t *restrict stacksize);
int pthread_attr_setstack(pthread_attr_t *attr, void *stackaddr,
    size_t stacksize);
```

DESCRIPTION

The *pthread_attr_getstack*( ) and *pthread_attr_setstack*( ) functions, respectively, shall get and set the thread creation stack attributes *stackaddr* and *stacksize* in the *attr* object.

The stack attributes specify the area of storage to be used for the created thread's stack. The base (lowest addressable byte) of the storage shall be *stackaddr*, and the size of the storage shall be *stacksize* bytes. The *stacksize* shall be at least {PTHREAD_STACK_MIN}. The *stackaddr* shall be aligned appropriately to be used as a stack; for example, *pthread_attr_setstack*( ) may fail with [EINVAL] if (*stackaddr* & 0x7) is not 0. All pages within the stack described by *stackaddr* and *stacksize* shall be both readable and writable by the thread.

RETURN VALUE

Upon successful completion, these functions shall return a value of 0; otherwise, an error number shall be returned to indicate the error.

The *pthread_attr_getstack*( ) function shall store the stack attribute values in *stackaddr* and *stacksize* if successful.

ERRORS

The *pthread_attr_setstack*( ) function shall fail if:

[EINVAL]   The value of *stacksize* is less than {PTHREAD_STACK_MIN} or exceeds an implementation-defined limit.

The *pthread_attr_setstack*( ) function may fail if:

[EINVAL]   The value of *stackaddr* does not have proper alignment to be used as a stack, or if (*stackaddr* + *stacksize*) lacks proper alignment.

[EACCES]   The stack page(s) described by *stackaddr* and *stacksize* are not both readable and writable by the thread.

These functions shall not return an error code of [EINTR].

EXAMPLES

None.

APPLICATION USAGE

These functions are appropriate for use by applications in an environment where the stack for a thread must be placed in some particular region of memory.

While it might seem that an application could detect stack overflow by providing a protected page outside the specified stack region, this cannot be done portably. Implementations are free to place the thread's initial stack pointer anywhere within the specified region to accommodate the machine's stack pointer behavior and allocation requirements. Furthermore, on some architectures, such as the IA-64, "overflow" might mean that two separate stack pointers allocated within the region will overlap somewhere in the middle of the region.

RATIONALE

None.

FUTURE DIRECTIONS

None.

SEE ALSO

pthread_attr_init( ), *pthread_attr_setdetachstate*( ), *pthread_attr_setstacksize*( ), *pthread_create*( ), the Base Definitions volume of IEEE Std 1003.1-2001, **<limits.h>**, **<pthread.h>**

CHANGE HISTORY

First released in Issue 6. Developed as an XSI extension and brought into the BASE by IEEE PASC Interpretation 1003.1 #101.

NAME

pthread_attr_getstackaddr, pthread_attr_setstackaddr — get and set the stackaddr attribute

SYNOPSIS

THR TSA `#include <pthread.h>`

OB
```
int pthread_attr_getstackaddr(const pthread_attr_t *restrict attr,
    void **restrict stackaddr);
int pthread_attr_setstackaddr(pthread_attr_t *attr, void *stackaddr);
```

DESCRIPTION

The *pthread_attr_getstackaddr*( ) and *pthread_attr_setstackaddr*( ) functions, respectively, shall get and set the thread creation *stackaddr* attribute in the *attr* object.

The *stackaddr* attribute specifies the location of storage to be used for the created thread's stack. The size of the storage shall be at least {PTHREAD_STACK_MIN}.

RETURN VALUE

Upon successful completion, *pthread_attr_getstackaddr*( ) and *pthread_attr_setstackaddr*( ) shall return a value of 0; otherwise, an error number shall be returned to indicate the error.

The *pthread_attr_getstackaddr*( ) function stores the *stackaddr* attribute value in *stackaddr* if successful.

ERRORS

No errors are defined.

These functions shall not return an error code of [EINTR].

EXAMPLES

None.

APPLICATION USAGE

The specification of the *stackaddr* attribute presents several ambiguities that make portable use of these interfaces impossible. The description of the single address parameter as a ''stack'' does not specify a particular relationship between the address and the ''stack'' implied by that address. For example, the address may be taken as the low memory address of a buffer intended for use as a stack, or it may be taken as the address to be used as the initial stack pointer register value for the new thread. These two are not the same except for a machine on which the stack grows ''up'' from low memory to high, and on which a ''push'' operation first stores the value in memory and then increments the stack pointer register. Further, on a machine where the stack grows ''down'' from high memory to low, interpretation of the address as the ''low memory'' address requires a determination of the intended size of the stack. IEEE Std 1003.1-2001 has introduced the new interfaces *pthread_attr_setstack*( ) and *pthread_attr_getstack*( ) to resolve these ambiguities.

RATIONALE

None.

FUTURE DIRECTIONS

None.

SEE ALSO

pthread_attr_destroy( ), *pthread_attr_getdetachstate*( ), *pthread_attr_getstack*( ), *pthread_attr_getstacksize*( ), *pthread_attr_setstack*( ), *pthread_create*( ), the Base Definitions volume of IEEE Std 1003.1-2001, **<limits.h>**, **<pthread.h>**

CHANGE HISTORY

First released in Issue 5. Included for alignment with the POSIX Threads Extension.

Issue 6

The *pthread_attr_getstackaddr*( ) and *pthread_attr_setstackaddr*( ) functions are marked as part of the Threads and Thread Stack Address Attribute options.

The **restrict** keyword is added to the *pthread_attr_getstackaddr*( ) prototype for alignment with the ISO/IEC 9899:1999 standard.

These functions are marked obsolescent.

NAME

pthread_attr_getstacksize, pthread_attr_setstacksize — get and set the stacksize attribute

SYNOPSIS

THR TSA `#include <pthread.h>`

```
int pthread_attr_getstacksize(const pthread_attr_t *restrict attr,
    size_t *restrict stacksize);
int pthread_attr_setstacksize(pthread_attr_t *attr, size_t stacksize);
```

DESCRIPTION

The *pthread_attr_getstacksize( )* and *pthread_attr_setstacksize( )* functions, respectively, shall get and set the thread creation *stacksize* attribute in the *attr* object.

The *stacksize* attribute shall define the minimum stack size (in bytes) allocated for the created threads stack.

RETURN VALUE

Upon successful completion, *pthread_attr_getstacksize( )* and *pthread_attr_setstacksize( )* shall return a value of 0; otherwise, an error number shall be returned to indicate the error.

The *pthread_attr_getstacksize( )* function stores the *stacksize* attribute value in *stacksize* if successful.

ERRORS

The *pthread_attr_setstacksize( )* function shall fail if:

[EINVAL]   The value of *stacksize* is less than {PTHREAD_STACK_MIN} or exceeds a system-imposed limit.

These functions shall not return an error code of [EINTR].

EXAMPLES

None.

APPLICATION USAGE

None.

RATIONALE

None.

FUTURE DIRECTIONS

None.

SEE ALSO

pthread_attr_destroy( ), *pthread_attr_getstackaddr( )*, *pthread_attr_getdetachstate( )*, *pthread_create( )*, the Base Definitions volume of IEEE Std 1003.1-2001, **<limits.h>**, **<pthread.h>**

CHANGE HISTORY

First released in Issue 5. Included for alignment with the POSIX Threads Extension.

Issue 6

The *pthread_attr_getstacksize( )* and *pthread_attr_setstacksize( )* functions are marked as part of the Threads and Thread Stack Address Attribute options.

The **restrict** keyword is added to the *pthread_attr_getstacksize( )* prototype for alignment with the ISO/IEC 9899:1999 standard.

NAME

pthread_attr_init — initialize the thread attributes object

SYNOPSIS

THR

```
#include <pthread.h>

int pthread_attr_init(pthread_attr_t *attr);
```

DESCRIPTION

Refer to *pthread_attr_destroy( )*.

NAME

pthread_attr_setdetachstate — set the detachstate attribute

SYNOPSIS

THR   `#include <pthread.h>`

`int pthread_attr_setdetachstate(pthread_attr_t *attr, int detachstate);`

DESCRIPTION

Refer to *pthread_attr_getdetachstate*( ).

NAME

   pthread_attr_setguardsize — set the thread guardsize attribute

SYNOPSIS

XSI   `#include <pthread.h>`

   ```
   int pthread_attr_setguardsize(pthread_attr_t *attr,
       size_t guardsize);
   ```

DESCRIPTION

   Refer to *pthread_attr_getguardsize( )*.

NAME

pthread_attr_setinheritsched — set the inheritsched attribute (**REALTIME THREADS**)

SYNOPSIS

THR TPS `#include <pthread.h>`

```
int pthread_attr_setinheritsched(pthread_attr_t *attr,
    int inheritsched);
```

DESCRIPTION

Refer to *pthread_attr_getinheritsched*( ).

NAME

pthread_attr_setschedparam — set the schedparam attribute

SYNOPSIS

THR   `#include <pthread.h>`

```
int pthread_attr_setschedparam(pthread_attr_t *restrict attr,
    const struct sched_param *restrict param);
```

DESCRIPTION

Refer to *pthread_attr_getschedparam*( ).

NAME

        pthread_attr_setschedpolicy — set the schedpolicy attribute (**REALTIME THREADS**)

SYNOPSIS

THR TPS `#include <pthread.h>`

        `int pthread_attr_setschedpolicy(pthread_attr_t *attr, int policy);`

DESCRIPTION

        Refer to *pthread_attr_getschedpolicy( )*.

pthread_attr_setscope()

NAME

pthread_attr_setscope — set the contentionscope attribute (**REALTIME THREADS**)

SYNOPSIS

THR TPS `#include <pthread.h>`

```
int pthread_attr_setscope(pthread_attr_t *attr, int contentionscope);
```

DESCRIPTION

Refer to *pthread_attr_getscope*( ).

NAME
   pthread_attr_setstack — set the stack attribute

SYNOPSIS
XSI   #include <pthread.h>

   int pthread_attr_setstack(pthread_attr_t *attr, void *stackaddr,
       size_t stacksize);

DESCRIPTION
   Refer to *pthread_attr_getstack*( ).

NAME

pthread_attr_setstackaddr — set the stackaddr attribute

SYNOPSIS

THR TSA `#include <pthread.h>`

OB `int pthread_attr_setstackaddr(pthread_attr_t *attr, void *stackaddr);`

DESCRIPTION

Refer to *pthread_attr_getstackaddr*( ).

NAME

pthread_attr_setstacksize — set the stacksize attribute

SYNOPSIS

THR TSA `#include <pthread.h>`

`int pthread_attr_setstacksize(pthread_attr_t *attr, size_t stacksize);`

DESCRIPTION

Refer to *pthread_attr_getstacksize( )*.

NAME

pthread_cancel — cancel execution of a thread

SYNOPSIS

THR
```
#include <pthread.h>

int pthread_cancel(pthread_t thread);
```

DESCRIPTION

The *pthread_cancel*( ) function shall request that *thread* be canceled. The target thread's cancelability state and type determines when the cancelation takes effect. When the cancelation is acted on, the cancelation cleanup handlers for *thread* shall be called. When the last cancelation cleanup handler returns, the thread-specific data destructor functions shall be called for *thread*. When the last destructor function returns, *thread* shall be terminated.

The cancelation processing in the target thread shall run asynchronously with respect to the calling thread returning from *pthread_cancel*( ).

RETURN VALUE

If successful, the *pthread_cancel*( ) function shall return zero; otherwise, an error number shall be returned to indicate the error.

ERRORS

The *pthread_cancel*( ) function may fail if:

[ESRCH]   No thread could be found corresponding to that specified by the given thread ID.

The *pthread_cancel*( ) function shall not return an error code of [EINTR].

EXAMPLES

None.

APPLICATION USAGE

None.

RATIONALE

Two alternative functions were considered for sending the cancelation notification to a thread. One would be to define a new SIGCANCEL signal that had the cancelation semantics when delivered; the other was to define the new *pthread_cancel*( ) function, which would trigger the cancelation semantics.

The advantage of a new signal was that so much of the delivery criteria were identical to that used when trying to deliver a signal that making cancelation notification a signal was seen as consistent. Indeed, many implementations implement cancelation using a special signal. On the other hand, there would be no signal functions that could be used with this signal except *pthread_kill*( ), and the behavior of the delivered cancelation signal would be unlike any previously existing defined signal.

The benefits of a special function include the recognition that this signal would be defined because of the similar delivery criteria and that this is the only common behavior between a cancelation request and a signal. In addition, the cancelation delivery mechanism does not have to be implemented as a signal. There are also strong, if not stronger, parallels with language exception mechanisms than with signals that are potentially obscured if the delivery mechanism is visibly closer to signals.

In the end, it was considered that as there were so many exceptions to the use of the new signal with existing signals functions it would be misleading. A special function has resolved this problem. This function was carefully defined so that an implementation wishing to provide the cancelation functions on top of signals could do so. The special function also means that implementations are not obliged to implement cancelation with signals.

FUTURE DIRECTIONS

None.

SEE ALSO

pthread_exit ( ), *pthread_cond_timedwait* ( ), *pthread_join* ( ), *pthread_setcancelstate* ( ), the Base Definitions volume of IEEE Std 1003.1-2001, **<pthread.h>**

CHANGE HISTORY

First released in Issue 5. Included for alignment with the POSIX Threads Extension.

Issue 6

The *pthread_cancel* ( ) function is marked as part of the Threads option.

NAME
pthread_cond_broadcast, pthread_cond_signal — broadcast or signal a condition

SYNOPSIS
THR   #include <pthread.h>

```
int pthread_cond_broadcast(pthread_cond_t *cond);
int pthread_cond_signal(pthread_cond_t *cond);
```

DESCRIPTION
These functions shall unblock threads blocked on a condition variable.

The *pthread_cond_broadcast*( ) function shall unblock all threads currently blocked on the specified condition variable *cond*.

The *pthread_cond_signal*( ) function shall unblock at least one of the threads that are blocked on the specified condition variable *cond* (if any threads are blocked on *cond*).

If more than one thread is blocked on a condition variable, the scheduling policy shall determine the order in which threads are unblocked. When each thread unblocked as a result of a *pthread_cond_broadcast*( ) or *pthread_cond_signal*( ) returns from its call to *pthread_cond_wait*( ) or *pthread_cond_timedwait*( ), the thread shall own the mutex with which it called *pthread_cond_wait*( ) or *pthread_cond_timedwait*( ). The thread(s) that are unblocked shall contend for the mutex according to the scheduling policy (if applicable), and as if each had called *pthread_mutex_lock*( ).

The *pthread_cond_broadcast*( ) or *pthread_cond_signal*( ) functions may be called by a thread whether or not it currently owns the mutex that threads calling *pthread_cond_wait*( ) or *pthread_cond_timedwait*( ) have associated with the condition variable during their waits; however, if predictable scheduling behavior is required, then that mutex shall be locked by the thread calling *pthread_cond_broadcast*( ) or *pthread_cond_signal*( ).

The *pthread_cond_broadcast*( ) and *pthread_cond_signal*( ) functions shall have no effect if there are no threads currently blocked on *cond*.

RETURN VALUE
If successful, the *pthread_cond_broadcast*( ) and *pthread_cond_signal*( ) functions shall return zero; otherwise, an error number shall be returned to indicate the error.

ERRORS
The *pthread_cond_broadcast*( ) and *pthread_cond_signal*( ) function may fail if:

[EINVAL]   The value *cond* does not refer to an initialized condition variable.

These functions shall not return an error code of [EINTR].

EXAMPLES
None.

APPLICATION USAGE
The *pthread_cond_broadcast*( ) function is used whenever the shared-variable state has been changed in a way that more than one thread can proceed with its task. Consider a single producer/multiple consumer problem, where the producer can insert multiple items on a list that is accessed one item at a time by the consumers. By calling the *pthread_cond_broadcast*( ) function, the producer would notify all consumers that might be waiting, and thereby the application would receive more throughput on a multi-processor. In addition, *pthread_cond_broadcast*( ) makes it easier to implement a read-write lock. The *pthread_cond_broadcast*( ) function is needed in order to wake up all waiting readers when a

writer releases its lock. Finally, the two-phase commit algorithm can use this broadcast function to notify all clients of an impending transaction commit.

It is not safe to use the *pthread_cond_signal( )* function in a signal handler that is invoked asynchronously. Even if it were safe, there would still be a race between the test of the Boolean *pthread_cond_wait( )* that could not be efficiently eliminated.

Mutexes and condition variables are thus not suitable for releasing a waiting thread by signaling from code running in a signal handler.

RATIONALE

Multiple Awakenings by Condition Signal

On a multi-processor, it may be impossible for an implementation of *pthread_cond_signal( )* to avoid the unblocking of more than one thread blocked on a condition variable. For example, consider the following partial implementation of *pthread_cond_wait( )* and *pthread_cond_signal( )*, executed by two threads in the order given. One thread is trying to wait on the condition variable, another is concurrently executing *pthread_cond_signal( )*, while a third thread is already waiting.

```
pthread_cond_wait(mutex, cond):
    value = cond->value; /* 1 */
    pthread_mutex_unlock(mutex); /* 2 */
    pthread_mutex_lock(cond->mutex); /* 10 */
    if (value == cond->value) { /* 11 */
        me->next_cond = cond->waiter;
        cond->waiter = me;
        pthread_mutex_unlock(cond->mutex);
        unable_to_run(me);
    } else
        pthread_mutex_unlock(cond->mutex); /* 12 */
    pthread_mutex_lock(mutex); /* 13 */

pthread_cond_signal(cond):
    pthread_mutex_lock(cond->mutex); /* 3 */
    cond->value++; /* 4 */
    if (cond->waiter) { /* 5 */
        sleeper = cond->waiter; /* 6 */
        cond->waiter = sleeper->next_cond; /* 7 */
        able_to_run(sleeper); /* 8 */
    }
    pthread_mutex_unlock(cond->mutex); /* 9 */
```

The effect is that more than one thread can return from its call to *pthread_cond_wait( )* or *pthread_cond_timedwait( )* as a result of one call to *pthread_cond_signal( )*. This effect is called "spurious wakeup". Note that the situation is self-correcting in that the number of threads that are so awakened is finite; for example, the next thread to call *pthread_cond_wait( )* after the sequence of events above blocks.

While this problem could be resolved, the loss of efficiency for a fringe condition that occurs only rarely is unacceptable, especially given that one has to check the predicate associated with a condition variable anyway. Correcting this problem would unnecessarily reduce the degree of concurrency in this basic building block for all higher-level synchronization operations.

An added benefit of allowing spurious wakeups is that applications are forced to code a predicate-testing-loop around the condition wait. This also makes the application tolerate superfluous condition broadcasts or signals on the same condition variable that may be coded in some other part of the application. The resulting applications are thus more robust. Therefore, IEEE Std 1003.1-2001 explicitly documents that spurious wakeups may occur.

FUTURE DIRECTIONS
None.

SEE ALSO
pthread_cond_destroy( ),   *pthread_cond_timedwait*( ),   the   Base   Definitions   volume   of IEEE Std 1003.1-2001, **<pthread.h>**

CHANGE HISTORY
First released in Issue 5. Included for alignment with the POSIX Threads Extension.

Issue 6
The *pthread_cond_broadcast*( ) and *pthread_cond_signal*( ) functions are marked as part of the Threads option.

The APPLICATION USAGE section is added.

NAME

pthread_cond_destroy, pthread_cond_init — destroy and initialize condition variables

SYNOPSIS

THR   `#include <pthread.h>`

```
int pthread_cond_destroy(pthread_cond_t *cond);
int pthread_cond_init(pthread_cond_t *restrict cond,
    const pthread_condattr_t *restrict attr);
pthread_cond_t cond = PTHREAD_COND_INITIALIZER;
```

DESCRIPTION

The *pthread_cond_destroy*( ) function shall destroy the given condition variable specified by *cond*; the object becomes, in effect, uninitialized. An implementation may cause *pthread_cond_destroy*( ) to set the object referenced by *cond* to an invalid value. A destroyed condition variable object can be reinitialized using *pthread_cond_init*( ); the results of otherwise referencing the object after it has been destroyed are undefined.

It shall be safe to destroy an initialized condition variable upon which no threads are currently blocked. Attempting to destroy a condition variable upon which other threads are currently blocked results in undefined behavior.

The *pthread_cond_init*( ) function shall initialize the condition variable referenced by *cond* with attributes referenced by *attr*. If *attr* is NULL, the default condition variable attributes shall be used; the effect is the same as passing the address of a default condition variable attributes object. Upon successful initialization, the state of the condition variable shall become initialized.

Only *cond* itself may be used for performing synchronization. The result of referring to copies of *cond* in calls to *pthread_cond_wait*( ), *pthread_cond_timedwait*( ), *pthread_cond_signal*( ), *pthread_cond_broadcast*( ), and *pthread_cond_destroy*( ) is undefined.

Attempting to initialize an already initialized condition variable results in undefined behavior.

In cases where default condition variable attributes are appropriate, the macro PTHREAD_COND_INITIALIZER can be used to initialize condition variables that are statically allocated. The effect shall be equivalent to dynamic initialization by a call to *pthread_cond_init*( ) with parameter *attr* specified as NULL, except that no error checks are performed.

RETURN VALUE

If successful, the *pthread_cond_destroy*( ) and *pthread_cond_init*( ) functions shall return zero; otherwise, an error number shall be returned to indicate the error.

The [EBUSY] and [EINVAL] error checks, if implemented, shall act as if they were performed immediately at the beginning of processing for the function and caused an error return prior to modifying the state of the condition variable specified by *cond*.

ERRORS

The *pthread_cond_destroy*( ) function may fail if:

[EBUSY]   The implementation has detected an attempt to destroy the object referenced by *cond* while it is referenced (for example, while being used in a *pthread_cond_wait*( ) or *pthread_cond_timedwait*( )) by another thread.

[EINVAL]   The value specified by *cond* is invalid.

The *pthread_cond_init*( ) function shall fail if:

[EAGAIN]   The system lacked the necessary resources (other than memory) to initialize another condition variable.

[ENOMEM]   Insufficient memory exists to initialize the condition variable.

The *pthread_cond_init*( ) function may fail if:

[EBUSY]   The implementation has detected an attempt to reinitialize the object referenced by *cond*, a previously initialized, but not yet destroyed, condition variable.

[EINVAL]   The value specified by *attr* is invalid.

These functions shall not return an error code of [EINTR].

EXAMPLES

A condition variable can be destroyed immediately after all the threads that are blocked on it are awakened. For example, consider the following code:

```
struct list {
    pthread_mutex_t lm;
    ...
}

struct elt {
    key k;
    int busy;
    pthread_cond_t notbusy;
    ...
}
/* Find a list element and reserve it. */
struct elt *
list_find(struct list *lp, key k)
{
    struct elt *ep;

    pthread_mutex_lock(&lp->lm);
    while ((ep = find_elt(1, k) != NULL) && ep->busy)
        pthread_cond_wait(&ep->notbusy, &lp->lm);
    if (ep != NULL)
        ep->busy = 1;
    pthread_mutex_unlock(&lp->lm);
    return(ep);
}

delete_elt(struct list *lp, struct elt *ep)
{
    pthread_mutex_lock(&lp->lm);
    assert(ep->busy);
    ... remove ep from list ...
    ep->busy = 0;   /* Paranoid. */
(A) pthread_cond_broadcast(&ep->notbusy);
    pthread_mutex_unlock(&lp->lm);
(B) pthread_cond_destroy(&rp->notbusy);
    free(ep);
}
```

In this example, the condition variable and its list element may be freed (line B) immediately after all threads waiting for it are awakened (line A), since the mutex and the code ensure that no other thread can touch the element to be deleted.

APPLICATION USAGE

None.

RATIONALE

See *pthread_mutex_init( )*; a similar rationale applies to condition variables.

FUTURE DIRECTIONS

None.

SEE ALSO

pthread_cond_broadcast( ), *pthread_cond_signal( )*, *pthread_cond_timedwait( )*, the Base Definitions volume of IEEE Std 1003.1-2001, **<pthread.h>**

CHANGE HISTORY

First released in Issue 5. Included for alignment with the POSIX Threads Extension.

Issue 6

The *pthread_cond_destroy( )* and *pthread_cond_init( )* functions are marked as part of the Threads option.

IEEE PASC Interpretation 1003.1c #34 is applied, updating the DESCRIPTION.

The **restrict** keyword is added to the *pthread_cond_init( )* prototype for alignment with the ISO/IEC 9899: 1999 standard.

NAME

pthread_cond_signal — signal a condition

SYNOPSIS

THR   `#include <pthread.h>`

`int pthread_cond_signal(pthread_cond_t *cond);`

DESCRIPTION

Refer to *pthread_cond_broadcast*( ).

NAME

pthread_cond_timedwait, pthread_cond_wait — wait on a condition

SYNOPSIS

THR   `#include <pthread.h>`

```
int pthread_cond_timedwait(pthread_cond_t *restrict cond,
    pthread_mutex_t *restrict mutex,
    const struct timespec *restrict abstime);
int pthread_cond_wait(pthread_cond_t *restrict cond,
    pthread_mutex_t *restrict mutex);
```

DESCRIPTION

The *pthread_cond_timedwait( )* and *pthread_cond_wait( )* functions shall block on a condition variable. They shall be called with *mutex* locked by the calling thread or undefined behavior results.

These functions atomically release *mutex* and cause the calling thread to block on the condition variable *cond*; atomically here means "atomically with respect to access by another thread to the mutex and then the condition variable". That is, if another thread is able to acquire the mutex after the about-to-block thread has released it, then a subsequent call to *pthread_cond_broadcast( )* or *pthread_cond_signal( )* in that thread shall behave as if it were issued after the about-to-block thread has blocked.

Upon successful return, the mutex shall have been locked and shall be owned by the calling thread.

When using condition variables there is always a Boolean predicate involving shared variables associated with each condition wait that is true if the thread should proceed. Spurious wakeups from the *pthread_cond_timedwait( )* or *pthread_cond_wait( )* functions may occur. Since the return from *pthread_cond_timedwait( )* or *pthread_cond_wait( )* does not imply anything about the value of this predicate, the predicate should be re-evaluated upon such return.

The effect of using more than one mutex for concurrent *pthread_cond_timedwait( )* or *pthread_cond_wait( )* operations on the same condition variable is undefined; that is, a condition variable becomes bound to a unique mutex when a thread waits on the condition variable, and this (dynamic) binding shall end when the wait returns.

A condition wait (whether timed or not) is a cancelation point. When the cancelability enable state of a thread is set to PTHREAD_CANCEL_DEFERRED, a side effect of acting upon a cancelation request while in a condition wait is that the mutex is (in effect) re-acquired before calling the first cancelation cleanup handler. The effect is as if the thread were unblocked, allowed to execute up to the point of returning from the call to *pthread_cond_timedwait( )* or *pthread_cond_wait( )*, but at that point notices the cancelation request and instead of returning to the caller of *pthread_cond_timedwait( )* or *pthread_cond_wait( )*, starts the thread cancelation activities, which includes calling cancelation cleanup handlers.

A thread that has been unblocked because it has been canceled while blocked in a call to *pthread_cond_timedwait( )* or *pthread_cond_wait( )* shall not consume any condition signal that may be directed concurrently at the condition variable if there are other threads blocked on the condition variable.

The *pthread_cond_timedwait( )* function shall be equivalent to *pthread_cond_wait( )*, except that an error is returned if the absolute time specified by *abstime* passes (that is, system time equals or exceeds *abstime*) before the condition *cond* is signaled or broadcasted, or if the absolute time specified by *abstime* has already been passed at the time of the call.

CS If the Clock Selection option is supported, the condition variable shall have a clock attribute which specifies the clock that shall be used to measure the time specified by the *abstime* argument. When such timeouts occur, *pthread_cond_timedwait*( ) shall nonetheless release and re-acquire the mutex referenced by *mutex*. The *pthread_cond_timedwait*( ) function is also a cancelation point.

If a signal is delivered to a thread waiting for a condition variable, upon return from the signal handler the thread resumes waiting for the condition variable as if it was not interrupted, or it shall return zero due to spurious wakeup.

RETURN VALUE

Except in the case of [ETIMEDOUT], all these error checks shall act as if they were performed immediately at the beginning of processing for the function and shall cause an error return, in effect, prior to modifying the state of the mutex specified by *mutex* or the condition variable specified by *cond*.

Upon successful completion, a value of zero shall be returned; otherwise, an error number shall be returned to indicate the error.

ERRORS

The *pthread_cond_timedwait*( ) function shall fail if:

[ETIMEDOUT]   The time specified by *abstime* to *pthread_cond_timedwait*( ) has passed.

The *pthread_cond_timedwait*( ) and *pthread_cond_wait*( ) functions may fail if:

[EINVAL]   The value specified by *cond*, *mutex*, or *abstime* is invalid.

[EINVAL]   Different mutexes were supplied for concurrent *pthread_cond_timedwait*( ) or *pthread_cond_wait*( ) operations on the same condition variable.

[EPERM]   The mutex was not owned by the current thread at the time of the call.

These functions shall not return an error code of [EINTR].

EXAMPLES

None.

APPLICATION USAGE

None.

RATIONALE

Condition Wait Semantics

It is important to note that when *pthread_cond_wait*( ) and *pthread_cond_timedwait*( ) return without error, the associated predicate may still be false. Similarly, when *pthread_cond_timedwait*( ) returns with the timeout error, the associated predicate may be true due to an unavoidable race between the expiration of the timeout and the predicate state change.

Some implementations, particularly on a multi-processor, may sometimes cause multiple threads to wake up when the condition variable is signaled simultaneously on different processors.

In general, whenever a condition wait returns, the thread has to re-evaluate the predicate associated with the condition wait to determine whether it can safely proceed, should wait again, or should declare a timeout. A return from the wait does not imply that the associated predicate is either true or false.

It is thus recommended that a condition wait be enclosed in the equivalent of a "while loop" that checks the predicate.

Timed Wait Semantics

An absolute time measure was chosen for specifying the timeout parameter for two reasons. First, a relative time measure can be easily implemented on top of a function that specifies absolute time, but there is a race condition associated with specifying an absolute timeout on top of a function that specifies relative timeouts. For example, assume that *clock_gettime*( ) returns the current time and *cond_relative_timed_wait*( ) uses relative timeouts:

```
clock_gettime(CLOCK_REALTIME, &now)
reltime = sleep_til_this_absolute_time -now;
cond_relative_timed_wait(c, m, &reltime);
```

If the thread is preempted between the first statement and the last statement, the thread blocks for too long. Blocking, however, is irrelevant if an absolute timeout is used. An absolute timeout also need not be recomputed if it is used multiple times in a loop, such as that enclosing a condition wait.

For cases when the system clock is advanced discontinuously by an operator, it is expected that implementations process any timed wait expiring at an intervening time as if that time had actually occurred.

Cancelation and Condition Wait

A condition wait, whether timed or not, is a cancelation point. That is, the functions *pthread_cond_wait*( ) or *pthread_cond_timedwait*( ) are points where a pending (or concurrent) cancelation request is noticed. The reason for this is that an indefinite wait is possible at these points—whatever event is being waited for, even if the program is totally correct, might never occur; for example, some input data being awaited might never be sent. By making condition wait a cancelation point, the thread can be canceled and perform its cancelation cleanup handler even though it may be stuck in some indefinite wait.

A side effect of acting on a cancelation request while a thread is blocked on a condition variable is to re-acquire the mutex before calling any of the cancelation cleanup handlers. This is done in order to ensure that the cancelation cleanup handler is executed in the same state as the critical code that lies both before and after the call to the condition wait function. This rule is also required when interfacing to POSIX threads from languages, such as Ada or C++, which may choose to map cancelation onto a language exception; this rule ensures that each exception handler guarding a critical section can always safely depend upon the fact that the associated mutex has already been locked regardless of exactly where within the critical section the exception was raised. Without this rule, there would not be a uniform rule that exception handlers could follow regarding the lock, and so coding would become very cumbersome.

Therefore, since *some* statement has to be made regarding the state of the lock when a cancelation is delivered during a wait, a definition has been chosen that makes application coding most convenient and error free.

When acting on a cancelation request while a thread is blocked on a condition variable, the implementation is required to ensure that the thread does not consume any condition signals directed at that condition variable if there are any other threads waiting on that condition variable. This rule is specified in order to avoid deadlock conditions that could occur if these two independent requests (one acting on a thread and the other acting on the condition variable) were not processed independently.

Performance of Mutexes and Condition Variables

Mutexes are expected to be locked only for a few instructions. This practice is almost automatically enforced by the desire of programmers to avoid long serial regions of execution (which would reduce total effective parallelism).

When using mutexes and condition variables, one tries to ensure that the usual case is to lock the mutex, access shared data, and unlock the mutex. Waiting on a condition variable should be a relatively rare situation. For example, when implementing a read-write lock, code that acquires a read-lock typically needs only to increment the count of readers (under mutual-exclusion) and return. The calling thread would actually wait on the condition variable only when there is already an active writer. So the efficiency of a synchronization operation is bounded by the cost of mutex lock/unlock and not by condition wait. Note that in the usual case there is no context switch.

This is not to say that the efficiency of condition waiting is unimportant. Since there needs to be at least one context switch per Ada rendezvous, the efficiency of waiting on a condition variable is important. The cost of waiting on a condition variable should be little more than the minimal cost for a context switch plus the time to unlock and lock the mutex.

Features of Mutexes and Condition Variables

It had been suggested that the mutex acquisition and release be decoupled from condition wait. This was rejected because it is the combined nature of the operation that, in fact, facilitates realtime implementations. Those implementations can atomically move a high-priority thread between the condition variable and the mutex in a manner that is transparent to the caller. This can prevent extra context switches and provide more deterministic acquisition of a mutex when the waiting thread is signaled. Thus, fairness and priority issues can be dealt with directly by the scheduling discipline. Furthermore, the current condition wait operation matches existing practice.

Scheduling Behavior of Mutexes and Condition Variables

Synchronization primitives that attempt to interfere with scheduling policy by specifying an ordering rule are considered undesirable. Threads waiting on mutexes and condition variables are selected to proceed in an order dependent upon the scheduling policy rather than in some fixed order (for example, FIFO or priority). Thus, the scheduling policy determines which thread(s) are awakened and allowed to proceed.

Timed Condition Wait

The *pthread_cond_timedwait*( ) function allows an application to give up waiting for a particular condition after a given amount of time. An example of its use follows:

```
(void) pthread_mutex_lock(&t.mn);
        t.waiters++;
    clock_gettime(CLOCK_REALTIME, &ts);
    ts.tv_sec += 5;
    rc = 0;
    while (! mypredicate(&t) && rc == 0)
        rc = pthread_cond_timedwait(&t.cond, &t.mn, &ts);
    t.waiters--;
    if (rc == 0) setmystate(&t);
(void) pthread_mutex_unlock(&t.mn);
```

By making the timeout parameter absolute, it does not need to be recomputed each time the program checks its blocking predicate. If the timeout was relative, it would have to be recomputed before each call. This would be especially difficult since such code would need to take into account the possibility of extra wakeups that result from extra broadcasts or signals on the condition variable that occur before either the predicate is true or the timeout is due.

FUTURE DIRECTIONS

None.

SEE ALSO

pthread_cond_signal( ), *pthread_cond_broadcast*( ), the Base Definitions volume of IEEE Std 1003.1-2001, **<pthread.h>**

CHANGE HISTORY

First released in Issue 5. Included for alignment with the POSIX Threads Extension.

Issue 6

The *pthread_cond_timedwait*( ) and *pthread_cond_wait*( ) functions are marked as part of the Threads option.

The Open Group Corrigendum U021/9 is applied, correcting the prototype for the *pthread_cond_wait*( ) function.

The DESCRIPTION is updated for alignment with IEEE Std 1003.1j-2000 by adding semantics for the Clock Selection option.

The ERRORS section has an additional case for [EPERM] in response to IEEE PASC Interpretation 1003.1c #28.

The **restrict** keyword is added to the *pthread_cond_timedwait*( ) and *pthread_cond_wait*( ) prototypes for alignment with the ISO/IEC 9899: 1999 standard.

NAME

pthread_condattr_destroy, pthread_condattr_init — destroy and initialize the condition variable attributes object

SYNOPSIS

THR   `#include <pthread.h>`

```
int pthread_condattr_destroy(pthread_condattr_t *attr);
int pthread_condattr_init(pthread_condattr_t *attr);
```

DESCRIPTION

The *pthread_condattr_destroy*( ) function shall destroy a condition variable attributes object; the object becomes, in effect, uninitialized. An implementation may cause *pthread_condattr_destroy*( ) to set the object referenced by *attr* to an invalid value. A destroyed *attr* attributes object can be reinitialized using *pthread_condattr_init*( ); the results of otherwise referencing the object after it has been destroyed are undefined.

The *pthread_condattr_init*( ) function shall initialize a condition variable attributes object *attr* with the default value for all of the attributes defined by the implementation.

Results are undefined if *pthread_condattr_init*( ) is called specifying an already initialized *attr* attributes object.

After a condition variable attributes object has been used to initialize one or more condition variables, any function affecting the attributes object (including destruction) shall not affect any previously initialized condition variables.

This volume of IEEE Std 1003.1-2001 requires two attributes, the *clock* attribute and the *process-shared* attribute.

Additional attributes, their default values, and the names of the associated functions to get and set those attribute values are implementation-defined.

RETURN VALUE

If successful, the *pthread_condattr_destroy*( ) and *pthread_condattr_init*( ) functions shall return zero; otherwise, an error number shall be returned to indicate the error.

ERRORS

The *pthread_condattr_destroy*( ) function may fail if:

[EINVAL]   The value specified by *attr* is invalid.

The *pthread_condattr_init*( ) function shall fail if:

[ENOMEM]   Insufficient memory exists to initialize the condition variable attributes object.

These functions shall not return an error code of [EINTR].

EXAMPLES

None.

APPLICATION USAGE

None.

RATIONALE

See *pthread_attr_init*( ) and *pthread_mutex_init*( ).

A *process-shared* attribute has been defined for condition variables for the same reason it has been defined for mutexes.

FUTURE DIRECTIONS
    None.

SEE ALSO
    pthread_attr_destroy( ), *pthread_cond_destroy*( ), *pthread_condattr_getpshared*( ), *pthread_create*( ), *pthread_mutex_destroy*( ), the Base Definitions volume of IEEE Std 1003.1-2001, **<pthread.h>**

CHANGE HISTORY
    First released in Issue 5. Included for alignment with the POSIX Threads Extension.

Issue 6
    The *pthread_condattr_destroy*( ) and *pthread_condattr_init*( ) functions are marked as part of the Threads option.

NAME

pthread_condattr_getclock, pthread_condattr_setclock — get and set the clock selection condition variable attribute (**ADVANCED REALTIME**)

SYNOPSIS

THR CS `#include <pthread.h>`

```
int pthread_condattr_getclock(const pthread_condattr_t *restrict attr,
    clockid_t *restrict clock_id);
int pthread_condattr_setclock(pthread_condattr_t *attr,
    clockid_t clock_id);
```

DESCRIPTION

The *pthread_condattr_getclock*( ) function shall obtain the value of the *clock* attribute from the attributes object referenced by *attr*. The *pthread_condattr_setclock*( ) function shall set the *clock* attribute in an initialized attributes object referenced by *attr*. If *pthread_condattr_setclock*( ) is called with a *clock_id* argument that refers to a CPU-time clock, the call shall fail.

The *clock* attribute is the clock ID of the clock that shall be used to measure the timeout service of *pthread_cond_timedwait*( ). The default value of the *clock* attribute shall refer to the system clock.

RETURN VALUE

If successful, the *pthread_condattr_getclock*( ) function shall return zero and store the value of the clock attribute of *attr* into the object referenced by the *clock_id* argument. Otherwise, an error number shall be returned to indicate the error.

If successful, the *pthread_condattr_setclock*( ) function shall return zero; otherwise, an error number shall be returned to indicate the error.

ERRORS

These functions may fail if:

[EINVAL]   The value specified by *attr* is invalid.

The *pthread_condattr_setclock*( ) function may fail if:

[EINVAL]   The value specified by *clock_id* does not refer to a known clock, or is a CPU-time clock.

These functions shall not return an error code of [EINTR].

EXAMPLES

None.

APPLICATION USAGE

None.

RATIONALE

None.

FUTURE DIRECTIONS

None.

SEE ALSO

pthread_cond_destroy( ), *pthread_cond_timedwait*( ), *pthread_condattr_destroy*( ), *pthread_condattr_getpshared*( ) (on page 1041),1 *pthread_condattr_init*( ), *pthread_condattr_setpshared*( ) (on page 1045),1 *pthread_create*( ), *pthread_mutex_init*( ), the Base Definitions volume of IEEE Std 1003.1-2001, **<pthread.h>**

CHANGE HISTORY

First released in Issue 6. Derived from IEEE Std 1003.1j-2000.

NAME

pthread_condattr_getpshared, pthread_condattr_setpshared — get and set the process-shared condition variable attributes

SYNOPSIS

THR TSH `#include <pthread.h>`

```
int pthread_condattr_getpshared(const pthread_condattr_t *restrict attr,
    int *restrict pshared);
int pthread_condattr_setpshared(pthread_condattr_t *attr,
    int pshared);
```

DESCRIPTION

The *pthread_condattr_getpshared*( ) function shall obtain the value of the *process-shared* attribute from the attributes object referenced by *attr*. The *pthread_condattr_setpshared*( ) function shall set the *process-shared* attribute in an initialized attributes object referenced by *attr*.

The *process-shared* attribute is set to PTHREAD_PROCESS_SHARED to permit a condition variable to be operated upon by any thread that has access to the memory where the condition variable is allocated, even if the condition variable is allocated in memory that is shared by multiple processes. If the *process-shared* attribute is PTHREAD_PROCESS_PRIVATE, the condition variable shall only be operated upon by threads created within the same process as the thread that initialized the condition variable; if threads of differing processes attempt to operate on such a condition variable, the behavior is undefined. The default value of the attribute is PTHREAD_PROCESS_PRIVATE.

RETURN VALUE

If successful, the *pthread_condattr_setpshared*( ) function shall return zero; otherwise, an error number shall be returned to indicate the error.

If successful, the *pthread_condattr_getpshared*( ) function shall return zero and store the value of the *process-shared* attribute of *attr* into the object referenced by the *pshared* parameter. Otherwise, an error number shall be returned to indicate the error.

ERRORS

The *pthread_condattr_getpshared*( ) and *pthread_condattr_setpshared*( ) functions may fail if:

[EINVAL]   The value specified by *attr* is invalid.

The *pthread_condattr_setpshared*( ) function may fail if:

[EINVAL]   The new value specified for the attribute is outside the range of legal values for that attribute.

These functions shall not return an error code of [EINTR].

EXAMPLES

None.

APPLICATION USAGE

None.

RATIONALE

None.

FUTURE DIRECTIONS

None.

SEE ALSO

pthread_create( ), *pthread_cond_destroy*( ), *pthread_condattr_destroy*( ), *pthread_mutex_destroy*( ), the Base Definitions volume of IEEE Std 1003.1-2001, **<pthread.h>**

CHANGE HISTORY

First released in Issue 5. Included for alignment with the POSIX Threads Extension.

Issue 6

The *pthread_condattr_getpshared*( ) and *pthread_condattr_setpshared*( ) functions are marked as part of the Threads and Thread Process-Shared Synchronization options.

The **restrict** keyword is added to the *pthread_condattr_getpshared*( ) prototype for alignment with the ISO/IEC 9899: 1999 standard.

NAME

pthread_condattr_init — initialize the condition variable attributes object

SYNOPSIS

THR   `#include <pthread.h>`

`int pthread_condattr_init(pthread_condattr_t *attr);`

DESCRIPTION

Refer to *pthread_condattr_destroy*( ).

NAME

pthread_condattr_setclock — set the clock selection condition variable attribute

SYNOPSIS

`#include <pthread.h>`

```
int pthread_condattr_setclock(pthread_condattr_t *attr,
    clockid_t clock_id);
```

DESCRIPTION

Refer to *pthread_condattr_getclock( )*.

NAME

pthread_condattr_setpshared — set the process-shared condition variable attribute

SYNOPSIS

THR TSH `#include <pthread.h>`

```
int pthread_condattr_setpshared(pthread_condattr_t *attr,
    int pshared);
```

DESCRIPTION

Refer to *pthread_condattr_getpshared*( ).

NAME

pthread_create — thread creation

SYNOPSIS

THR   `#include <pthread.h>`

```
int pthread_create(pthread_t *restrict thread,
    const pthread_attr_t *restrict attr,
    void *(*start_routine)(void*), void *restrict arg);
```

DESCRIPTION

The *pthread_create*( ) function shall create a new thread, with attributes specified by *attr*, within a process. If *attr* is NULL, the default attributes shall be used. If the attributes specified by *attr* are modified later, the thread's attributes shall not be affected. Upon successful completion, *pthread_create*( ) shall store the ID of the created thread in the location referenced by *thread*.

The thread is created executing *start_routine* with *arg* as its sole argument. If the *start_routine* returns, the effect shall be as if there was an implicit call to *pthread_exit*( ) using the return value of *start_routine* as the exit status. Note that the thread in which *main*( ) was originally invoked differs from this. When it returns from *main*( ), the effect shall be as if there was an implicit call to *exit*( ) using the return value of *main*( ) as the exit status.

The signal state of the new thread shall be initialized as follows:

- The signal mask shall be inherited from the creating thread.
- The set of signals pending for the new thread shall be empty.

The floating-point environment shall be inherited from the creating thread.

If *pthread_create*( ) fails, no new thread is created and the contents of the location referenced by *thread* are undefined.

TCT   If _POSIX_THREAD_CPUTIME is defined, the new thread shall have a CPU-time clock accessible, and the initial value of this clock shall be set to zero.

RETURN VALUE

If successful, the *pthread_create*( ) function shall return zero; otherwise, an error number shall be returned to indicate the error.

ERRORS

The *pthread_create*( ) function shall fail if:

[EAGAIN]   The system lacked the necessary resources to create another thread, or the system-imposed limit on the total number of threads in a process {PTHREAD_THREADS_MAX} would be exceeded.

[EINVAL]   The value specified by *attr* is invalid.

[EPERM]   The caller does not have appropriate permission to set the required scheduling parameters or scheduling policy.

The *pthread_create*( ) function shall not return an error code of [EINTR].

EXAMPLES
   None.

APPLICATION USAGE
   None.

RATIONALE

A suggested alternative to *pthread_create*( ) would be to define two separate operations: create and start. Some applications would find such behavior more natural. Ada, in particular, separates the "creation" of a task from its "activation".

Splitting the operation was rejected by the standard developers for many reasons:

- The number of calls required to start a thread would increase from one to two and thus place an additional burden on applications that do not require the additional synchronization. The second call, however, could be avoided by the additional complication of a start-up state attribute.

- An extra state would be introduced: "created but not started". This would require the standard to specify the behavior of the thread operations when the target has not yet started executing.

- For those applications that require such behavior, it is possible to simulate the two separate steps with the facilities that are currently provided. The *start_routine*( ) can synchronize by waiting on a condition variable that is signaled by the start operation.

An Ada implementor can choose to create the thread at either of two points in the Ada program: when the task object is created, or when the task is activated (generally at a "begin"). If the first approach is adopted, the *start_routine*( ) needs to wait on a condition variable to receive the order to begin "activation". The second approach requires no such condition variable or extra synchronization. In either approach, a separate Ada task control block would need to be created when the task object is created to hold rendezvous queues, and so on.

An extension of the preceding model would be to allow the state of the thread to be modified between the create and start. This would allow the thread attributes object to be eliminated. This has been rejected because:

- All state in the thread attributes object has to be able to be set for the thread. This would require the definition of functions to modify thread attributes. There would be no reduction in the number of function calls required to set up the thread. In fact, for an application that creates all threads using identical attributes, the number of function calls required to set up the threads would be dramatically increased. Use of a thread attributes object permits the application to make one set of attribute setting function calls. Otherwise, the set of attribute setting function calls needs to be made for each thread creation.

- Depending on the implementation architecture, functions to set thread state would require kernel calls, or for other implementation reasons would not be able to be implemented as macros, thereby increasing the cost of thread creation.

- The ability for applications to segregate threads by class would be lost.

Another suggested alternative uses a model similar to that for process creation, such as "thread fork". The fork semantics would provide more flexibility and the "create" function can be implemented simply by doing a thread fork followed immediately by a call to the desired "start routine" for the thread. This alternative has these problems:

- For many implementations, the entire stack of the calling thread would need to be duplicated, since in many architectures there is no way to determine the size of the calling frame.

- Efficiency is reduced since at least some part of the stack has to be copied, even though in most cases the thread never needs the copied context, since it merely calls the desired start routine.

FUTURE DIRECTIONS

None.

SEE ALSO

fork( ), *pthread_exit*( ), *pthread_join*( ), the Base Definitions volume of IEEE Std 1003.1-2001, **<pthread.h>**

CHANGE HISTORY

First released in Issue 5. Included for alignment with the POSIX Threads Extension.

Issue 6

The *pthread_create*( ) function is marked as part of the Threads option.

The following new requirements on POSIX implementations derive from alignment with the Single UNIX Specification:

- The [EPERM] mandatory error condition is added.

The thread CPU-time clock semantics are added for alignment with IEEE Std 1003.1d-1999.

The **restrict** keyword is added to the *pthread_create*( ) prototype for alignment with the ISO/IEC 9899: 1999 standard.

The DESCRIPTION is updated to make it explicit that the floating-point environment is inherited from the creating thread.

NAME

pthread_detach — detach a thread

SYNOPSIS

THR `#include <pthread.h>`

`int pthread_detach(pthread_t` *thread*`);`

DESCRIPTION

The *pthread_detach*( ) function shall indicate to the implementation that storage for the thread *thread* can be reclaimed when that thread terminates. If *thread* has not terminated, *pthread_detach*( ) shall not cause it to terminate. The effect of multiple *pthread_detach*( ) calls on the same target thread is unspecified.

RETURN VALUE

If the call succeeds, *pthread_detach*( ) shall return 0; otherwise, an error number shall be returned to indicate the error.

ERRORS

The *pthread_detach*( ) function shall fail if:

[EINVAL]   The implementation has detected that the value specified by *thread* does not refer to a joinable thread.

[ESRCH]   No thread could be found corresponding to that specified by the given thread ID.

The *pthread_detach*( ) function shall not return an error code of [EINTR].

EXAMPLES

None.

APPLICATION USAGE

None.

RATIONALE

The *pthread_join*( ) or *pthread_detach*( ) functions should eventually be called for every thread that is created so that storage associated with the thread may be reclaimed.

It has been suggested that a "detach" function is not necessary; the *detachstate* thread creation attribute is sufficient, since a thread need never be dynamically detached. However, need arises in at least two cases:

1. In a cancelation handler for a *pthread_join*( ) it is nearly essential to have a *pthread_detach*( ) function in order to detach the thread on which *pthread_join*( ) was waiting. Without it, it would be necessary to have the handler do another *pthread_join*( ) to attempt to detach the thread, which would both delay the cancelation processing for an unbounded period and introduce a new call to *pthread_join*( ), which might itself need a cancelation handler. A dynamic detach is nearly essential in this case.

2. In order to detach the "initial thread" (as may be desirable in processes that set up server threads).

FUTURE DIRECTIONS

None.

SEE ALSO

pthread_join ( ), the Base Definitions volume of IEEE Std 1003.1-2001, **<pthread.h>**

CHANGE HISTORY

First released in Issue 5. Included for alignment with the POSIX Threads Extension.

Issue 6

The *pthread_detach* ( ) function is marked as part of the Threads option.

NAME

pthread_equal — compare thread IDs

SYNOPSIS

THR
```
#include <pthread.h>

int pthread_equal(pthread_t t1, pthread_t t2);
```

DESCRIPTION

This function shall compare the thread IDs *t1* and *t2*.

RETURN VALUE

The *pthread_equal*( ) function shall return a non-zero value if *t1* and *t2* are equal; otherwise, zero shall be returned.

If either *t1* or *t2* are not valid thread IDs, the behavior is undefined.

ERRORS

No errors are defined.

The *pthread_equal*( ) function shall not return an error code of [EINTR].

EXAMPLES

None.

APPLICATION USAGE

None.

RATIONALE

Implementations may choose to define a thread ID as a structure. This allows additional flexibility and robustness over using an **int**. For example, a thread ID could include a sequence number that allows detection of "dangling IDs" (copies of a thread ID that has been detached). Since the C language does not support comparison on structure types, the *pthread_equal*( ) function is provided to compare thread IDs.

FUTURE DIRECTIONS

None.

SEE ALSO

pthread_create( ), *pthread_self*( ), the Base Definitions volume of IEEE Std 1003.1-2001, **<pthread.h>**

CHANGE HISTORY

First released in Issue 5. Included for alignment with the POSIX Threads Extension.

Issue 6

The *pthread_equal*( ) function is marked as part of the Threads option.

NAME

pthread_exit — thread termination

SYNOPSIS

THR
```
#include <pthread.h>

void pthread_exit(void *value_ptr);
```

DESCRIPTION

The *pthread_exit*( ) function shall terminate the calling thread and make the value *value_ptr* available to any successful join with the terminating thread. Any cancelation cleanup handlers that have been pushed and not yet popped shall be popped in the reverse order that they were pushed and then executed. After all cancelation cleanup handlers have been executed, if the thread has any thread-specific data, appropriate destructor functions shall be called in an unspecified order. Thread termination does not release any application visible process resources, including, but not limited to, mutexes and file descriptors, nor does it perform any process-level cleanup actions, including, but not limited to, calling any *atexit*( ) routines that may exist.

An implicit call to *pthread_exit*( ) is made when a thread other than the thread in which *main*( ) was first invoked returns from the start routine that was used to create it. The function's return value shall serve as the thread's exit status.

The behavior of *pthread_exit*( ) is undefined if called from a cancelation cleanup handler or destructor function that was invoked as a result of either an implicit or explicit call to *pthread_exit*( ).

After a thread has terminated, the result of access to local (auto) variables of the thread is undefined. Thus, references to local variables of the exiting thread should not be used for the *pthread_exit*( ) *value_ptr* parameter value.

The process shall exit with an exit status of 0 after the last thread has been terminated. The behavior shall be as if the implementation called *exit*( ) with a zero argument at thread termination time.

RETURN VALUE

The *pthread_exit*( ) function cannot return to its caller.

ERRORS

No errors are defined.

EXAMPLES

None.

APPLICATION USAGE

None.

RATIONALE

The normal mechanism by which a thread terminates is to return from the routine that was specified in the *pthread_create*( ) call that started it. The *pthread_exit*( ) function provides the capability for a thread to terminate without requiring a return from the start routine of that thread, thereby providing a function analogous to *exit*( ).

Regardless of the method of thread termination, any cancelation cleanup handlers that have been pushed and not yet popped are executed, and the destructors for any existing thread-specific data are executed. This volume of IEEE Std 1003.1-2001 requires that cancelation cleanup handlers be popped and called in order. After all cancelation cleanup handlers have been executed, thread-specific data destructors are called, in an unspecified order, for each item of thread-specific data that exists in the thread. This ordering is necessary because cancelation cleanup handlers may rely on thread-specific data.

As the meaning of the status is determined by the application (except when the thread has been canceled, in which case it is PTHREAD_CANCELED), the implementation has no idea what an illegal status value is, which is why no address error checking is done.

FUTURE DIRECTIONS

None.

SEE ALSO

exit( ), *pthread_create*( ), *pthread_join*( ), the Base Definitions volume of IEEE Std 1003.1-2001, **<pthread.h>**

CHANGE HISTORY

First released in Issue 5. Included for alignment with the POSIX Threads Extension.

Issue 6

The *pthread_exit*( ) function is marked as part of the Threads option.

pthread_getconcurrency( )

System Interfaces

NAME

pthread_getconcurrency, pthread_setconcurrency — get and set the level of concurrency

SYNOPSIS

XSI
```
#include <pthread.h>

int pthread_getconcurrency(void);
int pthread_setconcurrency(int new_level);
```

DESCRIPTION

Unbound threads in a process may or may not be required to be simultaneously active. By default, the threads implementation ensures that a sufficient number of threads are active so that the process can continue to make progress. While this conserves system resources, it may not produce the most effective level of concurrency.

The *pthread_setconcurrency*( ) function allows an application to inform the threads implementation of its desired concurrency level, *new_level*. The actual level of concurrency provided by the implementation as a result of this function call is unspecified.

If *new_level* is zero, it causes the implementation to maintain the concurrency level at its discretion as if *pthread_setconcurrency*( ) had never been called.

The *pthread_getconcurrency*( ) function shall return the value set by a previous call to the *pthread_setconcurrency*( ) function. If the *pthread_setconcurrency*( ) function was not previously called, this function shall return zero to indicate that the implementation is maintaining the concurrency level.

A call to *pthread_setconcurrency*( ) shall inform the implementation of its desired concurrency level. The implementation shall use this as a hint, not a requirement.

If an implementation does not support multiplexing of user threads on top of several kernel-scheduled entities, the *pthread_setconcurrency*( ) and *pthread_getconcurrency*( ) functions are provided for source code compatibility but they shall have no effect when called. To maintain the function semantics, the *new_level* parameter is saved when *pthread_setconcurrency*( ) is called so that a subsequent call to *pthread_getconcurrency*( ) shall return the same value.

RETURN VALUE

If successful, the *pthread_setconcurrency*( ) function shall return zero; otherwise, an error number shall be returned to indicate the error.

The *pthread_getconcurrency*( ) function shall always return the concurrency level set by a previous call to *pthread_setconcurrency*( ). If the *pthread_setconcurrency*( ) function has never been called, *pthread_getconcurrency*( ) shall return zero.

ERRORS

The *pthread_setconcurrency*( ) function shall fail if:

[EINVAL]   The value specified by *new_level* is negative.

[EAGAIN]   The value specific by *new_level* would cause a system resource to be exceeded.

These functions shall not return an error code of [EINTR].

EXAMPLES

None.

APPLICATION USAGE

Use of these functions changes the state of the underlying concurrency upon which the application depends. Library developers are advised to not use the *pthread_getconcurrency*( ) and *pthread_setconcurrency*( ) functions since their use may conflict with an applications use of these functions.

RATIONALE

None.

FUTURE DIRECTIONS

None.

SEE ALSO

The Base Definitions volume of IEEE Std 1003.1-2001, **<pthread.h>**

CHANGE HISTORY

First released in Issue 5.

NAME

pthread_getcpuclockid — access a thread CPU-time clock (**ADVANCED REALTIME THREADS**)

SYNOPSIS

THR TCT `#include <pthread.h>`
`#include <time.h>`

`int pthread_getcpuclockid(pthread_t `*`thread_id`*`, clockid_t *`*`clock_id`*`);`

DESCRIPTION

The *pthread_getcpuclockid*( ) function shall return in *clock_id* the clock ID of the CPU-time clock of the thread specified by *thread_id*, if the thread specified by *thread_id* exists.

RETURN VALUE

Upon successful completion, *pthread_getcpuclockid*( ) shall return zero; otherwise, an error number shall be returned to indicate the error.

ERRORS

The *pthread_getcpuclockid*( ) function may fail if:

[ESRCH]   The value specified by *thread_id* does not refer to an existing thread.

EXAMPLES

None.

APPLICATION USAGE

The *pthread_getcpuclockid*( ) function is part of the Thread CPU-Time Clocks option and need not be provided on all implementations.

RATIONALE

None.

FUTURE DIRECTIONS

None.

SEE ALSO

clock_getcpuclockid( ), *clock_getres*( ), *timer_create*( ), the Base Definitions volume of IEEE Std 1003.1-2001, **<pthread.h>**, **<time.h>**

CHANGE HISTORY

First released in Issue 6. Derived from IEEE Std 1003.1d-1999.

In the SYNOPSIS, the inclusion of **<sys/types.h>** is no longer required.

NAME

pthread_getschedparam, pthread_setschedparam — dynamic thread scheduling parameters access (**REALTIME THREADS**)

SYNOPSIS

THR TPS `#include <pthread.h>`

```
int pthread_getschedparam(pthread_t thread, int *restrict policy,
    struct sched_param *restrict param);
int pthread_setschedparam(pthread_t thread, int policy,
    const struct sched_param *param);
```

DESCRIPTION

The *pthread_getschedparam*( ) and *pthread_setschedparam*( ) functions shall, respectively, get and set the scheduling policy and parameters of individual threads within a multi-threaded process to be retrieved and set. For SCHED_FIFO and SCHED_RR, the only required member of the **sched_param** structure is the priority *sched_priority*. For SCHED_OTHER, the affected scheduling parameters are implementation-defined.

The *pthread_getschedparam*( ) function shall retrieve the scheduling policy and scheduling parameters for the thread whose thread ID is given by *thread* and shall store those values in *policy* and *param*, respectively. The priority value returned from *pthread_getschedparam*( ) shall be the value specified by the most recent *pthread_setschedparam*( ), *pthread_setschedprio*( ), or *pthread_create*( ) call affecting the target thread. It shall not reflect any temporary adjustments to its priority as a result of any priority inheritance or ceiling functions. The *pthread_setschedparam*( ) function shall set the scheduling policy and associated scheduling parameters for the thread whose thread ID is given by *thread* to the policy and associated parameters provided in *policy* and *param*, respectively.

The *policy* parameter may have the value SCHED_OTHER, SCHED_FIFO, or SCHED_RR. The scheduling parameters for the SCHED_OTHER policy are implementation-defined. The SCHED_FIFO and SCHED_RR policies shall have a single scheduling parameter, *priority*.

TSP If _POSIX_THREAD_SPORADIC_SERVER is defined, then the *policy* argument may have the value SCHED_SPORADIC, with the exception for the *pthread_setschedparam*( ) function that if the scheduling policy was not SCHED_SPORADIC at the time of the call, it is implementation-defined whether the function is supported; in other words, the implementation need not allow the application to dynamically change the scheduling policy to SCHED_SPORADIC. The sporadic server scheduling policy has the associated parameters *sched_ss_low_priority*, *sched_ss_repl_period*, *sched_ss_init_budget*, *sched_priority*, and *sched_ss_max_repl*. The specified *sched_ss_repl_period* shall be greater than or equal to the specified *sched_ss_init_budget* for the function to succeed; if it is not, then the function shall fail. The value of *sched_ss_max_repl* shall be within the inclusive range [1,{SS_REPL_MAX}] for the function to succeed; if not, the function shall fail.

If the *pthread_setschedparam*( ) function fails, the scheduling parameters shall not be changed for the target thread.

RETURN VALUE

If successful, the *pthread_getschedparam*( ) and *pthread_setschedparam*( ) functions shall return zero; otherwise, an error number shall be returned to indicate the error.

ERRORS

The *pthread_getschedparam*( ) function may fail if:

[ESRCH]	The value specified by *thread* does not refer to an existing thread.

The *pthread_setschedparam*( ) function may fail if:

[EINVAL]	The value specified by *policy* or one of the scheduling parameters associated with the scheduling policy *policy* is invalid.
[ENOTSUP]	An attempt was made to set the policy or scheduling parameters to an unsupported value.

TSP   [ENOTSUP]   An attempt was made to dynamically change the scheduling policy to SCHED_SPORADIC, and the implementation does not support this change.

[EPERM]	The caller does not have the appropriate permission to set either the scheduling parameters or the scheduling policy of the specified thread.
[EPERM]	The implementation does not allow the application to modify one of the parameters to the value specified.
[ESRCH]	The value specified by *thread* does not refer to a existing thread.

These functions shall not return an error code of [EINTR].

EXAMPLES
None.

APPLICATION USAGE
None.

RATIONALE
None.

FUTURE DIRECTIONS
None.

SEE ALSO
pthread_setschedprio( ), *sched_getparam*( ), *sched_getscheduler*( ), the Base Definitions volume of IEEE Std 1003.1-2001, **<pthread.h>**, **<sched.h>**

CHANGE HISTORY
First released in Issue 5. Included for alignment with the POSIX Threads Extension.

Issue 6

The *pthread_getschedparam*( ) and *pthread_setschedparam*( ) functions are marked as part of the Threads and Thread Execution Scheduling options.

The [ENOSYS] error condition has been removed as stubs need not be provided if an implementation does not support the Thread Execution Scheduling option.

The Open Group Corrigendum U026/2 is applied, correcting the prototype for the *pthread_setschedparam*( ) function so that its second argument is of type **int**.

The SCHED_SPORADIC scheduling policy is added for alignment with IEEE Std 1003.1d-1999.

The **restrict** keyword is added to the *pthread_getschedparam*( ) prototype for alignment with the ISO/IEC 9899: 1999 standard.

The Open Group Corrigendum U047/1 is applied.

IEEE PASC Interpretation 1003.1 #96 is applied, noting that priority values can also be set by a call to the *pthread_setschedprio*( ) function.

pthread_getspecific( )

NAME

pthread_getspecific, pthread_setspecific — thread-specific data management

SYNOPSIS

THR   `#include <pthread.h>`

```
void *pthread_getspecific(pthread_key_t key);
int pthread_setspecific(pthread_key_t key, const void *value);
```

DESCRIPTION

The *pthread_getspecific*( ) function shall return the value currently bound to the specified *key* on behalf of the calling thread.

The *pthread_setspecific*( ) function shall associate a thread-specific *value* with a *key* obtained via a previous call to *pthread_key_create*( ). Different threads may bind different values to the same key. These values are typically pointers to blocks of dynamically allocated memory that have been reserved for use by the calling thread.

The effect of calling *pthread_getspecific*( ) or *pthread_setspecific*( ) with a *key* value not obtained from *pthread_key_create*( ) or after *key* has been deleted with *pthread_key_delete*( ) is undefined.

Both *pthread_getspecific*( ) and *pthread_setspecific*( ) may be called from a thread-specific data destructor function. A call to *pthread_getspecific*( ) for the thread-specific data key being destroyed shall return the value NULL, unless the value is changed (after the destructor starts) by a call to *pthread_setspecific*( ). Calling *pthread_setspecific*( ) from a thread-specific data destructor routine may result either in lost storage (after at least PTHREAD_DESTRUCTOR_ITERATIONS attempts at destruction) or in an infinite loop.

Both functions may be implemented as macros.

RETURN VALUE

The *pthread_getspecific*( ) function shall return the thread-specific data value associated with the given *key*. If no thread-specific data value is associated with *key*, then the value NULL shall be returned.

If successful, the *pthread_setspecific*( ) function shall return zero; otherwise, an error number shall be returned to indicate the error.

ERRORS

No errors are returned from *pthread_getspecific*( ).

The *pthread_setspecific*( ) function shall fail if:

[ENOMEM]   Insufficient memory exists to associate the value with the key.

The *pthread_setspecific*( ) function may fail if:

[EINVAL]   The key value is invalid.

These functions shall not return an error code of [EINTR].

EXAMPLES
None.

APPLICATION USAGE
None.

RATIONALE
Performance and ease-of-use of *pthread_getspecific*( ) are critical for functions that rely on maintaining state in thread-specific data. Since no errors are required to be detected by it, and since the only error that could be detected is the use of an invalid key, the function to *pthread_getspecific*( ) has been designed to favor speed and simplicity over error reporting.

FUTURE DIRECTIONS
None.

SEE ALSO
pthread_key_create( ), the Base Definitions volume of IEEE Std 1003.1-2001, **<pthread.h>**

CHANGE HISTORY
First released in Issue 5. Included for alignment with the POSIX Threads Extension.

Issue 6
The *pthread_getspecific*( ) and *pthread_setspecific*( ) functions are marked as part of the Threads option.

IEEE PASC Interpretation 1003.1c #3 (Part 6) is applied, updating the DESCRIPTION.

pthread_join()

NAME

pthread_join — wait for thread termination

SYNOPSIS

THR
```
#include <pthread.h>

int pthread_join(pthread_t thread, void **value_ptr);
```

DESCRIPTION

The *pthread_join*( ) function shall suspend execution of the calling thread until the target *thread* terminates, unless the target *thread* has already terminated. On return from a successful *pthread_join*( ) call with a non-NULL *value_ptr* argument, the value passed to *pthread_exit*( ) by the terminating thread shall be made available in the location referenced by *value_ptr*. When a *pthread_join*( ) returns successfully, the target thread has been terminated. The results of multiple simultaneous calls to *pthread_join*( ) specifying the same target thread are undefined. If the thread calling *pthread_join*( ) is canceled, then the target thread shall not be detached.

It is unspecified whether a thread that has exited but remains unjoined counts against {PTHREAD_THREADS_MAX}.

RETURN VALUE

If successful, the *pthread_join*( ) function shall return zero; otherwise, an error number shall be returned to indicate the error.

ERRORS

The *pthread_join*( ) function shall fail if:

[EINVAL]   The implementation has detected that the value specified by *thread* does not refer to a joinable thread.

[ESRCH]   No thread could be found corresponding to that specified by the given thread ID.

The *pthread_join*( ) function may fail if:

[EDEADLK]   A deadlock was detected or the value of *thread* specifies the calling thread.

The *pthread_join*( ) function shall not return an error code of [EINTR].

EXAMPLES

An example of thread creation and deletion follows:

```
typedef struct {
    int *ar;
    long n;
} subarray;

void *
incer(void *arg)
{
    long i;

    for (i = 0; i < ((subarray *)arg)->n; i++)
        ((subarray *)arg)->ar[i]++;
}

int main(void)
{
    int         ar[1000000];
```

```
        pthread_t  th1, th2;
        subarray   sb1, sb2;

        sb1.ar = &ar[0];
        sb1.n  = 500000;
        (void) pthread_create(&th1, NULL, incer, &sb1);

        sb2.ar = &ar[500000];
        sb2.n  = 500000;
        (void) pthread_create(&th2, NULL, incer, &sb2);

        (void) pthread_join(th1, NULL);
        (void) pthread_join(th2, NULL);
        return 0;
    }
```

APPLICATION USAGE

None.

RATIONALE

The *pthread_join( )* function is a convenience that has proven useful in multi-threaded applications. It is true that a programmer could simulate this function if it were not provided by passing extra state as part of the argument to the *start_routine( )*. The terminating thread would set a flag to indicate termination and broadcast a condition that is part of that state; a joining thread would wait on that condition variable. While such a technique would allow a thread to wait on more complex conditions (for example, waiting for multiple threads to terminate), waiting on individual thread termination is considered widely useful. Also, including the *pthread_join( )* function in no way precludes a programmer from coding such complex waits. Thus, while not a primitive, including *pthread_join( )* in this volume of IEEE Std 1003.1-2001 was considered valuable.

The *pthread_join( )* function provides a simple mechanism allowing an application to wait for a thread to terminate. After the thread terminates, the application may then choose to clean up resources that were used by the thread. For instance, after *pthread_join( )* returns, any application-provided stack storage could be reclaimed.

The *pthread_join( )* or *pthread_detach( )* function should eventually be called for every thread that is created with the *detachstate* attribute set to PTHREAD_CREATE_JOINABLE so that storage associated with the thread may be reclaimed.

The interaction between *pthread_join( )* and cancelation is well-defined for the following reasons:

- The *pthread_join( )* function, like all other non-async-cancel-safe functions, can only be called with deferred cancelability type.

- Cancelation cannot occur in the disabled cancelability state.

Thus, only the default cancelability state need be considered. As specified, either the *pthread_join( )* call is canceled, or it succeeds, but not both. The difference is obvious to the application, since either a cancelation handler is run or *pthread_join( )* returns. There are no race conditions since *pthread_join( )* was called in the deferred cancelability state.

FUTURE DIRECTIONS

None.

SEE ALSO

pthread_create( ), *wait*( ), the Base Definitions volume of IEEE Std 1003.1-2001, **<pthread.h>**

CHANGE HISTORY

First released in Issue 5. Included for alignment with the POSIX Threads Extension.

Issue 6

The *pthread_join*( ) function is marked as part of the Threads option.

NAME

      pthread_kill — send a signal to a thread

SYNOPSIS

THR   `#include <signal.h>`

      `int pthread_kill(pthread_t thread, int sig);`

DESCRIPTION

      The *pthread_kill* () function shall request that a signal be delivered to the specified thread.

      As in *kill* (), if *sig* is zero, error checking shall be performed but no signal shall actually be sent.

RETURN VALUE

      Upon successful completion, the function shall return a value of zero. Otherwise, the function shall return an error number. If the *pthread_kill* () function fails, no signal shall be sent.

ERRORS

      The *pthread_kill* () function shall fail if:

      [ESRCH]   No thread could be found corresponding to that specified by the given thread ID.

      [EINVAL]   The value of the *sig* argument is an invalid or unsupported signal number.

      The *pthread_kill* () function shall not return an error code of [EINTR].

EXAMPLES

      None.

APPLICATION USAGE

      The *pthread_kill* () function provides a mechanism for asynchronously directing a signal at a thread in the calling process. This could be used, for example, by one thread to affect broadcast delivery of a signal to a set of threads.

      Note that *pthread_kill* () only causes the signal to be handled in the context of the given thread; the signal action (termination or stopping) affects the process as a whole.

RATIONALE

      None.

FUTURE DIRECTIONS

      None.

SEE ALSO

      kill (), *pthread_self* (), *raise* (), the Base Definitions volume of IEEE Std 1003.1-2001, **<signal.h>**

CHANGE HISTORY

      First released in Issue 5. Included for alignment with the POSIX Threads Extension.

Issue 6

      The *pthread_kill* () function is marked as part of the Threads option.

      The APPLICATION USAGE section is added.

pthread_mutex_destroy()

NAME

pthread_mutex_destroy, pthread_mutex_init — destroy and initialize a mutex

SYNOPSIS

THR
```
#include <pthread.h>

int pthread_mutex_destroy(pthread_mutex_t *mutex);
int pthread_mutex_init(pthread_mutex_t *restrict mutex,
    const pthread_mutexattr_t *restrict attr);
pthread_mutex_t mutex = PTHREAD_MUTEX_INITIALIZER;
```

DESCRIPTION

The *pthread_mutex_destroy*() function shall destroy the mutex object referenced by *mutex*; the mutex object becomes, in effect, uninitialized. An implementation may cause *pthread_mutex_destroy*() to set the object referenced by *mutex* to an invalid value. A destroyed mutex object can be reinitialized using *pthread_mutex_init*(); the results of otherwise referencing the object after it has been destroyed are undefined.

It shall be safe to destroy an initialized mutex that is unlocked. Attempting to destroy a locked mutex results in undefined behavior.

The *pthread_mutex_init*() function shall initialize the mutex referenced by *mutex* with attributes specified by *attr*. If *attr* is NULL, the default mutex attributes are used; the effect shall be the same as passing the address of a default mutex attributes object. Upon successful initialization, the state of the mutex becomes initialized and unlocked.

Only *mutex* itself may be used for performing synchronization. The result of referring to copies of *mutex* in calls to *pthread_mutex_lock*(), *pthread_mutex_trylock*(), *pthread_mutex_unlock*(), and *pthread_mutex_destroy*() is undefined.

Attempting to initialize an already initialized mutex results in undefined behavior.

In cases where default mutex attributes are appropriate, the macro PTHREAD_MUTEX_INITIALIZER can be used to initialize mutexes that are statically allocated. The effect shall be equivalent to dynamic initialization by a call to *pthread_mutex_init*() with parameter *attr* specified as NULL, except that no error checks are performed.

RETURN VALUE

If successful, the *pthread_mutex_destroy*() and *pthread_mutex_init*() functions shall return zero; otherwise, an error number shall be returned to indicate the error.

The [EBUSY] and [EINVAL] error checks, if implemented, act as if they were performed immediately at the beginning of processing for the function and shall cause an error return prior to modifying the state of the mutex specified by *mutex*.

ERRORS

The *pthread_mutex_destroy*() function may fail if:

[EBUSY]   The implementation has detected an attempt to destroy the object referenced by *mutex* while it is locked or referenced (for example, while being used in a *pthread_cond_timedwait*() or *pthread_cond_wait*()) by another thread.

[EINVAL]   The value specified by *mutex* is invalid.

The *pthread_mutex_init*() function shall fail if:

[EAGAIN]   The system lacked the necessary resources (other than memory) to initialize another mutex.

[ENOMEM]   Insufficient memory exists to initialize the mutex.

[EPERM]   The caller does not have the privilege to perform the operation.

The *pthread_mutex_init* ( ) function may fail if:

[EBUSY]   The implementation has detected an attempt to reinitialize the object referenced by *mutex*, a previously initialized, but not yet destroyed, mutex.

[EINVAL]   The value specified by *attr* is invalid.

These functions shall not return an error code of [EINTR].

EXAMPLES
 None.

APPLICATION USAGE
 None.

RATIONALE

Alternate Implementations Possible

This volume of IEEE Std 1003.1-2001 supports several alternative implementations of mutexes. An implementation may store the lock directly in the object of type **pthread_mutex_t**. Alternatively, an implementation may store the lock in the heap and merely store a pointer, handle, or unique ID in the mutex object. Either implementation has advantages or may be required on certain hardware configurations. So that portable code can be written that is invariant to this choice, this volume of IEEE Std 1003.1-2001 does not define assignment or equality for this type, and it uses the term "initialize" to reinforce the (more restrictive) notion that the lock may actually reside in the mutex object itself.

Note that this precludes an over-specification of the type of the mutex or condition variable and motivates the opaqueness of the type.

An implementation is permitted, but not required, to have *pthread_mutex_destroy* ( ) store an illegal value into the mutex. This may help detect erroneous programs that try to lock (or otherwise reference) a mutex that has already been destroyed.

Tradeoff Between Error Checks and Performance Supported

Many of the error checks were made optional in order to let implementations trade off performance *versus* degree of error checking according to the needs of their specific applications and execution environment. As a general rule, errors or conditions caused by the system (such as insufficient memory) always need to be reported, but errors due to an erroneously coded application (such as failing to provide adequate synchronization to prevent a mutex from being deleted while in use) are made optional.

A wide range of implementations is thus made possible. For example, an implementation intended for application debugging may implement all of the error checks, but an implementation running a single, provably correct application under very tight performance constraints in an embedded computer might implement minimal checks. An implementation might even be provided in two versions, similar to the options that compilers provide: a full-checking, but slower version; and a limited-checking, but faster version. To forbid this optionality would be a disservice to users.

By carefully limiting the use of "undefined behavior" only to things that an erroneous (badly coded) application might do, and by defining that resource-not-available errors are mandatory, this volume of IEEE Std 1003.1-2001 ensures that a fully-conforming application is portable across the full range of implementations, while not forcing all implementations to add overhead to check for numerous things that a correct program never does.

Why No Limits are Defined

Defining symbols for the maximum number of mutexes and condition variables was considered but rejected because the number of these objects may change dynamically. Furthermore, many implementations place these objects into application memory; thus, there is no explicit maximum.

Static Initializers for Mutexes and Condition Variables

Providing for static initialization of statically allocated synchronization objects allows modules with private static synchronization variables to avoid runtime initialization tests and overhead. Furthermore, it simplifies the coding of self-initializing modules. Such modules are common in C libraries, where for various reasons the design calls for self-initialization instead of requiring an explicit module initialization function to be called. An example use of static initialization follows.

Without static initialization, a self-initializing routine *foo* () might look as follows:

```
static pthread_once_t foo_once = PTHREAD_ONCE_INIT;
static pthread_mutex_t foo_mutex;

void foo_init()
{
    pthread_mutex_init(&foo_mutex, NULL);
}

void foo()
{
    pthread_once(&foo_once, foo_init);
    pthread_mutex_lock(&foo_mutex);
    /* Do work. */
    pthread_mutex_unlock(&foo_mutex);
}
```

With static initialization, the same routine could be coded as follows:

```
static pthread_mutex_t foo_mutex = PTHREAD_MUTEX_INITIALIZER;

void foo()
{
    pthread_mutex_lock(&foo_mutex);
    /* Do work. */
    pthread_mutex_unlock(&foo_mutex);
}
```

Note that the static initialization both eliminates the need for the initialization test inside *pthread_once*() and the fetch of *&foo_mutex* to learn the address to be passed to *pthread_mutex_lock*() or *pthread_mutex_unlock*().

Thus, the C code written to initialize static objects is simpler on all systems and is also faster on a large class of systems; those where the (entire) synchronization object can be stored in application memory.

Yet the locking performance question is likely to be raised for machines that require mutexes to be allocated out of special memory. Such machines actually have to have mutexes and possibly condition variables contain pointers to the actual hardware locks. For static initialization to work on such machines, *pthread_mutex_lock* () also has to test whether or not the pointer to the actual lock has been allocated. If it has not, *pthread_mutex_lock* () has to initialize it before use. The reservation of such resources can be made when the program is loaded, and hence return codes have not been added to mutex locking and condition variable waiting to indicate failure to complete initialization.

This runtime test in *pthread_mutex_lock* () would at first seem to be extra work; an extra test is required to see whether the pointer has been initialized. On most machines this would actually be implemented as a fetch of the pointer, testing the pointer against zero, and then using the pointer if it has already been initialized. While the test might seem to add extra work, the extra effort of testing a register is usually negligible since no extra memory references are actually done. As more and more machines provide caches, the real expenses are memory references, not instructions executed.

Alternatively, depending on the machine architecture, there are often ways to eliminate *all* overhead in the most important case: on the lock operations that occur *after* the lock has been initialized. This can be done by shifting more overhead to the less frequent operation: initialization. Since out-of-line mutex allocation also means that an address has to be dereferenced to find the actual lock, one technique that is widely applicable is to have static initialization store a bogus value for that address; in particular, an address that causes a machine fault to occur. When such a fault occurs upon the first attempt to lock such a mutex, validity checks can be done, and then the correct address for the actual lock can be filled in. Subsequent lock operations incur no extra overhead since they do not ''fault''. This is merely one technique that can be used to support static initialization, while not adversely affecting the performance of lock acquisition. No doubt there are other techniques that are highly machine-dependent.

The locking overhead for machines doing out-of-line mutex allocation is thus similar for modules being implicitly initialized, where it is improved for those doing mutex allocation entirely inline. The inline case is thus made much faster, and the out-of-line case is not significantly worse.

Besides the issue of locking performance for such machines, a concern is raised that it is possible that threads would serialize contending for initialization locks when attempting to finish initializing statically allocated mutexes. (Such finishing would typically involve taking an internal lock, allocating a structure, storing a pointer to the structure in the mutex, and releasing the internal lock.) First, many implementations would reduce such serialization by hashing on the mutex address. Second, such serialization can only occur a bounded number of times. In particular, it can happen at most as many times as there are statically allocated synchronization objects. Dynamically allocated objects would still be initialized via *pthread_mutex_init* () or *pthread_cond_init* ().

Finally, if none of the above optimization techniques for out-of-line allocation yields sufficient performance for an application on some implementation, the application can avoid static initialization altogether by explicitly initializing all synchronization objects with the corresponding *pthread_*_init* () functions, which are supported by all implementations. An implementation can also document the tradeoffs and advise which initialization technique is more efficient for that particular implementation.

Destroying Mutexes

A mutex can be destroyed immediately after it is unlocked. For example, consider the following code:

```
struct obj {
pthread_mutex_t om;
    int refcnt;
    ...
};

obj_done(struct obj *op)
{
    pthread_mutex_lock(&op->om);
    if (--op->refcnt == 0) {
        pthread_mutex_unlock(&op->om);
(A)     pthread_mutex_destroy(&op->om);
(B)     free(op);
    } else
(C)     pthread_mutex_unlock(&op->om);
}
```

In this case *obj* is reference counted and *obj_done*() is called whenever a reference to the object is dropped. Implementations are required to allow an object to be destroyed and freed and potentially unmapped (for example, lines A and B) immediately after the object is unlocked (line C).

FUTURE DIRECTIONS
None.

SEE ALSO
pthread_mutex_getprioceiling(), *pthread_mutex_lock*(), *pthread_mutex_timedlock*(), *pthread_mutexattr_getpshared*(), the Base Definitions volume of IEEE Std 1003.1-2001, **<pthread.h>**

CHANGE HISTORY
First released in Issue 5. Included for alignment with the POSIX Threads Extension.

Issue 6

The *pthread_mutex_destroy*() and *pthread_mutex_init*() functions are marked as part of the Threads option.

The *pthread_mutex_timedlock*() function is added to the SEE ALSO section for alignment with IEEE Std 1003.1d-1999.

IEEE PASC Interpretation 1003.1c #34 is applied, updating the DESCRIPTION.

The **restrict** keyword is added to the *pthread_mutex_init*() prototype for alignment with the ISO/IEC 9899: 1999 standard.

NAME

pthread_mutex_getprioceiling, pthread_mutex_setprioceiling — get and set the priority ceiling of a mutex (**REALTIME THREADS**)

SYNOPSIS

THR TPP `#include <pthread.h>`

```
int pthread_mutex_getprioceiling(const pthread_mutex_t *restrict mutex,
    int *restrict prioceiling);
int pthread_mutex_setprioceiling(pthread_mutex_t *restrict mutex,
    int prioceiling, int *restrict old_ceiling);
```

DESCRIPTION

The *pthread_mutex_getprioceiling*( ) function shall return the current priority ceiling of the mutex.

The *pthread_mutex_setprioceiling*( ) function shall either lock the mutex if it is unlocked, or block until it can successfully lock the mutex, then it shall change the mutex's priority ceiling and release the mutex. When the change is successful, the previous value of the priority ceiling shall be returned in *old_ceiling*. The process of locking the mutex need not adhere to the priority protect protocol.

If the *pthread_mutex_setprioceiling*( ) function fails, the mutex priority ceiling shall not be changed.

RETURN VALUE

If successful, the *pthread_mutex_getprioceiling*( ) and *pthread_mutex_setprioceiling*( ) functions shall return zero; otherwise, an error number shall be returned to indicate the error.

ERRORS

The *pthread_mutex_getprioceiling*( ) and *pthread_mutex_setprioceiling*( ) functions may fail if:

[EINVAL]   The priority requested by *prioceiling* is out of range.

[EINVAL]   The value specified by *mutex* does not refer to a currently existing mutex.

[EPERM]   The caller does not have the privilege to perform the operation.

These functions shall not return an error code of [EINTR].

EXAMPLES

None.

APPLICATION USAGE

None.

RATIONALE

None.

FUTURE DIRECTIONS

None.

SEE ALSO

pthread_mutex_destroy( ), *pthread_mutex_lock*( ), *pthread_mutex_timedlock*( ), the Base Definitions volume of IEEE Std 1003.1-2001, **<pthread.h>**

CHANGE HISTORY

First released in Issue 5. Included for alignment with the POSIX Threads Extension.

Marked as part of the Realtime Threads Feature Group.

Issue 6

The *pthread_mutex_getprioceiling* () and *pthread_mutex_setprioceiling* () functions are marked as part of the Threads and Thread Priority Protection options.

The [ENOSYS] error condition has been removed as stubs need not be provided if an implementation does not support the Thread Priority Protection option.

The [ENOSYS] error denoting non-support of the priority ceiling protocol for mutexes has been removed. This is because if the implementation provides the functions (regardless of whether _POSIX_PTHREAD_PRIO_PROTECT is defined), they must function as in the DESCRIPTION and therefore the priority ceiling protocol for mutexes is supported.

The *pthread_mutex_timedlock* () function is added to the SEE ALSO section for alignment with IEEE Std 1003.1d-1999.

The **restrict** keyword is added to the *pthread_mutex_getprioceiling* () and *pthread_mutex_setprioceiling* () prototypes for alignment with the ISO/IEC 9899:1999 standard.

NAME

pthread_mutex_init — initialize a mutex

SYNOPSIS

THR   `#include <pthread.h>`

```
int pthread_mutex_init(pthread_mutex_t *restrict mutex,
    const pthread_mutexattr_t *restrict attr);
pthread_mutex_t mutex = PTHREAD_MUTEX_INITIALIZER;
```

DESCRIPTION

Refer to *pthread_mutex_destroy* ( ).

NAME

pthread_mutex_lock, pthread_mutex_trylock, pthread_mutex_unlock — lock and unlock a mutex

SYNOPSIS

THR   `#include <pthread.h>`

```
int pthread_mutex_lock(pthread_mutex_t *mutex);
int pthread_mutex_trylock(pthread_mutex_t *mutex);
int pthread_mutex_unlock(pthread_mutex_t *mutex);
```

DESCRIPTION

The mutex object referenced by *mutex* shall be locked by calling *pthread_mutex_lock*(). If the mutex is already locked, the calling thread shall block until the mutex becomes available. This operation shall return with the mutex object referenced by *mutex* in the locked state with the calling thread as its owner.

XSI   If the mutex type is PTHREAD_MUTEX_NORMAL, deadlock detection shall not be provided. Attempting to relock the mutex causes deadlock. If a thread attempts to unlock a mutex that it has not locked or a mutex which is unlocked, undefined behavior results.

If the mutex type is PTHREAD_MUTEX_ERRORCHECK, then error checking shall be provided. If a thread attempts to relock a mutex that it has already locked, an error shall be returned. If a thread attempts to unlock a mutex that it has not locked or a mutex which is unlocked, an error shall be returned.

If the mutex type is PTHREAD_MUTEX_RECURSIVE, then the mutex shall maintain the concept of a lock count. When a thread successfully acquires a mutex for the first time, the lock count shall be set to one. Every time a thread relocks this mutex, the lock count shall be incremented by one. Each time the thread unlocks the mutex, the lock count shall be decremented by one. When the lock count reaches zero, the mutex shall become available for other threads to acquire. If a thread attempts to unlock a mutex that it has not locked or a mutex which is unlocked, an error shall be returned.

If the mutex type is PTHREAD_MUTEX_DEFAULT, attempting to recursively lock the mutex results in undefined behavior. Attempting to unlock the mutex if it was not locked by the calling thread results in undefined behavior. Attempting to unlock the mutex if it is not locked results in undefined behavior.

The *pthread_mutex_trylock*() function shall be equivalent to *pthread_mutex_lock*(), except that if the mutex object referenced by *mutex* is currently locked (by any thread, including the current thread), the call shall return immediately. If the mutex type is PTHREAD_MUTEX_RECURSIVE and the mutex is currently owned by the calling thread, the mutex lock count shall be incremented by one and the *pthread_mutex_trylock*() function shall immediately return success.

XSI   The *pthread_mutex_unlock*() function shall release the mutex object referenced by *mutex*. The manner in which a mutex is released is dependent upon the mutex's type attribute. If there are threads blocked on the mutex object referenced by *mutex* when *pthread_mutex_unlock*() is called, resulting in the mutex becoming available, the scheduling policy shall determine which thread shall acquire the mutex.

XSI   (In the case of PTHREAD_MUTEX_RECURSIVE mutexes, the mutex shall become available when the count reaches zero and the calling thread no longer has any locks on this mutex.)

If a signal is delivered to a thread waiting for a mutex, upon return from the signal handler the thread shall resume waiting for the mutex as if it was not interrupted.

RETURN VALUE

If successful, the *pthread_mutex_lock*() and *pthread_mutex_unlock*() functions shall return zero; otherwise, an error number shall be returned to indicate the error.

The *pthread_mutex_trylock*() function shall return zero if a lock on the mutex object referenced by *mutex* is acquired. Otherwise, an error number is returned to indicate the error.

ERRORS

The *pthread_mutex_lock*() and *pthread_mutex_trylock*() functions shall fail if:

[EINVAL]   The *mutex* was created with the protocol attribute having the value PTHREAD_PRIO_PROTECT and the calling thread's priority is higher than the mutex's current priority ceiling.

The *pthread_mutex_trylock*() function shall fail if:

[EBUSY]   The *mutex* could not be acquired because it was already locked.

The *pthread_mutex_lock*(), *pthread_mutex_trylock*(), and *pthread_mutex_unlock*() functions may fail if:

[EINVAL]   The value specified by *mutex* does not refer to an initialized mutex object.

XSI   [EAGAIN]   The mutex could not be acquired because the maximum number of recursive locks for *mutex* has been exceeded.

The *pthread_mutex_lock*() function may fail if:

[EDEADLK]   The current thread already owns the mutex.

The *pthread_mutex_unlock*() function may fail if:

[EPERM]   The current thread does not own the mutex.

These functions shall not return an error code of [EINTR].

EXAMPLES

None.

APPLICATION USAGE

None.

RATIONALE

Mutex objects are intended to serve as a low-level primitive from which other thread synchronization functions can be built. As such, the implementation of mutexes should be as efficient as possible, and this has ramifications on the features available at the interface.

The mutex functions and the particular default settings of the mutex attributes have been motivated by the desire to not preclude fast, inlined implementations of mutex locking and unlocking.

For example, deadlocking on a double-lock is explicitly allowed behavior in order to avoid requiring more overhead in the basic mechanism than is absolutely necessary. (More "friendly" mutexes that detect deadlock or that allow multiple locking by the same thread are easily constructed by the user via the other mechanisms provided. For example, *pthread_self*() can be used to record mutex ownership.) Implementations might also choose to provide such extended features as options via special mutex attributes.

Since most attributes only need to be checked when a thread is going to be blocked, the use of attributes does not slow the (common) mutex-locking case.

Likewise, while being able to extract the thread ID of the owner of a mutex might be desirable, it would require storing the current thread ID when each mutex is locked, and this could incur unacceptable levels of overhead. Similar arguments apply to a *mutex_tryunlock* operation.

FUTURE DIRECTIONS
None.

SEE ALSO
pthread_mutex_destroy( ),   *pthread_mutex_timedlock*( ),   the   Base   Definitions   volume   of IEEE Std 1003.1-2001, **<pthread.h>**

CHANGE HISTORY
First released in Issue 5. Included for alignment with the POSIX Threads Extension.

Issue 6

The *pthread_mutex_lock*( ), *pthread_mutex_trylock*( ), and *pthread_mutex_unlock*( ) functions are marked as part of the Threads option.

The following new requirements on POSIX implementations derive from alignment with the Single UNIX Specification:

- The behavior when attempting to relock a mutex is defined.

The *pthread_mutex_timedlock*( ) function is added to the SEE ALSO section for alignment with IEEE Std 1003.1d-1999.

NAME

pthread_mutex_setprioceiling — change the priority ceiling of a mutex (**REALTIME THREADS**)

SYNOPSIS

THR TPP `#include <pthread.h>`

```
int pthread_mutex_setprioceiling(pthread_mutex_t *restrict mutex,
    int prioceiling, int *restrict old_ceiling);
```

DESCRIPTION

Refer to *pthread_mutex_getprioceiling* ( ).

NAME

pthread_mutex_timedlock — lock a mutex (**ADVANCED REALTIME**)

SYNOPSIS

THR TMO
```
#include <pthread.h>
#include <time.h>

int pthread_mutex_timedlock(pthread_mutex_t *restrict mutex,
    const struct timespec *restrict abs_timeout);
```

DESCRIPTION

The *pthread_mutex_timedlock*() function shall lock the mutex object referenced by *mutex*. If the mutex is already locked, the calling thread shall block until the mutex becomes available as in the *pthread_mutex_lock*() function. If the mutex cannot be locked without waiting for another thread to unlock the mutex, this wait shall be terminated when the specified timeout expires.

The timeout shall expire when the absolute time specified by *abs_timeout* passes, as measured by the clock on which timeouts are based (that is, when the value of that clock equals or exceeds *abs_timeout*), or if the absolute time specified by *abs_timeout* has already been passed at the time of the call.

TMR   If the Timers option is supported, the timeout shall be based on the CLOCK_REALTIME clock; if the Timers option is not supported, the timeout shall be based on the system clock as returned by the *time*() function.

The resolution of the timeout shall be the resolution of the clock on which it is based. The **timespec** data type is defined in the **<time.h>** header.

Under no circumstance shall the function fail with a timeout if the mutex can be locked immediately. The validity of the *abs_timeout* parameter need not be checked if the mutex can be locked immediately.

As a consequence of the priority inheritance rules (for mutexes initialized with the PRIO_INHERIT protocol), if a timed mutex wait is terminated because its timeout expires, the priority of the owner of the mutex shall be adjusted as necessary to reflect the fact that this thread is no longer among the threads waiting for the mutex.

RETURN VALUE

If successful, the *pthread_mutex_timedlock*() function shall return zero; otherwise, an error number shall be returned to indicate the error.

ERRORS

The *pthread_mutex_timedlock*() function shall fail if:

[EINVAL]   The mutex was created with the protocol attribute having the value PTHREAD_PRIO_PROTECT and the calling thread's priority is higher than the mutex' current priority ceiling.

[EINVAL]   The process or thread would have blocked, and the *abs_timeout* parameter specified a nanoseconds field value less than zero or greater than or equal to 1 000 million.

[ETIMEDOUT]   The mutex could not be locked before the specified timeout expired.

The *pthread_mutex_timedlock*() function may fail if:

[EINVAL]   The value specified by *mutex* does not refer to an initialized mutex object.

XSI   [EAGAIN]   The mutex could not be acquired because the maximum number of recursive
                       locks for *mutex* has been exceeded.

[EDEADLK]   The current thread already owns the mutex.

This function shall not return an error code of [EINTR].

EXAMPLES

None.

APPLICATION USAGE

The *pthread_mutex_timedlock*() function is part of the Threads and Timeouts options and need
not be provided on all implementations.

RATIONALE

None.

FUTURE DIRECTIONS

None.

SEE ALSO

pthread_mutex_destroy(),   *pthread_mutex_lock*(),   *pthread_mutex_trylock*(),   *time*(),   the   Base
Definitions volume of IEEE Std 1003.1-2001, **<pthread.h>**, **<time.h>**

CHANGE HISTORY

First released in Issue 6. Derived from IEEE Std 1003.1d-1999.

pthread_mutex_trylock( )

NAME

pthread_mutex_trylock, pthread_mutex_unlock — lock and unlock a mutex

SYNOPSIS

THR
```
#include <pthread.h>

int pthread_mutex_trylock(pthread_mutex_t *mutex);
int pthread_mutex_unlock(pthread_mutex_t *mutex);
```

DESCRIPTION

Refer to *pthread_mutex_lock*( ).

NAME

pthread_mutexattr_destroy, pthread_mutexattr_init — destroy and initialize the mutex attributes object

SYNOPSIS

THR
```
#include <pthread.h>

int pthread_mutexattr_destroy(pthread_mutexattr_t *attr);
int pthread_mutexattr_init(pthread_mutexattr_t *attr);
```

DESCRIPTION

The *pthread_mutexattr_destroy*( ) function shall destroy a mutex attributes object; the object becomes, in effect, uninitialized. An implementation may cause *pthread_mutexattr_destroy*( ) to set the object referenced by *attr* to an invalid value. A destroyed *attr* attributes object can be reinitialized using *pthread_mutexattr_init*( ); the results of otherwise referencing the object after it has been destroyed are undefined.

The *pthread_mutexattr_init*( ) function shall initialize a mutex attributes object *attr* with the default value for all of the attributes defined by the implementation.

Results are undefined if *pthread_mutexattr_init*( ) is called specifying an already initialized *attr* attributes object.

After a mutex attributes object has been used to initialize one or more mutexes, any function affecting the attributes object (including destruction) shall not affect any previously initialized mutexes.

RETURN VALUE

Upon successful completion, *pthread_mutexattr_destroy*( ) and *pthread_mutexattr_init*( ) shall return zero; otherwise, an error number shall be returned to indicate the error.

ERRORS

The *pthread_mutexattr_destroy*( ) function may fail if:

[EINVAL]   The value specified by *attr* is invalid.

The *pthread_mutexattr_init*( ) function shall fail if:

[ENOMEM]   Insufficient memory exists to initialize the mutex attributes object.

These functions shall not return an error code of [EINTR].

EXAMPLES

None.

APPLICATION USAGE

None.

RATIONALE

See *pthread_attr_init*( ) for a general explanation of attributes. Attributes objects allow implementations to experiment with useful extensions and permit extension of this volume of IEEE Std 1003.1-2001 without changing the existing functions. Thus, they provide for future extensibility of this volume of IEEE Std 1003.1-2001 and reduce the temptation to standardize prematurely on semantics that are not yet widely implemented or understood.

Examples of possible additional mutex attributes that have been discussed are *spin_only*, *limited_spin*, *no_spin*, *recursive*, and *metered*. (To explain what the latter attributes might mean: recursive mutexes would allow for multiple re-locking by the current owner; metered mutexes would transparently keep records of queue length, wait time, and so on.) Since there is not yet wide agreement on the usefulness of these resulting from shared implementation and usage experience, they are not yet specified in this volume of IEEE Std 1003.1-2001. Mutex attributes objects, however, make it possible to test out these concepts for possible standardization at a later time.

Mutex Attributes and Performance

Care has been taken to ensure that the default values of the mutex attributes have been defined such that mutexes initialized with the defaults have simple enough semantics so that the locking and unlocking can be done with the equivalent of a test-and-set instruction (plus possibly a few other basic instructions).

There is at least one implementation method that can be used to reduce the cost of testing at lock-time if a mutex has non-default attributes. One such method that an implementation can employ (and this can be made fully transparent to fully conforming POSIX applications) is to secretly pre-lock any mutexes that are initialized to non-default attributes. Any later attempt to lock such a mutex causes the implementation to branch to the "slow path" as if the mutex were unavailable; then, on the slow path, the implementation can do the "real work" to lock a non-default mutex. The underlying unlock operation is more complicated since the implementation never really wants to release the pre-lock on this kind of mutex. This illustrates that, depending on the hardware, there may be certain optimizations that can be used so that whatever mutex attributes are considered "most frequently used" can be processed most efficiently.

Process Shared Memory and Synchronization

The existence of memory mapping functions in this volume of IEEE Std 1003.1-2001 leads to the possibility that an application may allocate the synchronization objects from this section in memory that is accessed by multiple processes (and therefore, by threads of multiple processes).

In order to permit such usage, while at the same time keeping the usual case (that is, usage within a single process) efficient, a *process-shared* option has been defined.

If an implementation supports the _POSIX_THREAD_PROCESS_SHARED option, then the *process-shared* attribute can be used to indicate that mutexes or condition variables may be accessed by threads of multiple processes.

The default setting of PTHREAD_PROCESS_PRIVATE has been chosen for the *process-shared* attribute so that the most efficient forms of these synchronization objects are created by default.

Synchronization variables that are initialized with the PTHREAD_PROCESS_PRIVATE *process-shared* attribute may only be operated on by threads in the process that initialized them. Synchronization variables that are initialized with the PTHREAD_PROCESS_SHARED *process-shared* attribute may be operated on by any thread in any process that has access to it. In particular, these processes may exist beyond the lifetime of the initializing process. For example, the following code implements a simple counting semaphore in a mapped file that may be used by many processes.

```
/* sem.h */
struct semaphore {
    pthread_mutex_t lock;
    pthread_cond_t nonzero;
    unsigned count;
};
typedef struct semaphore semaphore_t;

semaphore_t *semaphore_create(char *semaphore_name);
semaphore_t *semaphore_open(char *semaphore_name);
```

```
      void semaphore_post(semaphore_t *semap);
      void semaphore_wait(semaphore_t *semap);
      void semaphore_close(semaphore_t *semap);

      /* sem.c */
      #include <sys/types.h>
      #include <sys/stat.h>
      #include <sys/mman.h>
      #include <fcntl.h>
      #include <pthread.h>
      #include "sem.h"

      semaphore_t *
      semaphore_create(char *semaphore_name)
      {
      int fd;
          semaphore_t *semap;
          pthread_mutexattr_t psharedm;
          pthread_condattr_t psharedc;

          fd = open(semaphore_name, O_RDWR | O_CREAT | O_EXCL, 0666);
          if (fd < 0)
              return (NULL);
          (void) ftruncate(fd, sizeof(semaphore_t));
          (void) pthread_mutexattr_init(&psharedm);
          (void) pthread_mutexattr_setpshared(&psharedm,
              PTHREAD_PROCESS_SHARED);
          (void) pthread_condattr_init(&psharedc);
          (void) pthread_condattr_setpshared(&psharedc,
              PTHREAD_PROCESS_SHARED);
          semap = (semaphore_t *) mmap(NULL, sizeof(semaphore_t),
                  PROT_READ | PROT_WRITE, MAP_SHARED,
                  fd, 0);
          close (fd);
          (void) pthread_mutex_init(&semap->lock, &psharedm);
          (void) pthread_cond_init(&semap->nonzero, &psharedc);
          semap->count = 0;
          return (semap);
      }

      semaphore_t *
      semaphore_open(char *semaphore_name)
      {
          int fd;
          semaphore_t *semap;

          fd = open(semaphore_name, O_RDWR, 0666);
          if (fd < 0)
              return (NULL);
          semap = (semaphore_t *) mmap(NULL, sizeof(semaphore_t),
                  PROT_READ | PROT_WRITE, MAP_SHARED,
                  fd, 0);
          close (fd);
          return (semap);
      }
```

```
void
semaphore_post(semaphore_t *semap)
{
    pthread_mutex_lock(&semap->lock);
    if (semap->count == 0)
        pthread_cond_signal(&semapx->nonzero);
    semap->count++;
    pthread_mutex_unlock(&semap->lock);
}

void
semaphore_wait(semaphore_t *semap)
{
    pthread_mutex_lock(&semap->lock);
    while (semap->count == 0)
        pthread_cond_wait(&semap->nonzero, &semap->lock);
    semap->count--;
    pthread_mutex_unlock(&semap->lock);
}

void
semaphore_close(semaphore_t *semap)
{
    munmap((void *) semap, sizeof(semaphore_t));
}
```

The following code is for three separate processes that create, post, and wait on a semaphore in the file **/tmp/semaphore**. Once the file is created, the post and wait programs increment and decrement the counting semaphore (waiting and waking as required) even though they did not initialize the semaphore.

```
/* create.c */
#include "pthread.h"
#include "sem.h"

int
main()
{
    semaphore_t *semap;

    semap = semaphore_create("/tmp/semaphore");
    if (semap == NULL)
        exit(1);
    semaphore_close(semap);
    return (0);
}

/* post */
#include "pthread.h"
#include "sem.h"

int
main()
{
    semaphore_t *semap;
```

```
            semap = semaphore_open("/tmp/semaphore");
            if (semap == NULL)
                exit(1);
            semaphore_post(semap);
            semaphore_close(semap);
            return (0);
        }

        /* wait */
        #include "pthread.h"
        #include "sem.h"

        int
        main()
        {
            semaphore_t *semap;

            semap = semaphore_open("/tmp/semaphore");
            if (semap == NULL)
                exit(1);
            semaphore_wait(semap);
            semaphore_close(semap);
            return (0);
        }
```

FUTURE DIRECTIONS

None.

SEE ALSO

pthread_cond_destroy( ), *pthread_create*( ), *pthread_mutex_destroy*( ), *pthread_mutexattr_destroy*( ), the Base Definitions volume of IEEE Std 1003.1-2001, **<pthread.h>**

CHANGE HISTORY

First released in Issue 5. Included for alignment with the POSIX Threads Extension.

Issue 6

The *pthread_mutexattr_destroy*( ) and *pthread_mutexattr_init*( ) functions are marked as part of the Threads option.

IEEE PASC Interpretation 1003.1c #27 is applied, updating the ERRORS section.

NAME

pthread_mutexattr_getprioceiling, pthread_mutexattr_setprioceiling — get and set the prioceiling attribute of the mutex attributes object (**REALTIME THREADS**)

SYNOPSIS

THR TPP `#include <pthread.h>`

```
int pthread_mutexattr_getprioceiling(const pthread_mutexattr_t *
    restrict attr, int *restrict prioceiling);
int pthread_mutexattr_setprioceiling(pthread_mutexattr_t *attr,
    int prioceiling);
```

DESCRIPTION

The *pthread_mutexattr_getprioceiling*() and *pthread_mutexattr_setprioceiling*() functions, respectively, shall get and set the priority ceiling attribute of a mutex attributes object pointed to by *attr* which was previously created by the function *pthread_mutexattr_init*().

The *prioceiling* attribute contains the priority ceiling of initialized mutexes. The values of *prioceiling* are within the maximum range of priorities defined by SCHED_FIFO.

The *prioceiling* attribute defines the priority ceiling of initialized mutexes, which is the minimum priority level at which the critical section guarded by the mutex is executed. In order to avoid priority inversion, the priority ceiling of the mutex shall be set to a priority higher than or equal to the highest priority of all the threads that may lock that mutex. The values of *prioceiling* are within the maximum range of priorities defined under the SCHED_FIFO scheduling policy.

RETURN VALUE

Upon successful completion, the *pthread_mutexattr_getprioceiling*() and *pthread_mutexattr_setprioceiling*() functions shall return zero; otherwise, an error number shall be returned to indicate the error.

ERRORS

The *pthread_mutexattr_getprioceiling*() and *pthread_mutexattr_setprioceiling*() functions may fail if:

[EINVAL]   The value specified by *attr* or *prioceiling* is invalid.

[EPERM]   The caller does not have the privilege to perform the operation.

These functions shall not return an error code of [EINTR].

EXAMPLES

None.

APPLICATION USAGE

None.

RATIONALE

None.

FUTURE DIRECTIONS

None.

SEE ALSO

pthread_cond_destroy(), *pthread_create*(), *pthread_mutex_destroy*(), the Base Definitions volume of IEEE Std 1003.1-2001, **<pthread.h>**

CHANGE HISTORY

First released in Issue 5. Included for alignment with the POSIX Threads Extension.

Marked as part of the Realtime Threads Feature Group.

Issue 6

The *pthread_mutexattr_getprioceiling* ( ) and *pthread_mutexattr_setprioceiling* ( ) functions are marked as part of the Threads and Thread Priority Protection options.

The [ENOSYS] error condition has been removed as stubs need not be provided if an implementation does not support the Thread Priority Protection option.

The [ENOTSUP] error condition has been removed since these functions do not have a *protocol* argument.

The **restrict** keyword is added to the *pthread_mutexattr_getprioceiling* ( ) prototype for alignment with the ISO/IEC 9899: 1999 standard.

NAME

    pthread_mutexattr_getprotocol, pthread_mutexattr_setprotocol — get and set the protocol
    attribute of the mutex attributes object (**REALTIME THREADS**)

SYNOPSIS

THR   `#include <pthread.h>`

TPP|TPI `int pthread_mutexattr_getprotocol(const pthread_mutexattr_t *`
        `    restrict attr, int *restrict protocol);`
        `int pthread_mutexattr_setprotocol(pthread_mutexattr_t *attr,`
        `    int protocol);`

DESCRIPTION

    The *pthread_mutexattr_getprotocol*() and *pthread_mutexattr_setprotocol*() functions, respectively,
    shall get and set the protocol attribute of a mutex attributes object pointed to by *attr* which was
    previously created by the function *pthread_mutexattr_init*().

    The *protocol* attribute defines the protocol to be followed in utilizing mutexes. The value of
    protocol may be one of:

        PTHREAD_PRIO_NONE
TPI   PTHREAD_PRIO_INHERIT
TPP   PTHREAD_PRIO_PROTECT

    which are defined in the **<pthread.h>** header.

    When a thread owns a mutex with the PTHREAD_PRIO_NONE *protocol* attribute, its priority
    and scheduling shall not be affected by its mutex ownership.

TPI   When a thread is blocking higher priority threads because of owning one or more mutexes with
        the PTHREAD_PRIO_INHERIT *protocol* attribute, it shall execute at the higher of its priority or
        the priority of the highest priority thread waiting on any of the mutexes owned by this thread
        and initialized with this protocol.

TPP   When a thread owns one or more mutexes initialized with the PTHREAD_PRIO_PROTECT
        protocol, it shall execute at the higher of its priority or the highest of the priority ceilings of all
        the mutexes owned by this thread and initialized with this attribute, regardless of whether other
        threads are blocked on any of these mutexes or not.

    While a thread is holding a mutex which has been initialized with the
    PTHREAD_PRIO_INHERIT or PTHREAD_PRIO_PROTECT protocol attributes, it shall not be
    subject to being moved to the tail of the scheduling queue at its priority in the event that its
    original priority is changed, such as by a call to *sched_setparam*(). Likewise, when a thread
    unlocks a mutex that has been initialized with the PTHREAD_PRIO_INHERIT or
    PTHREAD_PRIO_PROTECT protocol attributes, it shall not be subject to being moved to the tail
    of the scheduling queue at its priority in the event that its original priority is changed.

    If a thread simultaneously owns several mutexes initialized with different protocols, it shall
    execute at the highest of the priorities that it would have obtained by each of these protocols.

TPI   When a thread makes a call to *pthread_mutex_lock*(), the mutex was initialized with the protocol
        attribute having the value PTHREAD_PRIO_INHERIT, when the calling thread is blocked
        because the mutex is owned by another thread, that owner thread shall inherit the priority level
        of the calling thread as long as it continues to own the mutex. The implementation shall update
        its execution priority to the maximum of its assigned priority and all its inherited priorities.
        Furthermore, if this owner thread itself becomes blocked on another mutex, the same priority

inheritance effect shall be propagated to this other owner thread, in a recursive manner.

RETURN VALUE

Upon successful completion, the *pthread_mutexattr_getprotocol*() and *pthread_mutexattr_setprotocol*() functions shall return zero; otherwise, an error number shall be returned to indicate the error.

ERRORS

The *pthread_mutexattr_setprotocol*() function shall fail if:

[ENOTSUP]   The value specified by *protocol* is an unsupported value.

The *pthread_mutexattr_getprotocol*() and *pthread_mutexattr_setprotocol*() functions may fail if:

[EINVAL]   The value specified by *attr* or *protocol* is invalid.

[EPERM]   The caller does not have the privilege to perform the operation.

These functions shall not return an error code of [EINTR].

EXAMPLES

None.

APPLICATION USAGE

None.

RATIONALE

None.

FUTURE DIRECTIONS

None.

SEE ALSO

pthread_cond_destroy(), *pthread_create*(), *pthread_mutex_destroy*(), the Base Definitions volume of IEEE Std 1003.1-2001, **<pthread.h>**

CHANGE HISTORY

First released in Issue 5. Included for alignment with the POSIX Threads Extension.

Marked as part of the Realtime Threads Feature Group.

Issue 6

The *pthread_mutexattr_getprotocol*() and *pthread_mutexattr_setprotocol*() functions are marked as part of the Threads option and either the Thread Priority Protection or Thread Priority Inheritance options.

The [ENOSYS] error condition has been removed as stubs need not be provided if an implementation does not support the Thread Priority Protection or Thread Priority Inheritance options.

The **restrict** keyword is added to the *pthread_mutexattr_getprotocol*() prototype for alignment with the ISO/IEC 9899: 1999 standard.

NAME

pthread_mutexattr_getpshared, pthread_mutexattr_setpshared — get and set the process-shared attribute

SYNOPSIS

THR TSH `#include <pthread.h>`

```
int pthread_mutexattr_getpshared(const pthread_mutexattr_t *
    restrict attr, int *restrict pshared);
int pthread_mutexattr_setpshared(pthread_mutexattr_t *attr,
    int pshared);
```

DESCRIPTION

The *pthread_mutexattr_getpshared*() function shall obtain the value of the *process-shared* attribute from the attributes object referenced by *attr*. The *pthread_mutexattr_setpshared*() function shall set the *process-shared* attribute in an initialized attributes object referenced by *attr*.

The *process-shared* attribute is set to PTHREAD_PROCESS_SHARED to permit a mutex to be operated upon by any thread that has access to the memory where the mutex is allocated, even if the mutex is allocated in memory that is shared by multiple processes. If the *process-shared* attribute is PTHREAD_PROCESS_PRIVATE, the mutex shall only be operated upon by threads created within the same process as the thread that initialized the mutex; if threads of differing processes attempt to operate on such a mutex, the behavior is undefined. The default value of the attribute shall be PTHREAD_PROCESS_PRIVATE.

RETURN VALUE

Upon successful completion, *pthread_mutexattr_setpshared*() shall return zero; otherwise, an error number shall be returned to indicate the error.

Upon successful completion, *pthread_mutexattr_getpshared*() shall return zero and store the value of the *process-shared* attribute of *attr* into the object referenced by the *pshared* parameter. Otherwise, an error number shall be returned to indicate the error.

ERRORS

The *pthread_mutexattr_getpshared*() and *pthread_mutexattr_setpshared*() functions may fail if:

[EINVAL]   The value specified by *attr* is invalid.

The *pthread_mutexattr_setpshared*() function may fail if:

[EINVAL]   The new value specified for the attribute is outside the range of legal values for that attribute.

These functions shall not return an error code of [EINTR].

EXAMPLES

None.

APPLICATION USAGE

None.

RATIONALE

None.

FUTURE DIRECTIONS

None.

SEE ALSO

pthread_cond_destroy ( ), *pthread_create* ( ), *pthread_mutex_destroy* ( ), *pthread_mutexattr_destroy* ( ), the Base Definitions volume of IEEE Std 1003.1-2001, **<pthread.h>**

CHANGE HISTORY

First released in Issue 5. Included for alignment with the POSIX Threads Extension.

Issue 6

The *pthread_mutexattr_getpshared* ( ) and *pthread_mutexattr_setpshared* ( ) functions are marked as part of the Threads and Thread Process-Shared Synchronization options.

The **restrict** keyword is added to the *pthread_mutexattr_getpshared* ( ) prototype for alignment with the ISO/IEC 9899: 1999 standard.

NAME

pthread_mutexattr_gettype, pthread_mutexattr_settype — get and set the mutex type attribute

SYNOPSIS

XSI   `#include <pthread.h>`

```
int pthread_mutexattr_gettype(const pthread_mutexattr_t *restrict attr,
    int *restrict type);
int pthread_mutexattr_settype(pthread_mutexattr_t *attr, int type);
```

DESCRIPTION

The *pthread_mutexattr_gettype*( ) and *pthread_mutexattr_settype*( ) functions, respectively, shall get and set the mutex *type* attribute. This attribute is set in the *type* parameter to these functions. The default value of the *type* attribute is PTHREAD_MUTEX_DEFAULT.

The type of mutex is contained in the *type* attribute of the mutex attributes. Valid mutex types include:

PTHREAD_MUTEX_NORMAL
> This type of mutex does not detect deadlock. A thread attempting to relock this mutex without first unlocking it shall deadlock. Attempting to unlock a mutex locked by a different thread results in undefined behavior. Attempting to unlock an unlocked mutex results in undefined behavior.

PTHREAD_MUTEX_ERRORCHECK
> This type of mutex provides error checking. A thread attempting to relock this mutex without first unlocking it shall return with an error. A thread attempting to unlock a mutex which another thread has locked shall return with an error. A thread attempting to unlock an unlocked mutex shall return with an error.

PTHREAD_MUTEX_RECURSIVE
> A thread attempting to relock this mutex without first unlocking it shall succeed in locking the mutex. The relocking deadlock which can occur with mutexes of type PTHREAD_MUTEX_NORMAL cannot occur with this type of mutex. Multiple locks of this mutex shall require the same number of unlocks to release the mutex before another thread can acquire the mutex. A thread attempting to unlock a mutex which another thread has locked shall return with an error. A thread attempting to unlock an unlocked mutex shall return with an error.

PTHREAD_MUTEX_DEFAULT
> Attempting to recursively lock a mutex of this type results in undefined behavior. Attempting to unlock a mutex of this type which was not locked by the calling thread results in undefined behavior. Attempting to unlock a mutex of this type which is not locked results in undefined behavior. An implementation may map this mutex to one of the other mutex types.

RETURN VALUE

Upon successful completion, the *pthread_mutexattr_gettype*( ) function shall return zero and store the value of the *type* attribute of *attr* into the object referenced by the *type* parameter. Otherwise, an error shall be returned to indicate the error.

If successful, the *pthread_mutexattr_settype*( ) function shall return zero; otherwise, an error number shall be returned to indicate the error.

ERRORS

The *pthread_mutexattr_settype*( ) function shall fail if:

[EINVAL]   The value *type* is invalid.

The *pthread_mutexattr_gettype*( ) and *pthread_mutexattr_settype*( ) functions may fail if:

[EINVAL]   The value specified by *attr* is invalid.

These functions shall not return an error code of [EINTR].

EXAMPLES

None.

APPLICATION USAGE

It is advised that an application should not use a PTHREAD_MUTEX_RECURSIVE mutex with condition variables because the implicit unlock performed for a *pthread_cond_timedwait*( ) or *pthread_cond_wait*( ) may not actually release the mutex (if it had been locked multiple times). If this happens, no other thread can satisfy the condition of the predicate.

RATIONALE

None.

FUTURE DIRECTIONS

None.

SEE ALSO

pthread_cond_timedwait( ), the Base Definitions volume of IEEE Std 1003.1-2001, **<pthread.h>**

CHANGE HISTORY

First released in Issue 5.

Issue 6

The Open Group Corrigendum U033/3 is applied. The SYNOPSIS for *pthread_mutexattr_gettype*( ) is updated so that the first argument is of type **const pthread_mutexattr_t ***.

The **restrict** keyword is added to the *pthread_mutexattr_gettype*( ) prototype for alignment with the ISO/IEC 9899: 1999 standard.

NAME

pthread_mutexattr_init — initialize the mutex attributes object

SYNOPSIS

THR   #include <pthread.h>

int pthread_mutexattr_init(pthread_mutexattr_t *attr);

DESCRIPTION

Refer to *pthread_mutexattr_destroy*( ).

NAME

pthread_mutexattr_setprioceiling — set the prioceiling attribute of the mutex attributes object **(REALTIME THREADS)**

SYNOPSIS

THR TPP `#include <pthread.h>`

```
int pthread_mutexattr_setprioceiling(pthread_mutexattr_t *attr,
    int prioceiling);
```

DESCRIPTION

Refer to *pthread_mutexattr_getprioceiling* ( ).

NAME

pthread_mutexattr_setprotocol — set the protocol attribute of the mutex attributes object **(REALTIME THREADS)**

SYNOPSIS

THR

```
#include <pthread.h>
```

TPP | TPI

```
int pthread_mutexattr_setprotocol(pthread_mutexattr_t *attr,
    int protocol);
```

DESCRIPTION

Refer to *pthread_mutexattr_getprotocol* ( ).

NAME

pthread_mutexattr_setpshared — set the process-shared attribute

SYNOPSIS

THR TSH `#include <pthread.h>`

```
int pthread_mutexattr_setpshared(pthread_mutexattr_t *attr,
    int pshared);
```

DESCRIPTION

Refer to *pthread_mutexattr_getpshared*().

pthread_mutexattr_settype( )

NAME

pthread_mutexattr_settype — set the mutex type attribute

SYNOPSIS

XSI   `#include <pthread.h>`

`int pthread_mutexattr_settype(pthread_mutexattr_t *attr, int type);`

DESCRIPTION

Refer to *pthread_mutexattr_gettype*( ).

NAME

pthread_once — dynamic package initialization

SYNOPSIS

THR   `#include <pthread.h>`

```
int pthread_once(pthread_once_t *once_control,
    void (*init_routine)(void));
pthread_once_t once_control = PTHREAD_ONCE_INIT;
```

DESCRIPTION

The first call to *pthread_once*() by any thread in a process, with a given *once_control*, shall call the *init_routine* with no arguments. Subsequent calls of *pthread_once*() with the same *once_control* shall not call the *init_routine*. On return from *pthread_once*(), *init_routine* shall have completed. The *once_control* parameter shall determine whether the associated initialization routine has been called.

The *pthread_once*() function is not a cancelation point. However, if *init_routine* is a cancelation point and is canceled, the effect on *once_control* shall be as if *pthread_once*() was never called.

The constant PTHREAD_ONCE_INIT is defined in the **<pthread.h>** header.

The behavior of *pthread_once*() is undefined if *once_control* has automatic storage duration or is not initialized by PTHREAD_ONCE_INIT.

RETURN VALUE

Upon successful completion, *pthread_once*() shall return zero; otherwise, an error number shall be returned to indicate the error.

ERRORS

The *pthread_once*() function may fail if:

[EINVAL]   If either *once_control* or *init_routine* is invalid.

The *pthread_once*() function shall not return an error code of [EINTR].

EXAMPLES

None.

APPLICATION USAGE

None.

RATIONALE

Some C libraries are designed for dynamic initialization. That is, the global initialization for the library is performed when the first procedure in the library is called. In a single-threaded program, this is normally implemented using a static variable whose value is checked on entry to a routine, as follows:

```
static int random_is_initialized = 0;
extern int initialize_random();

int random_function()
{
    if (random_is_initialized == 0) {
        initialize_random();
        random_is_initialized = 1;
    }
    ... /* Operations performed after initialization. */
}
```

To keep the same structure in a multi-threaded program, a new primitive is needed. Otherwise, library initialization has to be accomplished by an explicit call to a library-exported initialization function prior to any use of the library.

For dynamic library initialization in a multi-threaded process, a simple initialization flag is not sufficient; the flag needs to be protected against modification by multiple threads simultaneously calling into the library. Protecting the flag requires the use of a mutex; however, mutexes have to be initialized before they are used. Ensuring that the mutex is only initialized once requires a recursive solution to this problem.

The use of *pthread_once*( ) not only supplies an implementation-guaranteed means of dynamic initialization, it provides an aid to the reliable construction of multi-threaded and realtime systems. The preceding example then becomes:

```
#include <pthread.h>
static pthread_once_t random_is_initialized = PTHREAD_ONCE_INIT;
extern int initialize_random();

int random_function()
{
    (void) pthread_once(&random_is_initialized, initialize_random);
    ... /* Operations performed after initialization. */
}
```

Note that a **pthread_once_t** cannot be an array because some compilers do not accept the construct **&<array_name>**.

FUTURE DIRECTIONS

None.

SEE ALSO

The Base Definitions volume of IEEE Std 1003.1-2001, **<pthread.h>**

CHANGE HISTORY

First released in Issue 5. Included for alignment with the POSIX Threads Extension.

Issue 6

The *pthread_once*( ) function is marked as part of the Threads option.

The [EINVAL] error is added as a may fail case for if either argument is invalid.

NAME

pthread_rwlock_destroy, pthread_rwlock_init — destroy and initialize a read-write lock object

SYNOPSIS

THR   #include <pthread.h>

```
int pthread_rwlock_destroy(pthread_rwlock_t *rwlock);
int pthread_rwlock_init(pthread_rwlock_t *restrict rwlock,
    const pthread_rwlockattr_t *restrict attr);
```

DESCRIPTION

The *pthread_rwlock_destroy*( ) function shall destroy the read-write lock object referenced by *rwlock* and release any resources used by the lock. The effect of subsequent use of the lock is undefined until the lock is reinitialized by another call to *pthread_rwlock_init*( ). An implementation may cause *pthread_rwlock_destroy*( ) to set the object referenced by *rwlock* to an invalid value. Results are undefined if *pthread_rwlock_destroy*( ) is called when any thread holds *rwlock*. Attempting to destroy an uninitialized read-write lock results in undefined behavior.

The *pthread_rwlock_init*( ) function shall allocate any resources required to use the read-write lock referenced by *rwlock* and initializes the lock to an unlocked state with attributes referenced by *attr*. If *attr* is NULL, the default read-write lock attributes shall be used; the effect is the same as passing the address of a default read-write lock attributes object. Once initialized, the lock can be used any number of times without being reinitialized. Results are undefined if *pthread_rwlock_init*( ) is called specifying an already initialized read-write lock. Results are undefined if a read-write lock is used without first being initialized.

If the *pthread_rwlock_init*( ) function fails, *rwlock* shall not be initialized and the contents of *rwlock* are undefined.

Only the object referenced by *rwlock* may be used for performing synchronization. The result of referring to copies of that object in calls to *pthread_rwlock_destroy*( ), *pthread_rwlock_rdlock*( ), *pthread_rwlock_timedrdlock*( ), *pthread_rwlock_timedwrlock*( ), *pthread_rwlock_tryrdlock*( ), *pthread_rwlock_trywrlock*( ), *pthread_rwlock_unlock*( ), or *pthread_rwlock_wrlock*( ) is undefined.

RETURN VALUE

If successful, the *pthread_rwlock_destroy*( ) and *pthread_rwlock_init*( ) functions shall return zero; otherwise, an error number shall be returned to indicate the error.

The [EBUSY] and [EINVAL] error checks, if implemented, act as if they were performed immediately at the beginning of processing for the function and caused an error return prior to modifying the state of the read-write lock specified by *rwlock*.

ERRORS

The *pthread_rwlock_destroy*( ) function may fail if:

[EBUSY]   The implementation has detected an attempt to destroy the object referenced by *rwlock* while it is locked.

[EINVAL]   The value specified by *rwlock* is invalid.

The *pthread_rwlock_init*( ) function shall fail if:

[EAGAIN]   The system lacked the necessary resources (other than memory) to initialize another read-write lock.

[ENOMEM]   Insufficient memory exists to initialize the read-write lock.

[EPERM]   The caller does not have the privilege to perform the operation.

The *pthread_rwlock_init*( ) function may fail if:

[EBUSY]   The implementation has detected an attempt to reinitialize the object referenced by *rwlock*, a previously initialized but not yet destroyed read-write lock.

[EINVAL]   The value specified by *attr* is invalid.

These functions shall not return an error code of [EINTR].

EXAMPLES
None.

APPLICATION USAGE
None.

RATIONALE
None.

FUTURE DIRECTIONS
None.

SEE ALSO
pthread_rwlock_rdlock( ), *pthread_rwlock_timedrdlock*( ), *pthread_rwlock_timedwrlock*( ), *pthread_rwlock_tryrdlock*( ), *pthread_rwlock_trywrlock*( ), *pthread_rwlock_unlock*( ), *pthread_rwlock_wrlock*( ), the Base Definitions volume of IEEE Std 1003.1-2001, **<pthread.h>**

CHANGE HISTORY
First released in Issue 5.

Issue 6
The following changes are made for alignment with IEEE Std 1003.1j-2000:

- The margin code in the SYNOPSIS is changed to THR to indicate that the functionality is now part of the Threads option (previously it was part of the Read-Write Locks option in IEEE Std 1003.1j-2000 and also part of the XSI extension). The initializer macro is also deleted from the SYNOPSIS.

- The DESCRIPTION is updated as follows:

  — It explicitly notes allocation of resources upon initialization of a read-write lock object.

  — A paragraph is added specifying that copies of read-write lock objects may not be used.

- An [EINVAL] error is added to the ERRORS section for *pthread_rwlock_init*( ), indicating that the *rwlock* value is invalid.

- The SEE ALSO section is updated.

The **restrict** keyword is added to the *pthread_rwlock_init*( ) prototype for alignment with the ISO/IEC 9899: 1999 standard.

NAME

pthread_rwlock_rdlock, pthread_rwlock_tryrdlock — lock a read-write lock object for reading

SYNOPSIS

THR
```
#include <pthread.h>

int pthread_rwlock_rdlock(pthread_rwlock_t *rwlock);
int pthread_rwlock_tryrdlock(pthread_rwlock_t *rwlock);
```

DESCRIPTION

The *pthread_rwlock_rdlock*() function shall apply a read lock to the read-write lock referenced by *rwlock*. The calling thread acquires the read lock if a writer does not hold the lock and there are no writers blocked on the lock.

TPS
If the Thread Execution Scheduling option is supported, and the threads involved in the lock are executing with the scheduling policies SCHED_FIFO or SCHED_RR, the calling thread shall not acquire the lock if a writer holds the lock or if writers of higher or equal priority are blocked on the lock; otherwise, the calling thread shall acquire the lock.

TPS TSP
If the Threads Execution Scheduling option is supported, and the threads involved in the lock are executing with the SCHED_SPORADIC scheduling policy, the calling thread shall not acquire the lock if a writer holds the lock or if writers of higher or equal priority are blocked on the lock; otherwise, the calling thread shall acquire the lock.

If the Thread Execution Scheduling option is not supported, it is implementation-defined whether the calling thread acquires the lock when a writer does not hold the lock and there are writers blocked on the lock. If a writer holds the lock, the calling thread shall not acquire the read lock. If the read lock is not acquired, the calling thread shall block until it can acquire the lock. The calling thread may deadlock if at the time the call is made it holds a write lock.

A thread may hold multiple concurrent read locks on *rwlock* (that is, successfully call the *pthread_rwlock_rdlock*() function *n* times). If so, the application shall ensure that the thread performs matching unlocks (that is, it calls the *pthread_rwlock_unlock*() function *n* times).

The maximum number of simultaneous read locks that an implementation guarantees can be applied to a read-write lock shall be implementation-defined. The *pthread_rwlock_rdlock*() function may fail if this maximum would be exceeded.

The *pthread_rwlock_tryrdlock*() function shall apply a read lock as in the *pthread_rwlock_rdlock*() function, with the exception that the function shall fail if the equivalent *pthread_rwlock_rdlock*() call would have blocked the calling thread. In no case shall the *pthread_rwlock_tryrdlock*() function ever block; it always either acquires the lock or fails and returns immediately.

Results are undefined if any of these functions are called with an uninitialized read-write lock.

If a signal is delivered to a thread waiting for a read-write lock for reading, upon return from the signal handler the thread resumes waiting for the read-write lock for reading as if it was not interrupted.

RETURN VALUE

If successful, the *pthread_rwlock_rdlock*() function shall return zero; otherwise, an error number shall be returned to indicate the error.

The *pthread_rwlock_tryrdlock*() function shall return zero if the lock for reading on the read-write lock object referenced by *rwlock* is acquired. Otherwise, an error number shall be returned to indicate the error.

ERRORS

The *pthread_rwlock_tryrdlock* ( ) function shall fail if:

[EBUSY]   The read-write lock could not be acquired for reading because a writer holds the lock or a writer with the appropriate priority was blocked on it.

The *pthread_rwlock_rdlock* ( ) and *pthread_rwlock_tryrdlock* ( ) functions may fail if:

[EINVAL]   The value specified by *rwlock* does not refer to an initialized read-write lock object.

[EAGAIN]   The read lock could not be acquired because the maximum number of read locks for *rwlock* has been exceeded.

The *pthread_rwlock_rdlock* ( ) function may fail if:

[EDEADLK]   The current thread already owns the read-write lock for writing.

These functions shall not return an error code of [EINTR].

EXAMPLES

None.

APPLICATION USAGE

Applications using these functions may be subject to priority inversion, as discussed in the Base Definitions volume of IEEE Std 1003.1-2001, Section 3.285, Priority Inversion.

RATIONALE

None.

FUTURE DIRECTIONS

None.

SEE ALSO

pthread_rwlock_destroy ( ), *pthread_rwlock_timedrdlock* ( ), *pthread_rwlock_timedwrlock* ( ), *pthread_rwlock_trywrlock* ( ), *pthread_rwlock_unlock* ( ), *pthread_rwlock_wrlock* ( ), the Base Definitions volume of IEEE Std 1003.1-2001, **<pthread.h>**

CHANGE HISTORY

First released in Issue 5.

Issue 6

The following changes are made for alignment with IEEE Std 1003.1j-2000:

- The margin code in the SYNOPSIS is changed to THR to indicate that the functionality is now part of the Threads option (previously it was part of the Read-Write Locks option in IEEE Std 1003.1j-2000 and also part of the XSI extension).

- The DESCRIPTION is updated as follows:

  — Conditions under which writers have precedence over readers are specified.

  — Failure of *pthread_rwlock_tryrdlock* ( ) is clarified.

  — A paragraph on the maximum number of read locks is added.

- In the ERRORS sections, [EBUSY] is modified to take into account write priority, and [EDEADLK] is deleted as a *pthread_rwlock_tryrdlock* ( ) error.

- The SEE ALSO section is updated.

NAME

pthread_rwlock_timedrdlock — lock a read-write lock for reading

SYNOPSIS

THR TMO #include <pthread.h>
#include <time.h>

int pthread_rwlock_timedrdlock(pthread_rwlock_t *restrict *rwlock*,
        const struct timespec *restrict *abs_timeout*);

DESCRIPTION

The *pthread_rwlock_timedrdlock*( ) function shall apply a read lock to the read-write lock referenced by *rwlock* as in the *pthread_rwlock_rdlock*( ) function. However, if the lock cannot be acquired without waiting for other threads to unlock the lock, this wait shall be terminated when the specified timeout expires. The timeout shall expire when the absolute time specified by *abs_timeout* passes, as measured by the clock on which timeouts are based (that is, when the value of that clock equals or exceeds *abs_timeout*), or if the absolute time specified by *abs_timeout* has already been passed at the time of the call.

TMR If the Timers option is supported, the timeout shall be based on the CLOCK_REALTIME clock. If the Timers option is not supported, the timeout shall be based on the system clock as returned by the *time*( ) function. The resolution of the timeout shall be the resolution of the clock on which it is based. The **timespec** data type is defined in the **<time.h>** header. Under no circumstances shall the function fail with a timeout if the lock can be acquired immediately. The validity of the *abs_timeout* parameter need not be checked if the lock can be immediately acquired.

If a signal that causes a signal handler to be executed is delivered to a thread blocked on a read-write lock via a call to *pthread_rwlock_timedrdlock*( ), upon return from the signal handler the thread shall resume waiting for the lock as if it was not interrupted.

The calling thread may deadlock if at the time the call is made it holds a write lock on *rwlock*. The results are undefined if this function is called with an uninitialized read-write lock.

RETURN VALUE

The *pthread_rwlock_timedrdlock*( ) function shall return zero if the lock for reading on the read-write lock object referenced by *rwlock* is acquired. Otherwise, an error number shall be returned to indicate the error.

ERRORS

The *pthread_rwlock_timedrdlock*( ) function shall fail if:

[ETIMEDOUT]   The lock could not be acquired before the specified timeout expired.

The *pthread_rwlock_timedrdlock*( ) function may fail if:

[EAGAIN]   The read lock could not be acquired because the maximum number of read locks for lock would be exceeded.

[EDEADLK]   The calling thread already holds a write lock on *rwlock*.

[EINVAL]   The value specified by *rwlock* does not refer to an initialized read-write lock object, or the *abs_timeout* nanosecond value is less than zero or greater than or equal to 1 000 million.

This function shall not return an error code of [EINTR].

EXAMPLES

None.

APPLICATION USAGE

Applications using this function may be subject to priority inversion, as discussed in the Base Definitions volume of IEEE Std 1003.1-2001, Section 3.285, Priority Inversion.

The *pthread_rwlock_timedrdlock*( ) function is part of the Threads and Timeouts options and need not be provided on all implementations.

RATIONALE

None.

FUTURE DIRECTIONS

None.

SEE ALSO

pthread_rwlock_destroy( ), *pthread_rwlock_rdlock*( ), *pthread_rwlock_timedwrlock*( ), *pthread_rwlock_tryrdlock*( ), *pthread_rwlock_trywrlock*( ), *pthread_rwlock_unlock*( ), *pthread_rwlock_wrlock*( ), the Base Definitions volume of IEEE Std 1003.1-2001, **<pthread.h>**, **<time.h>**

CHANGE HISTORY

First released in Issue 6. Derived from IEEE Std 1003.1j-2000.

NAME

pthread_rwlock_timedwrlock — lock a read-write lock for writing

SYNOPSIS

THR TMO `#include <pthread.h>`
`#include <time.h>`

```
int pthread_rwlock_timedwrlock(pthread_rwlock_t *restrict rwlock,
    const struct timespec *restrict abs_timeout);
```

DESCRIPTION

The *pthread_rwlock_timedwrlock*() function shall apply a write lock to the read-write lock referenced by *rwlock* as in the *pthread_rwlock_wrlock*() function. However, if the lock cannot be acquired without waiting for other threads to unlock the lock, this wait shall be terminated when the specified timeout expires. The timeout shall expire when the absolute time specified by *abs_timeout* passes, as measured by the clock on which timeouts are based (that is, when the value of that clock equals or exceeds *abs_timeout*), or if the absolute time specified by *abs_timeout* has already been passed at the time of the call.

TMR If the Timers option is supported, the timeout shall be based on the CLOCK_REALTIME clock. If the Timers option is not supported, the timeout shall be based on the system clock as returned by the *time*() function. The resolution of the timeout shall be the resolution of the clock on which it is based. The **timespec** data type is defined in the **<time.h>** header. Under no circumstances shall the function fail with a timeout if the lock can be acquired immediately. The validity of the *abs_timeout* parameter need not be checked if the lock can be immediately acquired.

If a signal that causes a signal handler to be executed is delivered to a thread blocked on a read-write lock via a call to *pthread_rwlock_timedwrlock*(), upon return from the signal handler the thread shall resume waiting for the lock as if it was not interrupted.

The calling thread may deadlock if at the time the call is made it holds the read-write lock. The results are undefined if this function is called with an uninitialized read-write lock.

RETURN VALUE

The *pthread_rwlock_timedwrlock*() function shall return zero if the lock for writing on the read-write lock object referenced by *rwlock* is acquired. Otherwise, an error number shall be returned to indicate the error.

ERRORS

The *pthread_rwlock_timedwrlock*() function shall fail if:

[ETIMEDOUT]   The lock could not be acquired before the specified timeout expired.

The *pthread_rwlock_timedwrlock*() function may fail if:

[EDEADLK]   The calling thread already holds the *rwlock*.

[EINVAL]   The value specified by rwlock does not refer to an initialized read-write lock object, or the *abs_timeout* nanosecond value is less than zero or greater than or equal to 1 000 million.

This function shall not return an error code of [EINTR].

EXAMPLES

None.

APPLICATION USAGE

Applications using this function may be subject to priority inversion, as discussed in the Base Definitions volume of IEEE Std 1003.1-2001, Section 3.285, Priority Inversion.

The *pthread_rwlock_timedwrlock*( ) function is part of the Threads and Timeouts options and need not be provided on all implementations.

RATIONALE

None.

FUTURE DIRECTIONS

None.

SEE ALSO

pthread_rwlock_destroy( ), *pthread_rwlock_rdlock*( ), *pthread_rwlock_timedrdlock*( ), *pthread_rwlock_tryrdlock*( ), *pthread_rwlock_trywrlock*( ), *pthread_rwlock_unlock*( ), *pthread_rwlock_wrlock*( ), the Base Definitions volume of IEEE Std 1003.1-2001, **<pthread.h>**, **<time.h>**

CHANGE HISTORY

First released in Issue 6. Derived from IEEE Std 1003.1j-2000.

NAME

pthread_rwlock_tryrdlock — lock a read-write lock object for reading

SYNOPSIS

THR   `#include <pthread.h>`

`int pthread_rwlock_tryrdlock(pthread_rwlock_t *rwlock);`

DESCRIPTION

Refer to *pthread_rwlock_rdlock*().

NAME

pthread_rwlock_trywrlock, pthread_rwlock_wrlock — lock a read-write lock object for writing

SYNOPSIS

THR   `#include <pthread.h>`

```
int pthread_rwlock_trywrlock(pthread_rwlock_t *rwlock);
int pthread_rwlock_wrlock(pthread_rwlock_t *rwlock);
```

DESCRIPTION

The *pthread_rwlock_trywrlock*() function shall apply a write lock like the *pthread_rwlock_wrlock*() function, with the exception that the function shall fail if any thread currently holds *rwlock* (for reading or writing).

The *pthread_rwlock_wrlock*() function shall apply a write lock to the read-write lock referenced by *rwlock*. The calling thread acquires the write lock if no other thread (reader or writer) holds the read-write lock *rwlock*. Otherwise, the thread shall block until it can acquire the lock. The calling thread may deadlock if at the time the call is made it holds the read-write lock (whether a read or write lock).

Implementations may favor writers over readers to avoid writer starvation.

Results are undefined if any of these functions are called with an uninitialized read-write lock.

If a signal is delivered to a thread waiting for a read-write lock for writing, upon return from the signal handler the thread resumes waiting for the read-write lock for writing as if it was not interrupted.

RETURN VALUE

The *pthread_rwlock_trywrlock*() function shall return zero if the lock for writing on the read-write lock object referenced by *rwlock* is acquired. Otherwise, an error number shall be returned to indicate the error.

If successful, the *pthread_rwlock_wrlock*() function shall return zero; otherwise, an error number shall be returned to indicate the error.

ERRORS

The *pthread_rwlock_trywrlock*() function shall fail if:

[EBUSY]   The read-write lock could not be acquired for writing because it was already locked for reading or writing.

The *pthread_rwlock_trywrlock*() and *pthread_rwlock_wrlock*() functions may fail if:

[EINVAL]   The value specified by *rwlock* does not refer to an initialized read-write lock object.

The *pthread_rwlock_wrlock*() function may fail if:

[EDEADLK]   The current thread already owns the read-write lock for writing or reading.

These functions shall not return an error code of [EINTR].

EXAMPLES
None.

APPLICATION USAGE
Applications using these functions may be subject to priority inversion, as discussed in the Base Definitions volume of IEEE Std 1003.1-2001, Section 3.285, Priority Inversion.

RATIONALE
None.

FUTURE DIRECTIONS
None.

SEE ALSO
pthread_rwlock_destroy( ), *pthread_rwlock_rdlock*( ), *pthread_rwlock_timedrdlock*( ), *pthread_rwlock_timedwrlock*( ), *pthread_rwlock_tryrdlock*( ), *pthread_rwlock_unlock*( ), the Base Definitions volume of IEEE Std 1003.1-2001, **<pthread.h>**

CHANGE HISTORY
First released in Issue 5.

Issue 6
The following changes are made for alignment with IEEE Std 1003.1j-2000:

- The margin code in the SYNOPSIS is changed to THR to indicate that the functionality is now part of the Threads option (previously it was part of the Read-Write Locks option in IEEE Std 1003.1j-2000 and also part of the XSI extension).

- The [EDEADLK] error is deleted as a *pthread_rwlock_trywrlock*( ) error.

- The SEE ALSO section is updated.

NAME

pthread_rwlock_unlock — unlock a read-write lock object

SYNOPSIS

THR   ```
#include <pthread.h>
```

```
int pthread_rwlock_unlock(pthread_rwlock_t *rwlock);
```

DESCRIPTION

The *pthread_rwlock_unlock*( ) function shall release a lock held on the read-write lock object referenced by *rwlock*. Results are undefined if the read-write lock *rwlock* is not held by the calling thread.

If this function is called to release a read lock from the read-write lock object and there are other read locks currently held on this read-write lock object, the read-write lock object remains in the read locked state. If this function releases the last read lock for this read-write lock object, the read-write lock object shall be put in the unlocked state with no owners.

If this function is called to release a write lock for this read-write lock object, the read-write lock object shall be put in the unlocked state.

TPS   If there are threads blocked on the lock when it becomes available, the scheduling policy shall determine which thread(s) shall acquire the lock. If the Thread Execution Scheduling option is supported, when threads executing with the scheduling policies SCHED_FIFO, SCHED_RR, or SCHED_SPORADIC are waiting on the lock, they shall acquire the lock in priority order when the lock becomes available. For equal priority threads, write locks shall take precedence over read locks. If the Thread Execution Scheduling option is not supported, it is implementation-defined whether write locks take precedence over read locks.

Results are undefined if any of these functions are called with an uninitialized read-write lock.

RETURN VALUE

If successful, the *pthread_rwlock_unlock*( ) function shall return zero; otherwise, an error number shall be returned to indicate the error.

ERRORS

The *pthread_rwlock_unlock*( ) function may fail if:

[EINVAL]   The value specified by *rwlock* does not refer to an initialized read-write lock object.

[EPERM]   The current thread does not hold a lock on the read-write lock.

The *pthread_rwlock_unlock*( ) function shall not return an error code of [EINTR].

EXAMPLES

None.

APPLICATION USAGE

None.

RATIONALE

None.

FUTURE DIRECTIONS

None.
```

SEE ALSO

pthread_rwlock_destroy(), *pthread_rwlock_rdlock*(), *pthread_rwlock_timedrdlock*(),
pthread_rwlock_timedwrlock(), *pthread_rwlock_tryrdlock*(), *pthread_rwlock_trywrlock*(),
pthread_rwlock_wrlock(), the Base Definitions volume of IEEE Std 1003.1-2001, **<pthread.h>**

CHANGE HISTORY

First released in Issue 5.

Issue 6

The following changes are made for alignment with IEEE Std 1003.1j-2000:

- The margin code in the SYNOPSIS is changed to THR to indicate that the functionality is now part of the Threads option (previously it was part of the Read-Write Locks option in IEEE Std 1003.1j-2000 and also part of the XSI extension).

- The DESCRIPTION is updated as follows:

  — The conditions under which writers have precedence over readers are specified.

  — The concept of read-write lock owner is deleted.

- The SEE ALSO section is updated.

NAME

pthread_rwlock_wrlock — lock a read-write lock object for writing

SYNOPSIS

THR   `#include <pthread.h>`

`int pthread_rwlock_wrlock(pthread_rwlock_t *rwlock);`

DESCRIPTION

Refer to *pthread_rwlock_trywrlock*( ).

NAME

pthread_rwlockattr_destroy, pthread_rwlockattr_init — destroy and initialize the read-write lock attributes object

SYNOPSIS

THR `#include <pthread.h>`

```
int pthread_rwlockattr_destroy(pthread_rwlockattr_t *attr);
int pthread_rwlockattr_init(pthread_rwlockattr_t *attr);
```

DESCRIPTION

The *pthread_rwlockattr_destroy*( ) function shall destroy a read-write lock attributes object. A destroyed *attr* attributes object can be reinitialized using *pthread_rwlockattr_init*( ); the results of otherwise referencing the object after it has been destroyed are undefined. An implementation may cause *pthread_rwlockattr_destroy*( ) to set the object referenced by *attr* to an invalid value.

The *pthread_rwlockattr_init*( ) function shall initialize a read-write lock attributes object *attr* with the default value for all of the attributes defined by the implementation.

Results are undefined if *pthread_rwlockattr_init*( ) is called specifying an already initialized *attr* attributes object.

After a read-write lock attributes object has been used to initialize one or more read-write locks, any function affecting the attributes object (including destruction) shall not affect any previously initialized read-write locks.

RETURN VALUE

If successful, the *pthread_rwlockattr_destroy*( ) and *pthread_rwlockattr_init*( ) functions shall return zero; otherwise, an error number shall be returned to indicate the error.

ERRORS

The *pthread_rwlockattr_destroy*( ) function may fail if:

[EINVAL]   The value specified by *attr* is invalid.

The *pthread_rwlockattr_init*( ) function shall fail if:

[ENOMEM]   Insufficient memory exists to initialize the read-write lock attributes object.

These functions shall not return an error code of [EINTR].

EXAMPLES

None.

APPLICATION USAGE

None.

RATIONALE

None.

FUTURE DIRECTIONS

None.

SEE ALSO

pthread_rwlock_destroy( ), *pthread_rwlockattr_getpshared*( ), *pthread_rwlockattr_setpshared*( ), the Base Definitions volume of IEEE Std 1003.1-2001, **<pthread.h>**

CHANGE HISTORY

First released in Issue 5.

Issue 6

The following changes are made for alignment with IEEE Std 1003.1j-2000:

- The margin code in the SYNOPSIS is changed to THR to indicate that the functionality is now part of the Threads option (previously it was part of the Read-Write Locks option in IEEE Std 1003.1j-2000 and also part of the XSI extension).

- The SEE ALSO section is updated.

NAME

pthread_rwlockattr_getpshared, pthread_rwlockattr_setpshared — get and set the process-shared attribute of the read-write lock attributes object

SYNOPSIS

THR TSH `#include <pthread.h>`

```
int pthread_rwlockattr_getpshared(const pthread_rwlockattr_t *
    restrict attr, int *restrict pshared);
int pthread_rwlockattr_setpshared(pthread_rwlockattr_t *attr,
    int pshared);
```

DESCRIPTION

The *pthread_rwlockattr_getpshared*( ) function shall obtain the value of the *process-shared* attribute from the initialized attributes object referenced by *attr*. The *pthread_rwlockattr_setpshared*( ) function shall set the *process-shared* attribute in an initialized attributes object referenced by *attr*.

The *process-shared* attribute shall be set to PTHREAD_PROCESS_SHARED to permit a read-write lock to be operated upon by any thread that has access to the memory where the read-write lock is allocated, even if the read-write lock is allocated in memory that is shared by multiple processes. If the *process-shared* attribute is PTHREAD_PROCESS_PRIVATE, the read-write lock shall only be operated upon by threads created within the same process as the thread that initialized the read-write lock; if threads of differing processes attempt to operate on such a read-write lock, the behavior is undefined. The default value of the *process-shared* attribute shall be PTHREAD_PROCESS_PRIVATE.

Additional attributes, their default values, and the names of the associated functions to get and set those attribute values are implementation-defined.

RETURN VALUE

Upon successful completion, the *pthread_rwlockattr_getpshared*( ) function shall return zero and store the value of the *process-shared* attribute of *attr* into the object referenced by the *pshared* parameter. Otherwise, an error number shall be returned to indicate the error.

If successful, the *pthread_rwlockattr_setpshared*( ) function shall return zero; otherwise, an error number shall be returned to indicate the error.

ERRORS

The *pthread_rwlockattr_getpshared*( ) and *pthread_rwlockattr_setpshared*( ) functions may fail if:

[EINVAL]   The value specified by *attr* is invalid.

The *pthread_rwlockattr_setpshared*( ) function may fail if:

[EINVAL]   The new value specified for the attribute is outside the range of legal values for that attribute.

These functions shall not return an error code of [EINTR].

EXAMPLES

    None.

APPLICATION USAGE

    None.

RATIONALE

    None.

FUTURE DIRECTIONS

    None.

SEE ALSO

    pthread_rwlock_destroy(), *pthread_rwlockattr_destroy*(), *pthread_rwlockattr_init*(), the Base Definitions volume of IEEE Std 1003.1-2001, **<pthread.h>**

CHANGE HISTORY

    First released in Issue 5.

Issue 6

    The following changes are made for alignment with IEEE Std 1003.1j-2000:

- The margin code in the SYNOPSIS is changed to THR TSH to indicate that the functionality is now part of the Threads option (previously it was part of the Read-Write Locks option in IEEE Std 1003.1j-2000 and also part of the XSI extension).

- The DESCRIPTION notes that additional attributes are implementation-defined.

- The SEE ALSO section is updated.

The **restrict** keyword is added to the *pthread_rwlockattr_getpshared*() prototype for alignment with the ISO/IEC 9899: 1999 standard.

NAME

pthread_rwlockattr_init — initialize the read-write lock attributes object

SYNOPSIS

XSI

```
#include <pthread.h>

int pthread_rwlockattr_init(pthread_rwlockattr_t *attr);
```

DESCRIPTION

Refer to *pthread_rwlockattr_destroy*().

NAME

pthread_rwlockattr_setpshared — set the process-shared attribute of the read-write lock attributes object

SYNOPSIS

XSI
```
#include <pthread.h>
```
```
int pthread_rwlockattr_setpshared(pthread_rwlockattr_t *attr,
    int pshared);
```

DESCRIPTION

Refer to *pthread_rwlockattr_getpshared* ( ).

NAME

pthread_self — get the calling thread ID

SYNOPSIS

THR   #include <pthread.h>

pthread_t pthread_self(void);

DESCRIPTION

The *pthread_self*( ) function shall return the thread ID of the calling thread.

RETURN VALUE

Refer to the DESCRIPTION.

ERRORS

No errors are defined.

The *pthread_self*( ) function shall not return an error code of [EINTR].

EXAMPLES

None.

APPLICATION USAGE

None.

RATIONALE

The *pthread_self*( ) function provides a capability similar to the *getpid*( ) function for processes and the rationale is the same: the creation call does not provide the thread ID to the created thread.

FUTURE DIRECTIONS

None.

SEE ALSO

pthread_create( ), *pthread_equal*( ), the Base Definitions volume of IEEE Std 1003.1-2001, **<pthread.h>**

CHANGE HISTORY

First released in Issue 5. Included for alignment with the POSIX Threads Extension.

Issue 6

The *pthread_self*( ) function is marked as part of the Threads option.

NAME

pthread_setcancelstate, pthread_setcanceltype, pthread_testcancel — set cancelability state

SYNOPSIS

THR   #include <pthread.h>

```
int pthread_setcancelstate(int state, int *oldstate);
int pthread_setcanceltype(int type, int *oldtype);
void pthread_testcancel(void);
```

DESCRIPTION

The *pthread_setcancelstate*( ) function shall atomically both set the calling thread's cancelability state to the indicated *state* and return the previous cancelability state at the location referenced by *oldstate*. Legal values for *state* are PTHREAD_CANCEL_ENABLE and PTHREAD_CANCEL_DISABLE.

The *pthread_setcanceltype*( ) function shall atomically both set the calling thread's cancelability type to the indicated *type* and return the previous cancelability type at the location referenced by *oldtype*. Legal values for *type* are PTHREAD_CANCEL_DEFERRED and PTHREAD_CANCEL_ASYNCHRONOUS.

The cancelability state and type of any newly created threads, including the thread in which *main*( ) was first invoked, shall be PTHREAD_CANCEL_ENABLE and PTHREAD_CANCEL_DEFERRED respectively.

The *pthread_testcancel*( ) function shall create a cancelation point in the calling thread. The *pthread_testcancel*( ) function shall have no effect if cancelability is disabled.

RETURN VALUE

If successful, the *pthread_setcancelstate*( ) and *pthread_setcanceltype*( ) functions shall return zero; otherwise, an error number shall be returned to indicate the error.

ERRORS

The *pthread_setcancelstate*( ) function may fail if:

[EINVAL]   The specified state is not PTHREAD_CANCEL_ENABLE or PTHREAD_CANCEL_DISABLE.

The *pthread_setcanceltype*( ) function may fail if:

[EINVAL]   The specified type is not PTHREAD_CANCEL_DEFERRED or PTHREAD_CANCEL_ASYNCHRONOUS.

These functions shall not return an error code of [EINTR].

EXAMPLES

None.

APPLICATION USAGE

None.

RATIONALE

The *pthread_setcancelstate*( ) and *pthread_setcanceltype*( ) functions control the points at which a thread may be asynchronously canceled. For cancelation control to be usable in modular fashion, some rules need to be followed.

An object can be considered to be a generalization of a procedure. It is a set of procedures and global variables written as a unit and called by clients not known by the object. Objects may depend on other objects.

First, cancelability should only be disabled on entry to an object, never explicitly enabled. On exit from an object, the cancelability state should always be restored to its value on entry to the object.

This follows from a modularity argument: if the client of an object (or the client of an object that uses that object) has disabled cancelability, it is because the client does not want to be concerned about cleaning up if the thread is canceled while executing some sequence of actions. If an object is called in such a state and it enables cancelability and a cancelation request is pending for that thread, then the thread is canceled, contrary to the wish of the client that disabled.

Second, the cancelability type may be explicitly set to either *deferred* or *asynchronous* upon entry to an object. But as with the cancelability state, on exit from an object the cancelability type should always be restored to its value on entry to the object.

Finally, only functions that are cancel-safe may be called from a thread that is asynchronously cancelable.

FUTURE DIRECTIONS

None.

SEE ALSO

pthread_cancel ( ), the Base Definitions volume of IEEE Std 1003.1-2001, **<pthread.h>**

CHANGE HISTORY

First released in Issue 5. Included for alignment with the POSIX Threads Extension.

Issue 6

The *pthread_setcancelstate* ( ), *pthread_setcanceltype* ( ), and *pthread_testcancel* ( ) functions are marked as part of the Threads option.

NAME

pthread_setconcurrency — set the level of concurrency

SYNOPSIS

XSI   `#include <pthread.h>`

`int pthread_setconcurrency(int new_level);`

DESCRIPTION

Refer to *pthread_getconcurrency* ( ).

NAME

pthread_setschedparam — dynamic thread scheduling parameters access (**REALTIME THREADS**)

SYNOPSIS

THR TPS `#include <pthread.h>`

```
int pthread_setschedparam(pthread_t thread, int policy,
    const struct sched_param *param);
```

DESCRIPTION

Refer to *pthread_getschedparam* ( ).

NAME

pthread_setschedprio — dynamic thread scheduling parameters access (**REALTIME THREADS**)

SYNOPSIS

THR TPS `#include <pthread.h>`

`int pthread_setschedprio(pthread_t thread, int prio);`

DESCRIPTION

The *pthread_setschedprio*( ) function shall set the scheduling priority for the thread whose thread ID is given by *thread* to the value given by *prio*. See **Scheduling Policies** (on page 44) for a description on how this function call affects the ordering of the thread in the thread list for its new priority.

If the *pthread_setschedprio*( ) function fails, the scheduling priority of the target thread shall not be changed.

RETURN VALUE

If successful, the *pthread_setschedprio*( ) function shall return zero; otherwise, an error number shall be returned to indicate the error.

ERRORS

The *pthread_setschedprio*( ) function may fail if:

[EINVAL]	The value of *prio* is invalid for the scheduling policy of the specified thread.
[ENOTSUP]	An attempt was made to set the priority to an unsupported value.
[EPERM]	The caller does not have the appropriate permission to set the scheduling policy of the specified thread.
[EPERM]	The implementation does not allow the application to modify the priority to the value specified.
[ESRCH]	The value specified by *thread* does not refer to an existing thread.

The *pthread_setschedprio*( ) function shall not return an error code of [EINTR].

EXAMPLES

None.

APPLICATION USAGE

None.

RATIONALE

The *pthread_setschedprio*( ) function provides a way for an application to temporarily raise its priority and then lower it again, without having the undesired side effect of yielding to other threads of the same priority. This is necessary if the application is to implement its own strategies for bounding priority inversion, such as priority inheritance or priority ceilings. This capability is especially important if the implementation does not support the Thread Priority Protection or Thread Priority Inheritance options, but even if those options are supported it is needed if the application is to bound priority inheritance for other resources, such as semaphores.

The standard developers considered that while it might be preferable conceptually to solve this problem by modifying the specification of *pthread_setschedparam*( ), it was too late to make such a change, as there may be implementations that would need to be changed. Therefore, this new function was introduced.

FUTURE DIRECTIONS
     None.

SEE ALSO
     Scheduling Policies (on page 44), *pthread_getschedparam*( ), the Base Definitions volume of
     IEEE Std 1003.1-2001, **<pthread.h>**

CHANGE HISTORY
     First released in Issue 6. Included as a response to IEEE PASC Interpretation 1003.1 #96.

NAME

pthread_setspecific — thread-specific data management

SYNOPSIS

THR   `#include <pthread.h>`

`int pthread_setspecific(pthread_key_t key, const void *value);`

DESCRIPTION

Refer to *pthread_getspecific* ( ).

NAME

    pthread_testcancel — set cancelability state

SYNOPSIS

THR   `#include <pthread.h>`

       `void pthread_testcancel(void);`

DESCRIPTION

    Refer to *pthread_setcancelstate*( ).

POSIX Standard
for Process Management

This appendix contains sections from the POSIX Standard for Process Management. Portable Operating System Interface (POSIX) is the open operating system interface standard accepted worldwide. It is produced by IEEE and recognized by ISO and ANSI. Support of POSIX standards ensures code portability between systems and is increasingly mandated for commercial applications and government contracts. The POSIX Standard is the most widely available method for cross-platform multicore development. It is compatible with high-level libraries such as the Standard Template Adaptive Parallel Library (STAPL) and new Standard C++0x. The POSIX Standard is voluminous, containing thousands of pages. Here, for your convenience, are selected sections from the standard on process management. The API functions contained in these selected sections were either covered in this book or are of concern when developing multicore applications.

The following excerpts are reprinted with permission from *IEEE Std. 1003.1-2001, IEEE Standard for Information Technology - Portable Operating System Interface (POSIX)*, Copyright 2001, by IEEE. The IEEE disclaims any responsibility or liability resulting from the placement and use in the described manner.

NAME

posix_spawn, posix_spawnp — spawn a process (**ADVANCED REALTIME**)

SYNOPSIS

SPN   `#include <spawn.h>`

```
int posix_spawn(pid_t *restrict pid, const char *restrict path,
    const posix_spawn_file_actions_t *file_actions,
    const posix_spawnattr_t *restrict attrp,
    char *const argv[restrict], char *const envp[restrict]);
int posix_spawnp(pid_t *restrict pid, const char *restrict file,
    const posix_spawn_file_actions_t *file_actions,
    const posix_spawnattr_t *restrict attrp,
    char *const argv[restrict], char * const envp[restrict]);
```

DESCRIPTION

The *posix_spawn*() and *posix_spawnp*() functions shall create a new process (child process) from the specified process image. The new process image shall be constructed from a regular executable file called the new process image file.

When a C program is executed as the result of this call, it shall be entered as a C-language function call as follows:

`int main(int argc, char *argv[]);`

where *argc* is the argument count and *argv* is an array of character pointers to the arguments themselves. In addition, the following variable:

`extern char **environ;`

shall be initialized as a pointer to an array of character pointers to the environment strings.

The argument *argv* is an array of character pointers to null-terminated strings. The last member of this array shall be a null pointer and is not counted in *argc*. These strings constitute the argument list available to the new process image. The value in *argv*[0] should point to a filename that is associated with the process image being started by the *posix_spawn*() or *posix_spawnp*() function.

The argument *envp* is an array of character pointers to null-terminated strings. These strings constitute the environment for the new process image. The environment array is terminated by a null pointer.

The number of bytes available for the child process' combined argument and environment lists is {ARG_MAX}. The implementation shall specify in the system documentation (see the Base Definitions volume of IEEE Std 1003.1-2001, Chapter 2, Conformance) whether any list overhead, such as length words, null terminators, pointers, or alignment bytes, is included in this total.

The *path* argument to *posix_spawn*() is a pathname that identifies the new process image file to execute.

The *file* parameter to *posix_spawnp*() shall be used to construct a pathname that identifies the new process image file. If the *file* parameter contains a slash character, the *file* parameter shall be used as the pathname for the new process image file. Otherwise, the path prefix for this file shall be obtained by a search of the directories passed as the environment variable *PATH* (see the Base Definitions volume of IEEE Std 1003.1-2001, Chapter 8, Environment Variables). If this environment variable is not defined, the results of the search are implementation-defined.

If *file_actions* is a null pointer, then file descriptors open in the calling process shall remain open in the child process, except for those whose close-on-*exec* flag FD_CLOEXEC is set (see *fcntl* ( )). For those file descriptors that remain open, all attributes of the corresponding open file descriptions, including file locks (see *fcntl* ( )), shall remain unchanged.

If *file_actions* is not NULL, then the file descriptors open in the child process shall be those open in the calling process as modified by the spawn file actions object pointed to by *file_actions* and the FD_CLOEXEC flag of each remaining open file descriptor after the spawn file actions have been processed. The effective order of processing the spawn file actions shall be:

1. The set of open file descriptors for the child process shall initially be the same set as is open for the calling process. All attributes of the corresponding open file descriptions, including file locks (see *fcntl* ( )), shall remain unchanged.

2. The signal mask, signal default actions, and the effective user and group IDs for the child process shall be changed as specified in the attributes object referenced by *attrp*.

3. The file actions specified by the spawn file actions object shall be performed in the order in which they were added to the spawn file actions object.

4. Any file descriptor that has its FD_CLOEXEC flag set (see *fcntl* ( )) shall be closed.

The **posix_spawnattr_t** spawn attributes object type is defined in **<spawn.h>**. It shall contain at least the attributes defined below.

If the POSIX_SPAWN_SETPGROUP flag is set in the *spawn-flags* attribute of the object referenced by *attrp*, and the *spawn-pgroup* attribute of the same object is non-zero, then the child's process group shall be as specified in the *spawn-pgroup* attribute of the object referenced by *attrp*.

As a special case, if the POSIX_SPAWN_SETPGROUP flag is set in the *spawn-flags* attribute of the object referenced by *attrp*, and the *spawn-pgroup* attribute of the same object is set to zero, then the child shall be in a new process group with a process group ID equal to its process ID.

If the POSIX_SPAWN_SETPGROUP flag is not set in the *spawn-flags* attribute of the object referenced by *attrp*, the new child process shall inherit the parent's process group.

PS   If the POSIX_SPAWN_SETSCHEDPARAM flag is set in the *spawn-flags* attribute of the object referenced by *attrp*, but POSIX_SPAWN_SETSCHEDULER is not set, the new process image shall initially have the scheduling policy of the calling process with the scheduling parameters specified in the *spawn-schedparam* attribute of the object referenced by *attrp*.

If the POSIX_SPAWN_SETSCHEDULER flag is set in the *spawn-flags* attribute of the object referenced by *attrp* (regardless of the setting of the POSIX_SPAWN_SETSCHEDPARAM flag), the new process image shall initially have the scheduling policy specified in the *spawn-schedpolicy* attribute of the object referenced by *attrp* and the scheduling parameters specified in the *spawn-schedparam* attribute of the same object.

The POSIX_SPAWN_RESETIDS flag in the *spawn-flags* attribute of the object referenced by *attrp* governs the effective user ID of the child process. If this flag is not set, the child process shall inherit the parent process' effective user ID. If this flag is set, the child process' effective user ID shall be reset to the parent's real user ID. In either case, if the set-user-ID mode bit of the new process image file is set, the effective user ID of the child process shall become that file's owner ID before the new process image begins execution.

The POSIX_SPAWN_RESETIDS flag in the *spawn-flags* attribute of the object referenced by *attrp* also governs the effective group ID of the child process. If this flag is not set, the child process shall inherit the parent process' effective group ID. If this flag is set, the child process' effective group ID shall be reset to the parent's real group ID. In either case, if the set-group-ID mode bit of the new process image file is set, the effective group ID of the child process shall become that file's group ID before the new process image begins execution.

If the POSIX_SPAWN_SETSIGMASK flag is set in the *spawn-flags* attribute of the object referenced by *attrp*, the child process shall initially have the signal mask specified in the *spawn-sigmask* attribute of the object referenced by *attrp*.

If the POSIX_SPAWN_SETSIGDEF flag is set in the *spawn-flags* attribute of the object referenced by *attrp*, the signals specified in the *spawn-sigdefault* attribute of the same object shall be set to their default actions in the child process. Signals set to the default action in the parent process shall be set to the default action in the child process.

Signals set to be caught by the calling process shall be set to the default action in the child process.

Except for SIGCHLD, signals set to be ignored by the calling process image shall be set to be ignored by the child process, unless otherwise specified by the POSIX_SPAWN_SETSIGDEF flag being set in the *spawn-flags* attribute of the object referenced by *attrp* and the signals being indicated in the *spawn-sigdefault* attribute of the object referenced by *attrp*.

If the SIGCHLD signal is set to be ignored by the calling process, it is unspecified whether the SIGCHLD signal is set to be ignored or to the default action in the child process, unless otherwise specified by the POSIX_SPAWN_SETSIGDEF flag being set in the *spawn_flags* attribute of the object referenced by *attrp* and the SIGCHLD signal being indicated in the *spawn_sigdefault* attribute of the object referenced by *attrp*.

If the value of the *attrp* pointer is NULL, then the default values are used.

All process attributes, other than those influenced by the attributes set in the object referenced by *attrp* as specified above or by the file descriptor manipulations specified in *file_actions*, shall appear in the new process image as though *fork*( ) had been called to create a child process and then a member of the *exec* family of functions had been called by the child process to execute the new process image.

THR It is implementation-defined whether the fork handlers are run when *posix_spawn*( ) or *posix_spawnp*( ) is called.

RETURN VALUE

Upon successful completion, *posix_spawn*( ) and *posix_spawnp*( ) shall return the process ID of the child process to the parent process, in the variable pointed to by a non-NULL *pid* argument, and shall return zero as the function return value. Otherwise, no child process shall be created, the value stored into the variable pointed to by a non-NULL *pid* is unspecified, and an error number shall be returned as the function return value to indicate the error. If the *pid* argument is a null pointer, the process ID of the child is not returned to the caller.

ERRORS

The *posix_spawn*( ) and *posix_spawnp*( ) functions may fail if:

[EINVAL]   The value specified by *file_actions* or *attrp* is invalid.

If this error occurs after the calling process successfully returns from the *posix_spawn*( ) or *posix_spawnp*( ) function, the child process may exit with exit status 127.

If *posix_spawn*( ) or *posix_spawnp*( ) fail for any of the reasons that would cause *fork*( ) or one of the *exec* family of functions to fail, an error value shall be returned as described by *fork*( ) and *exec*, respectively (or, if the error occurs after the calling process successfully returns, the child process shall exit with exit status 127).

If POSIX_SPAWN_SETPGROUP is set in the *spawn-flags* attribute of the object referenced by *attrp*, and *posix_spawn*() or *posix_spawnp*() fails while changing the child's process group, an error value shall be returned as described by *setpgid*() (or, if the error occurs after the calling process successfully returns, the child process shall exit with exit status 127).

PS   If POSIX_SPAWN_SETSCHEDPARAM is set and POSIX_SPAWN_SETSCHEDULER is not set in the *spawn-flags* attribute of the object referenced by *attrp*, then if *posix_spawn*() or *posix_spawnp*() fails for any of the reasons that would cause *sched_setparam*() to fail, an error value shall be returned as described by *sched_setparam*() (or, if the error occurs after the calling process successfully returns, the child process shall exit with exit status 127).

If POSIX_SPAWN_SETSCHEDULER is set in the *spawn-flags* attribute of the object referenced by *attrp*, and if *posix_spawn*() or *posix_spawnp*() fails for any of the reasons that would cause *sched_setscheduler*() to fail, an error value shall be returned as described by *sched_setscheduler*() (or, if the error occurs after the calling process successfully returns, the child process shall exit with exit status 127).

If the *file_actions* argument is not NULL, and specifies any *close*, *dup2*, or *open* actions to be performed, and if *posix_spawn*() or *posix_spawnp*() fails for any of the reasons that would cause *close*(), *dup2*(), or *open*() to fail, an error value shall be returned as described by *close*(), *dup2*(), and *open*(), respectively (or, if the error occurs after the calling process successfully returns, the child process shall exit with exit status 127). An open file action may, by itself, result in any of the errors described by *close*() or *dup2*(), in addition to those described by *open*().

EXAMPLES

None.

APPLICATION USAGE

These functions are part of the Spawn option and need not be provided on all implementations.

RATIONALE

The *posix_spawn*() function and its close relation *posix_spawnp*() have been introduced to overcome the following perceived difficulties with *fork*(): the *fork*() function is difficult or impossible to implement without swapping or dynamic address translation.

- Swapping is generally too slow for a realtime environment.

- Dynamic address translation is not available everywhere that POSIX might be useful.

- Processes are too useful to simply option out of POSIX whenever it must run without address translation or other MMU services.

Thus, POSIX needs process creation and file execution primitives that can be efficiently implemented without address translation or other MMU services.

The *posix_spawn*() function is implementable as a library routine, but both *posix_spawn*() and *posix_spawnp*() are designed as kernel operations. Also, although they may be an efficient replacement for many *fork*()/*exec* pairs, their goal is to provide useful process creation primitives for systems that have difficulty with *fork*(), not to provide drop-in replacements for *fork*()/*exec*.

This view of the role of *posix_spawn*() and *posix_spawnp*() influenced the design of their API. It does not attempt to provide the full functionality of *fork*()/*exec* in which arbitrary user-specified operations of any sort are permitted between the creation of the child process and the execution of the new process image; any attempt to reach that level would need to provide a programming language as parameters. Instead, *posix_spawn*() and *posix_spawnp*() are process creation primitives like the *Start_Process* and *Start_Process_Search* Ada language bindings package *POSIX_Process_Primitives* and also like those in many operating systems that are not UNIX systems, but with some POSIX-specific additions.

To achieve its coverage goals, *posix_spawn* () and *posix_spawnp* () have control of six types of inheritance: file descriptors, process group ID, user and group ID, signal mask, scheduling, and whether each signal ignored in the parent will remain ignored in the child, or be reset to its default action in the child.

Control of file descriptors is required to allow an independently written child process image to access data streams opened by and even generated or read by the parent process without being specifically coded to know which parent files and file descriptors are to be used. Control of the process group ID is required to control how the child process' job control relates to that of the parent.

Control of the signal mask and signal defaulting is sufficient to support the implementation of *system* (). Although support for *system* () is not explicitly one of the goals for *posix_spawn* () and *posix_spawnp* (), it is covered under the "at least 50%" coverage goal.

The intention is that the normal file descriptor inheritance across *fork* (), the subsequent effect of the specified spawn file actions, and the normal file descriptor inheritance across one of the *exec* family of functions should fully specify open file inheritance. The implementation need make no decisions regarding the set of open file descriptors when the child process image begins execution, those decisions having already been made by the caller and expressed as the set of open file descriptors and their FD_CLOEXEC flags at the time of the call and the spawn file actions object specified in the call. We have been assured that in cases where the POSIX *Start_Process* Ada primitives have been implemented in a library, this method of controlling file descriptor inheritance may be implemented very easily.

We can identify several problems with *posix_spawn* () and *posix_spawnp* (), but there does not appear to be a solution that introduces fewer problems. Environment modification for child process attributes not specifiable via the *attrp* or *file_actions* arguments must be done in the parent process, and since the parent generally wants to save its context, it is more costly than similar functionality with *fork* ()/*exec*. It is also complicated to modify the environment of a multi-threaded process temporarily, since all threads must agree when it is safe for the environment to be changed. However, this cost is only borne by those invocations of *posix_spawn* () and *posix_spawnp* () that use the additional functionality. Since extensive modifications are not the usual case, and are particularly unlikely in time-critical code, keeping much of the environment control out of *posix_spawn* () and *posix_spawnp* () is appropriate design.

The *posix_spawn* () and *posix_spawnp* () functions do not have all the power of *fork* ()/*exec*. This is to be expected. The *fork* () function is a wonderfully powerful operation. We do not expect to duplicate its functionality in a simple, fast function with no special hardware requirements. It is worth noting that *posix_spawn* () and *posix_spawnp* () are very similar to the process creation operations on many operating systems that are not UNIX systems.

Requirements

The requirements for *posix_spawn* () and *posix_spawnp* () are:

* They must be implementable without an MMU or unusual hardware.
* They must be compatible with existing POSIX standards.

Additional goals are:

* They should be efficiently implementable.
* They should be able to replace at least 50% of typical executions of *fork* ().

- A system with *posix_spawn*() and *posix_spawnp*() and without *fork*() should be useful, at least for realtime applications.

- A system with *fork*() and the *exec* family should be able to implement *posix_spawn*() and *posix_spawnp*() as library routines.

Two-Syntax

POSIX *exec* has several calling sequences with approximately the same functionality. These appear to be required for compatibility with existing practice. Since the existing practice for the *posix_spawn**() functions is otherwise substantially unlike POSIX, we feel that simplicity outweighs compatibility. There are, therefore, only two names for the *posix_spawn**() functions.

The parameter list does not differ between *posix_spawn*() and *posix_spawnp*(); *posix_spawnp*() interprets the second parameter more elaborately than *posix_spawn*().

Compatibility with POSIX.5 (Ada)

The *Start_Process* and *Start_Process_Search* procedures from the *POSIX_Process_Primitives* package from the Ada language binding to POSIX.1 encapsulate *fork*() and *exec* functionality in a manner similar to that of *posix_spawn*() and *posix_spawnp*(). Originally, in keeping with our simplicity goal, the standard developers had limited the capabilities of *posix_spawn*() and *posix_spawnp*() to a subset of the capabilities of *Start_Process* and *Start_Process_Search*; certain non-default capabilities were not supported. However, based on suggestions by the ballot group to improve file descriptor mapping or drop it, and on the advice of an Ada Language Bindings working group member, the standard developers decided that *posix_spawn*() and *posix_spawnp*() should be sufficiently powerful to implement *Start_Process* and *Start_Process_Search*. The rationale is that if the Ada language binding to such a primitive had already been approved as an IEEE standard, there can be little justification for not approving the functionally-equivalent parts of a C binding. The only three capabilities provided by *posix_spawn*() and *posix_spawnp*() that are not provided by *Start_Process* and *Start_Process_Search* are optionally specifying the child's process group ID, the set of signals to be reset to default signal handling in the child process, and the child's scheduling policy and parameters.

For the Ada language binding for *Start_Process* to be implemented with *posix_spawn*(), that binding would need to explicitly pass an empty signal mask and the parent's environment to *posix_spawn*() whenever the caller of *Start_Process* allowed these arguments to default, since *posix_spawn*() does not provide such defaults. The ability of *Start_Process* to mask user-specified signals during its execution is functionally unique to the Ada language binding and must be dealt with in the binding separately from the call to *posix_spawn*().

Process Group

The process group inheritance field can be used to join the child process with an existing process group. By assigning a value of zero to the *spawn-pgroup* attribute of the object referenced by *attrp*, the *setpgid*() mechanism will place the child-process in a new process group.

Threads

Without the *posix_spawn* () and *posix_spawnp* () functions, systems without address translation can still use threads to give an abstraction of concurrency. In many cases, thread creation suffices, but it is not always a good substitute. The *posix_spawn* () and *posix_spawnp* () functions are considerably "heavier" than thread creation. Processes have several important attributes that threads do not. Even without address translation, a process may have base-and-bound memory protection. Each process has a process environment including security attributes and file capabilities, and powerful scheduling attributes. Processes abstract the behavior of non-uniform-memory-architecture multi-processors better than threads, and they are more convenient to use for activities that are not closely linked.

The *posix_spawn* () and *posix_spawnp* () functions may not bring support for multiple processes to every configuration. Process creation is not the only piece of operating system support required to support multiple processes. The total cost of support for multiple processes may be quite high in some circumstances. Existing practice shows that support for multiple processes is uncommon and threads are common among "tiny kernels". There should, therefore, probably continue to be AEPs for operating systems with only one process.

Asynchronous Error Notification

A library implementation of *posix_spawn* () or *posix_spawnp* () may not be able to detect all possible errors before it forks the child process. IEEE Std 1003.1-2001 provides for an error indication returned from a child process which could not successfully complete the spawn operation via a special exit status which may be detected using the status value returned by *wait* () and *waitpid* ().

The *stat_val* interface and the macros used to interpret it are not well suited to the purpose of returning API errors, but they are the only path available to a library implementation. Thus, an implementation may cause the child process to exit with exit status 127 for any error detected during the spawn process after the *posix_spawn* () or *posix_spawnp* () function has successfully returned.

The standard developers had proposed using two additional macros to interpret *stat_val*. The first, WIFSPAWNFAIL, would have detected a status that indicated that the child exited because of an error detected during the *posix_spawn* () or *posix_spawnp* () operations rather than during actual execution of the child process image; the second, WSPAWNERRNO, would have extracted the error value if WIFSPAWNFAIL indicated a failure. Unfortunately, the ballot group strongly opposed this because it would make a library implementation of *posix_spawn* () or *posix_spawnp* () dependent on kernel modifications to *waitpid* () to be able to embed special information in *stat_val* to indicate a spawn failure.

The 8 bits of child process exit status that are guaranteed by IEEE Std 1003.1-2001 to be accessible to the waiting parent process are insufficient to disambiguate a spawn error from any other kind of error that may be returned by an arbitrary process image. No other bits of the exit status are required to be visible in *stat_val*, so these macros could not be strictly implemented at the library level. Reserving an exit status of 127 for such spawn errors is consistent with the use of this value by *system* () and *popen* () to signal failures in these operations that occur after the function has returned but before a shell is able to execute. The exit status of 127 does not uniquely identify this class of error, nor does it provide any detailed information on the nature of the failure. Note that a kernel implementation of *posix_spawn* () or *posix_spawnp* () is permitted (and encouraged) to return any possible error as the function value, thus providing more detailed failure information to the parent process.

Thus, no special macros are available to isolate asynchronous *posix_spawn* () or *posix_spawnp* () errors. Instead, errors detected by the *posix_spawn* () or *posix_spawnp* () operations in the context of the child process before the new process image executes are reported by setting the child's exit status to 127. The calling process may use the WIFEXITED and WEXITSTATUS macros on the *stat_val* stored by the *wait*() or *waitpid*() functions to detect spawn failures to the extent that other status values with which the child process image may exit (before the parent can conclusively determine that the child process image has begun execution) are distinct from exit status 127.

FUTURE DIRECTIONS

None.

SEE ALSO

alarm(), *chmod*(), *close*(), *dup*(), *exec*, *exit*(), *fcntl*(), *fork*(), *kill*(), *open*(), *posix_spawn_file_actions_addclose*(), *posix_spawn_file_actions_adddup2*(), *posix_spawn_file_actions_addopen*(), *posix_spawn_file_actions_destroy*(), <REFERENCE UNDEFINED>(posix_spawn_file_actions_init), *posix_spawnattr_destroy*(), *posix_spawnattr_init*(), *posix_spawnattr_getsigdefault*(), *posix_spawnattr_getflags*(), *posix_spawnattr_getpgroup*(), *posix_spawnattr_getschedparam*(), *posix_spawnattr_getschedpolicy*(), *posix_spawnattr_getsigmask*(), *posix_spawnattr_setsigdefault*(), *posix_spawnattr_setflags*(), *posix_spawnattr_setpgroup*(), *posix_spawnattr_setschedparam*(), *posix_spawnattr_setschedpolicy*(), *posix_spawnattr_setsigmask*(), *sched_setparam*(), *sched_setscheduler*(), *setpgid*(), *setuid*(), *stat*(), *times*(), *wait*(), the Base Definitions volume of IEEE Std 1003.1-2001, **<spawn.h>**

CHANGE HISTORY

First released in Issue 6. Derived from IEEE Std 1003.1d-1999.

IEEE PASC Interpretation 1003.1 #103 is applied, noting that the signal default actions are changed as well as the signal mask in step 2.

IEEE PASC Interpretation 1003.1 #132 is applied.

NAME

posix_spawn_file_actions_addclose, posix_spawn_file_actions_addopen — add close or open action to spawn file actions object (**ADVANCED REALTIME**)

SYNOPSIS

SPN   `#include <spawn.h>`

```
int posix_spawn_file_actions_addclose(posix_spawn_file_actions_t *
    file_actions, int fildes);
int posix_spawn_file_actions_addopen(posix_spawn_file_actions_t *
    restrict file_actions, int fildes,
    const char *restrict path, int oflag, mode_t mode);
```

DESCRIPTION

These functions shall add or delete a close or open action to a spawn file actions object.

A spawn file actions object is of type **posix_spawn_file_actions_t** (defined in **<spawn.h>**) and is used to specify a series of actions to be performed by a *posix_spawn* ( ) or *posix_spawnp* ( ) operation in order to arrive at the set of open file descriptors for the child process given the set of open file descriptors of the parent. IEEE Std 1003.1-2001 does not define comparison or assignment operators for the type **posix_spawn_file_actions_t**.

A spawn file actions object, when passed to *posix_spawn* ( ) or *posix_spawnp* ( ), shall specify how the set of open file descriptors in the calling process is transformed into a set of potentially open file descriptors for the spawned process. This transformation shall be as if the specified sequence of actions was performed exactly once, in the context of the spawned process (prior to execution of the new process image), in the order in which the actions were added to the object; additionally, when the new process image is executed, any file descriptor (from this new set) which has its FD_CLOEXEC flag set shall be closed (see *posix_spawn* ( )).

The *posix_spawn_file_actions_addclose* ( ) function shall add a *close* action to the object referenced by *file_actions* that shall cause the file descriptor *fildes* to be closed (as if *close* (*fildes*) had been called) when a new process is spawned using this file actions object.

The *posix_spawn_file_actions_addopen* ( ) function shall add an *open* action to the object referenced by *file_actions* that shall cause the file named by *path* to be opened (as if *open* (*path*, *oflag*, *mode*) had been called, and the returned file descriptor, if not *fildes*, had been changed to *fildes*) when a new process is spawned using this file actions object. If *fildes* was already an open file descriptor, it shall be closed before the new file is opened.

The string described by *path* shall be copied by the *posix_spawn_file_actions_addopen* ( ) function.

RETURN VALUE

Upon successful completion, these functions shall return zero; otherwise, an error number shall be returned to indicate the error.

ERRORS

These functions shall fail if:

[EBADF]   The value specified by *fildes* is negative or greater than or equal to {OPEN_MAX}.

These functions may fail if:

[EINVAL]   The value specified by *file_actions* is invalid.

[ENOMEM]   Insufficient memory exists to add to the spawn file actions object.

It shall not be considered an error for the *fildes* argument passed to these functions to specify a file descriptor for which the specified operation could not be performed at the time of the call. Any such error will be detected when the associated file actions object is later used during a *posix_spawn* ( ) or *posix_spawnp* ( ) operation.

EXAMPLES
None.

APPLICATION USAGE
These functions are part of the Spawn option and need not be provided on all implementations.

RATIONALE
A spawn file actions object may be initialized to contain an ordered sequence of *close* ( ), *dup2* ( ), and *open* ( ) operations to be used by *posix_spawn* ( ) or *posix_spawnp* ( ) to arrive at the set of open file descriptors inherited by the spawned process from the set of open file descriptors in the parent at the time of the *posix_spawn* ( ) or *posix_spawnp* ( ) call. It had been suggested that the *close* ( ) and *dup2* ( ) operations alone are sufficient to rearrange file descriptors, and that files which need to be opened for use by the spawned process can be handled either by having the calling process open them before the *posix_spawn* ( ) or *posix_spawnp* ( ) call (and close them after), or by passing filenames to the spawned process (in *argv*) so that it may open them itself. The standard developers recommend that applications use one of these two methods when practical, since detailed error status on a failed open operation is always available to the application this way. However, the standard developers feel that allowing a spawn file actions object to specify open operations is still appropriate because:

1. It is consistent with equivalent POSIX.5 (Ada) functionality.

2. It supports the I/O redirection paradigm commonly employed by POSIX programs designed to be invoked from a shell. When such a program is the child process, it may not be designed to open files on its own.

3. It allows file opens that might otherwise fail or violate file ownership/access rights if executed by the parent process.

Regarding 2. above, note that the spawn open file action provides to *posix_spawn* ( ) and *posix_spawnp* ( ) the same capability that the shell redirection operators provide to *system* ( ), only without the intervening execution of a shell; for example:

```
system ("myprog <file1 3<file2");
```

Regarding 3. above, note that if the calling process needs to open one or more files for access by the spawned process, but has insufficient spare file descriptors, then the open action is necessary to allow the *open* ( ) to occur in the context of the child process after other file descriptors have been closed (that must remain open in the parent).

Additionally, if a parent is executed from a file having a "set-user-id" mode bit set and the POSIX_SPAWN_RESETIDS flag is set in the spawn attributes, a file created within the parent process will (possibly incorrectly) have the parent's effective user ID as its owner, whereas a file created via an *open* ( ) action during *posix_spawn* ( ) or *posix_spawnp* ( ) will have the parent's real ID as its owner; and an open by the parent process may successfully open a file to which the real user should not have access or fail to open a file to which the real user should have access.

File Descriptor Mapping

The standard developers had originally proposed using an array which specified the mapping of child file descriptors back to those of the parent. It was pointed out by the ballot group that it is not possible to reshuffle file descriptors arbitrarily in a library implementation of *posix_spawn* ( ) or *posix_spawnp* ( ) without provision for one or more spare file descriptor entries (which simply may not be available). Such an array requires that an implementation develop a complex strategy to achieve the desired mapping without inadvertently closing the wrong file descriptor at the wrong time.

It was noted by a member of the Ada Language Bindings working group that the approved Ada Language *Start_Process* family of POSIX process primitives use a caller-specified set of file actions to alter the normal *fork* ( )/*exec* semantics for inheritance of file descriptors in a very flexible way, yet no such problems exist because the burden of determining how to achieve the final file descriptor mapping is completely on the application. Furthermore, although the file actions interface appears frightening at first glance, it is actually quite simple to implement in either a library or the kernel.

FUTURE DIRECTIONS
None.

SEE ALSO
close ( ),   *dup* ( ),   *open* ( ),   *posix_spawn* ( ),   *posix_spawn_file_actions_adddup2* ( ), *posix_spawn_file_actions_destroy* ( ),   *posix_spawnp* ( ),   the   Base   Definitions   volume   of IEEE Std 1003.1-2001, **<spawn.h>**

CHANGE HISTORY
First released in Issue 6. Derived from IEEE Std 1003.1d-1999.

IEEE PASC Interpretation 1003.1 #105 is applied, adding a note to the DESCRIPTION that the string pointed to by *path* is copied by the *posix_spawn_file_actions_addopen* ( ) function.

NAME

posix_spawn_file_actions_adddup2 — add dup2 action to spawn file actions object
(**ADVANCED REALTIME**)

SYNOPSIS

SPN
```
#include <spawn.h>

int posix_spawn_file_actions_adddup2(posix_spawn_file_actions_t *
    file_actions, int fildes, int newfildes);
```

DESCRIPTION

The *posix_spawn_file_actions_adddup2*() function shall add a *dup2*() action to the object referenced by *file_actions* that shall cause the file descriptor *fildes* to be duplicated as *newfildes* (as if *dup2*(*fildes*, *newfildes*) had been called) when a new process is spawned using this file actions object.

A spawn file actions object is as defined in *posix_spawn_file_actions_addclose*().

RETURN VALUE

Upon successful completion, the *posix_spawn_file_actions_adddup2*() function shall return zero; otherwise, an error number shall be returned to indicate the error.

ERRORS

The *posix_spawn_file_actions_adddup2*() function shall fail if:

[EBADF]   The value specified by *fildes* or *newfildes* is negative or greater than or equal to {OPEN_MAX}.

[ENOMEM]   Insufficient memory exists to add to the spawn file actions object.

The *posix_spawn_file_actions_adddup2*() function may fail if:

[EINVAL]   The value specified by *file_actions* is invalid.

It shall not be considered an error for the *fildes* argument passed to the *posix_spawn_file_actions_adddup2*() function to specify a file descriptor for which the specified operation could not be performed at the time of the call. Any such error will be detected when the associated file actions object is later used during a *posix_spawn*() or *posix_spawnp*() operation.

EXAMPLES

None.

APPLICATION USAGE

The *posix_spawn_file_actions_adddup2*() function is part of the Spawn option and need not be provided on all implementations.

RATIONALE

Refer to the RATIONALE in *posix_spawn_file_actions_addclose*().

FUTURE DIRECTIONS

None.

SEE ALSO

dup(), *posix_spawn*(), *posix_spawn_file_actions_addclose*(), *posix_spawn_file_actions_destroy*(), *posix_spawnp*(), the Base Definitions volume of IEEE Std 1003.1-2001, **<spawn.h>**

CHANGE HISTORY

First released in Issue 6. Derived from IEEE Std 1003.1d-1999.

IEEE PASC Interpretation 1003.1 #104 is applied, noting that the [EBADF] error can apply to the *newfildes* argument in addition to *fildes*.

NAME

posix_spawn_file_actions_addopen — add open action to spawn file actions object
(ADVANCED REALTIME)

SYNOPSIS

SPN `#include <spawn.h>`

```
int posix_spawn_file_actions_addopen(posix_spawn_file_actions_t *
    restrict file_actions, int fildes,
    const char *restrict path, int oflag, mode_t mode);
```

DESCRIPTION

Refer to *posix_spawn_file_actions_addclose*( ).

NAME

posix_spawn_file_actions_destroy, posix_spawn_file_actions_init — destroy and initialize spawn file actions object (**ADVANCED REALTIME**)

SYNOPSIS

SPN   `#include <spawn.h>`

```
int posix_spawn_file_actions_destroy(posix_spawn_file_actions_t *
    file_actions);
int posix_spawn_file_actions_init(posix_spawn_file_actions_t *
    file_actions);
```

DESCRIPTION

The *posix_spawn_file_actions_destroy*() function shall destroy the object referenced by *file_actions*; the object becomes, in effect, uninitialized. An implementation may cause *posix_spawn_file_actions_destroy*() to set the object referenced by *file_actions* to an invalid value. A destroyed spawn file actions object can be reinitialized using *posix_spawn_file_actions_init*(); the results of otherwise referencing the object after it has been destroyed are undefined.

The *posix_spawn_file_actions_init*() function shall initialize the object referenced by *file_actions* to contain no file actions for *posix_spawn*() or *posix_spawnp*() to perform.

A spawn file actions object is as defined in *posix_spawn_file_actions_addclose*().

The effect of initializing an already initialized spawn file actions object is undefined.

RETURN VALUE

Upon successful completion, these functions shall return zero; otherwise, an error number shall be returned to indicate the error.

ERRORS

The *posix_spawn_file_actions_init*() function shall fail if:

[ENOMEM]   Insufficient memory exists to initialize the spawn file actions object.

The *posix_spawn_file_actions_destroy*() function may fail if:

[EINVAL]   The value specified by *file_actions* is invalid.

EXAMPLES

None.

APPLICATION USAGE

These functions are part of the Spawn option and need not be provided on all implementations.

RATIONALE

Refer to the RATIONALE in *posix_spawn_file_actions_addclose*().

FUTURE DIRECTIONS

None.

SEE ALSO

posix_spawn(), *posix_spawnp*(), the Base Definitions volume of IEEE Std 1003.1-2001, **<spawn.h>**

CHANGE HISTORY

First released in Issue 6. Derived from IEEE Std 1003.1d-1999.

In the SYNOPSIS, the inclusion of **<sys/types.h>** is no longer required.

NAME

posix_spawnattr_destroy, posix_spawnattr_init — destroy and initialize spawn attributes object **(ADVANCED REALTIME)**

SYNOPSIS

SPN
```
#include <spawn.h>

int posix_spawnattr_destroy(posix_spawnattr_t *attr);
int posix_spawnattr_init(posix_spawnattr_t *attr);
```

DESCRIPTION

The *posix_spawnattr_destroy*() function shall destroy a spawn attributes object. A destroyed *attr* attributes object can be reinitialized using *posix_spawnattr_init*(); the results of otherwise referencing the object after it has been destroyed are undefined. An implementation may cause *posix_spawnattr_destroy*() to set the object referenced by *attr* to an invalid value.

The *posix_spawnattr_init*() function shall initialize a spawn attributes object *attr* with the default value for all of the individual attributes used by the implementation. Results are undefined if *posix_spawnattr_init*() is called specifying an already initialized *attr* attributes object.

A spawn attributes object is of type **posix_spawnattr_t** (defined in **<spawn.h>**) and is used to specify the inheritance of process attributes across a spawn operation. IEEE Std 1003.1-2001 does not define comparison or assignment operators for the type **posix_spawnattr_t**.

Each implementation shall document the individual attributes it uses and their default values unless these values are defined by IEEE Std 1003.1-2001. Attributes not defined by IEEE Std 1003.1-2001, their default values, and the names of the associated functions to get and set those attribute values are implementation-defined.

The resulting spawn attributes object (possibly modified by setting individual attribute values), is used to modify the behavior of *posix_spawn*() or *posix_spawnp*(). After a spawn attributes object has been used to spawn a process by a call to a *posix_spawn*() or *posix_spawnp*(), any function affecting the attributes object (including destruction) shall not affect any process that has been spawned in this way.

RETURN VALUE

Upon successful completion, *posix_spawnattr_destroy*() and *posix_spawnattr_init*() shall return zero; otherwise, an error number shall be returned to indicate the error.

ERRORS

The *posix_spawnattr_init*() function shall fail if:

[ENOMEM]   Insufficient memory exists to initialize the spawn attributes object.

The *posix_spawnattr_destroy*() function may fail if:

[EINVAL]   The value specified by attr is invalid.

EXAMPLES

None.

APPLICATION USAGE

These functions are part of the Spawn option and need not be provided on all implementations.

RATIONALE

The original spawn interface proposed in IEEE Std 1003.1-2001 defined the attributes that specify the inheritance of process attributes across a spawn operation as a structure. In order to be able to separate optional individual attributes under their appropriate options (that is, the *spawn-schedparam* and *spawn-schedpolicy* attributes depending upon the Process Scheduling option), and also for extensibility and consistency with the newer POSIX interfaces, the attributes interface has been changed to an opaque data type. This interface now consists of the type **posix_spawnattr_t**, representing a spawn attributes object, together with associated functions to initialize or destroy the attributes object, and to set or get each individual attribute. Although the new object-oriented interface is more verbose than the original structure, it is simple to use, more extensible, and easy to implement.

FUTURE DIRECTIONS

None.

SEE ALSO

posix_spawn ( ), *posix_spawnattr_getsigdefault* ( ), *posix_spawnattr_getflags* ( ),
posix_spawnattr_getpgroup ( ), *posix_spawnattr_getschedparam* ( ), *posix_spawnattr_getschedpolicy* ( ),
posix_spawnattr_getsigmask ( ), *posix_spawnattr_setsigdefault* ( ), *posix_spawnattr_setflags* ( ),
posix_spawnattr_setpgroup ( ), *posix_spawnattr_setsigmask* ( ), *posix_spawnattr_setschedpolicy* ( ),
posix_spawnattr_setschedparam ( ), *posix_spawnp* ( ), the Base Definitions volume of
IEEE Std 1003.1-2001, **<spawn.h>**

CHANGE HISTORY

First released in Issue 6. Derived from IEEE Std 1003.1d-1999.

IEEE PASC Interpretation 1003.1 #106 is applied, noting that the effect of initializing an already initialized spawn attributes option is undefined.

NAME

posix_spawnattr_getflags, posix_spawnattr_setflags — get and set the spawn-flags attribute of a spawn attributes object (**ADVANCED REALTIME**)

SYNOPSIS

SPN
```
#include <spawn.h>
```

```
int posix_spawnattr_getflags(const posix_spawnattr_t *restrict attr,
    short *restrict flags);
int posix_spawnattr_setflags(posix_spawnattr_t *attr, short flags);
```

DESCRIPTION

The *posix_spawnattr_getflags*() function shall obtain the value of the *spawn-flags* attribute from the attributes object referenced by *attr*.

The *posix_spawnattr_setflags*() function shall set the *spawn-flags* attribute in an initialized attributes object referenced by *attr*.

The *spawn-flags* attribute is used to indicate which process attributes are to be changed in the new process image when invoking *posix_spawn*() or *posix_spawnp*(). It is the bitwise-inclusive OR of zero or more of the following flags:

POSIX_SPAWN_RESETIDS
POSIX_SPAWN_SETPGROUP
POSIX_SPAWN_SETSIGDEF
POSIX_SPAWN_SETSIGMASK
PS
POSIX_SPAWN_SETSCHEDPARAM
POSIX_SPAWN_SETSCHEDULER

These flags are defined in **<spawn.h>**. The default value of this attribute shall be as if no flags were set.

RETURN VALUE

Upon successful completion, *posix_spawnattr_getflags*() shall return zero and store the value of the *spawn-flags* attribute of *attr* into the object referenced by the *flags* parameter; otherwise, an error number shall be returned to indicate the error.

Upon successful completion, *posix_spawnattr_setflags*() shall return zero; otherwise, an error number shall be returned to indicate the error.

ERRORS

These functions may fail if:

[EINVAL]   The value specified by *attr* is invalid.

The *posix_spawnattr_setflags*() function may fail if:

[EINVAL]   The value of the attribute being set is not valid.

EXAMPLES
None.

APPLICATION USAGE
These functions are part of the Spawn option and need not be provided on all implementations.

RATIONALE
None.

FUTURE DIRECTIONS
None.

SEE ALSO
posix_spawn (), *posix_spawnattr_destroy* (), *posix_spawnattr_init* (), *posix_spawnattr_getsigdefault* (), *posix_spawnattr_getpgroup* (), *posix_spawnattr_getschedparam* (), *posix_spawnattr_getschedpolicy* (), *posix_spawnattr_getsigmask* (), *posix_spawnattr_setsigdefault* (), *posix_spawnattr_setpgroup* (), *posix_spawnattr_setschedparam* (), *posix_spawnattr_setschedpolicy* (), *posix_spawnattr_setsigmask* (), *posix_spawnp* (), the Base Definitions volume of IEEE Std 1003.1-2001, **<spawn.h>**

CHANGE HISTORY
First released in Issue 6. Derived from IEEE Std 1003.1d-1999.

NAME

posix_spawnattr_getpgroup, posix_spawnattr_setpgroup — get and set the spawn-pgroup attribute of a spawn attributes object (**ADVANCED REALTIME**)

SYNOPSIS

SPN   `#include <spawn.h>`

```
int posix_spawnattr_getpgroup(const posix_spawnattr_t *restrict attr,
    pid_t *restrict pgroup);
int posix_spawnattr_setpgroup(posix_spawnattr_t *attr, pid_t pgroup);
```

DESCRIPTION

The *posix_spawnattr_getpgroup*() function shall obtain the value of the *spawn-pgroup* attribute from the attributes object referenced by *attr*.

The *posix_spawnattr_setpgroup*() function shall set the *spawn-pgroup* attribute in an initialized attributes object referenced by *attr*.

The *spawn-pgroup* attribute represents the process group to be joined by the new process image in a spawn operation (if POSIX_SPAWN_SETPGROUP is set in the *spawn-flags* attribute). The default value of this attribute shall be zero.

RETURN VALUE

Upon successful completion, *posix_spawnattr_getpgroup*() shall return zero and store the value of the *spawn-pgroup* attribute of *attr* into the object referenced by the *pgroup* parameter; otherwise, an error number shall be returned to indicate the error.

Upon successful completion, *posix_spawnattr_setpgroup*() shall return zero; otherwise, an error number shall be returned to indicate the error.

ERRORS

These functions may fail if:

[EINVAL]   The value specified by *attr* is invalid.

The *posix_spawnattr_setpgroup*() function may fail if:

[EINVAL]   The value of the attribute being set is not valid.

EXAMPLES

None.

APPLICATION USAGE

These functions are part of the Spawn option and need not be provided on all implementations.

RATIONALE

None.

FUTURE DIRECTIONS

None.

SEE ALSO

posix_spawn(), *posix_spawnattr_destroy*(), *posix_spawnattr_init*(), *posix_spawnattr_getsigdefault*(), *posix_spawnattr_getflags*(), *posix_spawnattr_getschedparam*(), *posix_spawnattr_getschedpolicy*(), *posix_spawnattr_getsigmask*(), *posix_spawnattr_setsigdefault*(), *posix_spawnattr_setflags*(), *posix_spawnattr_setschedparam*(), *posix_spawnattr_setschedpolicy*(), *posix_spawnattr_setsigmask*(), *posix_spawnp*(), the Base Definitions volume of IEEE Std 1003.1-2001, **<spawn.h>**

CHANGE HISTORY

First released in Issue 6. Derived from IEEE Std 1003.1d-1999.

NAME

posix_spawnattr_getschedparam, posix_spawnattr_setschedparam — get and set the spawn-schedparam attribute of a spawn attributes object (**ADVANCED REALTIME**)

SYNOPSIS

SPN PS   `#include <spawn.h>`
`#include <sched.h>`

```
int posix_spawnattr_getschedparam(const posix_spawnattr_t *
    restrict attr, struct sched_param *restrict schedparam);
int posix_spawnattr_setschedparam(posix_spawnattr_t *restrict attr,
    const struct sched_param *restrict schedparam);
```

DESCRIPTION

The *posix_spawnattr_getschedparam*( ) function shall obtain the value of the *spawn-schedparam* attribute from the attributes object referenced by *attr*.

The *posix_spawnattr_setschedparam*( ) function shall set the *spawn-schedparam* attribute in an initialized attributes object referenced by *attr*.

The *spawn-schedparam* attribute represents the scheduling parameters to be assigned to the new process image in a spawn operation (if POSIX_SPAWN_SETSCHEDULER or POSIX_SPAWN_SETSCHEDPARAM is set in the *spawn-flags* attribute). The default value of this attribute is unspecified.

RETURN VALUE

Upon successful completion, *posix_spawnattr_getschedparam*( ) shall return zero and store the value of the *spawn-schedparam* attribute of *attr* into the object referenced by the *schedparam* parameter; otherwise, an error number shall be returned to indicate the error.

Upon successful completion, *posix_spawnattr_setschedparam*( ) shall return zero; otherwise, an error number shall be returned to indicate the error.

ERRORS

These functions may fail if:

[EINVAL]   The value specified by *attr* is invalid.

The *posix_spawnattr_setschedparam*( ) function may fail if:

[EINVAL]   The value of the attribute being set is not valid.

EXAMPLES

None.

APPLICATION USAGE

These functions are part of the Spawn and Process Scheduling options and need not be provided on all implementations.

RATIONALE

None.

FUTURE DIRECTIONS

None.

SEE ALSO

posix_spawn( ), *posix_spawnattr_destroy*( ), *posix_spawnattr_init*( ), *posix_spawnattr_getsigdefault*( ), *posix_spawnattr_getflags*( ), *posix_spawnattr_getpgroup*( ), *posix_spawnattr_getschedpolicy*( ), *posix_spawnattr_getsigmask*( ), *posix_spawnattr_setsigdefault*( ), *posix_spawnattr_setflags*( ), *posix_spawnattr_setpgroup* ( ), *posix_spawnattr_setschedpolicy* ( ), *posix_spawnattr_setsigmask* ( ), *posix_spawnp* ( ), the Base Definitions volume of IEEE Std 1003.1-2001, **<sched.h>**, **<spawn.h>**

CHANGE HISTORY

First released in Issue 6. Derived from IEEE Std 1003.1d-1999.

NAME

posix_spawnattr_getschedpolicy, posix_spawnattr_setschedpolicy — get and set the spawn-schedpolicy attribute of a spawn attributes object (**ADVANCED REALTIME**)

SYNOPSIS

SPN PS
```
#include <spawn.h>
#include <sched.h>

int posix_spawnattr_getschedpolicy(const posix_spawnattr_t *
    restrict attr, int *restrict schedpolicy);
int posix_spawnattr_setschedpolicy(posix_spawnattr_t *attr,
    int schedpolicy);
```

DESCRIPTION

The *posix_spawnattr_getschedpolicy*( ) function shall obtain the value of the *spawn-schedpolicy* attribute from the attributes object referenced by *attr*.

The *posix_spawnattr_setschedpolicy*( ) function shall set the *spawn-schedpolicy* attribute in an initialized attributes object referenced by *attr*.

The *spawn-schedpolicy* attribute represents the scheduling policy to be assigned to the new process image in a spawn operation (if POSIX_SPAWN_SETSCHEDULER is set in the *spawn-flags* attribute). The default value of this attribute is unspecified.

RETURN VALUE

Upon successful completion, *posix_spawnattr_getschedpolicy*( ) shall return zero and store the value of the *spawn-schedpolicy* attribute of *attr* into the object referenced by the *schedpolicy* parameter; otherwise, an error number shall be returned to indicate the error.

Upon successful completion, *posix_spawnattr_setschedpolicy*( ) shall return zero; otherwise, an error number shall be returned to indicate the error.

ERRORS

These functions may fail if:

[EINVAL]   The value specified by *attr* is invalid.

The *posix_spawnattr_setschedpolicy*( ) function may fail if:

[EINVAL]   The value of the attribute being set is not valid.

EXAMPLES

None.

APPLICATION USAGE

These functions are part of the Spawn and Process Scheduling options and need not be provided on all implementations.

RATIONALE

None.

FUTURE DIRECTIONS

None.

SEE ALSO

posix_spawn( ), *posix_spawnattr_destroy*( ), *posix_spawnattr_init*( ), *posix_spawnattr_getsigdefault*( ), *posix_spawnattr_getflags*( ), *posix_spawnattr_getpgroup*( ), *posix_spawnattr_getschedparam*( ), *posix_spawnattr_getsigmask*( ), *posix_spawnattr_setsigdefault*( ), *posix_spawnattr_setflags*( ), *posix_spawnattr_setpgroup*( ), *posix_spawnattr_setschedparam*( ), *posix_spawnattr_setsigmask*( ), *posix_spawnp* ( ), the Base Definitions volume of IEEE Std 1003.1-2001, **<sched.h>**, **<spawn.h>**

CHANGE HISTORY

First released in Issue 6. Derived from IEEE Std 1003.1d-1999.

Bibliography

Audi, Robert. *Action, Intention, and Reason*. Ithaca, NY: Cornell University Press, 1993.

Axford, Tom. *Concurrent Programming: Fundamental Techniques for Real-Time and Parallel Software Design*. Chichester: John Wiley & Sons, 1989.

Baase, Sarah. *Computer Algorithms: Introduction to Design and Analysis*. 2nd ed. Reading, MA: Addison-Wesley, 1988.

Barfield, Woodrow and Thomas A. Furness III. *Virtual Environments and Advanced Interface Design*. New York, NY: Oxford University Press, 1995.

Bergadano, Francesco and Daniele Gunetti. *Inductive Logic Programming: From Machine Learning to Software Engineering*. London, England: MIT Press, 1996.

Binkley, Robert, Richard Bronaugh, and Ausonio Marras. *Agent, Action, and Reason*. Britain: University of Toronto Press, 1971.

Booch, Grady, James Rumbaugh, and Ivar Jacobson. *The Unified Modeling Language User Guide*. Boston, MA: Addison Wesley, 1999.

Brewka, Gerhard, Jurgen Dix, and Kurt Konolige. *Nonmonotonic Reasoning*. Stanford, CA: CSLI Publications, 1997.

Carroll, Martin D. and Margaret A. Ellis. *Designing and Coding Reusable C++*. Reading, MA: Addison-Wesley, 1995.

Cassell, Justine, Joseph Sullivan, Scott Prevost, and Elizabeth Churchill. *Embodied Conversational Agents*. Cambridge, MA: The MIT Press, 2000.

Chellas, Brian F. *Modal Logic: An Introduction*. New York, NY: Cambridge University Press, 1980.

Bibliography

Conway, Pat and Bill Hughes. "The AMD Opteron Nothrbridge Architecture." *IEEE Micro*, March/April 2007 (Vol.27, No.2), pp.10–21.

Coplien, James O. *Multi-Paradigm Design for C++*. Reading, MA: Addison-Wesley, 1999.

Cormen, Thomas, Charles Leiserson, and Ronald Rivest. *Introduction to Algorithms*. Cambridge, MA: The MIT Press, 1995.

Deitel, H.M, P.J. Deitel, and D.R. Choffnes. *Operating Systems*. 3rd ed. Upper Saddle, NJ: Prentice Hall, 2004.

Englemore, Robert and Tony Morgan. *Blackboard Systems*. England: Addison-Wesley, 1988.

Fagin, Ronald, Joseph Halpern, Yoram Moses, and Moshe Vardi. *Reasoning About Knowledge*. London, England: MIT Press, 1995.

Geist, Al, Adam Beguelin, Jack Dongarra, Weicheng Jiang, Robert Manchek, and Vaidy Sinderman. *PVM: Parallel Virtual Machine*. London, England: MIT Press, 1994.

Goertzel, Ben and Cassio Pennachin, eds. *Artificial General Intelligence*. Berlin, Heidelberg: Springer-Verlag, 2007.

Goodheart, Berny and James Cox. *The Magic Garden Explained: The Internals of Unix System V Release 4*. New York, NY: Prentice Hall, 1994.

Gries, David and Fred B. Schneider. *A Logical Approach to Discrete Math*. New York, NY: Springer-Verlag, 1993.

Gshchwind, Michael, David Erb, Sid Manning, and Mark Nutter. "An Open Source Environment for Cell Broadband Engine System Software." *IEEE Computer*, June 2007 (Vol. 40, No.6): pp. 37–47.

Heath, Michael T. *Scientific Computing: An Introductory Survey*. New York, NY: McGraw Hill, 2002.

Hennessy, John L. and David A. Patterson. *Computer Architecture: A Quantitative Approach, Fourth Edition*. San Francisco, CA: Morgan Kaufman, 2007.

Hennessy, John L. and David A. Patterson. *Computer Architecture: A Quantitative Approach, 2nd Edition*. San Francisco, CA: Morgan Kaufman, 1996.

Hintikka, Jaakko and Merrill Hintikka. *The Logic of Epistemology and the Epistemology of Logic*. New York, NY: Springer-Verlag, 1989.

Horty, John F. *Agency and Deontic Logic*. New York, NY: Oxford University Press, 2001.

Hughes, Cameron and Tracey Hughes. *Linux Rapid Application Development*. Foster City, CA: M & T Books, 2000.

_____. *Object-Oriented Multithreading Using C++*. New York, NY: John Wiley & Sons, 1997.

_____. *Mastering the Standard C++ Classes: An Essential Reference*. New York, NY: John Wiley & Sons, 1990.

_____. *Parallel and Distributed Programming Using C++*. Boston, MA: Addison-Wesley, 2004.

Huth, Michael and Mark Ryan. *Logic in Computer Science: Modelling and Reasoning about Systems*, 2nd ed. Cambridge, England: Cambridge University Press, 2004.

ISO, *Information Technology: Portable Operating System Interface*. "System Interfaces." Std 1003.1 ANSI/IEEE. 2001.

Josuttis, Nicolai M. *The C++ Standard*. Boston, MA: Addison-Wesley, 1999.

Kaner, Cem. *Testing Computer Software*. Blue Ridge Summit, PA: Tab Professional and Reference Books, 1988.

Koeing, Andrew and Barbara Moo. *Ruminations on C++*. Reading, MA: Addison-Wesley, 1997.

Kraus, Sarit. *Strategic Negotiation in Multiagent Environments*. London: The MIT Press, 2001.

Krishnamoorthy, C.S. and S. Rajeev. *Artificial Intelligence and Expert Systems for Engineers*. Boca Raton, FL: CRC Press, Inc., 1996.

Luger, George F. *Artificial Intelligence*. 4th ed. England: Addison-Wesley, 2002.

Mandrioli, Dino and Carlo Ghezzi. *Theoretical Foundations of Computer Science*. New York, NY: John Wiley & Sons, 1987.

Meyer, Bertrand. *Object-Oriented Software Construction*. Upper Saddle River, NJ: Prentice Hall Press, 1988.

Meyer, J.-J. Ch. and W. van der Hoek. *Epistemic Logic for AI and Computer Science*. Cambridge, England: Cambridge University Press, 2004.

Nielsen, Michael A. and Isaac L. Chuang. *Quantum Computation and Quantum Information*. New York, NY: Cambridge University Press, 2000.

Patel, Mukesh J., Vasant Honavar, and Karthik Balakrishnan. *Advances in the Evolutionary Synthesis of Intelligent Agents*. Cambridge, MA: The MIT Press, 2001.

Picard, Rosalind. *Affective Computing*. England: The MIT Press, 1997.

Reinders, James. *Intel Threading Building Blocks: Outfitting C++ for Multi-core Processor Parallelism*. Sebastopol, CA: O'Reilly & Associates, 2007.

Rescher, Nicholas and Alasdir Urquhart. *Temporal Logic*. New York, NY: Springer-Verlag, 1971.

Robbins, Kay A. and Steven Robbins. *Practical Unix Programming*. Upper Saddle River, NJ: Prentice Hall, 1996.

Russell, Stuart and Peter Norvig. *Artificial Intelligence: A Modern Approach*, 2nd ed. Upper Saddle, New Jersey: Prentice Hall, 2003.

Saraswat, Vijay A. *Concurrent Constraint Programming*. Cambridge, MA: The MIT Press, 1993.

Schmucker, Kurt, Ander Weinand, and John M. Vlissides. *Object-Oriented Application Frameworks.* Greenwich, CT: Manning Publications Co., 1995.

Skillicorn, David. *Foundations of Parallel Programming.* New York, NY: Cambridge University Press, 1994.

Soukup, Jiri. *Taming C++: Pattern Classes and Persistence for Large Projects.* Reading, MA: Addison-Wesley, 1994.

Sterling, Thomas L., John Salmon, Donald J. Becker, and Daniel F. Savarese. *How to Build a Beowulf: A Guide to Implementation and Application of PC Clusters.* London: MIT Press, 1999.

Stevens, W. Richard. *UNIX Network Programming: Interprocess Communications, Vol. 2.* 2nd ed. Upper Saddle River, NJ: Prentice Hall, 1999.

Stroustrup, Bjarne. *The C++ Programming Language*, 3rd ed. Addison-Wesley, 1997.

Stroustrup, Bjarne. *The Design and Evolution of C++.* Reading, MA: Addison-Wesley, 1994.

Subrahmanian, V.S., Piero Bonatti, Jurgen Dix, Thomas Eiter, Sarit Kraus, Fatma Ozcan, and Robert Ross. *Heterogeneous Agent Systems.* Cambridge, MA: The MIT Press, 2000.

Tel, Gerard. *Introduction to Distributed Algorithms.* 2nd ed. New York, NY: Cambridge University Press, 2000.

Thompson, William J. *Computing for Scientists and Engineers.* New York, NY: John Wiley & Sons, 1992.

Tomas, Gerald and Christoph W. Ueberhuber. *Visualization of Scientific Parallel Programming.* New York, NY: Springer-Verlag, 1994.

Tracy, Kim W. and Peter Bouthoorn. *Object-Oriented: Artificial Intelligence Using C++.* New York, NY: Computer Science Press, 1997.

Weiss, Gerhard. *Multiagent Systems.* Cambridge, MA: The MIT Press, 1999.

Wooldridge, Michael. *Reasoning about Rational Agents.* London, England: The MIT Press, 2000.

Index

L